Philosophy
of
Woman

Philosophy of Woman

An Anthology of
Classic to Current Concepts

Third Edition

Edited by
Mary Briody Mahowald

Hackett Publishing Company, Inc.
Indianapolis/Cambridge

02 01 00 99 98 97 96 95 94 1 2 3 4 5 6 7 8 9

Printed in the United States of America

For further information, please address
Hackett Publishing Company, Inc.
P.O. Box 44937
Indianapolis, Indiana 46244-0937

Design by James N. Rogers

Production Coordination: Elizabeth Shaw Editorial and Publishing Services, Tucson, Arizona

Library of Congress Cataloging-in-Publication Data
Philosophy of woman: an anthology of classic to current concepts/
edited by Mary Briody Mahowald.—3rd ed.
p. cm.
Includes bibliographic references.
ISBN 0-87220-262-3. ISBN 0-87220-261-5 (pbk.)
1. Woman (Philosophy) I. Mahowald, Mary Briody.
HQ1206.P46 1994
305.42—dc20 94-25616
CIP

The paper used in this publication meets the minimum requirements of American National Standard for Information Sciences—Permanence of Paper for Printed Library Materials, ANSI Z39.48—1984.

∞

To my very dear friends
Maureen, Lisa, Michael, and Tony—
for the clarity and courage
to be who we are

Contents

Preface

"The proper study of mankind is man."
Alexander Pope, *Essay on Man*

Surely when Pope penned the above line, he intended "mankind" and "man" to be interpreted generically. Nonetheless, in most philosophical sources of the past, the concept of man has been construed primarily if not exclusively as male, while the concept of woman or women has been considered only peripherally, uncritically, or not at all. The main purpose of this book is to reduce the resultant conceptual gap by providing means to a clearer, more complete understanding of human beings. In other words, my purpose is largely remedial.

A second aim is pertinent to the problem of women's status in today's society. Undoubtedly, each of us has opinions regarding this issue. At the heart of any justification for these opinions is the need for clarification of concepts of woman or women. Similarly, at the heart of any defensible rejection of others' opinions is the need for clarification of their concepts. The material here assembled is meant to evoke such clarifications and assessment of the related concepts, and of their presuppositions and implications. In this sense, my purpose is propaedeutic to examination and determination of specific issues relevant to women.

The "proper study" for which this collection serves as source is appropriately pursuable by men as well as women. For either sex, analysis of concepts of woman may expose the inconsistencies that occur between those concepts and concepts of human nature, and elucidate the rational (or irrational) basis of behavior toward half the human race. It may be argued that it is more important for men than for women to undertake this study because men have no direct experience on which to base their understanding of women.

The selections that follow represent major philosophical orientations and influences. Some of the female authors are not as well known as others in philosophical circles; their inclusion also has a remedial goal. As in the previous edition, I have included biblical and psychoanalytical sources because current concepts may be better understood and evaluated in their light. Of course, any of the thinkers here represented may be studied in conjunction with a more extended concentration on her or his overall set of views. In fact, a comparison among these views is quite appropriate.

When this book first appeared in 1978, it included sections on "representative popular concepts" and "current philosophical articles." From the perspective of 1994, those concepts are no longer popular, and those articles are no longer current. In this edition, therefore, I have moved some of the philosophical articles into their appropriate topical category, and have added a section illustrating the philosophical versions of feminism that have developed over the last two decades. While explicitly representing different versions of feminism, the articles in the last section are also relatable to the topical sections that precede them.

Although courses about women have been taught for many years, some people still think that interest in the study of women is a fad. An optimistic implication of this notion is that someday the "specialness" or "unusualness" of studying women will disappear. While that goal is certainly appealing, my hope in making this material accessible is much more modest: to facilitate a less inadequate understanding of human beings.

Philosophy
of
Woman

Introduction

THE INEVITABILITY, USEFULNESS, AND INADEQUACY OF CONCEPTS OF WOMAN AND WOMEN

Imagine each of the following scenarios:

(1) a professor having an affair with a graduate student;
(2) a housekeeper calling the plumber to repair a leak;
(3) a corporation executive dictating a letter to a secretary;
(4) an operating room nurse assisting a surgeon.

For many people, the images evoked by these scenarios place men in the roles of professor, plumber, executive, and surgeon, and place women in each of the corresponding roles. Considering the words involved more carefully, however, it is obvious that none of the persons designated is identified by gender. Consequently, all of the relationships described could conceivably be the reverse of the gender arrangement envisioned, or they could occur between either men or women exclusively. Why, then, do we tend to assign genders where words fail to specify them? One plausible explanation is that our concepts of women fail to encompass activities or roles that are properly assignable to either gender. In other words, our concepts are unwarrantably restrictive.

As human beings, we cannot help but think, and thinking inevitably involves concepts. These concepts are generally derived from our experience of existent objects and their relationships, or indirectly from second-order objects or other concepts. Among the objects about which we inevitably develop concepts are human beings. Among the human beings about whom we inevitably develop concepts are men and women.

Since each individual's experiences of other human beings are influenced by his or her particular history, our concepts of human beings are bound to differ in some respects. Nonetheless, the fact that we distinguish between men and women as well as between human and other beings, and communicate successfully about differences and similarities we thereby observe, suggests that our thinking has a common basis in reality.

Concepts are useful if they contribute to our own or others' knowledge. To the extent that this knowledge reflects reality, it is valuable in its own right. But concepts also influence behavior. If we view some human beings as inferior to others, for example, we tend to treat them as inferior. If we view all human beings as equal, we tend to treat them as equals.

Concepts may be defined as instruments through which we think about the world; we combine our concepts through judgments whose truth or falsity may be measured by their degree of conformity with reality. Among other things, the world is comprised of a variety of unique human beings who are ongoingly related to one another and to the rest of the world. Our judgments about human beings are thus true to the extent that they reflect the reality of human beings living in the world; our judgments about women and men are true to the extent that they conform with the reality of individual women and men.

Just as the term "man" may be used generically to refer to all of humankind, both male and female, or to an individual male human being, the term "woman" may be used generically to refer to all of womankind or to an individual female human being. Nonetheless, because individual women are as unique as individual men, a generic meaning of woman that is applicable to every individual woman is a rather thin concept. Other generic concepts such as class, race, and culture may thicken one's concept of a particular female human being, but even when a number of generic concepts are applied to an individual, they cannot entirely capture the meaning of that individual. Accordingly, while concepts of woman are inevitable and useful, they are also inadequate. Their inadequacy can be reduced through further examination of experience and consideration of other concepts. A philosophy of woman attempts to extend our understanding of women and to clarify the concepts of woman and women that we inevitably formulate, so that the usefulness of these concepts and the truth status of our judgments about women will be maximized.

As a particular way of thinking about something, a concept is related to other ways of thinking about things. Concepts of woman or women are necessarily connected with other concepts such as those of man, men, and human nature. Because the term "man" may be interpreted to include *or* exclude female members of the species *Homo sapiens*, this term, along with its equivalents in other languages, has long been the source of ambiguity in oral as well as written discourse. Obviously, the mere fact that the term *may* be applied to women is not sufficient grounds for judging that it *is* applied to women. The authors of the selections in this book include many whose influential views on "man" have been construed as applicable to both sexes, yet whose remarks—on closer inspection—simply do not or cannot apply to those "men" who are women.

To facilitate correct interpretation of the selections, we subsequently distinguish between the concepts of man as male and the concepts of man as an individual of either sex or of humankind generally. Hereafter, then, the terms "man" and "men" should be construed as referring only to individual male persons, whereas the terms "human" and "person" are used for women or men, or both. Where the selections do not observe as clear a distinction, the different concepts may be distinguished through textual and contextual analyses.

Which concepts are essentially related and which are virtually unrelated depends upon the specific concepts and context under consideration. For example, concepts of woman or women seem totally unrelated to concepts of nuclear fission or of geometric progression. But some apparently unrelated concepts may be construed as essential to a particular concept of woman or women. For example, consider the concept of physical weight or mass: some specific quantitative range or average (of weight or mass) may be viewed as necessary to a concept of woman as a bodily being, particularly where such a concept is contrasted with a corresponding concept of man as a bodily being.

A cursory perusal of this book reveals such recurrent themes as freedom, equality, happiness, love, sex, marriage, femininity, and (in the last section) feminism. While these concepts are pertinent to concepts of women and their role in society, they are also subject to various interpretations. For example, John Stuart Mill's concept of happiness as an expected result of sex equality is quite different from the happiness Simone de Beauvoir suggests may be forfeited through human (including women's) liberation. The meaning of love criticized by Mary Wollstonecraft as an obstacle to women's virtue clearly contrasts with the meaning Thomas Aquinas attaches to love as the form of women's (and anyone's) virtue. While several of the feminist authors whose views are elaborated in the last section articulate philosophical orientations previously developed (for example, Marxism and liberalism), they also illustrate widely different concepts of feminism. In order to clarify and understand each author's concept of women, it is important both to identify the crucially related concepts and to elucidate their meanings as fully as possible.

The challenge of philosophy is to overcome what the Austrian philosopher Ludwig Wittgenstein called the "bewitchment of our intelligence by means of language."[1] The selections that follow contain many possibilities for such bewitchment. To discern and overcome them the reader will need (among other things) to recognize that conceptual disagreements are sometimes masked by equivocation, that is, through use of terms which take on different meanings in different contexts; and to recognize that, conversely, conceptual

1. Ludwig Wittgenstein, *Philosophical Investigations*, trans. by G. E. M. Anscombe (New York: Macmillan Publishing Company, 1968), p. 109.

agreements may be obscured by univocal use of terms which have conflicting meanings. For example, the term "woman" is typically used to designate any adult female person, yet in some contexts it is used as a synonym for "wife," from which its original meaning derives. Conceptual analysis entails careful scrutiny of such terms so that the underlying meanings may be discerned despite possible ambiguity and inconsistency of language. While concepts sometimes entail positions about the things we think about, such positions are logical rather than existential. It remains possible that a particular concept conflicts with experience or behavior—even when consistency between thought and action is considered desirable. Thus my concepts of women and of persons may be consistent with each other, while my actual behavior toward women conflicts with my view of persons. On the other hand, my concepts of human beings and of women may be inconsistent, while my behavior toward women accords with my concept of human beings.

In introducing the selections by philosophers of the past I have briefly indicated the author's overall approach to and views about human beings in general. These are crucial considerations in light of two legitimate assumptions: (1) that each author's concept of woman or women ought to be consistent with her or his generic concept of human beings, and (2) the author's basic philosophical orientation (for example, Plato's idealism, Hume's empiricism, Schopenhauer's voluntarism, Mill's utilitarianism) provides grounds for determining the validity of the corresponding views about humans, whether male or female. While both assumptions are surely defensible, it is appropriate to acknowledge their status as assumptions. In fact, a generally helpful question to ask as we assess our own and others' views is, What assumptions or set of assumptions lies at the root of these concepts or judgments? Although warrantable assumptions may not ultimately be provable, awareness of them may enlighten us about the values and priorities which infuse the premises of logical argument and rational behavior.

I

INFLUENCES FROM THE PAST

ANCIENT AND MEDIEVAL SOURCES

In this section we reach into the historical roots of our concepts of human nature and of woman. That these roots are still quite alive is apparent to anyone familiar with the history of Western philosophy and the Judaic-Christian tradition which links contemporary thought to its classical sources. While we may personally reject or challenge these sources, the ideas they express have undoubtedly influenced us through the world about us.

Among the Greeks of the fifth century B.C., Plato and Aristotle were principal contributors to an intellectual heritage utilized by medieval theologians in order to teach their religious beliefs. Foremost among the Christian theologians were Augustine and Thomas Aquinas. The former drew heavily upon Plato, the latter upon Aristotle; but both regarded the Bible as an utterly reliable source of truth about God, the world, and human nature.

PLATO

The principal writings of Plato (427–437 B.C.) are dialogues in which Socrates, his teacher, generally articulates the positions of the author. In the *Republic,* from which the following selection is excerpted (Book V, 451c–466d), Plato describes two worlds: a world of forms or ideas, and a world of physical objects or appearances. Since these two worlds are viewed as radically distinct, Plato is often called a dualist. His basic claim, made plausible through the Myth of the Cave (Book VI), is that the world of forms (of immaterial objects) is the real world, while the world of appearances (the world we perceive), is not.

Graphically, this *Weltanschauung* (worldview) of Plato may be represented as follows:

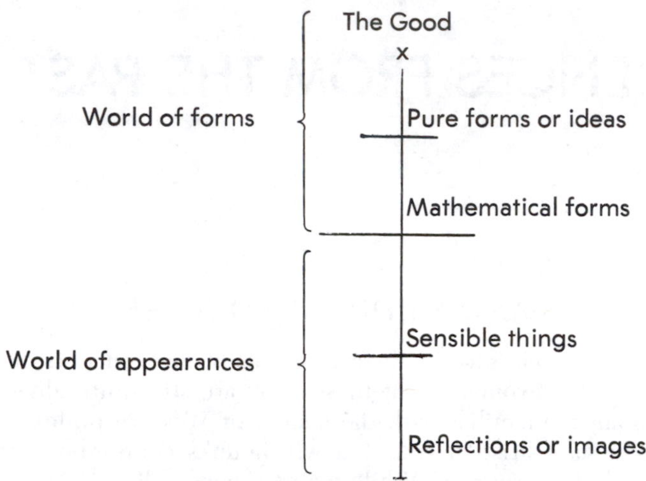

In Book VII of the *Republic,* Plato describes the division of each world: the world of appearances includes material objects (such as your body) and reflections (such as your mirror image); and the world of forms includes mathematical forms or quantitative abstractions (such as square or hypotenuse) and pure forms of qualitative abstractions (such as justice or gentleness). But Plato's dualism denies both reality and intelligibility to anything that is merely physical or material. We can only know that which is real, and reality is immaterial, universal, and unchanging. Our awareness of changing, particular appearances is not knowledge but opinion. As one advances toward the highest form (the Good), one increases in knowledge and reality; thus my body, while not belonging to the world of forms, is closer to that reality than is my shadow, and justice is a higher level of being or reality than a circle.

Since the real world for Plato is essentially immaterial, human reality is essentially immaterial, or soul. This soul comprises three parts: an appetitive part (desire for sensual fulfillment); a courageous and spirited part (pursuit of honor and fame); and a rational part (the reason, capable of controlling and ordering the other parts). Of these, the last is the immortal part of human nature. Plato regards the body as a kind of prison from which the soul may one day be released through death to live a purely rational life. If you were to find a place for yourself within Plato's world of forms and world of appearances, you might see yourself sitting on a line separating the two worlds, your head in one, and your feet dangling in the other; through your body you are merely appearance—unreal and unintelligible; through your soul you are truly human—real and rational.

Plato's Republic is an ideally just state, with a citizenry composed of workers, warriors, and philosopher-rulers or guardians. Each inhabitant is educated to fulfill the function for which he or she is best suited by nature. The term "nature" in the *Republic* is used in several ways: Plato speaks of the nature of an individual person (male or female), the nature of woman (in general), and the nature of humankind. For the good of the state, Plato insists on respecting the natural differences among individuals. The more universal good for Plato has priority over less universal goods; thus the good of one sex or class has a lower priority than the good of all humankind. The greater good is always the more rational, immaterial, and unchanging, when contrasted with other goods of nature. Radical practices such as those recommended for the Republic (for example, community of wives and children, and control of reproduction) should be assessed in light of this priority. Although Plato's later views concerning women were more conservative (e.g., in *The Laws*), his emphasis on the universal good remained consistent.

Republic

(Book V)

We must now, said I, go back to what should have been said
earlier in sequence. However, this may well be the right way: c
after we have completed the parts that men must play, we turn to those of women, especially as you call on me to do so.

For men of such a nature and education as we have described there is, in my opinion, no other right way to deal with wives and children than following the road upon which we started them. We attempted, in our argument, to establish the men as guardians of the flock. — Yes.

Let us then give them for the birth and upbringing of chil- d
dren a system appropriate to that function and see whether it suits us or not. — How?

Like this: do we think that the wives of our guardian watchdogs should join in whatever guardian duties the men fulfill, join them in the hunt, and do everything else in common, or should we keep the women at home as unable to do so because they must bear and rear their young, and leave to the men the labour and the whole care of the flock?

e All things, he said, should be done in common, except that
the women are physically weaker and the men stronger.

And is it possible, I asked, to make use of living creatures for the same purposes unless you give them the same upbringing and education? – It is not possible.

So if we use the women for the same tasks as the men, they
452 must be taught the same things. – Yes.

Now we gave the men artistic and physical culture. – Yes.

So we must give both also to the women, as well as training in war, and use them for the same tasks. – That seems to follow from what you say.

Perhaps, I said, many of the things we are saying, being contrary to custom, would stir up ridicule, if carried out in practice in the way we are telling them. – They certainly would, he said.

What, I asked, is the most ridiculous feature you see in
b this? Or is it obvious that women should exercise naked in
the palaestra along with the men, not only the young women
but the older women too, as the old men do in the gymnasia
when their bodies are wrinkled and not pleasant to look at
and yet they are fond of physical exercise? – Yes, by Zeus,
he said, it would appear ridiculous as things stand now.

Surely, I said, now that we have started on this argument,
c we must not be afraid of all the jokes of the kind that the wits
will make about such a change in physical and artistic culture, and not least about the women carrying arms and riding
horses. – You are right, he said.

As we have begun this discussion we must go on to the
tougher part of the law and beg these people not to practise
their own trade of comedy at our expense but to be serious
and to remember that it is not very long since the Greeks
thought it ugly and ridiculous, as the majority of barbarians
still do, for men to be seen naked. When first the cretans and
d then the Lacedaemonians started their physical training, the
wits of those days could have ridiculed it all, or do you not
think so? – I do.

But I think that after it was found in practice to be better
to strip than to cover up all those parts, then the spectacle
ceased to be looked on as ridiculous because reasonable argument had shown that it was best. This showed that it is foolish
to think anything ridiculous except what is bad, or to try to
e raise a laugh at any other spectacle than that of ignorance
and evil as being ridiculous, as it is foolish to be in earnest
about any other standard of beauty than that of the good. –
Most certainly.

Must we not first agree whether our proposals are possible

or not? And we must grant an opportunity for discussion to anyone who, in jest or seriously, wishes to argue the point 453
whether female human nature can share all the tasks of the male sex, or none at all, or some but not others, and to which of the two waging war belongs. Would this not be the best beginning and likely to lead to the best conclusion? – Certainly.

Do you then want us to dispute among ourselves on behalf of those others, lest the other side of the argument fall by default? – There is nothing to stop us. b

Let us then speak on their behalf: "Socrates and Glaucon, there is no need for others to argue with you. You yourselves, when you began to found your city, agreed that each person must pursue the one task for which he is fitted by nature." I think we did agree to this, of course. – "Can you deny that a woman is by nature very different from a man?" – Of course not. "And is it not proper to assign a different task to each according to their nature?" – Certainly. "How then are you c
not wrong and contradicting yourselves when you say that men and women must do the same things, when they have quite separate natures?" Do you have any defence against that argument, my good friend?

That is not very easy offhand, he said, but I ask and beg you to explain the argument on our side, whatever it is.

It is these and many other difficulties that I foresaw, Glaucon, I said, when I was afraid and hesitated to tackle the law d
concerning the acquiring of wives and the upbringing of children. – By Zeus, he said, it does not seem at all easy.

It is not, said I, but the fact is that whether a man falls into a small swimming pool or in the middle of the ocean, he must swim all the same. – Certainly.

So when we must swim too and try to save ourselves from the sea of our argument, hoping that a dolphin will pick us up or we may find some other miraculous deliverance. – It e
seems so.

Come now, said I, let us see if we can find a way out. We have agreed that a different nature must follow a different occupation and that the nature of man and woman is different, and we now say that different natures must follow the same pursuits. This is the accusation brought against us. – Surely.

How grand is the power of disputation, Glaucon. – Why? 454

Because, I said, many people fall into it unwittingly and think they are not disputing but conversing because they cannot analyze their subject into its parts, but they pursue mere verbal contradictions of what has been said, thus engaging in a dispute rather than in a conversation.

Many people, he said, have that experience, but does this also apply to us at the present moment?

b It most certainly does, I said. I am afraid we have indeed unwittingly fallen into disputation. — How?

We are bravely, but in a disputatious and verbal fashion, pursuing the principle that a nature which is not the same must not engage in the same pursuits, but when we assigned different tasks to a different nature and the same to the same nature, we did not examine at all what kind of difference and sameness of nature we had in mind and in what regard we were distinguishing them. — No, we did not look into that.

c We might therefore just as well, it seems, ask ourselves whether the nature of bald men and long-haired men is the same and not opposite, and then, agreeing that they are opposite, if we allow bald men to be cobblers, not allow long-haired men to be, or again if long-haired men are cobblers, not allow the others to be. — That would indeed be ridiculous.

Is it ridiculous for any other reason than because we did not fully consider their same or different natures in every
d respect but we were only watching the kind of difference and sameness which applied to those particular pursuits? For example, a male and a female physician, we said, have the same nature of soul, or do you not think so? — I do.

But a physician and a carpenter have a different nature? — Surely.

Therefore, I said, if the male and the female are seen to be different as regards a particular craft or other pursuit we shall say this must be assigned to one or the other. But if they seem to differ in this particular only, that the female bears children while the male begets them, we shall say that there
e has been no kind of proof that a woman is different from a man as regards the duties we are talking about, and we shall still believe that our guardians and their wives should follow the same pursuits. — And rightly so.

Next we shall bid anyone who holds the contrary view to
455 instruct us in this: with regard to what craft or pursuit concerned with the establishment of the city is the nature of man and woman not the same but different? — That is right.

Someone else might very well say what you said a short time ago, that it is not easy to give an immediate reply, but that it would not be at all difficult after considering the question. — He might say that.

Do you then want us to beg the one who raises these ob-
b jections to follow us to see whether we can show him that no

pursuit connected with the management of the city belongs in particular to a woman? – Certainly.

Come now, we shall say to him, give us an answer: did you
mean that one person had a natural ability for a certain pursuit, while another had not, when the first learned it easily,
the latter with difficulty? The one, after a brief period of instructions, was able to find things out for himself from what
he had learned, while the other, after much instruction, could
not even remember what he had learned; the former's body
adequately served his mind, while the other's physical reac- c
tions opposed his. Are there any other ways in which you distinguished the naturally gifted in each case from those who
were not? – No one will say anything else.

Do you know of any occupation practised by mankind in
which the male sex is not superior to the female in all these
respects? Or shall we pursue the argument at length by mentioning weaving, baking cakes, cooking vegetables, tasks in
which the female sex certainly seems to distinguish itself, and
in which it is most laughable of all for women to be inferior d
to men?

What you say is true, he said, namely that one sex is much superior to the other in almost everything, yet many women are better than many men in many things, but on the whole it is as you say.

There is therefore no pursuit connected with city management which belongs to woman because she is a woman, or to
a man because he is a man, but various natures are scattered
in the same way among both kinds of persons. Woman by nature shares all pursuits, and so does man, but in all of them
woman is a physically weaker creature than man. – Certainly. e

Shall we then assign them all to men, and none to a woman? – How can we?

One woman, we shall say, is a physician, another is not, one is by nature artistic, another is not. – Quite so.

One may be athletic or warlike, while another is not war- 456
like and has no love of athletics. – I think so.

Further, may not one woman love wisdom, another hate it, or one may be high-spirited, another be without spirit? – That too.

So one woman may have a guardian nature, the other not. Was it not a nature with these qualities which we selected among men for our male guardians too? – We did.

Therefore the nature of man and woman is the same as regards guarding the city, except in so far as she is physically weaker, and the man's nature stronger. – So it seems.

Such women must then be chosen along with such men to b

live with them and share their guardianship, since they are qualified and akin to them by nature. – Certainly.

Must we not assign the same pursuits to the same natures? – The same.

We have come round then to what we said before, and we agree that it is not against nature to give to the wives of the guardians an education in the arts and physical culture. – Definitely not.

We are not legislating against nature or indulging in mere
c wishful thinking since the law we established is in accord with nature. It is rather the contrary present practice which is against nature as it seems. – It appears so.

Now we were to examine whether our proposals were possible and the best. – We were.

That they are possible is now agreed? – Yes.

After this we must seek agreement whether they are the best. – Clearly.

With a view to having women guardians, we should not have one kind of education to fashion the men, and another
d for the women, especially as they have the same nature to begin with. – No, not another.

What is your opinion of this kind of thing? – Of what?

About thinking to yourself that one man is better and another worse, or do you think that they are all alike? – Certainly not.

In the city we were establishing, do you think the guardians are made better men by the education they have received, or the cobblers who were educated for their craft? – Your question is ridiculous.

e I know, said I. Well, are these guardians not the best of all the citizens? – By far.

Will then these women guardians not be the best of women? – That too by far.

Is there anything better for a city than to have the best possible men and women? – Nothing.

457 And it is the arts and physical culture, as we have described them, which will achieve this? – Of course.

So the institution we have established is not only possible but also the best. – That is so.

The women then must strip for their physical training, since they will be clothed in excellence. They must share in war and the other duties of the guardians about the city, and have no other occupation; the lighter duties will be assigned to them because of the weakness of their sex. The man
b who laughs at the sight of naked women exercising for the

best of reasons is "plucking the unripe fruit of laughter," he understands nothing of what he is laughing at, it seems, nor what he is doing. For it is and always will be a fine saying that what is beneficial is beautiful, what is harmful is ugly. – Very definitely.

Let us say then that we have escaped from one wave of criticism in our discussion of the law about women, and we have not been altogether swamped when we laid it down
that male and female guardians must share all their duties in c
common, and our argument is consistent when it states that this is both possible and beneficial. – It is, he said, certainly no small wave from which you are escaping.

You will not say this was a big one when you see the one that follows, I said. – Speak up, then, he said, and let me see it.

I think, I said, that the law follows from the last and those that have gone before. – What law?

All these women shall be wives in common to all the men, d
and not one of them shall live privately with any man; the children too should be held in common so that no parent shall know which is his own offspring, and no child shall know his parent.

This proposal raises far more doubts than the last, both as to its possibility and its usefulness, he said.

I do not think its usefulness will be disputed, I said, namely that it is not a great blessing to hold wives in common, and children too, provided it is possible. I think that most controversy will arise on the question of its possibility. – Both e
points, he said, will certainly be disputed.

You mean that I will have to fight a combination of arguments. I thought I could escape by running away from one of them, if you thought the proposal beneficial, and that it would only remain for me to argue its possibility. – I saw you running away, he said, but you must explain both.

Well, I said, I must take my punishment. Allow me, however, to indulge myself as if on holiday, as lazy-minded 458
people feast on their own thoughts whenever they take a walk alone. Instead of finding out how something they desire may become a reality, such people pass over that question to avoid wearying themselves by deliberating on what is possible and what is not; they assume that what they desire is available; they arrange the details and enjoy themselves thinking about all they will do when it has come to pass, thus
making a lazy mind ever lazier. I am myself at this moment b
getting soft, and I want to delay consideration of the feasi-

bility of our proposal until later. I will assume that it is feasible and examine, if you will allow me, how the rulers will arrange these things when they happen and I will argue that this will be most beneficial to the city and to the guardians. This I will try to examine along with you, and deal with the other question later, if you permit. – I permit it, he said, carry on with your examination.

I think that surely our rulers, if indeed they are worthy
c of the name, and their auxiliaries as well, will be willing,
the latter to do what they are told, the former to give the orders, in part by obeying the laws themselves, and in part, in such matters as we have entrusted to them, by imitating these laws. – That is likely.

You then, as their lawgiver, just as you chose the men, will in the same manner choose the women and provide as far as possible those of the same nature. Since they have their dwellings and meals together and none of them possess any-
d thing of the kind as private property, they will be together
and mix together both in the gymnasia and in the rest of their education and they will, I think, be driven by inborn necessity to have intercourse with one another. Or do you not think that what I say will of necessity happen?

The necessity is not of a mathematical but of an erotic kind, he said, and this is probably stronger in persuading and compelling the mass of the people.

Yes indeed, I said. The next point is, Glaucon, that promiscuity is impious in a city of fortunate people, nor will the
e rules allow it. – It is not right.

After this we must obviously make marriage as sacred as possible, and sacred marriages will be those which are the most beneficial. – Most certainly.

459 How then will they be most beneficial? Tell me, Glaucon:
I see that at home you have hunting dogs and quite a number of pedigree birds. Did you then, by Zeus, pay any attention to their unions and breeding? – In what way? he asked.

In the first place, though they are all of good stock, are there not some who are and prove themselves to be best? – There are.

Do you breed equally from them all, or are you anxious to breed most from the best? – From the best.

b Further, do you breed from the youngest, or from the
oldest, or from those in their prime? – From those in their prime.

And do you think that if they were not bred in this way, your stock of birds and dogs would deteriorate considerably? – I do.

Do you think things are any different in the case of horses
and the other animals? – That would indeed be absurd.

Good gracious, my friend, I said, how great is our need for
extremely able rulers if the same is true for the human race. – c
It is, but what about it?

Because they will need to use a good many drugs. For people who do not need drugs but are willing to follow a diet
even an inferior physician will be sufficient, but when drugs
are needed, we know that a bolder physician is required. –
True, but what do you have in mind?

This, I said: our rulers will probably have to make con-
siderable use of lies and deceit for the good of their subjects. d
We said that all such things are useful as a kind of drug. –
And rightly so.

This "rightly" will occur frequently in matters of marriage
and the bearing of children. – How so?

It follows from our previous agreement that the best men
must have intercourse with the best women as frequently as
possible, and the opposite is true of the very inferior men and
women; the offspring of the former must be reared, but not e
the offspring of the latter, if our herd is to be of the highest
possible quality. Only the rulers should know of these arrangements, if our herd of guardians is to avoid all dissension as far as possible. – Quite right.

Therefore certain festivals will be established by law at
which we shall bring the brides and grooms together; there 460
will also be sacrifices, and our poets must compose hymns to
celebrate the marriages. The number of marriages we shall
leave to the rulers to decide, in such a way as to keep the
number of males as stable as possible, taking into account
war, disease, and similar factors so that our city shall, as far
as possible, become neither too big nor too small. – Right.

There will have to be some clever lots introduced, so that
at each marriage celebration the inferior man we mentioned
will blame chance but not the rulers. – Quite so.

The young men who have distinguished themselves in war b
or in other ways must be given awards consisting of other
prizes and also more abundant permission to sleep with
women, so that we may have a good excuse to have as many
children as possible begotten by them. – Right.

As the children are born, officials appointed for the purpose – be they men or women or both, since our offices are
open to both women and men – will take them. – Yes.

The children of good parents they will take to a rearing c
pen in the care of nurses living apart in a certain section of
the city; the children of inferior parents, or any child of the

others born defective, they will hide, as is fitting, in a secret and unknown place. — Yes, he said, if the breed of the guardians is to remain pure.

The nurses will also see to it that the mothers are brought
d to the rearing pen when their breasts have milk, but take
every precaution that no mother shall know her own child;
they will provide wet nurses if the number of mothers is insufficient; they will take care that the mothers suckle the children for only a reasonable time; the care of sleepless children and all other troublesome duties will belong to the wet nurses and other attendants.

You are making it very easy, he said, for the wives of the guardians to have children.

And that is fitting, I said. Let us take up the next point of our proposal: We said that the children's parents should be in their prime. — True.

e Do you agree that a reasonable interpretation of this is
twenty years for a woman and thirty years for a man? — Which years?

A woman, I said, is to bear children for the state from the
age of twenty to the age of forty, a man after he has passed
461 "his peak as a racer" begets children for the state till he
reaches fifty. — This, he said, is the physical and mental peak for both.

If a man either younger or older than this meddles with procreation for the state, we shall declare his offence to be neither pious nor right as he begets for the city a child which, if he remains secret, will be born without benefit of the sacrifices and prayers which priests and priestesses and the whole city utter at every marriage festival, that the children of good
and useful parents may always prove themselves better and
b more useful; but this child is born in darkness, the result of
dangerous incontinence. — Right.

The same law will apply, I said, if a man still of begetting years unites with a woman of child-bearing age without the sanction of the rulers; we shall say that he brings to the city an unauthorized and unhallowed bastard. — Quite right.

However, I think that when women and men have passed
c the age of having children, we shall leave them free to have
intercourse with anyone they wish, with these exceptions: for a man, his daughter or mother, or the daughter's daughters, or his mother's female progenitors; for a woman, a son or father, their male issue or progenitors. Having received these instructions they should be very careful not to bring a single child into the light, but if one should be conceived, and forces

its way to the light, they must deal with it knowing that no
nurture is available for it.

This too, he said, is sensibly spoken, but how shall they
know their fathers and daughters and those other relation- d
ships you mentioned?

They have no means of knowing, I said, but all the children
who are born in the tenth and seventh month after a man
became a bridegroom he will call sons if they are male,
daughters if they are female, and they will call him father,
and so too he will call their offspring his grandchildren who
in turn will call the first group their grandfathers and grandmothers. Those born during the time when their fathers and
mothers were having children they will call their brothers
and sisters, so that, as I said, these groups will have no sexual
relations with each other. But the law will allow brothers and e
sisters to live together if the lot so falls and the Pythian ap-
proves. – Quite right.

This then is the holding in common of wives and children
for the guardians of your city. We must now confirm in our
argument that it conforms with the rest of our constitution 462
and is by far the best. Or how are we to proceed? – In that
way, by Zeus.

Is not the first step towards agreement to ask ourselves
what we say is the greatest good in the management of the
city? At this the lawgiver must aim in making his laws. Also
what is the greatest evil. Then we should examine whether
the system we have just described follows the tracks of the
good and not those of evil. – By all means.

Is there any greater evil we can mention for a city than
whatever tears it apart into many communities instead of b
one? – There is not.

Do not common feelings of pleasure and pain bind the
city together, when as nearly as possible all the citizens
equally rejoice or feel pain at the same successes and failures? – Most certainly.

For such feelings to be isolated and private dissolves the
city's unity, when some suffer greatly while others greatly c
rejoice at the same public or private events. – Of course.

And that sort of thing happens whenever such words as
"mine" and "not mine" – and so with "another's" – are not
used in unison. – Most certainly.

And the city which most closely resembles the individual?
When one of us hurts his finger, the whole organism which
binds body and soul together into the unitary system managed by the ruling part of it shares the pain at once through-

d out when one part suffers. This is why we say that the man has a pain in his finger, and the same can be said of any part of the man, both about the pain which any part suffers, and its pleasure when it finds relief.

Certainly, he said. As for your question, the best managed city certainly closely resembles such an organism.

And whenever anything good or bad happens to a single
e one of its citizens, such a city will certainly say that this citizen is a part of itself, and the whole city will rejoice or suffer with him. – That must be so, if it has good laws.

It is time now, I said, for us to return to our own city and to look there for the features we have agreed on, whether it, or any other city, possesses them to the greatest degree. – We must do so.

463 Well then. There are rulers and people in the other cities as well as in this one? – There are.

And they call each other fellow-citizens. – Of course.

Besides the word fellow-citizens, what do the people call the rulers in the other cities?

In many they call them masters, but in democracies they call them by this very name, rulers.

What do the people call them in our city? Besides fellow-
b citizens, what do they call the rulers? – Saviors and helpers.

And what do the rulers call the people? – Providers of food and wages.

What do the rulers call the people in other cities? – Slaves.

And what do the rulers call each other? – Fellow rulers.

And ours? – Fellow guardians.

Can you tell me whether a ruler in the other cities might address one of his fellow rulers as his kinsman and another as an outsider? – Certainly, many could.

He then considers his kinsman, and addresses him, as his
c own, but not the outsider? – That is so.

What about your guardians? Can any of them consider any other of his fellow guardians an outsider and address him as such?

Not in any way, he said, for when he meets any one of them he will think he is meeting a brother or a sister, a father or a mother, a son or a daughter, their offspring or progenitors.

You put that very well, I said, but, further, tell me this:
d will you legislate these family relationships as names only, or must they act accordingly in all they do? Must a man show to his fathers the respect, solicitude, and obedience to his parents required by law? Otherwise, if he acts differently, he will fare worse at the hands of gods and men as one whose actions are neither pious nor just. Will these be the sayings

that ring in his ears on the part of all citizens from childhood both about their fathers, those pointed out to them as such, and about their other kindred – or will there be other voices?

It will be those, he said; it would be absurd if their lips e
spoke these names of kindred without appropriate action
following.

So in our city more than any other, when any individual fares well or badly, they would all speak in unison the words we mentioned just now, namely that "mine" is doing well, or "mine" is doing badly. – That also is very true.

And we said that such a belief and its expression are fol- 464
lowed by common feelings of pleasure and pain. – And we
were right.

So our citizens will to the greatest extent share the same thing which they call "mine," with the result that they in highest degree share common feelings of pleasure and pain. – Surely.

And besides other arrangements, the reason for this is the holding of wives and children in common among the guardians. – More than anything else.

This we agreed was the greatest blessing for a city, and we b
compared a well run city to the body's reaction to pain or
pleasure in any part of it. – And we were right to agree
on that.

So then the cause of the greatest good for our city has been shown to be the common ownership of wives and children among the auxiliaries. – Certainly.

And in this we are consistent with what went before, for
we said somewhere that they must have no private houses
or land or any private possessions, that they receive their
upkeep from the other citizens as a wage for their guardian- c
ship, and that they must all spend it in common, if they are
to be real guardians. – Right.

Does now what we said before and what we are saying
now make them even more real guardians, and prevent them
from tearing the city apart by not calling the same thing
"mine," one man applying the word to one thing and another
to another? One man would then drag into his own house d
whatever he could get hold of away from the others; another
drag things into his different house to another wife and other
children. This would make for private pleasures and pains at
private events. Our people, on the other hand, will think of
the same thing as their own, aim at the same goal, and, as far
as possible, feel pleasure and pain in unison. – Most certainly.

What follows? Will not lawsuits and mutual accusations disappear from among them, one might say, since they own e nothing but their body, everything else being held in common? Hence they will be spared all the dissension which is due to the possession of wealth, children, and families? – They will inevitably be spared them.

Nor could cases of violence or assault rightly occur among them, for we shall declare that it is a fine and just thing to defend oneself against those of the same age, thus compelling them to keep in good physical condition. – Right.

465 The law is right in this also, that if an angry man satisfied his anger in a personal encounter of this kind, he is less likely to turn to more important quarrels. – Certainly.

An older man will have authority over all the young, and be allowed to chastise them. – Obviously.

It is surely also obvious that a younger man, except by order of the rulers, shall not apply violence of any kind to, nor strike, an older man, nor fail to respect him in other ways. There are two adequate guardians to prevent this, namely shame and fear; shame will prevent him laying hands on his
b parents, fear because the others will come to the rescue of the victim, some as his sons, some as his brothers, and some as his fathers. – That follows, he said.

So the laws will induce people to live at peace with each other. – Very much so.

And if there is no discord among the guardians there is no danger that the rest of the city will start factions against them or among themselves. – No danger.

c I hesitate to mention the petty evils they will escape: the poor man's flattery of the rich, the perplexities and sufferings involved in bringing up children and in making the necessary money to feed the household, sometimes borrowing, sometimes denying the debt, in one way or another providing enough money to hand over to their wives and household slaves to dispense; all the various troubles which men endure
d in these matters are quite obvious and sordid and not worth discussing. – They are clear even to the blind.

They will be free of all these, and they will live a life more blessed than that of Olympian victors. – How?

Olympian victors are considered happy on account of only a small part of the blessings available to our guardians, whose victory is even finer and their upkeep from public funds more complete. The victory they gain is the safety of the whole city and the victor's crown they and their children receive is their nurture and all the necessities of life; they
e receive rewards from their own city while they live, and at their death they are given a worthy funeral. – Certainly fine rewards.

Remember, said I, that earlier in our discussion someone –
I forget who – shocked us by saying that we did not make
our guardians happy, that while it was in their power to own
all the possessions of our citizens, yet they possessed nothing.
We said at the time that we would investigate later whether 466
this would happen, but that our concern at the time was to
make our guardians true guardians and the city as happy as
we could, and that we would not concentrate our attention
upon one group and make them happy in our city. – I remember.

Well now, if the life of the auxiliaries is indeed much finer
and better than that of Olympian victors, it is not to be compared to that of the cobblers or other craftsmen, or with that b
of the farmers? – I do not think so.

It is surely right to repeat here what I said then, that, if a
guardian seeks happiness in such a way as not even to be a
guardian nor to be satisfied with a life so stable and moderate
and, as we maintain, so much the best; if a silly and youthful
idea of happiness should come into his mind and set him off
to use his power to appropriate everything in the city as his
own, he will realize the true wisdom of Hesiod's saying that c
somehow "the half is more than the whole."

If he takes my advice, he said, he will stay with this kind of life.

You agree then, I said, that the women should be associated
with the men in the way we have described in matters of
education and child bearing, and in the guarding of the other
citizens. Both when they remain in the city and when they d
go to war they must share the guardians' duties, hunt with
them like hounds, share as far as possible in everything in
every way. In doing so they will be acting for the best, and in
no way contrary to woman's nature as compared with man's,
as they were born to associate with one another. – I agree.

It now remains, I said, for us to determine whether this association can be brought about among human beings as it can among animals, and how it can be brought about. – You took the words out of my mouth.

As far as war is concerned, I said, the way they will wage e
it is clear, I think. – How so?

Men and women will campaign together; moreover they
will take the sturdy among their children with them, in order
that, like the children of other craftsmen, they may observe
the actions which they will perform when they grow up. 467
Moreover, in addition to observing these, they can assist and
help in all the duties of war and attend upon their fathers and
mothers. Have you not noticed in the other crafts how the

children of potters for example assist and observe for a long time before they engage in making pots? — Yes indeed.

Should those craftsmen take more care than the guardians in training their children by suitable experience and observation? — That would be quite ridiculous.

b Besides, every living creature will fight better in the presence of its young. — That is true, but, Socrates, there is a considerable danger that, if they are defeated, as happens frequently in war, they will lose their children's lives as well as their own, thus making it impossible for the rest of the city to recover.

* * *

ARISTOTLE

Although his philosophy rests on the principles of logic which he developed and elaborated, Aristotle (384–322 B.C.), in contrast to his teacher Plato, is decidedly empiricist in his approach to knowledge. All things in nature, Aristotle asserts, act toward an end. Changes or motion in the physical world are explained through the principles of act and potency, and in individual existents these principles emerge as matter and form. Neither can exist separately; matter is a principle of individuation, and form a principle of intelligibility.

In living things, the form is soul, which Aristotle defines as "principle of life." Plants possess a vegetative soul which enables them to grow and reproduce; animals possess a sentient soul which enables them to propel themselves and respond to sense stimuli. In the Aristotelian hierarchy of souls, the higher organism subsumes capabilities of the lower organism, so that animals also grow and reproduce, and human beings fulfill vegetative and animal (as well as human) functions.

What makes a human being human, according to Aristotle, is his or her rational soul, the basis for faculties of intellect and will. As rational animals, human beings fulfill their nature, or act according to their proper end, to the extent that they exercise their reason and volition. Knowledge is acquired through a process of conceptualization, or abstraction of a universal essence from a multiplicity of sense experiences. Thus knowledge depends upon, but is not identical with, experience. Concepts are universal and immaterial; the objects of knowledge are individual and material. Since we only know forms, there is an inevitable gap between our knowledge of existent things and the things themselves.

The will, or rational appetite, inclines us to embrace an apprehended good. Where good is obtained, the result is happiness. On ethical as well as political levels, human beings act in pursuit of happiness. The universal good, which has priority over any merely individual good, produces some degree of happiness or satisfaction for everyone, since it applies to all individuals.

Human beings are also political animals. Their natural social interactions, according to Aristotle, arise from love of the useful, the pleasant, and the good. "Perfect friendship," Aristotle maintains, "is the friendship of men who are good, and alike in virtue; for these wish well alike to each other *qua* good, and they are good in themselves." While such friendships evoke pleasure without seeking it, they occur but rarely because "such men are rare," and there must be equality between the friends.

On the Generation of Animals

We may safely set down as the chief principles of generation the male [factor] and the female [factor]; the male as possessing the principle of movement and of generation, the female as possessing that of matter. One is most likely to be convinced of this by considering how the semen is formed and whence it comes; for although the things that are formed in the course of Nature no doubt take their rise out of semen, we must not fail to notice how the semen itself is formed from the male and the female, since it is because this part is secreted from the male and the female, and because its secretion takes place in them and out of them, that the male and the female are the principles of generation. By a "male" animal we mean one which generates in another, by "female" one which generates in itself. This is why in cosmology too they speak of the nature of the Earth as something female and call it "mother," while they give to the heaven and the sun and anything else of that kind the title of "generator," and "father."

Now male and female differ in respect of their *logos*, in that the power or faculty possessed by the one differs from that possessed by the other; but they differ also in bodily sense, in respect of certain physical parts. They differ in their *logos*, because the male is that which has the power to generate in another (as was stated above), while the female is that which can generate in itself, *i.e.*, it is that out of which the generated offspring, which is present in the generator, comes into being. Very well, then: they are distinguished in respect of their faculty, and this entails a certain function. Now for the exercise of every function instruments are needed, and the instruments for physical faculties are the parts of the body. Hence it is necessary that, for the purpose of copulation and procreation, certain parts should exist, parts that are different from each other, in respect of which the male will differ from the female; for although male and female are indeed used as epithets of the whole of the animal, it is not male or female in respect of the whole of itself, but only in respect of a particular faculty and a particular part—just as it is "seeing" and "walking" in respect of certain parts—and this part is one which is evident to the senses. . . .

. . . A woman is as it were an infertile male; the female, in fact, is female on account of inability of a sort, viz., it lacks the power to concoct semen out of the final state of the nourishment (this is either blood, or its counterpart in bloodless animals) because of the coldness of its nature. . . .

. . . The female, though it does not contribute any semen to generation, yet contributes something, viz., the substance constituting the menstrual fluid. But the same is apparent if we consider the matter generally, from the theoretical standpoint. Thus: there must be that which generates, and that out of which it generates; and even if these two be united in one, at any rate they must differ in kind, and in that the *logos* of each of them is distinct. In those animals in which these two faculties are separate, the body—that is to say the physical nature—of the active partner and of the passive must be different. Thus, if the male is the active partner, the one which originates the movement, and the female *qua* female is the passive one, surely what the female contributes to the semen of the male will be not semen but material. And this is in fact what we find happening; for the natural substance of the menstrual fluid is to be classed as "prime matter." . . .

. . . As for the reason why one comes to be formed, and is, male, and another female (*a*) in so far as this results from *necessity, i.e.*, from the proximate motive cause and from what sort of matter, our argument as it proceeds must endeavour to explain; (*b*) in so far as this occurs on account of what is *better, i.e.*, on account of the final cause (the Cause "for the sake of which"), the principle is derived from the upper cosmos. What I mean is this. Of the things which are, some are eternal and divine, others admit alike of being and not-being, and the beautiful and the divine acts always, in virtue of its own nature, as a cause which produces that which is *better* in the things which admit of it; while that which is not eternal admits of being [and not-being], and of acquiring a share both in the better and in the worse; also, Soul is better than body, and a thing which has Soul in it is better than one which has not, in virtue of that Soul; and being is better than not-being, and living than not living. These are the causes on account of which generation of animals takes place, because since the nature of a class of this sort is unable to be eternal, that which comes into being is eternal in the manner that is open to it. Now it is impossible for it to be so *numerically*, since the "being" of things is to be found in the particular, and if it really were so, then it would be eternal; it is, however, open to it to be so *specifically*. That is why there is always a *class* of men, of animals, of plants; and since the principle of these is "the male" and "the female," it will surely be for the sake of generation that "the male" and "the female" are present in the individuals which are male and female. And as the proximate motive cause, to which belong the *logos* and the Form, is *better* and more divine in its nature than the Matter, it is *better* also that the superior one should be separate from the inferior one. That is why wherever possible and so far as possible the male is separate from the female, since it is something *better* and more divine in that it is the principle of movement for generated things, while the female serves as their matter. The male, however, comes together with the female and mingles with it for the business of generation, because this is something that concerns both of them. . . .

. . . Just as it sometimes happens that deformed offspring are produced by deformed parents, and sometimes not, so the offspring produced by a female are sometimes female, sometimes not, but male. The reason is that the female is as it were a deformed male; and the menstrual discharge is semen, though in an impure condition; *i.e.*, it lacks one constituent, and one only, the principle of Soul. . . . This principle has to be supplied by the semen of the male, and it is when the female's residue secures this principle that a fetation is formed. . . .

. . . Why does this generative residue, then, not occur in all males, although it occurs in all females? The answer is that an animal is a living body, a body with Soul in it. The female always provides the material, the male provides that which fashions the material into shape; this, in our view, is the specific characteristic of each of the sexes: that is what it means to be male or to be female. Hence, necessity requires that the female should provide the physical part, *i.e.*, a quantity of material, but not that the male should do so, since necessity does not require that the tools should reside in the product that is being made, nor that the agent which uses them should do so. Thus the physical part, the body, comes from the female, and the Soul from the male, since the Soul is the essence of a particular body. . . .

. . . The male and the female are distinguished by a certain ability and inability. Male is that which is able to concoct, to cause to take shape, and to discharge, semen possessing the "principle" of the "form"; and by "principle" I do not mean that sort of principle out of which, as out of matter, an offspring is formed belonging to the same kind as its parent, but I mean the *first motive principle*, whether it is able to act thus in itself or in something else. Female is that which receives the semen, but is unable to cause semen to take shape or to discharge it. And all concoction works by means of heat. Assuming the truth of these two statements, it follows of necessity that male animals are hotter than female ones, since it is on account of coldness and inability that the female is more abundant in blood in certain regions of the body. . . .

Now as the one sex is able and the other is unable to secrete the residue in a pure condition; and as there is an instrument for every ability or faculty, for the one which yields its product in a more finished condition and for the one which yields the same product in a less finished condition; and as male and female stand opposed in this way ("able" and "unable" being used in more senses than one); therefore of necessity there must be an instrument both for the male and for the female; hence the male has the *perineos* and the female has the uterus. Nature gives each one its instrument simultaneously with its ability, since it is *better* done thus. Hence each of these regions of the body gets formed simultaneously with the corresponding secretions and abilities, just as the ability to see does not get perfected without eyes, nor the eye without the ability to see, and just as the gut and the bladder are perfected simultaneously with the ability to form the residues. Now as the stuff out of which the parts are formed is the same as that from which they derive their growth, namely the nourishment, we should expect each of the parts to be formed out of that sort of material and that sort of residue which it is fitted to receive. Secondly, and on the contrary, it is, as we hold, formed in a way out of its opposite. Thirdly, in addition, it must be laid down that, assuming the extinction of a thing means its passing into its opposite condition, then also that which does not get mastered by the agent which is fashioning it must of necessity change over into its opposite condition. With these as our premises it may perhaps be clearer why and by what cause one offspring becomes male and another female. It is this. When the "principle" is failing to gain the mastery and is unable to effect concoction owing to deficiency of heat, and does not succeed in reducing the material into its own proper form, but instead is worsted in the attempt, then of necessity the material must change over into its opposite condition. Now the opposite of the male is the female, and it is opposite in respect of that whereby one is male and the other female. And since it differs in the ability it possesses, so also it differs in the instrument which it possesses. Hence this is the condition into which the material changes over. And when one vital part changes, the whole make-up of the animal differs greatly in appearance and form. This may be observed in the case of eunuchs; the mutilation of just one part of them results in such a great alteration of their old semblance, and in close approximation to the appearance of the female. The reason for this is that some of the body's parts are "principles" and once a principle has been "moved" (*i.e.*, changed), many of the parts which cohere with it must of necessity change as well.

Let us assume then (1) that "the male" is a principle and is causal in its nature; (2) that a male is male in virtue of a particular ability, and a female in virtue of a particular inability; (3) that the line of determination between the ability and the inability is whether a thing effects or does not effect concoction of the ultimate nourishment; (4) that the reason for this lies in the "principle," *i.e.*, in the part of the body which possesses the principle of the natural heat. From this it follows of necessity that, in the blooded animals, a heart must take shape and that the creature formed is to be either male or female, and, in the other kinds which have male and female sexes, the counterpart of the heart. As far, then, as the principle and the cause of male and female is concerned, this is what it is and where it is situated; a creature, however, really is male or female only from the time when it has got the parts by which female differs from male, because it is not in virtue of some casual part that it is male or female, any more than it is in virtue of some casual part that it can see or hear.

To resume then: We repeat that semen has been posited to be the ultimate residue of the nourishment. (By "ultimate" I mean that which gets carried to each part of the body—and that too is why the offspring begotten takes after the parent which has begotten it, since it comes to exactly the same thing whether we speak of being drawn from every one of the parts or passing into every one of the parts, though the latter is more correct.) The semen of the male, however, exhibits a difference, inasmuch as the male possesses in itself a principle of such a kind as to set up movement [in the animal as well] and thoroughly to concoct the ultimate nourishment, whereas the female's semen contains material only. If [the male semen] gains the mastery, it brings [the material] over to itself; but if it gets mastered, it changes over either into its opposite or else into extinction. And the opposite of the male is the female, which is female in virtue of its inability to effect concoction, and of the coldness of its bloodlike nourishment. And Nature assigns to each of the residues the part which is fitted to receive it. Now the semen is a residue, and in the hotter of the blooded animals, *i.e.*, the males, this is manageable in size and amount, and therefore in males the parts which receive this residual product are passages; in females, however, on account of their failure to effect concoction, this residue is a considerable volume of bloodlike substance, because it has not been matured; hence there must of necessity be here too some part fitted to receive it, different from that in the male, and of a fair size. That is why the uterus has these characteristics; and that is the part wherein the female differs from the male. . . .

In human beings, more males are born deformed than females; in other animals, there is no preponderance either way. The reason is that in human beings the male is much hotter in its nature than the female. On that account male embryos tend to move about more than female ones, and owing to their moving about they get broken more, since a young creature can easily be destroyed owing to its weakness. And it is due to this self-same cause that the perfecting of female embryos is inferior to that of male ones, [since their uterus is inferior in condition. In other animals, however, the perfecting of female embryos is not inferior to that of male ones: they are not any later in developing than the males, as they *are* in women], for while still within the mother, the female takes longer to develop than the male does; though once birth has taken place everything reaches its perfection sooner in females than in males—*e.g.*, puberty, maturity, old age—because females are weaker and colder in their nature; and we should look upon the female state as being as it were a deformity, though one which occurs in the ordinary course of nature. While it is within the mother, then, it develops slowly on account of its coldness, since development is a sort of concoction, concoction is effected by heat, and if a thing is hotter its concoction is easy; when, however, it is free from the mother, on account of its weakness it quickly approaches its maturity and old age, since inferior things all reach their end more quickly, and this applies to those which take their shape under the hand of Nature just as much as to the products of the arts and crafts. The reason which I have just stated accounts also for the fact that (a) in human beings twins survive less well if one is male and the other female, but (b) in other animals they survive just as well: in human beings it is contrary to nature for the two sexes to keep pace with each other, male and female requiring unequal periods for their development to take place; the male is bound to be late or the female early; whereas in the other animals equal speed is not contrary to nature. There is also a difference between human beings and the other animals with regard to gestation. Other animals are most of the time in better physical condition, whereas the majority of women suffer discomfort in connexion with gestation. Now the cause of this is to some extent attributable to their manner of life, which is sedentary, and this means that they are full of residue; they have more of it than the other animals. This is borne out by the case of those tribes where the women live a life of hard work. With such women gestation is not so obvious, and they find delivery an easy business. And so do women everywhere who are used to hard work. The reason is that the effort of working uses up the residues, whereas sedentary women have a great deal of such matter in their bodies owing to the absence of effort, as well as to the cessation of the menstrual discharges during gestation, and they find the pains of delivery severe. Hard work, on the other hand, gives the breath (*pneuma*) exercise, so that they can hold it; and it is this which determines whether delivery is easy or difficult. . . .

* * *

Politics

It is by examining things in their growth from the very beginning that we shall in this, as in other matters, obtain the clearest view. Now, it is necessary, in the first place, to group in couples those elements that cannot exist without each other, such as the female and male united for the sake of reproduction of species (and this union does not come from the deliberate action of the will, but in them, as in the other animals and plants, the desire to leave behind such another as themselves is implanted by nature), and also that which naturally rules, and that which naturally is ruled, connected for the sake of security. For that which has the capacity, in virtue of its intelligence, of looking forward is by nature the ruling and master element, while that which has the capacity, in virtue of its body, of carrying out this will of the superior is the subject and slave by nature. And for this reason the interests of the master and the slave are identical. Now it is by *nature* that the woman and the slave have been marked as separate, for nature produces nothing in a niggard fashion . . . but she makes each individual thing for one end; for it is only thus that each instrument will receive its most perfect development, namely, by subserving not many functions, but one. But among the barbarians the female and slave have the same position as the man; and the reason is that these nations do not possess the naturally ruling element, but, instead, their association becomes that of slave-woman and slave-man: and on this account the poets say, 'It is proper that Greeks should rule over barbarians,' implying that the ideas of barbarian and slave are by nature the same. So from these two forms of association comes the *Family* in its original form. . . .

. . . Every state is composed of Households, and the parts of the Household are those elements of which the household in its turn consists. Now the Household, when complete, consists of slaves and free persons. . . .

There have been seen to be three elements of household government, the first being the rule of the master over slaves, of which we have spoken before, the second that of the father over children, and the third that of the husband over the wife; for to rule both his wife and his children as beings equally free, but not with the same character of rule. His rule over the wife is like that of a magistrate in a free state, over his children it is like that of a king. For both the male is naturally more qualified to lead than the female, unless where some unnatural case occurs, and also the older and more perfect than the younger and imperfect. Now in the government of free states in most cases the positions of ruler and ruled alternate, for there is a tendency that all should be naturally equal and differ in no respect; but, nevertheless, whenever one party rules and the other is ruled, there is a wish that there should be some difference made in garb, titles, honours. . . . But the relation of the male to the female is always of this character and unchanged. But the rule over the children is the rule of a king, for the father is ruler both through affection and seniority, and this is the character of a king's rule; and for this reason Homer was right in addressing Zeus as 'Father of Gods and Men'—Zeus the king of all these. For a king should differ in nature from his subjects, but be still the same in kind; and this is the relation of the elder to the younger, the father to the child.

It is clear, therefore, that the earnest attention of household management is more concerned with living men than with the acquisition of inanimate objects—with the excellence of the former rather than with that of property, to which we give the name of wealth—with the excellence of freemen rather than with that of slaves. Now, in the first place, some one may raise a difficulty with regard to slaves: whether a slave has any excellence beyond that of an instrument and an agent; any other more valuable than these, such as Temperance, Courage, Justice, and any of the other dispositions of that sort; or whether he has none at all beyond bodily services. There is a difficulty either way. For if slaves have such excellence, in what will they differ from freemen? and yet to say that they are not, if they are men with a share of reason, is absurd. The question is very nearly the same in the case of women and children, as to whether they too have excellences, and if a woman ought to be temperate and courageous and just, and if a child is utterly intemperate or wisely temperate or not. And to speak generally, we have now this consideration before us with regard to the natural subject and the natural ruler, have they the same excellence or a distinct kind? For if both ought to share in nobleness of character, why, once and for ever, should one be ruler and the other be subject? for it cannot be that they differ in the matter of greatness or less (i.e., of degree), for to be ruled and to rule differ in kind, but the greater and the less do not. On the other hand, if one ought to possess this nobleness, while the other ought not, it is a strange state of things. For if, on the one hand, the ruler is not to be temperate and just, how is he to be a good ruler? if, on the other, the subject (is to lack these qualities), how is he to be a good subject? For being, according to our supposition, utterly intemperate and cowardly, he will do none of those things that he should do. It is obvious, then, that while it is necessary for both parties to have their share of excellence, there must still be different kinds of excellence, just as there are also different kinds of those who are naturally subject to rule. And this has led us directly to the consideration of the Soul: for in the soul there is by nature an element that rules and also an element that is ruled; and in these we recognise distinction of excellence—the excellence, to wit, of that which possesses reason, and the excellence of that which lacks it. It is clear, then, that the same rule holds good in the other cases also, so that most things in the world are rulers or ruled by Nature's direction. For in different method does the free element rule the slave, the male the female, the man the child; and while in all of these are there present their separate shares of soul, these are present in each in a different manner. For the slave, speaking generally, has not the deliberative faculty, but the woman has it, though without power to be effective; the child has it, but in an imperfect degree. Similarly, then, must it necessarily be with regard to the moral virtues also. We must suppose that all ought to have some share in them, though not in the same way, but only so far as each requires for the fulfillment of his own function. Therefore the ruler should have moral excellence in its perfect form (for his function is strictly that of the master builder, and *reason* is the master builder), and each of the rest (the subordinates) should have just as much as falls to him. And so it is clear that moral excellence belongs to all the classes we have mentioned: and yet the same kind of temperance does not belong to woman and man, nor the same courage and justice (as Socrates thought), but the one is the courage of the ruler, the other the courage of the subject. And similarly with the other virtues. . . .

. . . Since every household is part of a state, . . . it is necessary that we should have our eye on the constitution in educating our children and wives; if so be that it is of importance towards the State being good that both the children should be good and the women good; and important it must necessarily be. For women are half the free population; and it is from children that grow the members of the constitution.

* * *

THE BIBLE

Most Scripture scholars concur that there are several authors for the Book of Genesis, and the selection below supports that judgment; for example, Chapters 1 and 2 present two different accounts of creation, and Chapters 4 and 5 provide differing genealogies. The Song of Songs is a series of love poems generally attributed to King Solomon.

The letters of Paul are primarily his response to particular situations in particular communities that he had converted to Christianity. One problem among the Corinthian Christians with which Paul was concerned was sexual immorality; Chapter 7 of his first letter to them forms a part of his response to that problem. Another issue was that of authority, both at home and at worship; Chapter 11 (below) gives Paul's advice on the question of authority in the husband/wife relationship. Although scholars do not all agree that the Letter to the Ephesians was authored by Paul, its content as here excerpted is basically in accord with Paul's sentiments in I Cor. 11.

To appreciate biblical conceptions of woman, man, and human nature, we need to be aware of the religious presuppositions that underlie these concepts. One such presupposition is the doctrine of creation, which maintains that all things owe their origin and continued existence to God. While this belief is also logically tenable for one who believes in biological evolution, it involves a confession that existence is ultimately contingent, that is, dependent upon a supreme being. In contrast with the Platonic tradition, the notion of creation implies a positive regard for the physical world, as the work of a Creator who "saw that it was good" (Gen. 1:25).

A second presupposition or belief is humankind's need for and hope of being saved. Leaving aside the question of what constitutes salvation, the "need" and "hope" are paradoxical aspects—the first involving an admission of human limitation, the second an expectation that the limitation is overcome through divine redemption. In this context human freedom is restricted from within through natural limitations and from without through ultimate dependence on God.

The selections from the Old Testament represent contrasting views of human sexuality. In Genesis, God's punishment to Eve, the prototypical woman, is her sexual desire for man, her domination by him, and the pain of childbirth. The Song of Solomon, on the other hand, extols the joy and beauty of sexual love, depicting both bride and bridegroom as aggressive, passionate lovers. The husband/wife relationship, as here described, is usually seen as an allegory for the relationship between God and Israel, or (for Christians) between Christ and the Church. Paul's letter to the Ephesians also employs this allegory, advising husbands to love their wives as Christ loved the Church.

That the human body is to be regarded with particular reverence among the works of creation is clear from both Testaments. In Genesis, for example, we read that God created "man" in his own image and gave "him" (or "them") dominion over other creatures (Gen. 1:26). Since it is the whole person that is God's creature, one does not *have* a body, but *is* the union of soul and body. In the New Testament, the idea of respect for the body is reinforced through the doctrine of the incarnation, of God assuming flesh in Christ, who was conceived by and born of a woman. Various passages indicate that every human body is deserving of reverence; for example, Paul's reminder to the Corinthians: "Your body, you know, is the temple of the Holy Spirit: (1 Cor. 6:19). Belief in "resurrection of the body" (i.e., its reunion with the soul sometime after death) also illustrates the essential connection between body and soul.

Genesis 1–5

1 In the beginning God created the heavens and the earth. The earth was without form and void, and darkness was upon the the face of the deep; and the Spirit of God was moving over the face of the waters.

3 And God said, "Let there be light"; and there was light. And God saw that the light was good; and God separated the light from the darkness. God called the light Day, and the darkness he called Night. And there was evening and there was morning, one day.

6 And God said, "Let there be a firmament in the midst of the waters, and let it separate the waters from the waters." And God made the firmament and separated the waters which were under the firmament from the waters which were above the firmament. And it was so. And God called the firmament Heaven. And there was evening and there was morning, a second day.

9 And God said, "Let the waters under the heavens be gathered together into one place, and let the dry land appear." And it was so. God called the dry land Earth, and the waters that were gathered together he called Seas. And God saw that it was good. And God said, "Let the earth put forth vegetation, plants yielding seed, and fruit trees bearing fruit in which is their seed, each according to its kind, upon the earth." And it was so. The earth brought forth vegetation, plants yielding seed according to their own kinds, and trees bearing fruit in which is their seed, each according to

its kind. And God saw that it was good. And there was evening and there was morning, a third day.

14 And God said, "Let there be lights in the firmament of the heavens to separate the day from the night; and let them be for signs and for seasons and for days and years, and let them be lights in the firmament of the heavens to give light upon the earth." And it was so. And God made the two great lights, the greater light to rule the day, and the lesser light to rule the night; he made the stars also. And God set them in the firmament of the heavens to give light upon the earth, to rule over the day and over the night, and to separate the light from the darkness. And God saw that it was good. And there was evening and there was morning, a fourth day.

20 And God said, "Let the waters bring forth swarms of living creatures, and let birds fly above the earth across the firmament of the heavens." So God created the great sea monsters and every living creature that moves, with which the waters swarm, according to their kinds, and every winged bird according to its kind. And God saw that it was good. And God blessed them, saying, "Be fruitful and multiply and fill the waters in the seas, and let birds multiply on the earth." And there was evening and there was morning, a fifth day.

24 And God said "Let the earth bring forth living creatures according to their kinds: cattle and creeping things and beasts of the earth according to their kinds." And it was so. And God made the beasts of the earth according to their kinds and the cattle according to their kinds, and everything that creeps upon the ground according to its kind. And God saw that it was good.

26 Then God said, "Let us make man in our image, after our likeness; and let them have dominion over the fish of the sea, and over the birds of the air, and over the cattle, and over all the earth, and over every creeping thing that creeps upon the earth." So God created man in his own image, in the image of God he created him; male and female he created them. And God blessed them, and God said to them, "Be fruitful and multiply, and fill the earth and subdue it; and have dominion over the fish of the sea and over the birds of the air and over every living thing that moves upon the earth." And God said, "Behold, I have given you every plant yielding seed which is upon the face of all the earth and every tree with seed in its fruit; you shall have them for food. And to every beast of the earth, and to every bird of the air, and to everything that creeps on the earth, everything that has the breath of life, I have given every green plant for food." And it was so. And God saw everything that he had made, and behold, it was very good. And there was evening and there was morning, a sixth day.

2 Thus the heavens and the earth were finished, and all the host of them. And on the seventh day God finished his work which he had done, and he rested on the seventh day from all his work which he had done. So God blessed the seventh day and hallowed it, because on it God rested from all his work which he had done in creation.

4 These are the generations of the heavens and the earth when they were created.

In the day that the LORD God made the earth and the heavens, when no plant of the field was yet in the earth and no herb of the field had yet sprung up–for the LORD God had not caused it to rain upon the earth, and there was no man to till the ground; but a mist went up from the earth and watered the whole face of the ground—then the Lord God formed man of dust from the ground, and breathed into his nostrils the breath of life; and man became a living being. And the LORD God planted a garden in Eden, in the east, and there he put the man whom he had formed. And out of the ground the LORD God made to grow every tree that is pleasant to the sight and good for food, the tree of life also in the midst of the garden, and the tree of the knowledge of good and evil. . . .

15 The LORD God took the man and put him in the garden of Eden to till it and keep it. And the LORD God commanded the man, saying, "You may freely eat of every tree of the garden; but of the tree of the knowledge of good and evil you shall not eat, for in the day that you eat of it you shall die."

18 Then the LORD God said, "It is not good that the man should be alone; I will make him a helper fit for him." So out of the ground the LORD God formed every beast of the field and every bird of the air, and brought them to the man to see what he would call them; and whatever the man called every living creature, that was its name. The man gave names to all cattle, and to the birds of the air, and to every beast of the field; but for the man there was not found a helper fit for him. So the LORD God caused a deep sleep to fall upon the man, and while he slept took one of his ribs and closed up its place with flesh; and the rib which the LORD God had taken from the man he made into a woman and brought her to the man. Then the man said,

"This at last is bone of my bones
and flesh of my flesh;
she shall be called Woman,
because she was taken out of
Man."

Therefore a man leaves his father and his mother and cleaves to his wife, and they become one flesh. And the man and his wife were both naked, and were not ashamed.

3 Now the serpent was more subtle than any other wild creature that the LORD God had made. He said to the woman, "Did God say, 'You shall not eat of any tree of the garden'?" And

the woman said to the serpent, "We may eat of the fruit of the trees of the garden; but God said, 'You shall not eat of the fruit of the tree which is in the midst of the garden, neither shall you touch it, lest you die.'" But the serpent said to the woman, "You will not die. For God knows that when you eat of it your eyes will be opened, and you will be like God, knowing good and evil." So when the woman saw that the tree was good for food, and that it was a delight to the eyes, and that the tree was to be desired to make one wise, she took of its fruit and ate; and she also gave some to her husband, and he ate. Then the eyes of both were opened, and they knew that they were naked; and they sewed fig leaves together and made themselves aprons.

8 And they heard the sound of the LORD God walking in the garden in the cool of the day, and the man and his wife hid themselves from the presence of the LORD God among the trees of the garden. But the LORD God called to the man, and said to him, "Where are you?" And he said, "I heard the sound of thee in the garden, and I was afraid, because I was naked; and I hid myself." He said, "Who told you that you were naked? Have you eaten of the tree of which I commanded you not to eat?" The man said, "The woman whom thou gavest to be with me, she gave me fruit of the tree, and I ate." Then the LORD God said to the woman, "What is this that you have done?" The woman said, "The serpent beguiled me, and I ate." The LORD God said to the serpent,

"Because you have done this,
cursed are you above all cattle,
and above all wild animals;
upon your belly you shall go,
and dust you shall eat
all the days of your life.
I will put enmity between you and the woman,
and between your seed and her seed;
he shall bruise your head,
and you shall bruise his heel."

To the woman he said,

"I will greatly multiply your pain in childbearing;
in pain you shall bring forth children,
yet your desire shall be for your husband,
and he shall rule over you."

And to Adam he said,

"Because you have listened to the voice of your wife,
and have eaten of the tree
of which I commanded you,
'You shall not eat of it,'
cursed is the ground because of you;
in toil you shall eat of it all the days of your life;
thorns and thistles it shall bring forth to you;
and you shall eat the plants of the field.
In the sweat of your face
you shall eat bread
till you return to the ground,
for out of it you were taken;
you are dust,

and to dust you shall
return."

20 The man called his wife's name Eve, because she was the mother of all living. And the LORD God made for Adam and for his wife garments of skins, and clothed them.

22 Then the LORD God said, "Behold, the man has become like one of us, knowing good and evil; and now, lest he put forth his hand and take also of the tree of life, and eat, and live for ever"— therefore the LORD God sent him forth from the garden of Eden, to till the ground from which he was taken. He drove out the man; and at the east of the garden of Eden he placed the cherubim, and a flaming sword which turned every way, to guard the way to the tree of life.

4 Now Adam knew Eve his wife, and she conceived and bore Cain, saying, "I have gotten a man with the help of the LORD." . . .

5 This is the book of the generations of Adam. When God created man, he made him in the likeness of God. Male and female he created them, and he blessed them and named them Man when they were created. When Adam had lived a hundred and thirty years, he became the father of a son in his own likeness, after his image, and named him Seth. The days of Adam after he became the father of Seth were eight hundred years; and he had other sons and daughters. Thus all the days that Adam lived were nine hundred and thirty years; and he died.

* * *

The Song of Solomon

2 I am a rose of Sharon,
a lily of the valleys.

As a lily among brambles,
so is my love among
maidens.

As an apple tree among the
trees of the wood,
so is my beloved among
young men.
With great delight I sat in his
shadow,
and his fruit was sweet to
my taste.
He brought me to the
banqueting house,
and his banner over me was
love.
Sustain me with raisins,
refresh me with apples;
for I am sick with love.
O that his left hand were
under my head,
and that his right hand
embraced me!
I adjure you, O daughters of
Jerusalem,
by the gazelles or the hinds
of the field,

that you stir not up nor
awaken love
until it please.

The voice of my beloved!
Behold, he comes,
leaping upon the mountains,
bounding over the hills.
My beloved is like a gazelle,
or a young stag.
Behold, there he stands
behind our wall,
gazing in at the windows,
looking through the lattice.
My beloved speaks and says
to me:
"Arise, my love, my fair one,
and come away;
for lo, the winter is past,
the rain is over and gone.
The flowers appear on the
earth,
the time of singing has
come,
and the voice of the
turtledove
is heard in our land.
The fig tree puts forth its figs,
and the vines are in
blossom;
they give forth fragrance.
Arise, my love, my fair one,
and come away.
3 Upon my bed by night
I sought him whom my soul
loves;
I sought him, but found him
not;
I called him, but he gave
no answer.
"I will rise now and go about
the city,
in the streets and in the
squares;
I will seek him whom my soul
loves."
I sought him, but found
him not.
The watchmen found me,
as they went about in the
city.
"Have you seen him whom
my soul loves?"
Scarcely had I passed them,
when I found him whom
my soul loves.
I held him, and would not let
him go
until I had brought him
into my mother's house,
and into the chamber of her
that conceived me.
I adjure you, O daughters of
Jerusalem,
by the gazelles or the hinds
of the field,
that you stir not up nor
awaken love
until it please.

What is that coming up from
the wilderness,
like a column of smoke,
perfumed with myrrh and
frankincense,
with all the fragrant
powders of the merchant?
Behold, it is the litter of
Solomon!
About it are sixty mighty men
of the mighty men of Israel.
all girt with swords
and expert in war,
each with his sword at his
thigh,
against alarms by night.
King Solomon made himself a
palanquin
from the wood of Lebanon.
He made its posts of silver,
its back of gold, its seat of
purple;

it was lovingly wrought
within
by the daughters of
Jerusalem.
Go forth, O daughters of Zion,
and behold King Solomon,
with the crown with which
his mother crowned him
on the day of his wedding,
on the day of the gladness
of his heart.

5 I come to my garden, my
sister, my bride,
I gather my myrrh with my
spice,
I eat my honeycomb with
my honey,
I drink my wine with my
milk.

Eat, O friends, and drink:
drink deeply, O lovers!

I slept, but my heart was
awake.
Hark! my beloved is knocking.
"Open to me, my sister, my
love,
my dove, my perfect one;
for my head is wet with dew,
my locks with the drops of
the night."
I had put off my garment,
how could I put it on?
I had bathed my feet,
how could I soil them?
My beloved put his hand to
the latch,
and my heart was thrilled
within me.
I arose to open to my beloved,
and my hands dripped with
myrrh,
my fingers with liquid myrrh,
upon the handles of the
bolt.
I opened to my beloved,
but my beloved had turned
and gone.
My soul failed me when he
spoke.
I sought him, but found him
not;
I called him, but he gave no
answer.
The watchmen found me,
as they went about in the
city;
they beat me, they wounded
me,
they took away my mantle,
those watchmen of the
walls.
I adjure you, O daughters of
Jerusalem,
if you find my beloved,
that you tell him
I am sick with love.

What is your beloved more
than another beloved,
O fairest among women?
What is your beloved more
than another beloved,
that you thus adjure us?

My beloved is all radiant and
ruddy,
distinguished among ten
thousand.
His head is the finest gold;
his locks are wavy,
black as a raven.
His eyes are like doves
beside springs of water,
bathed in milk,
fitly set.
His cheeks are like beds of
spices,
yielding fragrance.
His lips are lilies,
distilling liquid myrrh.

His arms are rounded gold,
set with jewels.
His body is ivory work,
encrusted with sapphires,
His legs are alabaster
columns,
set upon bases of gold.
His appearance is like
Lebanon,
choice as the cedars.
His speech is most sweet,
and he is altogether
desirable.
This is my beloved and this is
my friend,
O daughters of Jerusalem.

7 How graceful are your
feet in sandals,
O queenly maiden!
Your rounded thighs are like
jewels,
the work of a master hand.
Your navel is a rounded bowl
that never lacks mixed
wine.
Your belly is a heap of wheat,
encircled with lilies.
Your two breasts are like two
fawns,
twins of a gazelle.
Your neck is like an ivory
tower.
Your eyes are pools in
Heshbon,
by the gate of Bath-rab'bim.
Your nose is like a tower of
Lebanon,
overlooking Damascus.
Your head crowns you like
Carmel,
and your flowing locks are
like purple;
a king is held captive in
the tresses.

How fair and pleasant you
are,
O loved one, delectable
maiden!
You are stately as a palm tree,
and your breasts are like its
clusters.
I say I will climb the palm
tree
and lay hold of its branches.
Oh, may your breasts be like
clusters of the vine,
and the scent of your
breath like apples,
and your kisses like the best
wine
that goes down smoothly,
gliding over lips and teeth.

I am my beloved's,
and his desire is for me.
Come, my beloved,
let us go forth into the
fields,
and lodge in the villages;
let us go out early to the
vineyards,
and see whether the vines
have budded,
whether the grape blossoms
have opened
and the pomegranates are
in bloom.
There I will give you my love.
The mandrakes give forth
fragrance,
and over our doors are all
choice fruits,
new as well as old,
which I have laid up for
you, O my beloved.

8 O that you were like a
brother to me,
that nursed at my mother's
breast!

If I met you outside, I would kiss you,
and none would despise me.
I would lead you and bring you
into the house of my mother,
and into the chamber of her that conceived me.
I would give you spiced wine to drink,
the juice of my pomegranates.
O that his left hand were under my head,
and that his right hand embraced me!
I adjure you, O daughters of Jerusalem,
that you stir not up nor awaken love
until it please.

Who is that coming up from the wilderness,
leaning upon her beloved?
Under the apple tree I awakened you.
There your mother was in travail with you,
there she who bore you was in travail.

Set me as a seal upon your heart,
as a seal upon your arm;
for love is strong as death,
jealousy is cruel as the grave.
Its flashes are flashes of fire,
a most vehement flame.
Many waters cannot quench love,
neither can floods drown it.
If a man offered for love
all the wealth of his house,
it would be utterly scorned.

Ephesians 5

5 Therefore be imitators of
God, as beloved children.
And walk in love, as Christ
loved us and gave himself up
for us, a fragrant offering and
sacrifice to God. . . .
21 Be subject to one another
out of reverence for Christ.
Wives, be subject to your husband, as to the Lord. For the
husband is the head of the wife
as Christ is the head of the
church, his body, and is himself
its Savior. As the church is subject to Christ, so let wives also
be subject in everything to their
husbands. Husbands, love your
wives, as Christ loved the
church and gave himself up for
her, that he might sanctify her,
having cleansed her by the
washing of water with the word,
that he might present the church
to himself in splendor, without
spot or wrinkle or any such
thing, that she might be holy
and without blemish. Even so
husbands should love their
wives as their own bodies. He
who loves his wife loves himself.
For no man ever hates his own
flesh, but nourishes and cher-
ishes it, as Christ does the
church, because we are members of his body. "For this reason a man shall leave his father

and mother and be joined to his wife, and the two shall become one flesh." This mystery is a profound one, and I am saying that it refers to Christ and the church; however, let each one of you love his wife as himself, and let the wife see that she respects her husband.

* * *

1 Corinthians 7

7 Now concerning the matters about which you wrote. It is well for a man not to touch a woman. But because of the temptation to immorality, each man should have his own wife and each woman her own husband. The husband should give to his wife her conjugal rights, and likewise the wife to her husband. For the wife does not rule over her own body, but the husband does; likewise the husband does not rule over his own body, but the wife does. Do not refuse one another except perhaps by agreement for a season, that you may devote yourselves to prayer; but then come together again, lest Satan tempt you through lack of self-control. I say this by way of concession, not of command. I wish that all were as I myself am. But each has his own special gift from God, one of one kind and one of another.

8 To the unmarried and the widows I say that it is well for them to remain single as I do. But if they cannot exercise self-control, they should marry. For it is better to marry than to be aflame with passion.

10 To the married I give charge, not I but the Lord, that the wife should not separate from her husband (but if she does, let her remain single or else be reconciled to her husband)—and that the husband should not divorce his wife.

12 To the rest I say, not the Lord, that if any brother has a wife who is an unbeliever, and she consents to live with him, he should not divorce her. If any woman has a husband who is an unbeliever, and he consents to live with her, she should not divorce him. For the unbelieving husband is consecrated through his wife, and the unbelieving wife is consecrated through her husband. Otherwise, your children would be unclean, but as it is they are holy. But if the unbelieving partner desires to separate, let it be so; in such a case the brother or sister is not bound. For God has called us to peace. Wife, how do you know whether you will save your husband? Husband, how do you know whether you will save your wife?

17 Only, let every one lead the life which the Lord has assigned to him, and in which God has called him. This is my rule in all the churches. Was any one at the time of his call already circumcised? Let him not seek to remove the marks of circum-

cision. Was any one at the time of his call uncircumcised? Let him not seek circumcision. For neither circumcision counts for anything nor uncircumcision, but keeping the commandments of God. Every one should remain in the state in which he was called. Were you a slave when called? Never mind. But if you can gain your freedom, avail yourself of the opportunity. For he who was called in the Lord as a slave is a freedman of the Lord. Likewise he who was free when called is a slave of Christ. You were bought with a price; do not become slaves of men. So, brethren, in whatever state each was called, there let him remain with God.

25 Now concerning the unmarried, I have no command of the Lord, but I give my opinion as one who by the Lord's mercy is trustworthy. I think that in view of the present distress it is well for a person to remain as he is. Are you bound to a wife? Do not seek to be free. Are you free from a wife? Do not seek marriage. But if you marry, you do not sin, and if a girl marries she does not sin. Yet those who marry will have worldly troubles, and I would spare you that. I mean, brethren, the appointed time has grown very short; from now on, let those who have wives live as though they had none, and those who mourn as though they were not mourning, and those who rejoice as though they were not rejoicing, and those who buy as though they had no goods, and those who deal with the world as though they had no dealings with it. For the form of this world is passing away.

32 I want you to be free from anxieties. The unmarried man is anxious about the affairs of the Lord, how to please the Lord; but the married man is anxious about worldly affairs, how to please his wife, and his interests are divided. And the unmarried woman or girl is anxious about the affairs of the Lord, how to be holy in body and spirit; but the married woman is anxious about worldly affairs, how to please her husband. I say this for your own benefit, not to lay any restraint upon you, but to promote good order and to secure your individual devotion to the Lord.

36 If any one thinks that he is not behaving properly toward his betrothed, if his passions are strong, and it has to be, let him do as he wishes: let them marry —it is no sin. But whoever is firmly established in his heart, being under no necessity but having his desire under control, and has determined this in his heart, to keep her as his betrothed, he will do well. So that he who marries his betrothed does well; and he who refrains from marriage will do better.

39 A wife is bound to her husband as long as he lives. If the husband dies, she is free to be married to whom she wishes, only in the Lord. But in my judgment she is happier if she remains as she is. And I think that I have the Spirit of God.

1 Corinthians 11

11 Be imitators of me, as I am of Christ.

2 I commend you because you remember me in everything and maintain the traditions even as I have delivered them to you. But I want you to understand that the head of every man is Christ, the head of a woman is her husband, and the head of Christ is God. Any man who prays or prophesies with his head covered dishonors his head, but any woman who prays or prophesies with her head unveiled dishonors her head—it is the same as if her head were shaven. For if a woman will not veil herself, then she should cut off her hair; but if it is disgraceful for a woman to be shorn or shaven, let her wear a veil. For a man ought not to cover his head, since he is the image and glory of God; but woman is the glory of man. (For man was not made from woman, but woman from man. Neither was man created for woman, but woman for man.) That is why a woman ought to have a veil on her head, because of the angels. (Nevertheless, in the Lord woman is not independent of man nor man of woman; for as woman was made from man, so man is now born of woman. And all things are from God.) Judge for yourselves; is it proper for a woman to pray to God with her head uncovered? Does not nature itself teach you that for a man to wear long hair is degrading to him, but if a woman has long hair, it is her pride? For her hair is given to her for a covering. If any one is disposed to be contentious, we recognize no other practice, nor do the churches of God. . . .

* * *

AUGUSTINE

In the contribution of Greek philosophy to medieval thought, Plato was the most widespread and consistent influence, especially as interpreted through Plotinus by Augustine (354–430). Although Augustine considered faith superior to reason as a source of truth, his views also reflect Plato's rather disparaging attitudes toward the body, as well as Plato's insistence that truth is immutable and immaterial. Augustine's own experience may have been an impetus to the development of negative attitudes toward sex. In 386, after having parted from the woman with whom he had lived for over ten years and who bore him a son, Augustine was converted to Christianity. His conversion constituted a deliberate redirection of a natural inclination toward sensual and sexual gratification. While his taste for intellectual pursuits continued, his energies were thereafter channeled toward the fulfillment of religious and ascetic ideals.

Philosophically, Augustine's concept of human nature is platonic: to be human is to be a soul imprisoned by a body. Theologically, however, Augustine amended this view to accommodate the Scriptural data regarding creation. In his work *The Trinity* Augustine explains his concept of the *imago Dei* (image of God) in light of the statement in Genesis 1:27 that

> God created man in the image of himself, in the image of God he created him, male and female he created them.

As God is immaterial, the *imago Dei* is also immaterial, or soul. As God is Trinity (Father, Son, and Spirit), his human image is also trinitarian through its threefold spiritual powers of memory, understanding, and will. Human beings increase in their likeness to God and in fulfillment of their own human reality to the extent that these powers are directed toward God.

The famous Augustinian dictum "Love, and do what you will" can only be properly understood in the light of the preceding concept of human nature. So understood, it is relevant also to Augustine's description of peace: the "tranquillity of order," which is the goal of all societal relationships (including war). The order to be observed involves a notion of authority as service. In the family, for example,

> they who care for the rest rule—the husband the wife, the parents the children, the masters the servants; and they who are cared for obey—the women their husbands, the children their parents, the servants their masters. But in the family of the just man who lives by faith and is as yet a pilgrim journeying on to the celestial city, even those who rule serve those whom they seem to command. . . .

Only where familial roles and authority are so construed can "domestic peace" prevail.

The Trinity

(Book XII)

. . . .

Why . . . does Scripture make no mention except of male and female in the nature of man that has been made to the image of

God? For to complete the image of the Trinity the son should also be added, even though he was still placed in the loins of his father, as the woman was in his side. Or perhaps the woman, too, was already made, and Scripture has combined in a summary statement that of which it will explain more carefully later on, how it was done, and for this reason could not mention the son because he was not yet born? As if the Holy Spirit, who was later to describe the birth of the son in its proper place, could not have also included it in this brief account, just as He afterwards spoke about the woman in the proper place, who was taken from the side of the man, and yet has not failed to make mention of her here.

We ought . . . not to understand man as made to the image of the exalted Trinity, that is, to the image of God, in such a way that the same image is understood to be in three human beings; especially since the Apostle says that the man is the image of God, and consequently should remove the covering from his head, which he warns the woman to use, when he speaks as follows: 'A man indeed ought not to cover his head, because he is the image and glory of God. But the woman is the glory of the man.'

What, then, is to be said about this? If the woman according to her own person completes the image of the Trinity, why is the man still called that image when she has been taken from his side? Or if even one human person out of three can be called the image of God, as each person in the exalted Trinity itself is also God, why is not the woman also the image of God? For this is also the reason why she is commanded to cover her head, which he is forbidden to do because he is the image of God.

But we must see how the words spoken by the Apostle, that not the woman but the man is the image of God, are not contrary to that which is written in Genesis: 'God made man, to the image of God he made him; male and female he made them and blessed them.' For he says that human nature itself, which is complete in both sexes, has been made to the image of God, and he does not exclude the woman from being understood as the image of God. For after he had said that God made man to the image of God, he went on to say: 'He made him male and female,' or at any rate (if we punctuate this passage differently) 'male and female he made them.' In what sense, therefore, are we to understand the Apostle, that the man is the image of God, and consequently is forbidden to cover his head, but the woman is not, and on this account is commanded to do so? The solution lies, I think, in what I already said when discussing the nature of the human mind, namely, that the woman together with her husband is the image of God, so that that whole substance is one image. But when she is assigned as a help-mate, a function that pertains to her alone, then she is not the image of God; but as far as the man is concerned, he is by himself alone the image of God, just as fully and completely as when he and the woman are joined together into one.

As we said of the nature of the human mind, that if as a whole it contemplates the truth, it is the image of God; and when its functions are divided and something of it is diverted to the handling of temporal things, nevertheless that part which consults the truth is the image of God, but that other part, which is directed to the handling of inferior things, is not the image of God. And since the more it has extended itself towards that which is eternal, so much the more is it formed thereby to the image of God, and on that account it is not to be restrained so as to hold itself back and refrain from thence; therefore, the man ought not to cover his head.

But because an all too great advance towards the inferior things is dangerous to that rational knowledge which is concerned with corporeal and temporal things, it ought to have a power over its head; this is indicated by the veil which signifies that it ought to be kept in check. For a sacred and pious meaning is pleasing to the holy angels. For God does not see things according to the measure of time, nor is anything new wrought in His vision and knowledge when anything temporal and transitory takes place, as the senses are affected by such things, whether the carnal senses of animals and men, or even the heavenly senses of the angels.

That the Apostle Paul intended by this distinction between the male and female sex to signify the mystery of a more hidden truth can be understood from this, that he says in another place that she is indeed a widow, who is desolate, without sons and nephews, and yet that she ought to trust in the Lord and continue in prayers night and day; he here indicates that the woman having been seduced and brought into transgression will be saved through child-bearing, and then he has added: 'If they shall continue in faith and love and holiness with sobriety' [1 Tim. 2.15]. As if it could possibly harm a good widow if she did not have any children, or if those whom she had did not wish to continue in good works!

But because those which are called good works are, as it were, the sons of our life, according to the sense in which it is asked, what is a man's life? that is, how does he conduct himself in temporal things? and because these good works are wont to be practiced chiefly in the offices of mercy, but the works of mercy profit nothing either to the pagans or to the Jews, who do not believe in Christ, or to any heretics or schismatics, in whom faith, charity, and sober holiness are not found, what the Apostle meant to signify is evident, and it is expressed figuratively and mystically, because he was speaking about the veiling of the woman's head, which will remain an empty precept, unless it is referred to some hidden mystery.

For as not only the most true reason, but also the authority of the Apostle himself declares, man was made to the image of God, not according to the form of the body, but according to the rational mind. For it is a vain and degrading thought which represents God as circumscribed and limited by the outlines of corporeal members. Moreover, does not this same blessed Apostle say: 'Be renewed in the spirit of your mind, and put on the new man, him who is created according to God' [Eph. 4.23–24], and even more plainly in another place: 'Stripping yourselves of the old man with his deeds, put on the new, who is renewed unto the knowledge of God according to the image of him that created him' [cf. Col. 3.9–10]? If, therefore, we are renewed in the spirit of our mind, and it is precisely the new man who is renewed unto the knowledge of God, according to the image of Him who created him, then no one can doubt that man has been made to the image of Him who created him, not according to the body, nor according to any part of the mind, but according to the rational mind where the knowledge of God can reside.

But according to this renewal we are also made the sons of God through the Baptism of Christ, and when we put on the new man, we certainly put on Christ through faith. Who is it, then, that would exclude women from this fellowship, since they are with us co-heirs of grace, and since the same Apostle says in another place: 'For you are all children of God through faith in Christ Jesus. For whoever have been baptized in Christ, has put on Christ. There is neither Jew nor Greek, there is neither slave nor freeman, there is neither male nor female. For you are all one in Christ Jesus' [cf. Gal. 3.26–28]. Have the believing women, therefore, lost their bodily sex?

But because they are renewed there to the image of God, where there is no sex, man is made there to the image of God, where there is no sex, namely, in the spirit of his mind. Why, then, is the man on that account not bound to cover his head because he is the image and glory of God, but the woman must cover it because she is the glory of the man, just as if the woman were not renewed in the spirit of her mind, who is renewed unto the knowledge of God according to the image of Him who created him? But because she differs from the man by her bodily sex, that part of the reason which is turned aside to regulate temporal things, could be properly symbolized by her corporeal veil; so that the image of God does not remain except in that part of the mind of man in which it clings to the contemplation and consideration of the external reasons, which, as is evident, not only men but also women possess.

* * *

Treatises on Marriage and Other Subjects

THE GOOD OF MARRIAGE

. . . This is what we now say, that according to the present condition of birth and death, which we know and in which we were created, the marriage of male and female is something good. This union divine Scripture so commands that it is not permitted a woman who has been dismissed by her husband to marry again, as long as her husband lives, nor is it permitted a man who has been dismissed by his wife to marry again, unless she who left has died. Therefore, regarding the good of marriage, which even the Lord confirmed in the Gospel, not only because He forbade the dismissal of a wife except for fornication, but also because He came to the marriage when invited, there is merit in inquiring why it is a good.

This does not seem to me to be a good solely because of the procreation of children, but also because of the natural companionship between the two sexes. Otherwise, we could not speak of marriage in the case of old people, especially if they had either lost their children or had begotten none at all. But, in a good marriage, although one of many years, even if the ardor of youths has cooled between man and woman, the order of charity still flourishes between husband and wife. They are better in proportion as they begin the earlier to refrain by mutual consent from sexual intercourse, not that it would afterwards happen of necessity that they would not be able to do what they wished, but that it would be a matter of praise that they had refused beforehand what they were able to do. If, then, there is observed that promise of respect and of services due to each other by either sex, even though both members weaken in health and become almost corpse-like, the chastity of souls rightly joined together continues the purer, the more it has been proved, and the more secure, the more it has been calmed.

Marriage has also this good, that carnal or youthful incontinence, even if it is bad, is turned to the honorable task of begetting children, so that marital intercourse makes something good out of the evil of lust. Finally, the concupiscence of the flesh, which parental affection tempers, is repressed and becomes inflamed more modestly. For a kind of dignity prevails when, as husband and wife they unite in the marriage act, they think of themselves as mother and father. . . .

. . . If we compare the things themselves, in no way can it be doubted that the chastity of continence is better than the chastity of marriage. Although both, indeed, are a good, when we compare the men, the one who has the greater good than the other is the better. . . .

We must take this into account, too, that it is not right to compare men with men in some one good. For, it can happen that one does not have something that the other has, but he has something that is to be valued more highly. Greater, indeed, is the good of obedience than the good of continence. Marriage is nowhere condemned by the authority of our Scriptures; disobedience, however, is nowhere condoned. . . .

The right question is plainly not whether a virgin thoroughly disobedient should be compared with an obedient married woman, but a less obedient to a more obedient, for there is also nuptial chastity and it is indeed a good, but a lesser one than virginal chastity. Therefore, if the woman who is inferior in the good of obedience in proportion as she is greater in the good of chastity is compared with the other, then he who sees, when he compares chastity itself and obedience, that obedience in a certain way is the mother of all virtues, judges which woman is to be placed first. On this account, then, there can be obedience without virginity, because virginity is of counsel, not of precept. I am speaking of that obedience whereby precepts are obeyed. There can be obedience to precepts without virginity, but there cannot be this obedience without chastity. For it is of the essence of chastity not to commit fornication, not to commit adultery, not to be stained with any illicit intercourse. Whoever do not observe these precepts act against the commands of God and on this account are banished from the virtue of obedience. Virginity can exist by itself without obedience, since a woman can, although accepting the counsel of virginity and guarding her virginity, neglect the precepts; just as we know many sacred virgins who are garrulous, inquisitive, addicted to drink, contentious, greedy, proud. All these vices are against the precepts and destroy them through their sin of disobedience, like Eve herself. Therefore, not only is the obedient person to be preferred to the disobedient one, but the more obedient wife is to be preferred to the less obedient virgin.

ADULTEROUS MARRIAGES

. . . Since the husband and wife are equal as regards the marriage bond, just as 'The wife, while her husband is alive, will be called an adulteress, if she be with another man' [Rom. 7.3], so will the husband also be called an adulterer if, while his wife is living, he is with another woman. . . .

. . . I am making these observations about both sexes, but particularly on account of men who think themselves superior to women, lest they deem themselves their equals in the matter of chastity. They should have taken the lead in chastity, so that their wives would follow them as their heads. But, since the law forbids adultery, if weakness of the flesh should be admitted as an excuse of incontinence, an occasion for losing their souls is offered to many under the guise of a false impunity. Women also have flesh, to whom their husbands are unwilling to make some such allowance, as though it were granted them because they are men. Never believe that something is owed the stronger sex as an honor which is detrimental to chastity, since meet honor is owed to virtue and not to vice. On the contrary, when they demand such great chastity on the part of their wives, who assuredly have flesh, so that, when they go on long journeys away from their wives, they wish them to pass their glowing youth, untarnished by any adulterous relations—in fact, a great many women pass their days most virtuously, particularly the women of Syria, whose husbands, absorbed in business affairs, leave them as young men and hardly return to their old wives in their advanced age—by the very fact that they pretend that they are unable to practice continence they prove more clearly that it is not impossible. For, if the weakness of men could not accomplish this, much less could the weaker feminine sex.

* * *

Confessions

(Book XIII)

. . . Even as in his soul there is one power which is master by virtue of counsel and another made its subject so as to obey, so also for man in the corporeal order there was made woman. Because of her reasonable and intelligent mind she would have equality of nature, but as to bodily sex she would be subject to the male sex, just as the active appetite is made subject, so as to conceive right and prudent conduct from the rational mind.

* * *

The City of God

(Book XXII)

Chapter 17

There are some who think that in the resurrection all will be men, and that women will lose their sex. This view springs from an interpretation of the texts: 'Until we all attain to . . . perfect manhood, to the mature measure of the fullness of Christ' [Eph. 4.13] and 'conformed to the image of the Son of God' [Rom. 8.29]. The interpretation is based on the fact that the man alone was made by God out of the 'slime of the earth,' whereas the woman was made from the man. For myself, I think that those others are more sensible who have no doubt that both sexes will remain in the resurrection. After all, there will then be none of that lust which is the cause of shame in connection with sex, and so, all will be as before the first sin, when the man and the woman were naked and felt no shame. In the resurrection, the blemishes of the body will be gone, but the nature of the body will remain. And, certainly a woman's sex is her nature and no blemish; only, in the resurrection, there will be no conception or child-bearing associated with her nature. Her members will remain as before, with the former purpose sublimated to a newer beauty. There will be no concupiscence to arouse and none will be aroused, but her womanhood will be a hymn to the wisdom of God, who first made her a woman, and to the clemency of God, who freed her from the corruption into which she fell.

Even in the beginning, when woman was made from a rib in the side of the sleeping man, that had no less a purpose than to symbolize prophetically the union of Christ and His Church. . . . Therefore, woman is as much the creation of God as man is. If she was made from the man, this was to show her oneness with him; and if she was made in the way she was, this was to prefigure the oneness of Christ and the Church.

God, then, who made us man and woman will raise us up as man and woman. . . .

What our Lord said was that, in the resurrection, there would be no marriage. He did not say that there would be no women. In the context it would have been an easier answer to the question asked to have said that there would be no women–if that was to be the case in the resurrection. Actually, He affirmed that there would be women when He used the double expression: 'neither marry' (as men do) nor 'be given in marriage' (as in the case of women). In the resurrection, then, there will be those who on earth 'marry' and those who 'are given in marriage.' Only, in heaven there will be no marriage.

* * *

THOMAS AQUINAS

In contrast with most medieval theologians, Thomas Aquinas (1225–1274) used Aristotle rather than Plato as his main philosophical source. As a result, some of his views were considered sufficiently radical to warrant their official condemnation by church authorities. The influence of Aristotle is evident in Aquinas' emphases on experience as the basis of knowledge and on the essential unity of form and matter in individuals.

A crucial contribution of Aquinas himself to philosophy is his notion of the act of existence (sometimes called *esse*, which literally means "to be") as the principle of individual unity in all things, even God. For creatures, this concept involves a distinction between "what a thing is" (its general essence or nature or species; e.g., a human being's "humanness") and "that it is" (its particular existence as a unique individual). In the Creator, however, essence and existence are the same. Hence, God alone is utterly simple.

Since Aquinas construed his role as that of Christian theologian and teacher, his primary concern in his writings was to elicit an understanding of Christian beliefs. For example, his main work, from which the following selection is taken, is neither pure philosophy nor an apology (a rational defense of faith); it is rather, as its title implies (Summa Theologica means "highest theology"), a work written by a believer for believers. Accordingly, the starting point is faith data, or revelation (the Bible), and philosophy is used as a rational tool for understanding and explaining what is already believed.

Since Aquinas subscribed to the Aristotelian concept of human nature as an essential union of body and soul, he considered death the proof of human mortality, and held that the separated soul which continues to exist after death does not truly constitute a person. But Aquinas also believed in the Christian doctrine of resurrection of the body through reunion with the soul sometime after death. This belief supported his argument for personal immortality in a life subsequent to that resurrection.

For Aquinas, each human being is a union of his or her human essence (which includes soul and body) and existence (which is not to be identified with soul or body). "What you are" is not to be equated with "that you are" because your essence was conceived within the divine mind before it was given existence through creation. From the perspective of his Christian faith, Aquinas also considered human nature as oriented toward a supernatural end, that is, an end which can neither be conceived nor achieved through mere human capability. To Aquinas, then, to be a person is to be a rational animal whose origin and end is God.

On the First Man

Question XCII

THE PRODUCTION OF WOMAN

(In Four Articles)

We must next consider the production of the woman. Under this head there are four points of inquiry: (1) Whether woman should have been made in that first production of things? (2) Whether woman should have been made from man? (3) Whether of man's rib? (4) Whether woman was made immediately by God?

First Article

WHETHER WOMAN SHOULD HAVE BEEN MADE IN THE FIRST PRODUCTION OF THINGS?

We proceed thus to the First Article:–

Objection 1. It would seem that woman should not have been made in the first production of things. For the Philosopher says that the *female is a misbegotten male.*[1] But nothing misbegotten or defective should have been in the first production of things. Therefore woman should not have been made at that first production.

Obj. 2. Further, subjection and limitation were a result of sin, for to the woman was it said after sin (Gen. iii. 16): *Thou shalt be under the man's power;* and Gregory says that, *Where there is no sin, there is no inequality.*[2] But woman is naturally of less strength and dignity than man, *for the agent is always more honorable than the patient,* as Augustine says.[3] Therefore woman should not have been made in the first production of things before sin.

Obj. 3. Further, occasions of sin should be cut off. But God foresaw that woman would be an occasion of sin to man. Therefore He should not have made woman.

On the contrary, It is written (Gen. ii. 18): *It is not good for man to be alone; let us make him a helper like to himself.*

1. *De Gener. Anim.*, II, 3 (737a 27).

2. *Moral.* XXI, 15 (PL 76, 203).

3. *De Genesi ad Litt.*, XII, 16 (PL 34, 467).

I answer that, It was necessary for woman to be made, as the Scripture says, as *a helper* to man; not, indeed, as a helpmate in other works, as some say, since man can be more efficiently helped by another man in other works; but as a helper in the work of generation. This can be made clear if we observe the mode of generation carried out in various living things. Some living things do not possess in themselves the power of generation, but are generated by an agent of another species; and such are those plants and animals which are generated, without seed, from suitable matter through the active power of the heavenly bodies. Others possess the active and passive generative power together, as we see in plants which are generated from seed. For the noblest vital function in plants is generation, and so we observe that in these the active power of generation invariably accompanies the passive power. Among perfect animals, the active power of generation belongs to the male sex, and the passive power to the female. And as among animals there is a vital operation nobler than generation, to which their life is principally directed, so it happens that the male sex is not found in continual union with the female in perfect animals, but only at the time of coition; so that we may consider that by coition the male and female are one, as in plants they are always united, even though in some cases one of them preponderates, and in some the other. But man is further ordered to a still nobler work of life, and that is intellectual operation. Therefore there was greater reason for the distinction of these two powers in man; so that the female should be produced separately from the male, and yet that they should be carnally united for generation. Therefore directly after the formation of woman, it was said: *And they shall be two in one flesh* (Gen. ii. 24).

Reply Obj. 1. As regards the individual nature, woman is defective and misbegotten, for the active power in the male seed tends to the production of a perfect likeness according to the masculine sex; while the production of woman comes from defect in the active power, or from some material indisposition, or even from some external influence, such as that of a south wind, which is moist, as the Philosopher observes.[4] On the other hand, as regards universal human nature, woman is not misbegotten, but is included in nature's intention as directed to the work of generation. Now the universal intention of nature depends on God, Who is the universal Author of nature. Therefore, in producing nature, God formed not only the male but also the female.

Reply Obj. 2. Subjection is twofold. One is servile, by virtue of which a superior makes use of a subject for his own benefit; and this kind of subjection began after sin. There is another kind of

4. *De Gener. Anim.*, IV, 2 (766b 33).

subjection, which is called economic or civil, whereby the superior makes use of his subjects for their own benefit and good; and this kind of subjection existed even before sin. For the good of order would have been wanting in the human family if some were not governed by others wiser than themselves. So by such a kind of subjection woman is naturally subject to man, because in man the discernment of reason predominates. Nor is inequality among men excluded by the state of innocence, as we shall prove.

Reply Obj. 3. If God had deprived the world of all those things which proved an occasion of sin, the universe would have been imperfect. Nor was it fitting for the common good to be destroyed in order that individual evil might be avoided; especially as God is so powerful that He can direct any evil to a good end.

Second Article

WHETHER WOMAN SHOULD HAVE BEEN MADE FROM MAN?

We proceed thus to the Second Article:—

Objection 1. It would seem that woman should not have been made from man. For sex belongs both to man and animals. But in the other animals the female was not made from the male. Therefore neither should it have been so with man.

Obj. 2. Further, things of the same species are of the same matter. But male and female are of the same species. Therefore, as man was made of the slime of the earth, so woman should have been made of the same, and not from man.

Obj. 3. Further, woman was made to be a helpmate to man in the work of generation. But close relationship makes a person unfit for that office; and hence near relations are debarred from intermarriage, as is written (Lev. xviii. 6). Therefore woman should not have been made from man.

On the contrary, It is written (Eccles. xvii. 5): *He created for him,* that is, out of man, *a helpmate like to himself,* that is, woman.

I answer that, When all things were first made, it was more suitable for woman to be formed from man than for this to happen in other animals. First, in order thus to give the first man a certain dignity consisting in this, that as God is the principle of the whole universe, so the first man, in likeness to God, was the principle of the whole human race. Hence Paul says that *God made the whole human race from one* (Acts xvii. 26). Secondly, that man might love woman all the more, and cleave to her more closely, knowing her to be fashioned from himself. Hence it is written (Gen. ii. 23, 24): *She was taken out of man, wherefore a man shall leave father and mother, and shall cleave to his wife.* This was most necessary in the human species, in which the male and female live together for life; which is not the case with other animals. Thirdly, because, as the Philosopher says, the human male and female are united, not only for generation, as with other animals, but also for the purpose of domestic life, in which each has his or her particular duty, and in which the man is the head of the woman.[5] Therefore it was suitable for the woman to be made out of man, as out of her principle. Fourthly, there is a sacramental reason for this. For by this is signified that the Church takes her origin from Christ. Therefore the Apostle says (Ephes. v. 32): *This is a great sacrament; but I speak in Christ and in the Church.*

Reply Obj. 1. is clear from the foregoing.

Reply Obj. 2. Matter is that from which something is made. Now created nature has a determinate principle, and since it is determined to one thing, it has also a determinate mode of proceeding. Therefore from determinate matter it produces something in a determinate species. On the other hand, the divine power, being infinite, can produce things of the same species out of any matter, such as a man from the slime of the earth, and a woman from a man.

Reply Obj. 3. A certain affinity arises from natural generation, and this is an impediment to matrimony. Woman, however, was not produced from man by natural generation, but by the divine power alone. Hence Eve is not called the daughter of Adam. And so this argument does not prove.

Third Article

WHETHER THE WOMAN WAS FITTINGLY MADE FROM THE RIB OF MAN?

We proceed thus to the Third Article:—

Objection 1. It would seem that woman should not have been formed from the rib of man. For the rib was much smaller than the woman's body. Now from a smaller thing a larger thing can be made only—either by addition (and then the woman ought to have been described as made out of that which was added, rather than out of the rib itself);—or by rarefaction, because, as Augustine says: *A body cannot increase in bulk except by rarefaction.*[6] But woman's body is not more rarefied than man's—at least, not in the proportion of a rib to Eve's body. Therefore Eve was not formed from a rib of Adam.

Obj. 2. Further, in those things which were first created there was nothing superfluous. Therefore a rib of Adam belonged to the

5. *Eth.*, VIII, 12 (1162a 19).

6. *De Genesi ad Litt.*, X, 26 (PL 34, 428).

integrity of his body. So, if a rib was removed, his body remained imperfect; which is unreasonable to suppose.

Obj. 3. Further, a rib cannot be removed from man without pain. But there was no pain before sin. Therefore it was not right for a rib to be taken from the man, that Eve might be made from it.

On the contrary, It is written (Gen. ii. 22): *God built the rib, which He took from Adam, into a woman.*

I answer that, It was right for a woman to be made from a rib of man. First, to signify the social union of man and woman, for the woman should neither use authority over man, and so she was not made from his head; nor was it right for her to be subject to man's contempt as his slave, and so she was not made from his feet. Secondly, for the sacramental signification; for from the side of Christ sleeping on the Cross the Sacraments flowed—namely, blood and water—on which the Church was established.

Reply Obj. 1. Some say that woman's body was formed by a material increase, without anything being added, in the same way as our Lord multiplied the five loaves. But this is quite impossible. For such an increase of matter would either be by a change of the very substance of the matter itself, or by a change of its dimensions. It was not by a change of the substance of the matter, both because matter, considered in itself, is quite unchangeable, since it has a potential existence, and has nothing but the nature of a subject; and because multiplication and size are extraneous to the essence of matter itself. And so, the multiplication of matter is quite unintelligible, as long as the matter itself remains the same without anything added to it, unless it receives greater dimensions. This implies rarefaction, which is for the same matter to receive greater dimensions, as the Philosopher says.[7] To say, therefore, that the same matter is enlarged, without being rarefied, is to combine contradictories—viz., the definition without the absence of the thing defined.

Therefore, as no rarefaction is apparent in such multiplications of matter, we must admit an addition of matter, either by creation or, what is more probable, by conversion. Hence Augustine says that *Christ filled five thousand men with five loaves in the same way as from a few seeds He produces the harvest of corn*[8]—that is, by transformation of the nourishment. Nevertheless, we say that the crowds were fed with five loaves, or that woman was made from the rib, because an addition was made to the already existing matter of the loaves and of the rib.

Reply Obj. 2. The rib belonged to the integral perfection of Adam, not as an individual, but as the principle of the human

7. *Phys.,* IV, 9 (217a 25).

8. *Tract.* XXIV, super *Ioann.,* VI, 2 (PL 35, 1593).

race; just as the semen belongs to the perfection of the begetter, and is released by a natural and pleasurable operation. Much more, therefore, was it possible that by the divine power the body of woman should be produced from the man's rib.

From this it is clear how to answer the third objection.

Fourth Article

WHETHER WOMAN WAS FORMED IMMEDIATELY BY GOD?

We proceed thus to the Fourth Article:—

Objection 1. It would seem that woman was not formed immediately by God. For no individual is produced immediately by God from another individual alike in species. But woman was made from man, who is of the same species. Therefore she was not made immediately by God.

Obj. 2. Further, Augustine says that corporeal things are governed by God through the angels. But woman's body was formed from corporeal matter. Therefore it was made through the ministry of the angels, and not immediately by God.

Obj. 3. Further, those things which pre-exist in creatures in their causal principles are produced by the power of some creature, and not immediately by God. But woman's body was produced in its causal principles among the first created works, as Augustine says. Therefore it was not produced immediately by God.

On *the contrary,* Augustine says, in the same work: *God alone, to Whom all nature owes its existence, could form or fashion woman from man's rib.*[9]

I answer that, As was said above, the natural generation of every species is from some determinate matter. Now the matter whence man is naturally begotten is the human semen of man or woman. Therefore an individual of the human species cannot be generated naturally from any other matter. Now God alone, the author of nature, can bring an effect into being outside the ordinary course of nature. Therefore God alone could produce either man from the slime of the earth, or woman from the rib of man.

Reply Obj. 1. This argument is good when an individual is begotten, by natural generation, from that which is like it in species.

Reply Obj. 2. As Augustine says, we do not know whether the angels were employed by God in the formation of woman; but it is certain that, as the body of man was not formed by the angels from the slime of the earth, so neither was the body of woman formed by them from the man's rib.

9. *De Genesi ad Litt.,* IX, 15 (PL 34, 403).

Reply Obj. 3. As Augustine says: *The first creation of things did not demand that woman should be made thus; it made it possible for her to be thus made.*[10] Therefore the body of woman preexisted according to these causal principles in the first works of God, not according to an active potentiality, but according to a passive potentiality ordered to the active power of God.

. . . .

Question XCIII
Fourth Article

WHETHER THE IMAGE OF GOD IS FOUND IN EVERY MAN?

. . . .

Objection 1. It would seem that the image of God is not found in every man. For the Apostle says that *man is the image of God, but woman is the image of man* (I Cor. xi. 7). Therefore, as woman is an individual of the human species, it is clear that every individual is not an image of God. . . .

Reply Obj. 1. The image of God, in its principal signification, namely the intellectual nature, is found both in man and in woman. Hence after the words, *To the image of God He created him,* it is added, *Male and female He created them* (Gen. i. 27). Moreover it is said *them* in the plural, as Augustine remarks, lest it should be thought that both sexes were united in one individual. But in a secondary sense the image of God is found in man, and not in woman, for man is the beginning and end of woman, just as God is the beginning and end of every creature. So when the Apostle had said that *man is the image and glory of God, but woman is the glory of man,* he adds his reason for saying this: *For man is not of woman, but woman of man; and man was not created for woman, but woman for man.*

. . . .

Sixth Article

WHETHER THE IMAGE OF GOD IS IN MAN AS REGARDS THE MIND ONLY?

. . . *Obj.* 2. Further it is written (Gen. i. 27): *God created man to His own image; to the image of God He created him; male and*

10. *Op. cit.,* IX, 18 (PL 34, 407).

female He created them. But the distinction of male and female is in the body. Therefore the image of God is also in the body, and not only in the mind.

. . . *Reply Obj*. 2. As Augustine says, some have thought that the image of God was not in man individually, but severally. They held that *the man represents the Person of the Father; that those born of man denote the person of the Son; and that woman is a third person in likeness to the Holy Ghost, since she so proceeded from man as not to be his son or daughter*. All of this is manifestly absurd. First, because it would follow that the Holy Ghost is the principle of the Son, just as woman is the principle of man's offspring; secondly, because one man would be to the image of only one Person; thirdly, because in that case Scripture should not have mentioned the image of God in man until after the birth of offspring. Therefore we must observe that when Scripture had said, *to the image of God He created him*, it added, *male and female He created them*, not to imply that the image of God came through the distinction of sex, but that the image of God belongs to both sexes, since it is in the mind, wherein there is no distinction of sexes. Therefore the Apostle (Col. iii. 10), after saying *According to the image of Him that created him*, added, *Where there is neither male nor female*. . . .

Question XCIV
Fourth Article

WHETHER MAN IN HIS FIRST STATE COULD HAVE BEEN DECEIVED?

. . . .

Objection 1. It would seem that man in his first state could have been deceived. For the Apostle says (1 Tim. ii. 14) that *the woman being seduced was in the transgression*.

Obj. 2. Further, the Master of the *Sentences* says that *woman was not frightened at the serpent speaking, because she thought that he had received the faculty of speech from God*.[11] But this was untrue. Therefore before sin woman was deceived. . . .

Reply Obj. 1. Though woman was deceived before she sinned in deed, still it was not till she had already sinned by interior pride. For Augustine says that *woman would not have believed the words*

11. Peter Lombard, *Sent.*, II, xxi, 4 (I, 405).

of the serpent, had she not already acquiesced in the love of her own power, and in a presumption of self-conceit.[12]

Reply Obj. 2. Woman thought that the serpent had received this faculty, not as acting in accordance with nature, but by virtue of some supernatural operation. We need not, however, follow the Master of the *Sentences* in this point.

Question XCVI
Third Article

WHETHER IN THE STATE OF INNOCENCE MEN WOULD HAVE BEEN EQUAL?

. . . .

On the contrary, It is written (Rom. xiii. I): *The things which are of God, are well ordered.* But order consists chiefly in inequality, for Augustine says: *Order disposes things equal and unequal in their proper place.*[13] Therefore in the first state, which would have been most proper and orderly, inequality would exist.

I answer that, We must needs admit that in the first state there would have been some inequality, at least as regards sex, because generation depends upon diversity of sex; and likewise as regards age, for some would have been born of others, nor would sexual union have been sterile.

Moreover, as regards the soul, there would have been inequality as to justice and knowledge. For man worked, not of necessity, but of his own free choice, by virtue of which man can apply himself, more or less, to action, desire or knowledge. Hence some would have made a greater advance in justice and knowledge than others.

There could also have been bodily disparity. For the human body was not entirely exempt from the laws of nature, so as not to receive from exterior sources more or less advantage and help, since it was likewise dependent on food wherewith to sustain life.

So we may say that, according to the climate, or the movement of the stars, some would have been born more robust in body than others, and also greater, and more beautiful, and in all ways better disposed; so that, however, in those who were thus surpassed, there would have been no defect or fault either in soul or body.

12. *De Genesi ad Litt.,* XI, 30 (PL 34, 445).

13. *De Civit. Dei,* XIX, 13 (PL 41, 640).

SUGGESTIONS FOR FURTHER READING

Plato

Annas, Julia. "Plato's Republic and Feminism." *Philosophy* 51 (July 1976), pp. 307–21.

Atherton, Margaret. "Education for Equality." In *Women, Philosophy, and Sport*, ed. by Betsy C. Postow. Metuchen, N.J.: Scarecrow Press, Inc., 1983, pp. 233–45.

Bluestone, Natalie Harris. *Women and the Ideal Society: Plato's 'Republic' and Modern Myths of Gender*. Amherst: University of Massachusetts Press, 1987.

Brown, Wendy. "Supposing Truth Were a Woman: Plato's Subversion of Masculine Discourse." *Political Theory* 16 (Nov. 1988), pp. 594–616.

Darling, John. "Are Women Good Enough: Plato's Feminism Re-Examined." *Journal of Philosophy of Education* 20 (Summer 1986), pp. 123–28.

Dickason, Anne. "Anatomy and Destiny: The Role of Biology in Plato's Views of Women." In *Women and Philosophy*, ed. by Carol C. Gould and Marx W. Wartofsky. New York: G. P. Putnam's Sons, 1976, pp. 45–53.

Fortenbaugh, W. W. "On Plato's Feminism in Republic V." *Apeiron* 9 (Nov. 1975), pp. 1–4.

Garside, Christine. "Plato on Women." *Feminist Studies* 2 (1975), pp. 131–38.

Martin, Jane. "Sex Equality and Education in Plato's Just State." In *Femininity, Masculinity, and Androgyny*, ed. by Mary Vetterling-Braggin. Totowa, N.J.: Littlefield Adams, 1982, pp. 279–300.

Okin, Susan. "Philospher Queens and Private Wives: Plato on Women and the Family." *Philosophy and Public Affairs* 6 (Summer 1977), pp. 345–69.

Osborne, Martha Lee. "Plato's Unchanging View of Woman: A Denial that Anatomy Spells Destiny." *Philosophical Forum* 6 (Summer 1975), pp. 447–52.

Pierce, Christine. "Equality: Republic V." *The Monist* (Jan. 1973), pp. 1–11.

Pomeroy, Sarah. "Feminism in Book V of Plato's *Republic*." *Apeiron* 8 (1974), pp. 32–34.

Saxonhouse, Arlene W. "Eros and the Female in Greek Political Thought: An Interpretation of Plato's 'Symposium.'" *Political Theory* 12 (Fall 1984), pp. 5–28.

Smith, Janet Farrell. "Plato, Irony and Equality." *Hypatia* 1 (1983), pp. 597–607.

Spelman, Elizabeth V. "Woman as Body: Ancient and Contemporary Views." *Feminist Studies* 8 (Spring 1982), pp. 109–32.

Aristotle

Andic, Martin. "Were Plato and Aristotle Humanists?" In *The Question of Humanism: Challenges and Possibilities,* ed. by David Goicoechea. Buffalo: Prometheus, 1991, pp. 27–40.

Clark, Stephen. "Aristotle's Woman." *History of Political Thought* 3 (Summer 1982), pp. 177–92.

Fritz, Kurt von. "Aristotle's Anthropological Ethics and Its Relevance to Modern Problems." *Journal of the History of Ideas* 42 (April–June 1981), pp. 187–208.

Green, Judith. "Aristotle on Necessary Verticality, Body Heat, and Gendered Proper Places in the Polis: A Feminist Critique." *Hypatia* 7 (Winter 1992), pp. 70–96.

Jones, Ken. "Human Sexuality." *Irish Philosophical Journal* 4 (1987), pp. 153–60.

Lange, Lynda. "Woman Is Not a Rational Animal: On Aristotle's Biology of Reproduction." In *Discovering Reality,* ed. by Sandra Harding. Dordrecht: Reidel, 1983, pp. 1–16.

Matthews, Gareth B. "Gender and Essence in Aristotle." *Australasian Journal of Philosophy* Suppl. 64 (June 1986), pp. 16–25.

Okin, Susan Moller. *Women in Western Political Thought.* Princeton: Princeton University Press, 1979.

Price, A. W. *Love and Friendship in Plato and Aristotle.* New York: Clarendon / Oxford Press, 1989.

Scott, Robin. "Aristotle on Women." *Kinesis* 11 (Spring 1982), pp. 69–84.

Smith, Nicholas D., "Plato and Aristotle on the Nature of Women." *Journal of the History of Philosophy* 21 (Oct. 1983), pp. 467–78.

Spelman, Elizabeth V. "Aristotle and the Politicization of the Soul." In *Discovering Reality,* ed. by Sandra Harding. Dordrecht: Reidel, 1983, pp. 17–30.

Strikwerda, Robert A. and May, Larry (eds.). "Male Friendship and Intimacy." In *Rethinking Masculinity: Philosophical Explorations in Light of Feminism.* Lanham, Md.: Rowman and Littlefield, 1992.

Tumulty, Peter. "Aristotle, Feminism and Natural Law Theory." *New Scholasticism* 55 (Autumn 1981), pp. 450–64.

The Bible

Bassett, Marion Preston. *A New Sex Ethics and Marriage Structure; Discussed by Adam and Eve.* New York: Philosophical Library, 1961.

Boldrey, Richard and Boldrey, Joyce. *Chauvinist or Feminist? Paul's View of Women.* Grand Rapids: Baker Book House, 1976.

Borresen, Kari Elisabeth (ed.). *Image of God and Gender Models in Judaeo-Christian Tradition.* Atlantic Highlands, N.J.: Humanities Press, 1991.

Cadegan, Una M. and Heft, James L. "Mary of Nazareth, Feminism and the Tradition." *Thought* 65 (June 1990), pp. 169–89.

Christ, Carol and Plaskow, Judith. *Womanspirit Rising: A Feminist Reader in Religion.* New York: Harper and Row Publishing Company, 1979.

Cummings, Alan. "Pauline Christianity and Greek Philosophy: A Study of the Status of Women." *Journal of the History of Ideas* 34 (1973), pp. 517–28.

Daly, Mary. *Beyond God the Father.* Boston: Beacon Press, 1973.

Fischer, James A. *God Said: Let There Be Woman: A Study of Biblical Women.* New York: Alba House, 1979.

Kolton, Elizabeth (ed.). *The Jewish Woman.* New York: Schocken Books, 1976.

Lightfoot, Neil R. *The Role of Women: New Testament Perspectives.* Memphis: Student Association Press, 1978.

Maimonides, Moses. *The Code of Maimonides,* vol. 4, Book IV of the Code, "The Book of Women." New Haven: Yale University Press, 1972.

Mikhail, Mona N. *Images of Islamic Women: Fact and Fiction.* Metuchen, N.J.: Scarecrow Press, Inc., 1978.

Mollenkott, Virginia R. *Women, Men, and the Bible.* Nashville: Abingdon Press, 1977.

Ochs, Carol. *Behind the Sex of God.* Boston: Beacon Press, 1977.

Otwell, John H. *And Sarah Laughed: The Status of Woman in the Old Testament.* Philadelphia: Westminster Press, 1977.

Raccagni, Michelle. *The Modern Arab Woman.* Metuchen, N.J.: Scarecrow Press, Inc., 1978.

Ruether, Rosemary. *The Image of Women in the Judeo-Christian Tradition.* New York: Simon and Schuster, Inc., 1972.

———. (ed.). *Religion and Sexism.* Images of Women in the Jewish and Christian Traditions. New York: Simon and Schuster, Inc., 1974.

Russell, Letty. *The Liberating Word: A Guide to Non-Sexist Interpretation of the Bible.* Philadelphia: Westminster Press, 1976.

Scanzoni, Letha and Hardesty, Nancy. *All We're Meant to Be: A Biblical Approach to Women's Liberation.* Waco, Tex.: Word Books, 1975.

Stanton, Elizabeth Cady. *The Woman's Bible.* Seattle: Coalition on Women and Religion, 1974.

Augustine

Alexander, William M. "Sex and Philosophy in Augustine." *Augustinian Studies* 5 (1974), pp. 197–208.

Babcock, William S. "Augustine on Sin and Moral Agency." *Journal of Religious Ethics* 16 (Spring 1988), pp. 28–55.

Miles, Margaret R. "The Body and Human Values in Augustine of Hippo," in *Grace, Politics and Desire: Essays on Augustine*, ed. by Hugo Meynell. Calgary: University of Calgary Press, 1990.

O'Connor, William R. "The Concept of the Person in St. Augustine's De Trinitate." *Augustinian Studies* 13 (1982), pp. 33–44.

Power, Eileen Edna. *Medieval Women*. New York: Cambridge University Press, 1975.

Ramsey, Paul. "Human Sexuality in the History of Redemption." *Journal of Religious Ethics* 16 (Spring 1988), pp. 56–86.

Weaver, F. Ellen and Laporte, Jean. "Augustine and Women: Relationships and Teachings." *Augustinian Studies* 12 (1981), pp. 115–32.

Aquinas

Bell, Linda A. "Does Marriage Require a Head: Some Historical Arguments." *Hypatia* 4 (Spring 1989), pp. 139–54.

Borresen, Kari Elisabeth. *Subordination and Equivalence: The Nature and Role of Woman in Augustine and Thomas Aquinas*, trans. by Charles H. Talbot. Washington, D.C.: University Press of America, 1981.

Kelsey, David H. "Aquinas and Barth on the Human Body." *Thomist* 50 (Oct. 1986), pp. 643–89.

Ostheimer, Anthony. *The Family: A Thomistic Study in Social Philosophy*. Washington: Catholic University of America Press, 1939.

Postow, B. C. "Thomas on Sexism." *Ethics* 90 (Spring 1980), pp. 251–56.

Seidl, Horst. "The Concept of Person in St. Thomas Aquinas." *Thomist* 51 (July 1987), pp. 435–60.

Vadakkemuriyil, A. "Philosophers on Gender and Sexuality," *Journal of Dharma* (April–June 1991), pp. 106–14.

POST-ENLIGHTENMENT SOURCES

In general, the authors in this section exemplify the spirit of the Enlightenment through their concern with the human subject and with the moral and social life of that subject. However, their common concern is reflected through differing philosophies: empiricism, rationalism, and idealism, and consequently through differing views of human nature. Except in the case of Mary Wollstonecraft, specific remarks about women occur only peripherally or secondarily to the writer's main philosophical contributions, which include elaborations on the meaning of man. It is useful to compare or contrast concepts of person and of woman in the same writer, for such concepts have continued quite beyond the life span of their author.

Jean-Jacques Rousseau provides a link between the thinkers here presented. John Locke seems to have anticipated Rousseau's social contract theory in its view of primitive human nature. David Hume attempted, rather unsuccessfully, to befriend Rousseau by offering him sanctuary in England when his works had evoked hostile reaction in France and Switzerland. Immanuel Kant admits to having been greatly impressed by the works of Rousseau, whose *Emile* he had read before writing the *Observations* from which our selection is excerpted. Mary Wollstonecraft devotes much space in *The Vindication of the Rights of Women* to a critique of Rousseau's thoughts in *Emile*. G. W. F. Hegel read Rousseau's writings during his student days, and Arthur Schopenhauer cites Rousseau as an author whose views on women support his own.

JOHN LOCKE

Like other philosophers of his day, John Locke (1632–1704) was especially concerned with the problem of human knowledge. While he agreed with Cartesian criticism of the scholastic tradition as obscure and unproductive, he rejected the theory of innate ideas, insisting that the mind is a *tabula rasa* (blank slate) prior to experience. In his famous *Treatise concerning Human Understanding* Locke distinguishes between primary qualities, as powers inherent in real things, and secondary qualities, as the ways through which primary qualities are perceived by a subject. Sensation and reflection are the twin sources of experience, providing us with ideas that may be simple or complex. An idea is defined as "the *object* of the understanding when a man thinks," and knowledge consists in our perception of agreement or disagreement among ideas. Three kinds of knowledge are accessible to human beings: intuitive knowledge of oneself, demonstrative knowledge of God, and sensitive knowledge of the external world.

Locke defines a person as "a thinking, intelligent being, that has reason and reflection and can consider itself as itself, the same thinking thing in different times and places." The basis for one's sense of self is thus bodily continuity, as perceived by consciousness. In anticipation of Rousseau, Locke views the state of nature as a situation in which human beings are free and equal, with no common authority over them. They are also naturally prone to communicate with others; hence, language is "the great instrument and common tie of society."

According to Locke, the specific purpose for which people join together is "the material preservation of their lives, liberties and estates, which I call by the general name property." In other words our natural independence and desire for (as well as right to) property are bound to cause social conflicts which require the mediation of government for their resolution. Governments are thus designed to promote the common good. Since they represent the will of the majority of the people, the people retain the right to alter their mode of representation, even in extreme cases, through rebellion.

That Locke saw no need to avoid religious sources in philosophical writing is evident in the selection that follows. Among his peers this was intellectually acceptable, since the Bible was generally regarded as a source of truth not only about God but also about the world and human nature.

Of Paternal Power

It may perhaps be censured as an impertinent criticism, in a discourse of this nature, to find fault with words and names, that have obtained in the world: and yet possibly it may not be amiss to offer new ones, when the old are apt to lead men into mistakes, as this of *paternal power* probably has done, which seems so to place the power of parents over their children wholly in the *father*, as if the *mother* had no share in it; whereas, if we consult reason or revelation, we shall find, she has an equal title. This may give one reason to ask, whether this might not be more properly called *parental power?* for whatever obligation nature and the right of generation lays on children, it must certainly bind them equal to both the concurrent causes of it. And accordingly we see the positive law of God everywhere joins them together, without distinction, when it commands the obedience of children, *Honour thy father and thy mother,* Exod. xx. 12. *Whosoever curseth his father or his mother*, Lev. xx. 9. *Ye shall fear every man his mother and his father*, Lev. xix. 3. *Children, obey your parents*, &c. Eph. vi. 1. is the style of the Old and New Testament.

Had but this one thing been well considered, without looking any deeper into the matter, it might perhaps have kept men from running into those gross mistakes, they have made, about this power of parents; which, however it might, without any great harshness, bear the name of absolute dominion, and regal authority, when under the title of *paternal power* it seemed appropriated to the father, would yet have sounded but oddly, and in the very name shown the absurdity, if this supposed absolute power over children had been called *parental;* and thereby have discovered, that it belonged to the *mother* too: for it will but very ill serve the turn of those men, who contend so much for the absolute power and authority of the *fatherhood,* as they call it, that the mother should have any share in it; and it would have but ill supported the *monarchy* they contend for, when by the very name it appeared, that that fundamental authority, from whence they would derive their government of a single person only, was not placed in one, but two persons jointly. But to let this of names pass.

Though I have said above, *Chap. II. That all men by nature are equal,* I cannot be supposed to understand all sorts of *equality: age* or *virtue* may give men a just precedency: *excellency of parts* and *merit* may place others above the common level: *birth* may subject some, and *alliance* or *benefits* others, to pay an observance to those to whom nature, gratitude, or other respects, may have made it due: and yet all this consists with the *equality,* which all men are in, in respect of jurisdiction or dominion one over another; which was the *equality* I there spoke of, as proper to the business in hand, being that *equal right,* that every man hath, *to his natural freedom,* without being subjected to the will or authority of any other man. . . .

The *freedom* then of man, and liberty of acting according to his own will, is *grounded on* his having *reason,* which is able to instruct him in that law he is to govern himself by, and make him know how far he is left to the freedom of his own will. To turn him loose to an unrestrained liberty, before he has reason to guide him, is not the allowing him the privilege of his nature to be free; but to thrust him out amongst brutes, and abandon him to a state as wretched, and as much beneath that of a man, as theirs. This is that which puts the *authority* into the *parents'* hands to govern the *minority* of their children. God hath made it their business to employ this care on their offspring, and hath placed in them suitable inclinations of tenderness and concern to temper this power, to apply it, as his wisdom designed it, to the children's good, as long as they should need to be under it.

But what reason can hence advance this care of the *parents* due to their off-spring into an *absolute arbitrary dominion* of the father, whose power reaches no farther, than by such a discipline, as he finds most effectual, to give such strength and health to their bodies, such vigour and rectitude to their minds, as may best fit his children to be most useful to themselves and others; and, if it be necessary to his condition, to make them work, when they are able, for their own subsistence. But in this power the *mother* too has her share with the *father*.

Nay, this *power* so little belongs to the *father* by any peculiar right of nature, but only as he is guardian of his children, that when he quits his care of them, he loses his power over them, which goes along with their nourishment and education, to which it is inseparably annexed; and it belongs as much to the *foster-father* of an exposed child, as to the natural father of another. So little power does the bare *act of begetting* give a man over his issue; if all his care ends there, and this be all the title he hath to the name and authority of a father. And what will become of this *paternal power* in that part of the world, where one woman hath more than one husband at a time? or in those parts of *America*, where, when the husband and wife part, which happens frequently, the children are all left to the mother, follow her, and are wholly under her care and provision? If the father die whilst the children are young, do they not naturally everywhere owe the same obedience to their *mother*, during their minority, as to their father were he alive? and will any one say, that the mother hath a legislative power over her children? that she can make standing rules, which shall be of perpetual obligation, by which they ought to regulate all the concerns of their property, and bound their liberty all the course of their lives? or can she inforce the observation of them with capital punishments? for this is the proper *power of the magistrate*, of which the father hath not so much as the shadow. His command over his children is but temporary, and reaches not their life or property. . . .

* * *

Of Political and Civil Society

God having made man such a creature, that in his own judgment, it was not good for him to be alone, put him under strong obligations of necessity, convenience, and inclination to drive him into *society*, as well as fitted him with understanding and language to continue and enjoy it. The *first society* was between man and wife, which gave beginning to that between parents and children; to which, in time, that between master and servant came to be added: and though all these might, and commonly did meet together, and make up but one family, wherein the master or mistress of it had some sort of rule proper to a family; each of these, or all together, came short of *political society*, as we shall see, if we consider the different ends, ties, and bounds of each of these.

Conjugal society is made by a voluntary compact between man and woman; and tho' it consist chiefly in such a communion and right in one another's bodies as is necessary to its chief end, procreation; yet it draws with it mutual support and assistance, and a communion of interests too, as necessary not only to unite their care and affection, but also necessary to their common off-spring, who have a right to be nourished, and maintained by them, till they are able to provide for themselves.

For the end of *conjunction, between male and female,* being not barely procreation, but the continuation of the species; this conjunction betwixt male and female ought to last, even after procreation, so long as is necessary to the nourishment and support of the young ones, who are to be sustained by those that got them, till they are able to shift and provide for themselves. This rule, which the infinite wise maker hath set to the works of his hands, we find the inferior creatures steadily obey. In those viviparous animals which feed on grass, the *conjunction between male and female* lasts no longer than the very act of copulation; because the teat of the dam being sufficient to nourish the young, till it be able to feed on grass, the male only begets, but concerns not himself for the female or young, to whose sustenance he can contribute nothing. But in beasts of prey the *conjunction* lasts longer: because the dam not being able well to subsist herself, and nourish her numerous offspring by her own prey alone, a more laborious, as well as more dangerous way of living, than by feeding on grass, the assistance of the male is necessary to the maintenance of their common family, which cannot subsist till they are able to prey for themselves, but by the joint care of male and female. The same is to be observed in all birds (except some domestic ones, where plenty of food excuses the cock from feeding, and taking care of the young brood), whose young needing food in the nest, the cock and hen continue mates, till the young are able to use their wing, and provide for themselves.

And herein I think lies the chief, if not the only reason, *why the male and female in mankind are tied to a longer conjunction* than other creatures, *viz.* because the female is capable of conceiving, and *de facto* is commonly with child again, and brings forth too a new birth, long before the former is out of a dependency for support on his parents' help, and able to shift for himself, and has all the assistance that is due to him from his parents: whereby the father, who is bound to take care for those he hath begot, is under an obligation to continue in conjugal society with the same woman longer than other creatures, whose young being able to subsist of themselves, before the time of procreation returns again, the conjugal bond dissolves of itself, and they are at liberty, till *Hymen* at his usual anniversary season summons them again to choose new mates. Wherein one cannot but admire the wisdom of the great Creator, who having given to man foresight, and an ability to lay up for the future, as well as to supply the present necessity, hath made it necessary, that *society of man and wife should be more lasting*, than of male and female amongst other creatures; that so their industry might be encouraged, and their interest better united, to make provision and lay up goods for their common issue, which uncertain mixture, or easy and frequent solutions of conjugal society would mightily disturb.

But tho' these are ties upon *mankind*, which make the *conjugal bonds* more firm and lasting in man, than the other species of animals; yet it would give one reason to enquire, why this *compact*, where procreation and education are secured, and inheritance taken care for, may not be made determinable, either by consent, or at a certain time, or upon certain conditions, as well as any other voluntary compacts, there being no necessity in the nature of the thing, nor to the ends of it, that it should always be for life; I mean, to such as are under no restraint of any positive law, which ordains all such contracts to be perpetual.

But the husband and wife, though they have but one common concern, yet having different understandings, will unavoidably sometimes have different wills too; it therefore being necessary that the last determination, *i.e.*, the rule, should be placed somewhere; it naturally falls to the man's share, as the abler and the stronger. But this reaching but to the things of their common interest and property, leaves the wife in the full and free possession of what by contract is her peculiar right, and gives the husband no more power over her life than she has over his; the *power of the husband* being so far from that of an absolute monarch, that the *wife* has in many cases a liberty to separate from him, where natural right, or their contract allows it; whether that contract be made by themselves in the state of nature, or by the customs or laws of the country they live in; and the children upon such separation fall to the father or mother's lot, as such contract does determine.

For all the ends of *marriage* being to be obtained under politic government, as well as in the state of nature, the civil magistrate doth not abridge the right or power of either naturally necessary to those ends, *viz.* procreation and mutual support and assistance whilst they are together; but only decides any controversy that may arise between man and wife about them. If it were otherwise, and that absolute *sovereignty* and power of life and death naturally belonged to the husband, and were *necessary to the society between man and wife,* there could be no matrimony in any of those countries where the husband is allowed no such absolute authority. But the ends of matrimony requiring no such power in the husband, the condition of *conjugal society* put it not in him, it being not at all necessary to that state. *Conjugal society* could subsist and attain its ends without it; nay, community of goods, and the power over them, mutual assistance and maintenance, and other things belonging to *conjugal society,* might be varied and regulated by that contract which unites man and wife in that society, as far as may consist with procreation and the bringing up of children till they could shift for themselves; nothing being necessary to any society, that is not necessary to the ends for which it is made. . . .

Let us therefore consider a *master of a family* with all these subordinate relations of *wife, children, servants,* and *slaves,* united under the domestic rule of a family; which, what resemblance soever it may have in its order, offices, and number too, with a little common-wealth, yet is very far from it, both in its constitution, power and end: or if it must be thought a monarchy, and the *paterfamilias* the absolute monarch in it, absolute monarchy will have but a very shattered and short power, when it is plain, by what has been said before, that the *master of the family* has a very distinct and differently limited *power,* both as to time and extent, over those several persons that are in it; for excepting the slave (and the family is as much a family, and his power as *paterfamilias* as great, whether there be any slaves in his family or no) he has no legislative power of life and death over any of them, and none too but what a *mistress of a family* may have as well as he. And he certainly can have no absolute power over the whole *family,* who has but a very limited one over every individual in it. But how a *family,* or any other society of men, differ from that which is properly *political society,* we shall best see, by considering wherein *political society* itself consists.

* * *

DAVID HUME

The philosophy of David Hume (1711–1776), like that of Locke, is generally labeled as "empiricism" because of its emphasis on experience as the sole source of knowledge. Unlike other empiricists, however, Hume pursued the logic of their position to its radical implications: a critique of the principle of causality, and a denial of the possibility of certain or "scientific" knowledge about the world. Through association of ideas, Hume claimed, human beings tend to assign metaphysical causes to the data they experience. But such imputative judgments can never be entirely accounted for by reason, since the cause-effect relationship upon which they are based cannot be strictly demonstrated. Accordingly, even the most reliable scientific conclusions are mere statements of probability. Instead of interpreting such judgments as unfailing certitudes, we should, Hume maintains, preserve a healthy skepticism regarding all assertions about reality.

For Hume, the study of human nature constitutes the central concern of philosophy. The experimental method appropriate to this task is one based entirely on empirical data, including that of introspection, with conclusions that are open-ended. In light of this approach, Hume insisted that convictions about existence are not a matter of knowledge but of natural belief. Imagination, he maintained, is the source of belief in independent bodies, including our own, and memory plays a key role in establishing each one's sense of personal identity. As memory represents separate past perceptions in a chain of resemblance, imagination tends to (falsely) interpret their relation as a continuity which signifies identity of the self. According to Hume, "self or person is not any one impression, but that to which our several impressions and ideas *are supposed* to have a reference" (italics added). The supposition is natural but unwarranted, since there is no provable underlying identity in the succession of perceptions that constitutes the mind.

With regard to "liberty," Hume observes another instance of the tendency to attribute existential status to an unprovable cause of experienced effects. "By liberty," he asserts, "we can only mean *a power of acting or not acting according to the determinations of the will.*" The will is described as "the internal impression we feel and are conscious of, when we knowingly give rise to any new motion of our body, or new perception of our mind." Hume regards his definition of liberty as one "in which all men agree," and considers such liberty "also essential to morality."

As Hume uses it, the term "passion" refers to the entire sweep of human emotions and affections. Since reason alone is incapable of producing action or volition, he asserts that "[r]eason is, and ought only to be the slave of the passions" in questions of conduct. Hume seems to have thought that basic sentiments of morality were common to all individuals, and should be trusted. His moral ideal can readily be elaborated through epithets such as "*sociable, good-natured, humane, merciful, grateful, friendly, generous, beneficent,* or their equivalents." Such descriptives, Hume claims, "are known in all languages, and universally express the highest merit which human nature is capable of attaining."

Of Love and Marriage

I know not whence it proceeds, that women are so apt to take amiss every thing which is said in disparagement of the married state; and always consider a satyr upon matrimony as a satyr upon themselves. Do they mean, that they are the parties principally concerned, and that if a backwardness to enter into that state should prevail in the world, they would be the greatest sufferers? Or, are they sensible, that misfortunes and miscarriages of the married state are owing more to their sex than to ours? I hope they do not intend to confess either of these two particulars, or to give such an advantage to their adversaries, the men, as even to allow them to suspect it.

I have often had thoughts of complying with this humour of the fair sex, and of writing a panegyric upon marriage: But, in looking around for materials, they seemed to be of so mixed a nature, that at the conclusion of my reflections, I found that I was as much disposed to write a satyr, which might be placed on the opposite pages of the panegyric: And I am afraid, that as satyr is, on most occasions, thought to contain more truth than panegyric, I should have done their cause more harm than good by this expedient. To misrepresent facts is what, I know, they will not require of me. I must be more a friend to truth, than even to them, where their interests are opposite.

I shall tell the women what it is our sex complains of most in the married state; and if they be disposed to satisfy us in this particular, all the other differences will easily be accommodated. If I be not mistaken, 'tis their love of dominion, which is the ground of the quarrel; tho' 'tis very likely, that they will think it an unreasonable love of it in us, which makes us insist so much upon that point. However this may be, no passion seems to have more influence on female minds, than this for power; and there is a remarkable instance in history of its prevailing above another passion, which is the only one that can be supposed a proper counterpoise for it. We are told, that all the women in Scythia once conspired against the men, and kept the secret so well, that they executed their design before they were suspected. They surprised the men in drink, or asleep; bound them all fast in chains; and having called a solemn council of the whole sex, it was debated what expedient should be used to improve the present advantage, and prevent their falling again into slavery. To kill all the men did not seem to be the relish of any part of the assembly, notwithstanding the injuries formerly received; and they were afterwards pleased to make a great merit of this lenity of theirs. It was, therefore, agreed to put out the eyes of the whole male sex, and thereby resign in all future time the vanity which they could draw from their beauty, in order to secure their authority. We must no longer pretend to dress and show, said they; but then we shall be free from slavery. We shall hear no more tender sighs; but in return we shall hear no more imperious commands. Love must forever leave us; but he will carry subjection along with him.

'Tis regarded by some as an unlucky circumstance, since the women were resolved to maim the men, and deprive them of some of their senses, in order to render them humble and dependent, that the sense of hearing could not serve their purpose, since 'tis probable the females would rather have attacked that than the sight: And I think it is agreed among the learned, that, in a married state, 'tis not near so great an inconvenience to lose the former sense as the latter. However this may be, we are told by modern anecdotes, that some of the Scythian women did secretly spare their husbands' eyes; presuming, I suppose, that they could govern them as well by means of that sense as without it. But so incorrigible and untractable were these men, that their wives were all obliged, in a few years, as their youth and beauty decayed, to imitate the example of their sisters; which it was no difficult matter to do in a state where the female sex had once got the superiority.

I know not if our Scottish ladies derive any thing of this humour from their Scythian ancestors; but, I must confess that I have often been surprised to see a woman very well pleased to take a fool for her mate, that she might govern with the less control; and could not but think her sentiments, in this respect, still more barbarous than those of the Scythian women above-mentioned; as much as the eyes of the understanding are more valuable than those of the body.

But to be just, and to lay the blame more equally, I am afraid it is the fault of our sex, if the women be so fond of rule, and that if we did not abuse our authority, they would never think it worth while to dispute it. Tyrants, we know, produce rebels; and all history informs us, that rebels, when they prevail, are apt to become tyrants in their turn. For this reason, I could wish there were no pretensions to authority on either side; but that every thing was carried on with perfect equality, as between two equal members of the same body. And to induce both parties to embrace those amicable sentiments, I shall deliver to them Plato's account of the origin of love and marriage.

Mankind, according to that fanciful philosopher, were not, in their original, divided into male and female, as at present; but each individual person was a compound of both sexes, and was in himself both husband and wife, melted down into one living creature. This union, no doubt, was very entire, and the parts very well adjusted together, since there resulted a perfect harmony betwixt the male and female, altho' they were obliged to be inseparable companions. And so great were the harmony and happiness flowing from it, that the Androgynes (for so Plato calls them) or Men-Women, became insolent upon their prosperity, and rebelled against the Gods. To punish them for this temerity, Jupiter could contrive no better expedient, than to divorce the male-part from the female, and make two imperfect beings of the compound, which was before so perfect. Hence the origin of men and women, as distinct creatures. But notwithstanding this division, so lively is our remembrance of the happiness which we enjoyed in our primaeval state, that we are never at rest in this situation; but each of these halves is continually searching thro' the whole species to find the other half, which was broken from it: And when they meet, they join again with the greatest fondness and sympathy. But it often happens, that they are mistaken in this particular; that they take for their half what no way corresponds to them; and that the parts do not meet nor join in with each other, as is usual in fractures. In this case the union was soon dissolved, and each part is set loose again to hunt for its lost half, joining itself to every one whom it meets, by way of trial, and enjoying no rest till its perfect sympathy with its partner shows that it has at last been successful in its endeavours.

Were I disposed to carry on this fiction of Plato, which accounts for the mutual love betwixt the sexes in so agreeable a manner, I would do it by the following allegory.

When Jupiter had separated the male from the female, and had quelled their pride and ambition by so severe an operation, he could not but repent him of the cruelty of his vengeance, and take compassion on poor mortals, who were now become incapable of any repose or tranquility. Such cravings, such anxieties, such necessities arose, as made them curse their creation, and think existence itself a punishment. In vain had they recourse to every other occupation and amusement. In vain did they seek after every pleasure of sense, and every refinement of reason. Nothing could fill that void, which they felt in their hearts, or supply the loss of their partner, who was so fatally separated from them. To remedy this disorder, and to bestow some comfort, at least, on the human race in their forlorn situation, Jupiter sent down Love and Hymen, to collect the broken halves of human kind, and piece them together in the best manner possible. These two deities found such a prompt disposition in mankind to unite again in their primaeval state, that they proceeded on their work with wonderful success for some time; till at last, from many unlucky accidents, dissension arose betwixt them. The chief counsellor and favourite of Hymen was Care, who was continually filling his patron's head with prospects of futurity; a settlement, family, children, servants; so that little else was regarded in all the matches *they* made. On the other hand, *Love* had chosen Pleasure for his favourite, who was as pernicious a counsellor as the other, and would never allow *Love* to look beyond the present momentary gratification, or the satisfying of the prevailing inclination. These two favourites became, in a little time, irreconcilable enemies, and made it their chief business to undermine each other in all their undertakings. No sooner had *Love* fixed upon two halves, which he was cementing together, and forming to a close union, but *Care* insinuates himself; and bringing Hymen along with him, dissolves the union produced by love, and joins each half to some other half, which he had provided for it. To be revenged of this, *Pleasure* creeps in upon a pair already joined by Hymen; and calling *Love* to his assistance, they under hand contrive to join each half by secret links, to halves, which Hymen was wholly unacquainted with. It was not long before this quarrel was felt in its pernicious consequences; and such complaints arose before the throne of Jupiter, that he was obliged to summon the offending parties to appear before him, in order to give an account of their proceedings. After hearing the pleadings on both sides, he ordered an immediate reconcilement betwixt Love and Hymen, as the only expedient for giving happiness to mankind: And that he might be sure this reconcilement should be durable, he laid his strict injunctions on them never to join any halves without consulting their favourites *Care* and *Pleasure*, and obtaining the consent of both to the conjunction. Where this order is strictly observed, the *Androgyne* is perfectly restored, and the human race enjoy the same happiness as in their primaeval state. The seam is scarce perceived that joins the two beings; but both of them combine to form one perfect and happy creature.

* * *

Of Polygamy and Divorce

As marriage is an engagement entered into by mutual consent, and has for its end the propagation of the species, it is evident, that it must be susceptible of all the variety of conditions, which consent establishes, provided they be not contrary to this end.

A man, in conjoining himself to a woman, is bound to her according to the terms of his engagement: In begetting children, he is bound, by all the ties of nature and humanity, to provide for their subsistence and education. When he has performed these two parts of duty, no one can reproach him with injustice or injury. And as the terms of his engagement, as well as the methods of subsisting his offspring, may be various, it is mere superstition to imagine, that marriage can be entirely uniform, and will admit only of one mode or form. Did not human laws restrain the natural liberty of men, every particular marriage would be as different as contracts or bargains of any other kind or species.

As circumstances vary, and the laws purpose different advantages, we find, that, in different times and places, they impose different conditions on this important contract. In Tonquin, it is usual for the sailors, when the ships come into harbour, to marry for the season; and notwithstanding this precarious engagement, they are assured, it is said, of the strictest fidelity to their bed, as well as the whole management of their affairs, from those temporary spouses.

I cannot, at present, recollect my authorities; but I have somewhere read, that the republic of Athens, having lost many of its citizens by war and pestilence, allowed every man to marry two wives, in order the sooner to repair the waste which had been made by these calamities. The poet Euripides happened to be coupled to two noisy Vixens who so plagued him with their jealousies and quarrels, that he became ever after a professed *woman-hater;* and is the only theatrical writer, perhaps the only poet, that ever entertained an aversion to the sex.

In that agreeable romance, called *the History of the* Sevarambians, where a great many men and a few women are supposed to be shipwrecked on a desert coast; the captain of the troop, in order to obviate those endless quarrels which arose, regulates their marriages after the following manner: He takes a handsome female to himself alone; assigns one to every couple of inferior officers; and to five of the lowest rank he gives one wife in common.

The ancient Britons had a singular kind of marriage, to be met with among no other people. Any number of them, as ten or a dozen, joined in a society together, which was perhaps requisite for mutual defence in those barbarous times. In order to link this society the closer, they took an equal number of wives in common; and whatever children were born, were reputed to belong to all of them, and were accordingly provided for by the whole community.

Among the inferior creatures, nature herself, being the supreme legislator, prescribes all the laws which regulate their marriages, and varies those laws according to the different circumstances of the creature. Where she furnishes, with ease, food and defence to the newborn animal, the present embrace terminates the marriage; and the care of the offspring is committed entirely to the female. Where the food is of more difficult purchase, the marriage continues for one season, till the common progeny can provide for itself; and the union immediately dissolves, and leaves each of the parties free to enter into a new engagement at the ensuing season. But nature, having endowed man with reason, has not so exactly regulated every article of his marriage contract, but has left him to adjust them, by his own prudence, according to his particular circumstances and situation. Municipal laws are a supply to the wisdom of each individuual; and, at the same time, by restraining the natural liberty of men, make private interest submit to the interest of the public. All regulations, therefore, on this head are equally lawful, and equally conformable to the principles of nature; though they are not all equally convenient, or equally useful to society. The laws may allow of polygamy, as among the *Eastern* nations; or of voluntary divorces, as among the Greeks and Romans; or they may confine one man to one woman, during the whole course of their lives, as among the modern Europeans. It may not be disagreeable to consider the advantages and disadvantages, which result from each of these institutions.

The advocates for polygamy may recommend it as the only effectual remedy for the disorders of love, and the only expedient for freeing men from that slavery to the females, which the natural violence of our passions has imposed upon us. By this means alone can we regain our right of sovereignty; and, sating our appetite, re-establish the authority of reason in our minds, and, of consequence, our own authority in our families. Man, like a weak sovereign, being unable to support himself against the wiles and intrigues of his subjects, must play one faction against another, and become absolute by the mutual jealousy of the females. *To divide and to govern* is an universal maxim; and by neglecting it, the Europeans undergo a more grievous and a more ignominious slavery than the Turks or Persians, who are subjected indeed to a sovereign, that lies at a distance from them, but in their domestic affairs rule with an uncontrollable sway.

On the other hand, it may be urged with better reason, that this sovereignty of the male is a real usurpation, and destroys that nearness of rank, not to say equality, which nature has established between the sexes. We are, by nature, their lovers, their friends, their patrons: Would we willingly exchange such endearing appellations, for the barbarous title of master and tyrant?

In what capacity shall we gain by this inhuman proceeding? As lovers, or as husbands? The *lover,* is totally annihilated; and courtship, the most agreeable scene in life, can no longer have place, where women have not the free disposal of themselves, but are bought and sold, like the meanest animal. The *husband* is as little a gainer, having found the admirable secret of extinguishing every part of love, except its jealousy. No rose without its thorn; but he must be a foolish wretch indeed, that throws away the rose and preserves only the thorn.

But the Asiatic manners are as destructive to friendship as to love. Jealousy excludes men from all intimacies and familiarities with each other. No one dares bring his friend to his house or table, lest he bring a lover to his numerous wives. Hence all over the east, each family is as much separate from another, as if they were so many distinct kingdoms. No wonder then, that Solomon, living like an eastern prince, with his seven hundred wives, and three hundred concubines, without one friend, could write so pathetically concerning the vanity of the world. Had he tried the secret of one wife or mistress, a few friends, and a great many companions, he might have found life somewhat more agreeable. Destroy love and friendship; what remains in the world worth accepting?

The bad education of children, especially children of condition, is another unavoidable consequence of these eastern institutions. Those who pass the early part of life among slaves, are only qualified to be, themselves, slaves and tyrants; and in every future intercourse, either with their inferiors or superiors, are apt to forget the natural equality of mankind. What attention, too, can it be supposed a parent, whose seraglio affords him fifty sons, will give to instilling principles of morality or science into a progeny, with whom he himself is scarcely acquainted, and whom he loves with so divided an affection? Barbarism, therefore, appears, from reason as well as experience, to be the inseparable attendant of polygamy.

To render polygamy more odious, I need not recount the frightful effects of jealousy, and the constraint in which it holds the fair-sex all over the east. In those countries men are not allowed to have any commerce with the females, not even physicians, when sickness may be supposed to have extinguished all wanton passions in the bosoms of the fair, and, at the same time, has rendered them unfit objects of desire. . . .

. . . But it will, perhaps, appear strange, that, in a European country, jealousy can yet be carried to such a height, that it is indecent so much as to suppose that a woman of rank can have feet or legs. Witness the following story, which we have from very good authority. When the mother of the late king of Spain was on her road towards Madrid, she passed through a little town in Spain, famous for its manufactory of gloves and stockings. The magistrates of the place thought they could not better express their joy for the reception of their new queen, than by presenting her with a sample of those commodities, for which alone their town was remarkable. The *major domo*, who conducted the princess, received the gloves very graciously: But when the stockings were presented, he flung them away with great indignation, and severely reprimanded the magistrates for this egregious piece of indecency. *Know,* says he, *that a queen of Spain has no legs.* The young queen, who, at that time, understood the language but imperfectly, and had often been frightened with stories of Spanish jealousy, imagined that they were to cut off her legs. Upon which she fell a crying, and begged them to conduct her back to Germany; for that she never could endure the operation: And it was with some difficulty they could appease her. Philip IV. is said never in his life to have laughed heartily, but at the recital of this story.

Having rejected polygamy, and matched one man with one woman, let us now consider what duration we shall assign to their union, and whether we shall admit of those voluntary divorces, which were customary among the Greeks and Romans. Those who would defend this practice may employ the following reasons.

How often does disgust and aversion arise after marriage, from the most trivial accidents, or from an incompatibility of humour; where time, instead of curing the wounds, proceeding from mutual injuries, festers them every day the more, by new quarrels and reproaches? Let us separate hearts, which were not made to associate together. Each of them may, perhaps, find another for which it is better fitted. At least, nothing can be more cruel than to preserve, by violence, an union, which, at first, was made by mutual love, and is now, in effect, dissolved by mutual hatred.

But the liberty of divorces is not only a curet to hatred and domestic quarrels: It is also an admirable preservative against them, and the only secret for keeping alive that love, which first united the married couple. The heart of man delights in liberty: The very image of constraint is grievous to it: When you would confine it by violence, to what would otherwise have been its choice, the inclination immediately changes, and desire is turned into aversion. If the public interest will not allow us to enjoy in polygamy that *variety*, which is so agreeable in love: at least, deprive us not of that liberty, which is so essentially requisite. In vain you tell me, that I had my choice of the person, with whom I would conjoin myself. I had my choice, it is true, of my prison; but this is but a small comfort, since it must still be a prison.

Such are the arguments which may be urged in favour of divorces: But there seem to be these three unanswerable objections against them. *First*, What must become of the children, upon the separation of the parents? Must they be committed to the care of a step-mother; and instead of the fond attention and concern of a parent, feel all the indifference or hatred of a stranger or an enemy? These inconveniences are sufficiently felt, where nature has made the divorce by the doom inevitable to all mortals: And shall we seek to multiply those inconveniences, by multiplying divorces, and putting it in the power of parents, upon every caprice, to render their posterity miserable?

Secondly, If it be true, on the one hand, that the heart of man naturally delights in liberty, and hates every thing to which it is confined; it is also true, on the other, that the heart of man naturally submits to necessity, and soon loses an inclination, when there appears an absolute impossibility of gratifying it. These principles of human nature, you'll say, are contradictory: But what is man but a heap of contradictions! Though it is remarkable, that, where principles are, after this manner, contrary in their operation, they do not always destroy each other; but the one or the other may predominate on any particular occasion, according as circumstances are more or less favourable to it. For instance, love is a restless and impatient passion, full of caprices and variations: arising in a moment from a feature, from an air, from nothing, and suddenly extinguishing after the same manner. Such a passion requires liberty above all things; and therefore Eloisa had reason, when, in order to preserve this passion, she refused to marry her beloved Abelard.

> How oft, when prest to marriage, have I said,
> Curse on all laws but those which love has made;
> Love, free as air, at sight of human ties,
> Spreads his light wings, and in a moment flies.

But *friendship* is a calm and sedate affection, conducted by reason and cemented by habit; springing from long acquaintance and mutual obligations; without jealousies or fears, and without those feverish fits of heat and cold, which cause such an agreeable torment in the amorous passion. So sober an affection, therefore, as friendship, rather thrives under constraint, and never rises to such a height, as when any strong interest or necessity binds two persons together, and gives them some common object of pursuit. We need not, therefore, be afraid of drawing the marriage-knot, which chiefly subsists by friendship, the closest possible. The amity between the persons, where it is solid and sincere, will rather gain by it: And where it is wavering and uncertain, this is the best expedient for fixing it. How many frivolous quarrels and disgusts are there, which people of common prudence endeavour to forget, when they lie under a necessity of passing their lives together; but which would soon be inflamed into the most deadly hatred were they pursued to the utmost, under the prospect of an easy separation?

In the *third* place, we must consider, that nothing is more dangerous than to unite two persons so closely in all their interests and concerns, as man and wife, without rendering the union entire and total.

The least possibility of a separate interest must be the source of endless quarrels and suspicions. The wife, not secure of her establishment, will still be driving some separate end or project; and the husband's selfishness, being accompanied with more power, may be still more dangerous.

Should these reasons against voluntary divorces be deemed insufficient, I hope no body will pretend to refuse the testimony of experience. At the time when divorces were most frequent among the Romans, marriages were most rare; and Augustus was obliged, by penal laws, to force men of fashion into the married state: A circumstance which is scarcely to be found in any other age or nation. The more ancient laws of Rome, which prohibited divorces, are extremely praised by Dionysius Halycarnassaeus. Wonderful was the harmony, says the historian, which this inseparable union of interests produced between married persons; while each of them considered the inevitable necessity by which they were linked together, and abandoned all prospect of any other choice or establishment.

The exclusion of polygamy and divorces sufficiently recommends our present European practice with regard to marriage.

* * *

Of Chastity and Modesty

If any difficulty attend this system concerning the laws of nature and nations, 'twill be with regard to the universal approbation or blame, which follows their observance or transgression, and which some may not think sufficiently explain'd from the general interests of society. To remove, as far as possible, all scruples of this kind, I shall here consider another set of duties, *viz.* the *modesty* and *chastity* which belong to the fair sex: And I doubt not but these virtues will be found to be still more conspicuous instances of the operation of those principles, which I have insisted on.

There are some philosophers, who attack the female virtues with great vehemence, and fancy they have gone very far in detecting popular errors, when they can show, that there is no foundation in nature for all that exterior modesty, which we require in the expressions, and dress, and behaviour of the fair sex. I believe I may spare myself the trouble of insisting on so obvious a subject, and may proceed, without farther preparation, to examine after what manner such notions arise from education, from the voluntary conventions of men, and from the interest of society.

Whoever considers the length and feebleness of human infancy, with the concern which both sexes naturally have for their offspring, will easily perceive, that there must be an union of male and female for the education of the young, and that this union must be of considerable duration. But in order to induce the men to impose on themselves this restraint, and undergo cheerfully all the fatigues and expences, to which it subjects them, they must believe, that the children are their own, and that their natural instinct is not directed to a wrong object, when they give a loose to love and tenderness. Now if we examine the structure of the human body, we shall find, that this security is very difficult to be attain'd on our part; and that since, in the copulation of the sexes, the principle of generation goes from the man to the woman, an error may easily take place on the side of the former, tho' it be utterly impossible with regard to the latter. From this trivial and anatomical observation is deriv'd that vast difference betwixt the education and duties of the two sexes.

Were a philosopher to examine the matter *a priori*, he would reason after the following manner. Men are induc'd to labour for the maintenance and education of their children, by the persuasion that they are really their own; and therefore 'tis reasonable, and even necessary, to give them some security in this particular. This security cannot consist entirely in the imposing of severe punishments on any transgressions of conjugal fidelity on the part of the wife; since these public punishments cannot be inflicted without legal proof, which 'tis difficult to meet with in this subject. What restraint, therefore, shall we impose on women, in order to counterbalance so strong a temptation as they have to infidelity? There seems to be no restraint possible, but in the punishment of bad fame or reputation; a punishment, which has a mighty influence on the human mind, and at the same time is inflicted by the world upon surmises, and conjectures, and proofs, that would never be receiv'd in any court of judicature. In order, therefore, to impose a due restraint on the female sex, we must attach a peculiar degree of shame to their infidelity, above what arises merely from its injustice, and must bestow proportionable praises on their chastity.

But tho' this be a very strong motive to fidelity, our philosopher would quickly discover, that it would not alone be sufficient to that purpose. All human creatures, especially of the female sex, are apt to over-look remote motives in favour of any present temptation: The temptation is here the strongest imaginable: Its approaches are insensible and seducing: And a woman easily finds, or flatters herself she shall find, certain means of securing her reputation, and preventing all the pernicious consequences of her pleasures. 'Tis necessary, therefore, that, beside the infamy attending such licences, there should be some preceding backwardness or dread, which may prevent their first approaches, and may give the female sex a repugnance to all expressions, and postures, and liberties, that have an immediate relation to that enjoyment.

Such would be the reasonings of our speculative philosopher: But I am persuaded, that if he had not a perfect knowledge of human nature, he would be apt to regard them as mere chimerical speculations, and would consider the infamy attending infidelity, and backwardness to all its approaches, as principles that were rather to be wish'd than hop'd for in the world. For what means, would he say, of persuading mankind, that the transgressions of conjugal duty are more infamous than any other kind of injustice, when 'tis evident they are more excusable, upon account of the greatness of the temptation? And what possibility of giving a backwardness to the approaches of a pleasure, to which nature has inspir'd so strong a propensity; and a propensity that 'tis absolutely necessary in the end to comply with, for the support of the species?

But speculative reasonings, which cost so much pains to philosophers, are often form'd by the world naturally, and without reflection: As difficulties, which seem unsurmountable in theory, are easily got over in practice. Those, who have an interest in the fidelity of women, naturally disapprove of their infidelity, and all the approaches to it. Those, who have no interest, are carried along with the stream. Education takes possession of the ductile minds of the fair sex in their infancy. And when a general rule of this kind is once establish'd, men are apt to extend it beyond those principles, from which it first arose. Thus bachelors, however debauch'd, cannot choose but be shock'd with any instance of lewdness or impudence in women. And tho' all these maxims have a plain reference to generation, yet women past child-bearing have no more privilege in this respect, than those who are in the flower of their youth and beauty. Men have undoubtedly an implicit notion, that all those ideas of modesty and decency have a regard to generation; since they impose not the same laws, *with the same force,* on the male sex, where that reason takes not place. The exception is there obvious and extensive, and founded on a remarkable difference, which produces a clear separation and disjunction of ideas. But as the case is not the same with regard to the different ages of women, for this reason, tho' men know, that these notions are founded on the public interest, yet the general rule carries us beyond the original principle, and makes us extend the notions of modesty over the whole sex, from their earliest infancy to their extremest old-age and infirmity.

Courage, which is the point of honour among men, derives its merit, in a great measure, from artifice, as well as the chastity of women; tho' it has also some foundation in nature, as we shall see afterwards.

As to the obligations which the male sex lie under, with regard to chastity, we may observe, that according to the general notions of the world, they bear nearly the same proportion to the obligations of women, as the obligations of the law of nations do to those of the law of nature. 'Tis contrary to the interest of civil society, that men should have an *entire* liberty of indulging their appetites in venereal enjoyment: But as this interest is weaker than in the case of the female sex, the moral obligation, arising from it, must be proportionably weaker. And to prove this we need only appeal to the practice and sentiments of all nations and ages.

* * *

JEAN-JACQUES ROUSSEAU

The philosophy of Jean-Jacques Rousseau (1712–1778) emphasizes society as the means through which human beings are civilized. Ironically, Rousseau's own disposition, as reported by biographers, was extremely erratic and irascible. However, to dismiss his ideas simply on the basis of his personal flaws is to commit what logicians call the genetic fallacy. We ought instead to follow the example of Mary Wollstonecraft, who distinguished between the man and his ideas, evaluating the latter so as to discern what truth might be contained therein. Rousseau's principal philosophical contribution involves his focus on the individual and liberty, rather than on universal principles or changeless values.

In his *Discourse on the Origin of Inequality among Men,* Rousseau describes "primitive" man, or man "in the state of nature" as essentially free and good. Freedom, for Rousseau, is *the* fundamental difference between man and brute, more fundamental even than reason or understanding. But freedom is limited the minute an individual becomes socialized. Hence, primitive man is asocial, i.e., indifferent to others. Rousseau pictures such a person

> wandering up and down the forests, without industry, without speech and without hunger, an equal stranger to war and to all ties, neither standing in need of his fellow-creatures nor having any desire to hurt them.

Self-love is another trait of human nature in its primitive state. This is a passion which becomes good or evil according to the circumstances in which it develops. Compassion naturally arises through the extension of self-love to others; it is a virtue contributing to the preservation of the whole species. Conscience, which for Rousseau means a love of order, is an innate principle of justice and virtue and also derives from self-love. Egoism should not be identified with self-love, for "in the true state of nature, egoism does not exist."

Gradually, as free individuals claimed private property and required others to respect their ownership, the original natural equality of men disappeared. Rousseau describes the resulting social order as a "sacred right which serves as the basis of all other rights." Within that order *natural* freedom and equality are inevitably lost, but man gains *civil* liberty and equality by freely entering into a social contract. The "general will" defines the limit of civil liberty. Civil equality occurs to the extent that all citizens share the same duties and right. Within society, then, freedom and equality are *relative*, whereas for primitive man they were absolute. Summarily, Rousseau's contrasting concept can be put as follows:

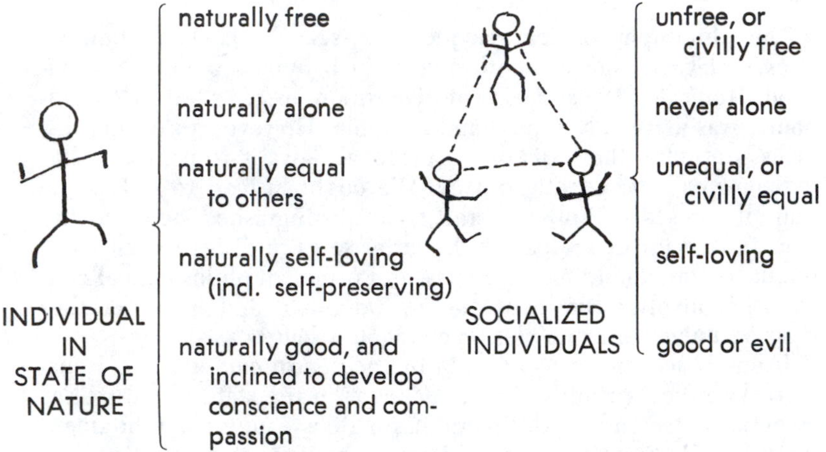

The following selection illustrates Rousseau's philosophy of education. Given the author's essentially positive view of primitive human nature, the responsibility of the educator is never to impede but always to facilitate the natural development of the individual. The task "to form the man of nature" is so comprehensive that a full-time private tutor is required. Rousseau sees the ideal tutor introducing his student to the best of life's experiences, fostering but never coercing the growth of virtue and reason. The education of Sophie is treated only with reference to preparing the ideal mate for Emile. Sophie represents any woman.

Marriage

Sophie should be as typically woman as Emile is man. She must possess all the characteristics of humanity and of womanhood which she needs for playing her part in the physical and the moral order. Let us begin by considering in what respects her sex and ours agree and differ.

In everything that does not relate to sex the woman is as the man: they are alike in organs, needs and capacities. In whatever way we look at them the difference is only one of less or more. In everything that relates to sex there are correspondences and differences. The difficulty is to determine what in their constitution is due to sex and what is not. All we know with certainty is that the common features are due to the species and the differences to sex. From this twofold point of view we find so many likenesses and so many contrasts that we cannot but marvel that nature has been able to create two beings so much alike with constitutions so different.

The sameness and the difference cannot but have an effect on mentality. This is borne out by experience and shows the futility of discussions about sex superiorities and inequalities. A perfect man and a perfect woman should no more resemble each other in mind than in countenance: and perfection does not admit of degrees.

In the mating of the sexes each contributes in equal measure to the common end but not in the same way. From this diversity comes the *first* difference which has to be noted in their personal relations. It is the part of the one to be active and strong, and of the other to be passive and weak. Accept this principle and it follows in the *second* place that woman is intended to please man. If the man requires to please the woman in turn the necessity is less direct. Masterfulness is his special attribute. He pleases by the very fact that he is strong. This is not the law of love, I admit. But it is the law of nature, which is more ancient than love.

If woman is made to please and to be dominated, she ought to make herself agreeable to man and avoid provocation. Her strength is in her charms and through them she should constrain him to discover his powers and make use of them. The surest way of bringing these powers into active operation is to make it necessary by her resistance.

In this way self-esteem is added to desire and the man triumphs in the victory which the woman has compelled him to achieve. Out of this relation comes attack and defence, boldness on the one side and timidity on the other, and in the end the modesty and sense of shame with which nature has armed the weak for the subjugation of the strong.

Hence as a *third* consequence of the different constitution of the sexes, the stronger may appear to be master, and yet actually be dependent on the weaker: not because of a superficial practice of gallantry or the prideful generosity of the protective sex, but by reason of an enduring law of nature. By giving woman the capacity to stimulate desires greater than can be satisfied, nature has made man dependent on woman's good will and constrained him to seek to please her as a condition of her submission. Always there remains for man in his conquest the pleasing doubt whether strength has mastered weakness, or there has been a willing subjection; and the woman has usually the guile to leave the doubt unresolved.

Men and women are unequally affected by sex. The male is only a male at times; the female is a female all her life and can never forget her sex.

Plato in his *Republic* gives women the same physical training as men. That is what might be expected. Having made an end of private families in his state and not knowing what to do with the women, he found himself compelled to make men of them. That wonderful genius provided for everything in his plans, and went out of his way to meet an objection that nobody was likely to make, while missing the real objection. I am not speaking about the so-called community of wives, so often charged against him by people who have not read him. What I refer to is the social promiscuity which ignored the differences of sex by giving men and women the same occupations, and sacrificed the sweetest sentiments of nature to the artificial sentiment of loyalty which could not exist without them. He did not realise that the bonds of convention always develop from some natural attachment: that the love one has for his neighbours is the basis of his devotion to the state; that the heart is linked with the great fatherland through the little fatherland of the home; that it is the good son, the good husband, the good father, that makes the good citizen.

Once it has been shown that men and women are essentially different in character and temperament, it follows that they ought not to have the same education. In accordance with the direction of nature they ought to co-operate in action, but not to do the same things. To complete the attempt we have been making to form the man of nature, we must now go on to consider how the fitting mate for him is to be formed.

If you want right guidance, always follow the leadings of nature. Everything that characterises sex should be respected as established by nature. Men's pride leads them astray when, comparing women with themselves, they say, as they are continually doing, that women have this or that defect, which is absent in men. What would be defects in men are good qualities in women, which are necessary to make things go on well. Women on their side never stop complaining that we men make coquettes of them and keep amusing them with trifles in order to maintain our ascendency. What a foolish idea! When have men ever had to do with the education of girls? Who prevents the mother bringing up their daughters as they please? Are we men to blame if girls please us by their beauty and attract us by the art they have learned from their mothers? Well, try to educate them like men. They will be quite willing. But the more they resemble men the less will be their power over men, and the greater their own subjection.

The faculties common to the sexes are not equally shared between them; but take them all in all, they are well balanced. The more womanly a woman is, the better. Whenever she exercises her own proper powers she gains by it: when she tries to usurp ours she becomes our inferior. Believe me, wise mother, it is a mistake to bring up your daughter to be like a good man. Make her a good woman, and you can be sure that she will be worth more for herself and for us. This does not mean that she should be brought up in utter ignorance and confined to domestic tasks. A man does not want to make his companion a servant and deprive himself of the peculiar charms of her company. That is quite against the teaching of nature, which has endowed women with quick pleasing minds. Nature means them to think, to judge, to love, to know and to cultivate the mind as well as the countenance. This is the equipment nature has given them to compensate for their lack of strength and enable them to direct the strength of men.

As I see it, the special functions of women, their inclinations and their duties, combine to suggest the kind of education they require. Men and women are made for each other but they differ in the measure of their dependence on each other. We could get on better without women than women could get on without us. To play their part in life they must earn our esteem. By the very law of nature women are at the mercy of men's judgments both for themselves and for their children. It is not enough that they should be estimable: they must be esteemed. It is not enough that they should be beautiful: they must be pleasing. It is not enough that they should be wise: their wisdom must be recognised. Their honour does not rest on their conduct but on their reputation. Hence the kind of education they get should be the very opposite of men's in this respect. Public opinion is the tomb of a man's virtue by the throne of a woman's.

On the good constitution of the mothers depends that of the children and the early education of men is in their hands. On women too depend the morals, the passions, the tastes, the pleasures, aye and the happiness of men. For this reason their education must be wholly directed to their relations with men. To give them pleasure, to be useful to them, to win their love and esteem, to train them in their childhood, to care for them when they grow up, to give them counsel and consolation, to make life sweet and agreeable for them: these are the tasks of women in all times for which they should be trained from childhood.

TRAINING FOR WOMANHOOD
(1) TO THE AGE OF TEN

From the beginning little girls are fond of dress. Not content with being pretty they want notice taken of them. It is evident from their little airs that they have already got this concern. Almost as soon as they can understand what is said to them they can be controlled by telling them what people think of them. It would be foolish to speak that way to little boys and it would not have the same effect. Provided they are left free to enjoy their games boys care very little about what anybody thinks of them. It takes much time and effort to bring them under the same control.

However girls get this first lesson, it is a very good one. The body, one might say is born before the mind and for that reason must be trained first. That applies to both sexes but with a difference. In the boys the object of the training is the development of strength, in the girls the development of graces. Not that these qualities should be confined to one sex or the other but that they should differ in the importance attached to them. Women should have enough strength to do all they have to do gracefully: men enough skill to do what they have to do with ease.

Excessive softness in women makes men soft. They should not be sturdy like men but for them, so that they may be the mothers of sturdy males. From this point of view convents and boarding schools where the children get homely food and can run about and play freely in the open air and garden are preferable to the home where a delicately nurtured girl, always seated in a stuffy room under her mother's eye, dare not get up to walk or talk or breathe and is never free for a moment to jump or run or shout or give way to the natural petulance of her age. This is against all reason. It can only result in the ruin of both heart and body.

Everything that checks and constrains nature is in bad taste. This applies to the finery that bedecks the body as much as to the ornaments of the mind. Life, health, sanity, comfort ought to come first. There can be no grace without freedom and no charm in languor and illness. Suffering excites pity but it is the bloom of health that gives pleasure and delight.

Children of the two sexes have many amusements in common, and that is right since it will be the same when they grow up. But they have also distinctive tastes. Boys like movement and noise: their toys are drums, tops and go-carts. Girls would rather have things that look well and serve for adornment: mirrors, jewels, dress materials and most of all dolls. The doll is the special plaything of the sex. Here the girls' liking is plainly directed towards her lifework. For her the art of pleasing finds its physical expression in dress. That is all a child can acquire of this art.

Look at the little girl, busy with her doll all day long, changing its trappings, dressing and undressing it hundreds of times, always on the outlook for new ways of decoration whether good or bad. Her fingers are clumsy and her taste unformed, but already her bent is evident. 'But,' you may say, 'she is dressing her doll, not herself.' No doubt! The fact is that she sees her doll and not herself. For the time being she herself does not matter. She is absorbed in the doll and her coquetry is expressed through it. But the time will come when she will be her own doll.

Here then right at the beginning is a well-marked taste. You have only to follow it up and give it direction. What the little one wishes most of all is to decorate her doll, to make bows, tippets, sashes, lacework for it. In all this she has to depend on the good will of others for help and it would be more convenient in every way if she could do it herself. Here is a motive for the first lessons given to her. They are not tasks prescribed for her but favours conferred. As a matter of fact nearly all little girls greatly dislike learning to read and write but they are always willing to learn to use the needle. They imagine themselves grown up and think happily of the time when they will be using their talents in adorning themselves.

The first open road is easy to follow. Tapestry which is the amusement of women is not much to the liking of girls, and furnishings, having nothing to do with the person, are remote from their interests. But needlework, embroidery and lacemaking come readily to them. The same willing progress leads on easily to drawing, for this art is not unrelated to that of dressing one's self with good taste. I would not have girls taught to draw landscape or to do figure painting. It will be enough if they draw leaves, flowers, fruit, draperies, anything that can add to the elegance of dress and enable them to make their own embroidery patterns. If it is important for men to confine their studies in the main to everyday knowledge, it is even more important for women whose way of life, though less laborious, does not permit them to devote themselves to the talent of their choice at the expense of their duties.

Whatever the humorists may say, good sense is common to the two sexes. Girls are generally more docile than boys and in any case have more need to be brought under authority. But this does not mean that they should be required to do things without seeing the use of them. The maternal art is to make evident the purpose of everything that is prescribed to them; and this is all the easier to do since the girl's intelligence is more precocious than the boy's. This principle excludes for both boys and girls not only studies which serve no obvious purpose but even those which only become useful at a later stage. If it is wrong to urge a boy to learn to read it is even worse to compel little girls to do so before making them realise the value of reading. After all what need have girls to read and write at an early age? They are not going to have a household to manage for a long time to come. All of them have curiosity enough to make sure that they will learn without compulsion when leisure and the occasion come. Possibly they should learn to count first of all.

Counting has an obvious utility at all stages and much practice is required to avoid errors in calculation. I guarantee that if a little girl does not get cherries at tea-time till she has performed some arithmetical exercise she will very soon learn to count.

Always justify the tasks you impose on young girls but impose them all the same. Idleness and indocility are their most dangerous faults and are most difficult to cure once they are contracted. Not only should girls be careful and industrious but they should be kept under control from an early age. This hardship, if it be a hardship, is inseparable from their sex. All their lives they will be under the hard, unceasing constraints of the proprieties. They must be disciplined to endure them till they come to take them as a matter of course and learn to overcome caprice and bow to authority. If they are inclined to be always busy they should sometimes be compelled to do nothing whatever. To save them from dissipation, caprice and fickleness they must learn above all to master themselves.

Do not let girls get bored with their occupations and turn too keen on their amusements, as happens in the ordinary education where, as Fénelon says, all the bordeom is on the one side and all the pleasure on the other. A girl will only be bored with her tasks if she gets on badly with the people around her. A little one who loves her mother or some darling friend will work in their company day in and day out and never become tired. The constraint put on the child, so far from weakening the affection she has for her mother, will make it stronger; for dependence is a state natural to women, and girls realise that they are made for obedience.

And just because they have, or ought to have, little freedom, they carry the freedom they have to excess. Extreme in all things, they devote themselves to their play with greater zeal than boys. This is the second defect. This zeal must be kept within bounds. It is the cause of several vices peculiar to women, among others the capricious changing of their tastes from day to day. Do not deprive them of mirth, laughter, noise and romping games, but prevent them tiring of one game and turning to another. They must get used to being stopped in the middle of their play and put to other tasks without protest on their part. This daily constraint will produce the docility that women need all their lives. The first and most important quality of a woman is sweetness. Being destined to obey a being so imperfect as man (often with many vices and always with many shortcomings), she must learn to submit uncomplainingly to unjust treatment and marital wrongs. Not for his sake but for her own she must preserve her sweetness.

Girls should always be submissive, but mothers should not always be inexorable. To make a young person docile there is no call to make her unhappy. Indeed I should not be sorry if sometimes she were allowed to exercise a little cunning, not to elude punishment but to escape having to obey. Guile is a natural gift of her sex; and being convinced that all natural dispositions are good and right in themselves I think that this one should be cultivated like the rest. The characteristic cunning with which women are endowed is an equitable compensation for their lesser strength. Without it women would not be the comrade of man but his slave. This talent gives her the superiority that keeps her his equal and enables her to rule him even while she obeys.

TRAINING FOR WOMANHOOD (2) AFTER THE AGE OF TEN

Fine dress may make a woman outstanding, but it is only the person herself that pleases. The attire that is least noticeable often makes its wearer most noticed. The education of young girls in this respect is utterly wrong. They are promised ornaments for rewards, and taught to love gorgeous apparel. 'How beautiful she is,' people say when a girl is all dressed up. This is quite wrong. Girls should learn that so much finery is only put on to hide defects, and that the triumph of beauty is to shine by itself. If I saw a young girl strutting like a peacock in gay garments I should show myself disturbed by this disguising of her figure. I should remark: 'What a pity she is so over-dressed. Do you not think she could do with something simpler? Is she pretty enough to dispense with this or that?' Perhaps she would then be the first to want the ornamentation removed so that she might be judged on her merits.

The first thing that young persons notice as they grow up is that external adornment is not enough, if they lack accomplishments of their own. They cannot make themselves beautiful, and it is too soon for them to play the coquette; but they are old enough to have graceful gestures, an attractive accent, a self-possessed bearing, a light step, and gracious manners. At this stage the voice improves in range, strength and tone, the arms develop, the movements become more confident; and with all this comes the discovery that there is an art by which they can win attention in any situation. From this point sewing and industry no longer suffice of themselves. New talents make their appearance and their usefulness is recognised.

I know that austere teachers are against teaching girls singing or dancing or any of the arts of pleasing. Secular songs, they say, are wicked. Dancing is an invention of the devil. A young girl should find entertainment enough in work and prayer. Strange entertainments these for a child of ten! For my part I greatly fear that the little saints who have been compelled to spend their childhood in prayer will occupy their youth in quite different ways and make up for what they missed in girlhood when they marry. We should consider what befits age as well as befits sex. A young girl should not live like her grandmother. She should be lively and merry. She should dance and sing as much as she likes and enjoy all the innocent pleasures of her age. . . .

The question is sometimes raised whether girls should be taught by masters or mistresses. Personally I would rather they had no need for either but should learn of themselves what they are strongly inclined to learn. In the arts which have pleasure as their object anyone can teach a young girl—father or mother, sister or brother, girl friends, governesses, her mirror, above all her own taste. Taste is formed by industry and the natural gifts. By its means the mind is gradually opened to the idea of beauty in all its forms, and ultimately to those moral notions allied to beauty. This is perhaps one reason why the sentiments of decency and propriety are acquired by girls sooner than by boys. They certainly do not come from their governesses.

The art of speech takes first place among the pleasing arts. It is the mind with its succession of feelings and ideas that imparts life and variety to the countenance and inspires the talk that keeps the attention fixed on one object. That, I believe, is why young girls so quickly learn to chatter agreeably and put expression into their talk, even before they feel it. And that is why men find it amusing to listen to them so soon: they are waiting for the first gleam of intelligence to break through feeling.

The chatter of girls should not be curbed by the hard question that one puts to boys: 'What's the good of that?' but rather by the other question that is no more easy to answer: 'What will be the effect of that?' In the early years before they can distinguish good and evil, or pass judgment on other people, girls should make it a rule for themselves to say only agreeable things to those with whom they are talking. What makes this rule difficult in practice is that it must always be kept subordinate to our first rule: 'Never tell a lie.'

It is obvious that if male children cannot form any true idea of religion it is still more beyond the comprehension of girls. For that very reason I would speak to them about it at an earlier age, for if it were necessary to wait till they were able to discuss these profound questions the chances are that they would never be mentioned at all. Just as a woman's conduct is subject to public opinion, so is her faith subject to authority. Every girl should have her mother's religion, and every woman her husband's. Not being able to judge for themselves in such matters, they should accept the conviction of fathers and husbands as they accept that of the church. . . .

It is of less consequence that girls should learn their religion young than that they should learn it well and still more that they love it. If you make it onerous and are always depicting God as angry with them, if in His name you impose on them a great many disagreeable duties which they never see you fulfil yourself, what can they think but that learning the catechism and praying to God are duties for little girls and will wish to be grown up like you to escape this obligation? Example is all important. Without it you will never make any impression on children.

When you explain the articles of faith let it be in the form of direct instruction and not by question and answer. Girls should only answer what they think themselves and not what has been prescribed for them. . . .

[M]etaphysical questions are not for a little girl to answer. . . . Don't make your girls theologians and dialecticians. Accustom them to feel themselves always under the eyes of God, and to live as they will be glad to have lived when they appear before Him. That is the true religion, the only one incapable of abuse, impiety or fanaticism. . . .

It is well to keep in mind that up to the age when reason becomes active and the growth of sentiment makes conscience speak, good or bad for young women is only what those around them so regard. What they are told to do is good: what they are forbidden is bad. That is all they have to know. From this it is evident how important is the choice of those who are to be with them and exercise authority over them, even more than in the case of boys. But in due course the moment will come when they begin to form their own judgment and then the plan of their education must be changed. We cannot leave them with social prejudices as the only law of their lives. For all human beings there is a rule of conduct which comes before public opinion. All other rules are subject to the inflexible direction of this rule. Even prejudices must be judged by it, and it is only in so far as the values of men are in accord with it that they are entitled to have authority over us. This rule is conscience, the inner conviction (*sentiment*). Unless the two rules are in concord in women's education, it is bound to be defective. Personal conviction without regard for public opinion will fail to give them that fineness of soul which puts the hallmark of worldly honour on good conduct; and public opinion lacking personal conviction will only make false, dishonest women with a sham virtue. For the co-ordination of the two guides to right living, women need to cultivate a faculty to arbitrate between them, to prevent conscience going astray on the one hand and correct the errors of prejudice on the other. This faculty is reason. But at the mention of reason all sorts of questions arise. Are women capable of sound reasoning? Is it necessary for them to cultivate it? If they do cultivate it, will it be of any use to them in the functions imposed on them? Is it compatible with a becoming simplicity?

The reason that brings a man to a knowledge of his duties is not very complex. The reason that brings a woman to hers is simpler still. The obedience and loyalty she owes to her husband and the tender care she owes her children are such obvious and natural consequences of her position that she cannot without bad faith refuse to listen to the inner sentiment which is her guide, nor fail to recognise her duty in her natural inclination. Since she depends on her own conscience and on the opinion of other people she must learn to compare and harmonise the two rules. This can best be done by cultivating her understanding and her reason.

SOPHIE

The Outcome of the Right Education

Let us now look at the picture of Sophie which has been put before Emile, the image he has of the woman who can make him happy.

Sophie is well born and has a good natural disposition. She has a feeling heart which sometimes makes her imagination difficult to control. Her mind is acute rather than precise: her temper easy but variable; her person ordinary but pleasing. Her countenance gives indication of a soul—with truth. Some girls have good qualities she lacks and others have the qualities she possesses in fuller measure; but none has these qualities better combined in a happy character. Without being very striking, she interests and charms, and it is difficult to say why.

Sophie is fond of dress and has taste enough to dress well. She dislikes rich clothes and her own always combine simplicity with elegance. She does not know which are the fashionable colours, but she knows to perfection those that suit herself. No girl gives less sign of careful dressing and yet no piece of hers has been selected casually. Her dress is modest in appearance but coquettish in effect. She does not display her charms, but hides them in such a way as to appeal to the imagination.

Sophie has natural talents. She is aware of them and has not neglected them. But not having been in a position to give much thought to their cultivation, she has been content to exercise her sweet voice in singing with truth and taste, and her little feet in walking with an easy grace. She has had no singing teacher but her father, and no dancing mistress but her mother. A neighbouring organist has given her a few lessons in playing accompaniments on the harpsichord, which she has practised alone. But music for her is a taste rather than a talent, and she cannot play a tune by note.

What Sophie knows best and has been most carefully taught are the tasks of her own sex, even those like dressmaking, not usually thought necessary. There is no kind of needlework she cannot do, but she has a special preference for lace-making because it calls for a pleasing pose, as well as grace and lightness in the fingers. She has also applied herself to all the details of the household. She understands cookery and kitchen work. She knows the prices of provisions and can judge their qualities. She can keep accounts and is her mother's housekeeper. At the same time, she does not take equal pleasure in all her duties. For example, though she likes nice food she is not fond of cooking, and is rather disgusted with some of its details. For the same reason she has always been unwilling to inspect the garden. The soil seems to her dirty, and when she sees the dunghill she imagines she feels a smell. This defect she owes to her mother, according to whom cleanliness is one of the first obligations imposed on a woman by nature. The result is that cleaning takes up an undue amount of Sophie's time.

Sophie's mind is pleasing but not brilliant, solid but not deep. She has always something attractive to say to those who talk with her, but lacks the conversational adornments we associate with cultured women. Her mind has been formed, not only by reading but by conversation with her father and mother and by her own reflections on the little bit of the world she has seen. She is too sensitive to preserve a perfect evenness of temper, but too sweet to allow this to be troublesome to other people. It is only herself that is hurt.

She is religious, but her religion is reasonable and simple, with few dogmas and still fewer observances. The essential observance for her is morality, and she devotes her life to the service of God by doing good. In all the instructions they have given her on this subject her parents have accustomed her to a respectful submission. 'My daughter,' they say to her, 'this knowledge is not for one of your age. When the time comes your husband will instruct you.' Apart from that, they are content to dispense with long pious talks, and only preach to her by their example.

The love of virtue is her ruling passion. She loves virtue, because it is the glory of a woman and the only road to true happiness; because, also, it is dear to her respected father and her tender mother. These sentiments inspire her with an enthusiasm that uplifts the soul and keeps all her young inclinations in subjection to the noble passion for virtue. She will be chaste and good till her last breath. . . .

A pupil of nature like Emile, she is better suited for him than any other woman. She is indeed his woman, his equal in birth and merit, his inferior in fortune. Her special charm only reveals itself gradually, as one comes to know her, and her husband will appreciate it more than anyone. Her education is in no way exceptional. She has taste without study, talents without art, judgment without knowledge. Her mind is still vacant but has been trained to learn: it is well-tilled land only waiting for the grain. What a pleasing ignorance! Happy is the man destined to instruct her. She will be her husband's disciple, not his teacher. Far from wanting to impose her tastes on him, she will share his. . . .

'My children,' I say to them as I take them both by the hand, . . . 'I have often thought that if it were possible to prolong the happiness of love in marriage we would have a heaven on earth. Would you like me to tell you what in my belief is the only way to secure that?' . . . 'It is to go on being lovers after you are married.' . . . 'Knots which are too tightly drawn break. That is what happens to the marriage tie when too great a strain is put on it. The faithfulness required of a married couple is the most sacred of all obligations but the power it gives one partner over the other is too great. Constraint and love go ill together, and the pleasures of marriage are not to be had on demand. It is impossible to make a duty of tender affection and to treat the sweetest pledges of love as a right. What right there is comes from mutual desire: nature knows no other. Neither belongs to the other except by his or her own good will. Both must remain master of their persons and their caresses.

'When Emile became your husband, Sophie, he became your head and by the will of nature you owe him obedience. But when the wife is like you it is good for the husband to be guided by her: that is also the law of nature and it gives you as much authority over his heart as his sex gives him over your person. Make yourself dear to him by your favours and respected by your refusals. On these terms you will get his confidence; he will listen to your advice and settle nothing without consulting you. After love has lasted a considerable time a sweet habit takes its place, and the attraction of confidence succeeds the transports of passion. When you cease to be Emile's mistress you will be his wife and sweetheart and the mother of his children, and you will enjoy the closest intimacy. Remember that if your husband lives happily with you, you will be a happy woman.'

'Dear Emile,' I say to the young husband, 'all through life a man has need of a counsellor and guide. . . . From this time on, Sophie is your tutor.'

* * *

IMMANUEL KANT

Although the life style of Immanuel Kant (1724–1804) was conservative and uneventful, his *Weltanschauung* (worldview) was a radical and thoroughly systematic innovation in philosophy. In developing his transcendental idealism he assimilated the fundamental emphases of both the rationalist and empiricist schools that preceded him. Basically, Kant distinguished between *noumena* or things-in-themselves, and *phenomena* or things-as-they-appear. Since experience is the only source of our knowledge, the phenomena or appearances are all that we know, while the noumena or the reality beyond appearance remains unknowable. We may make valid claims about reality, but these are postulates rather than certain judgments. The three fundamental ideas of reality which reason continually attempts to fathom are God, freedom, and immortality. Of these, freedom is the only idea whose corresponding reality can be known through experience (the experience of obligation provokes an awareness of freedom as the condition for our obligation); and even then, Kant maintains we can know *that* freedom is without knowing *what* it is.

The philosophy of Kant is elaborated most completely and clearly in his critical writings (mainly, his *Critique of Pure Reason, Critique of Practical Reason,* and *Critique of Judgment*), which were written later than the selection that follows. However, while the *Critiques* represent a difference in style, method, and content, they never contradict Kant's basic claims in the *Observations on the Feeling of the Beautiful and Sublime.*

For Kant, the only unconditioned good is the good will residing within a person. It is conditionless because its decisions are universalizable, which means that the goods chosen are intended to hold for all individuals. This leads to Kant's famous "categorical imperative": to act in whatever way you would will anyone in your situation to act. Persons ought always to be treated as ends in themselves, and never merely as means.

As its title implies, the *Observations* was never intended as an exhaustive systematic study of human nature. Nonetheless, its second section treats "Of the Attributes of the Beautiful and Sublime in Man in General." The two attributes refer to the chief kinds of finer human feelings. The "sublime" is that which arouses esteem and admiration; it is always great and simple. In contrast, the "beautiful" arouses love and joy; it may be small or ornamented. The sublime may be terrifying, noble, or splendid; the beautiful may be merely pretty (outwardly only), or properly beautiful (internally and externally). The sight of a snow-covered mountain peak is sublime; the sight of a flower-strewn meadow is beautiful.

Individuals are both beautiful and sublime. A melancholy person generally is more sublime in his makeup, while a sanguine person is more beautiful; a choleric person has the appearance rather than the substance of sublimity, while a phlegmatic person has neither attribute to a discernible degree. "Friendship," claims Kant, "has mainly the character of the sublime, but love between the sexes, that of the beautiful." The interplay between the two attributes affects the moral component of individual and social life.

Of the Distinction of the Beautiful and Sublime in the Interrelations of the Two Sexes

He who first conceived of woman under the name of the *fair sex* probably wanted to say something flattering, but he has hit upon it better than even he himself might have believed. For without taking into consideration that her figure in general is finer, her features more delicate and gentler, and her mien more engaging and more expressive of friendliness, pleasantry, and kindness than in the male sex, and not forgetting what one must reckon as a secret magic with which she makes our passion inclined to judgments favorable to her—even so, certain specific traits lie especially in the personality of this sex which distinguish it clearly from ours and chiefly result in making her known by the mark of the beautiful. On the other side, we could make a claim on the title of the *noble sex,* if it were not required of a noble disposition to decline honorific titles and rather to bestow than to receive them. It is not to be understood by this that woman lacks noble qualities, or that the male sex must do without beauty completely. On the contrary, one expects that a person of either sex brings both together, in such a way that all the other merits of a woman should unite solely to enhance the character of the beautiful, which is the proper reference point; and on the other hand, among the masculine qualities the sublime clearly stands out as the criterion of his kind. All judgments of the two sexes must refer to these criteria, those that praise as well as those that blame; all education and instruction must have these before its eyes, and all efforts to advance the moral perfection of the one or the other—unless one wants to disguise the charming distinction that nature has chosen to make between the two sorts of human being. For here it is not enough to keep in mind that we are dealing with human beings; we must also remember that they are not all alike.

Women have a strong inborn feeling for all that is beautiful, elegant, and decorated. Even in childhood they like to be dressed up, and take pleasure when they are adorned. They are cleanly and very delicate in respect to all that provokes disgust. They love pleasantry and can be entertained by trivialities if only these are merry and laughing. Very early they have a modest manner about themselves, know how to give themselves a fine demeanor and be self-possessed—and this at an age when our well-bred male youth is still unruly, clumsy, and confused. They have many sympathetic sensations, good-heartedness, and compassion, prefer the beautiful to the useful, and gladly turn abundance of circumstance into parsimony, in order to support expenditure on adornment and glitter. They have very delicate feelings in regard to the least offense, and are exceedingly precise to notice the most trifling lack of attention and respect toward them. In short, they contain the chief cause in human nature for the contrast of the beautiful qualities with the noble, and they refine even the masculine sex.

I hope the reader will spare me the reckoning of the manly qualities, so far as they are parallel to the feminine, and be content only to consider both in comparison with each other. The fair sex has just as much understanding as the male, but it is a *beautiful understanding,* whereas ours should be a *deep understanding*, an expression that signifies identity with the sublime.

To the beauty of all actions belongs above all the mark that they display facility, and appear to be accomplished without painful toil. On the other hand, strivings and surmounted difficulties arouse admiration and belong to the sublime. Deep meditation and a long-sustained reflection are noble but difficult, and do not well befit a person in whom unconstrained charms should show nothing else than a beautiful nature. Laborious learning or painful pondering, even if a woman should greatly succeed in it, destroy the merits that are proper to her sex, and because of their rarity they can make of her an object of cold admiration; but at the same time they will weaken the charms with which she exercises her great power over the other sex. A woman who has a head full of Greek . . . or carries on fundamental controversies about mechanics . . . might as well even have a beard; for perhaps that would express more obviously the mien of profundity for which she strives. The beautiful understanding selects for its objects everything closely related to the finer feeling, and relinquishes to the diligent, fundamental, and deep understanding abstract speculations or branches of knowledge useful but dry. A woman therefore will learn no geometry; of the principle of sufficient reason or the monads she will know only so much as is needed to perceive the salt in a satire which the insipid grubs of our sex have censured. The fair can leave Descartes his vortices to whirl forever without troubling themselves about them. . . . In history they will not fill their heads with battles, nor in geography with fortresses, for it becomes them just as little to reek of gunpowder as it does the males to reek of musk.

It appears to be a malicious stratagem of men that they have wanted to influence the fair sex to this perverted taste. For, well aware of their weakness before her natural charms and of the fact that a single sly glance sets them more in confusion than the most difficult problem of science, so soon as woman enters upon this taste they see themselves in a decided superiority and are at an advantage that otherwise they hardly would have, being able to succor their vanity in its weakness by a generous indulgence toward her. The content of woman's great science, rather, is humankind, and among humanity, men. Her philosophy is not to reason, but to sense. In the opportunity that one wants to give to women to cultivate their beautiful nature, one must always keep this relation before his eyes. One will seek to broaden their total moral feeling and not their memory, and that of course not by universal rules but by some judgment upon the conduct that they see about them. The examples one borrows from other times in order to examine the influence the fair sex has had in culture, the various relations to the masculine in which it has stood in other ages or in foreign lands, the character of both so far as it can be illustrated by these, and the changing taste in amusements—these comprise her whole history and geography. For the ladies, it is well to make it a pleasant diversion to see a map setting forth the entire globe or the principal parts of the world. This is brought about by showing it only with the intention of portraying the different characters of peoples that dwell there, and the differences of their taste and moral feeling, especially in respect to the effect these have upon the relations of the sexes—together with a few easy illustrations taken from the differences of their climates, or their freedom or slavery. It is of little consequence whether or not the women know the particular subdivisions of these lands, their industry, power, and sovereigns. Similarly, they will need to know nothing more of the cosmos than is necessary to make the appearance of the heavens on a beautiful evening a stimulating sight to them, if they can conceive to some extent that yet more worlds, and in them yet more beautiful creatures, are to be found. Feeling for expressive painting and for music, not so far as it manifests artistry but sensitivity—all this refines or elevates the taste of this sex, and always has some connection with moral impulses. Never a cold and speculative instruction but always feelings and those indeed which remain as close as possible to the situation of her sex. Such instruction is very rare because it demands talents, experience, and a heart full of feeling; and a woman can do very well without any other, as in fact without this she usually develops very well by her own efforts.

The virtue of a woman is a *beautiful virtue*. That of the male sex should be a *noble virtue*. Women will avoid the wicked not because it is unright, but because it is ugly; and virtuous actions mean to them such as are morally beautiful. Nothing of duty, nothing of compulsion, nothing of obligation! Woman is intolerant of all commands and all morose constraint. They do something only because it pleases them, and the art consists in making only that please them which is good. I hardly believe that the fair sex is capable of principles, and I hope by that not to offend, for these are also extremely rare in the male. But in place of it Providence has put in their breast kind and benevolent sensations, a fine feeling for propriety, and a complaisant soul. One should not at all demand sacrifices and generous self-restraint. A man must never tell his wife if he risks a part of his fortune on behalf of a friend. Why should he fetter her merry talkativeness by burdening her mind with a weighty secret whose keeping lies solely upon him? Even many of her weaknesses are, so to speak, *beautiful faults*. Offense or misfortune moves her tender soul to sadness. A man must never weep other than magnanimous tears. Those he sheds in pain or over circumstances of fortune make him contemptible. *Vanity*, for which one reproaches the fair sex so frequently, so far as it is a fault in that sex, yet is only a beautiful fault. For—not to mention that the men who so gladly flatter a woman would be left in a strait if she were not inclined to take it well—by that they actually enliven their charms. This inclination is an impulsion to exhibit pleasantness and good demeanor, to let her merry wit play, to radiate through the changing devices of dress, and to heighten her beauty. Now in this there is not at all any offensiveness toward others, but rather so much courtesy, if it is done with good taste, that to scold against it with peevish rebukes is very ill-bred. A woman who is too inconstant and deceitful is called a coquette; which expression yet has not so harsh a meaning as what, with a changed syllable, is applied to man, so that if we understand each other, it can sometimes indicate a familiar flattery. If vanity is a fault that in a woman much merits excuse, a *haughty bearing* is not only as reproachable in her as in people in general, but completely disfigures the character of her sex. For this quality is exceedingly stupid and ugly, and is set completely in opposition to her captivating, modest charms. Then such a person is in a slippery position. She will suffer herself to be judged sharply and without any pity; for whoever presumes an esteem invites all around him to rebuke. Each disclosure of even the least fault gives everyone a true joy, and the word *coquette* here loses its mitigated meaning. One must always distinguish between vanity and conceit. The first seeks approbation and to some extent honors those on whose account it gives itself the trouble. The second believes itself already in full possession of approbation, and because it never strives to gain any, it wins none.

If a few ingredients of vanity do not deform a woman in the eyes of the male sex, still, the more apparent they are, the more they serve to divide the fair sex among themselves. Then they judge one another very severely, because the one seems to obscure the charms of the other, and in fact, those who make strong presumptions of conquest actually are seldom friends of one another in a true sense.

Nothing is so much set against the beautiful as disgust, just as nothing sinks deeper beneath the sublime than the ridiculous. On this account no insult can be more painful to a man than being called a *fool*, and to a woman, than being called *disgusting*. The English *Spectator* maintains that no more insulting reproach could be made to a man than if he is considered a liar, and to a woman none more bitter than if she is held unchaste. I will leave this for what it is worth so far as it is judged according to strictness in morals. But here the question is not what of itself deserves the greatest rebuke, but what is actually felt as the harshest of all. And to that point I ask every reader whether, when he sets himself to thinking upon this matter, he must not assent to my opinion. . . .

[*N*]*eatness*, which of course well becomes any person, in the fair sex belongs among the virtues of first rank and can hardly be pushed too high among them, although in a man it sometimes rises to excess and then becomes trifling.

Sensitivity to *shame* is a secrecy of nature addressed to setting bounds to a very intractable inclination, and since it has the voice of nature on its side, seems always to agree with good moral qualities even if it yields to excess. Hence it is most needed, as a supplement to principles, for there is no instance in which inclination is so ready to turn Sophist, subtly to devise complaisant principles, as in this. But at the same time it serves to draw a curtain of mystery before even the most appropriate and necessary purposes of nature, so that a too familiar acquaintance with them might not occasion disgust, or indifference at least, in respect to the final purpose of an impulse onto which the finest and liveliest inclinations of human nature are grafted. This quality is especially peculiar to the fair sex and very becoming to it. There is also a coarse and contemptible rudeness in putting delicate modesty to embarrassment or annoyance by the sort of vulgar jests called obscenities. However, although one may go as far around the secret as one ever will, the sexual inclination still ultimately underlies all her remaining charms, and a woman, ever as a woman, is the pleasant object of a well-mannered conversation; and this might perhaps explain why otherwise polite men occasionally take the liberty to let certain fine allusions show through, by a little mischief in their jests, which make us call them *loose* or *waggish*. Because they neither affront by searching glances nor intend to injure anyone's esteem, they believe it justified to call the person who receives it with an indignant or brittle mien *a prude*. I mention this practice only because it is generally considered as a somewhat bold trait in polite conversation, and also because in point of fact much wit has been squandered upon it; however, judgment according to moral strictness does not belong here, because what I have to observe and explain in the sensing of the beautiful is only the appearances.

The noble qualities of this sex, which still, as we have already noted, must never disguise the feeling of the beautiful, proclaim themselves by nothing more clearly and surely than by *modesty*, a sort of noble simplicity and innocence in great excellences. Out of it shines a quiet benevolence and respect toward others, linked at the same time with a certain *noble trust* in oneself, and a reasonable self-esteem that is always to be found in a sublime disposition. Since this fine mixture at once captivates by charms and moves by respect, it puts all the remaining shining qualities in security against the mischief of censure and mockery. Persons of this temperament also have a heart for friendship, which in a woman can never be valued highly enough, because it is so rare and moreover must be so exceedingly charming.

As it is our purpose to judge concerning feelings, it cannot be unpleasant to bring under concepts, if possible, the difference of the impression that the form and features of the fair sex make on the masculine. This complete fascination is really overlaid upon the sex instinct. Nature pursues its great purpose, and all refinements that join together, though they may appear to stand as far from that as they will, are only trimmings and borrow their charm ultimately from that very source. A healthy and *coarse taste*, which always stays very close to this impulse, is little tempted by the charms of demeanor, of facial features, of eyes, and so on, in a woman, and because it really pertains only to sex, it oftentimes sees the delicacy of others as empty flirting.

If this taste is not fine, nevertheless it is not on that account to be disdained. For the largest part of mankind complies by means of it with the great order of nature, in a very simple and sure way. Through it the greatest number of marriages are brought about, and indeed by the most diligent part of the human race; and because the man does not have his head full of fascinating expressions, languishing eyes, noble demeanor, and so forth, and understands nothing of all this, he becomes that much the more attentive to householders' virtues, thrift and such, and to the dowry. As for what relates to the somewhat finer taste, one whose account it might be necessary to make a distinction among the exterior charms of women, this is fixed either upon what in the form and the expression of the face is moral, or upon what is non-moral. In respect to the last-named sort of pleasantness, a lady is called *pretty*. A well-proportioned figure, regular features, colors of eyes and face which contrast prettily, beauties pure and simple which are also pleasing in a bouquet and gain a cool approbation. The face itself says nothing, although it is pretty, and speaks not to the heart. What is moral in the expression of the features, the eyes, and mien pertains to the feeling either of the sublime or of the beautiful. A woman in whom the agreeableness beseeming her sex particularly makes manifest the moral expression of the sublime is called *beautiful* in the proper sense; so far as the moral composition makes itself discernible in the mien or facial features, she whose features show qualities of beauty is *agreeable*, and if she is that to a high degree, *charming*. The first, under a mien of composure and a noble demeanor, lets the glimmer of a beautiful understanding play forth through discreet glances, and as in her face she portrays a tender feeling and a benevolent heart, she seizes possession of the affection as well as the esteem of a masculine heart. The second exhibits merriment and wit in laughing eyes, something of fine mischief, the playfulness of jest and sly coyness. She charms, while the first moves; and the feeling of love of which she is capable and which she stimulates in others is fickle but beautiful, whereas the feeling of the first is tender, combined with respect, and constant. I do not want to engage in too detailed an analysis of this sort, for in doing so the author always appears to depict his own inclination. I shall still mention, however, that the liking many women have for a healthy but pale color can be explained here. For this generally accompanies a disposition of more inward feeling and delicate sensation, which belongs to the quality of the sublime; whereas the rosy and blooming complexion proclaims less of the first, but more of the joyful and merry disposition—but it is more suitable to vanity to move and to arrest, than to charm and to attract. On the other hand there can be very pretty persons completely without moral feeling and without any expression that indicates feeling; but they will neither move nor charm, unless it might be the coarse taste of which we have made mention, which sometimes grows somewhat more refined and then also selects after its fashion. It is too bad that this sort of beautiful creatures easily fall into the fault of *conceit*, through the consciousness of the beautiful figure their mirror shows them, and from a lack of finer sensations, for then they make all indifferent to them except the flatterer, who has ulterior motives and contrives intrigues.

Perhaps by following these concepts one can understand something of the different effect the figure of the same woman has upon the tastes of men. I do not concern myself with what in this impression relates too closely to the sex impulse and may be of a piece with the particular sensual illusion with which the feeling of everyone clothes itself, because it lies outside the compass of finer taste. Perhaps . . . the figure that makes the first impression, at the time when this impulse is still new and is beginning to develop, remains the pattern all feminine figures in the future must more or less follow so as to be able to stir the fanciful ardor, whereby a rather coarse inclination is compelled to choose among the different objects of a sex. Regarding the somewhat finer taste, I affirm that the sort of beauty we have called the *pretty figure* is judged by all men very much alike, and that opinions about it are not so different as one generally maintains. . . . [I]t appears that, as greatly as the caprice of taste in . . . different quarters of the world may diverge, still, whatever is once known in any of these as especially pretty will also be considered the same in all the others. But whenever what is moral in the features mingles in the judgment upon the fine figure, the taste of different men is always very different, both because their moral feeling itself is dissimilar, and also on account of the different meaning that the expression of the face may have in every fancy. One finds that those formations that at first glance do not have any particular effect, because they are not pretty in any decided way, generally appear far more to captivate and to grow constantly more beautiful as soon as they begin to please upon nearer acquaintance. On the other hand, the pretty appearance that proclaims itself at once is later received with greater indifference. This probably is because moral charms, when they are evident, are all the more arresting because they are set in operation only on the occasion of moral sensations, and let themselves be discovered in this way, each disclosure of a new charm causing one to suspect still more of these; whereas all the agreeable features that do not at all conceal themselves, after exercising their entire effect at the beginning, can subsequently do nothing more than to cool off the enamored curiosity and bring it gradually to indifference. . . .

Finally age, the great destroyer of beauty, threatens all these charms; and if it proceeds according to the natural order of things, gradually the sublime and noble qualities must take the place of the beautiful, in order to make a person always worthy of a greater respect as she ceases to be attractive. In my opinion, the whole perfection of the fair sex in the bloom of years should consist in the beautiful simplicity that has been brought to its height by a refined feeling toward all that is charming and noble. Gradually, as the claims upon charms diminish, the reading of books and the broadening of insight could refill unnoticed the vacant place of the Graces with the Muses, and the husband should be the first instructor. Nevertheless, when the epoch of growing old, so terrible to every woman, actually approaches, she still belongs to the fair sex, and that sex disfigures itself if in a kind of despair of holding this character longer, it gives way to a surly and irritable mood.

An aged person who attends a gathering with a modest and friendly manner, is sociable in a merry and sensible way, favors with a pleasant demeanor the pleasures of youth in which she herself no longer participates, and, as she looks after everything, manifests contentment and benevolence toward the joys that are going on around her, is yet a finer person than a man of like age and perhaps ever more attractive than a girl, although in another sense. Indeed the platonic love might well be somewhat too mystical, which an ancient philosopher asserted when he said of the object of his inclination, "The Graces reside in her wrinkles, and my soul seems to hover upon my lips when I kiss her withered mouth"; but such claims must be relinquished. An old man who acts infatuated is a fool, and the like presumptions of the other sex at that age are disgusting. It never is due to nature when we do not appear with a good demeanor, but rather to the fact that we turn her upside down.

In order to keep close to my text, I want to undertake a few reflections on the influence one sex can have upon the other, to beautify or ennoble its feeling. Woman has a superior feeling for the beautiful, so far as it pertains to herself; but for the noble, so far as it is encountered in the male sex. Man on the other hand has a decided feeling for the noble, which belongs to his qualities, but for the beautiful, so far as it is to be found in woman. From this it must follow that the purposes of nature are directed still more to ennoble man, by the sexual inclination, and likewise still more to beautify woman. A woman is embarrassed little that she does not possess certain high insights, that she is timid, and not fit for serious employments, and so forth; she is beautiful and captivates, and that is enough. On the other hand, she demands all these qualities in a man, and the sublimity of her soul shows itself only in that she knows to treasure these noble qualities so far as they are found in him. How else indeed would it be possible that so many grotesque male faces, whatever merits they may possess, could gain such well-bred and fine wives! Man on the other hand is much more delicate in respect to the beautiful charms of woman. By their fine figure, merry naiveté, and charming friendliness he is sufficiently repaid for the lack of book learning and for other deficiencies that he must supply by his own talents. Vanity and fashion can give these natural drives a false direction and make out of many a male a *sweet gentleman*, but out of a woman either a prude or an Amazon; but still nature always seeks to reassert her own order. One can thereby judge what powerful influences the sexual inclination could have especially upon the male sex, to ennoble it, if instead of many dry instructions the moral feeling of woman were seasonably developed to sense properly what belongs to the dignity and the sublime qualities of the other sex, and were thus prepared to look upon the trifling fops with disdain and to yield to no other qualities than the merits. It is also certain that the power of her charms on the whole would gain through that; for it is apparent that their fascination for the most part works only upon nobler souls; the others are not fine enough to sense them. Just as the poet Simonides said, when someone advised him to let the Thessalians hear his beautiful songs: "These fellows are too stupid to be beguiled by such a man as I am." It has been regarded moreover as an effect of association with the fair sex that men's customs have become gentler, their conduct more polite and refined, and their bearing more elegant; but the advantage of this is only incidental.[1] The principal object is that the man should become more perfect as a man, and the woman as a wife; that is, that the motives of the sexual inclination work according to the hint of nature, still more to ennoble the one and to beautify the qualities of the other. If all comes to the extreme, the man, confident in his merits, will be able to say: "Even if you do not love me, I will constrain you to esteem me," and the woman, secure in the might of her charms, will answer: "Even if you do not inwardly admire me, I will still constrain you to love me." In default of such principles one sees men take on femininity in order to please, and woman occasionally (although much more seldom) affect a masculine demeanor in order to stimulate esteem; but whatever one does contrary to nature's will, one always does very poorly.

In matrimonial life the united pair should, as it were, constitute a single moral person, which is animated and governed by the understanding of the man and the taste of the wife. For not only can one credit more insight founded on experience to the former, and more freedom and accuracy in sensation to the latter; but also, the more sublime a disposition is, the more inclined it is to place the greatest purpose of its exertions in the contentment of a beloved object, and likewise the more beautiful it is, the more it seeks to requite these exertions by complaisance. In such a relation, then, a dispute over precedence is trifling and, where it occurs, is the surest sign of a coarse or dissimilarly matched taste. If it comes to such a state that the question is of the right of the superior to command, then the case is already utterly corrupted; for where the whole union is in reality erected solely upon inclination, it is already half destroyed as soon as the "duty" begins to make itself heard. The presumption of the woman in this harsh tone is extremely ugly, and of the man is base and contemptible in the high-

1. This advantage itself is really much reduced by the observation that one will have made, that men who are too early and too frequently introduced into company where women set the tone generally become somewhat trifling, and in male society they are boring or even contemptible because they have lost the taste for conversation which must be merry, to be sure, but still of actual content—witty, to be sure, but also useful through its earnest discourse.

est degree. However, the wise order of things so brings it about that all these niceties and delicacies of feeling have their whole strength only in the beginning, but subsequently gradually become duller through association and domestic concerns, and then degenerate into familiar love. Finally, the great skill consists in still preserving sufficient remainders of those feelings so that indifference and satiety do not put an end to the whole value of the employment on whose account it has solely and alone been worth the trouble to enter such a union.

* * *

MARY WOLLSTONECRAFT

The name of Mary Wollstonecraft (1759–1797) is not generally included among the ranks of philosophers. Consequently, it may come as a surprise to someone reading her works for the first time to see how rich an intellectual source they provide. Unlike most philosophers, Wollstonecraft could draw on personal experience in describing the nature and role of woman, but her sex also exerted a limiting influence on her philosophical development. The little informal instruction she received was directed entirely toward fulfilment as a wife and mother. Moreover, she died at an age (thirty-eight years, of complications due to childbirth) when many major thinkers have yet to produce their greatest works (Kant's brilliant *Critiques*, for example, did not appear until he had passed fifty). The marvel is that, despite many obstacles and disadvantages, Wollstonecraft produced twelve books and numerous articles. Apparently, not only her words but her life contained the ideas she wanted to express.

Probably the work best calculated to prepare for a reading of the following selection is the earlier *A Vindication of the Rights of Men,* which was written in 1790 as a response to Edmund Burke's *Reflections on the Revolution in France.* Arguing against Burke's concept of rights and their underlying assumptions, Wollstonecraft maintained that

> The birthright of man [of humankind, or every individual regardless of sex] . . . is such a degree of liberty, civil and religious, as is compatible with the liberty of every other individual with whom he is united in a social compact. . . . It is necessary emphatically to repeat that there are rights which men inherit at their birth, as rational creatures, who were raised above the brute creation by their improvable faculties;

> and that, in receiving these, not from their forefathers but, from God, prescription can never undermine natural rights.

In his *Reflections* Burke had claimed that "a woman *is* but an animal, and an animal not of the highest order." Wollstonecraft's reply reveals her critical attitude toward the prevailing ("fashionable") feminine behavior:

> If beautiful weakness be interwoven in a woman's frame, if the chief business of her life be (as you insinuate) to inspire love, and Nature has made an eternal distinction between the qualities that dignify a rational being and this animal perfection, her duty and happiness in this life must clash with any preparation for a more exalted state.

A Vindication of the Rights of Men insists that a different concept of woman is both available and necessary to the liberty of humankind:

> But should experience prove that there is a beauty in virtue, a charm in order, which necessarily implies exertion, a depraved sensual taste may give way to a more manly one—and *melting* feelings to rational satisfactions. Both may be equally natural to man; the test is their moral difference, and that point reason alone can decide.
>
> Such a glorious change can only be produced by liberty. Inequality of rank must ever impede the growth of virtue, by vitiating the mind that submits or domineers; that is ever employed to procure nourishment for the body, or amusement for the mind.

Wollstonecraft's concept of human nature anticipates the utilitarian view of the essential freedom and intelligence of every individual. A situation of unequal rights demeans humanity in general, both those whose share of rights is greater as well as those whose rights are less or none.

A Vindication of the Rights of Woman

. . . I shall first consider women in the grand light of human creatures, who, in common with men, are placed on this earth to unfold their faculties; and afterwards I shall more particularly point out their peculiar designation. . . .

My own sex, I hope, will excuse me, if I treat them like rational creatures, instead of flattering their *fascinating* graces, and viewing them as if they were in a state of perpetual childhood, unable to stand alone. I earnestly wish to point out in what true dignity and human happiness consists—I wish to persuade women to endeavour to acquire strength, both of mind and body, and to convince them that the soft phrases, susceptibility of heart, delicacy of sentiment, and refinement of taste, are almost synonymous with epithets of weakness, and that those beings who are only the objects of pity and that kind of love, which has been termed its sister, will soon become objects of contempt.

Dismissing, then, those pretty feminine phrases, which the men condescendingly use to soften our slavish dependence, and despising that weak elegancy of mind, exquisite sensibility, and sweet docility of manners, supposed to be the sexual characteristics of the weaker vessel, I wish to shew that elegance is inferior to virtue, that the first object of laudable ambition is to obtain a character as a human being, regardless of the distinction of sex; and that secondary views should be brought to this simple touchstone.

. . . .

In the present state of society it appears necessary to go back to first principles in search of the most simple truths, and to dispute with some prevailing prejudice every inch of ground. To clear my way, I must be allowed to ask some plain questions, and the answers will probably appear as unequivocal as the axioms on which reasoning is built; though, when entangled with various motives of action, they are formally contradicted, either by the words or conduct of men.

In what does man's pre-eminence over the brute creation consist? The answer is as clear as that a half is less than the whole; in Reason.

What acquirement exalts one being above another? Virtue, we spontaneously reply.

For what purpose were the passions implanted? That man by struggling with them might attain a degree of knowledge denied to the brutes; whispers Experience.

Consequently the perfection of our nature and capability of happiness, must be estimated by the degree of reason, virtue, and knowledge, that distinguish the individual, and direct the laws which bind society: and that from the exercise of reason, knowledge and virtue naturally flow, is equally undeniable, if mankind be viewed collectively.

. . . .

[T]he most perfect education, in my opinion, is such an exercise of the understanding as is best calculated to strengthen the body and form the heart. Or, in other words, to enable the individual to attain such habits of virtue as will render it independent. In fact, it is a farce to call any being virtuous whose virtues do not result from the exercise of its own reason. This was Rousseau's opinion respecting men: I extend it to women, and confidently assert that they have been drawn out of their sphere by false refinement, and not by an endeavour to acquire masculine qualities. Still the regal homage which they receive is so intoxicating, that till the manners of the times are changed, and formed on more reasonable principles, it may be impossible to convince them that the illegitimate power, which they obtain, by degrading themselves, is a curse, and that they must return to nature and equality, if they wish to secure the placid satisfaction that unsophisticated affections impart. But for this epoch we must wait—wait, perhaps, till kings and nobles, enlightened by reason, and, preferring the real dignity of man to childish state, throw off their gaudy hereditary trappings: and if then women do not resign the arbitrary power of beauty—they will prove that they have *less* mind than man.

I may be accused of arrogance; still I must declare what I firmly believe, that all the writers who have written on the subject of female education and manners, from Rousseau to Dr. Gregory, have contributed to render women more artificial, weak characters, than they would otherwise have been; and consequently, more useless members of society. I might have expressed this conviction in a lower key; but I am afraid it would have been the whine of affectation, and not the faithful expression of my feelings, of the clear result which experience and reflection have led me to draw. When I come to that division of the subject, I shall advert to the passages that I more particularly disapprove of, in the works of the authors I have just alluded to; but it is first necessary to observe, that my objection extends to the whole purport of those books, which tend, in my opinion, to degrade one half of the human species, and render women pleasing at the expense of every solid virtue.

Though, to reason on Rousseau's ground, if man did attain a degree of perfection of mind when his body arrived at maturity, it might be proper, in order to make a man and his wife *one*, that she should rely entirely on his understanding; and the graceful ivy, clasping the oak that supported it, would form a whole in which strength and beauty would be equally conspicuous. But, alas! husbands, as well as their helpmates, are often only overgrown children; nay, thanks to early debauchery, scarcely men in their outward form—and if the blind lead the blind, one need not come from heaven to tell us the consequence.

Many are the causes that, in the present corrupt state of society, contribute to enslave women by cramping their understandings and sharpening their senses. One, perhaps, that silently does more mischief than all the rest, is their disregard of order.

To do everything in an orderly manner, is a most important precept, which women, who, generally speaking, receive only a disorderly kind of education, seldom attend to with that degree of exactness that men, who from their infancy are broken into method, observe. This negligent kind of guess-work, for what other epithet can be used to point out the random exertions of a sort of instinctive common sense, never brought to the test of reason? prevents their generalizing matters of fact—so that they do to-day, what they did yesterday, merely because they did it yesterday.

This contempt of the understanding in early life has more baneful consequences than is commonly supposed; for the little knowledge which women of strong minds attain, is, from various circumstances, of a more desultory kind than the knowledge of men, and it is acquired more by sheer observations on real life, than from comparing what has been individually observed with the results of experience generalized by speculation. Led by their dependent situation and domestic employments more into society, what they learn is rather by snatches; and as learning is with them, in general, only a secondary thing, they do not pursue any one branch with that persevering ardour necessary to give vigour to the faculties, and clearness to the judgment. In the present state of society, a little learning is required to support the character of a gentleman; and boys are obliged to submit to a few years of discipline. But in the education of women, the cultivation of the understanding is always subordinate to the acquirement of some corporeal accomplishment; even while enervated by confinement and false notions of modesty, the body is prevented from attaining that grace and beauty which relaxed half-formed limbs never exhibit. Besides, in youth their faculties are not brought forward by emulation; and having no serious scientific study, if they have natural sagacity it is turned too soon on life and manners. They dwell on effects, and modifications, without tracing them back to causes; and complicated rules to adjust behaviour are a weak substitute for simple principles.

As a proof that education gives this appearance of weakness to females, we may instance the example of military men, who are, like them, sent into the world before their minds have been stored with knowledge or fortified by principles. The consequences are similar; soldiers acquire a little superficial knowledge, snatched from the muddy current of conversation, and, from continually mixing with society, they gain, what is termed a knowledge of the world; and this acquaintance with manners and customs has frequently been confounded with a knowledge of the human heart. But can the crude fruit of casual observation, never brought to the test of judgment, formed by comparing speculation and experience, deserve such a distinction? Soldiers, as well as women, practice the minor virtues with punctilious politeness. Where is then the sexual difference, when the education has been the same? All the difference that I can discern, arises from the superior advantage of liberty, which enables the former to see more of life.

It is wandering from my present subject, perhaps, to make a political remark; but, as it was produced naturally by the train of my reflections, I shall not pass it silently over.

Standing armies can never consist of resolute robust men; they may be well disciplined machines, but they will seldom contain men under the influence of strong passions, or with very rigorous faculties. And as for any depth of understanding, I will venture to affirm, that it is as rarely to be found in the army as amongst women; and the cause, I maintain, is the same. It may be further observed, that officers are also particularly attentive to their persons, fond of dancing, crowded rooms, adventures, and ridicule. Like the *fair* sex, the business of their lives is gallantry. They were taught to please, and they only live to please. Yet they do not lose their rank in the distinction of sexes, for they are still reckoned superior to women, though in what their superiority consists, beyond what I have just mentioned, it is difficult to discover.

The great misfortune is this, that they both acquire manners before morals, and a knowledge of life before they have, from reflection, any acquaintance with the grand ideal outline of human nature. The consequence is natural; satisfied with common nature, they become a prey to prejudices, and taking all their opinions on credit, they blindly submit to authority. So that, if they have any sense, it is a kind of instinctive glance, that catches proportions, and decides with respect to manners; but fails when arguments are to be pursued below the surface, or opinions analyzed.

May not the same remarks be applied to women? Nay, the argument may be carried still further, for they are both thrown out of a useful station by the unnatural distinctions established in civilized life. Riches and hereditary honours have made cyphers of women to give consequence to the numerical figure; and idleness has produced a mixture of gallantry and despotism into society, which leads the very men who are the slaves of their mistresses to tyrannize over their sisters, wives, and daughters. This is only keeping them in rank and file, it is true. Strengthen the female mind by enlarging it, and there will be an end to blind obedience; but, as blind obedience is ever fought for by power, tyrants and sensualists are in the right when they endeavour to keep women in the dark, because the former only want slaves, and the latter a plaything. The sensualist, indeed, has been the most dangerous of tyrants, and women have been duped by their lovers, as princes by their ministers, whilst dreaming that they reigned over them.

I now principally allude to Rousseau, for his character of Sophia is, undoubtedly, a captivating one, though it appears to me grossly unnatural; however it is not the superstructure, but the foundation of her character, the principles on which her education was built, that I mean to attack; nay, warmly as I admire the genius of that able writer, whose opinions I shall often have occasion to cite, indignation always takes place of admiration, and the rigid frown of insulted virtue effaces the smile of complacency, which his eloquent periods are wont to raise, when I read his voluptuous reveries. Is this the man, who, in his ardour for virtue, would banish all the soft arts of peace, and almost carry us back to Spartan discipline? Is this the man who delights to paint the useful struggles of passion, the triumphs of good dispositions, and the heroic flights which carry the glowing soul out of itself?—How are these mighty sentiments lowered when he describes the pretty foot and enticing airs of his little favourite! But, for the present, I waive the subject, and, instead of severely reprehending the transient effusions of overweening sensibility, I shall only observe, that whoever has cast a benevolent eye on society, must often have been gratified by the sight of humble mutual love, not dignified by sentiment, or strengthened by a union in intellectual pursuits. The domestic trifles of the day have afforded matters for cheerful converse, and innocent caresses have softened toils which did not require great exercise of mind or stretch of thought: yet, has not the sight of this moderate felicity excited more tenderness than respect? An emotion similar to what we feel when children are playing, or animals sporting, whilst the contemplation of the noble struggles of suffering merit has raised admiration, and carried our thoughts to that world where sensation will give place to reason.

Women are, therefore, to be considered either as moral beings, or so weak that they must be entirely subjected to the superior faculties of men.

Let us examine this question. Rousseau declares that a woman should never, for a moment, feel herself independent, that she should be governed by fear to exercise her *natural* cunning, and made a coquettish slave in order to render her a more alluring object of desire, a *sweeter* companion to man, whenever he chooses to relax himself. He carries the arguments, which he pretends to draw from the indications of nature, still further, and insinuates that truth and fortitude, the corner stones of all human virtue, should be cultivated with certain restrictions, because, with respect to the female character, obedience is the grand lesson which ought to be impressed with unrelenting rigour.

What nonsense! when will a great man arise with sufficient strength of mind to puff away the fumes which pride and sensuality have thus spread over the subject! If women are by nature inferior to men, their virtues must be the same in quality, if not in degree, or virtue is a relative idea; consequently, their conduct should be founded on the same principles, and have the same aim.

Connected with man as daughters, wives, and mothers, their moral character may be estimated by their manner of fulfilling those simple duties; but the end, the grand end of their exertions should be to unfold their own faculties and acquire the dignity of conscious virtue. They may try to render their road pleasant; but ought never to forget, in common with man, that life yields not the felicity which can satisfy an immortal soul. I do not mean to insinuate that either sex should be so lost in abstract reflections or distant views, as to forget the affections and duties that lie before them, and are, in truth, the means appointed to produce the fruit of life: on the contrary, I would warmly recommend them, even while I assert, that they afford most satisfaction when they are considered in their true, sober light.

Probably the prevailing opinion, that woman was created for man, may have taken its rise from Moses's poetical story; yet, as very few, it is presumed, who have bestowed any serious thought on the subject, ever supposed that Eve was, literally speaking, one of Adam's ribs, the deduction must be allowed to fall to the ground; or, only be so far admitted as it proves that man, from the remotest antiquity, found it convenient to exert his strength to subjugate his companion, and his invention to show that she ought to have her neck bent under the yoke, because the whole creation was only created for his convenience or pleasure.

Let it not be concluded that I wish to invert the order of things; I have already granted, that, from the constitution of their bodies, men seem to be designed by Providence to attain a greater degree of virtue. I speak collectively of the whole sex; but I see not the shadow of a reason to conclude that their virtues should differ in respect to their nature. In fact, how can they, if virtue has only one eternal standard? I must therefore, if I reason consequentially, as strenuously maintain that they have the same simple direction, as that there is a God.

It follows then that cunning should not be opposed to wisdom, little cares to great exertions, or insipid softness, varnished over with the name of gentleness, to that fortitude which grand views alone can inspire.

I shall be told that woman would then lose many of her peculiar graces, and the opinion of a well-known poet might be quoted to refute my unqualified assertion. For Pope has said, in the name of the whole male sex,

"Yet ne'er so sure our passion to create,
As when she touch'd the brink of all we hate."

In what light this sally places men and women, I shall leave to the judicious to determine; meanwhile I shall content myself with observing, that I cannot discover why, unless they are mortal, females should always be degraded by being made subservient to love or lust.

To speak disrespectfully of love is, I know, high treason against sentiment and fine feelings; but I wish to speak the simple language of truth, and rather to address the head than the heart. To endeavour to reason love out of the world, would be to out Quixote Cervantes, and equally offend against common sense; but an endeavour to restrain this tumultuous passion, and to prove that it should not be allowed to dethrone superior powers, or to usurp the sceptre which the understanding should ever coolly wield, appears less wild.

Youth is the season for love in both sexes; but in those days of thoughtless enjoyment provision should be made for the more important years of life, when reflection takes place of sensation. But Rousseau, and most of the male writers who have followed his steps, have warmly inculcated that the whole tendency of female education ought to be directed to one point:—to render them pleasing.

Let me reason with the supporters of this opinion who have any knowledge of human nature, do they imagine that marriage can eradicate the habitude of life? The woman who has only been taught to please will soon find that her charms are oblique sunbeams, and that they cannot have much effect on her husband's heart when they are seen every day, when the summer is passed and gone. Will she then have sufficient native energy to look into herself for comfort, and cultivate her dormant faculties? or, is it not more rational to expect that she will try to please other men; and, in the emotions raised by the expectation of new conquests, endeavour to forget the mortification her love or pride has received? When the husband ceases to be a lover—and the time will inevitably come, her desire of pleasing will then grow languid, or become a spring of bitterness; and love, perhaps, the most evanescent of all passions, gives place to jealousy or vanity.

I now speak of women who are restrained by principle or prejudice; such women, though they would shrink from an intrigue with real abhorrence, yet, nevertheless, wish to be convinced by the homage of gallantry that they are cruelly neglected by their husbands; or, days and weeks are spent in dreaming of the happiness enjoyed by congenial souls till their health is undermined and their spirits broken by discontent. How then can the great art of pleasing be such a necessary study? it is only useful to a mistress; the chaste wife, and serious mother, should only consider her power to please as the polish of her virtues, and the affection of her husband as one of the comforts that render her talk less difficult and her life happier. But, whether she be loved or neglected, her first wish should be to make herself respectable, and not to rely for all her happiness on a being subject to like infirmities with herself.

The worthy Dr. Gregory fell into a similar error. . . . He advises them to cultivate a fondness for dress, because a fondness for dress, he asserts, is natural to them. I am unable to comprehend what either he or Rousseau mean, when they frequently use this indefinite term. If they told us that in a pre-existent state the soul was fond of dress, and brought this inclination with it into a new body, I should listen to them with a half smile, as I often do when I hear a rant about innate elegance. But if he only meant to say that the exercise of the faculties will produce this fondness—I deny it. It is not natural; but arises, like false ambition in men, from a love of power.

Dr. Gregory goes much further; he actually recommends dissimulation, and advises an innocent girl to give the lie to her feelings, and not dance with spirit, when gaiety of heart would make her feet eloquent without making her gestures immodest. In the name of truth and common sense, why should not one woman acknowledge that she can take more exercise than another? or, in other words, that she has a sound constitution; and why, to damp innocent vivacity, is she darkly to be told that men will draw conclusions which she little thinks of?—Let the libertine draw what inference he pleases; but, I hope, that no sensible mother will restrain the natural frankness of youth by instilling such indecent cautions. Out of the abundance of the heart the mother speaketh; and a wiser than Solomon hath said, that the heart should be made clean, and not trivial ceremonies observed, which it is not very difficult to fulfil with scrupulous exactness when vice reigns in the heart.

Women ought to endeavour to purify their heart; but can they do so when their uncultivated understandings make them entirely dependent on their senses for employment and amusement, when no noble pursuit sets them above the little vanities of the day, or enables them to curb the wild emotions that agitate a reed over which every passing breeze has power? To gain the affections of a virtuous man, is affectation necessary? Nature has given woman a weaker frame than man; but, to ensure her husband's affections, must a wife, who by the exercise of her mind and body whilst she was discharging the duties of a daughter, wife, and mother, has allowed her constitution to retain its natural strength, and her nerves a healthy tone, is she, I say, to condescend to use art and feign a sickly delicacy in order to secure her husband's affection? Weakness may excite tenderness, and gratify the arrogant pride of man; but the lordly caresses of a protector will not gratify a noble mind that pants for, and deserves to be respected. Fondness is a poor substitute for friendship!

In a seraglio, I grant, that all these arts are necessary; the epicure must have his palate tickled, or he will sink into apathy; but have women so little ambition as to be satisfied with such a condition? Can they supinely dream life away in the lap of pleasure, or the languor of weariness, rather than assert their claim to pursue reasonable pleasures and render themselves conspicuous by practising the virtues which dignify mankind? Surely she has not an immortal soul who can loiter life away merely employed to adorn her person, that she may amuse the languid hours, and soften the cares of a fellow-creature who is willing to be enlivened by her smiles and tricks, when the serious business of life is over.

Besides, the woman who strengthens her body and exercises her mind will, by managing her family and practising various virtues, become the friend, and not the humble dependent of her husband; and if she, by possessing such substantial qualities, merit his regard, she will not find it necessary to conceal her affection, not to pretend to an unnatural coldness of constitution to excite her husband's passions. In fact, if we revert to history, we shall find that the women who have distinguished themselves have neither been the most beautiful nor the most gentle of their sex.

Nature, or, to speak with strict propriety, God, has made all things right; but man has sought him out many inventions to mar the work. I now allude to that part of Dr. Gregory's treatise, where he advises a wife never to let her husband know the extent of her sensibility or affection. Voluptuous precaution, and as ineffectual as absurd. Love, from its very nature, must be transitory. To seek for a secret that would render it constant, would be as wild a search as for the philosopher's stone, or the grand panacea: and the discovery would be equally useless, or rather pernicious, to mankind. The most holy band of society is friendship. It has been well said, by a shrewd satirist, "that rare as true love is, true friendship is still rarer."

This is an obvious truth, and the cause not lying deep, will not elude a slight glance of inquiry.

Love, the common passion, in which chance and sensation take place of choice and reason, is, in some degree, felt by the mass of mankind; for it is not necessary to speak, at present, of the emotions that rise above or sink below love. This passion, naturally increased by suspense and difficulties, draws the mind out of its accustomed state, and exalts the affections; but the security of marriage, allowing the fever of love to subside, a healthy temperature is thought insipid only by those who have not sufficient intellect to substitute the calm tenderness of friendship, the confidence of respect, instead of blind admiration, and the sensual emotions of fondness.

This is, must be, the course of nature,—friendship or indifference inevitably succeeds love. And this constitution seems perfectly to harmonize with the system of government which prevails in the moral world. Passions are spurs to action, and open the mind; but they sink into mere appetites, become a personal and momentary gratification, when the object is gained, and the satisfied mind rests in enjoyment. . . .

If all the faculties of woman's mind are only to be cultivated as they respect her dependence on man; if, when a husband be obtained, she have arrived at her goal, and meanly proud rests satisfied with such a paltry crown, let her grovel contentedly, scarcely raised by her employments above the animal kingdom; but, if, struggling for the prize of her high calling, she look beyond the present scene, let her cultivate her understanding without stopping to consider what character the husband may have whom she is destined to marry. Let her only determine, without being too anxious about present happiness, to acquire the qualities that ennoble a rational being, and a rough inelegant husband may shock her taste without destroying her peace of mind. She will not model her soul to suit the frailties of her companion, but to bear with them: his character may be a trial, but not an impediment to virtue. . . .

I own it frequently happens that women who have fostered a romantic unnatural delicacy of feeling, waste their lives in *imagining* how happy they should have been with a husband who could love them with a fervid increasing affection every day, and all day. But they might as well pine married as single—and would not be a jot more unhappy with a bad husband than longing for a good one. That a proper education; or, to speak with more precision, a well stored mind, would enable a woman to support a single life with dignity, I grant; but that she should avoid cultivating her taste, lest her husband should occasionally shock it, is quitting a substance for a shadow. To say the truth, I do not know of what use is an improved taste, if the individual be not rendered more independent of the casualties of life; if new sources of enjoyment, only dependent on the solitary operations of the mind, are not opened. People of taste, married or single, without distinction, will ever be disgusted by various things that touch not less observing minds. . . .

How women are to exist in that state where there is to be neither marrying or giving in marriage, we are not told. For though moralists have agreed that the tenor of life seems to prove that *man* is prepared by various circumstances for a future state, they constantly concur in advising *woman* only to provide for the present. Gentleness, docility, and a spaniel-like affection are, on this ground, consistently recommended as the cardinal virtues of the sex; and, disregarding the arbitrary economy of nature, one writer has declared that it is masculine for a woman to be melancholy. She was created to be the toy of man, his rattle, and it must jingle in his ears whenever, dismissing reason, he chooses to be amused.

To recommend gentleness, indeed, on a broad basis is strictly philosophical. A frail being should labour to be gentle. But when forbearance confounds right and wrong, it ceases to be a virtue; and, however convenient it may be found in a companion—that companion will ever be considered as an inferior, and only inspire a vapid tenderness, which easily degenerates into contempt. Still, if advice could really make a being gentle, whose natural disposition admitted not of such a fine polish, something towards the advancement of order would be attained; but if, as might quickly be demonstrated, only affectation be produced by this indiscriminate counsel, which throws a stumbling-block in the way of gradual improvement, and true melioration of temper, the sex is not much benefited by sacrificing solid virtues to the attainment of superficial graces, though for a few years they may procure the individual's regal sway.

As a philosopher, I read with indignation the plausible epithets which men use to soften their insults; and, as a moralist, I ask what is meant by such heterogeneous associations, as fair defects, amiable weaknesses, &c? If there be but one criterion of morals, but one archetype for man, women appear to be suspended by destiny. . . , they have neither the unerring instinct of brutes, nor are allowed to fix the eye of reason on a perfect model. They were made to be loved, and must not aim at respect, lest they should be hunted out of society as masculine. . . .

[A]fter surveying the history of woman, I cannot help, agreeing with the severest satirist, considering the sex as the weakest as well as the most oppressed half of the species. What does history disclose but marks of inferiority, and how few women have emancipated themselves from the galling yoke of sovereign man?—So few, that the exceptions remind me of an ingenious conjecture respecting Newton: that he was probably a being of superior order, accidentally caged in a human body. Following the same train of thinking, I have been led to imagine that the few extraordinary women who have rushed in eccentrical directions out of the orbit prescribed to their sex, were *male* spirits, confined by mistake in female frames. But if it be not philosophical to think of sex when the soul is mentioned, the inferiority must depend on the organs;

or the heavenly fire, which is to ferment the clay, is not given in equal portions.

But avoiding, as I have hitherto done, any direct comparison of the two sexes collectively, or frankly acknowledging the inferiority of woman, according to the present appearance of things, I shall only insist that men have increased that inferiority till women are almost sunk below the standard of rational creatures. Let their faculties have room to unfold, and their virtues to gain strength, and then determine where the whole sex must stand in the intellectual scale. Yet let it be remembered, that for a small number of distinguished women I do not ask a place. . . .

[I]f they be really capable of acting like rational creatures, let them not be treated like slaves; or, like the brutes who are dependent on the reason of man, when they associate with him; but cultivate their minds, give them the salutary, sublime curb of principle, and let them attain conscious dignity by feeling themselves only dependent on God. Teach them, in common with man, to submit to necessity, instead of giving, to render them more pleasing, a sex to morals.

Further, should experience prove that they cannot attain the same degree of strength of mind, perseverance, and fortitude, let their virtues be the same in kind, though they may vainly struggle for the same degree; and the superiority of man will be equally clear, if not clearer; and truth, as it is a simple principle, which admits of no modification, would be common to both. Nay, the order of society as it is at present regulated, would not be inverted, for woman would then only have the rank that reason assigned her, and arts could not be practised to bring the balance even, much less to turn it.

These may be termed Utopian dreams. Thanks to that Being who impressed them on my soul, and gave me sufficient strength of mind to dare to exert my own reason, till, becoming dependent only on him for the support of my virtue, I view, with indignation, the mistaken notions that enslave my sex.

I love man as my fellow; but his sceptre, real or usurped, extends not to me, unless the reason of an individual demands my homage; and even then the submission is to reason, and not to man. In fact, the conduct of an unaccountable being must be regulated by the operations of its own reason; or on what foundation rests the throne of God?

It appears to me necessary to dwell on these obvious truths, because females have been insulated, as it were; and, while they have been stripped of the virtues that should clothe humanity, they have been decked with artificial graces that enable them to exercise a short-lived tyranny. Love, in their bosoms, taking place of every nobler passion, their sole ambition is to be fair, to raise emotion instead of inspiring respect; and this ignoble desire, like the servility in absolute monarchies, destroys all strength of character. Liberty is the mother of virtue, and if women be, by their very constitution, slaves, and not allowed to breathe the sharp invigorating air of freedom, they must ever languish like exotics, and be reckoned beautiful flaws in nature.

As to the argument respecting the subjection in which the sex has ever been held, it retorts on man. The many have always been enthralled by the few; and monsters, who scarcely have shewn any discernment of human excellence, have tyrannized over thousands of their fellow-creatures. Why have men of superior endowments submitted to such degradation? For, is it not universally acknowledged that kings, viewed collectively, have ever been inferior, in abilities and virtue, to the same number of men taken from the common mass of mankind—yet, have they not, and are they not still treated with a degree of reverence that is an insult to reason? China is not the only country where a living man has been made a God. *Men* have submitted to superior strength to enjoy with impunity the pleasure of the moment—*women* have only done the same, and therefore till it is proved that the courtier, who servilely resigns the birthright of a man, is not a moral agent, it cannot be demonstrated that woman is essentially inferior to man because she has always been subjugated. . . .

Bodily strength from being the distinction of heroes is now sunk into such unmerited contempt that men, as well as women, seem to think it unnecessary: the latter, as it takes from their feminine graces, and from that lovely weakness the source of their undue power; and the former, because it appears inimical to the character of a gentleman.

. . . Yet the contrary, I believe, will appear to be the fact; for, on diligent inquiry, I find that strength of mind has, in most cases, been accompanied by superior strength of body,—natural soundness of constitution,—not that robust tone of nerves and vigour of muscles, which arise from bodily labour, when the mind is quiescent, or only directs the hands. . . .

I will allow that bodily strength seems to give man a natural superiority over woman; and this is the only solid basis on which the superiority of the sex can be built. But I still insist, that not only the virtue, but the *knowledge* of the two sexes should be the same in nature, if not in degree, and that women, considered not only as moral, but rational creatures, ought to endeavour to acquire human virtues (or perfections) by the *same* means as men, instead of being educated like a fanciful kind of *half* being—one of Rousseau's wild chimeras.

But, if strength of body be, with some show of reason, the boast of men, why are women so infatuated as to be proud of a defect?

Rousseau has furnished them with a plausible excuse, which could only have occurred to a man, whose imagination had been allowed to run wild, and refine on the impressions made by exquisite senses;—that they might, forsooth, have a pretext for yielding to a natural appetite without violating a romantic species of modesty, which gratifies the price and libertinism of man.

. . . .

I have, probably, had an opportunity of observing more girls in their infancy than J. J. Rousseau—I can recollect my own feelings, and I have looked steadily around me; yet, so far from coinciding with him in opinion respecting the first dawn of the female character, I will venture to affirm, that a girl, whose spirits have not been damped by inactivity, or innocence tainted by false shame, will always be a romp, and the doll will never excite attention unless confinement allows her no alternative. Girls and boys, in short, would play harmlessly together, if the distinction of sex was not inculcated long before nature makes any difference. I will go further, and affirm, as an indisputable fact, that most of the women, in the circle of my observation, who have acted like rational creatures, or shown any vigour of intellect, have accidentally been allowed to run wild—as some of the elegant formers of the fair sex would insinuate. . . .

. . . .

I lament that women are systematically degraded by receiving the trivial attentions, which men think it manly to pay to the sex, when, in fact, they are insultingly supporting their own superiority. It is not condescension to bow to an inferior. So ludicrous, in fact, do these ceremonies appear to me, that I scarcely am able to govern my muscles, when I see a man start with eager and serious solicitude to lift a handkerchief, or shut a door, when the *lady* could have done it herself, had she only moved a pace or two. . . .

Women, commonly called Ladies, are not to be contradicted in company, are not allowed to exert any manual strength; and from them the negative virtues only are expected, when any virtues are expected, patience, docility, good-humour, and flexibility; virtues incompatible with any vigorous exertion of intellect.

. . . .

I wish to sum up what I have said in a few words, for I here throw down my gauntlet, and deny the existence of sexual virtues, not excepting modesty. For man and woman, truth, if I understand the meaning of the word, must be the same; yet the fanciful female character, so prettily drawn by poets and novelists, demanding the sacrifice of truth and sincerity, virtue becomes a relative idea, having no other foundation than utility, and of that utility men pretend arbitrarily to judge, shaping it to their own convenience.

Women, I allow, may have different duties to fulfil; but they are *human* duties, and the principles that should regulate the discharge of them, I sturdily maintain, must be the same.

To become respectable, the exercise of their understanding is necessary, there is no other foundation for independence of character; I mean explicitly to say that they must only bow to the authority of reason, instead of being the *modest* slaves of opinion.

In the superior ranks of life how seldom do we meet with a man of superior abilities, or even common acquirements? The reason appears to me clear, the state they are born in was an unnatural one. The human character has ever been formed by the employments the individual, or class, pursues; and if the faculties are not sharpened by necessity, they must remain obtuse. The argument may fairly be extended to women; for, seldom occupied by serious business, the pursuit of pleasure gives that insignificancy to their character which renders the society of the *great* so insipid. The same want of firmness, produced by a similar cause, forces them both to fly from themselves to noisy pleasures, and artificial passions, till vanity takes place of every social affection, and the characteristics of humanity can scarcely be discerned. Such are the blessings of civil governments, as they are at present organized, that wealth and female softness equally tend to debase mankind, and are produced by the same cause; but allowing women to be rational creatures, they should be incited to acquire virtues which they may call their own, for how can a rational being be ennobled by anything that is not obtained by its *own* exertions?

* * *

G. W. F. HEGEL

The problem bequeathed by Kant to his philosophical posterity was how to bridge the gap between *noumena* and *phenomena*. To Kant himself, as we have seen, the gap was unbridgeable, but to other idealists (e.g., Fichte, Schelling, and Schopenhauer as well as Hegel), a response to that problem was the foundation for each of their philosophies.

Georg Hegel's (1770–1831) basic response to the Kantian problem was a denial that the problem existed. As an absolute objective idealist, Hegel maintained that reality is ultimately rational, and thus accessible to reason. Reality is also dialectical, exhibiting its process character through ongoing syntheses of opposing (differing) elements. Through logic, philosophy of nature, and philosophy of spirit we study the dialectical unfolding of the Idea in thought, matter, and time. To Hegel, the more universal the idea, the more fully it presents reality. Since the Absolute Idea manifests itself gradually through us and in us, history discloses an inexorable and continuing progress towards the Absolute, which Hegel identifies with Spirit or Mind (*Geist*).

Human consciousness represents a link between nature and spirit. Unlike other natural organisms, human beings are capable of determining their own destinies through rational freedom. Such determination involves both cognitive and practical factors; among the former are intuition, imagination, and memory; among the latter are feeling, instincts, and will. According to Hegel, the free individual synthesizes these differing factors through reason, fulfilling his/her own subjective spirit through such free deliberations. In order to actualize the idea of rational freedom, however, spirit must pass over into the objective order of ethics and history.

The "march towards freedom" which Hegel defines as history consists in settling the conflict between particular wills and the universal Will of the Absolute. To the extent that particular agents identify their own interests with those of other individuals, they act both ethically and freely. The individual is related to the State through the family and through civil society. While Hegel did not view any particular state as complete embodiment of the Idea, he construed the State as the sovereign manifestation of Spirit at any given point in time.

The Ethical World

The divine law which holds sway in the family has also on its side distinctions within itself, the relations among which make up the living process of its realization. Amongst the three relationships, however, of husband and wife, parents and children, brothers and sisters, the relationship of husband and wife is to begin with the primary and immediate form in which one consciousness recognizes itself in another, and in which each knows that reciprocal recognition. Being natural self-knowledge, knowledge of self on the basis of nature and not on that of ethical life, it merely represents and typifies in a figure the life of spirit, and is not spirit itself actually realized. Figurative representation, however, has its reality in an other than it is. This relationship, therefore, finds itself realized not in itself as such, but in the child—an other, in whose coming into being that relationship consists, and with which it passes away. And this change from one generation onwards to another is permanent in and as the life of a nation.

The reverent devotion (*Pietät*) of husband and wife towards one another is thus mixed up with a natural relation and with feeling, and their relationship is not inherently self-complete; similarly, too, the second relationship, the reverent devotion of parents and children to one another. The devotion of parents towards their children is affected with emotion just by their being consciously realized in what is external to themselves (viz. the children), and by their seeing them become something on their own account without this returning to the parents; independent existence on the part of the children remains a foreign reality, a reality all their own. The devotion of children, again, towards their parents is conversely affected by their coming into being from, or having their essential nature in, what is external to themselves (viz. the parents) and passes away; and by their attaining independent existence and a self-consciousness of their own solely through separation from the source whence they came—a separation in which the spring gets exhausted.

Both these relationships are constituted by and hold within the transience and the dissimilarity of the two sides, which are assigned to them.

An unmixed intransitive form of relationship, however, holds between brother and sister. They are the same blood, which, however, in them has entered into a condition of stable equilibrium. They therefore stand in no such natural relation as husband and wife, they do not desire one another; nor have they given to one another, nor received from one another, this independence of individual being; they are free individualities with respect to each other. The feminine element, therefore, in the form of the sister, premonizes and foreshadows most completely the nature of ethical life (*sittliches Wesen*). She does not become conscious of it, and does not actualize it, because the law of the family is her inherent implicit inward nature, which does not lie open to the daylight of consciousness, but remains inner feeling and the divine element exempt from actuality. The feminine life is attached to these household divinities (*Penates*), and sees in them both her universal substance, and her particular individuality, yet so views them that this relation of her individuality to them is at the same time not the natural one of pleasure.

As a daughter, the woman must now see her parents pass away with natural emotion and yet with ethical resignation, for it is only at the cost of this condition that she can come to that individual existence of which she is capable. She thus cannot see her independent existence positively attained in her relation to her parents. The relationships of mother and wife, however, are individualized partly in the form of something natural, which brings pleasure; partly in the form of something negative, which finds simply its own evanescence in those relationships; partly again the individualization is just on that account something contingent which can be replaced by an other particular individuality. In a household of the ethical kind, a woman's relationships are not based on a reference to this particular husband, this particular child, but to *a* husband, to children *in general*,–not to feeling, but to the universal. The distinction between her ethical life (*Sittlichkeit*) (while it determines her particular existence and brings her pleasure) and that of her husband consists just in this, that it has always a directly universal significance for her, and is quite alien to the impulsive condition of mere particular desire. On the other hand, in the husband these two aspects get separated; and since he possesses, as a citizen, the self-conscious power belonging to the universal life, the life of the social whole, he acquires thereby the rights of desire, and keeps himself at the same time in detachment from it. So far, then, as particularity is implicated in this relationship in the case of the wife, her ethical life is not purely ethical; so far, however, as it is ethical, the particularity is a matter of indifference, and the wife is without the moment of knowing herself as *this* particular self in and through an other.

The brother, however, is in the eyes of the sister a being whose nature is unperturbed by desire and is ethically like her own; her recognition in him is pure and unmixed with any sexual relation. The indifference characteristic of particular existence and the ethical contingency thence arising are, therefore, not present in this relationship; instead, the moment of individual selfhood, recognizing and being recognized, can here assert its right, because it is bound up with the balance and equilibrium resulting from their being of the same blood, and from their being related in a way that involves no mutual desire. The loss of a brother is thus irreparable to the sister, and her duty towards him is the highest.[1]

This relationship at the same time is the limit, at which the circumscribed life of the family is broken up, and passes beyond itself. The brother is the member of the family in which its spirit becomes individualized, and enabled thereby to turn towards another sphere, towards what is other than and external to itself, and pass over into consciousness of universality. The brother leaves this immediate, rudimentary, and, therefore, strictly speaking, negative ethical life of the family, in order to acquire and produce the concrete ethical order which is conscious of itself.

He passes from the divine law, within whose realm he lived,

1. Cf. *Antigone*, 1. 910.

over to the human law. The sister, however, becomes, or the wife remains, director of the home and the preserver of the divine law. In this way both the sexes overcome their merely natural being, and become ethically significant, as diverse forms dividing between them the different aspects which the ethical substance assumes. Both these universal factors of the ethical world have their specific individuality in naturally distinct self-consciousnesses, for the reason that the spirit at work in the ethical order is the immediate unity of the substance [of ethical life] with self-consciousness—an immediacy which thus appears as the existence of a natural difference, at once as regards its aspect of reality and of difference. It is that aspect which, in the notion of spiritual reality, came to light as "original determinate nature", when we were dealing with the stage of "Individuality which is real to itself". This moment loses the indeterminateness which it still has there, and the contingent diversity of "constitution" and "capacities". It is now the specific opposition of the two sexes, whose natural character acquires at the same time the significance of their respective ethical determinations.

The distinction of the sexes and of their ethical content remains all the same within the unity of the ethical substance, and its process is just the constant development of that substance. The husband is sent forth by the spirit of the family into the life of the community, and finds there his self-conscious reality. Just as the family thereby finds in the community its universal substance and subsistence, conversely the community finds in the family the formal element of its own realization, and in the divine law its power and confirmation. Neither of the two is alone self-complete. Human law as a living and active principle proceeds from the divine, the law holding on earth from that of the nether world, the conscious from the unconscious, mediation from immediacy; and returns to whence it came. The power of the nether world, on the other hand, finds its realization upon earth; it comes through consciousness to have existence and efficacy.

The universal elements of the ethical life are thus the (ethical) substance *qua* universal, and that substance *qua* particular consciousness. Their universal actuality is the nation and the family; while they get their natural self, and their operative individuality, in man and woman. . . .

The ethical realm remains in this way permanently a world without blot or stain, a world untainted by any internal dissension. So, too, its process is an untroubled transition from one of its powers to the other, in such a way that each preserves and produces the other. We see it no doubt divided into two ultimate elements and their realization: but their opposition is rather the confirming and substantiation of one through the other; and where they directly come in contact with each other as actual factors, their mediating common element is the immediate permeation of the one with the other. The one extreme, universal spirit conscious of itself, becomes, through the individuality of man, linked together with its other extreme, its force and its element, with *unconscious* spirit. On the other hand, divine law is individualized, the unconscious spirit of the particular individual finds its existence, in woman, through the mediation of whom the unconscious spirit comes out of its unrealizedness into actuality, and rises out of the state of unknowing and unknown, into the conscious realm of universal spirit. The union of man with woman constitutes the operative mediating agency for the whole, and constitutes the element which, while separated into the extremes of divine and human law, is, at the same time, their immediate union. This union, again, turns both those first mediate connexions (*Schlusse*) into one and the same synthesis, and unites into one process the twofold movement in opposite directions—one from reality to unreality, the downward movement of human law, organized into independent members, to the danger and trial of death,—the other, from unreality to reality, the upward movement of the law of the nether world to the daylight of conscious existence. Of these movements the former falls to man, the latter to woman. . . .

* * *

Guilt and Destiny

Human law, then, in its universal mode of existence is the community, in its efficient operation in general is the manhood of the community, in its actual efficient operation is the government. It has its being, its process, and its subsistence by consuming and absorbing into itself the separatist action of the household gods (*Penates*), the individualization into insular independent families which are under the management of womankind, and by keeping them dissolved in the fluent continuum of its own nature. The family at the same time, however, is in general its element, the individual consciousness its universal operative basis. Since the community gets itself subsistence only by breaking in upon family happiness, and dissolving [individual] self-consciousness into the universal, it creates its enemy for itself within its own gates, creates it in what it suppresses, and what is at the same time essential to it —womankind in general. Womankind—the everlasting irony in the life of the community—changes by intrigue the universal purpose of government into a private end, transforms its universal activity into a work of this or that specific individual, and perverts the universal property of the state into a possession and ornament for the family. Woman in this way turns to ridicule the grave wisdom of maturity, which, being dead to all particular aims, to private pleasure, personal satisfaction, and actual activity as well, thinks of, and is concerned for, merely what is universal; she makes this wisdom the laughing-stock of raw and wanton youth, an object of derision and scorn, unworthy of their enthusiasm. She asserts that it is everywhere the force of youth that really counts; she upholds this as of primary significance; extols a son as one who is the lord and master of the mother who has borne him; a brother as one in whom the sister finds man on a level with herself; a youth as one through whom the daughter, freed from her dependence (on the family unity), acquires the satisfaction and the dignity of wifehood.

* * *

ARTHUR SCHOPENHAUER

Arthur Schopenhauer (1788–1860) is generally regarded as a philosopher of pessimism. This is an interesting designation because idealists such as he are more often construed as optimistic. Actually, there are reasons for both tendencies in Schopenhauer's background: the happy circumstances of his material wealth and gifts of mind, and the tragic circumstances of his father's suicide and the sustained hostility between his mother and himself.

Kant and Hegel exerted a significant influence upon the development of Schopenhauer's philosophy. From Kant he learned and applied the distinction between phenomena and noumena; from Hegel he learned and rejected an exclusively rationalistic interpretation of reality. For Schopenhauer, our "idea" of the world (the world as presented to us empirically or phenomenally) is diverse or many; but metaphysically or noumenally, the world is *one*. Its oneness is ascertained and maintained not through reason but through will. This will—a blind impulse, an incessant striving—is the driving force of the world. The title of Schopenhauer's main work, *The World as Will and Idea,* expresses his fundamental thesis in this regard.

According to Schopenhauer, all organisms possess a will to live. In human nature, the exercise of this will entails reason as a principal means of satisfying biological needs and wants. Knowledge is thus a servant of the human will to live.

The thought of Schopenhauer is called a voluntarism because of its emphasis on will, which is described as totally determinative of individuals and society. In our consciousness of acts already willed, we think ourselves free, but in fact our actions follow inexorably from our noumenal (real) character. Our sense of freedom is the effect of ignorance of the determining causes of our actions. Even apparently drastic changes in personality are traceable to character determination. Suppose, for example, an individual whose acts are generally motivated by desire for financial gain is persuaded that great treasure in heaven is obtainable through the fulfillment of certain "religious" observances. This new conviction may cause the person to behave in a manner radically different from past practice, yet entirely consistent with his or her character.

Schopenhauer's pessimism is evident in his discussion of the will to live as a striving to assert existence at the expense of others. Accordingly, he asserts that "[t]he chief source of the most serious evils which afflict man is man himself." In effect, the world is "a hell which surpasses that of Dante through the fact that one man must be the devil of another." Human desire is itself a form of pain, relieved only momentarily by snatches of happiness. Happiness is both transient and negative, for whatever quenches our desires soon turns into boredom, inclining us to seek one another's company for further relief. The greater our intellectual powers, the more we tend to experience isolation from others, and the greater our capacity for suffering.

Morality, for Schopenhauer, consists in overcoming our natural subservience to the will to live. The just man penetrates the illusion of individuality to the extent that he sets others on the same level with himself. Sympathy, or love, involves recognition that all individuals are really one, as differentiated phenomena of the same undivided will. "All true and pure love," Schopenhauer claims, "is sympathy, and all love which is not sympathy is selfishness."

On Women

Schiller's poem in honour of women, *Wurde der Frauen,* is the result of much careful thought, and it appeals to the reader by its antithetic style and its use of contrast; but as an expression of the true praise which should be accorded to them, it is, I think, inferior to these few words of Jouy's: *Without women the beginning of our life would be helpless; the middle, devoid of pleasure; and the end, of consolation.* The same thing is more feelingly expressed by Byron in *Sardanapalus:—*

The very first
Of human life must spring from woman's breast,
Your first small words are taught you from her lips,
Your first tears quench'd by her, and your last sighs
Too often breathed out in a woman's hearing,
When men have shrunk from the ignoble care
Of watching the last hour of him who led them.
(*Act* I. *Scene* 2.)

These two passages indicate the right standpoint for the appreciation of women.

You need only look at the way in which she is formed to see that woman is not meant to undergo great labour, whether of the mind or of the body. She pays the debt of life not by what she does but by what she suffers; by the pains of childbearing and care for the child, and by submission to her husband, to whom she should be a patient and cheering companion.

The keenest sorrows and joys are not for her, nor is she called upon to display a great deal of strength. The current of her life should be more gentle, peaceful and trivial than man's, without being essentially happier or unhappier.

Women are directly fitted for acting as the nurses and teachers of our early childhood by the fact that they are themselves childish, frivolous and short-sighted; in a word, they are big children all their life long—a kind of intermediate stage between the child and the full-grown man, who is man in the strict sense of the word. See how a girl will fondle a child for days together, dance with it and sing to it; and then think what a man, with the best will in the world, could do if he were put in her place.

With young girls Nature seems to have had in view what, in the language of the drama, is called *a coup de théâtre.* For a few years she dowers them with a wealth of beauty and is lavish in her gift of charm, at the expense of the rest of their life, in order that during those years they may capture the fantasy of some man to such a degree that he is hurried into undertaking the honourable care of them, in some form or other, as long as they live—a step for which there would not appear to be any sufficient warranty if reason only directed his thoughts. Accordingly Nature has equipped woman, as she does all her creatures, with the weapons and implements requisite for the safeguarding of her existence, and for just as long as it is necessary for her to have them. Here, as elsewhere, Nature proceeds with her usual economy; for just as the female ant, after fecundation, loses her wings, which are then superfluous, nay, actually a danger to the business of breeding; so, after giving birth to one or two children, a woman generally loses her beauty; probably, indeed, for similar reasons.

And so we find that young girls, in their hearts, look upon domestic affairs or work of any kind as of secondary importance, if not actually as a mere jest. The only business that really claims their earnest attention is love, making conquests, and everything connected with this—dress, dancing, and so on.

The nobler and more perfect a thing is, the later and slower it is in arriving at maturity. A man reaches the maturity of his reasoning powers and mental faculties hardly before the age of twenty-eight; a woman, at eighteen. And then, too, in the case of woman, it is only reason of a sort—very niggard in its dimensions. That is why women remain children their whole life long; never seeing anything but what is quite close to them, cleaving to the present moment, taking appearance for reality, and preferring trifles to matters of the first importance. For it is by virtue of his reasoning faculty that man does not live in the present only, like the brute, but looks about him and considers the past and the future; and this is the origin of prudence, as well as of that care and anxiety which so many people exhibit. Both the advantages and the disadvantages which this involves, are shared in by the woman to a smaller extent because of her weaker power of reasoning. She may, in fact, be described as intellectually short-sighted, because, while she has an intuitive understanding of what lies quite close to her, her field of vision is narrow and does not reach to what is remote: so that things which are absent or past or to come have much less effect upon women than upon men. This is the reason why women are more often inclined to be extravagant, and sometimes carry their inclination to a length that borders upon madness. In their hearts women think that it is men's business to earn money and theirs to spend it—if possible during their husband's life, but, at any rate, after his death. The very fact that their husband hands them over his earnings for purposes of housekeeping strengthens them in this belief.

However many disadvantages all this may involve, there is at least this to be said in its favour: that the woman lives more in the present than the man, and that, if the present is at all tolerable, she enjoys it more eagerly. This is the source of that cheerfulness which is peculiar to woman, fitting her to amuse man in his hours of recreation, and, in case of need, to console him when he is borne down by the weight of his cares.

It is by no means a bad plan to consult women in matters of difficulty, as the Germans used to do in ancient times; for their way of looking at things is quite different from ours, chiefly in the fact that they like to take the shortest way to their goal, and, in general, manage to fix their eyes upon what lies before them;

while we, as a rule, see far beyond it, just because it is in front of our noses. In cases like this, we need to be brought back to the right standpoint, so as to recover the near and simple view.

Then, again, women are decidedly more sober in their judgment than we are, so that they do not see more in things than is really there; whilst, if our passions are aroused, we are apt to see things in an exaggerated way, or imagine what does not exist.

The weakness of their reasoning faculty also explains why it is that women show more sympathy for the unfortunate than men do, and so treat them with more kindness and interest; and why it is that, on the contrary, they are inferior to men in point of justice, and less honourable and conscientious. For it is just because their reasoning power is weak that present circumstances have such a hold over them, and those concrete things which lie directly before their eyes exercise a power which is seldom counteracted to any extent by abstract principles of thought, by fixed rules of conduct, firm resolutions, or, in general, by consideration for the past and the future, or regard of what is absent and remote. Accordingly, they possess the first and main elements that go to make a virtuous character, but they are deficient in those secondary qualities which are often a necessary instrument in the formation of it.

Hence it will be found that the fundamental fault of the female character is that it has *no sense of justice*. This is mainly due to the fact, already mentioned, that women are defective in the powers of reasoning and deliberation; but it is also traceable to the position which Nature has assigned to them as the weaker sex. They are dependent, not upon strength, but upon craft; and hence their instinctive capacity for cunning, and their ineradicable tendency to say what is not true. For as lions are provided with claws and teeth, and elephants and boars with tusks, bulls with horns, and the cuttle fish with its cloud of inky fluid, so Nature has equipped woman, for her defence and protection, with the arts of dissimulation; and all the power which Nature has conferred upon man in the shape of physical strength and reason has been bestowed upon women in this form. Hence dissimulation is innate in woman, and almost as much a quality of the stupid as of the clever. It is as natural for them to make use of it on every occasion as it is for those animals to employ their means of defence when they are attacked; they have a feeling that in doing so they are only within their rights. Therefore a woman who is perfectly truthful and not given to dissimulation is perhaps an impossibility, and for this very reason they are so quick at seeing through dissimulation in others that it is not a wise thing to attempt it with them. But this fundamental defect which I have stated, with all that it entails, gives rise to falsity, faithlessness, treachery, ingratitude, and so on. Perjury in a court of justice is more often committed by women than by men. It may, indeed, be generally questioned whether women ought to be sworn at all. From time to time one finds repeated cases everywhere of ladies, who want for nothing, taking things from shop-counters when no one is looking and making off with them.

Nature has appointed that the propagation of the species shall be the business of men who are young, strong and handsome; so that the race may not degenerate. This is the firm will and purpose of Nature in regard to the species, and it finds its expression in the passions of women. There is no law that is older or more powerful than this. Woe, then, to the man who sets up claims and interests that will conflict with it; whatever he may say and do, they will be unmercifully crushed at the first serious encounter. For the innate rule that governs women's conduct, though it is secret and unformulated, nay, unconscious in its working, is this: *We are justified in deceiving those who think they have acquired rights over the species by paying little attention to the individual, that is, to us. The constitution and, therefore, the welfare of the species have been placed in our hands and committed to our care, through the control we obtain over the next generation, which proceeds from us; let us discharge our duties conscientiously.* But women have no abstract knowledge of this leading principle; they are conscious of it only as a concrete fact; and they have no other method of giving expression to it than the way in which they act when the opportunity arrives. And then their conscience does not trouble them so much as we fancy; for in the darkest recesses of their heart they are aware that, in committing a breach of their duty towards the individual, they have all the better fulfilled their duty towards the species, which is infinitely greater.[1]

And since women exist in the main solely for the propagation of the species, and are not destined for anything else, they live as a rule, more for the species than for the individual, and in their hearts take the affairs of the species more seriously than those of the individual. This gives their whole life and being a certain levity; the general bent of their character is in a direction fundamentally different from that of man; and it is this which produces that discord in married life which is so frequent, and almost the normal state.

The natural feeling between men is mere indifference, but between women it is actual enmity. The reason of this is that trade-jealousy—*odium figulinum*—which, in the case of men, does not go beyond the confines of their own particular pursuit but with women embraces the whole sex; since they have only one kind of business. Even when they meet in the street women look at one another like Guelphs and Ghibellines. And it is a patent fact that when two

1. A more detailed discussion of the matter in question may be found in my chief work, *Die Welt als Wille und Vorstellung*, vol. ii, ch. 44.

women make first acquaintance with each other they behave with more constraint and dissimulation than two men who would show in a like case; and hence it is that an exchange of compliments between two women is a much more ridiculous proceeding than between two men. Further, whilst a man will, as a general rule, always preserve a certain amount of consideration and humanity in speaking to others, even to those who are in a very inferior position, it is intolerable to see how proudly and disdainfully a fine lady will generally behave towards one who is in a lower social rank (I do not mean a woman who is in her service), whenever she speaks to her. The reason of this may be that, with women, differences of rank are much more precarious than with us; because, while a hundred considerations carry weight in our case, in theirs there is only one, namely, with which man they have found favour; as also that they stand in much nearer relations with one another than men do, in consequence of the one-sided nature of their calling. This makes them endeavour to lay stress upon differences of rank.

It is only the man whose intellect is clouded by his sexual impulses that could give the name of *the fair sex* to that undersized, narrow-shouldered, broad-hipped, and short-legged race: for the whole beauty of the sex is bound up with this impulse. Instead of calling them beautiful, there would be more warrant for describing women as the unaesthetic sex. Neither for music, nor for poetry, nor for fine art, have they really and truly any sense or susceptibility; it is a mere mockery if they make a pretence of it in order to assist their endeavour to please. Hence, as a result of this, they are incapable of taking a *purely objective interest* in anything; and the reason of it seems to me to be as follows. A man tries to acquire *direct* mastery over things, either by understanding them or by forcing them to do his will. But a woman is always and everywhere reduced to obtaining this mastery *indirectly*, namely through a man; and whatever direct mastery she may have is entirely confined to him. And so it lies in woman's nature to look upon everything only as a means for conquering man; and if she takes an interest in anything else it is simulated—a mere roundabout way of gaining her ends by coquetry and feigning what she does not feel. Hence even Rousseau declared: *Women have, in general, no love of any art; they have no proper knowledge of any; and they have no genius.*[2]

No one who sees at all below the surface can have failed to remark the same thing. You need only observe the kind of attention women bestow upon a concert, an opera, or a play—the childish simplicity, for example, with which they keep on chattering during

2. Lettre à d'Alembert.

the finest passages in the greatest masterpieces. If it is true that the Greeks excluded women from their theatres, they were quite right in what they did; at any rate you would have been able to hear what was said upon the stage. In our day, besides, or in lieu of saying, *Let a woman keep silence in the church,* it would be much to the point to say, *Let a woman keep silence in the theatre.* This might, perhaps, be put up in big letters on the curtain.

And you cannot expect anything else of women if you consider that the most distinguished intellects among the whole sex have never managed to produce a single achievement in the fine arts that is really great, genuine, and original; or given to the world any work of permanent value in any sphere. This is most strikingly shown in regard to painting, where mastery of techniques is at least as much within their power as within ours—and hence they are diligent in cultivating it; but still, they have not a single great painting to boast of, just because they are deficient in that objectivity of mind which is so directly indispensable in painting. They never get beyond a subjective point of view. It is quite in keeping with this that ordinary women have no real susceptibility for art at all; for Nature proceeds in strict sequence—*non facit saltum.* And Huarte in his *Examen de ingenios para las scienzias*—a book which has been famous for three hundred years—denies women the possession of all the higher faculties. The case is not altered by particular and partial exceptions; taken as a whole, women are, and remain, thorough-going philistines, and quite incurable. Hence, with that absurd arrangement which allows them to share the rank and title of their husbands, they are a constant stimulus to his ignoble ambitions. And, further, it is just because they are philistines that modern society, where they take the lead and set the tone, is in such a bad way. Napoleon's saying—that *women have no rank*—should be adopted as the right standpoint in determining their position in society; and as regards their other qualities Chamfort makes the very true remark: *They are made to trade with our own weaknesses and our follies, but not with our reason. The sympathies that exist between them and men are skin-deep only, and do not touch the mind or the feelings or the character.* They form the *sexus sequior*—the second sex, inferior in every respect to the first; their infirmities should be treated with consideration; but to show them great reverence is extremely ridiculous, and lowers us in their eyes. When Nature made two divisions of the human race, she did not draw the line exactly through the middle. These divisions are polar and opposed to each other, it is true; but the difference between them is not qualitative merely, it is also quantitative.

This is just the view which the ancients took of woman, and the view which people in the East take now; and their judgment as to her proper position is much more correct than ours, with our old French notions of gallantry and our preposterous system of reverence—that highest product of Teutonico-Christian stupidity. These notions have served only to make women more arrogant and overbearing; so that one is occasionally reminded of the holy apes in Benares, who in the consciousness of their sanctity and inviolable position think they can do exactly as they please.

But in the West the woman, and especially the *lady,* finds herself in a false position; for woman, rightly called by the ancients *sexus sequior,* is by no means fit to be the object of our honour and veneration, or to hold her head higher than man and be on equal terms with him. The consequences of this false position are sufficiently obvious. Accordingly it would be a very desirable thing if this Number Two of the human race were in Europe also relegated to her natural place, and an end put to that lady-nuisance, which not only moves all Asia to laughter, but would have been ridiculed by Greece and Rome as well. It is impossible to calculate the good effects which such a change would bring about in our social, civil and political arrangements. There would be no necessity for the Salic law: it would be a superfluous truism. In Europe the *lady,* strictly so-called, is a being who should not exist at all; she should be either a housewife or a girl who hopes to become one; and she should be brought up, not to be arrogant, but to be thrifty and submissive. It is just because there are such people as *ladies* in Europe that the women of the lower classes, that is to say, the great majority of the sex, are much more unhappy than they are in the East. And even Lord Byron says: *Thought of the state of women under the ancient Greeks—convenient enough. Present state, a remnant of the barbarism of the chivalric and the feudal ages—artificial and unnatural. They ought to mind home—and be well fed and clothed—but not mixed in society. Well educated, too, in religion—but to read neither poetry nor politics—nothing but books of piety and cookery. Music—drawing—dancing—also a little gardening and ploughing now and then. I have seen them mending the roads in Epirus with good success. Why not, as well as haymaking and milking?*

The laws of marriage prevailing in Europe consider the woman as the equivalent of the man—start, that is to say, from a wrong position. In our part of the world where monogamy is the rule, to marry means to have one's rights and double one's duties. Now when the laws gave women equal rights with man, they ought to have also endowed her with a masculine intellect. But the fact is that, just in proportion as the honours and privileges which the laws accord to women exceed the amount which Nature gives, there is a diminution in the number of women who really participate in these privileges; and all the remainder are deprived of their natural rights by just so much as is given to the others over and above their share. For the institution of monogamy, and the laws of marriage which it entails, bestow upon the woman an unnatural position of privilege, by considering her throughout as the full equivalent of the man, which is by no means the case; and seeing thus men who are shrewd and prudent very often scruple to make so great a sacrifice and to acquiesce in so unfair an arrangement.

Consequently, whilst among polygamous nations every woman is provided for, where monogamy prevails the number of married women is limited; and there remains over a large number of women without stay or support, who, in the upper classes, vegetate as useless old maids, and in the lower succumb to hard work for which they are not suited; or else become *filles de joie*, whose life is as destitute of joy as it is of honour. But under the circumstances they become a necessity; and their position is openly recognised as serving the special end of warding off temptation from those women favoured by fate, who have found, or may hope to find, husbands. In London alone there are 80,000 prostitutes. What are they but the women, who, under the institution of monogamy, have come off worst? Theirs is a dreadful fate: they are human sacrifices offered up on the altar of monogamy. The women whose wretched position is here described are the inevitable set-off to the European lady with her arrogance and pretension. Polygamy is therefore a real benefit to the female sex if it is taken as a whole. And, from another point of view, there is no true reason why a man whose wife suffers from chronic illness, or remains barren, or has gradually become too old for him, should not take a second. The motives which induce so many people to become converts to Mormonism appear to be just those which militate against the unnatural institution of monogamy.

Moreover, the bestowal of unnatural rights upon women has imposed upon them unnatural duties, and nevertheless a breach of these duties makes them unhappy. Let me explain. A man may often think that his social or financial position will suffer if he marries, unless he makes some brilliant alliance. His desire will then be to win a woman of his own choice under conditions other than those of marriage, such as will secure her position and that of the children. However fair, reasonable, fit and proper these conditions may be, if the woman consents by foregoing that undue amount of privilege which marriage alone can bestow, she to some extent loses her honour, because marriage is the basis of civic society; and she will lead an unhappy life, since human nature is so constituted that we pay an attention to the opinion of other people which is out of all proportion to its value. On the other hand, if she does not consent, she runs the risk either of having to be given in marriage to a man whom she does not like, or of being landed high and dry as an old maid; for the period during which she has a chance of being settled for life is very short. And in view of this aspect of the institution of monogamy, Thomasius' profoundly learned treatise *de Concubinatu* is well worth reading; for it shows that, amongst all nations and in all ages, down to the Lutheran Reformation, concubinage was permitted; nay, that it was an institution which was to a certain extent actually recognised by law, and attended with no dishonour. It was only the Lutheran Reformation that degraded it from this position. It was seen to be a further justification for the marriage of the clergy; and then, after that, the Catholic Church did not dare to remain behindhand in the matter.

There is no use arguing about polygamy; it must be taken as *de facto* existing everywhere, and the only question is as to how it shall be regulated. Where are there, then, any real monogamists? We all live, at any rate, for a time, and most of us, always, in polygamy. And so, since every man needs many women, there is nothing fairer than to allow him, nay, to make it incumbent upon him, to provide for many women. This will reduce woman to her true and natural position as a subordinate being; and the *lady*—that monster of European civilisation and Teutonico-Christian stupidity—will disappear from the world, leaving only *women*, but no more *unhappy women*, of whom Europe is now full.

In India no woman is ever independent, but in accordance with the law of Manu, she stands under the control of her father, her husband, her brother or her son. It is, to be sure, a revolting thing that a widow should immolate herself upon her husband's funeral pyre; but it is also revolting that she should spend her husband's money with her paramours—the money for which he toiled his whole life long, in the consoling belief that he was providing for his children. Happy are those who have kept the middle course—*medium tenuere beati.*

The first love of a mother for her child is, with the lower animals as with men, of a purely *instinctive* character, and so it ceases when the child is no longer in a physically helpless condition. After that, the first love should give way to one that is based on habit and reason; but this often fails to make its appearance, especially where the mother did not love the father. The love of a father for his child is of a different order, and more likely to last; because it has its foundation in the fact that in the child he recognises his own inner self; that is to say, his love for it is metaphysical in its origin.

In almost all nations, whether of the ancient or the modern world, even amongst the Hottentots, property is inherited by the male descendants alone; it is only in Europe that a departure has taken place; but not amongst the nobility, however. That the property which has cost men long years of toil and effort, and been won with so much difficulty, should afterwards come into the hands of women, who then, in their lack of reason, squander it in a short time, or otherwise fool it away, is a grievance and a wrong, as serious as it is common, which should be prevented by limiting the right of women to inherit. In my opinion the best arrangement would be that by which women, whether widows or daughters, should never receive anything beyond the interest for life on property secured by mortgage, and in no case the property itself, or the capital, except where all male descendants fail. The people who make money are men, not women; and it follows from this that women are neither justified in having unconditional possession of it, nor fit persons to be entrusted with its administration. When wealth, in any true sense of the word, that is to say, funds, houses or land, is to go to them as an inheritance, they should never be allowed the free disposition of it. In their case a guardian should always be appointed; and hence they should never be given the free control of their own children, wherever it can be avoided. The vanity of women, even though it should not prove to be greater than that of men, has this much danger in it that it takes an entirely material direction. They are vain, I mean, of their personal beauty, and then of finery, show and magnificence. That is just why they are so much in their element in society. It is this, too, which makes them so inclined to be extravagant, all the more as their reasoning power is low. Accordingly we find an ancient writer describing woman as in general of an extravagant nature—Γυνὴ τὸ σύνολον ἔστι δαπανηρὸν φύσει.[3] But with men vanity often takes the direction of non-material advantages, such as intellect, learning, courage.

In the *Politics*[4] Aristotle explains the great disadvantage which accrued to the Spartans from the fact that they conceded too much to their women, by giving them the right of inheritance and dower, and a great amount of independence; and he shows how much this contributed to Sparta's fall. May it not be the case in France that the influence of women, which went on increasing steadily from the time of Louis XIII., was to blame for that gradual corruption of the Court and the Government, which brought about the Revolution of 1789, of which all subsequent disturbances have been the fruit? However that may be, the false position which women occupy, demonstrated as it is, in the most glaring way, the institution of the *lady*, is a fundamental defect in our social scheme, and this

3. Brunck's *Gnomici poetae graeci* v. 115.

4. Bk. I, ch. 9.

defect, proceeding from the very heart of it, must spread its baneful influence in all directions.

That woman is by nature meant to obey may be seen by the fact that every woman who is placed in the unnatural position of complete independence, immediately attaches herself to some man, by whom she allows herself to be guided and ruled. It is because she needs a lord and master. If she is young, it will be a lover; if she is old, a priest.

SUGGESTIONS FOR FURTHER READING

Locke

Atherton, Margaret. "Locke's Theory of Personal Identity." *Midwest Studies in Philosophy* 8 (1983), pp. 273–94.

Clark, Lorenne. "Women and John Locke; Or, Who Owns the Apples in the Garden of Eden?" *Canadian Journal of Philosophy* 7 (Dec. 1977), pp. 699–724.

Helm, Paul. "Locke's Conditions for Personal Identity." *Locke News* 10 (Autumn 1979), pp. 43–51.

Simons, Martin. "Why Can't a Man Be More Like a Woman? (A Note on John Locke's Educational Thought.)" *Educational Theory* 40 (Winter 1990), pp. 135–45.

Squadrito, Kathy. "Locke on the Equality of the Sexes." *Journal of Social Philosophy* X, 1 (Jan. 1979), pp. 6–11.

Thornton, Mark. "Same Human Being, Same Person?" *Philosophy* 66 (Jan. 1991), pp. 115–18.

Hume

Baier, Annette. "Helping Hume to 'Compleat the Union.'" *Philosophy and Phenomenological Research* 41 (Sept.–Dec. 1980), pp. 167–86.

______. "Hume, the Women's Moral Theorist." In *Women and Moral Theory*, ed. by Eva Feder Kittay. Totowa, N.J.: Rowman & Littlefield, 1987, pp. 37–55.

Battersby, Christine. "An Enquiry Concerning the Humean Woman." *Philosophy* 56 (July 1981), pp. 303–12.

Berry, Christopher J. *Hume, Hegel and Human Nature*. Boston: Nijhoff, 1982.

Immerwahr, John. "David Hume, Sexism, and Sociobiology." *Southern Journal of Philosophy* 21 (Fall 1983), pp. 359–70.

McIntyre, Jane L. "Personal Identity and the Passions." *Journal of the History of Philosophy* 27 (Oct. 1989), pp. 545–57.

Mendus, Susan. "Personal Identity: The Two Analogies in Hume." *Philosophical Quarterly* 30 (Jan. 1980), pp. 61–68.

Richards, Janet Radcliffe. *The Skeptical Feminist: A Philosophical Enquiry*. Boston: Routledge & Kegan Paul, 1980.

Rousseau

Bloom, Allan. "Rousseau on the Equality of the Sexes." In *Justice and Equality Here and Now*, ed. by Frank S. Lucash. Ithaca: Cornell University Press, 1986, pp. 68–88.

Canovan, Margaret. "Rousseau's Two Concepts of Citizenship." In *Women in Western Political Philosophy: Kant to Nietzsche*, ed. by Ellen Kennedy and Susan Mendus. New York: St. Martin's Press, 1987, pp. 78–105.

Keohane, Nannerl O. "But for Her Sex: The Domestication of Sophie." *Review de l'Université d'Ottawa* 49 (July–Oct. 1979), pp. 390–400.

Kofman, Sarah. "Rousseau's Phallocratic Ends." *Hypatia* 3 (Winter 1989), pp. 123–36.

Lange, Lynda. "Women and 'The General Will.'" *Review de l'Université d'Ottawa* 49 (July–Oct. 1979), pp. 401–11.

———. "Rousseau and Modern Feminism." *Social Theory and Practice* 7 (Fall 1981), pp. 245–77.

Lloyd, Genevieve. "Rousseau on Reason, Nature and Women." *Metaphilosophy* 14 (July–Oct. 1983), pp. 308–26.

Martin, Jane Roland. "Taking Sophie Seriously." *Philosophy of Education, Proceedings of the Education Society* 39 (1983), pp. 53–56.

Misenheimer, Helen Evans. *Rousseau on the Education of Women*. Lanham, Md.: University Press of America, 1981.

Okin, Susan Moller. "Women and the Making of the Sentimental Family." *Philosophy and Public Affairs* 11 (Winter 1982), pp. 65–88.

Rapaport, Elizabeth. "On the Future of Love: Rousseau and the Radical Feminists." In *Women and Philosophy*, ed. by Carol C. Gould and Marx W. Wartofsky. New York: G. P. Putnam and Sons, 1976, pp. 185–205.

Schwartz, Joel. *The Sexual Politics of Jean-Jacques Rousseau*. Chicago: The University of Chicago Press, 1984.

Thomas, Paul. "Jean-Jacques Rousseau, Sexist?" *Feminist Studies* (Summer 1991), pp. 195–218.

Weiss, Penny A. "Rousseau, Antifeminism, and Woman's Nature." *Political Theory* 15 (Fall 1987), pp. 81–98.

Kant

Axelsen, Diana E. "Kant's Metaphors for Persons and Community." *Philosophy and Theology* 3 (Summer 1989), pp. 301–21.

Blum, Lawrence A. "Kant's and Hegel's Moral Rationalism: A Feminist Perspective." *Canadian Journal of Philosophy* 12 (June 1982), pp. 287–302.

Cooke, Vincent M. "Kant, Teleology, and Sexual Ethics." *International Philosophical Quarterly* (March 1991), pp. 3–13.

Hill, Thomas E., Fr. "Servility and Self-Respect." *The Monist* 57 (Jan. 1973), pp. 87–104.

Klein, Martha. "Morality and Justice in Kant." *Ratio* 3 (June 1990), pp. 1–20.

Kneller, Jane. "Kant's Concept of Beauty." *History of Philosophy Quarterly* 3 (July 1986), pp. 311–23.

Lo, P. C. *Treating Persons as Ends: An Essay on Kant's Moral Philosophy.* Lanham, Md.: University Press of America, 1987.

Rumsey, Jean P. "Agency, Human Nature and Character in Kantian Theory." *Journal of Value Inquiry* 24 (April 1990), pp. 109–21.

Sedgwick, Sally S. "Can Kant's Ethics Survive the Feminist Critique?" *Pacific Philosophical Quarterly* 71 (March, 1990), pp. 60–79.

Wollstonecraft

Barker-Benfield, G. J. "Mary Wollstonecraft: Eighteenth Century Commonwealthwoman." *Journal of the History of Ideas* 50 (Jan.–March 1989), pp. 95–115.

Flexner, Eleanor. *Mary Wollstonecraft; a Biography.* New York: Coward, McCann and Geoghegan, 1972.

Gatens, Moira. "Rousseau and Wollstonecraft: Nature vs. Reason." *Australasian Journal of Philosophy* Suppl. 64 (June 1986), pp. 1–15.

Grimshaw, Jean. "Mary Wollstonecraft and the Tensions in Feminist Philosophy." *Radical Philosophy* 52 (Summer 1989), pp. 11–17.

Kelso, Ruth. *Doctrine for the Lady of the Renaissance.* Urbana: University of Illinois Press, 1956.

Korsmeyer, Carolyn W. "Reason and Morals in the Early Feminist Movement: Mary Wollstonecraft." In *Women and Philosophy,* ed. by Carol C. Gould and Marx W. Wartofsky. New York: G. P. Putnam and Sons, 1976, pp. 97–111.

Larson, Elizabeth. "Mary Wollstonecraft and Women's Rights." *Free Inquiry* 12 (Spring 1992), pp. 45–48.

Nicholson, Mervyn. "The Eleventh Commandment: Sex and Spirit in Wollstonecraft and Malthus." *Journal of the History of Ideas* 51 (July–Sept. 1990), pp. 401–21.

Hegel

Bell, Linda A. and Alcoff, Linda. "Lordship, Bondage and the Dialectic of Work in Traditional Male/Female Relationships." *Cogito* 2 (Summer 1984), pp. 79–94.

Buckman, Kenneth L. "At the Crossroads: Inadequacy of Hegel's Familial Paradigm." *Kinesis* 15 (Summer 1986), pp. 107–24.

Dahlstrom, Daniel O. "The Sexual Basis of Moral Life." *American Catholic Philosophical Association, Proceedings* 62 (1988), pp. 202–11.

Hayim, Gila J. "Hegel's Critical Theory and Feminist Concerns." *Philosophy and Social Criticism* (1990), pp. 1–21.

Hodge, Joanna. "Women and the Hegelian State." In *Women in Western Political Philosophy: Kant to Nietzsche*, ed. by Ellen Kennedy and Susan Mendus. New York: St. Martin's Press, 1987. pp. 127–58.

Ravven, Heidi M. "Has Hegel Anything to Say to Feminists?" *Owl Minerva* 19 (Spring 1988), pp. 149–68.

Siebert, Rudolf J. "Hegel's Concept of Marriage and Family." In *Hegel's Social and Political Thought*, ed. by Donald Phillip Verene. Atlantic Highlands, N.J.: Humanities Press, 1980, pp. 177–214.

Stillman, Peter G. "Hegel's Idea of the Modern Family." *Thought* 56 (Summer 1981), pp. 342–52.

ver Eecke, Wilfried. "Fatherhood and Subjectivity." *Philosophy and Theology* 3 (Spring 1989), pp. 253–64.

Schopenhauer

Atwell, John. *Schopenhauer: The Human Character*. Philadelphia: Temple University Press, 1990.

Edman, Irwin (ed.). "The Metaphysics of the Love of the Sexes." In *The Philosophy of Schopenhauer*. New York: The Modern Library, Inc., 1928, pp. 337–76.

Gates, Eugene. "The Female Voice: Sexual Aesthetics Revisited." *Journal of Aesthetic Education* 22 (Winter 1988), pp. 59–68.

Stern, Karl. "Schopenhauer." In *The Flight from Woman*. New York: Farrar, Straus and Giroux, 1965, pp. 107–22.

II
RECENT INFLUENCES

Authors included in this section represent a number of philosophical methods or orientations: utilitarianism, existentialism, psychoanalysis, socialism, pragmatism, and philosophical analysis. While each orientation is separately describable, the different frameworks often overlap. Philosophical analysis, for example, provides a tool through which concepts and arguments developed in diverse philosophical traditions may be evaluated. In contrast to selections included in the previous section, the selections here place greater emphasis on the choices of, and relations between, individuals. Even within the same philosophical framework (e.g., existentialism), however, there are starkly contrasting views of women, and some authors present views of women that are incompatible with their generic view of humankind.

UTILITARIANISM

A utilitarian philosophy maintains that the total consequences of our actions are (or ought to be) the criteria according to which priorities are established for moral and political decisions. Despite the tension that this suggests, utilitarians generally uphold the value of both the individual and society. For John Stuart Mill and Harriet Taylor Mill, for example, social equality is essential to individual equality, and vice versa.

JOHN STUART MILL

Like Jeremy Bentham, his philosophical mentor, John Stuart Mill (1806–1873) affirmed that the greatest good for society is constituted by the greatest happiness or pleasure for the greatest number of individuals. Unlike Bentham, however, J. S. Mill maintained that the pleasures which may justify ethical action differ qualitatively as well as quantitatively. For example, merely sensual delights are in fact inferior to intellectual or aesthetic modes of pleasure. Moreover, it is futile to pursue happiness directly, or for oneself alone. "[P]aradoxical as the assertion may be," J. S. Mill claimed, "the conscious ability to do without happiness gives the best prospect of realizing such happiness as is attainable." To secure happiness for ourselves, then, we must seek primarily to promote the well-being of others.

J. S. Mill's personal life provides an intriguing example of consistency with his utilitarian ethics. Mill was a bachelor, and Harriett Taylor was a wife and mother of two when they met in their early twenties. Despite the deep rapport of intellect and sentiment which soon developed between them, it was not until twenty-one years later (two years after John Taylor's death) that they married. Harriet characterized her relationship both to her husband and to Mill during those years as that of a *Seelenfreundin* (a spiritual friend). Their decision not to break up the Taylor family through divorce seems to have been motivated by concern to promote the greatest happiness for the greatest number.

In his famous essay *On Liberty,* which Mill describes as a joint production with Harriet Taylor, the liberty defended is a liberty of conscience (of thought and feeling), of tastes and pursuits, and of association. The only grounds which justify limitation of any individual's liberty in these regards are self-protection and the prevention of harm to others. Since human nature is essentially free and fundamentally good, every individual has the right to seek happiness according to her or his own capacity, while respecting and supporting the right of others to do the same. Freedom, according to Mill, is a prerequisite for human happiness and progress. Contentment or satisfaction is possible for those who become inured to living in shackles, but such individuals cannot experience genuine happiness until they are actually free.

Before marrying Harriet Taylor, Mill formally renounced whatever legal advantages might accrue to him by reason of the marriage contract. "There is no natural inequality between the sexes, except perhaps in bodily strength; even that admits of doubt, and if bodily strength is to be the measure of superiority, mankind are no better than savages." Equality, however, should not be confused with sameness. The proper relationship between the sexes, as among all individuals, with their inevitable diversity, is one of complementarity, or "reciprocal superiority." Each of us has something unique and superior to contribute to one another.

The following is excerpted from an essay first published in 1869. Although Harriet had died eleven years earlier, Mill thus described her contribution to the work: "[A]ll that is most striking and profound belongs to my wife; coming from the fund of thought which had been made common to us both, by our innumerable conversations and discussions on a topic which filled so large a place in our minds."

The Subjection of Women

The object of this Essay is to explain as clearly as I am able, the grounds of an opinion which I have held from the very earliest period when I had formed any opinions at all on social or political matters, and which, instead of being weakened or modified, has been constantly growing stronger by the progress of reflection and the experience of life: That the principle which regulates the existing social relations between the two sexes—the legal subordination of one sex to the other—is wrong in itself, and now one of the chief hindrances to human improvement; and that it ought to be replaced by a principle of perfect equality, admitting no power or privilege on the one side, nor disability on the other. . . .

The generality of a practice is in some cases a strong presumption that it is, or at all events once was, conducive to laudable ends. This is the case, when the practice was first adopted, or afterwards kept up, as a means to such ends, and was grounded on experience of the mode in which they could be most effectually attained. If the authority of men over women, when first established, had been the result of a conscientious comparison between different modes of constituting the government of society; if, after trying various other modes of social organization—the government of women over men, equality between the two, and such mixed and divided modes of government as might be invented—it had been decided, on the testimony of experience, that the mode in which women are wholly under the rule of men, having no share at all in public concerns, and each in private being under the legal obligation of obedience to the man with whom she has associated her destiny, was the arrangement most conducive to the happiness and well being of both; its general adoption might then be fairly thought to be some evidence that, at the time when it was adopted, it was the best: though even then the considerations which recommended it may, like so many other primeval social facts of the greatest importance, have subsequently, in the course of ages, ceased to exist. But the state of the case is in every respect the reverse of this. In the first place, the opinion in favour of the present system, which entirely subordinates the weaker sex to the stronger, rests upon theory only; for there never has been trial made of any other: so that experience, in the sense in which it is vulgarly opposed to theory, cannot be pretended to have pronounced any verdict. And in the second place, the adoption of this system of inequality never was the result of deliberation, or forethought, or any social ideas, or any notion whatever of what conduced to the benefit of humanity or the good order of society. It arose simply from the fact that from the very earliest twilight of human society, every woman (owing to the value attached to her by men, combined with her inferiority in muscular strength) was found in a state of bondage to some man. Laws and systems of polity always begin by recognising the relations they find already existing between individuals. . . .

So true is it that unnatural generally means only uncustomary, and that everything which is usual appears natural. The subjection of women to men being a universal custom, any departure from it quite naturally appears unnatural. But how entirely, even in this case, the feeling is dependent on custom, appears by ample experience. Nothing so much astonishes the people of distant parts of the world, when they first learn anything about England, as to be told that it is under a queen: the thing seems to them so unnatural as to be almost incredible. To Englishmen this does not seem in the least degree unnatural, because they are used to it; but they do feel it unnatural that women should be soldiers or members of parliament. In the feudal ages, on the contrary, war and politics were not thought unnatural to women, because not unusual. . . .

But, it will be said, the rule of men over women differs from all these others in not being a rule of force: it is accepted voluntarily; women make no complaint, and are consenting parties to it.

In the first place, a great number of women do not accept it. Ever since there have been women able to make their sentiments known by their writings (the only mode of publicity which society permits to them), an increasing number of them have recorded protests against their present social condition. . . .

How many more women there are who silently cherish similar aspirations, no one can possibly know; but there are abundant tokens how many *would* cherish them, were they not so strenuously taught to repress them as contrary to the proprieties of their sex. It must be remembered, also, that no enslaved class ever asked for complete liberty at once. . . . It is a political law of nature that those who are under any power of ancient origin, never begin by complaining of the power itself, but only of its oppressive exercise. There is never any want of women who complain of ill usage by their husbands. There would be infinitely more, if complaint were not the greatest of all provocatives to a repetition and increase of the ill usage. . . .

Men do not want solely the obedience of women, they want their sentiments. All men, except the most brutish, desire to have, in the woman most nearly connected with them, not a forced slave but a willing one, not a slave merely, but a favourite. They have therefore put everything in practice to enslave their minds. . . .

All women are brought up from the earliest years in the belief that their ideal of character is the very opposite to that of men; not self-will, and government by self-control, but submission, and yielding to the control of others. All the moralities tell them that it is the duty of women, and all the current sentimentalities that it is their nature, to live for others; to make complete abnegation of themselves, and to have no life but in their affections. And by their affections are meant the only ones they are allowed to have—those to the men with whom they are connected, or to the children who constitute an additional and indefeasible tie between them and a man. When we put together three things—first, the natural attraction between opposite sexes; secondly, the wife's entire dependence on the husband, every privilege or pleasure she has being either his gift, or depending entirely on his will; and lastly, that the principal object of human pursuit, consideration, and all objects of social ambition, can in general be sought or obtained by her only through him, it would be a miracle if the object of being attractive to men had not become the polar star of feminine education and formation of character. And, this great means of influence over the minds of women have been acquired, an instinct of selfishness made men avail themselves of it to the utmost as a means of holding women in subjection, by representing to them meekness, submissiveness, and resignation of all individual will into the hands of a man, as an essential part of sexual attractiveness. . . .

The preceding considerations are amply sufficient to show that custom, however universal it may be, affords in this case no presumption, and ought not to create any prejudice, in favour of the arrangements which place women in social and political subjection to men. But I may go farther, and maintain that the course of history, and the tendencies of progressive human society, afford not only no presumption in favour of this system of inequality of rights, but a strong one against it; and that, so far as the whole course of human improvement up to this time, the whole stream of modern tendencies, warrants any inference on the subject, it is, that this relic of the past is discordant with the future, and must necessarily disappear. . . .

Neither does it avail anything to say that the *nature* of the two sexes adapts them to their present functions and position, and renders these appropriate to them. Standing on the ground of common sense and the constitution of the human mind, I deny that any one knows, or can know, the nature of the two sexes, as long as they have only been seen in their present relation to one another. If men had ever been found in society without women, or women without men, or if there had been a society of men and women in which the women were not under the control of the men, something might have been positively known about the mental and moral differences which may be inherent in the nature of each. What is now called the nature of women is an eminently artificial thing—the result of forced repression in some directions, unnatural stimulation in others. It may be asserted without scruple, that no other class of dependents have had their character so entirely distorted from its natural proportions by their relation with their masters. . . .

Even the preliminary knowledge, what the differences between the sexes now are, apart from all questions as to how they are made what they are, is still in the crudest and most incomplete state. . . . It is a subject on which nothing final can be known, as long as those who alone can really know it, women themselves, have given but little testimony, and that little, mostly suborned. . . .

It is only a man here and there who has any tolerable knowledge of the character even of the women of his own family. I do not mean, of their capabilities; these nobody knows, not even themselves, because most of them have never been called out. I mean their actually existing thoughts and feelings. Many a man thinks he perfectly understands women, because he has had amatory relations with several, perhaps with many of them. If he is a good observer, and his experience extends to quality as well as quantity, he may have learnt something of one narrow department of their nature—an important department, no doubt. But of all the rest of it, few persons are generally more ignorant, because there are few from whom it is so carefully hidden. The most favourable case which a man can generally have for studying the character of a woman, is that of his own wife: for the opportunities are greater, and the cases of complete sympathy not so unspeakably rare. And in fact, this is the source from which any knowledge worth having on the subject has, I believe, generally come. But most men have not had the opportunity of studying in this way more than a single case: accordingly one can, to an almost laughable degree, infer what a man's wife is like, from his opinions about women in general. . . .

[E]ven if he could study many women of one rank, or of one country, he would not thereby understand women of other ranks or countries; and even if he did, they are still only the women of a single period of history; we may safely assert that the knowledge which men can acquire of women, even as they have been and are, without reference to what they might be, is wretchedly imperfect and superficial, and always will be so, until women themselves have told all they have to tell. . . . One thing we may be certain of—that what is contrary to women's nature to do, they never will be made to do by simply giving their nature free play. . . . What women by nature cannot do, it is quite superfluous to forbid them from doing. What they can do, but not so well as the men who are their competitors, competition suffices to exclude them from. . . . If women have a greater natural inclination for some things than for others, there is no need of laws or social inculcation to make the majority of them do the former in preference to the latter. . . .

The general opinion of men is supposed to be, that the natural vocation of a woman is that of a wife and mother. I say, is supposed to be, because, judging from acts—from the whole of the present constitution of society—one might infer that their opinion was the direct contrary. They might be supposed to think that the alleged natural vocation of women was of all things the most repugnant to their nature; insomuch that if they are free to do anything else—if any other means of living, or occupation of their time and faculties, is open, which has any chance of appearing desirable to them—there will not be enough of them who will be willing to accept the condition said to be natural to them. If this is the real opinion of men in general, it would be well that it should be spoken out. I should like to hear somebody openly enunciating the doctrine (it is already implied in much that is written on the subject)—"It is necessary to society that women should marry and produce children. They will not do so unless they are compelled. Therefore it is necessary to compel them." . . .

I am far from pretending that wives are in general no better treated than slaves; but no slave is a slave to the same lengths, and in so full a sense of the word, as a wife is. Hardly any slave, except one immediately attached to the master's person, is a slave at all hours and all minutes; in general he has, like a soldier, his fixed task, and when it is done, or when he is off duty, he disposes within certain limits, of his own time, and has a family life into which the master rarely intrudes. . . .

Surely, if a woman is denied any lot in life but that of being the personal bodyservant of a despot, and is dependent for everything upon the chance of finding one who may be disposed to make a favourite of her instead of merely a drudge, it is a very cruel aggravation of her fate that she should be allowed to try this chance only once. The natural sequel and corollary from this state of things would be, that since her all in life depends upon obtaining a good master, she should be allowed to change again and again until she finds one. I am not saying that she ought to be allowed this privilege. That is a totally different consideration. The question of divorce, in the sense involving liberty of remarriage, is one into which it is foreign to my purpose to enter. All I now say, is that to those to whom nothing but servitude is allowed, the free choice of servitude is the only, though a most insufficient, alleviation. . . . If married life were all that it might be expected to be, looking to the laws alone, society would be a hell upon earth. Happily there are both feelings and interests which in many men exclude, and in most, greatly temper, the impulses and propensities which lead to tyranny. . . . [B]ecause men in general do not inflict, nor women suffer, all the misery which could be inflicted and suffered if the full power of tyranny with which the man is legally invested were acted on; the defenders of the existing form of the institution think that all its iniquity is justified, and that any complaint is merely quarrelling with the evil which is the price paid for every great good.

Meanwhile, laws and institutions require to be adapted, not to good men, but to bad. Marriage is not an institution designed for a select few. Men are not required, as a preliminary to the marriage ceremony, to prove by testimonials that they are fit to be trusted with the exercise of absolute power. . . . [T]here are all grades of goodness and wickedness in men, down to those whom no ties will bind, and on whom society has no action but through its *ultima ratio,* the penalties of the law. In every grade of this descending scale are men to whom are committed all the legal powers of a husband. The vilest malefactor has some wretched woman tied to him, against whom he can commit any atrocity except killing her, and, if tolerably cautious, can do that without much danger of the legal penalty. . . .

What is it then, which really tempers the corrupting effects of the power, and makes it compatible with such amount of good as we actually see? Mere feminine blandishments, though of great effect in individual instances, have very little effect in modifying the general tendencies of the situation; for their power only lasts while the woman is young and attractive, often only while her charm is new, and not dimmed by familiarity; and on many men they have not much influence at any time. The real mitigating causes are, the personal affection which is the growth of time, in so far as the man's nature is susceptible of it, and the woman's character sufficiently congenial with his to excite it; their common interests as regards the children, and their general community of interest as concerns third persons (to which however there are very great limitations); the real importance of the wife to his daily comforts and enjoyments, and the value he consequently attaches to her on his personal account, which, in a man capable of feeling for others, lays the foundation of caring for her on her own; and lastly, the influence naturally acquired over almost all human beings by those near to their persons. . . . Through these various means, the wife frequently exercises even too much power over the man; she is able to affect his conduct in things in which she may not be qualified to influence it for good—in which her influence may be not only unenlightened, but employed on the morally wrong side. . . .

But neither in the affairs of families nor in those of states is power a compensation for the loss of freedom. Her power often gives her what she has no right to, but does not enable her to assert her own rights. . . . There are, no doubt, women, as there are men, whom equality of consideration will not satisfy; with whom there is no peace while any will or wish is regarded but their own. Such persons are a proper subject for the law of divorce. They are only fit to live alone, and no human beings ought to be compelled to associate their lives with them.

[T]he true virtue of human beings is fitness to live together as equals; claiming nothing for themselves but what they as freely concede to every one else; regarding command of any kind as an exceptional necessity, and in all cases a temporary one; and preferring, whenever possible, the society of those with whom leading and following can be alternate and reciprocal. . . . The family, justly constituted, would be the real school of the virtues of freedom. . . . It will always be a school of obedience for the children, of command for the parents. What is needed is, that it should be a school of sympathy in equality, of living together in love, without power on one side or obedience on the other. This it ought to be between the parents. . . .

[W]hatever would be the husband's or wife's if they were not married, should be under their exclusive control during marriage; which need not interfere with the power to tie up property by settlement, in order to preserve it for children. Some people are sentimentally shocked at the idea of a separate interest in money matters, as inconsistent with the ideal fusion of two lives into one. For my own part, I am one of the strongest supporters of community of goods, when resulting from an entire unity of feeling in the owners, which makes all things common between them. But I have no relish for a community of goods resting on the doctrine, that what is mine is yours but what is yours is not mine; and I should prefer to decline entering into such a compact with any one, though I were myself the person to profit by it. . . .

When the support of the family depends, not on property, but on earnings, the common arrangement, by which the man earns the income and the wife superintends the domestic expenditure, seems to be in general the most suitable division of labour between the two persons. If, in addition to the physical suffering of bearing children, and the whole responsibility of their care and education in early years, the wife undertakes the careful and economical application of the husband's earnings to the general comfort of the family; she takes not only her fair share, but usually the larger share, of the bodily and mental exertion required by their joint existence. If she undertakes any additional portion, it seldom relieves her from this, but only prevents her from performing it properly. The care which she is herself disabled from taking of the children and the household, nobody else takes . . . .

In an otherwise just state of things, it is not, therefore, I think, a desirable custom, that the wife should contribute by her labour to the income of the family. In an unjust state of things, her doing so may be useful to her, by making her of more value in the eyes of the man who is legally her master; but, on the other hand, it enables him still farther to abuse his power, by forcing her to work, and leaving the support of the family to her exertions, while he spends most of his time in drinking and idleness. The *power* of earning is essential to the dignity of a woman, if she has not independent property. But if marriage were an equal contract . . . it would not be necessary for her protection, that during marriage she should make this particular use of her faculties. Like a man when he chooses a profession, so, when a woman marries, it may in general be understood that she makes choice of the management of a household, and the bringing up of a family, as the first call upon her exertions, during as many years of her life as may be required for the purpose; and that she renounces, not all other objects and occupations, but all which are not consistent with the requirements of this. . . . But the utmost latitude ought to exist for the adaptation of general rules to individual suitabilities; and there ought to be nothing to prevent faculties exceptionally adapted to any other pursuit, from obeying their vocation notwithstanding marriage: due provision being made for supplying otherwise any falling-short which might become inevitable, in her full performance of the ordinary functions of mistress of a family. These things, if once opinion were rightly directed on the subject, might with perfect safety be left to be regulated by opinion, without any interference of law.

. . . .

[T]he generality of the male sex cannot yet tolerate the idea of living with an equal. Were it not for that, I think that almost every one, in the existing state of opinion in politics and political economy, would admit the injustice of excluding half the human race from the greater number of lucrative occupations, and from almost all high social functions. . . . When anything is forbidden to women, it is thought necessary to say, and desirable to believe, that they are incapable of doing it, and that they depart from their real path of success and happiness when they aspire to it. But to make this reason plausible (I do not say valid), . . . [i]t is not sufficient to maintain that women on the average are less gifted than men on the average, with certain of the higher mental faculties, or that a smaller number of women than of men are fit for occupations and functions of the highest intellectual character. It is necessary to maintain that no women at all are fit for them, and that the most eminent women are inferior in mental faculties to the most mediocre of the men on whom those functions at present devolve. For if the performance of the function is decided either by competition, or by any mode of choice which secures regard to the public interest, there needs to be no apprehension that any important employments will fall into the hands of women inferior to average men, or to the average of their male competitors. The only result would be that there would be fewer women than men in such employments; a result certain to happen in any case, if only from the preference always likely to be felt by the majority of women for the one vocation in which there is nobody to compete with them. . . . [N]ot a few merely, but many women have proved themselves capable of everything, perhaps without a single exception, which is done by men, and of doing it successfully and creditably. The utmost that can be said is, that there are many things which none of them have succeeded in doing as well as they have been done by some men–many in which they have not reached the very highest rank. But there are extremely few, dependent only on mental faculties, in which they have not attained the rank next to the highest. . . .

Are we so certain of always finding a man made to our hands for any duty or function of social importance which falls vacant, that we lose nothing by putting a ban upon one-half of mankind, and refusing before hand to make their faculties available, however distinguished they may be? And even if we could do without them, would it be consistent with justice to refuse to them their fair share of honour and distinction, or to deny to them the equal moral right of all human beings to choose their occupation (short of injury to others) according to their own preferences, at their own risk? Nor is the injustice confined to them: it is shared by those who are in a position to benefit by their services. To ordain that any kind of persons shall not be physicians, or shall not be advocates, or shall not be members of parliament, is to injure not them only, but all who employ physicians or advocates, or elect members of parliament, and who are deprived of the stimulating effect of greater competition on the exertions of the competitors, as well as restricted to narrower range of individual choice.

[A]ny woman, who succeeds in an open profession, proves by that very fact that she is qualified for it. And in the case of public offices, if the political system of the country is such as to exclude unfit men, it will equally exclude unfit women: while if it is not, there is no additional evil in the fact that the unfit persons whom it admits may be either women or men. As long therefore as it is acknowledged that even a few women may be fit for these duties, the laws which shut the door on those exceptions cannot be justified by any opinion which can be held respecting the capacities of women in general. . . .

Let us consider the special nature of the mental capacities most characteristic of a woman of talent. They are all of a kind which fits them for practice, and makes them tend towards it. What is meant by a woman's capacity of intuitive perception? It means, a rapid and correct insight into present fact. . . . With equality of experience and of general faculties, a woman usually sees much more than a man of what is immediately before her. Now this sensibility to the present, is the main quality on which the capacity for practice, as distinguished from theory, depends. . . . I admit that there can be no good practice without principles, and that the predominant place which quickness of observation holds among a woman's faculties, makes her particularly apt to build over-hasty generalizations upon her own observation; though at the same time no less ready in rectifying those generalizations, as her observation takes a wider range. But the corrective to this defect, is access to the experience of the human race; general knowledge—exactly the thing which education can best supply. A woman's mistakes are specifically those of a clever self-educated man, who often sees what men trained in routine do not see, but falls into errors for want of knowing things which have long been known. . . .

[T]his gravitation of women's minds to the present, to the real, to actual fact, while in its exclusiveness it is a source of errors, is also a most useful counteractive of the contrary error. . . . A woman seldom runs wild after an abstraction. The habitual direction of her mind to dealing with things as individuals rather than in groups, and (what is closely connected with it) her more lively interest in the present feelings of persons, which makes her consider first of all, in anything which claims to be applied to practice, in what manner persons will be affected by it—these two things make her extremely unlikely to put faith in any speculation which loses sight of individuals, and deals with things as if they existed for the benefit of some imaginary entity, some mere creation of the mind, not resolvable into the feelings of living beings. Women's thoughts are thus as useful in giving reality to those of thinking men, as men's thoughts in giving width and largeness to those of women. In depth, as distinguished from breadth, I greatly doubt if even now, women, compared with men, are at any disadvantage.

Let us now consider another of the admitted superiorities of clever women, greater quickness of apprehension. . . . He who has not his faculties under immediate command, in the contingencies of action, might as well not have them at all. He may be fit to criticize, but he is not fit to act. Now it is in this that women, and the men who are most like women, confessedly excel. It will be said, perhaps, that the greater nervous susceptibility of women is a disqualification for practice, in anything but domestic life, by rendering them mobile, changeable, too vehemently under the influence of the moment, incapable of dogged perseverance, unequal and uncertain in the power of using their faculties. . . . Much of all this is the mere overflow of nervous energy run to waste, and would cease when the energy was directed to a definite end. Much is also the result of conscious or unconscious cultivation; as we see by the almost total disappearance of "hysterics" and fainting fits, since they have gone out of fashion.

Women who in their early years have shared in the healthful physical education and bodily freedom of their brothers, and who obtain a sufficiency of pure air and exercise in after-life, very rarely have any excessive susceptibility of nerves which can disqualify them for active pursuits. There is indeed a certain proportion of persons, in both sexes, in whom an unusual degree of nervous sensibility is constitutional, and of so marked a character as to be the feature of their organization which exercises the greatest influence over the whole character of the vital phenomena. . . . We will assume this as a fact: and let me then ask, are men of nervous temperament found to be unfit for the duties and pursuits usually followed by men? If not, why should women of the same temperament be unfit for them? The peculiarities of the temperament are, no doubt, within certain limits, an obstacle to success in some employments, though an aid to it in others. But when the occupation is suitable to the temperament, and sometimes even when it is unsuitable, the most brilliant examples of success are continually given by the men of high nervous sensibility. . . . [P]eople of this temperament are particularly apt for what may be called the executive department of the leadership of mankind. They are the material of great orators, great preachers, impressive diffusers of moral influences. . . .

To so ridiculous an extent are the notions formed of the nature of women, mere empirical generalizations, framed, without philosophy or analysis, upon the first instances which present themselves, that the popular idea of it is different in different countries, according as the opinions and social circumstances of the country have given to the women living in it any specialty of development or non-development. An Oriental thinks that women are by nature peculiarly voluptuous; see the violent abuse of them on this ground in Hindoo writings. An Englishman usually thinks that they are by nature cold. The sayings about women's fickleness are mostly of French origin; from the famous distich of Francis the First, upward and downward. In England it is a common remark, how much more constant women are than men. Inconstancy has been longer reckoned discreditable to a woman, in England than in France; and Englishwomen are besides, in their inmost nature, much more subdued to opinion. . . .

I have said that it cannot now be known how much of the existing mental differences between men and women is natural, and how much artificial; whether there are any natural differences at all; or, supposing all artificial causes of difference to be withdrawn, what natural character would be revealed. I am not about to attempt what I have pronounced impossible: but doubt does not forbid conjecture, and where certainty is unattainable, there may yet be the means of arriving at some degree of probability. . . .

Let us take, then, the only marked case which observation affords, of apparent inferiority of women to men, if we except the merely physical one of bodily strength. No production in philosophy, science, or art, entitled to the first rank, has been the work of a woman. Is there any mode of accounting for this, without supposing that women are naturally incapable of producing them?

In the first place, we may fairly question whether experience has afforded sufficient grounds for an induction. It is scarcely three generations since women, saving very rare exceptions, have begun to try their capacity in philosophy, science, or art. It is only in the present generation that their attempts have been at all numerous; and they are even now extremely few, everywhere but in England and France. It is a relevant question, whether a mind possessing the requisites of first-rate eminence in speculation or creative art could have been expected, on the mere calculation of chances, to turn up during that lapse of time, among the women whose tastes and personal position admitted of their devoting themselves to these pursuits. In all things which there has yet been time for—in all but the very highest grades in the scale of excellence, especially in the department in which they have been longest engaged, literature (both prose and poetry)—women have done quite as much, have obtained fully as high prizes as many of them, as could be expected from the length of time and the number of competitors. . . .

If we consider the works of women in modern times, and contrast them with those of men, either in the literary or the artistic department, such inferiority as may be observed resolves itself essentially into one thing: but that is a most material one; deficiency of originality. . . . Thoughts original, in the sense of being unborrowed—of being derived from the thinker's own observations or intellectual processes—are abundant in the writings of women. But they have not yet produced any of those great and luminous new ideas which form an era in thought, nor those fundamentally new conceptions in art, which open a vista of possible effects not before thought of, and found a new school. . . . This is the sort of inferiority which their works manifest: for in point of execution, in the detailed application of thought, and the perfection of style, there is no inferiority. . . .

It no doubt often happens that a person, who has not widely and accurately studied the thoughts of others on a subject, has by natural sagacity a happy intuition, which he can suggest, but cannot prove, which yet when matured may be an important addition to knowledge: but even then, no justice can be done to it until some other person, who does possess the previous acquirements, takes it in hand, tests it, gives it a scientific or practical form, and fits it into its place among the existing truths of philosophy or science. Is it supposed that such felicitous thoughts do not occur to women? They occur by hundreds to every woman of intellect. But they are mostly lost, for want of a husband or friend who has the other knowledge which can enable him to estimate them properly and bring them before the world: and even when they are brought before it, they generally appear as his ideas, not their real author's. Who can tell how many of the most original thoughts put forth by male writers, belong to a woman by suggestion, to themselves only by verifying and working out? If I may judge by my own case, a very large proportion indeed.

If we turn from pure speculation to literature in the narrow sense of the term, and the fine arts, there is a very obvious reason why women's literature is, in its general conception and in its main features, an imitation of men's. Why is the Roman literature, as critics proclaim to satiety, not original but an imitation of the Greek? Simply because the Greeks came first. If women lived in a different country from men, and had never read any of their writings, they would have had a literature of their own. As it is, they have not created one, because they found a highly advanced literature already created. . . . All women who write are pupils of the great male writers. . . . What years are to a gifted individual, generations are to a mass. If women's literature is destined to have a different collective character from that of men, depending on any difference of natural tendencies, much longer time is necessary than has yet elapsed, before it can emancipate itself from the influence of accepted models, and guide itself by its own impulses. But if, as I believe, there will not prove to be any natural tendencies common to women, and distinguishing their genius from that of men, yet every individual writer among them has her individual tendencies, which at present are still subdued by the influence of precedent and example: and it will require generations more, before their individuality is sufficiently developed to make head against the influence. . . .

There are other reasons, besides those which we have now given, that help to explain why women remain behind men, even in the pursuits which are open to both. For one thing, very few women have time for them. This may seem a paradox; it is an undoubted social fact. The time and thoughts of every woman have to satisfy great previous demands on them for things practical. There is, first, the superintendence of the family and the domestic expenditure, which. . . . presents questions for consideration and solution, foreseen and unforeseen, at every hour of the day. . . . If a woman is of a rank and circumstances which relieve her in a measure from these cares, she has still devolving on her the management for the whole family of its intercourse with others—of what is called society, and the less the call made on her by the former duty, the greater is always the development of the latter. . . .

There is another consideration to be added to all these . . . an ardent desire of celebrity. Nothing less is commonly a sufficient stimulus to undergo the long and patient drudgery, which, in the case even of the greatest natural gifts, is absolutely required for great eminence. . . . Now, whether the cause be natural or artificial, women seldom have this eagerness for fame. . . . The influence they seek is over those who immediately surround them. . . . I do not at all believe that it is inherent in women. It is only the natural result of their circumstances. The love of fame in men is encouraged by education and opinion, . . . and is stimulated by the access which fame gives to all objects of ambition, including even the favour of women; while to women themselves all these objects are closed, and the desire of fame itself considered daring and unfeminine. . . .

As for moral differences, considered as distinguished from intellectual, the distinction commonly drawn is to the advantage of women. They are declared to be better than men; an empty compliment, which must provoke a bitter smile from every woman of spirit, since there is no other situation in life in which it is the established order, and considered quite natural and suitable, that the better should obey the worse.

. . . .

What good are we to expect from the changes proposed in our customs and institutions? Would mankind be at all better off if women were free? If not, why disturb their minds, and attempt to make a social revolution in the name of an abstract right? . . . To which let me first answer, the advantage of having the most universal and pervading of all human relations regulated by justice instead of injustice. The vast amount of this gain to human nature, it is hardly possible, by any explanation or illustration, to place in a stronger light than it is placed by the bare statement, to any one who attaches a moral meaning to words. All the selfish propensities, the self-worship, the unjust self-preference, which exist among mankind, have their source and root in, and derive their principal nourishment from, the present constitution of the relation between men and women. Think what it is to a boy, to grow up to manhood in the belief that without any merit or any exertion of his own, . . . by the mere fact of being born a male he is by right the superior of all and every one of an entire half of the human race: including probably some whose real superiority to himself he has daily or hourly occasion to feel. . . . What must be the effect on his character, of this lesson? It is an exact parallel to the feeling of a hereditary king that he is excellent above others by being born a king, or a noble by being born a noble. . . . Above all, when the feeling of being raised above the whole of the other sex is combined with personal authority over one individual among them; the situation, if a school of conscientious and affectionate forbearance to those whose strongest points of character are conscience and affection, is to men of another quality a regularly constituted Academy or Gymnasium for training them in arrogance and overbearingness. . . .

The second benefit to be expected from giving to women the free use of their faculties, by leaving them the free choice of their employments, and opening to them the same field of occupation and the same prizes and encouragements as to other human beings, would be that of doubling the mass of mental faculties available for the higher service of humanity. Where there is now one person qualified to benefit mankind and promote the general improvement, as a public teacher, or an administrator of some branch of public or social affairs, there would then be a chance of two. . . .

This great accession to the intellectual power of the species, and to the amount of intellect available for the good management of its affairs, would be obtained, partly, through the better and more complete intellectual education of women, which would then improve *pari passu* with that of men. Women in general would be brought up equally capable of understanding business, public affairs, and the higher matters of speculation, with men in the same class of society; and the select few of the one as well as of the other sex, who were qualified not only to comprehend what is done or thought by others, but to think or do something considerable themselves, would meet with the same facilities for improving and training their capacities in the one sex as in the other. In this way the widening of the sphere of action for women would operate for good, by raising their education to the level of that of men, and making the one participate in all improvements made in the other. . . .

Besides the addition to the amount of individual talent available for the conduct of human affairs, which certainly are not at present so abundantly provided in that respect that they can afford to dispense with one-half of what nature proffers; the opinion of women would then possess a more beneficial, rather than a greater, influence upon the general mass of human belief and sentiment. I say a more beneficial, rather than a greater influence; for the influence of women over the general tone of opinion has always, or at least from the earliest known period, been very considerable. The influence of mothers on the early character of their sons, and the desire of young men to recommend themselves to young women, have in all recorded times been important agencies in the formation of character, and have determined some of the chief steps in the progress of civilization. . . . The other mode in which the effect of women's opinion has been conspicuous, is by giving a powerful stimulus to those qualities in men, which, not being themselves trained in, it was necessary for them that they should find in their protectors. Courage, and the military virtues generally, have at all times been greatly indebted to the desire which men felt of being admired by women: and the stimulus reaches far beyond this one class of eminent qualities, since, by a very natural effect of their position, the best passport to the admiration and favour of women has always been to be thought highly of by men. . . .

It is often said that in the classes most exposed to temptation, a man's wife and children tend to keep him honest and respectable, both by the wife's direct influence, and by the concern he feels for their future welfare. This may be so, and no doubt often is so, with those who are more weak than wicked; and this beneficial influence would be preserved and strengthened under equal laws. . . . But when we ascend higher in the scale, we come among a totally different set of moving forces. The wife's influence tends, as far as it goes, to prevent the husband from falling below the common standard of approbation of the country. It tends quite as strongly to hinder him from rising above it. The wife is the auxiliary of the common public opinion. . . . If he differs in his opinion from the mass—if he sees truths which have not yet dawned upon them, or if, feeling in his heart truths which they nominally recognize, he would like to act up to those truths more conscientiously than the generality of mankind—to all such thoughts and desires, marriage is the heaviest of drawbacks, unless he be so fortunate as to have a wife as much above the common level as he himself is. . . .

There is another very injurious aspect in which the effect, not of women's disabilities directly, but of the broad line of difference which those disabilities create between the education and character of a woman and that of a man, requires to be considered. Nothing can be more unfavourable to that union of thought and inclinations which is the ideal of married life. . . . While women are so unlike men, it is not wonderful that selfish men should feel the need of arbitrary power in their own hands, to arrest *in limine* the life-long conflict of inclinations, by deciding every question on the side of their own preference.

[T]hough it may stimulate the amatory propensities of men, it does not conduce to married happiness, to exaggerate by differences of education whatever may be the native differences of the sexes. . . .

What a difference there must be in the society which the two persons will wish to frequent, or be frequented by! Each will desire associates who share their own tastes: the persons agreeable to one, will be indifferent or positively disagreeable to the other. . . . They cannot help having different wishes as to the bringing up of the children: each will wish to see reproduced in them their own tastes and sentiments: and there is either a compromise, and only a half-satisfaction to either, or the wife has to yield—often with bitter suffering; and, with or without intention, her occult influence continues to counterwork the husband's purposes.

It would of course be extreme folly to suppose that these differences of feeling and inclination only exist because women are brought up differently from men, and that there would not be differences of taste under any imaginable circumstances. But there is nothing beyond the mark in saying that the distinction in bringing-up immensely aggravates those differences, and renders them wholly inevitable. . . .

[W]hen each of two persons, instead of being a nothing, is a something; when they are attached to one another, and are not too much unlike to begin with; the constant partaking in the same things, assisted by their sympathy, draws out the latent capacities of each for being interested in the things which were at first interesting only to the other; and works a gradual assimilation of the tastes and characters to one another, partly by the insensible modification of each, but more by a real enriching of the two natures, each acquiring the tastes and capacities of the other in addition to its own. . . .

What marriage may be in the case of two persons of cultivated faculties, identical in opinions and purposes, between whom there exists that best kind of equality, similarity of powers and capacities with reciprocal superiority in them—so that each can enjoy the luxury of looking up to the other, and can have alternately the pleasure of leading and of being led in the path of development—I will not attempt to describe. To those who can conceive it, there is no need; to those who cannot, it would appear the dream of an enthusiast. But I maintain, with the profoundest conviction, that this, and this only, is the ideal of marriage; and that all opinions, customs and institutions which favour any other notion of it, or turn the conceptions and aspirations connected with it into any other direction, by whatever pretences they may be coloured, are relics of primitive barbarism. The moral regeneration of mankind will only really commence, when the most fundamental of the social relations is placed under the rule of equal justice, and when human beings learn to cultivate their strongest sympathy with an equal in rights and in cultivation.

Thus far, the benefits which it has appeared that the world would gain by ceasing to make sex a disqualification for privileges and a badge of subjection, are social rather than individual; consisting in an increase of the general fund of thinking and acting power, and an improvement in the general conditions of the association of men with women. But it would be a grievous understatement of the case to omit the most direct benefit of all, the unspeakable gain in private happiness to the liberated half of the species; the difference to them between a life of subjection to the will of others, and a life of rational freedom. After the primary necessities of food and raiment, freedom is the first and strongest want of human nature.

* * *

HARRIET TAYLOR MILL

The writings of Harriet Taylor Mill (1807–1858) exemplify a utilitarian orientation through arguments based on an appeal to social consequences. The goal of sex equality, for example, is defended on grounds of its necessity for the good of men as well as women. She maintains that "the division of mankind into two castes, one born to rule over the other, . . . [forms] a bar . . . to any really vital improvement, either in the character or in the social condition of the human race." Inequality, according to Mill, corrupts men by giving them undeserved power; it corrupts women by encouraging women to be manipulative in resisting that power. Neither sex should be regarded as more virtuous than the other, for vices such as hatred, malice, and uncharitableness "are to be found among women fully as much as among men."

While acknowledging behavioral differences between the sexes, Mill makes no claim as to whether these are triggered by nature or nurture. Her view that most men "are sensualists more or less," whereas women are generally "exempt from this trait" may have been influenced by Victorian mores. Even so, Mill challenges any confinement of women to a "feminine" sphere of domesticity, claiming that the "proper sphere for all human beings is the largest and highest" to which they can attain. For some women, this attainment involves motherhood; for others, it does not. The same is true for men and fatherhood. In either case, maximization of liberty and education are requisite to the maximization of societal happiness.

Enfranchisement of Women

Women never have had equal rights with men. The claim in their behalf, of the common rights of mankind, is looked upon as barred by universal practice. This strongest of prejudices, the prejudice against what is new and unknown, has, indeed, in an age of changes like the present, lost much of its force; if it had not, there would be little hope of prevailing against it. Over three-fourths of the habitable world, even at this day, the answer, "it has always been so," closes all discussion. But it is the boast of modern Europeans, and of their American kindred, that they know and do many things which their forefathers neither knew nor did; and it is perhaps the most unquestionable point of superiority in the present above former ages, that habit is not now the tyrant it formerly was over opinions and modes of action, and that the worship of custom is a declining idolatry. An uncustomary thought, on a subject which touches the greater interests of life, still startles when first presented; but if it can be kept before the mind until the impression of strangeness wears off, it obtains a hearing, and as rational a consideration as the intellect of the hearer is accustomed to bestow on any other subject.

In the present case, the prejudice of custom is doubtless on the unjust side. Great thinkers, indeed, at different times, from Plato to Condorcet, besides some of the most eminent names of the present age, have made emphatic protests in favour of the equality of women. And there have been voluntary societies, religious or secular, of which the Society of Friends is the most known, by whom that principle was recognised. But there has been no political community or nation in which, by law, and usage, women have not been in a state of political and civil inferiority. In the ancient world the same fact was alleged, with equal truth, in behalf of slavery. It might have been alleged in favour of the mitigated form of slavery, serfdom, all through the middle ages. It was urged against freedom of industry, freedom of conscience, freedom of the press; none of these liberties were thought compatible with a well-ordered state, until they had proved their possibility by actually existing as facts. That an institution or a practice is customary is no presumption of its goodness, when any other sufficient cause can be assigned for its existence. There is no difficulty in understanding why the subjection of women has been a custom. No other explanation is needed than physical force.

That those who were physically weaker should have been made legally inferior, is quite conformable to the mode in which the world has been governed. Until very lately, the rule of physical strength was the general law of human affairs. Throughout history, the nations, races, classes, which found themselves the strongest, either in muscles, in riches, or in military discipline, have conquered and held in subjection the rest. If, even in the most improved nations, the law of the sword is at last discountenanced as unworthy, it is only since the calumniated eighteenth century. Wars of conquest have only ceased since democratic revolutions began. The world is very young, and has but just begun to cast off injustice. It is only now getting rid of negro slavery. It is only now getting rid of monarchical despotism. It is only now getting rid of hereditary feudal nobility. It is only now getting rid of disabilities on the ground of religion. It is only beginning to treat any *men* as citizens, except the rich and a favoured portion of the middle class. Can we wonder that it has not yet done as much for women? As society was constituted until the last few generations, inequality was its very basis; association grounded on equal rights scarcely existed; to be equals was to be enemies; two persons could hardly co-operate in anything, or meet in any amicable relation, without the law's appointing that one of them should be the superior of the other. Mankind have outgrown this state, and all things now tend to substitute, as the general principle of human relations, a just equality, instead of the dominion of the strongest. But of all relations, that between men and women being the nearest and most intimate, and connected with the greatest number of strong emotions, was sure to be the last to throw off the old rule and receive the new: for in proportion to the strength of a feeling, is the tenacity with which it clings to the forms and circumstances with which it has even accidentally become associated.

When a prejudice, which has any hold on the feelings, finds itself reduced to the unpleasant necessity of assigning reasons, it thinks it has done enough when it has re-asserted the very point in dispute, in phrases which appeal to the pre-existing feeling. Thus, many persons think they have sufficiently justified the restrictions on women's field of action, when they have said that the pursuits from which women are excluded are *unfeminine*, and that the *proper sphere* of women is not politics or publicity, but private and domestic life.

We deny the right of any portion of the species to decide for another portion, or any individual for another individual, what is and what is not their "proper sphere." The proper sphere for all human beings is the largest and highest which they are able to attain to. What this is, cannot be ascertained, without complete liberty of choice. The speakers at the Convention in America have therefore done wisely and right, in refusing to entertain the question of the peculiar aptitudes either of women or of men, or the limits within which this or that occupation may be supposed to be more adapted to the one or to the other. They justly maintain, that these questions can only be satisfactorily answered by perfect freedom. Let every occupation be open to all, without favour or discouragement to any, and employments will fall into the hands of those men or women who are found by experience to be most capable of worthily exercising them. There need be no fear that women will take out of the hands of men any occupation which men perform better than they. Each individual will prove his or her capacities, in the only way in which capacities can be proved—by trial; and the world will have the benefit of the best faculties of all its inhabitants. But to interfere beforehand by an arbitrary limit, and declare that whatever be the genius, talent, energy, or force of mind of an individual of a certain sex or class, those faculties shall not be exerted, or shall be exerted only in some few of the many modes in which others are permitted to use theirs, is not only an injustice to the individual, and a detriment to society, which loses what it can ill spare, but is also the most effectual mode of providing that, in the sex or class so fettered, the qualities which are not permitted to be exercised shall not exist. . . .

. . . [I]f those who assert that the "proper sphere" for women is the domestic, mean by this that they have not shown themselves qualified for any other, the assertion evinces great ignorance of life and of history. Women have shown fitness for the highest social functions, exactly in proportion as they have been admitted to them. . . .

Concerning the fitness, then, of women for politics, there can be no question: but the dispute is more likely to turn upon the fitness of politics for women. When the reasons alleged for excluding women from active life in all its higher departments, are stripped of their garb of declamatory phrases, and reduced to the simple expression of a meaning, they seem to be mainly three: the incompatibility of active life with maternity, and with the cares of a household; secondly, its alleged hardening effect on the character; and thirdly, the inexpediency of making an addition to the already excessive pressure of competition in every kind of professional or lucrative employment.

The first, the maternity argument, is usually laid most stress upon: although (it needs hardly be said) this reason, if it be one, can apply only to mothers. It is neither necessary nor just to make imperative on women that they shall be either mothers or nothing; or that if they have been mothers once, they shall be nothing else during the whole remainder of their lives. Neither women nor men need any law to exclude them from an occupation, if they have undertaken another which is incompatible with it. No one proposes to exclude the male sex from Parliament because a man may be a soldier or sailor in active service, or a merchant whose business requires all his time and energies. Nine-tenths of the occupations of men exclude them *de facto* from public life, as effectually as if they were excluded by law; but that is no reason for making laws to exclude even the nine-tenths, much less the remaining tenth. The reason of the case is the same for women as for men. There is no need to make provision by law that a woman shall not carry on the active details of a household, or of the education of children, and at the same time practise a profession or be elected to parliament. Where incompatibility is real, it will take care of itself: but there is gross injustice in making the incompatibility a pretence for the exclusion of those in whose case it does not exist. And these, if they were free to choose, would be a very large proportion. The maternity argument deserts its supporters in the case of single women, a large and increasing class of the population; a fact which, it is not irrelevant to remark, by tending to diminish the excessive competition of numbers, is calculated to assist greatly the prosperity of all. There is no inherent reason or necessity that all women should voluntarily choose to devote their lives to one animal function and its consequences. Numbers of women are wives and mothers only because there is no other career open to them, no other occupation for their feelings or their activities. Every improvement in their education, and enlargement of their faculties—everything which renders them more qualified for any other mode of life, increases the number of those to whom it is an injury and an oppression to be denied the choice. To say that women must be excluded from active life because maternity disqualifies them for it, is in fact to say, that every other career should be forbidden them in order that maternity may be their only resource.

But secondly, it is urged, that to give the same freedom of occupation to women as to men, would be an injurious addition to the crowd of competitors, by whom the avenues to almost all kinds of employment are choked up, and its remuneration depressed. This argument, it is to be observed, does not reach the political question. It gives no excuse for withholding from women the rights of citizenship. The suffrage, the jury-box, admission to the legislature and to office, it does not touch. It bears only on the industrial branch of the subject. Allowing it, then, in an economical point of view, its full force; assuming that to lay open to women the employments now monopolized by men, would tend, like the breaking down of other monopolies, to lower the rate of remuneration in those employments; let us consider what is the amount of this evil consequence, and what the compensation for it. The worst ever asserted, much worse than is at all likely to be realized, is that if women competed with men, a man and a woman could not together earn more than is now earned by the man alone. Let us make this supposition, the most unfavourable supposition possible:

the joint income of the two would be the same as before, while the woman would be raised from the position of a servant to that of a partner. Even if every woman, as matters now stand, had a claim on some man for support, how infinitely preferable is it that part of the income should be of the woman's earning, even if the aggregate sum were but little increased by it, rather than that she should be compelled to stand aside in order that men may be the sole earners, and the sole dispensers of what is earned. Even under the present laws respecting the property of women,[1] a woman who contributes materially to the support of the family, cannot be treated in the same contemptuously tyrannical manner as one who, however she may toil as a domestic drudge, is a dependent on the man for subsistence. As for the depression of wages by increase of competition, remedies will be found for it in time. Palliatives might be applied immediately; for instance, a more rigid exclusion of children from industrial employment, during the years in which they ought to be working only to strengthen their bodies and minds for after life. Children are necessarily dependent, and under the power of others; and their labour, being not for themselves but for the gain of their parents, is a proper subject for legislative regulation. With respect to the future, we neither believe that improvident multiplication, and the consequent excessive difficulty of gaining a subsistence, will always continue, nor that the division of mankind into capitalists and hired labourers, and the regulation of the reward of labourers mainly by demand and supply, will be for ever, or even much longer, the rule of the world. But so long as competition is the general law of human life, it is tyranny to shut out one-half of the competitors. All who have attained the age of self-government, have an equal claim to be permitted to sell whatever kind of useful labour they are capable of, for the price which it will bring.

The third objection to the admission of women to political or professional life, its alleged hardening tendency, belongs to an age now past, and is scarcely to be comprehended by people of the present time. There are still, however, persons who say that the world and its avocations render men selfish and unfeeling; that the struggles, rivalries, and collisions of business and of politics make them harsh and unamiable; that if half the species must unavoidably be given up to these things, it is the more necessary that the other half should be kept free from them; that to preserve women from the

1. The truly horrible effects of the present state of the law among the lowest of the working population, is exhibited in those cases of hideous maltreatment of their wives by working men, with which every newspaper, every police report, teems. Wretches unfit to have the smallest authority over any living thing, have a helpless woman for their household slave. These excesses could not exist if women both earned, and had the right to possess, a part of the income of the family.

bad influences of the world, is the only chance of preventing men from being wholly given up to them.

There would have been plausibility in this argument when the world was still in the age of violence; when life was full of physical conflict, and every man had to redress his injuries or those of others, by the sword or by the strength of his arm. Women, like priests, by being exempted from such responsibilities, and from some part of the accompanying dangers, may have been enabled to exercise a beneficial influence. But in the present condition of human life, we do not know where those hardening influences are to be found, to which men are subject and from which women are at present exempt. Individuals now-a-days are seldom called upon to fight hand to hand, even with peaceful weapons; personal enmities and rivalities count for little in worldly transactions; the general pressure of circumstances, not the adverse will of individuals, is the obstacle men now have to make head against. That pressure, when excessive, breaks the spirit, and cramps and sours the feelings, but not less of women than of men, since they suffer certainly not less from its evils. There are still quarrels and dislikes, but the sources of them are changed. The feudal chief once found his bitterest enemy in his powerful neighbour, the minister or courtier in his rival for place: but opposition of interest in active life, as a cause of personal animosity, is out of date; the enmities of the present day arise not from great things but small, from what people say of one another, more than from what they do; and if there are hatred, malice, and all uncharitableness, they are to be found among women fully as much as among men. In the present state of civilization, the notion of guarding women from the hardening influences of the world, could only be realized by secluding them from society altogether. The common duties of common life, as at present constituted, are incompatible with any other softness in women than weakness. Surely weak minds in weak bodies must ere long cease to be even supposed to be either attractive or amiable.

But, in truth, none of these arguments and considerations touch the foundations of the subject. The real question is, whether it is right and expedient that one-half of the human race should pass through life in a state of forced subordination to the other half. If the best state of human society is that of being divided into two parts, one consisting of persons with a will and a substantive existence, the other of humble companions to these persons, attached, each of them to one, for the purpose of bringing up *his* children, and making *his* home pleasant to him; if this is the place assigned to women, it is but kindness to educate them for this; to make them believe that the greatest good fortune which can befall them, is to be chosen by some man for his purpose; and that every other career which the world deems happy or honourable, is closed to them by the law, not of social institutions, but of nature and destiny.

When, however, we ask why the existence of one-half the species should be merely ancillary to that of the other—why each woman should be a mere appendage to a man, allowed to have no interests of her own, that there may be nothing to compete in her mind with his interests and his pleasure; the only reason which can be given is, that men like it. It is agreeable to them that men should live for their own sake, women for the sake of men: and the qualities and conduct in subjects which are agreeable to rulers, they succeed for a long time in making the subjects themselves consider as their appropriate virtues. Helvetius has met with much obloquy for asserting, that persons usually mean by virtues the qualities which are useful or convenient to themselves. How truly this is said of mankind in general, and how wonderfully the ideas of virtue set afloat by the powerful, are caught and imbibed by those under their dominion, is exemplified by the manner in which the world were once persuaded that the supreme virtue of subjects was loyalty to kings, and are still persuaded that the paramount virtue of womanhood is loyalty to men. Under a nominal recognition of a moral code common to both, in practice self-will and self-assertion form the type of what are designated as manly virtues, while abnegation of self, patience, resignation, and submission to power, unless when resistance is commanded by other interests than their own, have been stamped by general consent as pre-eminently the duties and graces required of women. The meaning being merely, that power makes itself the centre of moral obligation, and that a man likes to have his own will, but does not like that his domestic companion should have a will different from his.

We are far from pretending that in modern and civilized times, no reciprocity of obligation is acknowledged on the part of the stronger. Such an assertion would be very wide of the truth. But even this reciprocity, which has disarmed tyranny, at least in the higher and middle classes, of its most revolting features, yet when combined with the original evil of the dependent condition of women, has introduced in its turn serious evils.

In the beginning, and among tribes which are still in a primitive condition, women were and are the slaves of men for the purposes of toil. All the hard bodily labour devolves on them. The Australian savage is idle, while women painfully dig up the roots on which he lives. An American Indian, when he has killed a deer, leaves it, and sends a woman to carry it home. In a state somewhat more advanced, as in Asia, women were and are the slaves of men for the purposes of sensuality. In Europe there early succeeded a third and milder dominion, secured not by blows, nor by locks and bars, but by sedulous inculcation on the mind; feelings also of kindness, and ideas of duty, such as a superior owes to inferiors under his protection, became more and more involved in the relation. But it did not for many ages become a relation of companionship, even between unequals; the lives of the two persons were apart. The wife was part of the furniture of home, of the resting-place to which the man returned from business or pleasure. His occupations were, as they still are, among men; his pleasures and excitements also were, for the most part, among men—among his equals. He was a patriarch and a despot within four walls, and irresponsible power had its effect, greater or less according to his disposition, in rendering him domineering, exacting, self-worshipping, when not capriciously or brutally tyrannical. But if the moral part of his nature suffered, it was not necessarily so, in the same degree, with the intellectual or the active portion. He might have as much vigour of mind and energy of character as his nature enabled him, and as the circumstances of his times allowed. He might write the 'Paradise Lost," or win the battle of Marengo. This was the condition of the Greeks and Romans, and of the moderns until a recent date. Their relations with their domestic subordinates occupied a mere corner, though a cherished one, of their lives. Their education as men, the formation of their character and faculties, depended mainly on a different class of influences.

It is otherwise now. The progress of improvement has imposed on all possessors of power, and of domestic power among the rest, an increased and increasing sense of correlative obligation. No man now thinks that his wife has no claim upon his actions but such as he may accord to her. All men of any conscience believe that their duty to their wives is one of the most binding of their obligations. Nor is it supposed to consist solely in protection, which, in the present state of civilization, women have almost ceased to need: it involves care for their happiness and consideration of their wishes, with a not unfrequent sacrifice of their own to them. The power of husbands has reached the store which the power of kings had arrived at, when opinion did not yet question the rightfulness of arbitrary power, but in theory, and to a certain extent in practice, condemned the selfish use of it. This improvement in the moral sentiments of mankind, and increased sense of the consideration due by every man to those who have no one but himself to look to, has tended to make home more and more the centre of interest, and domestic circumstances and society a larger and larger part of life, and of its pursuits and pleasures. The tendency has been strengthened by the changes of tastes and manners which have so remarkably distinguished the last two or three generations. In days not far distant, men found their excitement and filled up their time in violent bodily exercises, noisy merriment, and intemperance.

They have now, in all but the very poorest classes, lost their inclination for these things, and for the coarser pleasures generally; they have now scarcely any tastes but those which they have in common with women, and, for the first time in the world, men and women are really companions. A most beneficial change, if the companionship were between equals; but being between unequals, it produces, what good observers have noticed, though without perceiving its cause, a progressive deterioration among men in what had hitherto been considered the masculine excellences. Those who are so careful that women should not become men, do not see that men are becoming, what they have decided that women should be—are falling into the feebleness which they have so long cultivated in their companions. Those who are associated in their lives, tend to become assimilated in character. In the present closeness of association between the sexes, men cannot retain manliness unless women acquire it.

There is hardly any situation more unfavourable to the maintenance of elevation of character or force of intellect, than to live in the society, and seek by preference the sympathy, of inferiors in mental endowments. Why is it that we constantly see in life so much of intellectual and moral promise followed by such inadequate performance, but because the aspirant has compared himself only with those below himself, and has not sought improvement or stimulus from measuring himself with his equals or superiors? In the present state of social life, this is becoming the general condition of men. They care less and less for any sympathies, and are less and less under any personal influences, but those of the domestic roof. Not to be misunderstood, it is necessary that we should distinctly disclaim the belief, that women are even now inferior in intellect to men. There are women who are the equals in intellect of any men who ever lived: and comparing ordinary women with ordinary men, the varied though petty details which compose the occupation of most women, call forth probably as much of mental ability, as the uniform routine of the pursuits which are the habitual occupation of a large majority of men. It is from nothing in the faculties themselves, but from the petty subjects and interests on which alone they are exercised, that the companionship of women, such as their present circumstances make them, so often exercises a dissolvent influence on high faculties and aspirations in men. If one of the two has no knowledge and no care about the great ideas and purposes which dignify life, or about any of its practical concerns save personal interests and personal vanities, her conscious, and still more her unconscious influence, will, except in rare cases, reduce to a secondary place in his mind, if not entirely extinguish, those interests which she cannot or does not share.

Our argument here brings us into collision with what may be termed the moderate reformers of the education of women; a sort of persons who cross the path of improvement on all great questions; those who would maintain the old bad principles, mitigating their consequences. These say, that women should be, not slaves, nor servants, but companions; and educated for that office (they do not say that men should be educated to be the companions of women). But since uncultivated women are not suitable companions for cultivated men, and a man who feels interest in things above and beyond the family circle wishes that his companion should sympathize with him in that interest, they therefore say, let women improve their understanding and taste, acquire general knowledge, cultivate poetry, art, even coquet with science, and some stretch their liberality so far as to say, inform themselves on politics; not as pursuits, but sufficiently to feel an interest in the subjects, and to be capable of holding a conversation on them with the husband, or at least of understanding and imbibing his wisdom. Very agreeable to him, no doubt, but unfortunately the reverse of improving. It is from having intellectual communion only with those to whom they can lay down the law, that so few men continue to advance in wisdom beyond the first stages. The most eminent men cease to improve, if they associate only with disciples. When they have overtopped those who immediately surround them, if they wish for further growth, they must seek for others of their own stature to consort with. The mental companionship which is improving, is communion between active minds, not mere contact between an active mind and a passive. This inestimable advantage is even now enjoyed, when a strong-minded man and a strong-minded woman are, by a rare chance, united: and would be had far oftener, if education took the same pains to form strong-minded women which it takes to prevent them from being formed. The modern, and what are regarded as the improved and enlightened modes of education of women, abjure, as far as words go, an education of mere show, and profess to aim at solid instruction, but mean by that expression, superficial information on solid subjects. Except accomplishments, which are now generally regarded as to be taught well if taught at all, nothing is taught to women thoroughly. Small portions only of what it is attempted to teach thoroughly to boys, are the whole of what it is intended or desired to teach to women. What makes intelligent beings is the power of thought: the stimuli which call forth that power are the interest and dignity of thought itself, and a field for its practical application. Both motives are cut off from those who are told from infancy that thought, and all its greater applications, are other people's business, while theirs is to make themselves agreeable to other people. High mental powers in women will be but an exceptional accident, until every career is open to them, and until they, as well as men, are educated for themselves and for the world—not one sex for the other.

In what we have said on the effect of the inferior position of women, combined with the present constitution of married life, we have thus far had in view only the most favourable cases, those in which there is some real approach to that union and blending of characters and of lives, which the theory of the relation contemplates as its ideal standard. But if we look to the great majority of cases, the effect of women's legal inferiority on the character both of women and of men must be painted in far darker colours. We do not speak here of the grosser brutalities, nor of the man's power to seize on the woman's earnings, or compel her to live with him against her will. We do not address ourselves to any one who requires to have it proved that these things should be remedied. We suppose average cases, in which there is neither complete union nor complete disunion of feelings and of character; and we affirm that in such cases the influence of the dependence on the woman's side, is demoralizing to the character of both.

The common opinion is, that whatever may be the case with the intellectual, the moral influence of women over men is almost always salutary. It is, we are often told, the great counteractive of selfishness. However the case may be as to personal influence, the influence of the position tends eminently to promote selfishness. The most insignificant of men, the man who can obtain influence or consideration nowhere else, finds one place where he is chief and head. There is one person, often greatly his superior in understanding, who is obliged to consult him, and whom he is not obliged to consult. He is judge, magistrate, ruler, over their joint concerns; arbiter of all differences between them. The justice or conscience to which her appeal must be made, is his justice and conscience: it is his to hold the balance and adjust the scales between his own claims or wishes and those of another. His is now the only tribunal, in civilized life, in which the same person is judge and party. A generous mind, in such a situation, makes the balance incline against its own side, and gives the other not less, but more, than a fair equality; and thus the weaker side may be enabled to turn the very fact of dependence into an instrument of power, and in default of justice, take an ungenerous advantage of generosity; rendering the unjust power, to those who make an unselfish use of it, a torment and a burthen. But how is it when average men are invested with this power, without reciprocity and without responsibility? Give such a man the idea that he is first in law and in opinion—that to will is his part, and hers to submit; it is absurd to suppose that this idea merely glides over his mind, without sinking into it, or having any effect on his feelings and practice. The propensity to make himself the first object of consideration, and others at most the second, is not so rare as to be wanting where everything seems purposely arranged for permitting its indulgence. If there is any self-will in the man, he becomes either the conscious or unconscious despot of his household. The wife, indeed, often succeeds in gaining her objects, but it is by some of the many various forms of indirectness and management.

Thus the position is corrupting equally to both; in the one it produces the vices of power, in the other those of artifice. Women, in their present physical and moral state, having stronger impulses, would naturally be franker and more direct than men; yet all the old saws and traditions represent them as artful and dissembling. Why? Because their only way to their objects is by indirect paths. In all countries where women have strong wishes and active minds, this consequence is inevitable: and if it is less conspicuous in England than in some other places, it is because Englishwomen, saving occasional exceptions, have ceased to have either strong wishes or active minds.

We are not now speaking of cases in which there is anything deserving the name of strong affection on both sides. That, where it exists, is too powerful a principle not to modify greatly the bad influences of the situation; it seldom, however, destroys them entirely. Much oftener the bad influences are too strong for the affection, and destroy it. The highest order of durable and happy attachments would be a hundred times more frequent than they are, if the affection which the two sexes sought from one another were that genuine friendship, which only exists between equals in privileges as in faculties. But with regard to what is commonly called affection in married life—the habitual and almost mechanical feeling of kindliness, and pleasure in each other's society, which generally grows up between persons who constantly live together, unless there is actual dislike—there is nothing in this to contradict or qualify the mischievous influence of the unequal relation. Such feelings often exist between a sultan and his favourites, between a master and his servants; they are merely examples of the pliability of human nature, which accommodates itself in some degree even to the worst circumstances, and the commonest natures always the most easily.

With respect to the influence personally exercised by women over men, it, no doubt, renders them less harsh and brutal; in ruder times, it was often the only softening influence to which they were accessible. But the assertion, that the wife's influence renders the man less selfish, contains, as things now are, fully as much error as truth. Selfishness towards the wife herself, and towards those in whom she is interested, the children, though favoured by their dependence, the wife's influence, no doubt, tends to counteract. But the general effect on him of her character, so long as her interests are concentrated in the family, tends but to substitute for individual selfishness a family selfishness, wearing an amiable guise, and putting on the mask of duty. How rarely is the wife's influence on the side of public virtue: how rarely does it do otherwise than discourage any effort of principle by which the private interests or worldly vanities of the family can be expected to suffer. Public spirit, sense of duty towards the public good, is of all virtues, as women are now educated and situated, the most rarely to be found among them; they have seldom even, what in men is often a partial substitute for public spirit, a sense of personal honour connected with any public duty. Many a man, whom no money or personal flattery would have bought, has bartered his political opinions against a title or invitations for his wife; and a still greater number are made mere hunters after the puerile vanities of society, because their wives value them. As for opinions; in Catholic countries, the wife's influence is another name for that of the priest: he gives her, in the hopes and emotions connected with a future life, a consolation for the sufferings and disappointments which are her ordinary lot in this. Elsewhere, her weight is thrown into the scale either of the most common-place, or of the most outwardly prosperous opinions: either those by which censure will be escaped, or by which worldly advancement is likeliest to be procured. In England, the wife's influence is usually on the illiberal and anti-popular side: this is generally the gaining side for personal interest and vanity; and what to her is the democracy or liberalism in which she has no part—which leaves her the Pariah it found her? The man himself, when he marries, usually declines into Conservatism; begins to sympathize with the holders of power, more than with its victims, and thinks it his part to be on the side of authority. As to mental progress, except those vulgarer attainments by which vanity or ambition are promoted, there is generally an end to it in a man who marries a woman mentally his inferior; unless, indeed, he is unhappy in marriage, or becomes indifferent. From a man of twenty-five or thirty, after he is married, an experienced observer seldom expects any further progress in mind or feelings. It is rare that the progress already made is maintained. Any spark of the *mens divinior* which might otherwise have spread and become a flame, seldom survives for any length of time unextinguished. For a mind which learns to be satisfied with what it already is—which does not incessantly look forward to a degree of improvement not yet reached—becomes relaxed, self-indulgent, and loses the spring and the tension which maintain it even at the point already attained. And there is no fact in human nature to which experience bears more invariable testimony than to this—that all social or sympathetic influences which do not raise up, pull down; if they do not tend to stimulate and exalt the mind, they tend to vulgarize it.

For the interest, therefore, not only of women but of men, and of human improvement in the widest sense, the emancipation of women, which the modern world often boasts of having effected, and for which credit is sometimes given to civilization, and sometimes to Christianity, cannot stop where it is. If it were either necessary or just that one portion of mankind should remain mentally and spiritually only half developed, the development of the other portion ought to have been made, as far as possible, independent of their influence. Instead of this, they have become the most intimate, and it may now be said, the only intimate associates of those to whom yet they are sedulously kept inferior; and have been raised just high enough to drag the others down to themselves. . . .

. . . The plea that women do not desire any change, is the same that has been urged, times out of mind, against the proposal of abolishing any social evil—"there is no complaint"; which is generally not true, and when true, only so because there is not that hope of success, without which complaint seldom makes itself audible to unwilling ears. How does the objector know that women do not desire equality and freedom? He never knew a woman who did not, or would not, desire it for herself individually. It would be very simple to suppose, that if they do desire it they will say so. Their position is like that of the tenants or labourers who vote against their own political interests to please their landlords or employers; with the unique addition, that submission is inculcated on them from childhood, as the peculiar attraction and grace of their character. They are taught to think, that to repel actively even an admitted injustice done to themselves, is somewhat unfeminine, and had better be left to some male friend or protector. To be accused of rebelling against anything which admits of being called an ordinance of society, they are taught to regard as an imputation of a serious offence, to say the least, against the proprieties of their sex. It requires unusual moral courage as well as disinterestedness in a woman, to express opinions favourable to women's enfranchisement, until, at least, there is some prospect of obtaining it. The comfort of her individual life, and her social consideration, usually depend on the good will of those who hold the undue power; and to possessors of power any complaint, however bitter, of the misuse of it, is a less flagrant act of insubordination than to protest against the power itself. The professions of women in this matter remind us of the state offenders of old, who, on the point of execution, used to protest their love and devotion to the sovereign by whose unjust mandate they suffered. . . .

But enough of this; especially as the fact which affords the occasion for this notice, makes it impossible any longer to assert the universal acquiescence of women (saving individual exceptions) in their dependent condition. In the United States at least, there are women, seemingly numerous, and now organised for action on the public mind, who demand equality in the fullest acceptation of the word, and demand it by a straightforward appeal to men's sense of justice, not plead for it with a timid deprecation of their displeasure. . . .

. . . The strength of the cause lies in the support of those who are influenced by reason and principle; and to attempt to recommend it by sentimentalities, absurd in reason, and inconsistent with the principle on which the movement is founded, is to place a good cause on a level with a bad one.

SUGGESTIONS FOR FURTHER READING

Utilitarianism

Ball, Terence. "Utilitarianism, Feminism and the Franchise: James Mill and His Critics." *History of Political Thought* 1 (Spring 1990), pp. 91–115.

Boralevi, Lea Campos. "Utilitarianism and Feminism." In *Women in Western Political Philosophy: Kant to Nietzsche*, ed. by Ellen Kennedy and Susan Mendus. New York: St. Martin's Press, 1987, pp. 159–78.

Donner, Wendy. "John Stuart Mill's Liberal Feminism." *Philosophical Studies* 69 (March 1993), pp. 155–66.

Goldstein, Leslie. "Mill, Marx, and Women's Liberation." *Journal of the History of Philosophy* 18 (July 1980), pp. 319–34.

Hayek, Friedrich A. *John Stuart Mill and Harriet Taylor: Their Friendship and Subsequent Marriage*. Chicago: The University of Chicago Press, 1951.

Hekman, Susan. "John Stuart Mill's 'The Subjection of Women': The Foundations of Liberal Feminism." *History of European Ideas* 15 (Aug. 1992), pp. 681–86.

Howes, John. "Mill on Women and Human Development." *Australasian Journal of Philosophy* Suppl. 64 (June 1986), pp. 66–74.

Mahowald, Mary B. "Freedom vs. Happiness, and 'Women's Lib.'" *Journal of Social Philosophy* VI, 2 (April 1975), pp. 10–13.

Mill, John Stuart. *Autobiography of John Stuart Mill*. New York: Columbia University Press, 1960.

Mill, John Stuart and Mill, Harriet Taylor. *Essays on Sex Equality*, ed. by Alice S. Rossi. Chicago: The University of Chicago Press, 1970.

Pappe, H. O. *John Stuart Mill and the Harriet Taylor Myth*. Parkville, Victoria: Melbourne University Press, 1961.

Pedersen, Joyce Senders. "Education, Gender and Social Change in Victorian Liberal Feminist Theory." *History of European Ideas* 8 (1987), pp. 503–19.

Robson, John M. "Harriet Taylor on Marriage: Two Fragments." *Mill News* 18 (Summer 1983), pp. 2–6.

———. "No Laughing Matter: John Stuart Mill's Establishment of Women's Suffrage as a Parliamentary Question." *Utilitas* 2 (May 1990), pp. 88–101.

Shanley, Mary Lyndon. "Marital Slavery and Friendship: John Stuart Mill's 'The Subjection of Women.'" *Political Theory* 9 (May 1981), pp. 229–47.

Soble, Alan. "The Epistemology of the Natural and the Social in Mill's 'The Subjection of Women.'" *Mill News* 16 (Summer 1991), pp. 3–10.

Stove, D. "The Subjection of John Stuart Mill." *Philosophy* 68 (Jan. 1993), pp. 5–14.

Urbinati, Nadia. "John Stuart Mill on Androgyny and Ideal Marriage." *Political Theory* (Nov. 1991), pp. 626–48.

Vicinus, Martha (ed.). *Suffer and Be Still/Women in the Victorian Age*. Bloomington: Indiana University Press, 1972.

Williford, Miriam. "Bentham on the Rights of Women." *Journal of the History of Ideas* 36 (1975), pp. 167–76.

EXISTENTIALISM

"Existentialism" is a term that can better be described than defined. Basically, the "existence" about which the existentialist is concerned is human existence, and the focus of that concern is human subjectivity or freedom. Historically, existentialism involves a reaction against an overemphasis on reason and the capability of reason for solving all human problems. Certain aspects of life, the existentialist insists, are entirely inexplicable by reason; certain values for the individual cannot and need not be rationally deduced or justified. Freedom is the assertion of power over reason and nature; it is the condition of life's responsibility and risk. Such an emphasis on freedom suggests an advocacy of liberation for women. But this is not the case for Kierkegaard and Nietzsche, as will be clear from the selections below. De Beauvoir's views on the issue seem to be more consistent with the existentialist position.

SØREN KIERKEGAARD

Søren Kierkegaard's (1813–1855) writings about woman may or may not have been influenced by a rigidly religious background and an extremely melancholy disposition. For a time his melancholy was lightened through love for and engagement to Regina Olsen. But Kierkegaard broke the engagement, even while claiming he still loved Regina. In subsequent writings he attempted to explain his decision to remain unmarried. For Kierkegaard, commitment to God required his renunciation of marriage.

For Kierkegaard, "existence" is a category relating to the free individual, actualized through the self-commitment to a radical choice between alternatives. To be human is to define oneself through such choices. The levels of alternatives constitute a progression from a subhuman level of existence (before choice) to a transcendence of reason, through faith. The first stage is that of the aesthetic, who has decided to live his life in pursuit of sensual enjoyment (Don Juan, for example). Inevitably, he cannot sustain the pleasure he seeks, and this leads him either to despair or to move to an ethical level of existence. If he chooses to live ethically his life is thereafter governed by reason. His acceptance of universal moral standards and obligations provides him with a sense of permanence, wholeness, and consistency. A typical instance of this decision is marriage, which necessarily involves renunciation and ordering of the sexual impulse. Eventually, however, the ethical person confronts the inadequacy of reason in grappling with life's problems. At that point, he is aware of a religious vocation: an invitation to live entirely by faith in the midst of objective uncertainty. If he chooses to take the "leap of faith," he fulfills his highest human capacity through his religious commitment. Unfortunately, claims Kierkegaard, woman is incapable of such commitment. "[T]o be able to be related to the Christian task," he writes, "it is necessary to be a man, [because] a man's hardness and strength are required to be able to bear just the stress of the task."

In the following selection, an aesthete named Johannes reflects on the meaning of woman. His "diary" recounts his successful seduction of Cordelia, whom he subsequently deserts. "When a girl has given away everything," he writes, "then she is weak, then she has lost everything. For a man guilt is a negative moment; for a woman it is the value of her being. Now all resistance is impossible, and only as long as that is present is it beautiful to love."

Diary of the Seducer

. . . .

Woman will always offer an inexhaustible fund of material for reflection, an eternal abundance for observation. The man who feels no impulse toward the study of woman may, as far as I am concerned, be what he will; one thing he certainly is not, he is no aesthetician. This is the glory and divinity of aesthetics, that it enters into relation only with the beautiful: it has to do essentially only with fiction and the fair sex. It makes me glad and causes my heart to rejoice when I represent to myself how the sun of feminine loveliness diffuses its rays into an infinite manifold, refracting itself in a confusion of tongues, where each individual woman has her little part of the whole wealth of femininity, yet so that her other characteristics harmoniously center about this point. In this sense feminine beauty is infinitely divisible. But the particular share of beauty which each one has must be present in a harmonious blending, for otherwise the effect will be disturbing, and it will seem as if Nature had intended something by this woman, but nothing ever came of it.

My eyes can never weary of surveying this peripheral manifold, these scattered emanations of feminine beauty. Each particular has its little share, and yet is complete in itself, happy, glad, beautiful. Every woman has her share: the merry smile, the roguish glance, the wistful eye, the pensive head, the exhuberant spirits, the quiet sadness, the deep foreboding, the brooding melancholy, the earthy homesickness, the unbaptized movements, the beckoning brows, the questioning lips, the mysterious forehead, the ensnaring curls, the concealing lashes, the heavenly pride, the earthly modesty, the angelic purity, the secret blush, the light step, the airy grace, the languishing posture, the dreamy yearning, the inexplicable sighs, the willowy form, the soft outlines, the luxuriant bosom, the swelling hips, the tiny foot, the dainty hand. —Each woman has her own traits, and the one does not merely repeat the other. And when I have gazed and gazed again, considered and again considered this multitudinous variety, when I have smiled, sighed, flattered, threatened, desired, tempted, laughed, wept, hoped, feared, won, lost—then I shut up my fan, and gather the fragments into a unity, the parts into a whole. Then my soul is glad, my heart beats, my passion is aflame. This one woman, the only woman in all the world, she must belong to me, she must be mine. Let God keep his heaven, if only I can keep her. I know full well what I choose; it is something so great that heaven itself must be the loser by such a division, for what would be left to heaven if I keep her? The faithful Mohammedans will be disappointed in their hopes when in their Paradise they embrace pale, weak shadows; for warm hearts they cannot find, since all the warmth of the heart is concentrated in her breast; they will yield themselves to be a comfortless despair when they find pale lips, lustreless eyes, a lifeless bosom, a limp pressure of the hand; for all the redness of the lips and the fire of the eye and the heaving of the bosom and the promise of the hand and the foreboding of the sigh and the seal of the kiss and the trembling of the touch and the passion of the embrace—all, all are concentrated in her, who lavishes on men a wealth sufficient for a whole world, both for time and eternity.

Thus I have often reflected upon this matter; but every time I conceive woman thus, I become warm, because I think of her as warm. And though in general, warmth is accounted a good sign, it does not follow that my mode of thinking will be granted the respectable predicate that it is solid. Hence I shall now for variety's sake attempt, myself being cold, to think coldly of woman. I shall attempt to think of woman in terms of her category. Under what category must she be conceived? Under the category of being for another. But this must not be understood in the bad sense, as if the woman who is for me is also for another. Here as always in abstract thinking, it is essential to refrain from every reference to experience; for otherwise as in the present case, I should find, in the most curious manner, that experience is both for and against me. Woman is therefore being for another. Here as always, experience is a most curious thing, because its nature is always to be both for and against. Here again, but from another side, it will be necessary not to let oneself be disturbed by experience, which teaches that it is a rare thing to find a woman who is in truth a being for another, since a great many are in general absolutely nothing, either for themselves or for others. Woman shares this category with Nature, and, in general, with everything feminine. Nature as a whole exists only for another; not in the teleological sense, so that one part of Nature exists for another part, but so that the whole of Nature is for an Other—for the Spirit. In the same way with the particulars.

The life of the plant, for example, unfolds in all naiveté its hidden charms and exists only for another. In the same way a mystery, a charade, a secret, a vowel, and so on, has being only for another. And from this it can be explained why, when God created Eve, he caused a deep sleep to fall upon Adam; for woman is the dream of man. In still another way the story teaches that woman is a being for another. It tells, namely, that Jehovah created Eve from a rib taken from the side of man. Had she been taken from man's brain, for example, woman would indeed still have been a being for another; but it was not the intention to make her a figment of the brain, but something quite different. She became flesh and blood, but this causes her to be included under the category of Nature, which is essentially being for another. She awakens first at the touch of love; before that time she is a dream, yet in her dream life we can distinguish two stages: in the first, love dreams about her; in the second, she dreams about love.

As being for another, woman is characterized by pure virginity. Virginity is, namely, a form of being, which, in so far as it is a being for itself, is really an abstraction, and only reveals itself to another. The same characterization also lies in the concept of female innocence. It is therefore possible to say that woman in this condition is invisible. As is well known, there existed no image of Vesta, the goddess who most nearly represented feminine virginity. This form of existence is, namely, jealous for itself aesthetically, just as Jehovah is ethically, and does not desire that there should be any image or even any notion of one. This is the contradiction, that the being which is for another *is* not, and only becomes visible, as it were, by the interposition of another. Logically, this contradiction will be found to be quite in order, and he who knows how to think logically will not be disturbed by it, but will be glad in it. But whoever thinks illogically will imagine that whatever is a being for another *is,* in the finite sense in which one can say about a particular thing: that is something for me.

This being of woman (for the word *existence* is too rich in meaning, since woman does not persist in and through herself) is rightly described as charm, an expression which suggests plant life; she is a flower, as the poets like to say, and even the spiritual in her is present in a vegetative manner. She is wholly subject to Nature, and hence only aesthetically free. In a deeper sense she first becomes free by her relation to man, and when man courts her properly, there can be no question of a choice. Woman chooses, it is true, but if this choice is thought of as the result of a long deliberation, then this choice is unfeminine. Hence it is, that it is a humiliation to receive a refusal, because the individual in question has rated himself too high, has desired to make another free without having the power.–In this situation there is deep irony. That which merely exists for another has the appearance of being predominant: man sues, woman chooses. The very concept of woman requires that she be the vanquished; the concept of man, that he be the victor; and yet the victor bows before the vanquished. And yet this is quite natural, and it is only boorishness, stupidity, and lack of erotic sensibility to take no notice of that which immediately yields in this fashion. It has also a deeper ground. Woman is, namely, substance, man is reflection. She does not therefore choose independently; man sues, she chooses. But man's courtship is a question, and her choice only an answer to a question. In a certain sense man is more than woman, in another sense he is infinitely less.

This being for another is the true virginity. If it makes an attempt to be a being for itself, in relation to another being which is being for it, then the opposition reveals itself in an absolute coyness; but this opposition shows at the same time that woman's essential being is being for another. The diametrical opposite to absolute devotion is absolute coyness, which in a converse sense is invisible as the abstraction against which everything breaks, without the abstraction itself coming to life. Femininity now takes on the character of an abstract cruelty, the caricature in its extreme form of the intrinsic feminine brittleness. A man can never be so cruel as a woman. Consult mythologies, fables, folk-tales, and you will find this view confirmed. If there is a description of a natural force whose mercilessness knows no limits, it will always be a feminine nature. Or one is horrified at reading about a young woman who callously allows all her suitors to lose their lives, as so often happens in the folk-tales of all nations. A Bluebeard slays all the women he has loved on their bridal night, but he does not find his happiness in slaying them; on the contrary, his happiness has preceded, and in this lies the concreteness; it is not cruelty for the sake of cruelty. A Don Juan seduces them and runs away, but he finds no happiness at all in running away from them, but rather in seducing them; consequently, it is by no means this abstract cruelty.

Thus, the more I reflect on this matter, I see that my practice is in perfect harmony with my theory. My practice has always been impregnated with the theory that woman is essentially a being for another. Hence it is that the moment has here such infinite significance; for a being for another is always the matter of a moment. It may take a longer, it may take a short time before the moment comes, but as soon as it has come, then that which was originally a being for another assumes the character of relative being, and then all is over. I know very well that husbands say that the woman is also in another sense a being for another, that she is everything to her husband through life. One must make allowance for husbands. I really believe that it is something which they mutually delude one another into thinking. Every class in society generally has certain conventional customs, and especially certain conventional lies. Among these must be reckoned this sailor's yarn. To be a good judge of the moment is not so easy a matter, and he who misjudges it is in for boredom for the rest of his life. The moment is everything, and in the moment, woman is everything; the consequences I do not understand. Among these consequences is the begetting of children. Now I fancy that I am a fairly consistent thinker, but if I were to think until I became crazy, I am not a man who could think this consequence; I simply do not understand it; to understand it requires a husband.

* * *

FRIEDRICH NIETZSCHE

Friedrich Nietzsche (1844–1900) was also brought up in a strongly religious household. After the death of his father, a Lutheran pastor, this household was composed entirely of women. In contrast to Kierkegaard, Nietzsche developed an antireligious attitude. To him (in *Joyful Wisdom*) we owe the popular antitheistic declaration: "God is dead."

For Nietzsche, man (male?) "is something which must be surpassed; man is a bridge and not a goal." He is "a rope stretched between animal and Superman—a rope over an abyss." The abyss is the irrationality of the world, which can only be transcended through the "Will to Power." This will is an intrinsic quality of the individual through which he affirms life—his life, rather than the life of humanity or another's life. Man's goal is to be "Superman," to acquire a personal individualistic excellence through fulfillment of his will to power. Since God is dead, this goal is now possible. The assertion of the will to power, which is the life of man, occurs only because certain individuals are thus controllable; they are controllable because they are naturally inferior.

Of Womenkind, Old and Young

Wherefore stealest thou so timidly through the twilight, Zarathustra? And what hidest thou so carefully beneath thy mantle?

Is it some treasure that hath been given thee? Or a child born unto thee? Or walkest thou now thyself in the ways of thieves, thou friend of the wicked?—

Verily, my brother! said Zarathustra, it is a treasure that hath been given me: a little truth it is that I carry.

But it is unruly as a young child, and if I hold not its mouth it crieth over-loud.

As this day I went my way alone at the hour of sunset I met a little old woman who spake thus to my soul:

Much hath Zarathustra spoken even unto us women, but never spake he unto us of woman.

And I answered her: Of woman must one speak only to men.

Speak also to me of woman, she said, I am old enough to forget it forthwith.

And I, assenting, spake thus to the little old woman:

All in woman is a riddle, and all in woman hath one answer—that is child-bearing.

Man is for woman a means: the end is ever the child. But what is woman for man?

Two things true man desireth: danger and play. Therefore desireth he woman as the most dangerous of playthings.

Man shall be trained for war, and woman for the recreation of the warrior: all else is folly.

Over-sweet fruits—the warrior loveth them not. Therefore he loveth woman; bitter is even the sweetest woman.

Woman understandeth children better than man, but man is more childlike than woman.

In true man a child lieth hidden: it longeth to play. Up, ye women, discover me the child in man!

Let woman be a plaything pure and delicate as a jewel, illumined with the virtues of a world that is yet to come.

Let the beam of a star shine in your love! Let your hope be, Would I might give birth to the Superman!

Let there be valour in your love! Assail with your love him that maketh you afraid.

In your love let your honour be! Little else knoweth woman of honour. But let it be your honour ever to love more than ye be loved, and never to be second.

Let man fear woman when she loveth: then will she sacrifice all, and naught else hath value for her.

Let man fear woman when she hateth: for in the depth of his soul man is but evil, but woman is base.

Whom hateth woman most?—Thus spake the iron to the loadstone: I hate thee most because thou drawest but are not strong enough to draw me to thee.

Man's happiness is, I will. Woman's happiness is, He will.

Behold, this moment hath the world been perfected;—thus deemeth every woman when she obeyeth with all her love.

Woman must obey and find depth to her surface. Surface is woman's nature, foam tossed to and fro on shallow water.

But deep is man's nature, his current floweth in subterranean caverns: woman divineth his power, but understandeth it not.

Then the little old woman answered me: Many fine things saith Zarathustra, and especially for them that are young enough.

A strange thing is this—Zarathustra knoweth little of women, and yet is he right regarding them! Is this because with women nothing is impossible?

And now take as thanks a little truth. I am old enough to speak it!

Wrap it well and keep its mouth shut: else will it cry over-loud, this little truth.

Give me, woman, thy little truth, I said. And thus spake the little old woman:

Thou goest to women? Remember thy whip!—

Thus spake Zarathustra.

* * *

Of Child and Marriage

I have a question for thee alone, my brother: I cast it as a plummet into thy soul that I may know how deep it be.

Thou art young and desirest child and marriage. But I ask thee, Art thou a man that *may* desire a child?

Art thou victor, self-subduer, master of thy senses, lord of thy virtues? Thus do I ask thee.

Or speak the beast and blind need in thy desire? Or loneliness? Or self-discord?

I would that thy victory and thy freedom desired a child. So thou shouldest build living monuments to thy victory and thy liberation.

Thou shalt build beyond thyself. But first I would have thee be built thyself—perfect in body and soul.

Thou shalt propagate thyself not only *onwards* but *upwards!* Thereto may the garden of marriage assist thee!

Thou shalt create a higher body, a primal motion, a self-rolling wheel—thou shalt create a creator.

Marriage: this call I the will of two to create that one which is more than they that created him. Marriage call I reverence of the one for the other as for them that possess such a will.

Let this be the meaning and truth of thy marriage. But that which the much-too-many call marriage, the superfluous ones—alas, what call I that?

Alas! this double poverty of soul! Alas! this double uncleanness of souls! Alas! this double despicable ease!

Marriage they call it; and they say their marriage is made in heaven.

As for me, I love it not, this heaven of the superfluous! Nay, I love them not, these beasts entrapped in heavenly snares!

Far from me also be the God that cometh halting to bless that He joined not together!

Laugh not at such marriages! What child hath not cause to weep over its parents?

Worthy meseemed such an one, and ripe for the meaning of earth, but when I beheld his wife earth seemed to me a madhouse.

Yea, I would the earth would quake whenever a saint mateth with a goose.

Such an one went forth in quest of truth like a hero, and his prize at length was a little dressed-up lie. He calleth it his marriage.

Such another was reserved in society and chose fastidiously. But suddenly he forever lowered his company: he calleth this his marriage.

A third sought a serving-wench with an angel's virtues. But suddenly he became the serving-wench of a woman, and now needeth himself to become an angel!

All buyers have I found cautious and cunning of eye. Yet even the most cunning buyeth his wife in a sack.

Many brief follies—that ye call love. And your marriage maketh an end of many brief follies with one long stupidity.

Your love for woman, and woman's love for man: alas, would they were sympathy for suffering and hidden deities! But commonly two beasts find one another out.

Even your best love is but a rapturous likeness, an anguished ardour. It is a torch to light you to higher paths.

Some day ye shall love beyond yourselves! *Learn,* then, how to love! To that end were ye compelled to drink the bitter cup of your love.

Bitterness is in the cup even of the best love: thus causeth it desire for the Superman: thus it maketh thee to thirst, the creator!

Creative thirst, an arrow of desire for the Superman: say, my brother, is this thy will to marriage?

Holy call I such a will and such a marriage.

Thus spake Zarathustra.

* * *

Our Virtues

231

Learning changes us; it does what all nourishment does which also does not merely "preserve"—as physiologists know. But at the bottom of us, really "deep down," there is, of course, something unteachable, some granite of spiritual *fatum,* of predetermined decision and answer to predetermined selected questions. Whenever a cardinal problem is at stake, there speaks an unchangeable "this is I"; about man and woman, for example, a thinker cannot relearn but only finish learning—only discover ultimately how this is "settled in him." At times we find certain solutions of problems that inspire strong faith in *us;* some call them henceforth *their* "convictions." Later—we see them only as steps to self-knowledge, sign-posts to the problem we *are*—rather, to the great stupidity we are, to our spiritual *fatum,* to what is *unteachable* very "deep down."

After this abundant civility that I have just evidenced in relation to myself I shall perhaps be permitted more readily to state a few truths about "woman as such"—assuming that it is now known from the outset how very much these are after all only—*my* truths.

232

Woman wants to become self-reliant—and for that reason she is beginning to enlighten men about "woman as such": *this* is one of the worst developments of the general *uglification* of Europe. For what must these clumsy attempts of women at scientific self-exposure bring to light! Woman has much reason for shame; so much pendantry, superficiality, schoolmarmishness, petty presumption, petty licentiousness and immodesty lies concealed in woman—one only needs to study her behavior with children!—and so far all this was at bottom best repressed and kept under control by *fear* of man. Woe when "the eternally boring in woman"—she is rich in that!—is permitted to venture forth! When she begins to unlearn thoroughly and on principle her prudence and art—of grace, of play, of chasing away worries, of lightening burdens and taking things lightly—and her subtle aptitude for agreeable desires!

Even now female voices are heard which—holy Aristophanes!—are frightening: they threaten with medical explicitness what woman *wants* from man, first and last. Is it not in the worst taste when woman sets about becoming scientific that way? So far enlightenment of this sort was fortunately man's affair, man's lot—we remained "among ourselves" in this; and whatever women write about "woman," we may in the end reserve a healthy suspicion whether woman really *wants* enlightenment about herself—whether she *can* will it—

Unless a woman seeks a new adornment for herself that way—I do think adorning herself is part of the Eternal-Feminine?—she surely wants to inspire fear of herself—perhaps she seeks mastery. But she does not *want* truth: what is truth to woman? From the beginning, nothing has been more alien, repugnant, and hostile to woman than truth—her great art is the lie, her highest concern is mere appearance and beauty. Let us men confess it: we honor and love precisely *this* art and *this* instinct in woman—we who have a hard time and for our relief like to associate with beings under whose hands, eyes, and tender follies our seriousness, our gravity and profundity almost appear to us like folly.

Finally I pose the question: has ever a woman conceded profundity to a woman's head, or justice to a woman's heart? And is it not true that on the whole "woman" has so far been despised most by woman herself—and by no means by us?

We men wish that woman should not go on compromising herself through enlightenment—just as it was man's thoughtfulness and consideration for woman that found expression in the church decree: *mulier taceat in ecclesia!*[1] It was for woman's good when Napoleon gave the all too eloquent Madame de Stael to understand: *mulier taceat in politicis!*[2] And I think it is a real friend of women that counsels them today: *mulier taceat de muliere!*[3]

233

It betrays a corruption of the instincts—quite apart from the fact that it betrays bad taste—when a woman adduces Madame Roland or Madame de Stael or Monsieur George Sand, of all people, as if they proved anything in *favor* of "woman as such." Among men these three are the three *comical* women as such—nothing more!—and precisely the best involuntary *counterarguments* against emancipation and feminine vainglory.

234

Stupidity in the kitchen; woman as cook: the gruesome thoughtlessness to which the feeding of the family and of the master of the house is abandoned! Woman does not understand what food *means*—and wants to be cook. If woman were a *thinking* creature, she, as cook for millennia, would surely have had to discover the greatest physiological facts, and she would have had to gain possession of the art of healing. Bad cooks—and the utter lack of reason in the kitchen—have delayed human development longest and impaired it most: nor have things improved much even today. A lecture for finishing-school girls.

1. Woman should be silent in church.

2. Woman should be silent when it comes to politics.

3. Woman should be silent about woman.

235

There are expressions and bull's-eyes of the spirit, there are epigrams, a little handful of words, in which a whole culture, a whole society is suddenly crystallized. Among these belongs the occasional remark of Madame de Lambert to her son: *"mon ami, ne vous permettez jamais que de folies, qui vous feront grand plaisir"*[4] —incidentally the most motherly and prudent word ever directed to a son.

236

What Dante and Goethe believed about woman—the former when he sang, *"ella guardava suso, ed io in lei,"*[5] and the latter when he translated this, "the Eternal-Feminine attracts us *higher*" —I do not doubt that every nobler woman will resist this faith, for she believes the same thing about the Eternal-Masculine—

237

SEVEN EPIGRAMS ON WOMAN

How the longest boredom flees, when a man comes on his knees!

Science and old age at length give weak virtue, too, some strength.

Black dress and a silent part make every woman appear—smart.

Whom I thank for my success? God;—and my dear tailoress.

Young: flower-covered den. Old: a dragon denizen.

Noble name, the legs are fine, man as well: that he were mine!

Ample meaning, speech concise—she-ass, watch for slippery ice!

237a

Men have so far treated women like birds who had strayed to them from some height: as something more refined and vulnerable, wilder, stranger, sweeter, and more soulful—but as something one has to lock up lest it fly away.

4. "My friend, permit yourself nothing but follies—that will give you great pleasure."

5. "She looked up, and I at her."

238

To go wrong on the fundamental problem of "man and woman," to deny the most abysmal antagonism between them and the necessity of an eternally hostile tension, to dream perhaps of equal rights, equal education, equal claims and obligations—that is a *typical* sign of shallowness, and a thinker who has proved shallow in this dangerous place—shallow in his instinct—may be considered altogether suspicious, even more—betrayed, exposed: probably he will be too "short" for all fundamental problems of life, of the life yet to come, too, and incapable of attaining *any* depth. A man, on the other hand, who has depth, in his spirit as well as in his desires, including that depth of benevolence which is capable of severity and hardness and easily mistaken for them, must always think about woman as *Orientals* do: he must conceive of woman as a possession, as property that can be locked, as something predestined for service and achieving her perfection in that. Here he must base himself on the tremendous reason of Asia, on Asia's superiority in the instincts, as the Greeks did formerly, who were Asia's best heirs and students: as is well known, from Homer's time to the age of Pericles, as their culture *increased* along with the range of their powers, they also gradually became *more severe*, in brief, more Oriental, against woman. *How* necessary, *how* logical, *how* humanely desirable even, this was—is worth pondering.

239

In no age has the weaker sex been treated with as much respect by men as in ours: that belongs to the democratic inclination and basic taste, just like disrespectfulness for old age. No wonder that this respect is immediately abused. One wants more, one learns to demand, finally one almost finds this tribute of respect insulting, one would prefer competition for rights, indeed even a genuine fight: enough, woman loses her modesty. Let us immediately add that she also loses taste. She unlearns her *fear* of man: but the woman who "unlearns fear" surrenders her most womanly instincts.

That woman ventures forth when the aspect of man that inspires fear—let us say more precisely, when the *man* in man is no longer desired and cultivated—that is fair enough, also comprehensible enough. What is harder to comprehend is that, by the same token—woman degenerates. This is what is happening today: let us not deceive ourselves about that.

Wherever the industrial spirit has triumphed over the military and aristocratic spirit, woman now aspires to the economic and legal self-reliance of a clerk: "woman as clerk" is inscribed on the gate to the modern society that is taking shape now. As she thus takes possession of new rights, aspires to become "master" and writes the "progress" of woman upon her standards and banners, the opposite development is taking place with terrible clarity: *woman is retrogressing.*

Since the French Revolution, woman's influence in Europe has *decreased* proportionately as her rights and claims have increased; and the "emancipation of woman," insofar as that is demanded and promoted by women themselves (and not merely by shallow males) is thus seen to be an odd symptom of the increasing weakening and dulling of the most feminine instincts. There is *stupidity* in this movement, an almost masculine stupidity of which a woman who had turned out well—and such women are always prudent—would have to be thoroughly ashamed.

To lose the sense for the ground on which one is most certain of victory; to neglect practice with one's proper weapons; to let oneself go before men, perhaps even "to the point of writing a book," when formerly one disciplined oneself to subtle and cunning humility; to work with virtuous audacity against men's faith in a basically different ideal that he takes to be *concealed* in woman, something Eternally-and-Necessarily-Feminine—to talk men emphatically and loquaciously out of their notion that woman must be maintained, taken care of, protected, and indulged like a more delicate, strangely wild, and often pleasant domestic animal; the awkward and indignant search for everything slavelike and serflike that has characterized woman's position in the order of society so far, and still does (as if slavery were a counterargument and not instead a condition of every higher culture, every enhancement of culture)—what is the meaning of all this if not a crumbling of feminine instincts, a defeminization?

To be sure, there are enough imbecilic friends and corrupters of woman among the scholarly asses of the male sex who advise woman to defeminize herself in this way and to imitate all the stupidities with which "man" in Europe, European "manliness," is sick: they would like to reduce woman to the level of "general education," probably even of reading the newspapers and talking about politics. Here and there they even want to turn women into freethinkers and scribblers—as if a woman without piety would not seem utterly obnoxious and ridiculous to a profound and godless man.

Almost everywhere one ruins her nerves with the most pathological and dangerous kind of music (our most recent German music) and makes her more hysterical by the day and more incapable of her first and last profession—to give birth to strong children. Altogether one wants to make her more "cultivated" and, as is said, make the weaker sex *strong* through culture—as if history did not teach us as impressively as possible that making men "cultivated" and making them weak—weakening, splintering, and sicklying over the *force of the will*—have always kept pace, and that the most powerful and influential women of the world (most recently Napolean's mother) owed their power and ascendancy over men to the force of their will—and not to schoolmasters!

What inspires respect for woman, and often enough even fear, is her *nature*, which is more "natural" than man's, the genuine, cunning suppleness of a beast of prey, the tiger's claw under the glove, the naiveté of her egoism, her uneducability and inner wildness, the incomprehensibility, scope, and movement of her desires and virtues—

What, in spite of all fear, elicits pity for this dangerous and beautiful cat "woman" is that she appears to suffer more, to be more vulnerable, more in need of love, and more condemned to disappointment than any other animal. Fear and pity: with these feelings man has so far confronted woman, always with one foot in tragedy which tears to pieces as it enchants.

What? And this should be the end? And the breaking of woman's magic spell is at work? The "borification" of woman is slowly dawning? O Europe! Europe! We know the horned animal you always found most attractive; it still threatens you! Your old fable could yet become "history"—once more an immense stupidity might become master over you and carry you off. And this time no god would hide in it; no, only an "idea," a "modern idea"!—

* * *

SIMONE DE BEAUVOIR

Simone de Beauvoir (1908–1986) draws upon her own experience in elaborating her concept of woman. Despite efforts of home and boarding school to mold her to the traditional feminine role (see her *Memoirs of a Dutiful Daughter*), she decided early in adult life to acquire and maintain a professional stature and independence through her teaching and writing, without the concomitant roles of wife and mother. It is now abundantly clear that she succeeded in that resolve. Among de Beauvoir's numerous works are the award-winning novel *The Mandarins* (1954), and a well-acclaimed critical analysis of society's maltreatment of the elderly, *The Coming of Age* (1972). In all her works, the social dimension of de Beauvoir's existentialist interpretation is apparent. As an author, she claims to have derived the greatest personal satisfaction from the book specifically addressed to the subject of woman, *The Second Sex*.

In *The Second Sex,* de Beauvoir defines her philosophical perspective as that of "existentialist ethics." From that perspective, human beings are necessarily viewed as unique individuals and subjects; as such, they live ethically to the degree that they realize their freedom. In an important earlier work, *The Ethics of Ambiguity,* de Beauvoir delineates the ways in which persons fall short of fulfilling their own humanity through apathy, childish submission, introversion, and extroversion. The ethical person recognizes that the human situation is irremediably ambiguous or absurd, but refuses to acquiesce or surrender to the ambiguity. Instead, the moral man or woman transcends the ambiguity through the activity of freedom. According to de Beauvoir, "freedom must project itself toward its own reality through a content whose value it establishes." Through the choices we make, we create our own values. To abstain from or avoid these choices by merely conforming to the values of others is to be immoral.

A rather common argument against the existentialist emphasis on individual freedom is that it implies an anarchic society, a chaos of clashes among egoistic pursuers of values. In the thought of de Beauvoir, this argument cannot be sustained, for freedom requires that (a) we assume full responsibility for our choices, and (b) we treat other persons as free also. In fact, "no existence can be validly fulfilled," de Beauvoir writes, "if it is limited to itself." Hence, "to will oneself free is also to will others free." In the following passage de Beauvoir explains her concept rather succinctly:

> to be free is not to have the power to do anything you like; it is to be able to surpass the given towards an open future; the existence of others as a freedom defines my situation and is even the condition of my own freedom. I am oppressed if I am thrown into prison, but not if I am kept from throwing my neighbor into prison.

The Second Sex

. . . [W]hat is a woman?

To state the question is, to me, to suggest, at once, a preliminary answer. The fact that I ask it is in itself significant. A man would never get the notion of writing a book on the peculiar situation of the human male.[1] But if I wish to define myself, I must first of all say: "I am a woman"; on this truth must be based all further discussion. A man never begins by presenting himself as an individual of a certain sex; it goes without saying that he is a man. The terms *masculine* and *feminine* are used symmetrically only as a matter of form, as on legal papers. In actuality the relation of the two sexes is not quite like that of two electrical poles, for man represents both the positive and the neutral, as is indicated by the common use of *man* to designate human beings in general; whereas woman represents only the negative, defined by limiting criteria, without reciprocity. In the midst of an abstract discussion it is vexing to hear a man say: "You think thus and so because you are a woman"; but I know that my only defense is to reply: "I think thus and so because it is true," thereby removing my subjective self from the argument. It would be out of the question to reply: "And you think the contrary because you are a man," for it is understood that the fact of being a man is no peculiarity. A man is in the right in being a man; it is the woman who is in the wrong. It amounts to this: just as for the ancients there was an absolute vertical with reference to which the oblique was defined, so there is an absolute human type, the masculine. Woman has ovaries, a uterus; these peculiarities imprison her in her subjectivity, circumscribe her within the limits of her own nature. It is often said that she thinks with her glands. Man superbly ignores the fact that his anatomy also includes glands, such as the testicles, and that they secrete hormones. He thinks of his body as a direct and normal connection with the world, which he believes he apprehends objectively, whereas he regards the body of woman as a hindrance, a prison, weighed down by everything peculiar to it. "The female is a female by virtue of a certain *lack* of qualities," said Aristotle; "we should regard the female nature as afflicted with a natural defectiveness." And St. Thomas for his part pronounced woman to be an "imperfect man," an "incidental" being. This is symbolized in Genesis where Eve is depicted as made from what Bossuet called "a supernumerary bone" of Adam.

Thus humanity is male and man defines woman not in herself but as relative to him; she is not regarded as an autonomous being. Michelet writes: "Woman, the relative being. . . ." And Benda is most positive in his *Rapport d'Uriel:* "The body of man makes sense in itself quite apart from that of woman, whereas the latter seems

1. The Kinsey Report [Alfred C. Kinsey and others: *Sexual Behavior in the Human Male* (W. B. Saunders Co., 1948)] is no exception, for it is limited to describing the sexual characteristics of American men, which is quite a different matter.

wanting in significance by itself. . . . Man can think of himself without woman. She cannot think of herself without man." And she is simply what man decrees; thus she is called "the sex," by which is meant that she appears essentially to the male as a sexual being. For him she is sex—absolute sex, no less. She is defined and differentiated with reference to man and not he with reference to her; she is the incidental, the inessential as opposed to the essential. He is the Subject, he is the Absolute—she is the Other.[2]

The category of the *Other* is as primordial as consciousness itself. In the most primitive societies, in the most ancient mythologies, one finds the expression of a duality—that of the Self and the Other. This duality was not originally attached to the division of the sexes; it was not dependent upon any empirical facts. . . .

. . . Otherness is a fundamental category of human thought.

Thus it is that no group ever sets itself up as the One without at once setting up the Other over against itself. If three travelers chance to occupy the same compartment, that is enough to make vaguely hostile "others" out of all the rest of the passengers on the train. In small-town eyes all persons not belonging to the village are "strangers" and suspect; to the native of a country all who inhabit other countries are "foreigners"; Jews are "different" for the anti-Semite, Negroes are "inferior" for American racists, aborigines are "natives" for colonists, proletarians are the "lower class" for the privileged. . . . No subject will readily volunteer to become the object, the inessential; it is not the Other who, in defining himself as the Other, establishes the One. The Other is posed as such by the One in defining himself as the One. But if the Other is not to regain the status of being the One, he must be submissive enough to accept this alien point of view.

. . . If woman seems to be the inessential which never becomes

2. E. Lévinas expresses this idea most explicitly in his essay *Temps et l'Autre*. "Is there not a case in which otherness, alterity [altérité], unquestionably marks the nature of a being, as its essence, an instance, of otherness not consisting purely and simply in the opposition of two species of the same genus? I think that the feminine represents the contrary in its absolute sense, this contrariness being in no wise affected by any relation between it and its correlative and thus remaining absolutely other. Sex is not a certain specific difference . . . no more is the sexual difference a mere contradiction. . . . Nor does this difference lie in the duality of two complementary terms, for two complementary terms imply a preexisting whole. . . . Otherness reaches its full flowering in the feminine, a term of the same rank as consciousness but of opposite meaning."

I suppose that Lévinas does not forget that woman, too, is aware of her own consciousness, or ego. But it is striking that he deliberately takes a man's point of view, disregarding the reciprocity of subject and object. When he writes that woman is mystery, he implies that she is mystery for man. Thus his description, which is intended to be objective, is in fact an assertion of masculine privilege.

the essential, it is because she herself fails to bring about this change. Proletarians say "We"; Negroes also. Regarding themselves as subjects, they transform the bourgeois, the whites, into "others." But women do not say "We," except at some congress of feminists or similar formal demonstration; men say "women," and women use the same word in referring to themselves. They do not authentically assume a subjective attitude. The proletarians have accomplished the revolution in Russia, the Negroes in Haiti, the Indo-Chinese are battling for it in Indo-China; but the women's effort has never been anything more than a symbolic agitation. They have gained only what men have been willing to grant; they have taken nothing, they have only received.

The reason for this is that women lack concrete means for organizing themselves into a unit which can stand face to face with the correlative unit. They have no past, no history, no religion of their own; and they have no such solidarity of work and interest as that of the proletariat. They are not even promiscuously herded together in the way that creates community feeling among the American Negroes, the ghetto Jews, the workers of Saint-Denis, or the factory hands of Renault. They live dispersed among the males, attached through residence, housework, economic condition, and social standing to certain men—fathers or husbands—more firmly than they are to other women. If they belong to the bourgeoisie, they feel solidarity with men of that class, not with proletarian women; if they are white, their allegiance is to white men, not to Negro women. The proletariat can propose to massacre the ruling class, and a sufficiently fanatical Jew or Negro might dream of getting sole possession of the atomic bomb and making humanity wholly Jewish or black; but woman cannot even dream of exterminating the males. The bond that unites her to her oppressors is not comparable to any other. The division of the sexes is a biological fact, not an event in human history. Male and female stand opposed within a primordial *Mitsein,* and woman has not broken it. The couple is a fundamental unity with its two halves riveted together, and the cleavage of society along the line of sex is impossible. Here is to be found the basic trait of woman: she is the Other in a totality of which the two components are necessary to one another.

. . . To decline to be the Other, to refuse to be a party to the deal —this would be for women to renounce all the advantages conferred upon them by their alliance with the superior caste. Man-the-sovereign will provide woman-the-liege with material protection and will undertake the moral justification of her existence; thus she can evade at once both economic risk and the metaphysical risk of a liberty in which ends and aims must be contrived without assistance. Indeed, along with the ethical urge of each individual to affirm his subjective existence, there is also the temptation to forgo liberty and become a thing. This is an inauspicious road, for he who takes it—passive, lost, ruined—becomes henceforth the creature of another's will, frustrated in his transcendence and deprived of every value. But it is an easy road; on it one avoids the strain involved in undertaking an authentic existence. When man makes of woman the *Other*, he may, then, expect her to manifest deep-seated tendencies toward complicity. Thus, woman may fail to lay claim to the status of subject because she lacks definite resources, because she feels the necessary bond that ties her to man regardless of reciprocity, and because she is often very well pleased with her role as the *Other*. . . . People have tirelessly sought to prove that woman is superior, inferior, or equal to man. Some say that, having been created after Adam, she is evidently a secondary being; others say on the contrary that Adam was only a rough draft and that God succeeded in producing the human being in perfection when He created Eve. Woman's brain is smaller; yes, but it is relatively larger. Christ was made a man; yes, but perhaps for his greater humility. Each argument at once suggests its opposite, and both are often fallacious. If we are to gain understanding, we must get out of these ruts; we must discard the vague notions of superiority, inferiority, equality which have hitherto corrupted every discussion of the subject and start afresh. . . .

But it is doubtless impossible to approach any human problem with a mind free from bias. The way in which questions are put, the points of view assumed, presuppose a relativity of interest; all characteristics imply values, and every objective description, so called, implies an ethical background. Rather than attempt to conceal principles more or less definitely implied, it is better to state them openly at the beginning. This will make it unnecessary to specify on every page in just what sense one uses such words as *superior, inferior, better, worse, progress, reaction,* and the like. If we survey some of the works on woman, we note that one of the points of view most frequently adopted is that of the public good, the general interest; and one always means by this the benefit of society as one wishes it to be maintained or established. For our part, we hold that the only public good is that which assures the private good of the citizens; we shall pass judgment on institutions according to their effectiveness in giving concrete opportunities to individuals. But we do not confuse the idea of private interest with that of happiness, although that is another common point of view. Are not women of the harem more happy than women voters? Is not the housekeeper happier than the working-woman? It is not too clear just what the word *happy* really means and still less what true values it may mask. There is no possibility of measuring the happiness of others, and it is always easy to describe as happy the situation in which one wishes to place them.

In particular those who are condemned to stagnation are often pronounced happy on the pretext that happiness consists in being at rest. This notion we reject, for our perspective is that of existentialist ethics. Every subject plays his part as such specifically through exploits or projects that serve as a mode of transcendence; he achieves liberty only through a continual reaching out toward other liberties. There is no justification for present existence other than its expansion into an indefinitely open future. Every time transcendence falls back into immanence, stagnation, there is a degradation of existence into the *"en-soi"*—the brutish life of subjection to given conditions—and of liberty into constraint and contingence. This downfall represents a moral fault if the subject consents to it; if it is inflicted upon him, it spells frustration and oppression. In both cases it is an absolute evil. Every individual concerned to justify his existence feels that his existence involves an undefined need to transcend himself, to engage in freely chosen projects.

Now, what peculiarly signalizes the situation of woman is that she—a free and autonomous being like all human creatures—nevertheless finds herself living in a world where men compel her to assume the status of the Other. They propose to stabilize her as object and to doom her to immanence since her transcendence is to be overshadowed and forever transcended by another ego (*conscience*) which is essential and sovereign. The drama of woman lies in this conflict between the fundamental aspirations of every subject (*ego*)—who always regards the self as the essential—and the compulsions of a situation in which she is the inessential. How can a human being in woman's situation attain fulfillment? What roads are open to her? Which are blocked? How can independence be recovered in a state of dependency? What circumstances limit woman's liberty and how can they be overcome? These are the fundamental questions on which I would fain throw some light. This means that I am interested in the fortunes of the individual as defined not in terms of happiness but in terms of liberty.

Quite evidently this problem would be without significance if we were to believe that woman's destiny is inevitably determined by physiological, psychological, or economic forces. Hence I shall discuss first of all the light in which woman is viewed by biology, psychoanalysis, and historical materialism. Next I shall try to show exactly how the concept of the "truly feminine" has been fashioned —why woman has been defined as the Other—and what have been the consequences from man's point of view. Then from woman's point of view I shall describe the world in which women must live; and thus we shall be able to envisage the difficulties in their way as, endeavoring to make their escape from the sphere hitherto assigned them, they aspire to full membership in the human race.

. . . .

We have seen that in spite of legends no physiological destiny imposes an eternal hostility upon Male and Female as such; even the famous praying mantis devours her male only for want of other food and for the good of the species: it is to this, the species, that all individuals are subordinated, from the top to the bottom of the scale of animal life. Moreover, humanity is something more than a mere species: it is a historical development; it is to be defined by the manner in which it deals with its natural, fixed characteristics, its *facticité*. Indeed, even with the most extreme bad faith in the world, it is impossible to demonstrate the existence of a rivalry between the human male and female of a truly physiological nature. Further, their hostility may be allocated rather to that intermediate terrain between biology and psychology: psychoanalysis. Woman, we are told, envies man his penis and wishes to castrate him; but the childish desire for the penis is important in the life of the adult woman only if she feels her femininity as a mutilation; and then it is as a symbol of all the privileges of manhood that she wishes to appropriate the male organ. We may readily agree that her dream of castration has this symbolic significance: she wishes, it is thought, to deprive the male of his transcendence.

But her desire, as we have seen, is much more ambiguous: she wishes, in a contradictory fashion, *to have* this transcendence, which is to suppose that she at once respects it and denies it, that she intends at once to throw herself into it and keep it within herself. This is to say that the drama does not unfold on a sexual level; further, sexuality has never seemed to us to define a destiny, to furnish in itself the key to human behavior, but to express the totality of a situation that it only helps to define. The battle of the *sexes* is not immediately implied in the anatomy of man and woman. The truth is that when one evokes it, one takes for granted that in the timeless realm of Ideas a battle is being waged between those vague essences the Eternal Feminine and the Eternal Masculine; and one neglects the fact that this titanic combat assumes on earth two totally different forms, corresponding with two different moments of history.

The woman who is shut up in immanence endeavors to hold man in that prison also; thus the prison will be confused with the world, and woman will no longer suffer from being confined there: mother, wife, sweetheart are the jailers. Society, being codified by man, decrees that woman is inferior: she can do away with this inferiority only by destroying the male's superiority. She sets about mutilating, dominating man, she contradicts him, she denies his truth and his values. But in doing this she is only defending herself; it was neither a changeless essence nor a mistaken choice that doomed her to immanence, to inferiority. They were imposed upon her. All oppression creates a state of war. And this is no exception. The existent who is regarded as inessential cannot fail to demand the re-establishment of her sovereignty.

Today the combat takes a different shape; instead of wishing to put man in a prison, woman endeavors to escape from one; she no longer seeks to drag him into the realms of immanence but to emerge, herself, into the light of transcendence. Now the attitude of the males creates a new conflict; it is with a bad grace that the man lets her go. He is very well pleased to remain the sovereign subject, the absolute superior, the essential being; he refuses to accept his companion as an equal in any concrete way. She replies to his lack of confidence in her by assuming an aggressive attitude. It is no longer a question of a war between individuals each shut up in his or her sphere: a caste claiming its rights goes over the top and it is resisted by the privileged caste. Here two transcendences are face to face; instead of displaying mutual recognition, each free being wishes to dominate the other.

This difference of attitude is manifest on the sexual plane as on the spiritual plane. The "feminine" woman in making herself prey tries to reduce man, also, to her carnal passivity; she occupies herself in catching him in her trap, in enchanting him by means of the desire she arouses in him in submissively making herself a thing. The emancipated woman, on the contrary, wants to be active, a taker, and refuses the passivity man means to impose on her. Thus Elise and her emulators deny the values of the activities of virile type; they put the flesh above the spirit, contingence above liberty, their routine wisdom above creative audacity. But the "modern" woman accepts masculine values: she prides herself on thinking, taking action, working, creating, on the same terms as men; instead of seeking to disparage them, she declares herself their equal. In so far as she expresses herself in definite action, this claim is legitimate, and male insolence must then bear the blame. But in men's defense it must be said that women are wont to confuse the issue. A Mabel Dodge Luhan intended to subjugate D. H. Lawrence by her feminine charms so as to dominate him spiritually thereafter; many women, in order to show by their successes their equivalence to men, try to secure male support by sexual means; they play on both sides, demanding old-fashioned respect and modern esteem, banking on their old magic and their new rights. It is understandable that a man becomes irritated and puts himself on the defensive; but he is also double-dealing when he requires women to play the game fairly while he denies them the indispensable trump cards through distrust and hostility. Indeed, the struggle cannot be clearly drawn between them, since woman is opaque in her very being; she stands before man not as a subject but as an object paradoxically endued with subjectivity; she takes herself simultaneously as *self* and as *other*, a contradiction that entails baffling consequences. When she makes weapons at once of her weakness and of her strength, it is not a matter of designing calculation: she seeks salvation spontaneously in the way that has been imposed on her, that of passivity, at the same time when she is actively demanding her sovereignty; and no doubt this procedure is unfair tactics, but it is dictated to her by the ambiguous situation assigned her. Man, however, becomes indignant when he treats her as a free and independent being and then realizes that she is still a trap for him; if he gratifies and satisfies her in her posture as prey, he finds her claims to autonomy irritating; whatever he does, he feels tricked and she feels wronged.

The quarrel will go on as long as men and women fail to recognize each other as peers; that is to say, as long as femininity is perpetuated as such. Which sex is the more eager to maintain it? Woman, who is being emancipated from it, wishes none the less to retain its privileges; and man, in that case, wants her to assume its limitations. "It is easier to accuse one sex than to excuse the other," says Montaigne. It is vain to apportion praise and blame. The truth is that if the vicious circle is so hard to break, it is because the two sexes are each the victim at once of the other and of itself. Between two adversaries confronting each other in their pure liberty, an agreement could be easily reached: the more so as the war profits neither. But the complexity of the whole affair derives from the fact that each camp is giving aid and comfort to the enemy; woman is pursuing a dream of submission, man a dream of identification. Want of authenticity does not pay: each blames the other for the unhappiness he or she has incurred in yielding to the temptations of the easy way; what man and woman loathe in each other is the shattering frustration of each one's own bad faith and baseness.

We have seen why men enslaved women in the first place; the devaluation of femininity has been a necessary step in human evolution, but it might have led to collaboration between the two sexes; oppression is to be explained by the tendency of the existent to flee from himself by means of identification with the other, whom he oppresses to that end. In each individual man that tendency exists today; and the vast majority yield to it. The husband wants to find himself in his wife, the lover in his mistress, in the form of a stone image; he is seeking in her the myth of his virility, of his sovereignty, of his immediate reality. "My husband never goes to the movies," says his wife, and the dubious masculine opinion is graved in the marble of eternity. But he is himself the slave of his double: what an effort to build up an image in which he is always in danger! In spite of everything his success in this depends upon the capricious freedom of women: he must constantly try to keep this propitious to him. Man is concerned with the effort to appear male, important, superior; he pretends so as to get pretense in return; he, too, is aggressive, uneasy; he feels hostility for women because he is afraid of them, he is afraid of them because he is afraid of the personage, the image, with which he identifies himself. What time and strength he squanders in liquidating, sublimating, transferring complexes, in talking about women, in seducing them, in fearing them! He would be liberated himself in their liberation. But this is precisely what he dreads. And so he obstinately persists in the mystifications intended to keep woman in her chains.

That she is being tricked, many men have realized. "What a misfortune to be a woman! And yet the misfortune, when one is a woman, is at bottom not to comprehend that it is one," says Kierkegaard.[3] For a long time there have been efforts to disguise this misfortune. For example, guardianship has been done away with: women have been given "protectors," and if they are invested with the rights of the old-time guardians, it is in woman's own interest. To forbid her working, to keep her at home, is to defend her against herself and to assure her happiness. We have seen what poetic veils are thrown over her monotonous burdens of housekeeping and maternity: in exchange for her liberty she has received the false treasures of her "femininity." Balzac illustrates this maneuver very well in counseling man to treat her as a slave while persuading her that she is a queen. Less cynical, many men try to convince themselves that she is really privileged. There are American sociologists who seriously teach today the theory of "low-class gain." In France, also, it has often been proclaimed—although in a less scientific manner—that the workers are very fortunate in not being obliged to "keep up appearances" and still more so the bums who can dress in rags and sleep on the sidewalks, pleasures forbidden to the Count de Beaumont and the Wendels. Like the carefree wretches gaily scratching at their vermin, like the merry Negroes laughing under the lash and those joyous Tunisian Arabs burying their starved children with a smile, woman enjoys that incomparable privilege: irresponsibility. Free from troublesome burdens and cares, she obviously has "the better part." But it is disturbing that with an obstinate perversity—connected no doubt with original sin—down through the centuries and in all countries, the people who

3. *In Vino Veritas.* He says further: "Politeness is pleasing—essentially—to woman, and the fact that she accepts it without hesitation is explained by nature's care for the weaker, for the unfavored being, and for one to whom an illusion means more than a material compensation. But this illusion, precisely, is fatal to her. . . . To feel oneself freed from distress thanks to something imaginary, to be the dupe of something imaginary, is that not a still deeper mockery? . . . Woman is very far from being *verwahrlost* (neglected), but in another sense she is, since she can never free herself from the illusion that nature has used to console her."

have the better part are always crying to their benefactors: "It is too much! I will be satisfied with yours!" But the munificent capitalists, the generous colonists, the superb males, stick to their guns: "Keep the better part, hold on to it!"

It must be admitted that the males find in woman more complicity than the oppressor usually finds in the oppressed. And in bad faith they take authorization from this to declare that she has *desired* the destiny they have imposed on her. We have seen that all the main features of her training combine to bar her from the roads of revolt and adventure. Society in general—beginning with her respected parents—lies to her by praising the lofty values of love, devotion, the gift of herself, and then concealing from her the fact that neither lover nor husband nor yet her children will be inclined to accept the burdensome charge of all that. She cheerfully believes these lies because they invite her to follow the easy slope: in this others commit their worst crime against her; throughout her life from childhood on, they damage and corrupt her by designating as her true vocation this submission, which is the temptation of every existent in the anxiety of liberty. If a child is taught idleness by being amused all day long and never being led to study, or shown its usefulness, it will hardly be said, when he grows up, that he chose to be incapable and ignorant; yet this is how woman is brought up, without ever being impressed with the necessity of taking charge of her own existence. So she readily lets herself come to count on the protection, love, assistance, and supervision of others, she lets herself be fascinated with the hope of self-realization without *doing* anything. She does wrong in yielding to the temptation; but man is in no position to blame her, since he has led her into the temptation. When conflict arises between them, each will hold the other responsible for the situation; she will reproach him with having made her what she is: "No one taught me to reason or to earn my own living"; he will reproach her with having accepted the consequences: "You don't know anything, you are an incompetent," and so on. Each sex thinks it can justify itself by taking the offensive; but the wrongs done by one do not make the other innocent.

The innumerable conflicts that set men and women against one another come from the fact that neither is prepared to assume all the consequences of this situation which the one has offered and the other accepted. The doubtful concept of "equality in inequality," which the one uses to mask his despotism and the other to mask her cowardice, does not stand the test of experience: in their exchanges, woman appeals to the theoretical equality she has been guaranteed, and man the concrete inequality that exists. The result is that in every association an endless debate goes on concerning the ambiguous meaning of the words *give* and *take:* she complains of giving her all, he protests that she takes his all. Woman has to learn that exchanges—it is a fundamental law of political economy—are based on the value the merchandise offered has for the buyer, and not for the seller: she has been deceived in being persuaded that her worth is priceless. The truth is that for man she is an amusement, a pleasure, company, an inessential boon; he is for her the meaning, the justification of her existence. The exchange, therefore, is not of two items of equal value.

This inequality will be especially brought out in the fact that the time they spend together—which fallaciously seems to be the same time—does not have the same value for both partners. During the evening the lover spends with his mistress he could be doing something of advantage to his career, seeing friends, cultivating business relationships, seeking recreation; for a man normally integrated in society, time is a positive value: money, reputation, pleasure. For the idle, bored woman, on the contrary, it is a burden she wishes to get rid of; when she succeeds in killing time, it is a benefit to her: the man's presence is pure profit. In a liaison what most clearly interests the man, in many cases, is the sexual benefit he gets from it: if need be, he can be content to spend no more time with his mistress than is required for the sexual act; but—with exceptions—what she, on her part, wants is to kill all the excess time she has on her hands; and—like the storekeeper who will not sell potatoes unless the customer will take turnips also—she will not yield her body unless her lover will take hours of conversation and "going out" into the bargain. A balance is reached if, on the whole, the cost does not seem too high to the man, and this depends, of course, on the strength of his desire and the importance he gives to what is to be sacrificed. But if the woman demands—offers—too much time, she becomes wholly intrusive, like the river overflowing its banks, and the man will prefer to have nothing rather than too much. Then she reduces her demands; but very often the balance is reached at the cost of a double tension: she feels that the man has "had" her at a bargain, and he thinks her price is too high. This analysis, of course, is put in somewhat humorous terms; but—except for those affairs of jealous and exclusive passions in which the man wants total possession of the woman—this conflict constantly appears in cases of affection, desire, and even love. He always has "other things to do" with his time; whereas she has time to burn; and he considers much of the time she gives him not as a gift but as a burden.

As a rule he consents to assume the burden because he knows very well that he is on the privileged side, he has a bad conscience; and if he is of reasonable good will he tries to compensate for the inequality by being generous. He prides himself on his compassion, however, and at the first clash he treats the woman as ungrateful and thinks, with some irritation: "I'm too good for her." She feels she is behaving like a beggar when she is convinced of the high value of her gifts, and that humiliates her.

Here we find the explanation of the cruelty that woman often shows she is capable of practicing; she has a good conscience because she is on the unprivileged side; she feels she is under no obligation to deal gently with the favored caste, and her only thought is to defend herself. She will even be very happy if she has occasion to show her resentment to a lover who has not been able to satisfy all her demands: since he does not give her enough, she takes savage delight in taking back everything from him. At this point the wounded lover suddenly discovers the value *in toto* of a liaison each moment of which he held more or less in contempt: he is ready to promise her everything, even though he will feel exploited again when he has to make good. He accuses his mistress of blackmailing him: she calls him stingy; both feel wronged.

Once again it is useless to apportion blame and excuses: justice can never be done in the midst of injustice. A colonial administrator has no possibility of acting rightly toward the natives, nor a general toward his soldiers; the only solution is to be neither colonist nor military chief; but a man could not prevent himself from being a man. So there he is, culpable in spite of himself and laboring under the effects of a fault he did not himself commit; and here she is, victim and shrew in spite of herself. Sometimes he rebels and becomes cruel, but then he makes himself an accomplice of the injustice, and the fault becomes really his. Sometimes he lets himself be annihilated, devoured, by his demanding victim; but in that case he feels duped. Often he stops at a compromise that at once belittles him and leaves him ill at ease. A well-disposed man will be more tortured by the situation than the woman herself: in a sense it is always better to be on the side of the vanquished; but if she is well-disposed also, incapable of self-sufficiency, reluctant to crush the man with the weight of her destiny, she struggles in hopeless confusion.

In daily life we meet with an abundance of these cases which are incapable of satisfactory solution because they are determined by unsatisfactory conditions. A man who is compelled to go on materially and morally supporting a woman whom he no longer loves feels he is victimized; but if he abandons without resources the woman who has pledged her whole life to him, she will be quite as unjustly victimized. The evil originates not in the perversity of individuals—and bad faith first appears when each blames the other—it originates rather in a situation against which all individual action is powerless. Women are "clinging," they are a dead weight, and they suffer for it; the point is that their situation is like that of a parasite sucking out the living strength of another organism. Let them be provided with living strength of their own, let them have the means to attack the world and wrest from it their own subsistence, and their dependence will be abolished—that of man also. There is no doubt that both men and women will profit greatly from the new situation.

A world where men and women would be equal is easy to visualize, for that precisely is what the Soviet Revolution *promised:* women raised and trained exactly like men were to work under the same conditions[4] and for the same wages. Erotic liberty was to be recognized by custom, but the sexual act was not to be considered a "service" to be paid for; woman was to be *obliged* to provide herself with other ways of earning a living; marriage was to be based on a free agreement that the spouses could break at will; maternity was to be voluntary, which meant that contraception and abortion were to be authorized and that, on the other hand, all mothers and their children were to have exactly the same rights, in or out of marriage; pregnancy leaves were to be paid for by the State, which would assume charge of the children, signifying not that they would be *taken away* from their parents, but that they would not be *abandoned* to them.

But is it enough to change laws, institutions, customs, public opinion, and the whole social context, for men and women to become truly equal? "Women will always be women," say the skeptics. Other seers prophesy that in casting off their femininity they will not succeed in changing themselves into men and they will become monsters. This would be to admit that the woman of today is a creation of nature; it must be repeated once more that in human society nothing is natural and that woman, like much else, is a product elaborated by civilization. The intervention of others in her destiny is fundamental: if this action took a different direction, it would produce a quite different result. Woman is determined not by her hormones or by mysterious instincts, but by the manner in which her body and her relation to the world are modified through the action of others than herself. The abyss that separates the adolescent boy and girl has been deliberately opened out between them since earliest childhood; later on, woman could not be other than what she *was made,* and that past was bound to shadow her for life. If we appreciate its influence, we see clearly that her destiny is not predetermined for all eternity.

We must not believe, certainly, that a change in woman's economic condition alone is enough to transform her, though this fac-

4. That certain too laborious occupations were to be closed to women is not in contradiction to this project. Even among men there is an increasing effort to obtain adaptation to profession; their varying physical and mental capacities limit their possibilities of choice; what is asked is that, in any case, no line of sex or caste be drawn.

tor has been and remains the basic factor in her evolution; but until it has brought about the moral, social, cultural, and other consequences that it promises and requires, the new woman cannot appear. At this moment they have been realized nowhere, in Russia no more than in France or the United States; and this explains why the woman of today is torn between the past and the future. She appears most often as a "true woman" disguised as a man, and she feels herself as ill at ease in her flesh as in her masculine garb. She must shed her old skin and cut her own new clothes. This she could do only through a social evolution. No single educator could fashion a *female human being* today who would be the exact homologue of the *male human being;* if she is raised like a boy, the young girl feels she is an oddity and thereby she is given a new kind of sex specification. Stendhal understood this when he said: "The forest must be planted all at once." But if we imagine, on the contrary, a society in which the equality of the sexes would be concretely realized, this equality would find new expression in each individual.

If the little girl were brought up from the first with the same demands and rewards, the same severity and the same freedom, as her brothers, taking part in the same studies, the same games, promised the same future, surrounded with women and men who seemed to her undoubted equals, the meanings of the castration complex and of the Oedipus complex would be profoundly modified. Assuming on the same basis as the father the material and moral responsibility of the couple, the mother would enjoy the same lasting prestige; the child would perceive around her an androgynous world and not a masculine world. Were she emotionally more attracted to her father—which is not even sure—her love for him would be tinged with a will to emulation and not a feeling of powerlessness; she would not be oriented toward passivity. Authorized to test her powers in work and sports, competing actively with the boys, she would not find the absence of the penis —compensated by the promise of a child—enough to give rise to an inferiority complex; correlatively, the boy would not have a superiority complex if it were not instilled into him and if he looked up to women with as much respect as to men.[5] The little girl would not seek sterile compensation in narcissism and dreaming, she would not take her fate for granted; she would be interested in what she was *doing,* she would throw herself without reserve into undertakings.

5. I knew a little boy of eight who lived with his mother, aunt, and grandmother, all independent and active women, and his weak old half-crippled grandfather. He had a crushing inferiority complex in regard to the feminine sex, although he made efforts to combat it. At school he scorned comrades and teachers because they were miserable males.

I have already pointed out how much easier the transformation of puberty would be if she looked beyond it, like the boys, toward a free adult future: menstruation horrifies her only because it is an abrupt descent into femininity. She would also take her young eroticism in much more tranquil fashion if she did not feel a frightened disgust for her destiny as a whole; coherent sexual information would do much to help her over this crisis. And thanks to coeducational schooling, the august mystery of Man would have no occasion to enter her mind: it would be eliminated by everyday familiarity and open rivalry.

Objections raised against this system always imply respect for sexual taboos; but the effort to inhibit all sex curiosity and pleasure in the child is quite useless; one succeeds only in creating repressions, obsessions, neuroses. The excessive sentimentality, homosexual fervors, and platonic crushes of adolescent girls, with all their train of silliness and frivolity, are much more injurious than a little childish sex play and a few definite sex experiences. It would be beneficial above all for the young girl not to be influenced against taking charge herself of her own existence, for then she would not seek a demigod in the male—merely a comrade, a friend, a partner. Eroticism and love would take on the nature of free transcendence and not that of resignation; she could experience them as a relation between equals. There is no intention, of course, to remove by a stroke of the pen all the difficulties that the child has to overcome in changing into an adult; the most intelligent, the most tolerant education could not relieve the child of experiencing things for herself; what could be asked is that obstacles should not be piled gratuitously in her path. Progress is already shown by the fact that "vicious" little girls are no longer cauterized with a red-hot iron. Psychoanalysis has given parents some instruction, but the conditions under which, at the present time, the sexual training and initiation of woman are accomplished are so deplorable that none of the objections advanced against the idea of a radical change could be considered valid. It is not a question of abolishing in woman the contingencies and miseries of the human condition, but of giving her the means for transcending them.

Woman is the victim of no mysterious fatality; the peculiarities that identify her as specifically a woman get their importance from the significance placed upon them. They can be surmounted, in the future, when they are regarded in new perspectives. Thus, as we have seen, through her erotic experience woman feels—and often detests—the domination of the male; but this is no reason to conclude that her ovaries condemn her to live forever on her knees. Virile aggressiveness seems like a lordly privilege only within a system that in its entirety conspires to affirm masculine sovereignty; and woman *feels* herself profoundly passive in the sexual act only because she already *thinks* of herself as such. Many modern women who lay claim to their dignity as human beings still envisage their erotic life from the standpoint of a tradition of slavery: since it seems to them humiliating to lie beneath the man, to be penetrated by him, they grow tense in frigidity. But if the reality were different, the meaning expressed symbolically in amorous gestures and postures would be different, too: a woman who pays and dominates her lover can, for example, take pride in her superb idleness and consider that she is enslaving the male who is actively exerting himself. And here and now there are many sexually well-balanced couples whose notions of victory and defeat are giving place to the idea of an exchange.

As a matter of fact, man, like woman, is flesh, therefore passive, the plaything of his hormones and of the species, the restless prey of his desires. And she, like him, in the midst of the carnal fever, is a consenting, a voluntary gift, an activity; they live out in their several fashions the strange ambiguity of existence made body. In those combats where they think they confront one another, it is really against the self that each one struggles, projecting into the partner that part of the self which is repudiated; instead of living out the ambiguities of their situation, each tries to make the other bear the abjection and tries to reserve the honor for the self. If, however, both should assume the ambiguity with a clear-sighted modesty, correlative of an authentic pride, they could see each other as equals and would live out their erotic drama in amity. The fact that we are human beings is infinitely more important than all the peculiarities that distinguish human beings from one another; it is never the given that confers superiorities: "virtue," as the ancients called it, is defined at the level of "that which depends on us." In both sexes is played out the same drama of the flesh and the spirit, of finitude and transcendence; both are gnawed away by time and laid in wait for by death, they have the same essential need for one another; and they can gain from their liberty the same glory. If they were to taste it, they would no longer be tempted to dispute fallacious privileges, and fraternity between them could then come into existence.

I shall be told that all this is utopian fancy, because woman cannot be "made over" unless society has first made her really the equal of man. Conservatives have never failed in such circumstances to refer to that vicious circle; history, however, does not revolve. If a caste is kept in a state of inferiority, no doubt it remains inferior; but liberty can break the circle. Let the Negroes vote and they become worthy of having the vote; let woman be given responsibilities and she is able to assume them. The fact is that oppressors cannot be expected to make a move of gratuitous generosity; but at one time the revolt of the oppressed, at another time even the very evolution of the privileged caste itself, creates new situations; thus men have been led, in their own interest, to give partial emancipation to women: it remains only for women to continue their ascent, and the successes they are obtaining are an encouragement for them to do so. It seems almost certain that sooner or later they will arrive at complete economic and social equality, which will bring about an inner metamorphosis.

However this may be, there will be some to object that if such a world is possible it is not desirable. When woman is "the same" as her male, life will lose its salt and spice. This argument, also, has lost its novelty: those interested in perpetuating present conditions are always in tears about the marvelous past that is about to disappear, without having so much as a smile for the young future. It is quite true that doing away with the slave trade meant death to the great plantations, magnificent with azaleas and camellias, it meant ruin to the whole refined Southern civilization. The attics of time have received its rare odd laces along with the clear pure voices of the Sistine *castrati,* and there is a certain "feminine charm" that is also on the way to the same dusty repository. I agree that he would be a barbarian indeed who failed to appreciate exquisite flowers, rare lace, the crystal-clear voice of the eunuch, and feminine charm.

When the "charming woman" shows herself in all her splendor, she is a much more exalting object than the "idiotic paintings, overdoors, scenery, showman's garish signs, popular chromos," that excited Rimbaud; adorned with the most modern artifices, beautified according to the newest techniques, she comes down from the remoteness of the ages, from Thebes, from Crete, from Chichén-Itzá; and she is also the totem set up deep in the African jungle; she is a helicopter and she is a bird; and there is this, the greatest wonder of all: under her tinted hair the forest murmur becomes a thought, and words issue from her breasts. Men stretch forth avid hands toward the marvel, but when they grasp it it is gone; the wife, the mistress, speak like everybody else through their mouths: their words are worth just what they are worth; their breasts also. Does such a fugitive miracle—and one so rare—justify us in perpetuating a situation that is baneful for both sexes? One can appreciate the beauty of flowers, the charm of women, and appreciate them at their true value; if these treasures cost blood or misery, they must be sacrificed.

But in truth this sacrifice seems to men a peculiarly heavy one; few of them really wish in their hearts for woman to succeed in making it; those among them who hold woman in contempt see in the sacrifice nothing for them to gain, those who cherish her see too much that they would lose. And it is true that the evolution now in progress threatens more than feminine charm alone: in beginning to exist for herself, woman will relinquish the function as double and mediator to which she owes her privileged place in the masculine universe; to man, caught between the silence of nature and the demanding presence of other free beings, a creature who is at once his like and a passive thing seems a great treasure. The guise in which he conceives his companion may be mythical, but the experiences for which she is the source or the pretext are none the less real: there are hardly any more precious, more intimate, more ardent. There is no denying that feminine dependence, inferiority, woe, give women their special character; assuredly woman's autonomy, if it spares men many troubles, will also deny them many conveniences; assuredly there are certain forms of the sexual adventure which will be lost in the world of tomorrow. But this does not mean that love, happiness, poetry, dream, will be banished from it.

Let us not forget that our lack of imagination always depopulates the future; for us it is only an abstraction; each one of us secretly deplores the absence there of the one who was himself. But the humanity of tomorrow will be living in its flesh and in its conscious liberty; that time will be its present and it will in turn prefer it. New relations of flesh and sentiment of which we have no conception will arise between the sexes; already, indeed, there have appeared between men and women friendships, rivalries, complicities, comradeships—chaste or sensual—which past centuries could not have conceived. To mention one point, nothing could seem to me more debatable than the opinion that dooms the new world to uniformity and hence to boredom. I fail to see that this present world is free from boredom or that liberty ever creates uniformity.

To begin with, there will always be certain differences between man and woman; her eroticism, and therefore her sexual world, have a special form of their own and therefore cannot fail to engender a sensuality, a sensitivity, of a special nature. This means that her relations to her own body, to that of the male, to the child, will never be identical with those the male bears to his own body, to that of the female, and to the child; those who make much of "equality in difference" could not with good grace refuse to grant me the possible existence of differences in equality. Then again, it is institutions that create uniformity. Young and pretty, the slaves of the harem are always the same in the sultan's embrace; Christianity gave eroticism its savor of sin and legend when it endowed the human female with a soul; if society restores her sovereign individuality to woman, it will not thereby destroy the power of love's embrace to move the heart.

It is nonsense to assert that revelry, vice, ecstasy, passion, would become impossible if man and woman were equal in concrete matters; the contradictions that put the flesh in opposition to the spirit, the instant to time, the swoon of immanence to the challenge of transcendence, the absolute of pleasure to the nothingness of forgetting, will never be resolved; in sexuality will always be materialized the tension, the anguish, the joy, the frustration, and the triumph of existence. To emancipate woman is to refuse to confine her to the relations she bears to man, not to deny them to her; let her have her independent existence and she will continue none the less to exist for him *also:* mutually recognizing each other as subject, each will yet remain for the other an *other*. The reciprocity of their relations will not do away with the miracles—desire, possession, love, dream, adventure—worked by the division of human beings into two separate categories; and the words that move us—giving, conquering, uniting—will not lose their meaning. On the contrary, when we abolish the slavery of half of humanity, together with the whole system of hypocrisy that it implies, then the "division" of humanity will reveal its genuine significance and the human couple will find its true form. "The direct, natural, necessary relation of human creatures is the *relation of man to woman,*" Marx has said.[6] "The nature of this relation determines to what point man himself is to be considered as a *generic being*, as mankind; the relation of man to woman is the most natural relation of human being to human being. By it is shown, therefore, to what point the *natural* behavior of man has become *human* or to what point the *human* being has become his *natural* being, to what point his *human nature* has become his *nature*."

The case could not be better stated. It is for man to establish the reign of liberty in the midst of the world of the given. To gain the supreme victory, it is necessary, for one thing, that by and through their natural differentiation men and women unequivocally affirm their brotherhood.

* * *

SUGGESTIONS FOR FURTHER READING

Existentialism

Allen, Jeffner and Young, Iris Marion (eds.). *The Thinking Muse: Feminism and Modern French Philosophy.* Bloomington: Indiana University Press, 1989.

Becker-Theye, Betty. *The Seducer as Mythic Figure in Richardson, Laclos and Kierkegaard.* New York: Garland, 1988.

Berfoffen, Debra B. "On the Advantage and Disadvantage of Nietzsche for Women." In *The Question of the Other: Essays in Contemporary Continental Philosophy*, ed. by Arleen B. Dallery

6. *Philosophical Works,* Vol. VI (Marx's italics).

and Charles E. Scott. Albany: State University of New York Press, 1989, pp. 77–88.

Bertram, Maryanne J. "God's 'Second' Blunder—Serpent Woman and the 'Gestalt' in Nietzsche's Thought." *Southern Journal of Philosophy* 19 (Fall 1981), pp. 259–78.

Card, Claudia. "Lesbian Attitudes and 'The Second Sex.'" *Hypatia* 3 (1985), pp. 209–14.

Collins, Margery L. and Pierce, Christine. "Holes and Slime: Sexism in Sartre's Psychoanalysis." In *Women and Philosophy*, ed. by Carol C. Gould and Marx W. Wartofsky. New York: G. P. Putnam and Sons, 1976, pp. 112–27.

Dallery, Arleen B. "Sexual Embodiment: Beauvoir and French Feminism (*Ecriture Feminine*)." *Hypatia* 3 (1985), pp. 197–202.

de Beauvoir, Simone. *Memoirs of a Dutiful Daughter*, trans. by James Kirkup. Baltimore: Penguin Books, 1974.

Diethe, Carol. "Nietzsche and the Woman Question." *History of European Ideas* (1989), pp. 865–75.

Diprose, Rosalyn. "Nietzsche, Ethics and Sexual Difference." *Radical Philosophy* 52 (Summer 1989), pp. 27–33.

Felsteiner, Mary Lowenthal. "Seeing 'The Second Sex' Through the Second Wave." *Feminist Studies* 6 (Summer 1980), pp. 247–76.

Ferguson, Ann. "Lesbian Identity: Beauvoir and History." *Hypatia* 3 (1985), pp. 203–8.

Frisbe, Sandra. "Women and the Will to Power." *Gnosis* 1 (Spring 1975), pp. 1–10.

Fuchs, Jo-Ann P. "Female Eroticism in 'The Second Sex.'" *Feminist Studies* 6 (Summer 1980), pp. 304–13.

Graybeal, Jean. *Language and 'the Feminine' in Nietzsche and Heidegger*. Bloomington: Indiana University Press, 1990.

Hatab, Lawrence J. "Nietzsche on Woman." *Southern Journal of Philosophy* 19 (Fall 1981), pp. 333–46.

Kainz, Howard P. "The Relationship of Dread to Spirit in Man and Woman, according to Kierkegaard." *The Modern Schoolman* 47, 1 (Nov. 1969), pp. 1–13.

Kennedy, Ellen. "Nietzsche: Women as 'Untermensch.'" In *Women in Western Political Philosophy: Kant to Nietzsche*, ed. by Ellen Kennedy and Susan Mendus. New York: St. Martin's Press, 1987, pp. 179–201.

Krell, David Farrell. *Postponements: Woman, Sensuality, and Death in Nietzsche*. Bloomington: Indiana University Press, 1986.

Lazaro, Reyes. "Feminism and Motherhood: O'Brien vs. Beauvoir." *Hypatia* 1 (Fall 1986), pp. 87–102.

Le Doeuff, Michele. "Simone de Beauvoir and Existentialism." *Feminist Studies* 6 (Summer 1980), pp. 277–89.

Leighton, Jean, *Simone de Beauvoir on Woman*. Rutherford, N.J.: Fairleigh Dickinson University Press, 1975.

Leon, Celine T., "Simone de Beauvoir's Woman: Eunuch or Male?" *Ultimate Reality and Meaning* 11 (Summer 1988), pp. 196–211.

Oliver, Kelly A., "Woman as Truth in Nietzsche's Writing." *Social Theory and Practice* 10 (Summer 1984), pp. 185–200.

______. "Nietzsche's Woman." *Radical Philosophy* 48 (Spring 1988), pp. 25–29.

Parsons, Katherine. "Nietzsche and Moral Change." *Feminist Studies* 2 (1974), pp. 57–76.

Pilardi, Jo-Ann. "The Changing Critical Fortunes of 'The Second Sex.'" *History and Theory* 32 (1993), pp. 51–73.

Shapiro, Gary. *Alcyone: Nietzsche on Gifts, Noise, and Women.* Albany: State University of New York Press, 1991.

Sijkstra, Sandra. "Simone de Beauvoir and Betty Friedan." *Feminist Studies* 6 (Summer 1980), pp. 290–303.

Simons, Margaret A. "Sexism and the Philosophical Canon: On Reading Beauvoir's 'The Second Sex.'" *Journal of the History of Ideas* 51 (1990), pp. 487–504.

Starrett, Shari Neller. "Nietzsche: Women and Relationships of Strength." *Southwest Philosophy Review* 6 (Jan. 1990), pp. 73–79.

Stern, Karl. "Kierkegaard." In *The Flight from Woman.* New York: Farrar, Straus and Giroux, 1965, pp. 199–226.

Thompson, J. L. "Nietzsche on Woman." *International Journal of Moral and Social Studies* (Autumn 1990), pp. 207–20.

Walsh, Sylvia I. "On 'Feminine' and 'Masculine' Forms of Despair." In *The Sickness Unto Death,* ed. by Robert L. Perkins. Macon, Ga.: Mercer University Press, 1987, pp. 121–34.

______. "Forming the Heart: The Role of Love in Kierkegaard's Thought." In *The Grammar of the Heart: New Essays in Moral Philosophy and Theology,* ed. by Richard H. Bell. San Francisco: Harper & Row, 1988, pp. 234–35.

PSYCHOANALYSIS

While there are diverse interpretations of psychoanalytic theory, these share certain claims about human nature and about a method for explaining mental functioning and human behavior. Basic to this theory is the role of the unconscious in psychic determinism. The human psyche is generally viewed as consisting of three structures: the id, the ego, and the superego, which interact and overlap in processes such as repression, projection, and transference. For each individual there are psychosexual stages of development: oral, anal, and genital, each describing an area of the body which is particularly responsive to pleasurable stimulation for a certain period; these correspond with stages of personality development in both sexes. Psychoanalytic therapy is designed to assist the individual to recall episodes of the past that lie buried in the unconscious. Supposedly, where such events have triggered undesirable behavior, recognition of their occurrence facilitates the overcoming of their debilitating influence.

SIGMUND FREUD

As founder of psychoanalysis, Sigmund Freud (1856–1939) not only elaborated its key concepts but precipitated much controversy because of the novelty and boldness of his ideas. In Freud's view the task of the ego is to reconcile the individual demands of the id with the social/moral demands of the superego; the healthy individual is one for whom as many demands as possible are fulfilled in light of the reality principle. Two basic human impulses, sexuality and aggression, account for personality differences from infancy through adulthood. An Oedipus complex explains how the initial bonding between infant and mother leads to repression of rivalry felt toward the parent of the same sex. The concept of penis envy is Freud's way of characterizing a little girl's reaction to her realization that she lacks the sexual organ of her male counterpart. Obviously this concept is suggestive of a broader level of application regarding female/male relations.

Femininity

To-day's lecture . . . brings forward nothing but observed facts, almost without any speculative additions, and it deals with a subject which has a claim on your interest second almost to no other.

Throughout history people have knocked their heads against the riddle of the nature of femininity—

> Häupter in Hieroglyphenmützen,
> Häupter in Turban und schwarzem Barett,
> Perückenhäupter und tausend andre
> Arme, schwitzende Menschenhäupter. . . .[1]

Nor will *you* have escaped worrying over this problem—those of you who are men; to those of you who are women this will not apply—you are yourselves the problem. When you meet a human being, the first distinction you make is 'male or female?' and you are accustomed to make the distinction with unhesitating certainty. Anatomical science shares your certainty at one point and not much further. The male sexual product, the spermatozoon, and its vehicle are male; the ovum and the organism that harbours it are female. In both sexes organs have been formed which serve exclusively for the sexual functions; they were probably developed from the same [innate] disposition into two different forms. Besides this, in both sexes the other organs, the bodily shapes and tissues, show the influence of the individual's sex, but this is inconstant and its amount variable; these are what are known as secondary sexual characters. Science next tells you something that runs counter to your expectations and is probably calculated to confuse your feelings. It draws your attention to the fact that portions of the male sexual apparatus also appear in women's bodies, though in an atrophied state, and vice versa in the alternative case. It regards their occurrence as indications of *bisexuality*, as though an individual is not a man or a woman but always both—merely a certain amount more the one than the other. You will then be asked to make yourselves familiar with the idea that the proportion in which masculine and feminine are mixed in an individual is subject to quite considerable fluctuations. Since, however, apart from the very rarest cases, only one kind of sexual product—ova or semen—is nevertheless present in one person, you are bound to have doubts as to the decisive significance of those elements and must conclude that what constitutes masculinity or femininity is an unknown characteristic which anatomy cannot lay hold of.

Can psychology do so perhaps? We are accustomed to employ 'masculine' and 'feminine' as mental qualities as well, and have in the same way transferred the notion of bisexuality to mental life.

1. Heads in hieroglyphic bonnets,
Heads in turbans and black birettas,
Heads in wigs and thousand other
Wretched, sweating heads of humans. . . .
(Heine, *Nordsee* [Second Cycle, VII, 'Fragen'].)

Thus we speak of a person, whether male or female, as behaving in a masculine way in one connection and in a feminine way in another. But you will soon perceive that this is only giving way to anatomy or to convention. You cannot give the concepts of 'masculine' and 'feminine' *any* new connotation. The distinction is not a psychological one; when you say 'masculine', you usually mean 'active', and when you say 'feminine', you usually mean 'passive'. Now it is true that a relation of the kind exists. The male sex-cell is actively mobile and searches out the female one, and the latter, the ovum, is immobile and waits passively. This behaviour of the elementary sexual organisms is indeed a model for the conduct of sexual individuals during intercourse. The male pursues the female for the purpose of sexual union, seizes hold of her and penetrates into her. But by this you have precisely reduced the characteristic of masculinity to the factor of aggressiveness so far as psychology is concerned. You may well doubt whether you have gained any real advantage from this when you reflect that in some classes of animals the females are the stronger and more aggressive and the male is active only in the single act of sexual union. This is so, for instance, with the spiders. Even the functions of rearing and caring for the young, which strike us as feminine *par excellence*, are not invariably attached to the female sex in animals. In quite high species we find that the sexes share the task of caring for the young between them or even that the male alone devotes himself to it. Even in the sphere of human sexual life you soon see how inadequate it is to make masculine behaviour coincide with activity and feminine with passivity. A mother is active in every sense towards her child; the act of lactation itself may equally be described as the mother suckling the baby or as her being sucked by it. The further you go from the narrow sexual sphere the more obvious will the 'error of superimposition'[2] become. Women can display great activity in various directions, men are not able to live in company with their own kind unless they develop a large amount of passive adaptability. If you now tell me that these facts go to prove precisely that both men and women are bisexual in the psychological sense, I shall conclude that you have decided in your own minds to make 'active' coincide with 'masculine' and 'passive' with 'feminine'. But I advise you against it. It seems to me to serve no useful purpose and adds nothing to our knowledge.

One might consider characterizing femininity psychologically as giving preference to passive aims. This is not, of course, the same thing as passivity; to achieve a passive aim may call for a large amount of activity. It is perhaps the case that in a woman, on the basis of her share in the sexual function, a preference for passive

2. [I.e., mistaking two different things for a single one.]

behaviour and passive aims is carried over into her life to a greater or lesser extent, in proportion to the limits, restricted or far-reaching, within which her sexual life thus serves as a model. But we must beware in this of underestimating the influence of social customs, which similarly force women into passive situations. All this is still far from being cleared up. There is one particularly constant relation between femininity and instinctual life which we do not want to overlook. The suppression of women's aggressiveness which is prescribed for them constitutionally and imposed on them socially favours the development of powerful masochistic impulses, which succeed, as we know, in binding erotically the destructive trends which have been diverted inwards. Thus masochism, as people say, is truly feminine. But if, as happens so often, you meet with masochism in men, what is left to you but to say that these men exhibit very plain feminine traits?

And now you are already prepared to hear that psychology too is unable to solve the riddle of femininity. The explanation must no doubt come from elsewhere, and cannot come till we have learnt how in general the differentiation of living organisms into two sexes came about. We know nothing about it, yet the existence of two sexes is a most striking characteristic of organic life which distinguishes it sharply from inanimate nature. However, we find enough to study in those human individuals who, through the possession of female genitals, are characterized as manifestly or predominantly feminine. In conformity with its peculiar nature, psychoanalysis does not try to describe what a woman is—that would be a task it could scarcely perform—but sets about enquiring how she comes into being, how a woman develops out of a child with a bisexual disposition. In recent times we have begun to learn a little about this, thanks to the circumstance that several of our excellent women colleagues in analysis have begun to work at the question. The discussion of this has gained special attractiveness from the distinction between the sexes. For the ladies, whenever some comparison seemed to turn out unfavourable to their sex, were able to utter a suspicion that we, the male analysts, had been unable to overcome certain deeply-rooted prejudices against what was feminine, and that this was being paid for in the partiality of our researches. We, on the other hand, standing on the ground of bisexuality, had no difficulty in avoiding impoliteness. We had only to say: 'This doesn't apply to *you*. You're the exception; on this point you're more masculine than feminine.'

We approach the investigation of the sexual development of women with two expectations. The first is that here once more the constitution will not adapt itself to its function without a struggle. The second is that the decisive turning-points will already have been prepared for or completed before puberty. Both expectations are promptly confirmed. Furthermore, a comparison with what happens with boys tells us that the development of a little girl into a normal woman is more difficult and more complicated, since it includes two extra tasks, to which there is nothing corresponding in the development of a man. Let us follow the parallel lines from their beginning. Undoubtedly the material is different to start with in boys and girls: it did not need psycho-analysis to establish that. The difference in the structure of the genitals is accompanied by other bodily differences which are too well known to call for mention. Differences emerge too in the instinctual disposition which give a glimpse of the later nature of women. A little girl is as a rule less aggressive, defiant and self-sufficient; she seems to have a greater need for being shown affection and on that account to be more dependent and pliant. It is probably only as a result of this pliancy that she can be taught more easily and quicker to control her excretions: urine and faeces are the first gifts that children make to those who look after them, and controlling them is the first concession to which the instinctual life of children can be induced. One gets an impression, too, that little girls are more intelligent and livelier than boys of the same age; they go out more to meet the external world and at the same time form stronger object-cathexes. I cannot say whether this lead in development has been confirmed by exact observations, but in any case there is no question that girls cannot be described as intellectually backward. These sexual differences are not, however, of great consequence: they can be outweighed by individual variations. For our immediate purposes they can be disregarded.

Both sexes seem to pass through the early phases of libidinal development in the same manner. It might have been expected that in girls there would already have been some lag in aggressiveness in the sadistic-anal phase, but such is not the case. Analysis of children's play has shown our women analysts that the aggressive impulses of little girls leave nothing to be desired in the way of abundance and violence. With their entry into the phallic phase the differences between the sexes are completely eclipsed by their agreements. We are now obliged to recognize that the little girl is a little man. In boys, as we know, this phase is marked by the fact that they have learnt how to derive pleasurable sensations from their small penis and connect its excited state with their ideas of sexual intercourse. Little girls do the same thing with their still smaller clitoris. It seems that with them all their masturbatory acts are carried out on this penis-equivalent, and that the truly feminine vagina is still undiscovered by both sexes. It is true that there are a few isolated reports of early vaginal sensations as well, but it could not be easy to distinguish these from sensations in the anus or vestibulum; in any case they cannot play a great part. We are entitled to keep to our view that in the phallic phase of girls the clitoris is the leading erotogenic zone. But it is not, of course, going to remain so. With the change to femininity the clitoris should wholly or in part hand over its sensitivity, and at the same time its importance, to the vagina. This would be one of the two tasks which a woman has to perform in the course of her development, whereas the more fortunate man has only to continue at the time of his sexual maturity the activity that he has previously carried out at the period of the early efflorescence of his sexuality.

We shall return to the part played by the clitoris; let us now turn to the second task with which a girl's development is burdened. A boy's mother is the first object of his love, and she remains so too during the formation of his Oedipus complex and, in essence, all through his life. For a girl too her first object must be her mother (and the figures of wet-nurses and foster-mothers that merge into her). The first object-cathexes occur in attachment to the satisfaction of the major and simple vital needs, and the circumstances of the care of children are the same for both sexes. But in the Oedipus situation the girl's father has become her love-object, and we expect that in the normal course of development she will find her way from this paternal object to her final choice of an object. In the course of time, therefore, a girl has to change her erotogenic zone and her object—both of which a boy retains. The question then arises of how this happens: in particular, how does a girl pass from her mother to an attachment to her father? or, in other words, how does she pass from her masculine phase to the feminine one to which she is biologically destined?

It would be a solution of ideal simplicity if we could suppose that from a particular age onwards the elementary influence of the mutual attraction between the sexes makes itself felt and impels the small woman towards men, while the same law allows the boy to continue with his mother. We might suppose in addition that in this the children are following the pointer given them by the sexual preference of their parents. But we are not going to find things so easy; we scarcely know whether we are to believe seriously in the power of which poets talk so much and with such enthusiasm but which cannot be further dissected analytically. We have found an answer of quite another sort by means of laborious investigations, the material for which at least was easy to arrive at. For you must know that the number of women who remain till a late age tenderly dependent on a paternal object, or indeed on their real father, is very great. We have established some surprising facts about these women with an intense attachment of long duration to their father. We knew, of course, that there had been a preliminary stage of attachment to the mother, but we did not know that it could be so rich in content and so long-lasting, and could leave behind so many opportunities for fixations and dispositions. During this time the girl's father is only a troublesome rival; in some cases the attachment to her mother lasts beyond the fourth year of life. Almost everything that we find later in her relation to her father was already present in this earlier attachment and has been transferred subsequently on to her father. In short, we get an impression that we cannot understand women unless we appreciate this phase of their pre-Oedipus attachment to their mother.

We shall be glad, then, to know the nature of the girl's libidinal relations to her mother. The answer is that they are of very many different kinds. Since they persist through all three phases of infantile sexuality, they also take on the characteristics of the different phases and express themselves by oral, sadistic-anal and phallic wishes. These wishes represent active as well as passive impulses; if we relate them to the differentiation of the sexes which is to appear later—though we should avoid doing so as far as possible—we may call them masculine and feminine. Besides this, they are completely ambivalent, both affectionate and of a hostile and aggressive nature. The latter often only come to light after being changed into anxiety ideas. It is not always easy to point to a formulation of these early sexual wishes; what is most clearly expressed is a wish to get the mother with child and the corresponding wish to bear her a child—both belonging to the phallic period and sufficiently surprising, but established beyond doubt by analytic observation. The attractiveness of these investigations lies in the surprising detailed findings which they bring us. Thus, for instance, we discover the fear of being murdered or poisoned, which may later form the core of a paranoic illness, already present in this pre-Oedipus period, in relation to the mother. Or another case: you will recall an interesting episode in the history of analytic research which caused me many distressing hours. In the period in which the main interest was directed to discovering infantile sexual traumas, almost all my women patients told me that they had been seduced by their father. I was driven to recognize in the end that these reports were untrue and so came to understand that hysterical symptoms are derived from phantasies and not from real occurrences. It was only later that I was able to recognize in this phantasy of being seduced by the father the expression of the typical Oedipus complex in women. And now we find the phantasy of seduction once more in the pre-Oedipus prehistory of girls; but the seducer is regularly the mother. Here, however, the phantasy touches the ground of reality, for it was really the mother who by her activities over the child's bodily hygiene inevitably stimulated, and perhaps even roused for the first time, pleasurable sensations in her genitals.

I have no doubt you are ready to suspect that this portrayal of the abundance and strength of a little girl's sexual relations with her mother is very much overdrawn. After all, one has opportunities of seeing little girls and notices nothing of the sort. But the objection is not to the point. Enough can be seen in the children if one knows how to look. And besides, you should consider how little of its sexual wishes a child can bring to preconscious expression or communicate at all. Accordingly we are only within our rights if we study the residues and consequences of this emotional world in retrospect, in people in whom these processes of development had attained a specially clear and even excessive degree of expansion. Pathology has always done us the service of making discernible by isolation and exaggeration conditions which would remain concealed in a normal state. And since our investigations have been carried out on people who were by no means seriously abnormal, I think we should regard their outcome as deserving belief.

We will now turn our interest on to the single question of what it is that brings this powerful attachment of the girl to her mother to an end. This, as we know, is its usual fate: it is destined to make room for an attachment to her father. Here we come upon a fact which is a pointer to our further advance. This step in development does not involve only a simple change of object. The turning away from the mother is accompanied by hostility; the attachment to the mother ends in hate. A hate of that kind may become very striking and last all through life; it may be carefully overcompensated later on; as a rule one part of it is overcome while another part persists. Events of later years naturally influence this greatly. We will restrict ourselves, however, to studying it at the time at which the girl turns to her father and to enquiring into the motives for it. We are then given a long list of accusations and grievances against the mother which are supposed to justify the child's hostile feelings; they are of varying validity which we shall not fail to examine. A number of them are obvious rationalizations and the true sources of enmity remain to be found. I hope you will be interested if on this occasion I take you through all the details of a psycho-analytic investigation.

The reproach against the mother which goes back furthest is that she gave the child too little milk—which is construed against her as lack of love. Now there is some justification for this reproach in our families. Mothers often have insufficient nourishment to give their children and are content to suckle them for a few months, for half or three-quarters of a year. Among primitive peoples children are fed at their mother's breast for two or three years. The figure of the wet-nurse who suckles the child is as a rule merged into the mother; when this has not happened, the reproach is turned into another one—that the nurse, who fed the child so willingly, was sent away by the mother too early. But whatever the true state of affairs may have been, it is impossible that the child's reproach can be justified as often as it is met with. It seems, rather, that the child's avidity for its earliest nourishment is altogether insatiable, that it never gets over the pain of losing its mother's breast. I should not be surprised if the analysis of a primitive child, who could still suck at its mother's breast when it was already able to run about and talk, were to bring the same reproach to light. The fear of being poisoned is also probably connected with the withdrawal of the breast. Poison is nourishment that makes one ill. Perhaps children trace back their early illnesses too to this frustration. A fair amount of intellectual education is a prerequisite for believing in chance; primitive people and uneducated ones, and no doubt children as well, are able to assign a ground for everything that happens. Perhaps originally it was a reason on animistic lines. Even to-day in some strata of our population no one can die without having been killed by someone else—preferably by the doctor. And the regular reaction of a neurotic to the death of someone closely connected with him is to put the blame on himself for having caused the death.

The next accusation against the child's mother flares up when the next baby appears in the nursery. If possible the connection with oral frustration is preserved: the mother could not or would not give the child any more milk because she needed the nourishment for the new arrival. In cases in which the two children are so close in age that lactation is prejudiced by the second pregnancy, this reproach acquires a real basis, and it is a remarkable fact that a child, even with an age difference of only 11 months, is not too young to take notice of what is happening. But what the child grudges the unwanted intruder and rival is not only the suckling but all the other signs of maternal care. It feels that it has been dethroned, despoiled, prejudiced in its rights; it casts a jealous hatred upon the new baby and develops a grievance against the faithless mother which often finds expression in a disagreeable change in its behaviour. It becomes 'naughty', perhaps, irritable and disobedient and goes back on the advances it has made towards controlling its excretions. All of this has been very long familiar and is accepted as self-evident; but we rarely form a correct idea of the strength of these jealous impulses, of the tenacity with which they persist and of the magnitude of their influence on later development. Especially as this jealousy is constantly receiving fresh nourishment in the later years of childhood and the whole shock is repeated with the birth of each new brother or sister. Nor does it make much difference if the child happens to remain the mother's preferred favourite. A child's demands for love are immoderate, they make exclusive claims and tolerate no sharing.

An abundant source of a child's hostility to its mother is provided by its multifarious sexual wishes, which alter according to the phase of the libido and which cannot for the most part be satisfied. The strongest of these frustrations occur at the phallic period, if the mother forbids pleasurable activity with the genitals—often with severe threats and every sign of displeasure—activity to which, after all, she herself had introduced the child. One would think these were reasons enough to account for a girl's turning away from her mother. One would judge, if so, that the estrangement follows inevitably from the nature of children's sexuality, from the immoderate character of their demand for love and the impossibility of fulfilling their sexual wishes. It might be thought indeed that this first love-relation of the child's is doomed to dissolution for the very reason that it is the first, for these early object-cathexes are regularly ambivalent to a high degree. A powerful tendency to aggressiveness is always present beside a powerful love, and the more passionately a child loves its object the more sensitive does it become to disappointments and frustrations from that object; and in the end the love must succumb to the accumulated hostility. Or the idea that there is an original ambivalence such as this in erotic cathexes may be rejected, and it may be pointed out that it is the special nature of the mother-child relation that leads, with equal inevitability, to the destruction of the child's love; for even the mildest upbringing cannot avoid using compulsion and introducing restrictions, and any such intervention in the child's liberty must provoke as a reaction an inclination to rebelliousness and aggressiveness. A discussion of these possibilities might, I think, be most interesting; but an objection suddenly emerges which forces our interest in another direction. All these factors—the slights, the disappointments in love, the jealousy, the seduction followed by prohibition—are, after all, also in operation in the relation of a *boy* to his mother and are yet unable to alienate him from the maternal object. Unless we can find something that is specific for girls and is not present or not in the same way present in boys, we shall not have explained the termination of the attachment of girls to their mother.

I believe we have found this specific factor, and indeed where we expected to find it, even though in a surprising form. Where we expected to find it, I say, for it lies in the castration complex. After all, the anatomical distinction [between the sexes] must express itself in psychical consequences. It was, however, a surprise to learn from analyses that girls hold their mother responsible for their lack of a penis and do not forgive her for their being thus put at a disadvantage.

As you hear, then, we ascribe a castration complex to women as well. And for good reasons, though its content cannot be the same as with boys. In the latter the castration complex arises after they have learnt from the sight of the female genitals that the organ which they value so highly need not necessarily accompany the body. At this the boy recalls to mind the threats he brought on himself by his doings with that organ, he begins to give credence to them and falls under the influence of fear of castration, which will be the most powerful motive force in his subsequent development. The castration complex of girls is also started by the sight of the genitals of the other sex. They at once notice the difference and, it must be admitted, its significance too. They feel seriously wronged, often declare that they want to 'have something like it too', and fall a victim to 'envy for the penis', which will leave ineradicable traces on their development and the formation of their character and which will not be surmounted in even the most favourable cases without a severe expenditure of psychical energy. The girl's recognition of the fact of her being without a penis does not by any means imply that she submits to the fact easily. On the contrary, she continues to hold on for a long time to the wish to get something like it herself and she believes in that possibility for improbably long years; and analysis can show that, at a period when knowledge of reality has long since rejected the fulfillment of the wish as unattainable, it persists in the unconscious and retains a considerable cathexis of energy. The wish to get the longed-for penis eventually in spite of everything may contribute to the motives that drive a mature woman to analysis, and what she may reasonably expect from analysis—a capacity, for instance, to carry on an intellectual profession—may often be recognized as a sublimated modification of this repressed wish.

One cannot very well doubt the importance of envy for the penis. You may take it as an instance of male injustice if I assert that envy and jealousy play an even greater part in the mental life of women than of men. It is not that I think these characteristics are absent in men or that I think they have no other roots in women than envy for the penis; but I am inclined to attribute their greater amount in women to this latter influence. Some analysts, however, have shown an inclination to depreciate the importance of this first instalment of penis-envy in the phallic phase. They are of opinion that what we find of this attitude in women is in the main a secondary structure which has come about on the occasion of later conflicts by regression to this early infantile impulse. This, however, is a general problem of depth psychology. In many pathological—or even unusual—instinctual attitudes (for instance, in all sexual perversions) the question arises of how much of their strength is to be attributed to early infantile fixations and how much to the influence of later experiences and developments. In such cases it is almost always a matter of complemental series such as we put forward in our discussion of the aetiology of the neuroses. Both factors play a part in varying amounts in the causation; a less on the one side is balanced by a more on the other. The infantile factor sets the pattern in all cases but does not always determine the issue, though it often does. Precisely in the case of penis-envy I should argue decidedly in favour of the preponderance of the infantile factor.

The discovery that she is castrated is a turning-point in a girl's growth. Three possible lines of development start from it: one leads to sexual inhibition or to neurosis, the second to change of character in the sense of a masculinity complex, the third, finally, to normal femininity. We have learnt a fair amount, though not everything, about all three.

The essential content of the first is as follows: the little girl has hitherto lived in a masculine way, has been able to get pleasure by the excitation of her clitoris and has brought this activity into relation with her sexual wishes directed towards her mother, which are often active ones; now, owing to the influence of her penis-envy, she loses her enjoyment in her phallic sexuality. Her self-love is mortified by the comparison with the boy's far superior equipment and in consequence she renounces her masturbatory satisfaction from her clitoris, repudiates her love for her mother and at the same time not infrequently represses a good part of her sexual trends in general. No doubt her turning away from her mother does not occur all at once, for to begin with the girl regards her castration as an individual misfortune, and only gradually extends it to other females and finally to her mother as well. Her love was directed to her *phallic* mother; with the discovery that her mother is castrated it becomes possible to drop her as an object, so that the motives for hostility, which have long been accumulating, gain the upper hand. This means, therefore, that as a result of the discovery of women's lack of a penis they are debased in value for girls just as they are for boys and later perhaps for men.

You all know the immense aetiological importance attributed by our neurotic patients to their masturbation. They make it responsible for all their troubles and we have the greatest difficulty in persuading them that they are mistaken. In fact, however, we ought to admit to them that they are right, for masturbation is the executive agent of infantile sexuality, from the faulty development of which they are indeed suffering. But what neurotics mostly blame is the masturbation of the period of puberty; they have mostly forgotten that of early infancy, which is what is really in question. I wish I might have an opportunity some time of explaining to you at length how important all the factual details of early masturbation become for the individual's subsequent neurosis or character: whether or not it was discovered, how the parents struggled against it or permitted it, or whether he succeeded in suppressing it himself. All of this leaves permanent traces on his development. But I am on the whole glad that I need not do this. It would be a hard and tedious task and at the end of it you would put me in an embarrassing situation by quite certainly asking me to give you some practical advice as to how a parent or educator should deal with the masturbation of small children. From the development of girls, which is what my present lecture is concerned with, I can give you the example of a child herself trying to get free from masturbating. She does not always succeed in this. If envy for the penis has provoked a powerful impulse against clitoridal masturbation but this nevertheless refuses to give way, a violent struggle for liberation ensues in which the girl, as it were, herself takes over the role of her deposed mother and gives expression to her entire dissatisfaction with her inferior clitoris in her efforts against obtaining satisfaction from it. Many years later, when her masturbatory activity has long since been suppressed, an interest still persists which we must interpret as a defence against a temptation that is still dreaded. It manifests itself in the emergence of sympathy for those to whom similar difficulties are attributed, it plays a part as a motive in contracting a marriage and, indeed, it may determine the choice of a husband or lover. Disposing of early infantile masturbation is truly no easy or indifferent business.

Along with the abandonment of clitoridal masturbation a certain amount of activity is renounced. Passivity now has the upper hand, and the girl's turning to her father is accomplished principally with the help of passive instinctual impulses. You can see that a wave of development like this, which clears the phallic activity out of the way, smooths the ground for femininity. If too much is not lost in the course of it through repression, this femininity may turn out to be normal. The wish with which the girl turns to her father is no doubt originally the wish for the penis which her mother has refused her and which she now expects from her father. The feminine situation is only established, however, if the wish for a penis is replaced by one for a baby, if, that is, a baby takes the place of a penis in accordance with an ancient symbolic equivalence. It has not escaped us that the girl has wished for a baby earlier, in the undisturbed phallic phase: that, of course, was the meaning of her playing with dolls. But that play was not in fact an expression of her femininity; it served as an identification with her mother with the intention of substituting activity for passivity. *She* was playing the part of her mother and the doll was herself: now she could do with the baby everything that her mother used to do with her. Not until the emergence of the wish for a penis does the doll-baby become a baby from the girl's father, and thereafter the aim of the most powerful feminine wish. Her happiness is great if later on this wish for a baby finds fulfilment in reality, and quite especially so if the baby is a little boy who brings the longed-for penis with him. Often enough in her combined picture of 'a baby from her father' the emphasis is laid on the baby and her father left unstressed. In this way the ancient masculine wish for the possession of a penis is still faintly visible through the femininity now achieved. But perhaps we ought rather to recognize this wish for a penis as being *par excellence* a feminine one.

With the transference of the wish for a penis-baby on to her father, the girl has entered the situation of the Oedipus complex. Her hostility to her mother, which did not need to be freshly created, is now greatly intensified, for she becomes the girl's rival, who receives from her father everything that she desires from him. For a long time the girl's Oedipus complex concealed her pre-Oedipus attachment to her mother from our view, though it is nevertheless so important and leaves such lasting fixations behind it. For girls the Oedipus situation is the outcome of a long and difficult development; it is a kind of preliminary solution, a position of rest which is not soon abandoned, especially as the beginning of the latency period is not far distant. And we are now struck by a difference between the two sexes, which is probably momentous, in regard to the relation of the Oedipus complex to the castration complex. In a boy the Oedipus complex, in which he desires his mother and would like to get rid of his father as being a rival, develops naturally from the phase of his phallic sexuality. The threat of castration compels him, however, to give up that attitude. Under the impression of the danger of losing his penis, the Oedipus complex is abandoned, repressed and, in the most normal cases, entirely destroyed, and a severe super-ego is set up as its heir. What happens with a girl is almost the opposite. The castration complex prepares for the Oedipus complex instead of destroying it; the girl is driven out of her attachment to her mother through the influence of her envy for the penis and she enters the Oedipus situation as though into a haven of refuge. In the absence of fear of castration the chief motive is lacking which leads boys to surmount the Oedipus complex. Girls remain in it for an indeterminate length of time; they demolish it late and, even so, incompletely. In these circumstances the formation of the super-ego must suffer; it cannot attain the strength and independence which give it its cultural significance, and feminists are not pleased when we point out to them the effects of this factor upon the average feminine character.

To go back a little. We mentioned as the second possible reaction to the discovery of female castration the development of a powerful masculinity complex. By this we mean that the girl refuses, as it were, to recognize the unwelcome fact and, defiantly rebellious, even exaggerates her previous masculinity, clings to her clitoridal activity and takes refuge in an identification with her phallic mother or her father. What can it be that decides in favour of this outcome? We can only suppose that it is a constitutional factor, a greater amount of activity, such as is ordinarily characteristic of a male. However that may be, the essence of this process is that at this point in development the wave of passivity is avoided which opens the way to the turn towards femininity. The extreme achievement of such a masculinity complex would appear to be the influencing of the choice of an object in the sense of manifest homosexuality. Analytic experience teaches us, to be sure, that female homosexuality is seldom or never a direct continuation of infantile masculinity. Even for a girl of this kind it seems necessary that she should take her father as an object for some time and enter the Oedipus situation. But afterwards, as a result of her inevitable disappointments from her father, she is driven to regress into her early masculinity complex. The significance of these disappointments must not be exaggerated; a girl who is destined to become feminine is not spared them, though they do not have the same effect. The predominance of the constitutional factor seems indisputable; but the two phases in the development of female homosexuality are well mirrored in the practices of homosexuals, who play the parts of mother and baby with each other as often and as clearly as those of husband and wife. . . .

. . . [T]he development of femininity remains exposed to disturbance by the residual phenomena of the early masculine period. Regressions to the fixations of the pre-Oedipus phases very frequently occur; in the course of some women's lives there is a repeated alternation between periods in which masculinity or femininity gains the upper hand. Some portion of what we men call 'the enigma of women' may perhaps be derived from this expression of bisexuality in women's lives. But another question seems to have become ripe for judgement in the course of these researches. We have called the motive force of sexual life 'the libido'. Sexual life is dominated by the polarity of masculine-feminine; thus the notion suggests itself of considering the relation of the libido to this antithesis. It would not be surprising if it were to turn out that each sexuality had its own special libido appropriated to it, so that one sort of libido would pursue the aims of a masculine sexual life and another sort those of a feminine one. But nothing of the kind is true. There is only one libido, which serves both the masculine and the feminine sexual functions. To it itself we cannot assign any sex; if, following the conventional equation of activity and masculinity, we are inclined to describe it as masculine, we must not forget that it also covers trends with a passive aim. Nevertheless the juxtaposition 'feminine libido' is without any justification. Furthermore, it is our impression that more constraint has been applied to the libido when it is pressed into the service of the feminine function, and that—to speak teleologically—Nature takes less careful account of its [that function's] demands than in the case of masculinity. And the reason for this may lie—thinking once again teleologically—in the fact that the accomplishment of the aim of biology has been entrusted to the aggressiveness of men and has been made to some extent independent of women's consent.

The sexual frigidity of women, the frequency of which appears to confirm this disregard, is a phenomenon that is still insufficiently understood. Sometimes it is psychogenic and in that case accessible to influence; but in other cases it suggests the hypothesis of its being constitutionally determined and even of there being a contributory anatomical factor.

I have promised to tell you of a few more psychical peculiarities of mature femininity, as we come across them in analytic observation. We do not lay claim to more than an average validity for these assertions; nor is it always easy to distinguish what should be ascribed to the influence of the sexual function and what to social breeding. Thus, we attribute a larger amount of narcissism to femininity, which also affects women's choice of object, so that to be loved is a stronger need for them than to love. The effect of penis-envy has a share, further, in the physical vanity of women, since they are bound to value their charms more highly as a late compensation for their original sexual inferiority. Shame, which is considered to be a feminine characteristic *par excellence* but is far more a matter of convention than might be supposed, has as its purpose, we believe, concealment of genital deficiency. We are not forgetting that at a later time shame takes on other functions. It seems that women have made few contributions to the discoveries and inventions in the history of civilization; there is, however, one technique which they may have invented—that of plaiting and weaving. If that is so, we should be tempted to guess the unconscious motive for the achievement. Nature herself would seem to have given the model which this achievement imitates by causing the growth at maturity of the pubic hair that conceals the genitals. The step that remained to be taken lay in making the threads adhere to one another, while on the body they stick into the skin and are only matted together. If you reject this idea as fantastic and regard my belief in the influence of lack of a penis on the configuration of femininity as an *idée fixe*, I am of course defenceless.

The determinants of women's choice of an object are often made unrecognizable by social conditions. Where the choice is able to show itself freely, it is often made in accordance with the narcissistic ideal of the man whom the girl had wished to become. If the girl has remained in her attachment to her father—that is, in the Oedipus complex—her choice is made according to the paternal type. Since, when she turned from her mother to her father, the hostility of her ambivalent relation remained with her mother, a choice of this kind should guarantee a happy marriage. But very often the outcome is of a kind that presents a general threat to such a settlement of the conflict due to ambivalence. The hostility that has been left behind follows in the train of the positive attachment and spreads over on to the new object. The woman's husband, who to begin with inherited from her father, becomes after a time her mother's heir as well. So it may easily happen that the second half of a woman's life may be filled by the struggle against her husband, just as the shorter first half was filled by her rebellion against her mother. When this reaction has been lived through, a second marriage may easily turn out very much more satisfying. Another alteration in a woman's nature, for which lovers are unprepared, may occur in a marriage after the first child is born. Under the influence of a woman's becoming a mother herself, an identification with her own mother may be revived, against which she had striven up till the time of her marriage, and this may attract all the available libido to itself, so that the compulsion to repeat reproduces an unhappy marriage between her parents. The difference in a mother's reaction to the birth of a son or a daughter shows that the old factor of lack of a penis has even now not lost its strength. A mother is only brought unlimited satisfaction by her relation to a son; this is altogether the most perfect, the most free from ambivalence of all human relationships. A mother can transfer to her son the ambition which she has been obliged to suppress in herself, and she can expect from him the satisfaction of all that has been left over in her of her masculinity complex. Even a marriage is not made secure until the wife has succeeded in making her husband her child as well and in acting as a mother to him.

A woman's identification with her mother allows us to distinguish two strata: the pre-Oedipus one which rests on her affectionate attachment to her mother and takes her as a model, and the later one from the Oedipus complex which seeks to get rid of her mother and take her place with her father. We are no doubt justified in saying that much of both of them is left over for the future and that neither of them is adequately surmounted in the course of development. But the phase of the affectionate pre-Oedipus attachment is the decisive one for a woman's future: during it preparations are made for the acquisition of the characteristics with which she will later fulfil her role in the sexual function and perform her invaluable social tasks. It is in this identification too that she acquires her attractiveness to a man, whose Oedipus attachment to his mother it kindles into passion. How often it happens, however, that it is only his son who obtains what he himself aspired to! One gets an impression that a man's love and a woman's are a phase apart psychologically.

The fact that women must be regarded as having little sense of justice is no doubt related to the predominance of envy in their mental life; for the demand for justice is a modification of envy and lays down the condition subject to which one can put envy aside. We also regard women as weaker in their social interests and as having less capacity for sublimating their instincts than men. The former is no doubt derived from the dissocial quality which unquestionably characterizes all sexual relations. Lovers find sufficiency in each other, and families too resist inclusion in more comprehensive associations. The aptitude for sublimation is subject to the greatest individual variations. On the other hand I cannot help mentioning an impression that we are constantly receiving during analytic practice. A man of about thirty strikes us as a youthful, somewhat unformed individual, whom we expect to make powerful use of the possibilities for development opened up to him by analysis. A woman of the same age, however, often frightens us by her psychical rigidity and unchangeability. Her libido has taken up final positions and seems incapable of exchanging them for others. There are no paths open to further development; it is as though the whole process had already run its course and remains thenceforward insusceptible to influence—as though, indeed, the difficult development to femininity had exhausted the possibilities of the person concerned. As therapists we lament this state of things, even if we succeed in putting an end to our patient's ailment by doing away with her neurotic conflict.

That is all I had to say to you about femininity. It is certainly incomplete and fragmentary and does not always sound friendly. But do not forget that I have only been describing women in so far as their nature is determined by their sexual function. It is true that that influence extends very far; but we do not overlook the fact that an individual woman may be a human being in other respects as well. If you want to know more about femininity, enquire from your own experiences of life, or turn to the poets, or wait until science can give you deeper and more coherent information.

* * *

C. G. JUNG

After several years of friendly collaboration, Carl Gustave Jung (1875–1961) broke with Freud to found his own school of analytical psychology. Jung's approach involved distinctions between predominantly extroverted and introverted personalities, and between four functions of personality—sensation, thinking, feeling, and intuition, which are present in differing proportions in different people. Each individual possesses a "persona" (cf. superego), i.e., a socially imposed mask behind which the true ego resides, and a "shadow" (cf. id), i.e., a rejected set of desires, emotions, and attitudes imprisoned in the unconscious. A third major force in personality is the "image," which determines how the opposite sex is perceived. In man this image of the feminine is called the *anima;* in woman the image of the masculine is the *animus.* Jung viewed the anima as particularly related to the function of feeling, and the animus to thinking, supposing that feeling is generally more dominant in woman, and thinking in man.

Marriage as a Psychological Relationship

Every man carries within him the eternal image of woman, not the image of this or that particular woman, but a definite feminine image. This image is fundamentally unconscious, an hereditary factor of primordial origin engraved in the living organic system of the man, an imprint or "archetype" of all the ancestral experiences of the female, a deposit, as it were, of all the impressions ever made by woman—in short, an inherited system of psychic adaptation. Even if no women existed, it would still be possible, at any given time, to deduce from this unconscious image exactly how a woman would have to be constituted psychically. The same is true of the woman: she too has her inborn image of man. Actually, we know from experience that it would be more accurate to describe it as an image of *men,* whereas in the case of the man it is rather the image of *woman.* Since this image is unconscious, it is always unconsciously projected upon the person of the beloved, and is one of the chief reasons for passionate attraction or aversion. I have called this image the "anima," and I find the scholastic question *Habet mulier animam?* especially interesting, since in my view it is an intelligent one inasmuch as the doubt seems justified. Woman has no anima, no soul, but she has an *animus.* The anima has an erotic, emotional character, the animus a rationalizing one. Hence most of what men say about feminine eroticism, and particularly about the emotional life of women, is derived from their own anima projections and distorted accordingly. On the other hand, the astonishing assumptions and fantasies that women make about men come from the activity of the animus, who produces an inexhaustible supply of illogical arguments and false explanations.

Anima and animus are both characterized by an extraordinary many-sidedness. In a marriage it is always the contained who projects this image upon the container, while the latter is only partially able to project his unconscious image upon his partner. The more unified and simple this partner is, the less complete the projection. In which case, this highly fascinating image hangs as it were in mid air, as though waiting to be filled out by a living person. There are certain types of women who seem to be made by nature to attract anima projections; indeed one could almost speak of a definite "anima type." The so-called "sphinx-like" character is an indispensable part of their equipment, also an equivocalness, an intriguing elusiveness—not an indefinite blur that offers nothing, but an indefiniteness that seems full of promises, like the speaking silence of a Mona Lisa. A woman of this kind is both old and young, mother and daughter, of more than doubtful chastity, childlike, and yet endowed with a naïve cunning that is extremely disarming to men. Not every man of real intellectual power can be an animus, for the animus must be a master not so much of fine ideas as of fine words—words seemingly full of meaning which purport to leave a great deal unsaid. He must also belong to the "misunderstood" class, or be in some way at odds with his environment, so that the idea of self-sacrifice can insinuate itself. He must be a rather questionable hero, a man with possibilities, which is not to say that an animus projection may not discover a real hero long before he has become perceptible to the sluggish wits of the man of "average intelligence."

For man as well as for woman, in so far as they are "containers," the filling out of this image is an experience fraught with consequences, for it holds the possibility of finding one's own complexities answered by a corresponding diversity. Wide vistas seem to open up in which one feels oneself embraced and contained. I say "seem" advisedly, because the experience may be two-faced. Just as the animus projection of a woman can often pick on a man of real significance who is not recognized by the mass, and can actually help him to achieve his true destiny with her moral support, so a man can create for himself a *femme inspiratrice* by his anima projection. But more often it turns out to be an illusion with destructive consequences, a failure because his faith was not sufficiently strong. To the pessimists I would say that these primordial psychic images have an extraordinarily positive value, but I must warn the optimists against blinding fantasies and the likelihood of the most absurd aberrations.

One should on no account take this projection for an individual and conscious relationship. In its first stages it is far from that, for it creates a compulsive dependence based on unconscious motives other than the biological ones. Rider Haggard's *She* gives some indication of the curious world of ideas that underlies the anima projection. They are in essence spiritual contents, often in erotic disguise, obvious fragments of a primitive mythological mentality that consists of archetypes, and whose totality constitutes the collective unconscious. Accordingly, such a relationship is at bottom collective and not individual. (Benoît, who created in *L'Atlantide* a fantasy figure similar even in details to "She," denies having plagiarized Rider Haggard.)

If such a projection fastens on to one of the marriage partners, a collective spiritual relationship conflicts with the collective biological one and produces in the container the division or disintegration I have described above. If he is able to hold his head above water, he will find himself through this very conflict. In that case the projection, though dangerous in itself, will have helped him to pass from a collective to an individual relationship. This amounts to full conscious realization of the relationship that marriage brings. Since the aim of this paper is a discussion of the psychology of marriage, the psychology of projection cannot concern us here. It is sufficient to mention it as a fact.

One can hardly deal with the psychological marriage relationship without mentioning, even at the risk of misunderstanding, the nature of its critical transitions. As is well known, one understands nothing psychological unless one has experienced it oneself. Not that this ever prevents anyone from feeling convinced that his own judgment is the only true and competent one. This disconcerting fact comes from the necessary over-valuation of the momentary content of consciousness, for without this concentration of attention one could not be conscious at all. Thus it is that every period of life has its own psychological truth, and the same applies to every stage of psychological development. There are even stages which only the few can reach, it being a question of race, family, education, talent, and passion. Nature is aristocratic. The normal man is a fiction, although certain generally valid laws do exist. Psychic life is a development that can easily be arrested on the lowest levels. It is as though every individual had a specific gravity, in accordance with which he either rises, or sinks down, to the level where he reaches his limit. His views and convictions will be determined accordingly. No wonder, then, that by far the greater number of marriages reach their upper psychological limit in fulfilment of the biological aim, without injury to spiritual or moral health. Relatively few people fall into deeper disharmony with themselves. Where there is a great deal of pressure from outside, the conflict is unable to develop much dramatic tension for sheer lack of energy. Psychological insecurity, however, increases in proportion to social security, unconsciously at first, causing neuroses, then consciously, bringing with it separations, discord, divorces, and other marital disorders. On still higher levels, new possibilities of psychological development are discerned, touching on the sphere of religion where critical judgment comes to a halt.

Progress may be permanently arrested on any of these levels, with complete unconsciousness of what might have followed at the next stage of development. As a rule graduation to the next stage is barred by violent prejudices and superstitious fears. This, however, serves a most useful purpose, since a man who is compelled by accident to live at a high level too high for him becomes a fool and a menace.

Nature is not only aristocratic, she is also esoteric. Yet no man of understanding will thereby be induced to make a secret of what he knows, for he realizes only too well that the secret of psychic development can never be betrayed, simply because that development is a question of individual capacity.

* * *

KAREN HORNEY

After fifteen years of consistently attempting to apply Freud's theories in behalf of her patients, Karen Horney (1885–1952) publicly articulated her points of disagreement with the founder of psychoanalysis. Like Jung, Horney rejects Freud's insistence on the centrality of the sexual drive in determining human personality. "When we relinquish this one-sided emphasis on genesis," she writes,

> we recognize that the connection between later peculiarities and earlier experiences is more complicated than Freud assumes: there is no such thing as an isolated repetition of isolated experiences; but the entirety of infantile experiences combines to form a certain character structure. . . .

To Horney the character structure that determines human personality is not the inevitable outcome of instinctual impulses, modified by the environment; rather it involves the activity of the ego in response to all of life's conditions, both internal and external. Instead of the pleasure principle, Horney speaks of a "striving for safety" as the motivation for human behavior. The "new therapeutic goal" which she endorses is "to restore the individual to himself, to help him regain his spontaneity and find his center of gravity in himself."

Feminine Psychology

Freud believes that psychic peculiarities and difficulties in the two sexes are engendered by bisexual trends in both of them. His contention is, briefly, that many psychic difficulties in man are due to his rejection of "feminine" trends in himself, and that many peculiarities in woman are due to her essential wish to be a man. Freud has elaborated this thought in more detail for the psychology of woman than for that of man, and therefore I shall discuss only his views of feminine psychology.

According to Freud the most upsetting occurrence in the development of the little girl is the discovery that other human beings have a penis, while she has none. "The discovery of her castration is the turning point in the life of the girl."[1] She reacts to this discovery with a definite wish to have a penis too, with the hope that it will still grow, and with an envy of those more fortunate beings who possess one. In the normal development penis-envy does not continue as such; after recognizing her "deficiency" as an unalterable fact, the girl transfers the wish for a penis to a wish for a child. "The hoped-for possession of a child is meant as a compensation for her bodily defect."[2]

Penis-envy is originally a merely narcissistic phenomenon, the girl feeling offended because her body is less completely equipped than the boy's. But it has also a root in object relations. According to Freud the mother is the first sexual object for the girl as well as for the boy. The girl wishes to have a penis not only for the sake of narcissistic pride, but also because of her libidinal desires for the mother, which, in so far as they are genital in nature, have a masculine character. Not recognizing the elemental power of heterosexual attraction, Freud raises the question as to why the girl has any need at all to change her attachment to the father. He gives two reasons for this change in affection: hostility toward the mother, who is held responsible for the lack of a penis, and a wish

1. Sigmund Freud, *New Introductory Lectures on Psychoanalysis* (1933), chapter on "The Psychology of Women." The following interpretation of Freud's point of view is based primarily on this source.

2. Karl Abraham, "Ausserungsformen des weiblichen Kastrationskomplexes" in *Internationale Zeitschrift für Psychoanalyse* (1921).

to obtain this desired organ from the father. "The wish with which girls turn to their father is, no doubt, ultimately the wish for the penis." Thus originally both boys and girls know only one sex: the masculine.

Penis-envy is assumed to leave ineradicable traces in woman's development; even in the most normal development it is overcome only by a great expenditure of energy. Woman's most significant attitudes or wishes derive their energy from her wish for a penis. Some of Freud's principal contentions intended to illustrate this may be briefly enumerated.

Freud considers the wish for a male child to be woman's strongest wish, because the wish for a child is heir to the wish for a penis. The son represents a sort of wish-fulfillment in the sense of penis possession. "The only thing that brings a mother undiluted satisfaction is her relation to a son: the mother can transfer to her son all the ambition which she has had to suppress in herself and she can hope to get from him the satisfaction of all that has remained to her of her masculinity complex."

Happiness during pregnancy, particularly when neurotic disturbances that are otherwise present subside during this time, is referred to as symbolic gratification in the possession of a penis (the penis being the child). When the delivery is delayed for functional reasons, it is suspected that the woman does not want to separate herself from the penis-child. On the other hand, motherhood may be rejected because it is a reminder of femininity. Similarly, depressions and irritations occurring during menstruation are regarded as the result of menstruation being a reminder of femininity. Cramps in menstruation are often interpreted as the result of fantasies in which the father's penis has been swallowed.

Disturbances in the relationship to men are regarded as ultimate results of penis-envy. As women turn to men mainly in the expectation of receiving a gift (penis-child), or in the expectation of having all their ambitions fulfilled, they easily turn against men if they fail to live up to such expectations. Envy of men may show itself also in the tendency to surpass them or in any kind of disparaging or in a striving for independence in so far as it implies disregarding man's help. In the sexual sphere the refutation of the feminine role may appear openly after defloration; the latter may arouse animosity to the partner because it is experienced as a castration.

In fact, there is scarcely any character trait in woman which is not assumed to have an essential root in penis-envy. Feminine inferiority feelings are regarded as an expression of contempt for the woman's own sex because of the lack of a penis. Freud believes that woman is more vain than man and attributes this to her necessity for compensation for the lack of a penis. Woman's physical modesty is born ultimately of a wish to hide the "deficiency" of her genitals. The greater role of envy and jealousy in woman's character is a direct outcome of penis-envy. Her tendency toward envy accounts for woman having "too little sense of justice," as well as for her "preference for mental and occupational interests belonging to the sphere of men."[3] Practically all of woman's ambitious strivings suggest to Freud her wish for a penis as the ultimate driving force. Also ambitions which are usually regarded as specifically feminine, such as the wish to be the most beautiful woman or the wish to marry the most prominent man, are, according to Abraham, expressions of penis-envy.

Although the concept of penis-envy is related to anatomical differences it is nevertheless contradictory to biological thinking. It would require tremendous evidence to make it plausible that woman, physically built for specifically female functions, should be psychically determined by a wish for attributes of the other sex. But actually the data presented for this contention are scant, consisting of three main observations.

First, it is pointed out that little girls often express the wish to have a penis or the hope that it will still grow. There is no reason, however, to think that this wish is any more significant than their equally frequent wish to have a breast; moreover the wish for a penis may be accompanied by a kind of behavior which in our culture is regarded as feminine.

It is also pointed out that some girls before puberty not only may wish to be a boy, but through their tomboyish behavior may indicate that they really mean it. Again, however, the question is whether we are justified in taking these tendencies at their face value; when they are analyzed we may find good reasons for the apparently masculine wishes: opposition, despair at not being attractive as a girl, and the like. As a matter of fact, since girls have been brought up with greater freedom this kind of behavior has become rare.

Finally, it is pointed out that adult women may express a wish to be a man, sometimes explicitly, sometimes by presenting themselves in dreams with a penis or penis symbol; they may express contempt for women and attribute existing inferiority feelings to being a woman; castrative tendencies may be manifest or may be expressed in dreams, in disguised or undisguised form. These latter data, however, though their occurrence is beyond doubt, are not as frequent as is suggested in some analytical writings. Also they are true only of neurotic women. Finally, they permit of a different interpretation and hence are far from proving the contention beyond dispute. Before discussing them critically let us first try to

3. Karl Abraham, *op. cit.*

understand how it is that Freud and many other analysts see such overwhelming evidence for the decisive influence of penis-envy on woman's character.

In my estimation two main factors account for this conviction. On the basis of theoretical biases—which coincide to some extent with existing cultural prejudices—the analyst regards the following trends in women patients as off-hand suggestive of underlying penis-envy: tendencies to boss man, to berate him, to envy his success, to be ambitious themselves, to be self-sufficient, to dislike accepting help. I suspect that these trends are sometimes imputed to underlying penis-envy without further evidence. Further evidence may easily be found, however, in simultaneous complaints about feminine functions (such as menstruation) or frigidity, or in complaints about a brother having been preferred, or in a tendency to point out certain advantages of man's social position, or in dream symbols (a woman carrying a stick, slicing a sausage).

In reviewing these trends, it is obvious that they are characteristic of neurotic men as well as of neurotic women. Tendencies toward dictatorial power, toward egocentric ambition, toward envying and berating others are never-failing elements in present-day neuroses though the role they assume in a neurotic structure varies.

Furthermore, observation of neurotic women shows that all the trends in question appear toward other women or toward children as well as toward men. It appears dogmatic to assume that their expression in relation to others is merely a radiation from their relation to men.

Finally, as to dream symbols, any expression of wishes for masculinity is taken at its face value instead of being regarded skeptically for a possible deeper meaning. This procedure is contrary to the customary analytical attitude and can be ascribed only to the determining power of theoretical preconceptions.

Another source feeding the analyst's conviction of the significance of penis-envy lies not in himself but in his women patients. While some women patients are not impressed by interpretations which point to penis-envy as the origin of their troubles, others take them up readily and quickly learn to talk about their difficulties in terms of femininity and masculinity, or even to dream in symbols fitting this kind of thinking. These are not necessarily patients who are particularly gullible. Every experienced analyst will notice whether a patient is docile and suggestible and by analyzing these trends will diminish errors springing from that source. And some patients view their problems in terms of masculinity and femininity without any suggestion from the analyst, for naturally one cannot exclude the influence of literature. But there is a deeper reason why many patients gladly seize upon explanations offered in terms of penis-envy: these explanations present comparatively harmless and simple solutions. It is so much easier for a woman to think that she is nasty to her husband because, unfortunately, she was born without a penis and envies him for having one than to think, for instance, that she has developed an attitude of righteousness and infallibility which makes it impossible to tolerate any questioning or disagreement. It is so much easier for a patient to think that nature has given her an unfair deal than to realize that she actually makes excessive demands on the environment and is furious whenever they are not complied with. It seems thus that the theoretical bias of the analyst may coincide with the patient's tendency to leave her real problems untouched.

If wishes for masculinity may screen repressed drives, what then renders them fit to serve in this way?

Here we come to see cultural factors. The wish to be a man, as Alfred Adler has pointed out, may be the expression of a wish for all those qualities or privileges which in our culture are regarded as masculine, such as strength, courage, independence, success, sexual freedom, right to choose a partner. To avoid misunderstanding let me state explicitly that I do not mean to say that penis-envy is nothing but a symbolic expression of the wish to have the qualities regarded as masculine in our culture. This would not be plausible, because wishes to have these qualities need not be repressed and hence do not require a symbolic expression. A symbolic expression is necessary only for tendencies or feelings shoved out of awareness.

What then are the repressed strivings which are covered up by the wish for masculinity? The answer is not an all-embracing formula but must be discovered from an analysis of each patient and each situation. In order to discover the repressed strivings it is necessary not to take at face value a woman's tendency in one way or another to base her inferiority feelings on the fact that she is a woman; rather it must be pointed out to her that every person belonging to a minority group or to a less privileged group tends to use that status as a cover for inferiority feelings of various sources, and that the important thing is to try to find out these sources. According to my experience, one of the most frequent and effective sources is a failure to live up to certain inflated notions about the self, notions which in turn are necessary because various unrecognized pretenses have to be covered up.

Furthermore, it is necessary to bear in mind the possibility that the wish to be a man may be a screen for repressed ambition. In neurotic persons ambition may be so destructive that it becomes loaded with anxiety and hence has to be repressed. This is true of men as well as of women but as a result of the cultural situation a repressed destructive ambition in a woman may express itself in the comparatively harmless symbol of a wish to be a man. What is required of psychoanalysis is to uncover the egocentric and destructive elements in the ambition and to analyze not only what led up to this kind of ambition but also what consequences it has for the personality in the way of inhibitions to love, inhibitions to work, envy of competitors, self-belittling tendencies, fear of failure and of success.[4] The wish to be a man drops out of the patient's associations as soon as we tackle the underlying problems of her ambition and exalted opinion about what she is or should be. It is then no longer possible for her to hide behind the symbolic screen of masculinity wishes.

In short, interpretations in terms of penis-envy bar the way to an understanding of fundamental difficulties, such as ambition, and of the whole personality structure linked up with them. That such interpretations befog the real issue is my most stringent objection to them, particularly from the therapeutic angle. And I have the same objection to the assumed importance of bisexuality in man's psychology. Freud believes that in man's psychology what corresponds to penis-envy is his "struggle against the passive or feminine attitude toward other men."[5] He calls this fear the "repudiation of femininity" and makes it responsible for various difficulties which in my estimation belong to the structure of types who need to appear perfect and superior.

Freud has made two other suggestions, closely interrelated, concerning inherent feminine characteristics. One is that femininity has "some secret relationship with masochism."[6] The other is that the basic fear in woman is that of losing love, and that this fear corresponds to the fear of castration in man.

Helene Deutsch has elaborated Freud's assumption and generalized it in calling masochism the elemental power in feminine mental life. She contends that what woman ultimately wants in intercourse is to be raped and violated; what she wants in mental life is to be humiliated; menstruation is significant to the woman because it feeds masochistic fantasies; childbirth represents the climax of masochistic satisfaction. The pleasures of motherhood, inasmuch as they include certain sacrifices and a concern for the children, constitute a long drawn out masochistic gratification. Because of these masochistic strivings women, according to Deutsch, are more or less doomed to be frigid unless in intercourse they are

4. *Cf.* Karen Horney, *The Neurotic Personality of Our Time* (1937), chs. 10–12.

5. Sigmund Freud, "Analysis Terminable and Interminable," in *International Journal of Psychoanalysis* (1937).

6. Sigmund Freud, *New Introductory Lectures.*

or feel raped, injured or humiliated.[7] Rado holds that woman's preference for masculinity is a defense against feminine masochistic strivings.[8]

Since according to psychoanalytic theory psychic attitudes are molded after sexual attitudes, the contentions concerning a specifically feminine basis of masochism have far-reaching implications. They entail the postulate that women in general, or at least the majority of them, essentially desire to be submissive and dependent. In support of these views is the impression that in our culture masochistic trends are more frequent in women than in men. But it must be remembered that the available data concern only neurotic women.

Many neurotic women have masochistic notions about intercourse, such as that women are prey to man's animal desires, that they have to sacrifice themselves and are debased by the sacrifice. There may be fantasies about being physically injured by intercourse. A few neurotic women have fantasies of masochistic satisfaction in childbirth. The great number of mothers who play the role of martyr and continually emphasize how much they are sacrificing themselves for the children may certainly be proof that motherhood can offer a masochistic satisfaction to neurotic women. There are also neurotic girls who shrink from marriage because they visualize themselves as enslaved and abused by the potential husband. Finally, masochistic fantasies about the sexual role of woman may contribute to a rejection of the female role and a preference for the masculine one.

Assuming that there is indeed a greater frequency of masochistic trends in neurotic women than in neurotic men, how may it be accounted for? Rado and Deutsch try to show that specific factors in feminine development are responsible. I refrain from discussing these attempts because both authors introduce as the basic factor the lack of a penis, or the girl's reactions to the discovery of this fact, and I believe this to be a wrong presupposition. In fact, I do not believe it is possible at all to find specific factors in feminine development which lead to masochism, for all such attempts rest on the premise that masochism is essentially a sexual phenomenon. It is true that the sexual aspect of masochism, as it appears in masochistic fantasies and perversions, is its most conspicuous part and was the first to attract the attention of psychiatrists. I hold, however —and this contention will be elaborated later on—that masochism

7. Helene Deutsch, "The Significance of Masochism in the Mental Life of Women" (Part I, "Feminine Masochism in Its Relation to Frigidity") in *International Journal of Psychoanalysis* (1930).

8. Sandor Rado, "Fear of Castration in Women" in *Psychoanalytic Quarterly* (1933).

is not a primarily sexual phenomenon, but is rather the result of certain conflicts in interpersonal relations. When masochistic tendencies are once established they may prevail also in the sexual sphere and here may become the condition for satisfaction. From this point of view masochism cannot be a specifically feminine phenomenon, and the analytical writers who have tried to find specific factors in feminine development accounting for masochistic attitudes in women are not to be blamed for the failure to find them.

In my opinion, one has to look not for biological reasons but for cultural ones. The question then is whether there are cultural factors which are instrumental in developing masochistic trends in women. The answer to this question depends on what one holds to be essential in the dynamics of masochism. My concept, briefly, is that masochistic phenomena represent the attempt to gain safety and satisfaction in life through inconspicuousness and dependency. As will be discussed later on, this fundamental attitude toward life determines the way in which individual problems are dealt with; it leads, for instance, to gaining control over others through weakness and suffering, to expressing hostility through suffering, to seeking in illness an alibi for failure.

If these presuppositions are valid there are indeed cultural factors fostering masochistic attitudes in women. They were more relevant for the past generation than for the present one, but they still throw their shadow today. They are, briefly, the greater dependency of woman; the emphasis on woman's weakness and frailty; the ideology that it is in woman's nature to lean on someone and that her life is given content and meaning only through others: family, husband, children. These factors do not in themselves bring about masochistic attitudes. History has shown that women can be happy, contented and efficient under these conditions. But factors like these, in my judgment, are responsible for the prevalence of masochistic trends in feminine neuroses when neuroses do develop.

Freud's contention that woman's basic fear is that of losing love is in part not separate from, for it is implicitly contained in, the postulate that there are specific factors in feminine development leading to masochism. Inasmuch as masochistic trends, among other characteristics, signify an emotional dependence on others, and inasmuch as one of the predominant masochistic means of reassurance against anxiety is to obtain affection, a fear of losing love is a specific masochistic feature.

It seems to me, however, that in contrast to Freud's other two contentions concerning feminine nature—that of penis-envy and that of a specifically feminine basis for masochism—this last one has some validity also for the healthy woman in our culture. There are no biological reasons but there are significant cultural factors which lead women to overvalue love and thus to dread losing it.

Woman lived for centuries under conditions in which she was kept away from great economic and political responsibilities and restricted to a private emotional sphere of life. This does not mean that she did not carry responsibility and did not have to work. But her work was done within the confines of the family circle and therefore was based only on emotionalism, in contradistinction to more impersonal, matter of fact relations. Another aspect of the same situation is that love and devotion came to be regarded as specifically feminine ideals and virtues. Still another aspect is that to woman—since her relations to men and children were her only gateway to happiness, security and prestige—love represented a realistic value, which in man's sphere can be compared with his activities relating to earning capacities. Thus not only were pursuits outside the emotional sphere factually discouraged, but in woman's own mind they assumed only secondary importance.

Hence there were, and to some extent still are, realistic reasons in our culture why woman is bound to over-rate love and to expect more from it than it can possibly give, and why she is more afraid of losing love than man is.

The cultural situation which has led woman to regard love as the only value that counts in life has implications which may throw light on certain characteristics of modern woman. One of them is the attitude toward aging: woman's age phobia and its implications. Since for such a long time woman's only attainable fulfillments—whether they involved love, sex, home or children—were obtained through men, it necessarily became of paramount importance to please men. The cult of beauty and charm resulting from this necessity might be registered, at least in some respects, as a good effect. But such a concentration on the importance of erotic attractiveness implies an anxiety for the time when it might eventually diminish in value. We should consider it neurotic if men became frightened or depressed when they approached the fifth decade. In a woman this is regarded as natural, and in a way it is natural so long as attractiveness represents a unique value. While age is a problem to everyone it becomes a desperate one if youthfulness is the center of attention.

This fear is not limited to the age which is regarded as ending woman's attractiveness, but throws its shadow over her entire life and is bound to create a great feeling of insecurity toward life. It accounts for the jealousy often existing between mothers and adolescent daughters, and not only helps to spoil their personal relationships but may leave a remnant of hostility toward all women. It prevents woman from evaluating qualities which are outside the erotic sphere, qualities best characterized by the terms maturity, poise, independence, autonomy in judgment, wisdom. Woman can scarcely take the task of the development of her personality as seriously as she does her love life if she constantly entertains a devaluating attitude toward her mature years, and considers them as her declining years.

The all-embracing expectations that are joined to love account to some extent for that discontentment with the female role which Freud ascribes to penis-envy. From this point of view the discontentment has two main reasons. One is that in a culture in which human relationships are so generally disturbed it is difficult to attain happiness in love life (by that I do *not* mean sexual relations). The other is that this situation is likely to create inferiority feelings. Sometimes the question is raised whether in our culture men or women suffer more from inferiority feelings. It is difficult to measure psychic quantities, but there is this difference: as a rule man's feeling of inferiority does not arise from the fact that he is a man; but woman often feels inferior merely because she is a woman. As mentioned before, I believe that feelings of inadequacy have nothing to do with femininity but use cultural implications of femininity as a disguise for other sources of inferiority feelings which, in essence, are identical in men and women. There remain, however, certain cultural reasons why woman's self-confidence is easily disturbed.

A sound and secure self-confidence draws upon a broad basis of human qualities, such as initiative, courage, independence, talents, erotic values, capacity to master situations. As long as homemaking was a really big task involving many responsibilities, and as long as the number of children was not restricted, woman had the feeling of being a constructive factor in the economic process; thus she was provided with a sound basis for self-esteem. This basis, however, has gradually vanished, and in its departure woman has lost one foundation for feeling herself valuable.

As far as the sexual basis of self-confidence is concerned, certainly the puritanical influences, however one may evaluate them, have contributed toward the debasement of women by giving sexuality the connotation of something sinful and low. In a patriarchal society this attitude was bound to make woman into the symbol of sin; many such allusions may be found in early Christian literature. This is one of the great cultural reasons why woman, even today, considers herself debased and soiled by sexuality and thus lowered in her own self-esteem.

There remains, finally, the emotional basis of self-confidence. If, however, one's self-confidence is dependent on giving or receiving love, then one builds on a foundation which is too small and too shaky—too small because it leaves out too many personality values, and too shaky because it is dependent on too many external factors, such as finding adequate partners. Beside, it very easily leads to an emotional dependence on other people's affection and appreciation, and results in a feeling of unworthiness if one is not loved or appreciated.

As far as the alleged given inferiority of woman is concerned, Freud has, to be sure, made a remark which it is quite a relief to hear from him: "You must not forget, however, that we have only described women in so far as their natures are determined by their sexual function. The influence of this factor is, of course, very far-reaching, but we must remember that *an individual woman may be a human being apart from this*" (italics mine). I am convinced that he really means it, but one would like to have this opinion of his assume a broader place in his theoretical system. Certain sentences in Freud's latest paper on feminine psychology indicate that in comparison with his earlier studies he is giving additional consideration to the influence of cultural factors on women's psychology: "But we must take care not to underestimate the influence of social conventions, which also force women into passive situations. The whole thing is still very obscure. We must not overlook one particularly constant relation between femininity and instinctual life. The repression of their aggressiveness, which is imposed upon women by their constitutions and by society, favors the development of strong masochistic impulses, which have the effect of binding erotically the destructive tendencies which have been turned inwards."

But since he has a primarily biological orientation Freud does not, and on the basis of his premises cannot, see the whole significance of these factors. He cannot see to what extent they mold wishes and attitudes, nor can he evaluate the complexity of interrelations between cultural conditions and feminine psychology.

I suppose everyone agrees with Freud that differences in sexual constitution and functions influence mental life. But it seems unconstructive to speculate on the exact nature of this influence. The American woman is different from the German woman; both are different from certain Pueblo Indian women. The New York society woman is different from the farmer's wife in Idaho. The way specific cultural conditions engender specific qualities and faculties, in women as in men—this is what we may hope to understand.

JULIET MITCHELL

Juliet Mitchell (1940–) is a psychoanalyst who was born in New Zealand. Since 1971 she has also been a freelance writer, broadcaster, and frequent lecturer. During the 1960s, she taught English at the University of Leeds and the University of Reading. Most of her work is explicitly feminist, combining her knowledge of psychoanalysis and literature with a critique of the oppression of women.

Mitchell explicitly links the oppression of women to capitalist ideology. "The social nature of work under capitalism," she writes, "fragments the unitary family," producing "an increased number of contradictions for the woman within it." Although she believes that psychological and behavioral differences between the sexes are partially explicable within a psychoanalytic framework, she insists that this does not imply "an acceptance of the present patriarchal practice of psychoanalysis, nor of the many patriarchal judgments found within Freud's own work." Mitchell's view of men, women, and society thus combines a socialist critique with psychoanalytic theory.

Femininity

. . . [O]ur mental life also reflects, in a transformed way, what culture has already done with our biological needs and constitutions. It was with this *transformation* that Freud was concerned. What we could, and should, criticize him for is that he never makes his repeated statements to this effect forcefully enough in the context of his accounts of psychological sexual differences. To the contrary, disastrously as it turned out for the future of the psychoanalysis of femininity, it is just at these points that he most frequently turned back from the problem, leaving the reader with a nasty feeling that Freud's last word on the subject referred her to biology or anatomy.

But clearly it was just such a taste of biology that 'post'-Freudian analysts savoured. As a criticism of this aspect of *their* work, the condemnations of Freud hold good. If any analysis of feminine psychology is to take place, it is high time that a decisive break was made both with biologism in general and with the specific contribution it makes here: that a so-called biological dualism between the sexes is reflected in mental life. Psychoanalysis is about the inheritance and acquisition of the human order. The fact that it has been used to induce conformity to specific social mores is a further abuse of it that largely has been made possible on the theoretical level by the same biological preoccupation of some post-Freudians. If anatomy were indeed destiny, as Freud once disastrously remarked, then we might as well all get on with it and give up, for *nothing* would distinguish man from the animals. But Freud made this fatal remark in the context of a science concerned with exploring human social laws as they are represented in the unconscious mind.

Both Reich and the feminist critics attack Freud for his ignorance of the determining effects of patriarchal culture, but ironically, in their own analyses, they forget exactly what they have remembered in their denunciatory rhetoric. In all the accounts the asymmetrical specific of a *father-dominated* social structure is forgotten in favour of male-female opposition with male domination. The general notion of opposition and social dualism is likewise an important feature of Laing's work. If such social dualism replaces biological dualism, circularity will be the inevitable result of the debate. The principle of dialectics is *contradiction,* not simple unity: elements contradict one another, resolve themselves, join together, and enter into further contradictions with other aspects—any 'unity' is a complex one containing contradictions. Even looking at the concept from a simplified, formalistic viewpoint, there must be at least *three* elements and the third cannot be the simple unity of the two, as Reich, Firestone and Laing (the authors who are interested in dialectics) would have it.

Freud's analysis of the psychology of women takes place within a concept that it is neither socially nor biologically dualistic. It takes place within an analysis of patriarchy. His theories give us the beginnings of an explanation of the inferiorized and 'alternative' (second sex) psychology of women under patriarchy. Their concern is with how the human animal with a bisexual psychological disposition becomes the sexed social creature—the man or the woman.

In his speculative works on the origins of human culture and man's phylogenesis, in particular in *Totem and Taboo* and *Moses and Monotheism,* Freud shows quite explicitly that the psychoanalytic concept of the unconscious is a concept of mankind's transmission and inheritance of his social (cultural) laws. In each man's unconscious lies all mankind's 'ideas' of his history; a history that cannot start afresh with each individual but must be acquired and contributed to over time. Understanding the laws of the unconscious thus amounts to a start in understanding how ideology functions, how we acquire and live the ideas and laws within which we must exist. A primary aspect of the law is that we live according to our sexed identity, our ever imperfect 'masculinity' or 'femininity'.

The determining feature of Freud's reconstruction of mankind's history is the murder of the primal father in a prehistorical period. It is this dead father that is the mark of patriarchy. In an imagined pre-social epoch, the father had *all* the power and *all* rights over *all* the women of the clan; a band of sons—all brothers, weak on their own, but strong together, murdered the father to get at his rights. Of course, they could not all have his rights and, of course, they must feel ambivalent about the deed they had committed. Totemism and exogamy are the dual signs of their response: in the totem, or symbolic substitute for the father, is guaranteed that no one else may kill him, or by then his heirs (each one of the brothers). Furthermore, not one of the brothers can inherit this father's right to all the women. For as they cannot *all* inherit, none shall. This is the start of social law and morality. The brothers identify with the father they have killed, and internalize the guilt which they feel along with the pleasure in his death. The father thus becomes far more powerful in death than in life; it is in death that he institutes human history. The dead, symbolic father is far more crucial than any actual living father who merely transmits his name. This is the story of the origins of patriarchy. It is against this symbolic mark of the dead father that boys and girls find their cultural place within the instance of the Oedipus complex.

In the situation of the Oedipus complex (which reiterates the rules of the totem and of exogamy) the little boy learns his place as the heir to this law of the father and the little girl learns her place within it. The Oedipus complex is certainly a patriarchal myth and, though he never said so, the importance of this fact was doubtless behind Freud's repudiation of a parallel myth for women—a so-called Electra complex. Freud always opposed any idea of symmetry in the cultural 'making' of men and women. A myth for women would have to bear most dominantly the marks of the Oedipus complex because it is a man's world into which a woman enters; complementarity or parallelism are out of the question. At first both sexes want to take the place of both the mother and the father, but as they cannot take *both* places, each sex has to learn to repress the characteristics of the other sex. But both, as they learn to speak and live within society, want to take the father's place, and *only the boy will one day be allowed to do so.* Furthermore both sexes are born into the desire of the mother, and as, through cultural heritage, what the mother desires is the phallus-turned-baby, *both* children desire to be the phallus for the mother. Again, *only the boy can fully recognize himself in his mother's desire.* Thus *both* sexes repudiate the implications of femininity. Femininity is, therefore, in part a repressed condition that can only be secondarily acquired in a distorted form. It is because it is repressed that femininity is so hard to comprehend both within and without psychoanalytic investigation—it returns in symptoms, such as hysteria. In the body of the hysteric, male and female, lies the feminine protest against the law of the father.[1] But what is repressed is both the representation of the desire and the prohibition against it: there is nothing 'pure' or 'original' about it.

1. It is the language or graphology of the body symptomatology, the traces of repressed femininity in hysteria, that the French women's liberation group, *Psychanalyse et Politique*, is deciphering. It was here in the analysis of the hysterical symptom in his earliest psychoanalytic days that, they consider, Freud stopped short. I am not sure that I would agree with the stress that I understand they put on the father's Oedipal 'rape' of his daughter, as it seems to me that the girl precisely has to learn the arts of seduction, of *winning* love.

The girl only acquires her secondary feminine identity within the law of patriarchy in her positive Oedipus complex when she is seduced/raped by, and/or seduces the father. As the boy becomes heir to the law with his acceptance of symbolic castration from the father, the girl learns her feminine destiny with this symbolic seduction. But it is less important than the boy's 'castration', because she has to some extent perceived her situation before it is thus confirmed by the father's intervention. She has already acquired the information that as she is not heir to the phallus she does not need to accept symbolic castration (she is already 'castrated'). But without the father's role in her positive Oedipus complex she could remain locked in pre-Oedipal dilemmas (and hence would become psychotic), for the Oedipus complex is her entry into her human heritage of femininity. Freud always said that a woman was 'more bisexual' than a man. By this he seems to have been hinting at the fact that within patriarchy her desire to take the father's place and be the phallus for the mother is as strong as is the boy's ultimate right to do so. The bisexual disposition of her pre-Oedipal moment remains strong and her Oedipus complex is a poor, secondary affair. An affair in which she learns that her subjugation to the law of the father entails her becoming the representative of 'nature' and 'sexuality', a chaos of spontaneous, intuitive creativity. As she cannot receive the 'touch' of the law, her submission to it must be in establishing herself as its opposite—as all that is loving and irrational. Such is the condition of patriarchal human history.

With the ending of his Oedipus complex and the internalizing of the 'castrating' father as his authoritative superego, the boy enters into the prospect of his future manhood. The girl, on the contrary, has almost to build her Oedipus complex out of the impossibilities of her bisexual pre-Oedipal desires. Instead of internalizing the mark of the law in a superego to which she will live up, she can only develop her narcissistic ego-ideal. She must confirm her pre-Oedipal identification (as opposed to attachment) with the mother, and instead of taking on qualities of aggression and control she acquires the art of love and conciliation. Not being heir to the law of culture, her task is to see that mankind reproduces itself within the circularity of the supposedly natural family. The family is, of course, no more 'natural' than the woman, but its place within the law is to take on 'natural' functions. For sexuality, which supposedly unites the couple, disrupts the kingdom if uncontrolled; it, too, must be contained and organized. Woman becomes, in her nineteenth-century designation, 'the sex'. Hers is the sphere of reproduction.

This is the place of all women in patriarchal culture. To put the matter in a most generalizing fashion: men enter into the class-dominated structures of history while women (as women, whatever their actual work in production) remain defined by the kinship patterns of organization. In our society the kinship system is harnessed into the family—where a woman is formed in such a way that that is where she will stay. Differences of class, historical epoch, specific social situations alter the expression of femininity; but in relation to the law of the father, women's position across the board is a comparable one. When critics condemn Freud for not taking account of social reality, their concept of that reality is too limited. The social reality that he is concerned with elucidating is the mental representation of the reality of society. . . .

As we have seen, Freud often longed for a satisfactory biological base on which to rest his psychological theories, and yet the wish was no sooner uttered than forgotten. From the work of Ernest Jones through to that of contemporary feminist analysts such as Mary Jane Sherfy,[2] the biological base of sexual dualism has been sought. Although there is an obvious *use* of the biological base in any social formation, it would seem dubious to stress this. For there seems little evidence of any biological priority. Quite the contrary; we are confronted with a situation that is determinately social. This situation is the initial *transformation* of biology by the exchange system expressed by kinship structures and the *social* taboos on incest that set up the differential conditions for the formation of men and women. This is not, of course, to deny that, as in all mammalian species, there is a difference between the reproductive roles of each sex, but it is to suggest that in *no* human society do these take precedence in an untransformed way. The establishment of human society relegates them to a secondary place, though their ideological reimportation may make them appear dominant.

It is not simply a question of the by-now familiar thesis that mankind, in effecting the move from nature to culture, 'chose' to preserve women within a natural ('animal') role for the sake of the propagation and nurturing of the species, for this suggestion sets up too simple a split between nature and culture and consequently too simple a division between the fate of the sexes. The very inauguration of 'culture' necessitated a different role. It is not that women are confined to a natural function but that they are given a specialized role in the formation of civilization. *It is thus not on account of their 'natural' procreative possibilities but on account of their cultural utilization as exchange-objects (which involves an exploitation of their role as propagators) that women acquire their feminine definition.* The situation, then, into which boys and girls are born is the same, the place to which they are assigned is clearly different. As it stands now, that place is in most important respects

2. See Mary Jane Sherfy, 'A Theory on Female Sexuality', in *Sisterhood Is Powerful*, ed. by Robin Morgan (New York: Random House, 1970).

the same that it has always been: boys are to take over from fathers, girls are to want to produce babies. Any biological urge to do so is buried beneath the cultural demand that makes the way this wish is acquired coincident with human society itself. The technological conquest of the biological distinction between the sexes that Firestone and others recommend is redundant; in this instance, biology is no longer relevant. In an important sense, on this question, it has not been relevant since the foundation of human society. That foundation itself distinguished between the sexes.

In what way does this emphatic change of terrain affect the tasks of feminism? If we identify patriarchy with human history, the solution to the question of the oppression of women at first seems far less accessible than if we were to explore other theories. It has been suggested that we struggle for an 'ecological revolution'—a *humanized* brave new world of extra-uterine babies—or that in the power games of all men we locate and challenge the enemy. In the first proposition, technology conquers the biological handicap of women—their greater physical weakness and painful ability to give birth. In the second, a sociological analysis matches the perceived actuality of male superiority—men as such *do* have greater economic and political power and thus social equality should right the injustice. One or [the] other, or a combination of both of these technological and sociological answers has held sway in all demands for change and all hopes for equity. Neither socialist practice nor Marxist theory in this field have been exempt from these essentially social-democratic visions.

It is no surprise that in these circumstances the feminist revolution has nowhere come about, and that women, in vastly differing ways and degrees remain 'oppressed'. Even if important details of these theories are correct, the posing of a biological problem and its technological solution or the sociological explanation of *male* domination and its overcoming (by consent or violence) are *both* at base misleading suggestions. It is the specific feature of patriarchy—the law of the hypothesized prehistoric murdered father—that defines the relative places of men and women in human history. This 'father' and his representatives—all fathers—are the crucial expression of patriarchal society. It is *fathers* not *men* who have the determinate power. And it is a question neither of biology nor of a specific society, but of *human* society itself.

Such a proposition possibly seems *more* generalized and its solution *less* available than the biological-technological and sociological theories. But I don't think this need be the case. Patriarchy describes the universal culture—however, each specific economic mode of production must express this in different ideological forms. The universal aspects of patriarchy set in motion by 'the death of the father' are the exchange of women and the cultural taboo on incest, but these are rehearsed diversely in the mind of man in different societies. It would seem to me that with capitalist society something new has happened to the culture that is patriarchy.

The complexity of capitalist society makes archaic the kinship structures and incest taboos for the majority of the people and yet it preserves them through thick and thin. Freud gave the name of the Oedipus complex to the universal law by which men and women learn their place in the world, but the universal law has specific expression in the capitalist family. (Anthropological arguments that make the Oedipus complex general without demarcating its specificity are inadequate; political suggestions that it is only to be found in capitalist societies are incorrect. What Freud was deciphering was our human heritage—but he deciphered it in a particular time and place.) *The capitalist economy implies that for the masses demands of exogamy and the social taboo on incest are irrelevant; but nevertheless it must preserve both these and the patriarchal structure that they imply.* Furthermore, it would seem that the specifically capitalist ideology of a supposedly natural nuclear family would be in harsh contradiction to the kinship structure as it is articulated in the Oedipus complex, which in this instance is expressed within this nuclear family. It is, I believe, this contradiction, which is already being powerfully felt, that must be analysed and then made use of for the overthrow of patriarchy.

Freud considered that 'discontent' (roughly, the sublimation and repression of desires) was a condition of civilization. It would seem indeed to be a condition, but one that Freud may well have been able to perceive precisely because it had reached a sort of 'ultimate'. Before I elaborate this point, I wish to distinguish it from one to which at first it seems to bear some resemblances. Herbert Marcuse, a Marxist who has consistently used psychoanalysis in the formation of his theories, claims that capitalist society demands a surplus repression—more repression than is needed by society in order to function. Marcuse argues that the reign of actual scarcity is all but over (or could be so), hence liberation from exploitative toil is possible; but capitalism, to retain its own nature (the exploitation of surplus-value), must create new needs, demand new 'performances' and thus institute unnecessary repression of the potentially liberated desires. It seems to me that this argument, although it welds together psychoanalytic and Marxist theory, in fact traps psychoanalysis within Marxist *economics*. In doing so it also casts, like Freud's own presentation of the progress of civilization, too evolutionary a light over the course of human history. Despite appearances and despite its important insights, this theory retains some of the worst aspects of both the sciences that it would use: an economism from Marxism and an evolutionary tinge from psychoanalysis. It is not that civilization has passed beyond the point where it needs its discontents but that there is a *contradiction* between the mode of the immediate expression-repression of these desires and the laws which forbid them as the very basis of culture. The ban on incest and the demand for exogamy howl so loudly in the contemporary Oedipus complex because they are reinforced precisely when they are no longer needed. It is only in this highly specific sense that capitalist society institutes a surplus repression; it is only the concept of *contradiction* (not that of *degree* implied by Marcuse's term 'surplus') that is of use in foreseeing any political transformation.

We can approach this proposition more concretely. Wars in no way change the basic relations of production but they do offer a different political situation and one that foreshadows the future. We can learn certain things from the last world war. Taking Britain as an example, we can see that in the period 1940–45 the family as we present it in our dominant ideologies virtually ceased to exist. In wartime the industrial employment of women was once more predominant and fathers were absent. For the first time there was planned alternative social organization to the family. Compulsory education was extended, pre-school crèches were provided, large-scale evacuation of children was organized, the state took care of food rations and ensured the basic necessary nourishment of small children and provided communal restaurants—all tasks normally left to the nuclear family. After a monumental post-war reaction, a repeat of certain of these trends is becoming visible today. With government plans for pre-school and nursery centres and the continual raising of the school leaving age, the school could rapidly become the main ideological institution into which the child is inserted. Of course such a development happens in an uneven and socially brutal fashion, but it is against such 'massifications' as the vast comprehensive school and the modern automated factory that romantics of the family and of the intimate and the private hold their own. Like the home-sweet-home songsters of the nineteenth century, they think they are looking back to a pre-capitalist golden age, but in fact they are only humming the descant. Capitalist society establishes the family in the context of its redundancy. The restoration or abolition of the family is not in itself important except as a symptom of this redundancy. It is the stress both in reactionary and in revolutionary arguments (such as Reich's) on the family and on its own contradictory nature under capitalism that has obscured the more fundamental contradiction between the specific conditions of the family and the demands of the law of human culture.

With capitalism (in its variant forms: imperialism, fascism, etc.), man reaches the limit of a historical development based throughout on class conflict. In the mass social work that man undertakes for the first time, the conditions of its own dissolution are powerfully present within capitalism. So, too, it would appear, are the conditions needed for a transformation of all previous ideology, the previous conditions of human culture. However, too often, while we acknowledge that the contradictions of capitalism as an economic system will only be resolved and released with its overthrow (and then in no straightforward manner), we forget that something similar holds true for its prevailing ideology. Why do we make this omission?

One important reason, I would suggest, is that we have tended to subject ideological analysis to economic analysis. (Although it seems to be doing the opposite, Marcuse's work is a case in point.) Or perhaps it would be more accurate to propose that the two spheres have become inextricably mingled, and theoretical progress depends not on amalgamation but on specification. However, such a commingling has still more serious consequences. Though, of course, ideology and a given mode of production are interdependent, one cannot be reduced to the other nor can the same laws be found to govern one as govern the other. To put the matter schematically, in analysing contemporary Western society we are (as elsewhere) dealing with two autonomous areas: the economic mode of capitalism and the ideological mode of patriarchy. The interdependence between them is found in the particular expression of patriarchal ideology—in this case the kinship system that defines patriarchy is forced into the straightjacket of the nuclear family. But if we analyse the economic and the ideological situation only at the point of their interpenetration, we shall never see the means to their transformation.

Under capitalism, just as the economic mode of production contains its own contradiction, so too does the ideological mode of reproduction. The social conditions of work under capitalism potentially contain the overthrow of the exploitative conditions into which they are harnessed and it is these *same* social conditions of work that make potentially redundant the laws of patriarchal culture. The working class has the power to take back to itself (for mankind) the products of the labour which are not taken from it; but no simple extension of this position can be taken to apply to patriarchal ideology. The same capitalist conditions of labour (the mass of people working together) create the conditions of change in both spheres, but because of their completely different origins, the change will come about in different ways. It is the working class as a class that has the products of its social labour privately appropriated by the capitalist class; it is women who stand at the heart of the contradiction of patriarchy under capitalism.

The controlled exchange of women that defines human culture is reproduced in the patriarchal ideology of every form of society. It goes alongside and is interlinked with class conflict, but it is not the same thing. It is not only in the ideology of their roles as mothers and procreators but above all in the very psychology of femininity that women bear witness to the patriarchal definition of human society. But today this patriarchal ideology, while it poses as the ultimate rationalization, is, in fact, in the slow death throes of its own irrationality; in this it is like the capitalist economy itself. But in both cases only a *political* struggle will bring their surcease. Neither can die a natural death; capitalism will, as it is all the time doing, intervene at a political level, to ensure their survival.

It is because it appears as the ultimate rationality, that critics mistake the Oedipus complex for the nuclear family itself. On the contrary, it is the contradiction between the internalized law of patriarchal human order described by Freud as the Oedipus complex, and its embodiment in the nuclear family, that is significant.

The patriarchal law speaks to and through each person in his unconscious; the reproduction of the ideology of human society is thus assured in the acquisition of the law by each individual. The unconscious that Freud analysed could thus be described as the domain of the reproduction of culture or ideology. The contradiction that exists between this law that is now essentially redundant but that of course still continues to speak in the unconscious, and the form of the nuclear family is therefore crucial. The bourgeois family was so to speak created to give that law a last hearing. Naturally enough, it is not very good at its job, so capitalist society offers a stop-go programme of boosting or undermining this family. It is because it is so obviously a point of weakness that so much revolutionary theory and strategy has concentrated on attacking it. But, as we have seen, its importance lies not *within* it so much as *between* it and the patriarchal law it is supposed to express. Of greater importance still is the contradiction between patriarchal law and the social organization of work—a contradiction held in check by the nuclear family.

It is at this moment, when the very structure of patriarchal culture becomes redundant, that with necessary perversity a vogue for man-as-animal comes into its own. Throughout history man has made strenuous intellectual efforts to distinguish himself from the beasts—this was always a dominant feature of his ideology; now, when the basis of his differential culture is in need of transformation, the only possible rearguard action is to consider that that culture was never in any case very significant. In the human zoo the male 'naked-ape' is naturally aggressive and the female naturally nurturative, they must regain their instinctive animal nature and forget what man has made of man. Such absurdities are a symptom of the dilemma of patriarchal human order. A symptom of a *completely different order* is the feminist movements of the nineteenth and twentieth centuries.

Under patriarchal order women are oppressed in their very psychologies of femininity; once this order is retained only in a highly contradictory manner this oppression manifests itself. Women have to organize themselves as a group to effect a change in the basic ideology of human society. To be effective, this can be no righteous challenge to the simple domination of men (though this plays a tactical part), but a struggle based on a theory of the social non-necessity at this stage of development of the laws instituted by patriarchy.

The overthrow of the capitalist economy and the political challenge that effects this, do not in themselves mean a transformation of patriarchal ideology. This is the implication of the fact that the ideological sphere has a certain autonomy. The change to a socialist economy does not by itself suggest that the end of patriarchy comfortably follows suit. A specific struggle against patriarchy—a cultural revolution—is requisite. The battles too must have their own autonomy. It seems to follow that women within revolutionary feminism can be the spearhead of general ideological change as the working class is the agent of the overthrow of the specifically capitalist mode of production. Neither contingent—women nor the working class—can act in such a role without a theory and a political practice. But there need be no order of priority here—it will depend on the conditions in which they have to take place. Because patriarchy is by no means identical with capitalism, the successes and strengths of the two revolutionary movements will not follow along neatly parallel paths. It is perfectly possible for feminism to make more intermediate gains under social democracy than it does in the first years of socialism. Nor, alternatively, because a socialist economy is achieved, does that mean that the struggle against patriarchy must cease. There is no question of either political movement taking precedence, or of either revolutionary group being mutually exclusive or even of each group containing only its own denominational membership. By this I mean that just as when the working class becomes revolutionary, people who do not actually come from the working class can make a political transformation of their own class origins and join it, so *when* the feminist movement has a revolutionary theory and practice, men too (if with difficulty) can give up their patriarchal privileges and become feminists. This is not to say that they can become members of the movement where it operates at the level of feminist consciousness any more than Marxist intellectuals can join the trade union movement which is the equivalent organization of working-class consciousness—they can merely support it in a practical fashion. I am making these comparisons only to help us situate ourselves in current debates on the left about political practice.

When the potentialities of the complexities of capitalism—both economic and ideological—are released by its overthrow, new structures will gradually come to be represented in the unconscious. It is the task of feminism to insist on their birth. Some other expression of the entry into culture than the implications for the unconscious of the exchange of women will have to be found in non-patriarchal society. We should also recognize that no society has yet existed—or existed for a sufficient length of time—for the 'eternal' unconscious to have shed its immortal nature. While matrilineages are certainly to be found, it seems as though matriarchies can be ruled out. Matrilineages only present us with a variation on the theme of the law-of-the-father. Socialist societies have had too little time on earth to have achieved anything as radical as a change in man's unconscious. And a sense of this can be read into a recent conversation between Mao Tse-tung and the late Edgar Snow. In this Mao claimed that despite collective work, egalitarian legislation, social care of children, etc., it was too soon for the Chinese really deeply and irrevocably to have changed their *attitudes* towards women. Or as he had told André Malraux: 'Of course it was necessary to give [women] legal equality to begin with! But from there on everything still remains to be done. The thought, culture, and customs which brought China to where we found her must disappear, and the thought, customs, and culture of proletarian China, which does not yet exist, must appear. The Chinese woman doesn't yet exist either, among the masses: but she is beginning to want to exist. And then to liberate women is not to manufacture washing-machines.' It is with understanding how thoughts, customs, and culture operate that psychoanalysis is concerned. We have to resist the temptation to neglect the analysis for a dream, for just as pre-Marxist nineteenth-century visions perceived communism as primitive communism, so too there is today a tendency to wish to see a post-patriarchal society in terms of a primitive matriarchy: the reign of nurturing, emotionality, and non-repression. Clearly neither vision has much to do with the reality of the past or of the future.

Today, our specific ideology of a natural, biological family (our 'holy family') re-expresses as a repressed Oedipal saga the kinship structure to which it is in contradiction, and the problems of learning differences. Some way of establishing distinctions will always be crucial; that it should be this way is quite another question. However, in the meantime, entering into what would seem to be only a revamped patriarchal society, the little girl has to acquire, and quickly too, her cultural destiny which is made to appear misleadingly coincident with a biological one.

It is not a question of changing (or ending) who has or how one has babies. It is a question of overthrowing patriarchy. As the end of 'eternal' class conflict is visible within the contradictions of capitalism, so too, it would seem, is the swan-song of the 'immortal' nature of patriarchal culture to be heard.

SUGGESTIONS FOR FURTHER READING

Psychoanalysis

Cadwallader, Eva H. "A Jungian Analysis of Current Tensions among Philosophers." *Philosophy Today* 24 (Winter 1980), pp. 349–59.

Chesler, Phyllis. *Women and Madness.* New York: Avon Books, 1972.

Donchin, Anne. "Concepts of Women in Psychoanalytic Theory: The Nature-Nurture Controversy Revisited." In *Beyond Domination*, ed. by Carol C. Gould. Totowa, N.J.: Rowman & Allanheld, 1984, pp. 89–106.

DuBois, Page. *Sowing the Body: Psychoanalysis and Ancient Representations of Women.* Chicago: The University of Chicago Press, 1988.

Flax, Jane. *Thinking Fragments: Psychoanalysis, Feminism, and Postmodernism in the Contemporary West.* Berkeley: University of California Press, 1989.

Grünbaum, Adolf. *The Foundations of Psychoanalysis.* Berkeley: University of California Press, 1984.

Hayes, John. "Freud's Philosophical Roots." *Irish Philosophical Journal* 5 (1988), pp. 46–71.

Horney, Karen. *The Collected Works of Karen Horney*, 2 vols. New York: W. W. Norton & Company, 1945, 1950.

Kelman, Harold. *Helping People. Karen Horney's Psychoanalytic Approach.* New York: Science House, 1971.

Kittay, Eva Feder. "Rereading Freud on 'Femininity' or Why Not 'Womb' Envy." *Hypatia* 2 (1984), pp. 385–91.

Miller, Jean. *Toward a New Psychology of Women.* Boston: Beacon Press, 1977.

Mitchell, Juliet. *The Longest Revolution: Essays on Feminism, Literature and Psychoanalysis.* London: Virago, 1966, 1984.

———. *Women's Estate.* New York: Pantheon Books, 1971, 1972.

———. *Psychoanalysis and Feminism.* New York: Pantheon Books, 1974.

Nagera, Humberto. *Female Sexuality and the Oedipus Complex.* New York: Aronson Jason, Inc., 1975.

Nissim-Sabat, Marilyn. "Freud, Feminism, and Faith." *Listening* 20 (Fall 1985), pp. 208–20.

Rawlinson, Mary C. "Psychiatric Discourse and the Feminine Voice." *Journal of Medicine and Philosophy* 7 (May 1982), pp. 153–78.

Rubins, Jack L. *Karen Horney. Gentle Rebel of Psychoanalysis.* New York: The Dial Press, 1978.

Sayers, Janet. *Mothers of Psychoanalysis: Helene Deutsch, Karen Horney, Anna Freud, Melanie Klein.* New York: W. W. Norton & Company, 1991.

Tapper, Marion E. "The Superego of Women." *Social Theory and Practice* 12 (Spring 1986), pp. 61–74.

Ulanov, Ann B. *The Feminine in Jungian Psychology and in Christian Theology.* Evanston: Northwestern University Press, 1971.

Weisstein, Naomi. "Psychology Constructs the Female." In *Sex Equality,* ed. by Jane English. Englewood Cliffs, N.J.: Prentice-Hall, Inc., 1977, pp. 205–15.

Westkott, Marcia. *The Feminist Legacy of Karen Horney.* New Haven: Yale University Press, 1986.

SOCIALISM

In general, Marxist theory involves a greater emphasis upon society than upon the individual. It would be a mistake, however, to construe that emphasis as denying rights and freedom to the individual, even though some supposedly Marxist instances of modern government seem to support that interpretation. Totalitarian regimes are basically inconsistent with the social teachings of Marx, particularly in his early writings. While some scholars consider the later writings a departure from the earlier ones, the majority insist that Marx was consistent, and that the politically radical views of the later period such as those expressed in *Capital* can only be understood correctly in the light of his earlier humanistic concepts.

FRIEDRICH ENGELS

Both Karl Marx (1818–1883) and Friedrich Engels (1820–1895) were products of German bourgeois society. Their life-long friendship began in 1844 in Paris, where Marx had gone to escape political pressures evoked by his radical writings. A key theme in Marx's manuscripts of this period is his denunciation of previous philosophers for having engaged exclusively in speculation about the world, thereby neglecting their primary responsibility for effecting social change. Through his own study of history, Marx had become convinced that the most effective way to improve society was through economics; he therefore embarked upon a thorough study of that subject as a tool through which to fulfill what he believed to be the proper function of philosophy.

Subsequently both Marx and Engels lived in England, where Marx labored long years in the composition of *Capital*. He supported his family on the pittance received from occasional articles, supplemented by the generosity of Engels, who managed his father's textile business in London. In fundamental agreement with Marx's ideas, Engels thus sought to contribute financially to their actualization. His writings also reflect his accord with Marx's theory.

One of the most influential converts to Marxism was another product of the bourgeoisie—Vladimir Lenin (1870–1924). As a youth in Russia, Lenin had become involved in the "intelligentsia," a politically radical discussion circle, for whom the writings of Marx and Engels were an important source and inspiration. Two early events are revealing with regard to Lenin's later social attitudes: (1) When his older brother Alex was arrested and executed for involvement in a plot to kill the tsar, Lenin refused to seek personal retribution or revenge; only universal interests, i.e., those of every member of society, could justify retaliation for such an act;

(2) In 1887 Lenin was expelled from law school for his part in a minor student demonstration. Without benefit of teachers or classes, he studied on his own and passed the required examinations with the highest possible grades: he thus exhibited a determined will as well as a keen intellect, powers he fully utilized in behalf of the oppressed.

As a result of his efforts to form a Russian Marxist organization, Lenin was arrested and imprisoned first at St. Petersburg, then in Siberia, for over four years. Upon his release he continued his subversive efforts from exile, principally by writings and building up a political party. Not until 1917, when revolution in Russia erupted spontaneously through the downfall of the tsar, did Lenin return to his native land, where he eventually succeeded in establishing and leading the Communist Party. In all these activities, Lenin saw himself as applying to Russia the ideas and idealism of Marx.

Marx's philosophy is sometimes called a dialectical materialism. The dialectic derives from Hegel; basically, it means a view of reality and history as a progressive process of interaction between opposing forces. Society is continually advancing through its varying forms, toward the fullest realization of our human potential. The materialism of Marx involves the claim that all reality is matter or nature, even human reality. This does not imply a denial of human consciousness, but allows that this consciousness be defined as a complex arrangement of matter. In other words, human beings are composed of the same "stuff" (matter) as are plants and animals and minerals, but they differ from those instances of matter in that they exhibit consciousness.

Hence, to be human, for Marx, is to be a very special kind of "dialectical matter"; it is to be a being whose consciousness allows him or her to affect as well as be affected by the world. To be human is to be a producer, and not a mere product, in the midst of nature. Marx's use of the term "production" extends to any work of human beings, including works of art and intellect. To be human is also to be related to other persons in a truly human, that is, a free and intelligent, manner. Dehumanization of individuals or society occurs wherever human beings are treated as products or means of production rather than as producers, or whenever they are alienated, or cut off from free interaction with other persons. According to Marx, such dehumanization inevitably occurs within the capitalistic economic system.

In his early writings, Marx had described the man-woman relationship as a gauge for the level of humanization achieved by a society. For example, wherever prostitution is practiced, women are used as objects of pleasure for men; similarly, capitalistic producers use the working class as means of obtaining economic profit for themselves. The following selection, written by Engels after Marx's death, applies Marx's criterion to a critique of the modern family.

Origin of the Family

If we consider the most primitive known forms of family . . . the form of sexual intercourse can only be described as promiscuous—promiscuous in so far as the restrictions later established by custom did not yet exist. . . .

According to Morgan,[1] from this primitive state of promiscuous intercourse there developed, probably very early:

1. THE CONSANGUINE FAMILY, THE FIRST STAGE OF THE FAMILY

Here the marriage groups are separated according to generations: all the grandfathers and grandmothers within the limits of the family are all husbands and wives of one another; so are also their children, the fathers and mothers; the latter's children will form a third circle of common husbands and wives; and their children, the great-grandchildren of the first group, will form a fourth. In this form of marriage, therefore, only ancestors and progeny, and parents and children, are excluded from the rights and duties (as we should say) of marriage with one another. . . .

2. THE PUNALUAN FAMILY

If the first advance in organization consisted in the exclusion of parents and children from sexual intercourse with one another, the second was the exclusion of sister and brother. On account of the greater nearness in age, this second advance was infinitely more important, but also more difficult, than the first. It was effected gradually, beginning probably with the exclusion from sexual intercourse of one's own brothers and sisters (children of the same mother) first in isolated cases and then by degrees as a general rule (even in this century exceptions were found in Hawaii), and ending with the prohibition of marriage even between collateral brothers and sisters, or, as we should say, between first, second, and third cousins. It affords, says Morgan, "a good illustration of the operation of the principle of natural selection." There can be no question that the tribes among whom inbreeding was restricted

1. Lewis H. Morgan, *Ancient Society or Researches in the Lines of Human Progress from Savagery through Barbarism to Civilization* (Chicago: Charles H. Kerr & Company, 1877).

by this advance were bound to develop more quickly and more fully than those among whom marriage between brothers and sisters remained the rule and the law. . . .

In all forms of group family, it is uncertain who is the father of a child; but it is certain who its mother is. Though she calls *all* the children of the whole family her children and has a mother's duties toward them, she nevertheless knows her own children from the others. It is therefore clear that in so far as group marriage prevails, descent can only be proved on the *mother's* side and that therefore only the *female* line is recognized. And this is in fact the case among all peoples in the period of savagery or in the lower stage of barbarism. It is the second great merit of Bachofen that he was the first to make this discovery. To denote this exclusive recognition of descent through the mother and the relations of inheritance which in time resulted from it, he uses the term "mother right," which for the sake of brevity I retain. The term is, however, ill-chosen, since at this stage of society there cannot yet be any talk of "right" in the legal sense. . . .

3. THE PAIRING FAMILY

A certain amount of pairing, for a longer or shorter period, already occurred in group marriage or even earlier; the man had a chief wife among his many wives (one can hardly yet speak of a favorite wife), and for her he was the most important among her husbands. . . . [T]hese customary pairings were bound to grow more stable as the gens developed and the classes of "brothers" and "sisters" between whom marriage was impossible became more numerous. The impulse given by the gens to the prevention of marriage between blood relatives extended still further.

. . . The increasing complication of these prohibitions made group marriages more and more impossible; they were displaced by the *pairing family*. In this stage, one man lives with one woman, but the relationship is such that polygamy and occasional infidelity remain the right of the men, even though for economic reasons polygamy is rare, while from the woman the strictest fidelity is generally demanded throughout the time she lives with the man and adultery on her part is cruelly punished. The marriage tie can, however, be easily dissolved by either partner; after separation, the children still belong as before to the mother alone. . . .

Thus the history of the family in primitive times consists in the progressive narrowing of the circle, originally embracing the whole tribe, within which the two sexes have a common conjugual relation. The continuous exclusion, first of nearer, then of more and more remote relatives, and at last even of relatives by marriage, ends by making any kind of group marriage practically impossible.

Finally, there remains only the single, still loosely linked pair, the molecule with whose dissolution marriage itself ceases. This in itself shows what a small part individual sex love, in the modern sense of the word, played in the rise of monogamy. . . .

The pairing family, itself too weak and unstable to make an independent household necessary or even desirable, in no wise destroys the communistic household inherited from earlier times. Communistic housekeeping, however, means the supremacy of women in the house; just as the exclusive recognition of the female parent, owing to the impossibility of recognizing the male parent with certainty, means that the women—the mothers—are held in high respect. One of the most absurd notions taken over from 18th century enlightenment is that in the beginning of society woman was the slave of man. Among all savages and all barbarians of the lower and middle stages, and to a certain extent of the upper stage also, the position of women is not only free, but honorable. . . .

The communistic household, in which most or all of the women belong to one and the same gens, while the men come from various gentes, is the material foundation of that supremacy of the women which was general in primitive times. . . . The reports of travelers and missionaries, I may add, to the effect that women among savages and barbarians are overburdened with work in no way contradict what has been said. The division of labor between the two sexes is determined by quite other causes than by the position of woman in society. Among peoples where the women have to work far harder than we think suitable, there is often much more real respect for women than among our Europeans. The lady of civilization, surrounded by false homage and estranged from all real work, has an infinitely lower social position than the hard-working woman of barbarism, who was regarded among her people as a real lady (lady, *frowa, Frau*—mistress) and who was also a lady in character.

. . . In the single pair the group was already reduced to its final unit, its two-atom molecule: one man and one woman. Natural selection, with its progressive exclusions from the marriage community, had accomplished its task; there was nothing more for it to do in this direction. Unless new, *social* forces came into play, there was no reason why a new form of family should arise from the single pair. But these new forces did come into play. . . . [T]he domestication of animals and the breeding of herds had developed a hitherto unsuspected source of wealth and created entirely new social relations. . . .

Once it had passed into the private possession of families and there rapidly begun to augment, this wealth dealt a severe blow to the society founded on pairing marriage and the matriarchal gens. Pairing marriage had brought a new element into the family. By the side of the natural mother of the child is placed its natural and attested father with a better warrant of paternity, probably, than that of many a "father" today. According to the division of labor within the family at that time, it was the man's part to obtain food and the instruments of labor necessary for the purpose. He therefore also owned the instruments of labor, and in the event of husband and wife separating, he took them with him, just as she retained her household goods. Therefore, according to the social custom of the time, the man was also the owner of the new source of subsistence, the cattle, and later of the new instruments of labor, the slaves. But according to the custom of the same society, his children could not inherit from him. . . .

Thus on the one hand, in proportion as wealth increased it made the man's position in the family more important than the woman's, and on the other hand created an impulse to exploit this strengthened position in order to overthrow, in favor of his children, the traditional order of inheritance. This, however, was impossible so long as descent was reckoned according to mother right. Mother right, therefore, had to be overthrown, and overthrown it was. . . .

The overthrow of mother right was the *world historical defeat of the female sex.* The man took command in the home also; the woman was degraded and reduced to servitude; she became the slave of his lust and a mere instrument for the production of children. This degraded position of the woman, especially conspicuous among the Greeks of the heroic and still more of the classical age, has gradually been palliated and glossed over, and sometimes clothed in a milder form; in no sense has it been abolished.

The establishment of the exclusive supremacy of the man shows its effects first in the patriarchal family, which now emerges as an intermediate form. Its essential characteristic is not polygyny, of which more later, but [according to Morgan] "the organization of a number of persons, bond and free, and into a family under paternal power for the purpose of holding lands and for the care of flocks and herds. . . . (In the Semitic form) the chiefs, at least, lived in polygamy. . . . Those held to servitude and those employed as servants lived in the marriage relation."

Its essential features are the incorporation of unfree persons and paternal power; hence the perfect type of this form of family is the Roman. The original meaning of the word "family" (*familia*) is not that compound of sentimentality and domestic strife which forms the ideal of the present-day philistine; among the Romans it did not at first even refer to the married pair and their children but only to the slaves. *Famulus* means domestic slave, and *familia* is the total number of slaves belonging to one man. As late as the time of Gaius, the *familia, id est patrimonium* (family, that is, the patrimony, the inheritance) was bequeathed by will. The term was invented by the Romans to denote a new social organism whose head ruled over wife and children and a number of slaves, and was invested under Roman paternal power with rights of life and death over them all. [Morgan states:]

> This term, therefore, is no older than the ironclad family system of the Latin tribes, which came in after field agriculture and after legalized servitude, as well as after the separation of the Greeks and Latins.

Marx adds:

> The modern family contains in germ not only slavery (*servitus*) but also serfdom, since from the beginning it is related to agricultural services. It contains *in miniature* all the contradictions which later extend throughout society and its state.

Such a form of family shows the transition of the pairing family to monogamy. In order to make certain of the wife's fidelity and therefore of the paternity of the children, she is delivered over unconditionally into the power of the husband; if he kills her, he is only exercising his rights.

With the patriarchal family, we enter the field of written history, a field where comparative jurisprudence can give valuable help. And it has in fact brought an important advance in our knowledge. We owe to Maxim Kovalevsky (*Tableau, etc.* 60–100) the proof that the patriarchal household community, as we still find it today among the Serbs and the Bulgars under the name of *zádruga* (which may be roughly translated "bond of friendship") or *bratstvo* (brotherhood), and in a modified form among the Oriental peoples, formed the transitional stage between the matriarchal family deriving from group marriage and the single family of the modern world. . . .

4. THE MONOGAMOUS FAMILY

It develops out of the pairing family, as previously shown, in the transitional period between the upper and middle stages of barbarism; its decisive victory is one of the signs that civilization is beginning. It is based on the supremacy of the man, the express purpose being to produce children of undisputed paternity; such paternity is demanded because these children are later to come into their father's property as his natural heirs. It is distinguished from pairing marriage by the much greater strength of the marriage tie, which can no longer be dissolved at either partner's wish. As a rule, it is now only the man who can dissolve it and put away his wife. The right of conjugal infidelity also remains secured to him, at any rate by custom (the *Code Napoléon* explicitly accords it to the husband as long as he does not bring his concubine into the house), and as social life develops he exercises his right more and more; should the wife recall the old form of sexual life and attempt to revive it, she is punished more severely than ever. . . .

This is the origin of monogamy as far as we can trace it back among the most civilized and highly developed people of antiquity. It was not in any way the fruit of individual sex love, with which it had nothing whatever to do; marriages remained as before marriages of convenience. It was the first form of the family to be based not on natural but on economic conditions—on the victory of private property over primitive, natural communal property. The Greeks themselves put the matter quite frankly: the sole exclusive aims of monogamous marriage were to make the man supreme in the family and to propagate, as the future heirs to his wealth, children indisputably his own. Otherwise, marriage was a burden, a duty which had to be performed whether one liked it or not to gods, state, and one's ancestors. In Athens the law exacted from the man not only marriage but also the performance of a minimum of so-called conjugal duties.

Thus when monogamous marriage first makes its appearance in history, it is not as the reconciliation of man and woman, still less as the highest form of such a reconciliation. Quite the contrary, monogamous marriage comes on the scene as the subjugation of the one sex by the other; it announces a struggle between the sexes unknown throughout the whole previous prehistorical period. In an old unpublished manuscript written by Marx and myself in 1846, I find the words: "The first division of labor is that between man and woman for the propagation of children." And today I can add: The first class opposition that appears in history coincides with the development of the antagonism between man and woman in monogamous marriage, and the first class oppression coincides with that of the female sex by the male. Monogamous marriage was a great historical step forward; nevertheless, together with slavery and private wealth, it opens the period that has lasted until today in which every step forward is also relatively a step backward, in which prosperity and development for some is won through the misery and frustration of others. It is the cellular form of civilized society in which the nature of the oppositions and contradictions fully active in that society can be already studied.

The old comparative freedom of sexual intercourse by no means disappeared with the victory of pairing marriage or even of monogamous marriage:

> The old conjugal system, now reduced to narrower limits by the gradual disappearance of the punaluan groups, still environed the advancing family, which it was to follow to the verge of civilization. . . . It finally disappeared in the new form of hetaerism, which still follows mankind in civilization as a dark shadow upon the family.

By "hetaerism" Morgan understands the practice, *coexistent with monogamous marriage,* of sexual intercourse between men and unmarried women outside marriage, which, as we know, flourishes in the most varied forms throughout the whole period of civilization and develops more and more into open prostitution. . . .

But a second contradiction thus develops within monogamous marriage itself. At the side of the husband who embellishes his existence with hetaerism stands the neglected wife. And one cannot have one side of this contradiction without the other, any more than a man has a whole apple in his hand after eating half. But that seems to have been the husbands' notion, until their wives taught them better. With monogamous marriage, two constant social types, unknown hitherto, make their appearance on the scene—the wife's attendant lover and the cuckold husband. The husbands had won the victory over the wives, but the vanquished magnanimously provided the crown. Together with monogamous marriage and hetaerism, adultery became an unavoidable social institution—denounced, severely penalized, but impossible to suppress. At best, the certain paternity of the children rested on moral conviction as before, and to solve the insoluble contradiction the *Code Napoléon*, Article 312, decreed: *"L'enfant conçu pendant le mariage a pour père le mari,"* the father of a child conceived during marriage is—the husband. Such is the final result of three thousand years of monogamous marriage.

Thus, wherever the monogamous family remains true to its historical origin and clearly reveals the antagonism between the man and the woman expressed in the man's exclusive supremacy, it exhibits in miniature the same oppositions and contradictions as those in which society has been moving, without power to resolve or overcome them, ever since it split into classes at the beginning of civilization. I am speaking here, of course, only of those cases of monogamous marriage where matrimonial life actually proceeds according to the original character of the whole institution but where the wife rebels against the husband's supremacy. Not all marriages turn out thus, as nobody knows better than the German philistine who can no more assert his rule in the home than he can in the state and whose wife, with every right, wears the trousers he is unworthy of. . . .

[I]f monogamy was the only one of all the known forms of the family through which modern sex love could develop, that does not mean that within monogamy modern sexual love developed exclusively or even chiefly as the love of husband and wife for each other. That was precluded by the very nature of strictly monogamous marriage under the rule of the man. Among all historically active classes—that is, among all ruling classes—matrimony remained what it had been since the pairing marriage, a matter of convenience which was arranged by the parents. The first historical form of sexual love as passion, a passion recognized as natural to all human beings (at least if they belonged to the ruling classes), and as the highest form of the sexual impulse—and that is what constitutes its specific character—this first form of individual sexual love, the chivalrous love of the middle ages, was by no means conjugal. Quite the contrary, in its classic form among the Provençals, it heads straight for adultery, and the poets of love celebrated adultery. . . .

Nowadays there are two ways of concluding a bourgeois marriage. In Catholic countries the parents, as before, procure a suitable wife for their young bourgeois son, and the consequence is, of course, the fullest development of the contradiction inherent in monogamy: the husband abandons himself to hetaerism and the wife to adultery. Probably the only reason why the Catholic Church abolished divorce was because it had convinced itself that there is no more a cure for adultery than there is for death. In Protestant countries, on the other hand, the rule is that the son of a bourgeois family is allowed to choose a wife from his own class with more or less freedom; hence there may be a certain element of love in the marriage as, indeed, in accordance with Protestant hypocrisy is always assumed for decency's sake. Here the husband's hetaerism is a more sleepy kind of business, and adultery by the wife is less the rule. But since in every kind of marriage people remain what they were before and since the bourgeois of Protestant countries are mostly philistines, all that this Protestant monogamy achieves, taking the average of the best cases, is a conjugal partnership of leaden boredom, known as "domestic bliss." . . .

In both cases, however, the marriage is conditioned by the class position of the parties and is to that extent always a marriage of convenience. In both cases this marriage of convenience turns often enough into the crassest prostitution—sometimes of both partners, but far more commonly of the woman, who only differs from the ordinary courtesan in that she does not let out her body on piecework as a wage worker but sells it once and for all into slavery.

And of all marriages of convenience Fourier's words hold true: "As in grammar two negatives make an affirmative, so in matrimonial morality two prostitutions pass for a virtue."[2] Sex love in the relationship with a woman becomes and can only become the real rule among the oppressed classes, which means today among the proletariat—whether this relation is officially sanctioned or not. But here all the foundations of typical monogamy are cleared away. Here there is no property, for the preservation and inheritance of which monogamy and male supremacy were established; hence there is no incentive to make this male supremacy effective. What is more, there are no means of making it so. Bourgeois law, which protects this supremacy, exists only for the possessing class and their dealings with the proletarians. The law costs money and, on account of the worker's poverty, it has no validity for his relation to his wife. Here quite other personal and social conditions decide. And now that large-scale industry has taken the wife out of the home onto the labor market and into the factory, and made her often the breadwinner of the family, no basis for any kind of male supremacy is left in the proletarian household, except, perhaps, for something of the brutality toward women that has spread since the introduction of monogamy. The proletarian family is therefore no longer monogamous in the strict sense, even where there is passionate love and firmest loyalty on both sides and maybe all the blessings of religious and civil authority. Here, therefore, the eternal attendants of monogamy, hetaerism and adultery, play only an almost vanishing part. The wife has in fact regained the right to dissolve the marriage, and if two people cannot get on with one another, they prefer to separate. In short, proletarian marriage is monogamous in the etymological sense of the word, but not at all in its historical sense.

Our jurists, of course, find that progress in legislation is leaving women with no further ground of complaint. Modern civilized systems of law increasingly acknowledge first, that for a marriage to be legal it must be a contract freely entered into by both partners and secondly, that also in the married state both partners must stand on a common footing of equal rights and duties. If both these demands are consistently carried out, say the jurists, women have all they can ask.

This typically legalist method of argument is exactly the same as that which the radical republican bourgeois uses to put the proletarian in his place. The labor contract is to be freely entered into by both partners. But it is considered to have been freely entered into as soon as the law makes both parties equal on *paper*. The power conferred on the one party by the difference of class position, the pressure thereby brought to bear on the other party—the real economic position of both—that is not the law's business. Again,

2. Charles Fourier, *Théorie de l'Unité Universelle,* Paris, 1841–45, III, 120.

for the duration of the labor contract, both parties are to have equal rights in so far as one or the other does not expressly surrender them. That economic relations compel the worker to surrender even the last semblance of equal rights—here again, that is no concern of the law.

In regard to marriage, the law, even the most advanced, is fully satisfied as soon as the partners have formally recorded that they are entering into the marriage of their own free consent. What goes on in real life behind the juridical scenes, how this free consent comes about—that is not the business of the law and the jurist. . . .

As regards the legal equality of husband and wife in marriage, the position is no better. The legal inequality of the two partners bequeathed to us from earlier social conditions is not the cause but the effect of the economic oppression of the woman. In the old communistic household, which comprised many couples and their children, the task entrusted to the women of managing the household was as much a public, a socially necessary industry as the procuring of food by the men. With the patriarchal family and still more with the single monogamous family, a change came. Household management lost its public character. It no longer concerned society. It became a *private service;* the wife became the head servant, excluded from all participation in social production. Not until the coming of modern large-scale industry was the road to social production opened to her again—and then only to the proletarian wife. But it was opened in such a manner that, if she carries out her duties in the private service of her family, she remains excluded from public production and unable to earn; and if she wants to take part in public production and earn independently, she cannot carry out family duties. And the wife's position in the factory is the position of women in all branches of business, right up to medicine and the law. The modern individual family is founded on the open or concealed domestic slavery of the wife, and modern society is a mass composed of these individual families as its molecules.

In the great majority of cases today, at least in the possessing classes, the husband is obliged to earn a living and support his family, and that in itself gives him a position of supremacy without any need for special legal titles and privileges. Within the family he is the bourgeois, and the wife represents the proletariat. In the industrial world, the specific character of the economic oppression burdening the proletariat is visible in all its sharpness only when all special legal privileges of the capitalist class have been abolished and complete legal equality of both classes established. The democratic republic does not do away with the opposition of the two classes; on the contrary, it provides the clear field on which the fight can be fought out. And in the same way, the peculiar character of the supremacy of the husband over the wife in the modern family, the necessity of creating real social equality between them and the way to do it, will only be seen in the clear light of day when both possess legally complete equality of rights. Then it will be plain that the first condition for the liberation of the wife is to bring the whole female sex back into public industry, and that this in turn demands that the characteristic of the monogamous family as the economic unit of society be abolished.

We thus have three principal forms of marriage which correspond broadly to the three principal stages of human development: for the period of savagery, group marriage; for barbarism, pairing marriage; for civilization, monogamy supplemented by adultery and prostitution. Between pairing marriage and monogamy intervenes a period in the upper stage of barbarism when men have female slaves at their command and polygamy is practiced.

As our whole presentation has shown, the progress which manifests itself in these successive forms is connected with the peculiarity that women, but not men, are increasingly deprived of the sexual freedom of group marriage. In fact, for men group marriage actually still exists even to this day. What for the woman is a crime entailing grave legal and social consequences is considered honorable in a man or, at the worse, a slight moral blemish which he cheerfully bears. But the more the hetaerism of the past is changed in our time by capitalist commodity production and brought into conformity with it, the more, that is to say, it is transformed into undisguised prostitution, the more demoralizing are its effects. And it demoralizes men far more than women. Among women, prostitution degrades only the unfortunate ones who become its victims, and even these by no means to the extent commonly believed. But it degrades the character of the whole male world. A long engagement particularly is in nine cases out of ten a regular preparatory school for conjugal infidelity.

We are now approaching a social revolution in which the economic foundations of monogamy as they have existed hitherto will disappear just as surely as those of its complement—prostitution. Monogamy arose from the concentration of considerable wealth in the hands of a single individual—a man—and from the need to bequeath this wealth to the children of that man and of no other. For this purpose, the monogamy of the woman was required, not that of the man, so this monogamy of the woman did not in any way interfere with open or concealed polygamy on the part of the man. But by transforming by far the greater portion, at any rate, of permanent, heritable wealth—the means of production—into social property, the coming social revolution will reduce to a minimum all this anxiety about bequeathing and inheriting. Having arisen from economic causes, will monogamy then disappear when these causes disappear?

One might answer, not without reason: far from disappearing, it will on the contrary begin to be realized completely. For with the transformation of the means of production into social property there will disappear also wage labor, the proletariat, and therefore the necessity for a certain—statistically calculable—number of women to surrender themselves for money. Prostitution disappears; monogamy, instead of collapsing, at last becomes a reality—also for men.

In any case, therefore, the position of men will be very much altered. But the position of women, of *all* women, also undergoes significant change. With the transfer of the means of production into common ownership, the single family ceases to be the economic unit of society. Private housekeeping is transformed into a social industry. The care and education of the children becomes a public affair; society looks after all children alike, whether they are legitimate or not. This removes all the anxiety about the "consequences," which today is the most essential social—moral as well as economic—factor that prevents a girl from giving herself completely to the man she loves. Will not that suffice to bring about the gradual growth of unconstrained sexual intercourse and with it a more tolerant public opinion in regard to a maiden's honor and a woman's shame? And finally, have we not seen that in the modern world monogamy and prostitution are indeed contradictions, but inseparable contradictions, poles of the same state of society? Can prostitution disappear without dragging monogamy with it into the abyss?

Here a new element comes into play, an element which at the time when monogamy was developing existed at most in embryo—individual sex love. . . .

Our sex love differs essentially from the simple sexual desire, the Eros, of the ancients. In the first place, it assumes that the person loved returns the love; to this extent the woman is on an equal footing with the man, whereas in the Eros of antiquity she was often not even asked. Secondly, our sex love has a degree of intensity and duration which makes both lovers feel that non-possession and separation are a great, if not the greatest, calamity; to possess one another, they risk high stakes, even life itself. In the ancient world this happened only, if at all, in adultery. And finally, there arises a new moral standard in the judgment of a sexual relationship. We do not only ask, was it within or outside marriage, but also, did it spring from love and reciprocated love or not? Of course, this new standard has fared no better in feudal or bourgeois practice than all the other standards of morality—it is ignored. But neither does it fare any worse. It is recognized, like all the rest, in theory, on paper. And for the present more than this cannot be expected. . . .

In the vast majority of cases . . . marriage remained up to the close of the middle ages what it had been from the start—a matter which was not decided by the partners. In the beginning, people were already born married—married to an entire group of the opposite sex. In the later forms of group marriage similar relations probably existed, but with the group continually contracting. In the pairing marriage it was customary for the mothers to settle the marriages of their children; here, too, the decisive considerations are the new ties of kinship which are to give the young pair a stronger position in the gens and tribe. And when, with the preponderance of private over communal property and the interest in its bequeathal father right and monogamy gained supremacy, the dependence of marriages on economic considerations became complete. The *form* of marriage by purchase disappears; the actual practice is steadily extended until not only the woman but also the man acquires a price—not according to his personal qualities but according to his property. That the mutual affection of the people concerned should be the one paramount reason for marriage, outweighing everything else, was and always had been absolutely unheard of in the practice of the ruling classes; that sort of thing only happened in romance—or among the oppressed classes, who did not count.

Such was the state of things encountered by capitalist production when it began to prepare itself, after the epoch of geographical discoveries, to win world power by world trade and manufacture. One would suppose that this manner of marriage exactly suited it, and so it did. And yet—there are no limits to the irony of history—capitalist production itself was to make the decisive breach in it. By changing all things into commodities, it dissolved all inherited and traditional relationships, and in place of time-honored custom and historic right, it set up purchase and sale, "free" contract. And the English jurist H. S. Maine thought he had made a tremendous discovery when he said that our whole progress in comparison with former epochs consisted in the fact that we had passed "from status to contract," from inherited to freely contracted conditions—which, in so far as it is correct was already in *The Communist Manifesto* [Chapter II].

But a contract requires people who can dispose freely of their persons, actions, and possessions and meet each other on the footing of equal rights. To create these "free" and "equal" people was one of the main tasks of capitalist production. Even though at the start it was carried out only half-consciously, and under a religious disguise at that, from the time of the Lutheran and Calvinist Reformation the principle was established that man is only fully responsible for his actions when he acts with complete freedom of will, and that it is a moral duty to resist all coercion to an immoral act. But how did this fit in with the hitherto existing practice in the arrangement of marriages? Marriage according to the bourgeois conception was a contract, a legal transaction, and the most important one of all because it disposed of two human beings, body and mind, for life. Formally, it is true, the contract at that time was entered into voluntarily; without the assent of the persons concerned, nothing could be done. But everyone knew only too well how this assent was obtained and who were the real contracting parties in the marriage. But if real freedom of decision was required for all other contracts, then why not for this? Had not the two young people to be coupled also the right to dispose freely of themselves, of their bodies and organs? Had not chivalry brought sex love into fashion, and was not its proper bourgeois form, in contrast to chivalry's adulterous love, the love of husband and wife? And if it was the duty of married people to love each other, was it not equally the duty of lovers to marry each other and nobody else? Did not this right of the lovers stand higher than the right of parents, relations, and other traditional marriage brokers and match-makers? . . .

So it came about that the rising bourgeoisie, especially in Protestant countries where existing conditions had been most severely shaken, increasingly recognized freedom of contract also in marriage, and carried it into effect in the manner described. Marriage remained class marriage, but within the class the partners were conceded a certain degree of freedom of choice. And on paper, in ethical theory and in poetic description, nothing was more immutably established than that every marriage is immoral which does not rest on mutual sexual love and really free agreement of husband and wife. In short, the love marriage was proclaimed as a human right, and indeed not only as a *droit de l'homme,* one of the rights of man, but also, for once in a way, as *droit de la femme,* one of the rights of woman.

This human right, however, differed in one respect from all other so-called human rights. While the latter in practice remain restricted to the ruling class (the bourgeoisie) and are directly or indirectly curtailed for the oppressed class (the proletariat), in the case of the former the irony of history plays another of its tricks. The ruling class remains dominated by the familiar economic influences and therefore only in exceptional cases does it provide instances of really freely contracted marriages, while among the oppressed class, as we have seen, these marriages are the rule.

Full freedom of marriage can therefore only be generally established when the abolition of capitalist production and of the property relations created by it has removed all the accompanying economic considerations which still exert such a powerful influence on the choice of a marriage partner. For then there is no other motive left except mutual inclination.

And as sexual love is by its nature exclusive—although at present this exclusiveness is fully realized only in the woman—the marriage based on sexual love is by its nature individual marriage. We have seen how right Bachofen was in regarding the advance from group marriage to individual marriage as primarily due to the women. Only the step from pairing marriage to monogamy can be put down to the credit of the men, and historically the essence of this was to make the position of the women worse and the infidelities of the men easier. If now the economic considerations also disappear which made women put up with the habitual infidelity of their husbands—concern for their own means of existence and still more for their children's future—then, according to all previous experience, the equality of woman thereby achieved will tend infinitely more to make men really monogamous than to make women polyandrous.

But what will quite certainly disappear from monogamy are all the features stamped upon it through its origin in property relations; these are, in the first place, supremacy of the man and secondly, the indissolubility of marriage. The supremacy of the man in marriage is the simple consequence of his economic supremacy, and with the abolition of the latter will disappear of itself. The indissolubility of marriage is partly a consequence of the economic situation in which monogamy arose, partly tradition from the period when the connection between this economic situation and monogamy was not fully understood and was carried to extremes under a religious form. Today it is already broken through at a thousand points. If only the marriage based on love is moral, then also only the marriage is moral in which love continues. But the intense emotion of individual sex love varies very much in duration from one individual to another, especially among men, and if affection definitely comes to an end or is supplanted by a new passionate love, separation is a benefit for both partners as well as for society—only people will then be spared having to wade through the useless mire of a divorce case.

What we can now conjecture about the way in which sexual relations will be ordered after the impending overthrow of capitalist production is mainly of a negative character, limited for the most part to what will disappear. But what will there be new? That will be answered when a new generation has grown up: a generation of men who never in their lives have known what it is to buy a woman's surrender with money or any other social instrument of power; a generation of women who have never known what it is to give themselves to a man from any other considerations than real love or to refuse to give themselves to their lover from fear of the economic consequences. When these people are in the world, they will care precious little what anybody today thinks they ought to do; they will make their own practice and their corresponding public opinion about the practice of each individual—and that will be the end of it.

* * *

V. I. LENIN

Like Marx and Engels, Lenin (1870–1924) viewed human nature from a materialistic perspective. Although human beings are comprised of mind and matter, the former is dependent upon the latter. Each person is essentially a social being, having a primary moral responsibility to promote the egalitarian interests of every member of society. In pursuing that end, the responsibility of the individual is proportionate to an awareness of obstacles to the universal interests, and to the varying competence of each individual for overcoming those obstacles. For example, Lenin himself, because of the advantages of his bourgeois background, natural talent, and education, considered himself more responsible for correcting the inequities of society than the typically uneducated proletarian peasant, who had become inured to oppression.

For Lenin, the ideal of an egalitarian society is so good in itself that it justifies revolution as means to its accomplishment. Nonetheless, violence and bloodshed are permitted only where indispensable for implementing the ideal, and never for the sake of merely procuring or maintaining dictatorial power. History discloses Lenin's effort, during the last few months of his life, to prevent Josef Stalin's assumption of the party's leadership. It appears that Lenin anticipated and disapproved the excessive exercise of power that followed in the Stalinist purges. Lenin wrote and spoke often about the necessity and means for emancipating women in society. His comments, spread over a range of years and documents, are collected in a book entitled *The Emancipation of Women*. The following selection is drawn from that collection; its main part is an interview with Lenin on the "*Woman Question*," conducted by the German communist, Clara Zetkin.

* * *

The Emancipation of Women

CAPITALISM AND FEMALE LABOUR

Modern capitalist society is the hiding place of numerous cases of poverty and oppression that are not immediately visible. The scattered families of middle class people, artisans, factory workers, clerks and the lower civil servants, are indescribably poor and barely make ends meet in the *best* of times. Millions and millions of women in such families live (or rather drag out an existence) as household slaves, striving with a desperate daily effort to feed and clothe their families on a few coppers, economising in everything except their own labour.

It is from among these women that the capitalists are most eager to engage workers who work at home and who are prepared for a monstrously low wage to "earn" an extra crust of bread for themselves and their families. It is from among them that the capitalists of all countries (like the slave owners of antiquity and the feudal lords of the Middle Ages) choose any number of concubines at the most "favourable" price. No "moral indignation" (hypocritical in ninety-nine cases out of a hundred) about prostitution can do anything to prevent this commerce in women's bodies; as long as wage slavery exists, prostitution must inevitably continue. Throughout the history of society all the oppressed and exploited classes have always been compelled (their exploitation consists in this) to hand over to the oppressors, first, their unpaid labour and, secondly, their women to be the concubines of the "masters".

Slavery, feudalism and capitalism are alike in this respect. Only the *form* of the exploitation changes, the exploitation remains.

. . . .

The conditions that make it impossible for the oppressed classes to "exercise" their democratic rights are not the exception under capitalism; they are typical of the system. In most cases the right of divorce will remain unrealisable under capitalism, for the oppressed sex is subjugated economically. No matter how much democracy there is under capitalism, the woman remains a "domestic slave", a slave locked up in the bedroom, nursery, kitchen. . . . The fuller the freedom of divorce, the clearer will women see that the source of their "domestic slavery" is capitalism, not lack of rights.

. . . .

SOVIET POWER AND THE STATUS OF WOMEN

The status of women makes clear in the most striking fashion the difference between bourgeois and socialist democracy. . . .

In a bourgeois republic (i.e., where there is private ownership of land, factories, shares, etc.), be it the most democratic republic, women have never had equal rights, *anywhere in the world, in any one of the more advanced countries*. And this despite the fact that more than 125 years passed since the French (bourgeois-democratic) Revolution.

In words bourgeois democracy promises equality and freedom, but in practice *not a single* bourgeois republic, even the more advanced, has granted women (half the human race) and men complete equality in the eyes of the law, or delivered women from dependence on and the oppression of the male.

Bourgeois democracy is the democracy of pompous phrases, solemn words, lavish promises and high-sounding slogans about *freedom and equality*, but in practice all this cloaks the lack of freedom and the inequality of women, the lack of freedom and the inequality for the working and exploited people.

. . . .

[N]ot a single democratic party in the world, not even in the most advanced bourgeois republic, has done in decades so much as a hundredth part of what we did in our very first year in power. We actually razed to the ground the infamous laws placing women in a position of inequality, restricting divorce and surrounding it with disgusting formalities, denying recognition to children born out of wedlock, enforcing a search for their fathers, etc., laws numerous survivals of which, to the shame of the bourgeoisie and of capitalism, are to be found in all civilised countries. We have a thousand times the right to be proud of what we have done in this field. But the more *thoroughly* we clear the ground of the lumber of the old, bourgeois laws and institutions, the more we realise that we have only cleared the ground to build on, but are not yet building.

Notwithstanding all the laws emancipating woman, she continues to be a *domestic slave*, because *petty housework* crushes, strangles, stultifies and degrades her, chains her to the kitchen and the nursery, and she wastes her labour on barbarously unproductive, petty, nerve-racking, stultifying and crushing drudgery. The real *emancipation of women*, real communism, will begin only where and when an all-out struggle begins (led by the proletariat wielding the state power) against this petty housekeeping, or rather when its *wholesale transformation* into a large-scale socialist economy begins.

Do we in practice pay sufficient attention to this question, which in theory every Communist considers indisputable? Of course not. Do we take proper care of the *shoots* of communism which already exist in this sphere? Again the answer is *no*. Public catering establishments, nurseries, kindergartens—here we have examples of these shoots, here we have the simple, everyday means, involving nothing pompous, grandiloquent or ceremonial, which can *really eman-*

cipate women, really lessen and abolish their inequality with men as regards their role in social production and public life. These means are not new, they (like all the material prerequisites for socialism) were created by large-scale capitalism. But under capitalism they remained, first, a rarity, and secondly—which is particularly important—either *profit-making* enterprises, with all the worst features of speculation, profiteering, cheating and fraud, or "acrobatics of bourgeois charity", which the best workers rightly hated and despised.

. . . .

AN INTERVIEW ON THE WOMAN QUESTION

"The first proletarian dictatorship is truly paving the way for the complete social equality of women. . . . I understand that in Hamburg a gifted Communist woman is bringing out a newspaper for prostitutes, and is trying to organise them for the revolutionary struggle. Now Rosa, a true Communist, felt and acted like a human being when she wrote an article in defence of prostitutes who have landed in jail for violating a police regulation concerning their sad trade. They are unfortunate double victims of bourgeois society. Victims, first, of its accursed system of property and, secondly, of its accursed moral hypocrisy. There's no doubt about this. Only a coarse-grained and short-sighted person could forget this. To understand this is one thing, but it is quite another thing—how shall I put it?—to organise the prostitutes as a special revolutionary guild contingent and publish a trade union paper for them. Are there really no industrial working women left in Germany who need organising, who need a newspaper, who should be enlisted in your struggle? This is a morbid deviation. It strongly reminds me of the literary vogue which made a sweet madonna out of every prostitute. Its origin was sound too: social sympathy, and indignation against the moral hypocrisy of the honourable bourgeoisie. But the healthy principle underwent bourgeois corrosion and degenerated. The question of prostitution will confront us even in our country with many a difficult problem. Return the prostitute to productive work, find her a place in the social economy—that is the thing to do. . . . I have been told that at the evenings arranged for reading and discussion with working women, sex and marriage problems come first. . . . Freud's theory has now become a fad. I mistrust sex theories expounded in articles, treatises, pamphlets, etc.—in short, the theories dealt with in that specific literature which sprouts so luxuriantly on the dung heap of bourgeois society. I mistrust those who are always absorbed in the sex problems, the way an Indian saint is absorbed in the contemplation of his navel. It seems to me that this superabundance of sex theories, which for the most part are mere hypotheses, and often quite arbitrary ones, stems from a personal need. It springs from the desire to justify one's own abnormal or excessive sex life before bourgeois morality and to plead for tolerance towards oneself. This veiled respect for bourgeois morality is as repugnant to me as rooting about in all that bears on sex. No matter how rebellious and revolutionary it may be made to appear, it is in the final analysis thoroughly bourgeois. Intellectuals and others like them are particularly keen on this. There is no room for it in the Party, among the class-conscious, fighting proletariat."

". . . Why is the approach to this problem inadequate and un-Marxist? Because sex and marriage problems are not treated as only part of the main social problem. Conversely, the main social problem is presented as a part, an appendage to the sex problem. The important point recedes into the background. Thus not only is this question obscured, but also thought, and the class-consciousness of working women in general, is dulled.

"Besides, and this isn't the least important point, Solomon the Wise said there is a time for everything. I ask you, is this the time to keep working women busy for months at a stretch with such questions as how to love or be loved, how to woo or be wooed? This, of course, with regard to the 'past, present and future', and among the various races. And it is proudly styled historical material. Nowadays all the thoughts of Communist women, of working women, should be centred on the proletarian revolution, which will lay the foundation, among other things, for the necessary revision of material and sexual relations. . . .

"I was also told that sex problems are a favourite subject in your youth organisations too, and that there are hardly enough lecturers on this subject. This nonsense is especially dangerous and damaging to the youth movement. It can easily lead to sexual excesses, to overstimulation of sex life and to wasted health and strength of young people. You must fight that too. There is no lack of contact between the youth movement and the women's movement. Our Communist women everywhere should cooperate methodically with young people. This will be a continuation of motherhood, will elevate it and extend it from the individual to the social sphere. Women's incipient social life and activities must be promoted, so that they can outgrow the narrowness of their philistine, individualistic psychology centred on home and family. But this is incidental.

"In our country, too, considerable numbers of young people are busy 'revising bourgeois conceptions and morals' in the sex question. And let me add that this involves a considerable section of our best boys and girls, of our truly promising youth. It is as you have just said. In the atmosphere created by the aftermath of war and by the revolution which has begun, old ideological values, finding themselves in a society whose economic foundations are undergoing a radical change, perish, and lose their restraining force. New values crystallise slowly, in the struggle. With regard to relations between people, and between man and woman, feelings and thoughts are also becoming revolutionised. New boundaries are being drawn between the rights of the individual and those of the community, and hence also the duties of the individual. Things are still in complete, chaotic ferment. The direction and potentiality of the various contradictory tendencies can still not be seen clearly enough. It is a slow and often very painful process of passing away and coming into being. All this applies also to the field of sexual relations, marriage, and the family. The decay, putrescence, and filth of bourgeois marriage with its difficult dissolution, its licence for the husband and bondage for the wife, and its disgustingly false sex morality and relations fill the best and most spiritually active of people with the utmost loathing.

"The coercion of bourgeois marriage and bourgeois legislation on the family enhance the evil and aggravate the conflicts. It is the coercion of 'sacrosanct' property. It sanctifies venality, baseness, and dirt. The conventional hypocrisy of 'respectable' bourgeois society takes care of the rest. People revolt against the prevailing abominations and perversions. And at a time when mighty nations are being destroyed, when the former power relations are being disrupted, when a whole social world is beginning to decline, the sensations of the individual undergo a rapid change. A stimulating thirst for different forms of enjoyment easily acquires an irresistible force. Sexual and marriage reforms in the bourgeois sense will not do. In the sphere of sexual relations and marriage, a revolution is approaching—in keeping with the proletarian revolution. Of course, women and young people are taking a deep interest in the complex tangle of problems which have arisen as a result of this. Both the former and the latter suffer greatly from the present messy state of sex relations. Young people rebel against them with the vehemence of their years. This is only natural. Nothing could be falser than to preach monastic self-denial and the sanctity of the filthy bourgeois morals to young people. However, it is hardly a good thing that sex, already strongly felt in the physical sense, should at such a time assume so much prominence in the psychology of young people. The consequences are nothing short of fatal. . . .

"Youth's altered attitude to questions of sex is of course 'fundamental', and based on theory. Many people call it 'revolutionary' and 'communist'. They sincerely believe that this is so. I am an old man, and I do not like it. I may be a morose ascetic, but quite often this so-called 'new sex life' of young people—and frequently of the adults too—seems to me purely bourgeois and simply an extension of the good old bourgeois brothel. All this has nothing in common with free love as we Communists understand it. No doubt you have heard about the famous theory that in communist society satisfying sexual desire and the craving for love is as simple and trivial as 'drinking a glass of water'. A section of our youth has gone mad, absolutely mad, over this 'glass-of-water theory'. It has been fatal to many a young boy and girl. Its devotees assert that it is a Marxist theory. I want no part of the kind of Marxism which infers all phenomena and all changes in the ideological superstructure of society directly and blandly from its economic basis, for things are not as simple as all that. A certain Frederick Engels has established this a long time ago with regard to historical materialism.

"I consider the famous 'glass-of-water' theory as completely un-Marxist and, moreover, as anti-social. It is not only what nature has given but also what has become culture, whether of a high or low level, that comes into play in sexual life. Engels pointed out in his *Origin of the Family* how significant it was that the common sexual relations had developed into individual sex love and thus became purer. The relations between the sexes are not simply the expression of a mutual influence between economics and a physical want deliberately singled out for physiological examination. It would be rationalism and not Marxism to attempt to refer the change in these relations directly to the economic basis of society in isolation from its connection with the ideology as a whole. To be sure, thirst has to be quenched. But would a normal person normally lie down in the gutter and drink from a puddle? Or even from a glass whose edge has been greased by many lips? But the social aspect is more important than anything else. The drinking of water is really an individual matter. But it takes two people to make love, and a third person, a new life, is likely to come into being. This deed has a social complexion and constitutes a duty to the community.

"As a Communist I have no liking at all for the 'glass-of-water' theory, despite its attractive label: 'emancipation of love'. Besides, emancipation of love is neither a novel nor a communistic idea. You will recall that it was advanced in fine literature around the middle of the past century as 'emancipation of the heart'. In bourgeois practice it materialised into emancipation of the flesh. It was preached with greater talent than now, though I cannot judge how it was practised. Not that I want my criticism to breed asceticism. That is farthest from my thoughts. Communism should not bring asceticism, but joy and strength, stemming, among other things, from a consummate love life. Whereas today, in my opinion, the obtaining plethora of sex life yields neither joy nor strength. On the contrary, it impairs them. This is bad, very bad, indeed, in the epoch of revolution.

"Young people are particularly in need of joy and strength. Healthy sports, such as gymnastics, swimming, hiking, physical exercises of every description and a wide range of intellectual interests is what they need, as well as learning, study and research, and as far as possible collectively. This will be far more useful to young people than endless lectures and discussions on sex problems and the so-called living by one's nature. *Mens sana in corpore sano.* Be neither monk nor Don Juan, but not anything in between either, like a German philistine. . . . I will not vouch for the reliability or the endurance of women whose love affair is intertwined with politics, or for the men who run after every petticoat and let themselves in with every young female. No, no, that does not go well with revolution. . . .

"The revolution calls for concentration and rallying of every nerve by the masses and by the individual. It does not tolerate orgiastic conditions so common among d'Annunzio's decadent heros and heroines. Promiscuity in sexual matters is bourgeois. It is a sign of degeneration. The proletariat is a rising class. It does not need an intoxicant to stupefy or stimulate it, neither the intoxicant of sexual laxity or of alcohol. It should and will not forget the vileness, the filth and the barbarity of capitalism. It derives its strongest inspiration to fight from its class position, from the communist ideal. What it needs is clarity, clarity, and more clarity. Therefore, I repeat, there must be no weakening, no waste and no dissipation of energy. Self-control and self-discipline are not slavery; not in matters of love either. . . . We want to separate organisations of communist women! She who is a Communist belongs as a member to the Party, just as he who is a Communist. They have the same rights and duties. There can be no difference of opinion on that score. However, we must not shut our eyes to the facts. The Party must have organs—working groups, commissions, committees, sections or whatever else they may be called—with the specific purpose of rousing the broad masses of women, bringing them into contact with the Party and keeping them under its influence. This naturally requires that we carry on systematic work among the women. We must teach the awakened women, win them over for the proletarian class struggle under the leadership of the Communist Party, and equip them for it. When I say this I have in mind not only proletarian women, whether they work in mills or cook the family meal. I also have in mind the peasant women and the women of the various sections of the lower middle class. They, too, are victims of capitalism, and more than ever since the war. The lack of interest in politics and the otherwise anti-social and backward psychology of these masses of women, the narrow scope of their activities and the whole pattern of their lives are undeniable facts. It would be silly to ignore them, absolutely silly. We must have our own groups to work among them, special methods of agitation, and special forms of organisation. This is not bourgeois 'feminism'; it is a practical revolutionary expediency. . . .

"We cannot exercise the dictatorship of the proletariat without having millions of women on our side. Nor can we engage in communist construction without them. We must find a way to reach them. We must study and search in order to find this way.

"It is therefore perfectly right for us to put forward demands for the benefit of women. This is not a minimum programme, nor a programme of reform in the Social-Democratic sense, in the sense of the Second International. It does not go to show that we believe the bourgeoisie and its state will last forever, or even for a long time. Nor is it an attempt to pacify the masses of women with reforms and to divert them from the path of revolutionary struggle. It is nothing of the sort, and not any sort of reformist humbug either. Our demands are no more than practical conclusions, drawn by us from the crying needs and disgraceful humiliations that weak and underprivileged woman must bear under the bourgeois system. We demonstrate thereby that we are aware of these needs and of the oppression of women, that we are conscious of the privileged position of the men, and that we hate—yes, hate—and want to remove whatever oppresses and harasses the working woman, the wife of the worker, the peasant woman, the wife of the little man, and even in many respects the woman of the propertied classes. The rights and social measures we demand of bourgeois society for women are proof that we understand the position and interests of women and that we will take note of them under the proletarian dictatorship. Naturally, not as soporific and patronising reformists. No, by no means. But as revolutionaries who call upon the women to take a hand as equals in the reconstruction of the economy and of the ideological superstructure.

". . . [I]n our propaganda we must not make a fetish out of our demands for women. No, we must fight now for these and now for other demands, depending on the existing conditions, and naturally always in association with the general interests of the proletariat.

"Every tussle of this kind sets us at loggerheads with the respectable bourgeois clique and its no less respectable reformist lackeys. This compels the latter either to fight under our leadership—which they do not want—or to drop their disguise. Thus, the struggle fences us off from them and shows our communist face. It wins us the confidence of the mass of women, who feel themselves exploited, enslaved and crushed by the domination of the man, by the power of their employers and by bourgeois society as a whole.

Betrayed and abandoned by all, working women come to realise that they must fight together with us. Must I avow, or make you avow, that the struggle for women's rights must also be linked with our principal aim—the conquest of power and the establishment of the dictatorship of the proletariat? At present, this is, and will continue to be, our alpha and omega. That is clear, absolutely clear. But the broad masses of working women will not feel irresistibly drawn to the struggle for state power if we harp on just this one demand, even though we may blare it forth on the trumpets of Jericho. No, a thousand times no! We must combine our appeal politically in the minds of the female masses with the sufferings, the needs and the wishes of the working women. They should all know what the proletarian dictatorship will mean to them—complete equality of rights with men, both legal and in practice, in the family, the state and in society, and that it also spells the annihilation of the power of the bourgeoisie. . . .

"Soviet Russia casts a new light on our demands for women. Under the dictatorship of the proletariat they are no longer an object of struggle between the proletariat and the bourgeoisie. Once they are carried out, they serve as bricks for the building of communist society. This shows the women on the other side of the border the decisive importance of the conquest of power by the proletariat. The difference between their status here and there must be demonstrated in bold relief in order to win the support of the masses of women in the revolutionary class struggles of the proletariat. Mobilisation of the female masses, carried out with a clear understanding of principles and a firm organisational basis, is a vital question for the Communist Parties and their victories. But let us not deceive ourselves. Our national sections still lack the proper understanding of this question. They adopt a passive, wait-and-see attitude when it comes to creating a mass movement of working women under communist leadership. They do not realize that developing and leading such a mass movement is an important part of all Party activity, as much as half of all the Party work. Their occasional recognition of the need and value of a purposeful, strong and numerous communist women's movement is but platonic lip-service rather than a steady concern and task of the Party.

"They regard agitation and propaganda among women and the task of rousing and revolutionising them as of secondary importance, as the job of just the women Communists. None but the latter are rebuked because the matter does not move ahead more quickly and strongly. This is wrong, fundamentally wrong! It is outright separatism. It is equality of women *à rebours*, as the French say, i.e., equality reversed. What is at the bottom of the incorrect attitude of our national sections? (I am not speaking of Soviet Russia.) In the final analysis, it is an underestimation of women and of their accomplishments. That's just what it is! Unfortunately, we may still say of many of our comrades, 'Scratch the Communist and a philistine appears'. To be sure, you have to scratch the sensitive spots,—such as their mentality regarding women. Could there be any more palpable proof than the common sight of a man calmly watching a woman wear herself out with trivial, monotonous, strength- and time-consuming work, such as her housework, and watching her spirit shrinking, her mind growing dull, her heartbeat growing faint, and her will growing slack? It goes without saying that I am not referring to the bourgeois ladies who dump all housework and the care for their children on the hired help. What I say applies to the vast majority of women, including the wives of workers, even if these spend the day at the factory and earn money.

"Very few husbands, not even the proletarians, think of how much they could lighten the burdens and worries of their wives, or relieve them entirely, if they lent a hand in this 'women's work'. But no, that would go against the 'privilege and dignity of the husband'. He demands that he have rest and comfort. The domestic life of the woman is a daily sacrifice of self to a thousand insignificant trifles. The ancient rights of her husband, her lord and master, survive unnoticed. Objectively, his slave takes her revenge. Also in concealed form. Her backwardness and her lack of understanding for her husband's revolutionary ideals act as a drag on his fighting spirit, on his determination to fight. They are like tiny worms, gnawing and undermining imperceptibly, slowly but surely. I know the life of the workers, and not only from books. Our communist work among the masses of women, and our political work in general, involves considerable educational work among the men. We must root out the old slave-owner's point of view, both in the Party and among the masses. That is one of our political tasks, a task just as urgently necessary as the formation of a staff composed of comrades, men and women, with thorough theoretical and practical training for Party work among working women. . . .

"The government of the proletarian dictatorship—jointly with the Communist party and the trade unions of course—makes every effort to overcome the backward views of men and women and thus uproot the old, non-communist psychology. It goes without saying that men and women are absolutely equal before the law. A sincere desire to give effect to this equality is evident in all spheres. We are enlisting women to work in the economy, the administration, legislation and government. All courses and educational institutions are open to them, so that they can improve their professional and social training. We are organising community kitchens and public dining-rooms, laundries and repair shops, crèches, kindergartens, children's homes and educational institutions of every kind. In brief, we are quite in earnest about carrying out the requirements of our programme to shift the functions of housekeeping and education from the individual household to society. Woman is thus being relieved from her old domestic slavery and all dependence on her husband. She is enabled to give her capabilities and inclinations full play in society. Children are offered better opportunities for their development than at home. We have the most progressive female labour legislation in the world, and it is enforced by authorised representatives of organised labour. We are establishing maternity homes, mother-and-child homes, mothers' health centres, courses for infant and child care, exhibitions of mother and child care, and the like. We are making every effort to provide for needy and unemployed women.

"We know perfectly well that all this is still too little, considering the needs of the working women, and that it is still far from sufficient for their real emancipation. Yet it is an immense stride forward from what there was in tsarist and capitalist Russia. Moreover, it is a lot as compared with the state of affairs where capitalism still holds undivided sway. It is a good start in the right direction, and we shall continue to develop it consistently, and with all available energy, too. . . . Because with each day that passes it becomes clearer that we cannot make progress without the millions of women. Think what this means in a country where the peasants comprise a solid 80% of the population. Small peasant farming implies individual housekeeping and the bondage of women. You will be far better off than we are in this respect, provided your proletarians at last grasp that the time is historically ripe for seizure of power, for revolution. In the meantime, we are not giving way to despair, despite the great difficulties. Our forces grow as the latter increase. Practical necessity will also impel us to find new ways of emancipating the masses of women. In combination with the Soviet state, comradely solidarity will accomplish wonders. To be sure, I mean comradely solidarity in the communist, not in the bourgeois, sense, in which it is preached by the reformists, whose revolutionary enthusiasm has evaporated like the smell of cheap vinegar. Personal initiative, which grows into, and fuses with collective activity, should accompany comradely solidarity. Under the proletarian dictatorship the emancipation of women through the realisation of communism will proceed also in the countryside. In this respect I expect much from the electrification of our industry and agriculture. That is a grand scheme! The difficulties in its way are great, monstrously great. Powerful forces latent in the masses will have to be released and trained to overcome them. Millions of women must take part in this".

* * *

CHARLOTTE PERKINS GILMAN

Charlotte Perkins Gilman (1860–1935) was born into a rich cultural heritage in New England. Her childhood was marred by her parents' separation and by the economic difficulties and overwork this caused for her mother as a single head of household. As a young adult Gilman experienced depression, a nervous breakdown following the birth of her daughter, and a divorce necessitated by "temporary insanity." By her thirties, she had recovered her health and begun to articulate publicly her criticisms of inequalities within society. By forty Gilman had married again, this time to a man who remained a faithful, supportive companion through the remainder of her life.

Although Gilman's egalitarian ideal was best supported by socialist theory, she also drew on the writings of economists, theologians, historians, anthropologists, and sociologists in her critique of patriarchal power as the primary oppressive force in women's lives. The family, she maintained, ensured women's economic dependence, nonvoluntary domestic service, emotional subservience, and sexual submission. Gilman advised women to overcome their oppression by pressing for full economic equality, satisfying work outside the home, and sexual equality in love relationships. Equality is a necessary condition for the full development of human beings. "That is human," she wrote, "which belongs to the human species as such, *without regard to sex*."

Women and Economics

. . . We are the only animal species in which the female depends on the male for food, the only animal species in which the sex-relation is also an economic relation. With us an entire sex lives in a relation of economic dependence upon the other sex, and the economic relation is combined with the sex relation. The economic status of the human female is relative to the sex-relation.

It is commonly assumed that this condition also obtains among other animals, but such is not the case. There are many birds among which, during the nesting season, the male helps the female feed the young, and partially feeds her; and, with certain of the higher carnivora, the male helps the female feed the young, and partially feeds her. In no case does she depend on him absolutely, even during this season, save in that of the hornbill, where the female, sitting on her nest in a hollow tree, is walled in with clay by the male, so that only her beak projects; and then he feeds her while the eggs are developing. But even the female hornbill does not expect to be fed at any other time. The female bee and ant are economically dependent, but not on the male. The workers are females, too, specialized to economic functions solely. And with the carnivora, if the young are to lose one parent, it might far better be the father: the mother is quite competent to take care of them herself. With many species, as in the case of the common cat, she not only feeds herself and her young, but has to defend the young against the male as well. In no case is the female throughout her life supported by the male.

In the human species the condition is permanent and general, though there are exceptions, and though the present century is witnessing the beginnings of a great change in this respect. We have not been accustomed to face this fact beyond our loose generalization that it was "natural," and that other animals did so, too.

To many this view will not seem clear at first; and the case of working peasant women or females of savage tribes, and the general household industry of women, will be instanced against it. Some careful and honest discrimination is needed to make plain to ourselves the essential facts of the relation, even in these cases. The horse, in his free natural condition, is economically independent. He gets his living by his own exertions, irrespective of any other creature. The horse, in his present condition of slavery, is economically dependent. He gets his living at the hands of his master; and his exertions, though strenuous, bear no direct relation to his living. In fact, the horses who are the best fed and cared for and the horses who are the hardest worked are quite different animals. The horse works, it is true; but what he gets to eat depends on the power and will of his master. His living comes through another. He is economically dependent. So with the hard-worked savage or peasant women. Their labor is the property of another: they work under another will; and what they receive depends not on their labor, but on the power and will of another. They are economically dependent. This is true of the human female both individually and collectively.

In studying the economic position of the sexes collectively, the difference is most marked. As a social animal, the economic status of man rests on the combined and exchanged services of vast numbers of progressively specialized individuals. The economic progress of the race, its maintenance at any period, its continued advance, involve the collective activities of all the trades, crafts, arts, manufactures, inventions, discoveries, and all the civil and military institutions that go to maintain them. The economic status of any race at any time, with its involved effect on all the constituent individuals, depends on their world-wide labors and their free exchange. Economic progress, however, is almost exclusively masculine. Such economic processes as women have been allowed to exercise are of the earliest and most primitive kind. Were men to perform no economic services save such as are still performed by women, our racial status in economics would be reduced to most painful limitations.

To take from any community its male workers would paralyze it economically to a far greater degree than to remove its female workers. The labor now performed by the women could be performed by the men, requiring only the setting back of many advanced workers into earlier forms of industry; but the labor now performed by the men could not be performed by the women without generations of effort and adaptation. Men can cook, clean, and sew as well as women; but the making and managing of the great engines of modern industry, the threading of earth and sea in our vast systems of transportation, the handling of our elaborate machinery of trade, commerce, government,—these things could not be done so well by women in their present degree of economic development.

This is not owing to lack of the essential human faculties necessary to such achievements, nor to any inherent disability of sex, but to the present condition of woman, forbidding the development of this degree of economic ability. The male human being is thousands of years in advance of the female in economic status. Speaking collectively, men produce and distribute wealth; and women receive it at their hands. As men hunt, fish, keep cattle, or raise corn, so do women eat game, fish, beef, or corn. As men go down to the sea in ships, and bring coffee and spices and silks and gems from far away, so do women partake of the coffee and spices and silks and gems the men bring.

The economic status of the human race in any nation, at any time, is governed mainly by the activities of the male: the female obtains her share in the racial advance only through him.

Studied individually, the facts are even more plainly visible, more open and familiar. From the day laborer to the millionnaire, the wife's worn dress or flashing jewels, her low roof or her lordly one, her weary feet or her rich equipage,—these speak of the economic ability of the husband. The comfort, the luxury, the necessities of life itself, which the woman receives, are obtained by the husband, and given her by him. And, when the woman, left alone with no man to "support" her, tries to meet her own economic necessities, the difficulties which confront her prove conclusively what the general economic status of the woman is. None can deny these patent facts,—that the economic status of women generally depends upon that of men generally, and that the economic status of women individually depends upon that of men individually, those men to whom they are related. But we are instantly confronted by the commonly received opinion that, although it must be admitted that men make and distribute the wealth of the world, yet women earn their share of it as wives. This assumes either that the husband is in the position of employer and the wife as employee, or that marriage is a "partnership," and the wife an equal factor with the husband in producing wealth.

Economic independence is a relative condition at best. In the broadest sense, all living things are economically dependent upon others,—the animals upon the vegetables, and man upon both. In a narrower sense, all social life is economically interdependent, man producing collectively what he could by no possibility produce separately. But, in the closest interpretation, individual economic independence among human beings means that the individual pays for what he gets, works for what he gets, gives to the other an equivalent for what the other gives him. I depend on the shoemaker for shoes, and the tailor for coats; but, if I give the shoemaker and the tailor enough of my own labor as a house-builder to pay for the shoes and coats they give me, I retain my personal independence. I have not taken of their product, and given nothing of mine. As long as what I get is obtained by what I give, I am economically independent.

Women consume economic goods. What economic product do they give in exchange for what they consume? The claim that marriage is a partnership, in which the two persons married produce wealth which neither of them, separately, could produce, will not bear examination. A man happy and comfortable can produce more than one unhappy and uncomfortable, but this is as true of a father or son as of a husband. To take from a man any of the conditions which make him happy and strong is to cripple his industry, generally speaking. But those relatives who make him happy are not therefore his business partners, and entitled to share his income.

Grateful return for happiness conferred is not the method of exchange in a partnership. The comfort a man takes with his wife is not in the nature of a business partnership, nor are her frugality and industry. A housekeeper, in her place, might be as frugal, as industrious, but would not therefore be a partner. Man and wife are partners truly in their mutual obligation to their children,—their common love, duty, and service. But a manufacturer who marries, or a doctor, or a lawyer, does not take a partner in his business, when he takes a partner in parenthood, unless his wife is also a manufacturer, a doctor, or a lawyer. In his business, she cannot even advise wisely without training and experience. To love her husband, the composer, does not enable her to compose; and the loss of a man's wife, though it may break his heart, does not cripple his business, unless his mind is affected by grief. She is in no sense a business partner, unless she contributes capital or experience or labor, as a man would in like relation. Most men would hesitate very seriously before entering a business partnership with any woman, wife or not.

If the wife is not, then, truly a business partner, in what way does she earn from her husband the food, clothing, and shelter she receives at his hands? By house service, it will be instantly replied. This is the general misty idea upon the subject,—that women earn all they get, and more, by house service. Here we come to a very practical and definite economic ground. Although not producers of wealth, women serve in the final processes of preparation and distribution. Their labor in the household has a genuine economic value.

For a certain percentage of persons to serve other persons, in order that the ones so served may produce more, is a contribution not to be overlooked. The labor of women in the house, certainly, enables men to produce more wealth than they otherwise could; and in this way women are economic factors in society. But so are horses. The labor of horses enables men to produce more wealth than they otherwise could. The horse is an economic factor in society. But the horse is not economically independent, nor is the woman. If a man plus a valet can perform more useful service than he could minus a valet, then the valet is performing useful service. But, if the valet is the property of the man, is obliged to perform this service, and is not paid for it, he is not economically independent.

The labor which the wife performs in the household is given as part of her functional duty, not as employment. The wife of the poor man, who works hard in a small house, doing all the work for the family, or the wife of the rich man, who wisely and gracefully manages a large house and administers its functions, each is entitled to fair pay for services rendered.

To take this ground and hold it honestly, wives, as earners through domestic service, are entitled to the wages of cooks, housemaids, nursemaids, seamstresses, or housekeepers, and to no more. This would of course reduce the spending money of the wives of the rich, and put it out of the power of the poor man to "support" a wife at all, unless, indeed, the poor man faced the situation fully, paid his wife her wages as house servant, and then she and he combined their funds in the support of their children. He would be keeping a servant: she would be helping keep the family. But nowhere on earth would there be "a rich woman" by these means. Even the highest class of private housekeeper, useful as her services are, does not accumulate a fortune. She does not buy diamonds and sables and keep a carriage. Things like these are not earned by house service.

But the salient fact in this discussion is that, whatever the economic value of the domestic industry of women is, they do not get it. The women who do the most work get the least money, and the women who have the most money do the least work. Their labor is neither given nor taken as a factor in economic exchange. It is held to be their duty as women to do this work; and their economic status bears no relation to their domestic labors, unless an inverse one. Moreover, if they were thus fairly paid,—given what they earned, and no more,—all women working in this way would be reduced to the economic status of the house servant. Few women—or men either—care to face this condition. The ground that women earn their living by domestic labor is instantly forsaken, and we are told that they obtain their livelihood as mothers. This is a peculiar position. We speak of it commonly enough, and often with deep feeling, but without due analysis.

In treating of an economic exchange, asking what return in goods or labor women make for the goods and labor given them,—either to the race collectively or to their husbands individually,—what payment women make for their clothes and shoes and furniture and food and shelter, we are told that the duties and services of the mother entitle her to support.

If this is so, if motherhood is an exchangeable commodity given by women in payment for clothes and food, then we must of course find some relation between the quantity or quality of the motherhood and the quantity and quality of the pay. This being true, then the women who are not mothers have no economic status at all; and the economic status of those who are must be shown to be relative to their motherhood. This is obviously absurd. The childless wife has as much money as the mother of many,—more; for the children of the latter consume what would otherwise be hers; and the inefficient mother is no less provided for than the efficient one. Visibly, and upon the face of it, women are not maintained in economic prosperity proportioned to their motherhood. Motherhood bears no relation to their economic status. Among primitive races, it is true, —in the patriarchal period, for instance,—there was some truth in this position. Women being of no value whatever save as bearers of children, their favor and indulgence did bear direct relation to maternity; and they had reason to exult on more grounds than one when they could boast a son. To-day, however, the maintenance of the woman is not conditioned upon this. A man is not allowed to discard his wife because she is barren. The claim of motherhood as a factor in economic exchange is false to-day. But suppose it were true. Are we willing to hold this ground, even in theory? Are we willing to consider motherhood as a business, a form of commercial exchange? Are the cares and duties of the mother, her travail and her love, commodities to be exchanged for bread?

It is revolting so to consider them; and, if we dare face our own thoughts, and force them to their logical conclusion, we shall see that nothing could be more repugnant to human feeling, or more socially and individually injurious, than to make motherhood a trade. Driven off these alleged grounds of women's economic independence; shown that women, as a class, neither produce nor distribute wealth; that women, as individuals, labor mainly as house servants, are not paid as such, and would not be satisfied with such an economic status if they were so paid; that wives are not business partners or co-producers of wealth with their husbands, unless they actually practise the same profession; that they are not salaried as mothers, and that it would be unspeakably degrading if they were, —what remains to those who deny that women are supported by men? This (and a most amusing position it is),—that the function of maternity unfits a woman for economic production, and, therefore, it is right that she should be supported by her husband.

The ground is taken that the human female is not economically independent, that she is fed by the male of her species. In denial of this, it is first alleged that she is economically independent, —that she does support herself by her own industry in the house. It being shown that there is no relation between the economic status of woman and the labor she performs in the home, it is then alleged that not as house servant, but as mother, does woman earn her living. It being shown that the economic status of woman bears no relation to her motherhood, either in quantity or quality, it is then alleged that motherhood renders a woman unfit for economic production, and that, therefore, it is right that she be supported by her husband. Before going farther, let us seize upon this admission,—that she *is* supported by her husband.

Without going into either the ethics or the necessities of the case, we have reached so much common ground: the female of genus homo is supported by the male. Whereas, in other species of animals, male and female alike graze and browse, hunt and kill, climb, swim, dig, run, and fly for their livings, in our species the female does not seek her own living in the specific activities of our race, but is fed by the male.

Now as to the alleged necessity. Because of her maternal duties, the human female is said to be unable to get her own living. As the maternal duties of other females do not unfit them for getting their own living and also the livings of their young, it would seem that the human maternal duties require the segregation of the entire energies of the mother to the service of the child during her entire adult life, or so large a proportion of them that not enough remains to devote to the individual interests of the mother.

Such a condition, did it exist, would of course excuse and justify the pitiful dependence of the human female, and her support by the male. As the queen bee, modified entirely to maternity, is supported, not by the male, to be sure, but by her co-workers, the "old maids," the barren working bees, who labor so patiently and lovingly in their branch of the maternal duties of the hive, so would the human female, modified entirely to maternity, become unfit for any other exertion, and a helpless dependant.

Is this the condition of human motherhood? Does the human mother, by her motherhood, thereby lose control of brain and body, lose power and skill and desire for any other work? Do we see before us the human race, with all its females segregated entirely to the uses of motherhood, consecrated, set apart, specially developed, spending every power of their nature on the service of their children?

We do not. We see the human mother worked far harder than a mare, laboring her life long in the service, not of her children only, but of men; husbands, brothers, fathers, whatever male relatives she has; for mother and sister also; for the church a little, if she is allowed; for society, if she is able; for charity and education and reform,—working in many ways that are not the ways of motherhood.

It is not motherhood that keeps the housewife on her feet from dawn till dark; it is house service, not child service. Women work longer and harder than most men, and not solely in maternal duties. The savage mother carries the burdens, and does all menial service for the tribe. The peasant mother toils in the fields, and the workingman's wife in the home. Many mothers, even now, are wage-earners for the family, as well as bearers and rearers of it. And the women who are not so occupied, the women who belong to rich men,—here perhaps is the exhaustive devotion to maternity which is supposed to justify an admitted economic dependence. But we do not find it even among these. Women of ease and wealth provide for their children better care than the poor woman can; but they do not spend more time upon it themselves, nor more care and effort. They have other occupation.

In spite of her supposed segregation to maternal duties, the human female, the world over, works at extra-maternal duties for hours enough to provide her with an independent living, and then is denied independence on the ground that motherhood prevents her working!

If this ground were tenable, we should find a world full of women who never lifted a finger save in the service of their children, and of men who did *all* the work besides, and waited on the women whom motherhood prevented from waiting on themselves. The ground is not tenable. A human female, healthy, sound, has twenty-five years of life before she is a mother, and should have twenty-five years more after the period of such maternal service as is expected of her has been given. The duties of grandmotherhood are surely not alleged as preventing economic independence.

The working power of the mother has always been a prominent factor in human life. She is the worker *par excellence*, but her work is not such as to affect her economic status. Her living, all that she gets,—food, clothing, ornaments, amusements, luxuries,—these bear no relation to her power to produce wealth, to her services in the house, or to her motherhood. These things bear relation only to the man she marries, the man she depends on,—to how much he has and how much he is willing to give her. The women whose splendid extravagance dazzles the world, whose economic goods are the greatest, are often neither houseworkers nor mothers, but simply the women who hold most power over the men who have the most money. The female of genus homo is economically dependent on the male. He is her food supply.

HERBERT MARCUSE

The three leading influences on the thought of Herbert Marcuse (1898–1979) are Hegel, Marx, and Freud. Although he rejected Hegel's vision of the Absolute Spirit, together with its "spiritualistic" view of human nature and society, Marcuse embraced the Hegelian dialectic and concept of history as a march toward freedom. On the whole Marcuse endorsed Marx's criticisms of philosophy and society, but extended his own critique to various expressions of Marxism as well as capitalism. For Marcuse the working class "no longer appears to be the living contradiction of the established society." Rather, the source of exploitation is the very concept of, and instinct toward, domination—a domination which dehumanizes not only the oppressed but also the oppressor. From Freud, Marcuse draws his notion that the overcoming of repression through the "rationality of gratification" is the ideal of individuals and for society.

In *One-Dimensional Man,* Marcuse describes the caricature of human nature which oppressive and repressive forces within society have created. Basically, one-dimensionality means the reduction of human nature to the dimension of objectivity; in other words, it is the denial of subjectivity or freedom to individuals. Marcuse maintains that human nature is in reality dialectical, i.e., it consists of the interaction between the free subject and the objective world, including other subjects. Such a view tends to identify the real and the ideal, invoking the latter as criterion for critique of dehumanizing conditions in society.

Dehumanization occurs not only through deprivation of freedom but also through denial of human capacities for rationality and happiness. Both are crucial factors for Marcuse. Accordingly, he construes the *eros* which impels us toward pleasure as entirely compatible with the *logos* of human reason. Indeed, he speculates about the possibility of a

> knowledge [which] will no longer disturb pleasure. Perhaps it can even become pleasure, which the ancient idea of *nous* had dared to see.

Such a goal is one which Marcuse himself views as achievable, but only insofar as we succeed in overcoming one-dimensionality through freedom.

Nature and Revolution

The novel historical pattern of the coming revolution is perhaps best reflected in the role played by a new sensibility in radically changing the "style" of the opposition. I have sketched out this new dimension in *An Essay on Liberation;* here I shall attempt to indicate what is at stake, namely, a new relation between man and nature—his own, and external nature. The radical transformation of nature becomes an integral part of the radical transformation of society. Far from being a mere "psychological" phenomenon in groups or individuals, the new sensibility is the medium in which social change becomes an individual need, the mediation between the political practice of "changing the world" and the drive for personal liberation.

What is happening is the discovery (or rather, rediscovery) of nature as an ally in the struggle against the exploitative societies in which the violation of nature aggravates the violation of man. The discovery of the liberating forces of nature and their vital role in the construction of a free society becomes a new force in social change.

What is involved in the liberation of nature as a vehicle of the liberation of man?

This notion refers to (1) *human* nature: man's primary impulses and senses as foundation of his rationality and experience and (2) *external* nature: man's existential environment, the "struggle with nature" in which he forms his society. It must be stressed from the beginning that, in both of these manifestations, nature is a historical entity: man encounters nature as transformed by society, subjected to a specific rationality which became, to an ever-increasing extent, technological, instrumentalist rationality, bent to the requirements of capitalism. And this rationality was also brought to bear on man's own nature, on his primary drives. To recall only two characteristic contemporary forms of the adaptation of primary drives to the needs of the established system: the social steering of *aggressiveness* through transferring the aggressive act to technical instruments, thus reducing the sense of guilt; and the social steering of *sexuality* through controlled desublimation, the plastic beauty industry, which leads to a reduction of the sense of guilt and thus promotes "legitimate" satisfaction.

Nature is a part of history, an object of history; therefore, "liberation of nature" cannot mean returning to a pretechnological stage, but advancing to the use of the achievements of technological civilization for freeing man and nature from the destructive abuse of science and technology in the service of exploitation. Then, certain lost qualities of artisan work may well reappear on the new technological base.

In the established society, nature itself, ever more effectively controlled, has in turn become another dimension for the control of man: the extended arm of society and its power. Commercialized nature, polluted nature, militarized nature cut down the life environment of man, not only in an ecological but also in a very existential sense. It blocks the erotic cathexis (and transformation) of his environment: it deprives man from finding himself in nature, beyond and this side of alienation; it also prevents him from recognizing nature as a *subject* in its own right—a subject with which to live in a common human universe. This deprivation is not undone by the opening of nature to massive fun and togetherness, spontaneous as well as organized—a release of frustration which only adds to the violation of nature.

Liberation of nature is the recovery of the life-enhancing forces in nature, the sensuous aesthetic qualities which are foreign to a life wasted in unending competitive performances: they suggest the new qualities of *freedom.* No wonder then that the "spirit of capitalism" rejects or ridicules the idea of liberated nature, that it relegates this idea to the poetic imagination. Nature, if not left alone and protected as "reservation," is treated in an aggressively scientific way: it is there for the sake of domination; it is value-free matter, material. This notion of nature is a *historical* a priori, pertaining to a specific form of society. A free society may well have a very different a priori and a very different object; the development of the scientific concepts may be grounded in an experience of nature as a totality of life to be protected and "cultivated," and technology would apply this science to the reconstruction of the environment of life.

Domination of man through the domination of nature: the concrete link between the liberation of man and that of nature has become manifest today in the role which the ecology drive plays in the radical movement. The pollution of air and water, the noise, the encroachment of industry and commerce on open natural space have the physical weight of enslavement, imprisonment. The struggle against them is a political struggle; it is obvious to what extent the violation of nature is inseparable from the economy of capitalism. At the same time, however, the political function of ecology is easily "neutralized" and serves the beautification of the Establishment. Still, the physical pollution practiced by the system must be combated here and now—just as its mental pollution. To drive ecology to the point where it is no longer containable within the capitalist framework means first extending the drive *within* the capitalist framework.[1]

The relation between nature and freedom is rarely made explicit in social theory. In Marxism too, nature is predominantly an object, the adversary in man's "struggle with nature," the field for the ever more rational development of the productive forces.[2] But in this form, nature appears as that which capitalism has *made* of nature: matter, raw material for the expanding and exploiting administration of men and things. Does this image of nature conform to that of a free society? Is nature only a productive force—or does it also exist *"for its own sake"* and, in *this* mode of existence, for *man?*

In the treatment of *human* nature, Marxism shows a similar tendency to minimize the role of the natural basis in social change—a tendency which contrasts sharply with the earlier writings of Marx. To be sure, "human nature" would be different under socialism to the degree to which men and women would, for the first time in history, develop and fulfill their own needs and faculties in association with each other. But this change is to come about almost as a by-product of the new socialist institutions. Marxist emphasis on the development of political consciousness shows little concern with the roots of liberation in individuals, i.e., with the roots of social relationships there where individuals most directly and profoundly experience their world and themselves: in their *sensibility*, in their instinctual needs.

In *An Essay on Liberation,* I suggested that without a change in this dimension, the old Adam would be reproduced in the new society, and that the construction of a free society *presupposes* a

1. See Murray Bookchin, "Ecology and Revolutionary Thought" and "Towards a Liberatory Technology," in *Post-Scarcity Anarchism* (Berkeley: Ramparts Press, 1971).

2. See Alfred Schmidt, *Der Begriff der Natur in der Lehre von Marx* (Frankfurt: Europäische Verlagsanstalt, 1962).

break with the familiar experience of the world: with the mutilated sensibility. Conditioned and "contained" by the rationality of the established system, sense experience tends to "immunize" man against the very unfamiliar experience of the possibilities of human freedom. The development of a radical, nonconformist sensibility assumes vital political importance in view of the unprecedented extent of social control perfected by advanced capitalism: a control which reaches down into the instinctual and physiological level of existence. Conversely, resistance and rebellion, too, tend to activate and operate on this level.

"Radical sensibility": the concept stresses the active, constitutive role of the senses in shaping reason, that is to say, in shaping the categories under which the world is ordered, experienced, changed. The senses are not merely passive, receptive: they have their own "syntheses" to which they subject the primary data of experience. And these syntheses are not only the pure "forms of intuition" (space and time) which Kant recognized as an inexorable a priori *ordering* of sense data. There are perhaps also other syntheses, far more concrete, far more "material," which may constitute an empirical (i.e., historical) a priori of experience. Our world emerges not only in the pure forms of time and space, but also, and *simultaneously,* as a totality of sensuous qualities—object not only of the eye (synopsis) but of *all* human senses (hearing, smelling, touching, tasting). It is this qualitative, elementary, unconscious, or rather preconscious, constitution of the world of experience, it is this primary experience itself which must change radically if social change is to be radical, qualitative change.

II

The subversive potential of the sensibility, and nature as a field of liberation are central themes in Marx's *Economic and Philosophic Manuscripts*. They have been reread and reinterpreted again and again, but these themes have been largely neglected. Recently, the Manuscripts served to justify the concept of "humanistic socialism" in opposition to the bureaucratic-authoritarian Soviet model; they provided a powerful impetus in the struggle against Stalinism and post-Stalinism. I believe that in spite of their "pre-scientific" character, and in spite of the prevalence of Feuerbach's philosophic naturalism, these writings espouse the most radical and integral idea of socialism, and that precisely here, "nature" finds its place in the theory of revolution.

I recall briefly the principal conception of the Manuscripts. Marx speaks of the "complete emancipation of all human senses and qualities"[3] as the feature of socialism: only this emancipation is the "transcendence of private property." This means the emergence of a new type of man, different from the human subject of class society in his very nature, in his physiology: "the *senses* of the social man are *other* than those of the non-social man."[4]

"*Emancipation of the senses*" implies that the senses become "practical" in the reconstruction of society, that they generate new (socialist) relationships between man and man, man and things, man and nature. But the senses become also "sources" of a new (socialist) *rationality:* freed from that of exploitation. The emancipated senses would repel the instrumentalist rationality of capitalism while preserving and developing its achievements. They would attain this goal in two ways: *negatively*—inasmuch as the Ego, the other, and the object world would no longer be experienced in the context of aggressive acquisition, competition, and defensive possession; *positively*—through the "human appropriation of nature," i.e., through the transformation of nature into an environment (medium) for the human being as "species being"; free to develop the specifically human faculties: the creative, aesthetic faculties.

"Only through the objectively unfolded richness of man's essential being is the richness of subjective human sensibility (a musical ear, an eye for beauty of form—in short, *senses* capable of human gratification, senses affirming themselves as essential powers of man) either cultivated or brought into being."[5] The emancipated senses, in conjunction with a natural science proceeding on their basis, would guide the "human appropriation" of nature. Then, nature would have "lost its mere utility,"[6] it would appear not merely as stuff—organic or inorganic matter—but as life force in its own right, as subject-object;[7] the striving for life is the substance common to man and nature. Man would then form a living object. The senses would "relate themselves to the thing for the sake of the thing. . . ."[8] And they can do so only inasmuch as the thing itself is

3. Karl Marx, *The Economic and Philosophic Manuscripts of 1844,* Dirk J. Struik, ed. (New York: International Publishers, 1964), p. 139.

4. *Ibid.,* p. 141.

5. *Ibid.,* p. 141.

6. *Ibid.,* p. 139.

7. "The sun is the object of the plant . . . just as the plant is an object for the sun. . . ." *Ibid.,* p. 181.

8. *Ibid.,* p. 139.

objectified human *Verhalten:* objectification of human relationships and is thus itself humanly related to man.[9]

This outrageously unscientific, metaphysical notion foreshadows the mature materialistic theory: it grasps the world of things as objectified human labor, shaped by human labor. Now if this forming human activity produces the technical and natural environment of an acquisitive and repressive society, it will also produce a dehumanized nature; and radical social change will involve a radical transformation of nature.

Also of the *science* of nature? Nature as manifestation of subjectivity: the idea seems inseparable from teleology—long since taboo in Western science. Nature as object per se fitted all too well into the universe of the capitalist treatment of matter to allow discarding the taboo. It seemed entirely justified by the increasingly effective and profitable mastery of nature which was achieved under this taboo.

Is it true that the recognition of nature as a subject is metaphysical teleology incompatible with scientific objectivity? Let us take Jacques Monod's statement of the meaning of objectivity in science:

> What I have tried to show . . . is that the scientific attitude implies what I call the postulate of objectivity—that is to say, the fundamental postulate that there is no plan, that there is no intention in the universe.[10]

The idea of the liberation of nature stipulates no such plan or intention in the universe: liberation is the possible plan and intention of human beings, brought to bear upon nature. However, it does stipulate that nature is susceptible to such an undertaking, and that there are forces in nature which have been distorted and suppressed—forces which could support and enhance the liberation of man. This capacity of nature may be called "chance," or "blind freedom," and it may give good meaning to the human effort to redeem this blindness—in Adorno's words: to help nature "to open

9. For the sake of the thing—an illustration:
In Yugoslavia, they sell wooden cutting boards which, on one side, are painted with very colorful, pretty flower patterns; the other side is unpainted. The boards bear the imprint: "don't hurt my pretty face, use other side." Childish anthropomorphism? Certainly. But can we perhaps imagine that the people who had this idea, and those users who pay attention to it, have a quite natural, instinctual aversion against violence and destruction, that they have indeed a "human relation" to matter, that matter to them is part of the *life* environment and thus assumes traits of a living object?

10. Interview with the *New York Times*, March 15, 1971.

its eyes," to help it "on the poor earth to become what perhaps it would like to be."[11]

Nature as subject without teleology, without "plan" and "intention": this notion goes well with Kant's "purposiveness without purpose." The most advanced concepts of the Third Critique have not yet been explored in their truly revolutionary significance. The aesthetic form in art has the aesthetic form in nature (*das Naturschöne*) as its correlate, or rather desideratum. If the idea of beauty pertains to nature as well as to art, this is not merely an analogy, or a human idea imposed on nature—it is the insight that the aesthetic form, as a token of freedom, is a mode (or moment?) of existence of the human as well as the natural universe, an objective quality. Thus Kant attributes the beautiful in nature to nature's "capacity to form itself, in its freedom, also in an aesthetically purposive way, according to chemical laws. . . ."[12]

The Marxian conception understands nature as a universe which becomes the congenial medium for human gratification to the degree to which nature's *own* gratifying forces and qualities are recovered and released. In sharp contrast to the capitalist exploitation of nature, its "human appropriation" would be nonviolent, nondestructive: oriented on the life-enhancing, sensuous, aesthetic qualities inherent in nature. Thus transformed, "humanized," nature would respond to man's striving for fulfillment, nay, the latter would not be possible without the former. Things have their "inherent measure" (*inhärentes Mass*):[13] this measure is *in* them, is the potential enclosed in them; only man can free it and, in doing so, free his own human potential. Man is the only being who can "form things in accordance with the laws of beauty."[14]

Aesthetics of liberation, beauty as a "form" of freedom: it looks as if Marx has shied away from this anthropomorphist, idealistic conception. Or is this apparently idealistic notion rather the *enlargement of the materialistic base?* For "man is directly a *natural being;* he is a corporeal, living, real, sensuous, objective being" who has "real, sensuous objects" as the objects of his life.[15] And his senses ("like those organs which are directly social in their form")[16]

11. Theodor W. Adorno, *Aesthetische Theorie* (Frankfurt/Main: Suhrkamp, 1970), pp. 100, 107.

12. *Critique of Judgment,* S 58.

13. Marx, *loc. cit.,* p. 114.

14. *Ibid.*

15. *Ibid.,* p. 181.

16. *Ibid.,* p. 139.

are active, practical in the "appropriation" of the object world; they express the social existence of man, his "objectification." This is no longer Feuerbach's "naturalism" but, on the contrary, the extension of Historical Materialism to a dimension which is to play a vital role in the liberation of man.

There is, however, a definite internal limit to the idea of the liberation of nature through "human appropriation." True, the aesthetic dimension is a vital dimension of freedom; true, it repels violence, cruelty, brutality, and by this token will become an essential quality of a free society, not as a separate realm of "higher culture," but as a driving force and *motive* in the *construction* of such a society. And yet, certain brute facts, unconquered and perhaps unconquerable facts, call for skepticism. Can the human appropriation of nature ever achieve the elimination of violence, cruelty, and brutality in the daily sacrifice of animal life for the physical reproduction of the human race? To treat nature "for its own sake" sounds good, but it is certainly not for the sake of the animal to be eaten, nor probably for the sake of the plant. The end of this war, the perfect peace in the animal world—this idea belongs to the Orphic myth, not to any conceivable historical reality. In the face of the suffering inflicted by man on man, it seems terribly "premature" to campaign for universal vegetarianism or synthetic foodstuffs; as the world is, priority must be on *human* solidarity among human beings. And yet, no free society is imaginable which does not, under its "regulative idea of reason," make the concerted effort to reduce consistently the suffering which man imposes on the animal world.

Marx's notion of a human appropriation of nature retains something of the *hubris* of domination. "Appropriation," no matter how human, remains appropriation of a (living) object by a subject. It offends that which is essentially other than the appropriating subject, and which exists precisely as object in its own right—that is, as subject! The latter may well be hostile to man, in which case the relation would be one of struggle; but the struggle may also subside and make room for peace, tranquillity, fulfillment. In this case, not appropriation but rather its negation would be the nonexploitative relation: surrender, "letting-be," acceptance. . . . But such surrender meets with the impenetrable resistance of matter; nature is not a manifestation of "spirit," but rather its essential *limit*.

III

Although the historical concept of nature as a dimension of social change does not imply teleology and does not attribute a "plan" to nature, it does conceive of nature as subject-object: as a *cosmos* with its own potentialities, necessities, and chances. And these potentialities can be, not only in the sense of their value-free function in theory and practice, but also as bearers of *objective values.* These are envisaged in such phrases as "violation of nature," "suppression of nature." Violation and suppression then mean that human action against nature, man's interrelation with nature, offends against certain objective *qualities* of nature—qualities which are essential to the enhancement and fulfillment of life. And it is on such objective grounds that the liberation for man to his own humane faculties is linked to the liberation of nature—that "truth" is attributable to nature not only in a mathematical but also in an existential sense. The emancipation of man involves the recognition of such truth in things, in nature. The Marxian vision recaptures the ancient theory of knowledge as *recollection:* "science" as the *re*discovery of the true *Forms* of things, distorted and denied in the established reality, the perpetual *materialistic core of idealism.* The "idea," as the term for these Forms, is not a "mere" idea, but an image illuminating what is false, distorted in the way in which things are "given," what is missing in their familiar perception, in the mutilated experience which is the work of society.

Recollection thus is not remembrance of a Golden Past (which never existed), of childhood innocence, primitive man, et cetera. Recollection as epistemological faculty rather is synthesis, reassembling the bits and fragments which can be found in the distorted humanity and distorted nature. This recollected material has become the domain of the imagination, it has been sanctioned by the repressive societies in art, and as "poetic truth"—poetic truth only, and therefore not much good in the actual transformation of society. These images may well be called "innate ideas" inasmuch as they cannot possibly be given in the immediate experience which prevails in the repressive societies. They are given rather as the *horizon* of experience under which the immediately given forms of things appear as "negative," as denial of their inherent possibilities, their truth. But in this sense, they are "innate" in man as *historical* being; they are themselves historical because the possibilities of liberation are always and everywhere historical possibilities. Imagination, *as knowledge*, retains the insoluble tension between idea and reality, the potential and the actual. This is the *idealistic core* of dialectical materialism: the transcendence of freedom beyond the given forms. In this sense too, Marxian theory is the historical heir of German idealism.

Freedom thus becomes a "regulative concept of reason" guiding the practice of changing reality in accordance with its "idea," i.e., its own potentialities—to make reality free for its truth. Dialectical materialism understands freedom as historical, empirical transcendence, as a force of social change, transcending its immediate form also in a socialist society—not toward ever more production, not toward Heaven or Paradise, but toward an ever more peaceful, joyful struggle with the inexorable resistance of society and nature. This is the philosophical core of the theory of the permanent revolution.

As such force, freedom is rooted in the primary drives of men and women, it is the vital need to enhance their life instincts. Prerequisite is the capacity of the senses to experience not only the "given" but also the "hidden" qualities of things which would make for the betterment of life. The radical redefinition of sensibility as "practical" desublimates the idea of freedom without abandoning its transcendent content: the senses are not only the basis for the *epistemological* constitution of reality, but also for its *transformation*, its *subversion* in the interest of liberation.

Human freedom is thus rooted in the human *sensibility:* the senses do not only "receive" what is given to them, in the form in which it appears, they do not "delegate" the transformation of the given to another faculty (the understanding); rather, they discover or *can* discover by themselves, in their "practice," new (more gratifying) possibilities and capabilities, forms and qualities of things, and can urge and guide their realization. The emancipation of the senses would make freedom what it is not yet: a sensuous need, an objective of the Life Instincts (*Eros*).

In a society based on alienated labor, human sensibility is *blunted:* men perceive things only in the forms and functions in which they are given, made, used by the existing society; and they perceive only the possibilities of transformation as defined by, and confined to, the existing society.[17] Thus, the existing society is *reproduced* not only in the mind, the consciousness of men, but *also in their senses;* and no persuasion, no theory, no reasoning can break this prison, unless the fixed, petrified *sensibility* of the individuals is *"dissolved," opened to a new dimension of history,* until the oppressive familiarity with the given object world is broken—broken in a *second alienation:* that from the alienated society.

Today, in the revolt against the "consumer society," sensibility strives to become "practical," the vehicle for radical reconstruction, for new ways of life. It has become a force in the *political* struggle for liberation.[18] And that means: the individual emancipation of the senses is supposed to be the beginning, even the foundation, of *universal* liberation, the free society is to take roots in

17. For the following see my *An Essay on Liberation* (Boston: Beacon Press, 1969), pp. 36ff.

18. The fight for the Peoples Park in Berkeley, which was met with brute force by the armed guardians of law and order, shows the explosion of sensibility in political action.

new instinctual needs. How is this possible? How can "humanity," human solidarity as *"concrete universal"* (and not as abstract value), as real force, as "praxis," originate in the individual sensibility; how can objective freedom originate in the most subjective faculties of man?

We are faced with the *dialectic* of the universal and the particular: how can the human sensibility, which is *principium individuationis,* also generate a *universalizing* principle?

I refer again to the philosophical treatment of this problem in German idealism: here is the intellectual origin of the Marxian concept. For *Kant:* a universal sensorium (the pure forms of intuition) constitutes the one unified framework of sense experience, thus validating the universal categories of the understanding. For *Hegel:* reflection on the content and mode of *my* immediate sense certainty reveals the "We" in the "I" of intuition and perception. When the still unreflected consciousness has reached the point where it becomes conscious of itself and its relation to its objects, where it has experienced a "trans-sensible" world "behind" the sensuous appearance of things, it discovers that *we* ourselves are behind the curtain of appearance. And this "we" unfolds as social reality in the struggle between Master and Servant for "mutual recognition."

This is the turning point on the road that leads from Kant's effort to reconcile man and nature, freedom and necessity, universal and particular, to Marx's materialistic solution: Hegel's *Phenomenology* breaks with Kant's transcendental conception: history and society enter into the theory of knowledge (and into the very structure of knowledge) and do away with the "purity" of the a priori; the materialization of the idea of freedom begins. But a closer look shows that the same tendency was already present in Kant's philosophy: in the development from the First to the Third Critique.

1) In the *First Critique,* the freedom of the subject is present only in the epistemological syntheses of the sense data; freedom is relegated to the transcendental Ego's pure syntheses: it is the power of the a priori by virtue of which the transcendental subject constitutes the objective world of experience; theoretical knowledge.

2) In the *Second Critique,* the realm of *praxis* is reached with the stipulation of the autonomy of the moral person: his power to *originate* causation without breaking the universal causation which governs nature: necessity. The price: subjection of the sensibility to the categorical imperative of reason. The relation between human freedom and natural necessity remains obscure.

3) In the *Third Critique,* man and nature are joined in the aesthetic dimension, the rigid "otherness" of nature is reduced, and Beauty appears as "symbol of morality." The union of the realm of

freedom and that of necessity is here conceived not as the mastery of nature, not as bending nature to the purposes of man, but as attributing to nature an ideal purposiveness "of its own: a purposiveness without purpose."

But it is only the *Marxian* conception which, while preserving the critical, transcendent element of idealism, uncovers the material, historical ground for the reconciliation of human freedom and natural necessity; subjective and objective freedom. This union presupposes liberation: the revolutionary *praxis* which is to abolish the institutions of capitalism and to replace them by socialist institutions and relationships. But in this transition, the emancipation of the senses must accompany the emancipation of consciousness, thus involving the *totality* of human existence. The individuals themselves must change in their very instincts and sensibilities if they are to build, in association, a *qualitatively* different society. But why the emphasis on *aesthetic* needs in this reconstruction?

IV

It is not just in passing and out of exuberance that Marx speaks of the formation of the object world "in accordance with the laws of beauty" as a feature of free human practice. Aesthetic qualities are essentially nonviolent, nondomineering. . . .—qualities which, in the domain of the arts, and in the repressive use of the term "aesthetic" as pertaining to the sublimated "higher culture" only, are divorced from the social reality and from "practice" as such. The revolution would undo this repression and recapture aesthetic needs as a subversive force, capable of counteracting the dominating aggressiveness which has shaped the social and natural universe. The faculty of being "receptive," "passive," is a precondition of freedom: it is the ability to see things in their own right, to experience the joy enclosed in them, the erotic energy of nature—an energy which is there to be liberated; nature, too, awaits the revolution! This receptivity is itself the soil of creation: it is opposed, not to productivity, but to *destructive* productivity.

The latter has been the ever more conspicuous feature of male domination: inasmuch as the "male principle" has been the ruling mental and physical force, a free society would be the "definite negation" of this principle–it would be a *female* society. In this sense, it has nothing to do with matriarchy of any sort; the image of the woman as mother is itself repressive; it transforms a biological fact into an ethical and cultural value and thus it supports and justifies her social repression. At stake is rather the ascent of Eros over aggression, in men *and* women; and this means, in a male-dominated civilization, the "femalization" of the male. It would express the decisive change in the instinctual structure: the weakening of primary aggressiveness which, by a combination of biological and social factors, has governed the patriarchal culture.

In this transformation, the Women's Liberation Movement becomes a radical force to the degree to which it transcends the entire sphere of aggressive needs and performances, the entire social organization and division of functions. In other words, the movement becomes radical to the degree to which it aims, not only at equality *within* the job and value structure of the *established* society (which would be the equality of dehumanization) but rather at a change in the structure itself (the basic demands of equal opportunity, equal pay, and release from full-time household and child care are a prerequisite). Within the established structure, neither men nor women are free—and the dehumanization of men may well be greater than that of women since the former suffer not only the conveyor belt and assembly line but also the standards and "ethics" of the "business community."

And yet, the liberation of women would be more sweeping than that of men because the repression of women has been constantly fortified by the social use of their biological constitution. The bearing of children, being a mother, is supposed to be not only their natural function but also the fulfillment of their "nature"—and so is being a wife, since the reproduction of the species occurs within the framework of the monogamous patriarchal family. Outside this framework, the woman is still predominantly a plaything or a temporary outlet for sexual energy not consummated in marriage.

Marxian theory considers sexual exploitation as the primary, original exploitation, and the Women's Liberation Movement fights the degradation of the woman to a "sexual object." But it is difficult to overcome the feeling that here, repressive qualities characteristic of the bourgeois-capitalist organization of society enter into the fight against this organization. Historically, the image of the woman as sexual object, and her exchange value on the market, devalue the earlier repressive images of the woman as mother and wife. These earlier images were essential to the bourgeois ideology during a period of capitalist development now left behind: the period where some "inner-worldly asceticism" was still operative in the dynamic of the economy. In comparison, the present image of the woman as sexual object is a *desublimation* of bourgeois morality—characteristic of a "higher stage" of capitalist development. Here, too, the commodity form is universalized: it now invades formerly sanctified and protected realms. The (female) body, as seen and plastically idealized by *Playboy*, becomes desirable merchandise with a high exchange value. Disintegration of bourgeois morality, perhaps—but *cui bono?* To be sure, this new body image promotes sales, and the plastic beauty may not be the real thing, but they stimulate aesthetic-sensuous needs which, in their development, must become incompatible with the body as instrument of alienated labor. The male body, too, is made the object of sexual image creation—also plasticized and deodorized . . . clean exchange value. After the secularization of religion, after the transformation of ethics into Orwellian hypocrisy—is the "socialization" of the body as sexual object perhaps one of the last decisive steps toward the completion of the exchange society: the completion which is the beginning of the end?

Still, the publicity with the body (at present, the female body) as object is dehumanizing, the more so since it plays up to the dominant male as the aggressive subject for whom the female is there, to be taken, to be laid. It is in the nature of sexual relationships that both, male and female, are object *and* subject at the same time; erotic and aggressive energy are fused in both. The surplus-aggression of the male is socially conditioned—as is the surplus-passivity of the female. But beneath the social factors which determine male aggressiveness and female receptivity, a *natural* contrast exists: it is the woman who "embodies," in a literal sense, the promise of peace, of joy, of the end of violence. Tenderness, receptivity, sensuousness have become features (or mutilated features) of her body—features of her (repressed) humanity. These female qualities may well be socially determined by the development of capitalism. The process is truly dialectical.[19] Although the reduction of the concrete individual faculties to abstract labor power established an abstract equality between men and women (equality before the machine), this abstraction was less complete in the case of women. They were employed in the material process of production to a lesser extent than men. Women were fully employed in the household, the family, which was supposed to be the sphere of realization for the bourgeois individual. However, this sphere was isolated from the productive process and thus contributed to the women's mutilation. And yet, this isolation (separation) from the alienated work world of capitalism enabled the woman to remain less brutalized by the Performance Principle, to remain closer to her sensibility: more human than men. That this image (and reality) of the woman has been determined by an aggressive, male-dominated society does not mean that this determination must be rejected, that the liberation of women must overcome the female "nature." The equalization of male and female would be regressive: it would be a new form of female acceptance of a male principle. Here too the historical process is dialectical: the patriarchal society has created a female image, a female counter-force, which may still be-

19. This dialectic is the center of Angela Davis's paper *Marxism and Women's Liberation*. Written in jail, this paper is the work of a great woman, militant, intellectual.

come one of the gravediggers of patriarchal society. In this sense too, the woman holds the promise of liberation. It is the woman who, in Delacroix' painting, holding the flag of the revolution, leads the people on the barricades. She wears no uniform; her breasts are bare, and her beautiful face shows no trace of violence. But she has a rifle in her hand—for the end of violence is still to be fought for. . . .

* * *

SUGGESTIONS FOR FURTHER READING

Socialism

Bebel, August. *Women and Socialism*, trans. by H. B. Adams Walther. New York: AMS Press, 1976.

Carver, Terrell. "Engels' Feminism." *History of Political Thought* 6 (Winter 1985), pp. 479–90.

Dixler, Elsa. "Women and Socialist Movements: A Review Essay." *Feminist Studies* 10 (Summer 1984), pp. 315–22.

Gilman, Charlotte Perkins. *The Living of Charlotte Perkins Gilman*. New York: D. Appleton-Century Company, 1935.

______. *Herland*. New York: Pantheon Books, 1979.

Guettel, Charnie. *Marxism and Feminism*. Toronto: Women's Press, 1974.

Held, Virginia. "Marx, Sex, and the Transformation of Society." In *Women and Philosophy*, ed. by Carol C. Gould and Marx W. Wartofsky. New York: G. P. Putnam and Sons, 1976, pp. 168–84.

Holmstrom, Nancy. "A Marxist Theory of Women's Nature." *Ethics* 94 (April 1984), pp. 456–73.

Honeycutt, Karen. "Clara Zetkin: A Socialist Approach to the Problem of Women's Oppression." *Feminist Studies* 3 (Spring–Summer 1976), pp. 131–44.

Jenness, Linda (ed.). *Feminism and Socialism*. New York: Pathfinder Press, 1972.

Jones, Kathleen B. "Socialist-Feminist Theories of the Family." *Praxis International* 8 (Oct. 1988), pp. 284–300.

Kessler-Harris, Alice. "The Just Price, the Free Market, and the Value of Women." *Feminist Studies* 14 (Summer 1988), pp. 235–50.

Kollontai, Alexandra. *Sexual Relations and the Class Struggle*, trans. by Alix Holt. Bristol: The Falling Wall Press, 1972.

Marcuse, Herbert. "Marxism and Feminism." *Women's Studies* 2 (1974), pp. 279–88.

Marx, Karl et al. *The Woman Question. Selections from the Writings of Marx, Lenin and Stalin.* New York: International Publishers, 1951.

Middleton, Peter. "Socialism, Feminism and Men." *Radical Philosophy* 53 (Autumn 1989), pp. 8–19.

Mitchell, Juliet. "Marxism and Women's Liberation." *Social Praxis* 1 (1973), pp. 11–22.

Nicholson, Linda. "Feminism and Marx: Integrating Kinship with the Economic." *Praxis International* 5 (Jan. 1986), pp. 367–80.

Perrin, Ronald. "Marcuse and the Meaning of Radical Philosophy." In *Continuity and Change in Marxism,* ed. by Norman Fischer, N. Georgopoulas, and Louis Patsouras. Atlantic Highlands, N.J.: Humanities Press, 1982, pp. 114–30.

Reed, Evelyn. *Problems of Women's Liberation.* New York: Pathfinder Press, 1969.

———. *Is Biology Woman's Destiny?* New York: Pathfinder Press, 1972.

Rowbotham, Sheila. *Women, Resistance and Revolution.* London: Allen Lane Imprint, The Penguin Press, 1972.

Scott, Hilda. *Does Socialism Liberate Women?* Boston: Beacon Press, 1974.

Stern, Bernhard J. "Engels on the Family." In *A Centenary of Marxism,* ed. by Samuel Bernstein. New York: Science and Society, 1948, pp. 42–64.

Trotsky, Leon. *Women and the Family.* New York: Pathfinder Press, 1970.

Upin, Jane S. "Charlotte Perkins Gilman: Instrumentalism Beyond Dewey." *Hypatia* 8 (Spring 1993), pp. 38–63.

Vogel, Lise. *Marxism and the Oppression of Women: Toward a Unitary Theory.* Leichhardt: Pluto Press, 1984.

PRAGMATISM

The term "pragmatism" was coined by the American philosopher and physicist Charles Sanders Peirce in 1878 to describe a method of clarifying ideas or abstract concepts by looking to their consequences. John Dewey later defined pragmatism as an extension of historical empiricism. To the pragmatist, experience is not only the source but also the end of knowledge, which thus involves an essential orientation toward future experience. The acquisition of knowledge is a social or collaborative process, yielding beliefs as plans of action.

Philosophers who have been identified as "classical American pragmatists" wrote very little about women or about issues specifically relevant to women. In contrast, the authors chosen for this section not only embraced and developed a pragmatic perspective in their writings, but wrote substantially about women and about social issues associated with gender differences.

JESSIE TAFT

The dissertation of Jessie Taft (1882–1961) on "The Woman Movement from the Point of View of Social Consciousness" was written for the University of Chicago's Department of Philosophy and directed by George Herbert Mead. In a prefatory note Taft acknowledges her indebtedness to Mead and to James H. Tufts, another Chicago pragmatist, for their advice and counsel. Not until twenty-one years later, however, did Taft succeed in finding a regular academic position, and that was in the School for Social Work at the University of Pennsylvania, where her philosophical background provided her with a theoretical framework for addressing everyday problems. In the intervening years, Taft worked as an assistant superintendent of the New York State Reformatory for Women and as a part-time psychology instructor in extension courses.

Like other pragmatists, Taft viewed relationships as real rather than theoretical constructs. And like the pragmatists, she also rejected the view that selves exist in isolation from one another. "Selfhood," she wrote, "is made, not born." Affirming "a social environment as an absolute prerequisite for consciousness of self," Taft declared that "the self thus developed continues to take on more highly conscious forms according to the increasing extent and complexity of the social relations which it actively maintains." The socialization process, she observed, has led to a double standard in relations between men and women. Men, for example, may advance in the public domain without having tasks to perform in the private domain as well; women, in contrast, are preempted from achieving economic independence because of their duties to home, husbands, and children. In sexual matters, a "standard of absolute physical chastity" prevails for women, whereas "almost unlimited license is taken for granted" for men. Overcoming this double standard requires reconstruction of society through reconstruction of selves.

The Woman Movement from the Point of View of Social Consciousness

We are now in a position to take a final survey of the woman movement in its relation to the larger stream of social evolution. The course of the preceding argument has been very briefly as follows: first, the woman movement is the expression of very genuine problems both for the individual woman and for society as a whole; second, those problems are the result of an unavoidable conflict of impulses and habits, values and standards, due to the effort of trying to combine, without deliberate and conscious adjustment on the part of society itself, two dissimilar worlds; third, such conflicts are, as a matter of fact, equally real for men and for women as the labor movement testifies, and give evidence of a real dualism of self and social environment, of a genuine inequality between the kind of consciousness actually developed and the type of consciousness required to deal with the complexities of modern social relations; and finally, the restoration of equality between self and environment depends on the possibility of developing a higher type of self-consciousness whose perfect comprehension of its relations to other selves would make possible a controlled adjustment of those relations from the point of view of all concerned. We endeavored to show that such a conception rests upon a social and dynamic theory of personality and pointed out an actual development in personality throughout history up to the present moment when the wished-for type is not only desired but is being actualized. In this concluding section, the attempt will be to leave an impression of the woman movement stripped bare of the detail of argument as it appears in perspective to one who looks at it from the point of view indicated in the preceding discussion.

The woman movement, viewed not as an isolated phenomenon but as an integral part of the vaster social evolution, is seen to be only the woman's side of what from the man's angle is called the labor movement. It is a reaction against the same conditions and a demand for changes in the social order such that life will once more become harmonious. The accident of modern civilization has brought about inevitable conflict in the fundamental human impulses for both men and women. It has apparently allowed for complete, almost over expression of one set of impulses; at the expense of a partial or sometimes complete repression of the other. This has meant, of course, that the set of impulses which was allowed to develop unchecked by the other set was as abnormal and as far from a well-balanced rounded fulfilment as were the unexpressed impulses. The industrial and economic system of today, which has come into being more or less unconsciously and accidentally, has so divorced the economic and the social that it is only with a tremendous struggle for more inclusive forms of consciousness that we shall be able to recognize that the split is only apparent and that a system which not only believes in, but insists on, such a separation results in irreconcilable dualism in the lives of the men and women involved, persisting to the point of gigantic social problems, agitations, and movements. Thus the labor movement symbolizes the impossibility of choosing between the fulfilment of the economic impulse and the fulfilment of the impulse to live. Men are granted unlimited opportunities to work, but no provision is made by the system for intelligent parenthood, for good citizenship, for a thoughtful development and use of the sex impulse. A man's parental expression is limited to caring for the economic welfare of his family. His own growth as a person must be sacrificed to the necessity of supporting himself and family. Work must be combined with life, but our system makes little provision for such a combination, hence, forcing into opposition fundamental impulses clamoring for expression. The labor movement demands a new society in which creative, sexual, parental, and other social impulses will have an unquestioned right to fulfilment.

With women, on the other hand, social impulses are the only ones which are overtly recognized. Women are constantly forced into the economic world, but the system ignores that fact and provides in no way for combining the peculiar social function of women with any economic function which they may find desirable or necessary. Such economic expression as has been conceded to them is confined to the home. Likewise, the other impulses, even the maternal, have no recognized place outside the limits of the individual home. For the woman, the system has no avenues of fulfilment foreseen and provided beforehand for any impulse whatsoever outside the home itself. Everything which has opened up has been at best, even after long and patient effort, only makeshift and haphazard. Society is always emphasizing the obligation of the woman to carry out the sex and maternal impulses at all costs and minimizing the need or value of the economic so far as she is concerned. In the conditions of living which are forced upon her, she is compelled to make the sorry choice of a limited sex and maternal expression or a doubtful and hazardous attempt on the economic side. In either case, she loses so far as society's aid or provision is concerned. Only by the extraordinary force of a powerful personality will she make a signal success at either venture. Society no more makes a thoughtful attempt to give the maternal interests the most complete development and employment possible than it makes any pretense at all of using intelligently the natural impulse of the woman to be of economic value in the world. Much less does it offer a rational scheme for combining both motives within a possible form of living for the average normal woman. Thus the woman, even more than the man, faces a perfectly hopeless alternative. Neither side at the present moment is overwhelmingly attractive in itself even apart from the sacrifice of other impulses which its choice involves. What woman would willingly abandon love and children? What normal woman would accept a life in which she gave up all effort at serious work of genuine economic value to society? What woman would attempt without shrinking the almost impossible task of combining the two as affairs stand today? Above all, what woman would undertake wifehood and motherhood with the limitations placed on it by our present social system and feel that those two fundamental parts of herself could ever reach a satisfactory and adequate fulfilment?

That the peculiarly unhappy position of the woman is a reality and not an illusion can be detected in the arguments used to convince woman of her obligation to bear and rear. The element of sacrifice is so obvious that it is even seized upon and treated as a virtue, an added glory for the crown of the wife and mother. Moreover, this notion of necessary sacrifice on the part of the woman and the bare fact of motherhood itself have grown into a sort of fetish. The experiences of motherhood are exalted to the point where they are assumed to be a sufficient compensation for any and all sacrifices. To silence our own doubts and justify our procedure, we have come to believe in the inherent and absolute value to the woman of the mere fact of giving birth to a child, even though the emotions and purposes thus originated are never carried past the instinctive or intuitive level to a rationalized and socialized expression. We are afraid to face the fact that the home in its present unrelated, individual form does demand of women, and men too for that matter, a sacrifice so great as to have lost a large part of its value for spiritual growth, an overwhelming and crushing sacrifice of the possibilities of motherhood and fatherhood that defeats its own end.

All of this hopeless conflict among impulses which the woman feels she has legitimate right, even a moral obligation, to express, all of the rebellion against stupid, meaningless sacrifice of powers that ought to be used by society, constitutes the force, conscious or unconscious, which motivates the woman movement and will continue to vitalize it until some adjustment is made.

The labor movement and the woman movement do not understand always how close is their relationship, nor do they see clearly that the reason why the obviously stupid and unsuitable social conditions which they combat are so difficult to alter is because human beings have not yet arrived at the stage where they know how to attack and solve social problems. The real goal of both movements is a society whose consciousness shall have reached the social stage and hence is capable of dealing scientifically with social as well as physical problems, a society which no longer leaves the social forms and relationships whereby human impulses are expressed to chance or physical force, but subjects them to rational control.

In the physical world we have at last become conscious of our method and hence have acquired a control over physical conditions which promises to become more and more complete. If the desire arises in a community to do something for which present physical conditions make no allowance, it becomes instantly a problem for the experts and it is only a question of time when a way will be found for the gratification of the felt need. The very basis of the physical problem is the thwarted desire of human beings to do something and the method of obtaining the end is, of course, a full and free admission of the inherent right and value of the desire, a deliberate searching for every element involved in the physical conditions of the problem, and a careful experimental attempt to find the combination which will satisfy all the conditions. We should not consider our problem solved if the scientist said to us, "You do not really want this thing, you only imagine it, and in any case it would be bad for you to have it. You have managed to live all these years without it, why complain now?" Imagine such an answer to the determination to fly in the air. But, supposing, if we persisted in our wish to fly and began to talk about it and clamor for a way to be opened, the authorities were to turn on us, demand silence on pain of arrest and imprisonment, label us socialists or anarchists, and tell us we were rebelling against the fixed and righteous order of things as they are. Should we consider that any attempt had been made at solving our problem of how to make a machine that would fly in the air? Yet, impossible as it may seem, that is thus far the favorite method of dealing with any unsatisfied, insufficiently expressed set of human wants, whose fulfilment would mean change of the social order. First, deny the existence of the want; second, call it wicked, foolish, or injurious to individual and society; third, suppress it by force—and you have dealt with it adequately.[1]

The chief task of all social movements, then, must be at first to impress upon the rest of society the right of unsatisfied and unexpressed human impulses to constitute a real problem worthy of the same amount of expert attention whether they demand a new way of crossing the Atlantic Ocean or a new combination of work and social expression in the lives of men and women. This they will never bring about until there is a sufficient number of people who are so socially sensitive and adaptable that they feel within themselves as their own the impulses and points of view of all classes and both sexes. Such individuals will be the social scientists who will offer solutions to our social problems because they are able to place themselves at the very heart of these problems and thus to comprehend the conditions, the unsatisfied, conflicting impulses, upon the harmonization and fulfilment of which any solution that has the right to the name must be based. The fundamental purpose of the woman movement, therefore, as of any great social movement, is bound to be the producing of social scientists who will be capable of offering hypotheses that are based on the actual data constituting the problems, and the bringing about of an increasing social consciousness among all people such that they too will become sufficiently aware of the real content of social relationships to be willing to undergo the adjustments of the social order necessary to make actual the theories which promise salvation.

JANE ADDAMS

Although Jane Addams (1860–1935) was forced to drop out of medical school because of her own medical problems, she was highly respected for her intellectual strengths by the academic pragmatists William James, John Dewey, and George Herbert Mead. Addams was eventually awarded an honorary degree from the University of Chicago, but was more closely affiliated with Hull House, a residence and education center for the poor in Chicago, which she started and sustained. The logical and practical extension of these efforts was her commitment to pacifism, based on the view that peace is a necessary condition for solving the problem of world hunger. In 1915 Addams helped to found the Women's International League for Peace and Freedom, serving as its international president for the next twenty years.

1. For a complete presentation of this failure of our civilization to handle its social problems see Walter Lippmann's *Preface to Politics*.

Addams viewed women as more natural nurturers than men, but considered all human beings as naturally inclined to be peacemakers rather than warriors. It is "abnormal, both from the biological and ethical point of view," she wrote, "that large masses of men should fight against other large masses." What is natural to men and women alike is that they form "friendly relationships with ever larger and larger groups, and to live constantly a more extended life."

Democracy and Social Ethics

It is always difficult for the family to regard the daughter otherwise than as a family possession. From her babyhood she has been the charm and grace of the household, and it is hard to think of her as an integral part of the social order, hard to believe that she has duties outside of the family, to the state and to society in the larger sense. This assumption that the daughter is solely an inspiration and refinement to the family itself and its own immediate circle, that her delicacy and polish are but outward symbols of her father's protection and prosperity, worked very smoothly for the most part so long as her education was in line with it. When there was absolutely no recognition of the entity of woman's life beyond the family, when the outside claims upon her were still wholly unrecognized, the situation was simple, and the finishing school harmoniously and elegantly answered all requirements. She was fitted to grace the fireside and to add lustre to that social circle which her parents selected for her. But this family assumption has been notably broken into, and educational ideas no longer fit it. Modern education recognizes woman quite apart from family or society claims, and gives her the training which for many years has been deemed successful for highly developing a man's individuality and freeing his powers for independent action. Perplexities often occur when the daughter returns from college and finds that this recognition has been but partially accomplished. When she attempts to act upon the assumption of its accomplishment, she finds herself jarring upon ideals which are so entwined with filial piety, so rooted in the tenderest affections of which the human heart is capable, that both daughter and parents are shocked and startled when they discover what is happening, and they scarcely venture to analyze the situation. The ideal for the education of woman has changed under the pressure of a new claim. The family has responded to the extent of granting the education, but they are jealous of the new claim and assert the family claim as over against it.

The modern woman finds herself educated to recognize a stress of social obligation which her family did not in the least anticipate when they sent her to college. She finds herself, in addition, under an impulse to act her part as a citizen of the world. She accepts her family inheritance with loyalty and affection, but she has entered into a wider inheritance as well, which, for lack of a better phrase, we call the social claim. This claim has been recognized for four years in her training, but after her return from college the family claim is again exclusively and strenuously asserted. The situation has all the discomfort of transition and compromise. The daughter finds a constant and totally unnecessary conflict between the social and the family claims. In most cases the former is repressed and gives way to the family claim, because the latter is concrete and definitely asserted, while the social demand is vague and unformulated. In such instances the girl quietly submits, but she feels wronged whenever she allows her mind to dwell upon the situation. She either hides her hurt, and splendid reserves of enthusiasm and capacity go to waste, or her zeal and emotions are turned inward, and the result is an unhappy woman, whose heart is consumed by vain regrets and desires.

If the college woman is not thus quietly reabsorbed, she is even reproached for her discontent. She is told to be devoted to her family, inspiring and responsive to her social circle, and to give the rest of her time to further self-improvement and enjoyment. She expects to do this, and responds to these claims to the best of her ability, even heroically sometimes. But where is the larger life of which she has dreamed so long? That life which surrounds and completes the individual and family life? She has been taught that it is her duty to share this life, and her highest privilege to extend it. This divergence between her self-centered existence and her best convictions becomes constantly more apparent. But the situation is not even so simple as a conflict between her affections and her intellectual convictions, although even that is tumultuous enough, also the emotional nature is divided against itself. The social claim is a demand upon the emotions as well as upon the intellect, and in ignoring it she represses not only her convictions but lowers her springs of vitality. Her life is full of contradictions. She looks out into the world, longing that some demand be made upon her powers, for they are too untrained to furnish an initiative. When her health gives way under this strain, as it often does, her physician invariably advises a rest. But to be put to bed and fed on milk is not what she requires. What she needs is simple, health-giving activity, which, involving the use of all her faculties, shall be a response to all the claims which she so keenly feels.

It is quite true that the family often resents her first attempts to be part of a life quite outside their own, because the college woman frequently makes these first attempts most awkwardly; her faculties have not been trained in the line of action. She lacks the ability to apply her knowledge and theories to life itself and to its complicated situations. This is largely the fault of her training and of the one-sidedness of educational methods. The colleges have long been full of the best ethical teaching, insisting that the good of the whole must ultimately be the measure of effort, and that the individual can only secure his own rights as he labors to secure those of others. But while the teaching has included an ever-broadening range of obligation and has insisted upon the recognition of the claims of human brotherhood, the training has been singularly individualistic; it has fostered ambitions for personal distinction, and has trained the faculties almost exclusively in the direction of intellectual accumulation. Doubtless, woman's education is at fault, in that it has failed to recognize certain needs, and has failed to cultivate and guide the larger desires of which all generous young hearts are full.

During the most formative years of life, it gives the young girl no contact with the feebleness of childhood, the pathos of suffering, or the needs of old age. It gathers together crude youth in contact only with each other and with mature men and women who are there for the purpose of their mental direction. The tenderest promptings are bidden to bide their time. This could only be justifiable if a definite outlet were provided when they leave college. Doubtless the need does not differ widely in men and women, but women not absorbed in professional or business life, in the years immediately following college, are baldly brought face to face with the deficiencies of their training. Apparently every obstacle is removed, and the college woman is at last free to begin the active life, for which, during so many years, she has been preparing. But during this so-called preparation, her faculties have been trained solely for accumulation, and she has learned to utterly distrust the finer impulses of her nature, which would naturally have connected her with human interests outside of her family and her own immediate social circle. All through school and college the young soul dreamed of self-sacrifice, of succor to the helpless and of tenderness to the unfortunate. We persistently distrust these desires, and, unless they follow well-defined lines, we repress them with every device of convention and caution.

Peace and Bread in Time of War

. . . The newspapers daily reported the changing fortunes of war on both fronts and our souls turned sick with anxiety and foreboding because all that the modern world held dear hung upon the hazards of battle. But certainly the labor for bread, which to me was more basic and legitimate than war, was still going on everywhere. In my desire to uncover it, to make clear woman's traditional activity with something of its poetry and significance, I read endlessly in Fraser's "Golden Bough," two large volumes of which are given over to the history and interpretation of the innumerable myths dealing with the Spirits of the Corn. These spirits are always feminine and are usually represented by a Corn Mother and her daughter, vaguely corresponding to the Greek Demeter—the always fostering Earth, and her child Persephone.

At the risk of breaking into the narrative of this book, so far as there is one, I am venturing to repeat some of the material which brought a touch of comfort to me and which, so far as I was able at that moment, I handed on to other women. Fraser discovers that relics of the Corn Mother and the Corn Maiden are found in nearly all the harvest fields of Europe; among many tribes of North American Indians; the Eastern world has its Rice Mother, for whom there are solemn ceremonies when the seed rice, believed to contain "soul stuff," is gathered. These deities are always feminine, as is perhaps natural from the association with fecundity and growth, and about them has gathered much of the poetry and song in the sowing of the grain and the gathering of the harvest, and those saddest plaints of all, expressing the sorrows of famine.

Myths centering about the Corn Mother but dimly foreshadowed what careful scientific researches have later verified and developed. Students of primitive society believe that women were the first agriculturists and were for a long time the only inventors and developers of its processes. The men of the tribe did little for cultivating the soil beyond clearing the space and sometimes surrounding it by a rough protection. The woman as consistently supplied all cereals and roots eaten by the tribe as the man brought in the game and fish, and in early picture writing the short hoe became as universally emblematic of woman as the spear of the hunter, or the shield and battle axe of the warrior. In some tribes it became a fixed belief that seeds would not grow if planted by a man, and apparently all primitive peoples were convinced that seeds would grow much better if planted by women. In Central Africa to this day a woman may obtain a divorce from her husband and return to her father's tribe, if the former fails to provide her with a garden and a hoe.

It is said that every widespread myth has its counterpart in the world of morals. This is certainly true of the "fostering Mother." Students in the origin of social customs contend that the gradual change from the wasteful manner of nomadic life to a settled and much more economic mode of existence may be fairly attributed to these primitive agricultural women. Mothers in order to keep their children alive had transplanted roots from the forest or wild grains from the plains, into patches of rudely cultivated ground. We can easily imagine when the hunting was poor or when the flocks needed a new pasture, that the men of the tribe would be for moving on, but that the women might insist that they could not possibly go until their tiny crops were garnered; and that if the tribe were induced to remain in the same caves or huts until after harvest the women might even timidly hope that they could use the same fields next year, and thus avert the loss of their children, sure to result from the alternation of gorging when the hunt was good and of starving when it was poor. The desire to grow food for her children led to a fixed abode and to the beginning of a home, from which our domestic morality and customs are supposed to have originated.

With such a historic background, it seemed to me that women might, in response to the food saving and food production appeals issued in one country after another, so enlarge their conception of duty that the consciousness of the world's needs for food should become the actual impulse of their daily activities.

It also presented another interesting aspect; from the time we were little children we have all of us, at moments at least, cherished overwhelming desires to be of use in the great world, to play a conscious part in its progress. The difficulty has always been in attaching our vague purposes to the routine of our daily living, in making a synthesis between our ambitions to cure the ills of the world on the one hand, and the need to conform to household requirements on the other.

It was a very significant part of the situation, therefore, that at this world's crisis the two had become absolutely essential to each other. A great world purpose could not be achieved without woman's participation founded upon an intelligent understanding and upon the widest sympathy, at the same time the demand could be met only if it were attached to her domestic routine, its very success depending upon a conscious change and modification of her daily habits.

It was no slight undertaking to make this synthesis, it afforded probably the most compelling challenge which has been made upon woman's constructive powers for centuries. It required all her human affection and all her clarity of mind to make the kind of adjustment which the huge scale of the situation demanded.

It is quite understandable that there was no place for woman and her possible contribution in international affairs under the old diplomacy. Such things were indeed not "woman's sphere." But it was possible that as women entered into politics when clean milk and the premature labor of children became factors in political life, so they might be concerned with international affairs when these at last were dealing with such human and poignant matters as food for starving peoples who could be fed only through international activities.

I recall a great audience in Hot Springs, Arkansas, made up of the members of the General Federation of Women's Clubs. It seemed to me that every woman there might influence her community "back home," not only to produce and to save more food, but to pour into the war torn world such compassion as would melt down its animosities and bring back into it a gregarious instinct older and more human than the motives responsible for war. I believed that a generous response to this world situation might afford an opportunity to lay over again the foundations for a wider, international morality, as woman's concern for feeding her children had made the beginnings of an orderly domestic life. We are told that when the crops of grain and roots so painstakingly produced by primitive women began to have a commercial value their production and exchange were taken over by the men, as men later turned the manufacturing of pottery and other of woman's early industries into profit making activities. Such a history, suggested that this situation might be woman's opportunity if only because foods were, during the war, no longer considered primarily in regard to their money-making value but from the point of view of their human use. Because the production of food was, for the moment, dependent upon earlier motives, it had fallen back into woman's hands. There had developed a wide concern for the feeding of hungry people, an activity with which women were normally connected.

As I had felt the young immigrant conscripts caught up into a great world movement, which sent them out to fight, so it seemed to me the millions of American women might be caught up into a great world purpose, that of conservation of life; there might be found an antidote to war in woman's affection and all-embracing pity for helpless children.

Certainly compassion is not without its social utility. Up to the present moment the nations, in their foreign policies, have conspicuously lacked that humane quality which has come in their domestic policies through the increasing care for the poor, and the protection of children. These have been responsible for all sorts of ameliorative legislation during the later years, in one nation after another. In their relations to each other, however, nations have been without such motives of humanitarian action until the Allied nations, during the war, evolved a strikingly new foreign policy in their efforts to relieve the starvation and distress throughout widespread areas.

There are such unexpected turnings in the paths of moral evolution that it would not be without precedent that a new and powerful force might be unloosed in the world when the motive for producing and shipping food on the part of great nations was no longer a commercial one but had for the moment shifted to a desire to feed hungry people with whose governments they had entered into obligations. Such a force might in the future have to be reckoned with as a factor in international affairs.

SUGGESTIONS FOR FURTHER READING

Pragmatism

Aboulafia, Mitchell. "Was George Herbert Mead a Feminist?" *Hypatia* 8 (Spring 1993), pp. 145–58.

Addams, Jane. *The Long Road of Woman's Memory.* New York: Macmillan, 1916.

Curti, Merle. "Jane Addams on Human Nature." *Journal of the History of Ideas* 22 (1961), pp. 240–53.

Deegan, Mary Jo. "The Clinical Sociology of Jessie Taft." *Clinical Sociology Review* 4 (1986), pp. 30–45.

Diner, Steven J. "George Herbert Mead's Ideas on Women and Careers." *Signs* 4 (1978), pp. 407–9.

Duran, Jane. "The Intersection of Feminism and Pragmatism." *Hypatia* 8 (Spring 1993), pp. 159–71.

Giarelli, James M. "Dewey and the Feminist Successor Pragmatism Project." *Free Inquiry* 13 (Winter 1992/1993), pp. 30–31.

Heldke, Lisa. "John Dewey and Evelyn Fox Keller: A Shared Epistemological Tradition." *Hypatia* 2 (1987), pp. 129–40.

Laird, Susan. "Women and Gender in John Dewey's Philosophy of Education." *Educational Theory* 38, 1 (1988), pp. 110–24.

Lasch, Christopher (ed.). *The Social Thought of Jane Addams.* Indianapolis: Bobbs-Merrill, 1965.

Leffers, M. Regina. "Pragmatists Jane Addams and John Dewey Inform the Ethic of Care." *Hypatia* 8 (Spring 1993), pp. 64–77.

Mahowald, Mary B. "A Majority Perspective: Feminine and Feminist Elements in American Philosophy." *Cross Currents* 36 (1987), pp. 410–17.

Miller, Marjorie C. "Feminism and Pragmatism." *The Monist* 75 (Oct. 1992), pp. 445–57.

Moen, Marcia K. "Peirce's Pragmatism as Resource for Feminism." *Charles S. Peirce Society, Transactions* (Fall 1991), pp. 435–50.

Pappas, Gregory Fernando. "Dewey and Feminism: The Affective and Relationships in Dewey's Ethics." *Hypatia* 8 (Spring 1993), pp. 78–95.

Radin, Margaret Jane. "The Pragmatist and the Feminist." *Southern California Law Review* 63 (1990), pp. 1699–726.

———. "The Pragmatist and the Feminist." In *Pragmatism in Law and Society*, ed. by Michael Brint. Boulder, Co.: Westview Press, 1991.

Randall, M. M. *John Dewey and Jane Addams.* Jane Addams House, Philadelphia: Women's International League for Peace and Freedom, 1959.

Robinson, Virginia P. (ed.). *Jessie Taft, Therapist and Social Worker Educator.* Philadelphia: University of Philadelphia Press, 1962.

Rorty, Richard. "Feminism and Pragmatism." In *The Tanner Lectures on Human Values*, vol. 13, ed. by Grethe B. Peterson. Salt Lake City: University of Utah Press, 1992.

______. "Feminism, Ideology, and Deconstruction: A Pragmatist View." *Hypatia* 8 (Spring 1993), pp. 96–103.

Rudnick, Lois. "A Feminist American Success Myth: Jane Addams's Twenty Years at Hull-House." In *Traditions and the Talents of Women*, ed. by Florence Howe. Urbana: University of Illinois Press, 1991.

Seigfried, Charlene Haddock. "Shared Communities of Interest: Feminism and Pragmatism." *Hypatia* 8 (Spring 1993), pp. 1–14.

______. "The Missing Perspective: Feminist Pragmatism." *Charles S. Peirce Society, Transactions* (Fall 1991), pp. 405–16.

______. "Where Are All the Pragmatist Feminists?" *Hypatia* 6 (Summer 1991), pp. 1–20.

Skillen, Tony. "Reply to Richard Rorty's 'Feminism and Pragmatism': Richard Rorty—Knight Errant." *Radical Philosophy* 62 (Autumn 1992), pp. 24–26.

Thayer, H. S. *Meaning and Action: A Critical History of Pragmatism.* Indianapolis: Hackett Publishing Company, Inc., 1981.

West, Cornel. *The American Evasion of Philosophy: A Geneaology of Pragmatism.* Madison: University of Wisconsin Press, 1989.

Wilson, Catherine. "Reply to Richard Rorty's 'Feminism and Pragmatism': How Did the Dinosaurs Die Out? How Did the Poets Survive?" *Radical Philosophy* 62 (Autumn 1992), pp. 20–23.

PHILOSOPHICAL ANALYSIS

In contrast to existentialism, which has been strongly influenced by Descartes and the German idealists, modern analytic philosophy derives largely from the empirical tradition of Hume. Its method, which has given rise to diverse interpretations and applications, describes the predominant philosophical approach in the United States and other English-speaking countries.

The method of analysis starts with data obtained through experience, and commonly accepted as knowledge. In order to explicate this complex bulk of data, the analytic philosopher formulates propositions (expressed judgments). Within any set of related propositions, a recognition of logical interdependence and redundancies enables the philosopher to reduce the propositions to their simplest formulation. The propositions are then arranged according to the inferential relationship that one bears to the other, so that their appropriate deductive sequence is manifest. ("Deductive" describes a process of reasoning from a general proposition to a less general proposition.) Formal syllogisms illustrate the deductive sequence. Each deductive chain of inference depends logically upon some initial premise or premises, which may or may not be provable. "The discovery of these premisses," writes Bertrand Russell, "belongs to philosophy." In other words, the philosophical method of logical analysis entails reasoning from complex and relatively concrete propositions to those that are simpler and more abstract.

BERTRAND RUSSELL

Like his godfather, John Stuart Mill, Bertrand Russell (1872–1970) was a financially independent aristocrat whose early focus on mathematics influenced a life-long devotion to logic. In his *Principia Mathematica* of 1910, Russell attempted (with his co-author Alfred North Whitehead) to show that pure mathematics is reducible to logic, because its primary principles are logical premises, and its concepts definable in logical terms or symbols. As Russell extended his study of logic to the philosophical arena, he insisted on recognition of philosophy's limits, especially by distinguishing between judgments that are empirically or logically demonstrable, and those that are ultimately reliant upon opinion or taste. The latter group includes metaphysical judgments, much of ethics, and social and political theory. Although Russell did not refrain from making statements in these areas, he considered them quite outside the scope of philosophy.

Another point of similarity with Mill is Russell's persistent dedication to the cause of individual rights and freedom. Not only did Russell write extensively on particular social issues; he also actively campaigned in support of his convictions. For example, in 1907 he ran for Parliament on behalf of women's suffrage; in 1918 he was imprisoned for six months because of his public opposition to the war. The latter issue also illustrates Russell's willingness to alter his views where further thought or evidence suggested he should do so. Despite his earlier pacifism, he concurred with efforts to resist Hitler's dominating influence in Europe. Once hostilities had ceased, his predominant interest was the promotion of world government and nuclear disarmament.

Russell categorized his own views on human nature and society as beliefs rather than knowledge. Belief, for Russell, describes the status of judgments that are not obtained through certainly reliable methods. What Russell purports to believe is that

> Man is a part of Nature. . . . His body, like other matter, is composed of electrons and protons, which, so far as we know, obey the same laws as those forming part of animals or plants. . . . Electrons and protons, like the soul, are logical fictions; each is really a history, a series of events, not a single persistent entity.[1]

"What we call our 'thoughts,'" Russell observes,

> seem to depend upon the organization of tracks in the brain in the same sort of way in which journeys depend upon roads and railways. . . . All the evidence goes to show that what we regard as our mental life is bound up with brain structure and organized bodily energy.

Although human beings are part of Nature, they are nonetheless capable of transcending Nature through the determination of values. In this respect, persons are greater than Nature. "Nature in itself," Russell claims, "is neutral, neither good nor bad." Only human beings can create or confer value so as to make their lives "good." For Russell himself, "[t]he good life is one inspired by love and guided by knowledge." It is a life conditioned by freedom and productive of happiness for individuals as well as for society. The function of the state is to facilitate "the good life" for all persons. An essential criterion in fulfilling this function is justice; that is, "the recognition of the equal claims of all human beings."

1. This quote, and the three that follow, come from "What I Believe," in *The Basic Writings of Bertrand Russell*, ed. by Robert E. Egner and Lester E. Dennon (New York: Simon and Schuster, A Clarion Books, 1967), pp. 367–90.

Marriage and Morals

The emancipation of women is part of the democratic movement; it begins with the French Revolution, which, as we have already seen, altered the laws of inheritance in a sense favourable to daughters. Mary Wollstonecraft's "Vindication of the Rights of Women" (1792) is a product of the ideas that caused and were caused by the French Revolution. From her time down to the present day the claim of women to equality with men has been asserted with continually increasing emphasis and success. John Stuart Mill's "Subjection of Women" is a very persuasive and well-reasoned book, which had a great influence upon the more thoughtful members of the generation immediately following his own. My father and mother were disciples of his, and my mother used to make speeches in favour of votes for women in the sixties.

. . . [T]he rapidity with which women in most civilized countries have acquired their political rights is without parallel in the past, considering the immense magnitude of the change in outlook that has been involved. The abolition of slavery is more or less analogous, but after all slavery did not exist in European countries in modern times, and did not concern anything so intimate as the relations of men and women.

The causes of this sudden change are, I think, twofold: on the one hand there was the direct influence of democratic theory, which made it impossible to find any logical answer to the demands of women; on the other hand there was the fact that a continually increasing number of women were engaged in making their own living outside the home, and did not depend for the comfort of their daily lives upon the favour of fathers and husbands. This situation, of course, reached its height during the war, when a very large part of the work usually performed by men had to be undertaken by women. Before the war one of the objections commonly urged against votes for women was that women would tend to be pacifists. During the war they gave a large-scale refutation of this charge, and the vote was given to them for their share in the bloody work. To the idealistic pioneers, who had imagined that women were going to raise the moral tone of politics, this issue may have been disappointing, but it seems to be the fate of idealists to obtain what they have struggled for in a form which destroys their ideals. The rights of women did not, of course, in fact depend upon any belief that women were morally or in any other way superior to men; they depended solely upon their rights as human beings, or rather upon the general argument in favour of democracy. But as always happens when an oppressed class or nation is claiming its rights, advocates sought to strengthen the general argument by the contention that women had peculiar merits, and these merits were generally represented as belonging to the moral order.

The political emancipation of women, however, concerns our theme only indirectly; it is their social emancipation that is important in connection with marriage and morals. In early days, and in the East down to our own time, the virtue of women was secured by segregating them. No attempt was made to give them inward self-control, but everything was done to take away all opportunity for sin. In the West this method was never adopted wholeheartedly, but respectable women were educated from their earliest years so as to have a horror of sexual intercourse outside marriage. As the methods of this education became more and more perfected, the outward barriers were more and more removed. Those who did most to remove the outward barriers were convinced that the inward barriers would be sufficient. It was thought, for example, that the chaperon was unnecessary, since a nice girl who had been well brought up would never yield to the advances of young men whatever opportunities of yielding might be allowed her. It was generally held by respectable women when I was young that sexual intercourse was displeasing to the great majority of women, and was only endured within marriage from a sense of duty; holding this view, they were not unwilling to risk a greater degree of freedom for their daughters than had seemed wise in more realistic ages. The results have perhaps been somewhat different from what was anticipated, and the difference has existed equally as regards wives and as regards unmarried women. The women of the Victorian age were, and a great many women still are, in a mental prison. This prison was not obvious to consciousness, since it consisted of subconscious inhibitions. The decay of inhibitions, which has taken place among the young of our own time, has led to the reappearance in consciousness of instinctive desires which has been buried beneath mountains of prudery. This is having a very revolutionary effect upon sexual morality, not only in one country or in one class, but in all civilized countries and in all classes.

The demand for equality between men and women concerned itself from the first not only with political matters but also with sexual morality. The attitude of Mary Wollstonecraft was thoroughly modern, but she was not imitated in this respect by the subsequent pioneers of women's rights. They, on the contrary, were for the most part very rigid moralists, whose hope was to impose upon men the moral fetters which hitherto had only been endured by women. Ever since 1914, however, young women, without much theorizing, have taken a different line. The emotional excitement of the war was no doubt the precipitating cause of this new departure, but it would have come before very long in any case. The motives of female virtue in the past were chiefly the fear of hell-fire and fear of pregnancy; the one was removed by the decay of theological orthodoxy, the other by contraceptives. For some time traditional morality managed to hold out through the force of custom and mental inertia, but the shock of the war caused these barriers to fall. Modern feminists are no longer so anxious as the feminists of thirty years ago to curtail the "vices" of men; they ask rather that what is permitted to men shall be permitted also to them. Their predecessors sought equality in moral slavery, whereas they seek equality in moral freedom.

This whole movement is as yet in a very early phase, and it is impossible to say how it will develop. Its adherents and practitioners as yet are mostly quite young. They have very few champions among persons of weight and importance. The police, the law, the Church and their parents are against them whenever the facts come to the knowledge of these repositories of power, but in general the young have the kindness to conceal the facts from those to whom they would cause pain. Writers who . . . proclaim the facts are thought by the old to be libelling the young, though the young remain unconscious of being libelled.

A situation of this sort is, of course, very unstable. It is a question which of two things will happen first: either the old will become aware of the facts and will set to work to deprive the young of their new-won freedom, or the young, growing up, will themselves acquire positions of dignity and importance, which will make it possible to give the sanction of authority to the new morality. . . .

Let us, however, pause a moment to consider the logical implications of the demand that women should be the equals of men. Men have from time immemorial been allowed in practice, if not in theory, to indulge in illicit sexual relations. It has not been expected of a man that he should be a virgin on entering marriage, and even after marriage, infidelities are not viewed very gravely if they never come to the knowledge of a man's wife and neighbours. The possibility of this system has depended upon prostitution. This institution, however, is one which it is difficult for a modern to defend, and few will suggest that women should acquire the same rights as men through the establishment of a class of male prostitutes for the satisfaction of women who wish, like their husbands, to seem virtuous without being so. Yet it is quite certain that in these days of late marriage only a small percentage of men will remain continent until they can afford to set up house with a woman of their own class. And if unmarried men are not going to be continent, unmarried women, on the ground of equal rights will claim that they also need not be continent. To the moralists this situation is no doubt regrettable. Every conventional moralist who takes the trouble to think it out will see that he is committed in practice to what is called the double standard, that is to say, the view that sexual virtue is more essential in a woman than in a man. It is all very well to argue that his theoretical ethic demands continence of men also. To this there is the obvious retort that the demand cannot be enforced on the men since it is easy for them to sin secretly. The conventional moralist is thus committed against his will not only to an inequality as between men and women, but also to the view that it is better for a young man to have intercourse with prostitutes than with girls of his own class, in spite of the fact that with the latter, though not with the former, his relations are not mercenary and may be affectionate and altogether delightful. Moralists, of course, do not think out the consequences of advocating a morality which they know will not be obeyed; they think that so long as they do not advocate prostitution they are not responsible for the fact that prostitution is the inevitable outcome of their teaching. This, however, is only another illustration of the well-known fact that the professional moralist in our day is a man of less than average intelligence.

In view of the above circumstances, it is evident that so long as many men for economic reasons find early marriage impossible, while many women cannot marry at all, equality as between men and women demands a relaxation in the traditional standards of feminine virtue. If men are allowed prenuptial intercourse (as in fact they are), women must be allowed it also. And in all countries where there is an excess of women it is an obvious injustice that those women who by arithmetical necessity must remain unmarried should be wholly debarred from sexual experience. Doubtless the pioneers of the women's movement had no such consequences in view, but their modern followers perceive them clearly, and whoever opposes these deductions must face the fact that he or she is not in favour of justice to the female sex.

A very clear-cut issue is raised by this question of the new morality versus the old. If the chastity of girls and the faithfulness of wives is no longer to be demanded, it becomes necessary either to have new methods of safeguarding the family or else to acquiesce in the breakup of the family. It may be suggested that the procreation of children should only occur within marriage, and that all extra-marital sexual intercourse should be rendered sterile by the use of contraceptives. In that case husbands might learn to be as tolerant of lovers as Orientals are of eunuchs. The difficulty of such a scheme as yet is that it requires us to place more reliance on the efficacy of contraceptives and the truthfulness of wives than seems rational; this difficulty may, however, be diminished before long.

The other alternative compatible with the new morality is the decay of fatherhood as an important social institution, and the taking over of the duties of the father by the State. In particular cases where a man felt sure of his paternity and fond of the child, he might, of course, voluntarily undertake to do what fathers now normally do in the way of financial support for the mother and child; but he would not be obliged to do so by law. Indeed all children would be in the position in which illegitimate children of unknown paternity are now, except that the State, regarding this as the normal case, would take more trouble with their nurture than it does at present.

If, on the other hand, the old morality is to be reestablished, certain things are essential; some of them are already done, but experience shows that these alone are not effective. The first essential is that the education of girls should be such as to make them stupid and superstitious and ignorant; this requisite is already fulfilled in schools over which the churches have any control. The next requisite is a very severe censorship upon all books giving information on sex subjects; this condition also is coming to be fulfilled in England and in America, since the censorship, without change in the law, is being tightened up by the increasing zeal of the police. These conditions, however, since they exist already, are clearly insufficient. The only thing that will suffice is to remove from younger women all opportunity of being alone with men: girls must be forbidden to earn their living by work outside the home; they must never be allowed an outing unless accompanied by their mother or an aunt; the regrettable practice of going to dances without a chaperon must be sternly stamped out. It must be illegal for an unmarried woman under fifty to possess a motor-car, and perhaps it would be wise to subject all unmarried women once a month to medical examination by police doctors, and to send to a penitentiary all such as were found to be not virgins. The use of contraceptives must, of course, be eradicated, and it must be illegal in conversation with unmarried women to throw doubt upon the dogma of eternal damnation. These measures, if carried out vigorously for a hundred years or more, may perhaps do something to stem the rising tide of immorality. I think, however, that in order to avoid the risk of certain abuses, it would be necessary that all policemen and all medical men should be castrated. Perhaps it would be wise to carry this policy a step further, in view of the inherent depravity of the male character. I am inclined to think that moralists would be well advised to advocate that all men should be castrated, with the exception of ministers of religion.

It will be seen that there are difficulties and objections whichever course we adopt. If we are to allow the new morality to take its course, it is bound to go further than it has done, and to raise difficulties hardly as yet appreciated. If, on the other hand, we attempt in the modern world to enforce restrictions which were possible in a former age, we are led into an impossible stringency of regulation, against which human nature would soon rebel. This is so clear that, whatever the dangers or difficulties, we must be content to let the world go forward rather than back. For this purpose we shall need a genuinely new morality. I mean by this that obligations and duties will still have to be recognized, though they may be very different from the obligations and duties recognized in the past.

. . . .

In a rational ethic, marriage would not count as such in the absence of children. A sterile marriage should be easily dissoluble, for it is through children alone that sexual relations become of importance to society, and worthy to be taken cognizance of by a legal institution. This, of course, is not the view of the Church, which, under the influence of St. Paul, still views marriage rather as the alternative to fornication than as the means to the procreation of children.

. . . .

It is . . . possible for a civilized man and woman to be happy in marriage, although if this is to be the case a number of conditions must be fulfilled. There must be a feeling of complete equality on both sides; there must be no interference with mutual freedom; there must be the most complete physical and mental intimacy; and there must be a certain similarity in regard to standards of values. (It is fatal, for example, if one values only money while the other values only good work.) Given all these conditions, I believe marriage to be the best and most important relation that can exist between two human beings. If it has not often been realized hitherto, that is chiefly because husband and wife have regarded themselves as each other's policeman. If marriage is to achieve its possibilities, husbands and wives must learn to understand that whatever the law may say, in their private lives they must be free.

. . . .

The importance of the family, as it exists at present, in the psychology of mothers is very difficult to estimate. I think that during pregnancy and lactation a woman has, as a rule, a certain instinctive tendency to desire a man's protection—a feeling, no doubt, inherited from the anthropoid apes. Probably a woman who, in our present rather harsh world, has to dispense with this protection tends to become somewhat unduly combative and self-assertive. These feelings, however, are only in part instinctive. They would be greatly weakened, and in some cases wholly abolished, if the State gave adequate care to expectant and nursing mothers and to young children. I think perhaps the chief harm that would be done to women by abolition of the father's place in the home would be the diminution in the intimacy and seriousness of their relations with the male sex. Human beings are so constructed that each sex has much to learn from the other, but mere sex relations, even when they are passionate, do not suffice for these lessons. Cooperation in the serious business of rearing children, and companionship through the long years involved, bring about a relation more important and more enriching to both parties than any that would exist if men had no responsibility for their children. And I do not think that mothers who live in a purely feminine atmosphere, or whose contacts with men are trivial, will, except in a minority of cases, be quite so good for their children from the point of view of emotional education as those who are happily married and cooperating at each stage with their husbands. One must, however, in a great many cases set other considerations over against these. If a woman is actively unhappy in her marriage—and this, after all, is by no means an uncommon occurrence—her unhappiness makes it very difficult for her to have the right kind of emotional poise in dealing with her children. In such cases she could undoubtedly be a better mother if she were quit of the father. We are thus led to the entirely trivial conclusion that happy marriages are good, while unhappy ones are bad.

. . . There is a theory that the desire for children is commoner among women than among men, but my own impression, for what it is worth, is exactly the contrary. In a very large number of modern marriages, the children are a concession on the part of the woman to the man's desires. A woman, after all, has to face labour and pain and possible loss of beauty in order to bring a child into the world, whereas a man has no such grounds for anxiety. A man's reasons for wishing to limit his family are generally economic; these reasons operate equally with the woman, but she has her own special reasons as well. The strength of the desire men feel for children is evident when one considers the loss of material comfort that professional men deliberately incur when they undertake to educate a family in the expensive manner that their class considers necessary.

. . . My belief, is, . . . though I put it forward with some hesitation, that the elimination of paternity as a recognized social relation would tend to make men's emotional life trivial and thin, causing in the end a slowly growing boredom and despair. . . .

. . . .

[T]he development of feminism among married women is likely, in the not distant future, even within the framework of capitalist society, to lead to the elimination of one if not both parents from the care of the young in the wage-earning class.

The revolt of women against the domination of men is a movement which, in its purely political sense, is practically completed, but in its wider aspects is still in its infancy. Gradually its remoter effects will work themselves out. The emotions which women are supposed to feel are still, as yet, a reflection of the interests and sentiments of men. You will read in the works of male novelists that women find physical pleasure in suckling their young; you can learn by asking any mother of your acquaintance that this is not the case, but until women had votes no man ever thought of doing so. Maternal emotions altogether have been so long slobbered over by men who saw in them subconsciously the means to their own domination that a considerable effort is required to arrive at what women sincerely feel in this respect. Until very recently, all decent women were supposed to desire children, but to hate sex. Even now, many men are shocked by women who frankly state that they do not desire children. Indeed, it is not uncommon for men to take it upon themselves to deliver homilies to such women. So long as women were in subjection, they did not dare to be honest about their own emotions, but professed those which were pleasing to the male. We cannot, therefore, argue from what has been hitherto supposed to be women's normal attitude towards children, for we may find that as women become fully emancipated their emotions turn out to be, in general, quite different from what has hitherto been thought. I think that civilization, at any rate as it has hitherto existed, tends greatly to diminish women's material feelings. It is probable that a high civilization will not in future be possible to maintain unless women are paid such sums for the production of children as to make them feel it is worth while as a money-making career. If that were done, it would, of course, be unnecessary that all women, or even a majority, should adopt this profession. It would be one profession among others, and would have to be undertaken with professional thoroughness. These, however, are speculations. The only point in them that seems fairly certain is that feminism in its later developments is likely to have a profound influence in breaking up the patriarchal family, which represents man's triumph over woman in prehistoric times.

* * *

JOYCE TREBILCOT

Joyce Trebilcot (1933–), one of the founders and long-time coordinator of the Women's Studies Program at Washington University, taught women's studies and philosophy there from 1970 to 1994. Although trained in analytic philosophy, she has for a number of years been struggling to put some distance between herself and that methodology, particularly its positivistic aspects. Since the late seventies she has regarded her work as radical lesbian feminist.

The essay included here was written before the author began to move away from analytic philosophy. Her concept of what it means to be human stresses that individuals differ with regard to their expression of characteristics attributed to sex roles. What is natural to a particular person may thus be at odds with what is natural to most persons of that sex. In this context, Trebilcot maintains that no matter how human beings "naturally" are, that issue should be subordinated to the moral question of whether they are treated justly in society.

Sex Roles: the Argument from Nature

I am concerned here with the normative question of whether, in an ideal society, certain roles should be assigned to females and others to males. In discussions of this issue, a great deal of attention is given to the claim that there are natural psychological differences between the sexes. Those who hold that at least some roles should be sex roles generally base their view primarily on an appeal to such natural differences, while many of those advocating a society without sex roles argue either that the sexes do not differ in innate psychological traits or that there is no evidence that they do.[1] In this paper I argue that whether there are natural psychological differences between females and males has little bearing on the issue of whether society should reserve certain roles for females and others for males.

Let me begin by saying something about the claim that there are natural psychological differences between the sexes. The issue we are dealing with arises, of course, because there are biological differences among human beings which are bases for designating some as females and others as males. Now it is held by some that,

1. For support of sex roles, see, for example, Aristotle, *Politics,* book 1; and Erik Erikson, "Womanhood and the Inner Space," *Identity: Youth and Crisis* (New York: W. W. Norton & Co., 1968). Arguments against sex roles may be found, for example, in J. S. Mill, "The Subjection of Women," in *Essays on Sex Equality: John Stuart Mill and Harriet Taylor Mill,* ed. Alice S. Rossi (Chicago: University of Chicago Press, 1970), and Naomi Weisstein, "Psychology Constructs the Female," in *Women in Sexist Society,* ed. Vivian Gornick and Barbara K. Moran (New York: Basic Books, 1971).

in addition to biological differences between the sexes, there are also natural differences in temperament, interests, abilities, and the like. In this paper I am concerned only with arguments which appeal to these psychological differences as bases of sex roles. Thus I exclude, for example, arguments that the role of jockey should be female because women are smaller than men or that boxers should be male because men are more muscular than women. Nor do I discuss arguments which appeal directly to the reproductive functions peculiar to each sex. If the physiological process of gestation or of depositing sperm in a vagina are, apart from any psychological correlates they may have, bases for sex roles, these roles are outside the scope of the present discussion.

It should be noted, however, that virtually all those who hold that there are natural psychological differences between the sexes assume that these differences are determined primarily by differences in biology. According to one hypothesis, natural psychological differences between the sexes are due at least in part to differences between female and male nervous systems. As the male fetus develops in the womb, the testes secrete a hormone which is held to influence the growth of the central nervous system. The female fetus does not produce this hormone, nor is there an analogous female hormone which is significant at this stage. Hence it is suggested that female and male brains differ in structure, that this difference is due to the prenatal influence of testicular hormone, and that the difference in brains is the basis of some later differences in behavior.[2]

A second view about the origin of allegedy natural psychological differences between the sexes, a view not incompatible with the first, is psychoanalytical. It conceives of feminine or masculine behavior as, in part, the individual's response to bodily structure. On this view, one's more or less unconscious experience of one's own body (and in some versions, of the bodies of others) is a major factor in producing sex-specific personality traits. The classic theories of this kind are, of course, Freud's; penis envy and the castration complex are supposed to arise largely from perceptions of differences between female and male bodies. Other writers make much of the analogies between genitals and genders: the uterus is passive and receptive, and so are females; penises are active and penetrating, and so are males.[3] But here we are con-

2. See John Money and Anke A. Ehrhardt, *Man and Woman, Boy and Girl* (Baltimore: Johns Hopkins Press, 1973).

3. For Freud, see, for example, "Some Psychological Consequences of the Anatomical Distinctions between the Sexes," in *Sigmund Freud: Collected Papers,* ed. James Strachey (New York: Basic Books, 1959), 5:186–97. See also Karl Stern, *The Flight from Woman* (New York: Farrar, Straus & Giroux, 1965), chap. 2; and Erikson.

cerned not with the etiology of allegedly natural differences between the sexes but rather with the question of whether such differences, if they exist, are grounds for holding that there should be sex roles.

That a certain psychological disposition is natural only to one sex is generally taken to mean in part that members of that sex are more likely to have the disposition, or to have it to a greater degree, than persons of the other sex. The situation is thought to be similar to that of height. In a given population, females are on the average shorter than males, but some females are taller than some males, as suggested by figure 1. The shortest members of the population are all females, and the tallest are all males, but there is an area of overlap. For psychological traits, it is usually assumed that there is some degree of overlap and that the degree of overlap is different for different characteristics. Because of the difficulty of identifying natural psychological characteristics, we have of course little or no data as to the actual distribution of such traits.

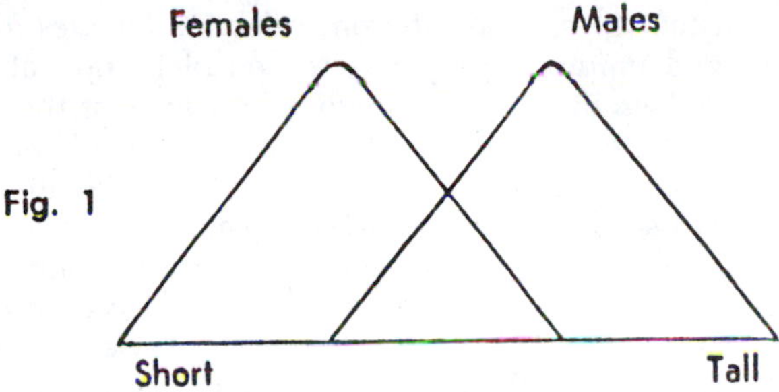

Fig. 1

I shall not undertake here to define the concept of role, but examples include voter, librarian, wife, president. A broad concept of role might also comprise, for example, being a joker, a person who walks gracefully, a compassionate person. The genders, femininity and masculinity, may also be conceived as roles. On this view, each of the gender roles includes a number of more specific sex roles, some of which may be essential to it. For example, the concept of femininity may be construed in such a way that it is necessary to raise a child in order to be fully feminine, while other feminine roles—teacher, nurse, charity worker—are not essential to gender. In the arguments discussed below, the focus is on sex roles rather than genders, but, on the assumption that the genders are roles, much of what is said applies, *mutatis mutandis*, to them.

A sex role is a role performed only or primarily by persons of a particular sex. Now if this is all we mean by "sex role," the problem of whether there should be sex roles must be dealt with as two separate issues: "Are sex roles a good thing?" and "Should society enforce sex roles?" One might argue, for example, that sex roles have value but that, even so, the demands of individual autonomy and freedom are such that societal institutions and practices should not enforce correlations between roles and sex. But the debate over sex roles is of course mainly a discussion about the second question, whether society should enforce these correlations. The judgment that there should be sex roles is generally taken to mean not just that sex-exclusive roles are a good thing, but that society should promote such exclusivity.

In view of this, I use the term "sex role" in such a way that to ask whether there should be sex roles is to ask whether society should direct women into certain roles and away from others, and similarly for men. A role is a sex role then (or perhaps an "institutionalized sex role") only if it is performed exclusively or primarily by persons of a particular sex *and* societal factors tend to encourage this correlation. These factors may be of various kinds. Parents guide children into what are taken to be sex-appropriate roles. Schools direct students into occupations according to sex. Marriage customs prescribe different roles for females and males. Employers and unions may refuse to consider applications from persons of the "wrong" sex. The media carry tales of the happiness of those who conform and the suffering of the others. The law sometimes penalizes deviators. Individuals may ridicule and condemn role crossing and smile on conformity. Societal sanctions such as these are essential to the notion of sex role employed here.

I turn now to a discussion of the three major ways the claim that there are natural psychological differences between the sexes is held to be relevant to the issue of whether there should be sex roles.

1. *Inevitability*.—It is sometimes held that if there are innate psychological differences between females and males, sex roles are inevitable. The point of this argument is not, of course, to urge that there should be sex roles, but rather to show that the normative question is out of place, that there will be sex roles, whatever we decide. The argument assumes first that the alleged natural differences between the sexes are inevitable; but if such differences are inevitable, differences in behavior are inevitable; and if differences in behavior are inevitable, society will inevitably be structured so as to enforce role differences according to sex. Thus, sex roles are inevitable.

For the purpose of this discussion, let us accept the claim that natural psychological differences are inevitable. We assume that there are such differences and ignore the possibility of their being altered, for example, by evolutionary change or direct biological intervention. Let us also accept the second claim, that behavioral differences are inevitable. Behavioral differences could perhaps be eliminated even given the assumption of natural differences in disposition (for example, those with no natural inclination to a certain kind of behavior might nevertheless learn it; but let us waive this point). We assume then that behavioral differences, and hence also role differences, between the sexes are inevitable. Does it follow that there must be sex roles, that is, that the institutions and practices of society must enforce correlations between roles and sex?

Surely not. Indeed, such sanctions would be pointless. Why bother to direct women into some roles and men into others if the pattern occurs regardless of the nature of society? Mill makes the point elegantly in *The Subjection of Women:* "The anxiety of mankind to interfere in behalf of nature, for fear lest nature should not succeed in effecting its purpose, is an altogether unnecessary solicitude."[4]

It may be objected that if correlations between sex and roles are inevitable, societal sanctions enforcing these correlations will develop because people will expect the sexes to perform different roles and these expectations will lead to behavior which encourages their fulfillment. This can happen, of course, but it is surely not inevitable. One need not act so as to bring about what one expects. Indeed, there could be a society in which it is held that there are inevitable correlations between roles and sex but institutionalization of these correlations is deliberately avoided. What is inevitable is presumably not, for example, that every woman will perform a certain role and no man will perform it, but rather that most women will perform the role and most men will not. For any individual, then, a particular role may not be inevitable. Now suppose it is a value in the society in question that people should be free to choose roles according to their individual needs and interests. But then there should not be sanctions enforcing correlations between roles and sex, for such sanctions tend to force some individuals into roles for which they have no natural inclination and which they might otherwise choose against.

I conclude then that, even granting the assumptions that natural psychological differences, and therefore role differences, between the sexes are inevitable, it does not follow that there must be sanctions enforcing correlations between roles and sex. Indeed, if individual freedom is valued, those who vary from the statistical norm should not be required to conform to it.

2. *Well-being.*—The argument from well-being begins with the claim that, because of natural psychological differences between the sexes, members of each sex are happier in certain roles than in

4. Mill, p. 154.

others, and the roles which tend to promote happiness are different for each sex. It is also held that if all roles are equally available to everyone regardless of sex, some individuals will choose against their own well-being. Hence, the argument concludes, for the sake of maximizing well-being there should be sex roles: society should encourage individuals to make "correct" role choices.

Suppose that women, on the average, are more compassionate than men. Suppose also that there are two sets of roles, "female" and "male," and that because of the natural compassion of women, women are happier in female than in male roles. Now if females and males overlap with respect to compassion, some men have as much natural compassion as some women, so they too will be happier in female than in male roles. Thus, the first premise of the argument from well-being should read: Suppose that, because of natural psychological differences between the sexes, *most* women are happier in female roles and *most* men in male roles. The argument continues: If all roles are equally available to everyone, some of the women who would be happier in female roles will choose against their own well-being, and similarly for men.

Now if the conclusion that there should be sex roles is to be based on these premises, another assumption must be added—that the loss of potential well-being resulting from societally produced adoption of unsuitable roles by individuals in the overlapping areas of the distribution is *less* than the loss that would result from "mistaken" free choices if there were no sex roles. With sex roles, some individuals who would be happier in roles assigned to the other sex perform roles assigned to their own sex, and so there is a loss of potential happiness. Without sex roles, some individuals, we assume, choose against their own well-being. But surely we are not now in a position to compare the two systems with respect to the number of mismatches produced. Hence, the additional premise required for the argument, that overall well-being is greater with sex roles than without them, is entirely unsupported.

Even if we grant, then, that because of innate psychological differences between the sexes members of each sex achieve greater well-being in some roles than in others, the argument from well-being does not support the conclusion that there should be sex roles. In our present state of knowledge, there is no reason to suppose that a sex role system which makes no discriminations within a sex would produce fewer mismatches between individuals and roles than a system in which all roles are open equally to both sexes.

3 *Efficiency.*—If there are natural differences between the sexes in the capacity to perform socially valuable tasks, then, it is sometimes argued, efficiency is served if these tasks are assigned to the sex with the greatest innate ability for them. Suppose, for example, that females are naturally better than males at learning

foreign languages. This means that, if everything else is equal and females and males are given the same training in a foreign language, females, on the average, will achieve a higher level of skill than males. Now suppose that society needs interpreters and translators and that in order to have such a job one must complete a special training program whose only purpose is to provide persons for these roles. Clearly, efficiency is served if only individuals with a good deal of natural ability are selected for training, for the time and effort required to bring them to a given level of proficiency is less than that required for the less talented. But suppose that the innate ability in question is normally distributed within each sex and that the sexes overlap (see fig. 2).

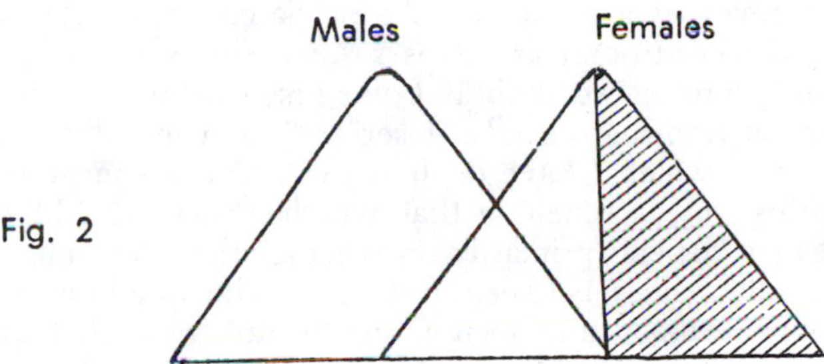

Fig. 2

If we assume that a sufficient number of candidates can be recruited by considering only persons in the shaded area, they are the only ones who should be eligible. There are no men in this group. Hence, although screening is necessary in order to exclude nontalented women, it would be inefficient even to consider men, for it is known that no man is as talented as the talented women. In the interest of efficiency, then, the occupational roles of interpreter and translator should be sex roles; men should be denied access to these roles but women who are interested in them, especially talented women, should be encouraged to pursue them.

This argument is sound. That is, if we grant the factual assumptions and suppose also that efficiency for the society we are concerned with has some value, the argument from efficiency provides one reason for holding that some roles should be sex roles. This conclusion of course is only prima facie. In order to determine whether there should be sex roles, one would have to weigh efficiency, together with other reasons for such roles, against reasons for holding that there should not be sex roles. The reasons against sex roles are very strong. They are couched in terms of individual rights—in terms of liberty, justice, equality of opportunity. Efficiency by itself does not outweigh these moral values. Nevertheless, the appeal to nature, if true, combined with an appeal to the value of efficiency, does provide one reason for the view that there should be sex roles.

The arguments I have discussed here are not the only ones which appeal to natural psychological differences between the sexes in defense of sex roles, but these three arguments—from inevitability, well-being, and efficiency—are, I believe, the most common and the most plausible ones. The argument from efficiency alone, among them, provides a reason—albeit a rather weak reason—for thinking that there should be sex roles. I suggest, therefore, that the issue of natural psychological differences between women and men does not deserve the central place it is given, both traditionally and currently, in the literature on this topic.

It is frequently pointed out that the argument from nature functions as a cover, as a myth to make patriarchy palatable to both women and men. Insofar as this is so, it is surely worthwhile exploring and exposing the myth. But of course most of those who use the argument from nature take it seriously and literally, and this is the spirit in which I have dealt with it. Considering the argument in this way, I conclude that whether there should be sex roles does not depend primarily on whether there are innate psychological differences between the sexes. The question is, after all, not what women and men naturally are, but what kind of society is morally justifiable. In order to answer this question, we must appeal to the notions of justice, equality, and liberty. It is these moral concepts, not the empirical issue of sex differences, which should have pride of place in the philosophical discussion of sex roles.

* * *

CHRISTINE PIERCE

Christine Pierce (1940–) has taught philosophy at North Carolina State University since 1983. One of the earliest contributors to feminist philosophy in the United States, she has used her analytic skills to show that the natural law tradition in ethics and theology functions to mystify and justify the restriction of women to predetermined social "places." Natural law arguments, she maintains, contribute "not only to bad law but to bad science."

Beyond the selection included here, Pierce's analysis and critique of the natural law tradition can be found in her writings on Plato and Sartre. With Margery Collins, she has challenged the sexism of Sartre's psychoanalysis, but she has defended Plato against widespread feminist criticisms. Pierce argues that Plato's views about sex equality in *Republic* V and about *eros* in the

Phaedrus and the *Symposium* are consistent "with the feminist and anti-heterosexist themes of his work." Recently, Pierce's philosophical interests have extended to environmental issues.

Natural Law Language and Women

"Nature" or "human nature" must be among the most enigmatic concepts ever used. Often, when the "natural" is invoked, we are left in the dark as to whether it is meant as an explanation, a recommendation, a claim for determinism, or simply a desperate appeal, as if the "natural" were some sort of metaphysical glue that could hold our claims or values together.

For centuries people have appealed to the "natural" to back up their moral and social recommendations. The ordinary uses of the term which everyone hears from time to time demonstrate that such efforts are still very much with us. We are told, for example, that suicide, birth control and homosexuality are wrong because they are unnatural. Now and then the use takes a positive form; motherhood is natural and hence the duty of women.

My major intent is to examine the language of "proper sphere," role, or function, showing its relationship to the language of natural law and pointing out problems in this kind of reasoning that are overlooked in the discussions of those who use this type of argument against women.

The following three examples characterize in a more extensive way the type of argument to be analyzed here. [1] in 1872, Myra Bradwell was refused admission to the Illinois bar by the state supreme court even though she had passed the bar entrance examination. Her suit, based upon the supposed right of every person, man or woman, to engage in any lawful employment for a livelihood, was denied. Justice Bradley, in his concurring opinion, opposed the idea that women might be attorneys on grounds that both God and nature disapprove.

> The civil law, as well as nature herself, has always recognized a wide difference in the respective spheres and destinies of man and woman. Man is, or should be, woman's protector and defender. The natural and proper timidity and delicacy which belongs to the female sex evidently unfits it for many of the occupations of civil life. The constitution of the family organization, which is founded in the divine ordinance, as well as in the nature of things, indicates the domestic sphere as that which properly belongs to the domain and functions of womanhood.[1]

1. *Bradwell v. The State,* 83 U.S. 130, 141 (1872).

[2] In a statement denouncing abortion, Pope Pius XI assumed that nature assigns duties to women. "However much we may pity the mother whose health and even life is gravely imperiled in the performance of *the duty allotted to her by nature,* nevertheless what could ever be a sufficient reason for excusing in any way the direct murder of the innocent?"[2] [3] A paragraph from Étienne Gilson's commentary on Aquinas illustrates the incredible implications of a well-known view that identifies natural sexuality with the reproductive function. On this concept of nature, rape is preferable to masturbation.

> . . . To violate nature is to set oneself against God who has ordained nature. Now the worst way of violating nature is to carry corruption into its very principle. Fornication, rape, adultery, incest, respect nature's order in the performing of the sexual act. Unnatural vice, however, refuses to respect this order. The worst form of luxury is bestiality, and after it, sodomy, irregularities in the sexual act and onanism. . . .[3]

Rape, a violent action, is not recommended, but it is not as bad as consensual sodomy or interrupting heterosexual intercourse, because heterosexual rape allows for the possibility of fulfilling the purpose of sexuality, namely, procreation. At the very least, it seems somewhat peculiar to prefer sexual acts which are by definition unloving, violent abuses of persons to acts which need not be, and may be quite the contrary. Here we see the natural defined as function or purpose and applied to the sexual organs. It is assumed that procreation is the only purpose of sexual activity, and that fulfilling its function is what makes an act morally good and deviating from that function is what makes an act morally bad.

As a preface to analyzing these kinds of arguments, it is important to stress how difficult it is for anyone in any social or moral context to say what they mean by "natural" and why it recommends itself as good. Two distinct steps are involved here: defining what is meant by "natural" and arguing that what is natural is good. . . .

It is often assumed that the word "natural" has an automatic "plus" value tag which does not have to be argued for on independent grounds. In other words, it is taken for granted that if one persuades us that " 'X' is natural," he has also persuaded us that " 'X' is good." The Vatican's position on birth control reflects this: *Humanae Vitae* assumes that it is sufficient to point out that artificial means of birth control interrupt the natural order of things.

2. *Encyclical Letter of Pope Pius XI on Christian Marriage,* St. Paul Editions (Boston, n.d.), p. 32. Emphasis added.

3. Étienne Gilson, *The Christian Philosophy of Saint Thomas Aquinas,* trans. L. K. Shook (New York: Random House, 1956), p. 298.

The most significant question of all, "Why is 'natural order' a good thing?" is never asked. Apparently, what the "natural order" means in this case is that which will happen if untouched by human invention. This definition, however, yields absurd consequences if we try to use it as a prescription. If "natural order" is a good thing, and we must assume it is because we are told not to interrupt it, why isn't shaving a moral issue? Clearly, it is natural for hair to grow on a man's face, and shaving introduces an artificial means to disrupt the natural order of things.

One thing is evident: we cannot discuss whether the natural is good until we are able to state what we mean by the term. "Natural" can mean "untouched by human invention," but this use is not a coherent basis for normative judgments. A second meaning of "natural" sometimes applied to human beings is that human nature is everything that human beings do. As an explanation, this use is simply vacuous; if meant as a justification, however, it would justify everything. If things are morally right because they are natural, and if everything human beings do is natural, then everything human beings do is morally justified. The third and fourth meanings that I want to consider are particularly interesting, not only because of their relevance to arguments for women's inequality, but because both definitions are currently in use and yet clearly incompatible. Human nature is construed to be either what human beings have in common with the rest of the animal world or what distinguishes human beings from the rest of the animal world.

One of the most amusing efforts to make the third use work against women is the following comment by Mary Hemingway: "Equality, what does it mean? What's the use for it? I've said it before and I'll repeat: Women are second-class citizens and not only biologically. A female's first duty is to bear children and rear them. With the exception of a few fresh water fish, most animals follow this basic rule."[4] Unfortunately, the most obvious consequence of Hemingway's argument is that a few fresh water fish are immoral! What she meant to say, however, was that human duties somehow can be determined by observing animal behavior. *Prima facie*, it seems odd to claim that the meaningfulness of moral terminology could be derived from a realm to which moral vocabulary does not apply. We must insist that people who talk this way be able to make sense of it. What does it mean, for example, to say that nature intends for us to do certain things? We know what it means to say that "I intend to pack my suitcase," but what sense can it make to say that nature intends for us to do one thing rather than another? The above use of "natural" reduces to saying "this is what most animals do." To the extent that this is the meaning of

4. Mary Hemingway, *Look*, September 6, 1966, p. 66.

the term, it will be hard to get a notion of value out of it. The fact that something happens a lot does not argue for or against it.

Interchanging words like "normal" and "natural" illustrates prejudice for the statistically prevalent as opposed to the unusual, the exception. The unusual *qua* unusual, however, cannot be ruled out as bad; it can be alternatively described as "deviant" or "original," depending on whether or not we like it. Nothing prevents describing the so-called sexual deviant as a sexual original except most people's inability to tolerate any unusual behavior in this area; hence, they use statistical concepts with bad connotations (unnatural, abnormal) to discuss it, instead of those with good connotations (original, exceptional).

The fourth meaning of "natural," that which distinguishes human beings from the rest of the (animal) world, reaches back to Plato. For Plato, to state the nature of any given class of things was to state the features of that class which distinguished it from all other classes of things. Although Plato did not claim that men and women have different natures, but rather referred to human beings as the class with the capacity to reason, his use of "natural" lends itself to the defining of classes of things according to function or role that is frequently used to restrict women. In order to understand how similar our way of talking and explaining things is to the Platonic view, it is first necessary to grasp how the latter has been historically conceived. An increased awareness of the natural law basis of the language of function should help us to be more critical of the language we take for granted, and to see what kinds of philosophical commitment we perhaps unwittingly make.

The Greek method of explanation for questions of the sort, "What is the nature of 'X'?" was teleological; explanations were given in terms of function, role, end or purpose, as opposed to mechanistic explanations. The difference between these explanations can easily be illustrated by comparing their answers to a simple question such as "What is a lawnmower?" A teleologist will explain: a lawnmower is something that is used to cut grass; a mechanist will explain about pulleys, plugs, and metal "teeth." Manufactured items lend themselves to the former type of explanation because hopefully we have in mind what the function of something is going to be before we start making any of it. Such explanation, however, is not so easily forthcoming for questions like, "What is the nature of human beings?" However, Plato was interested in this type of question; he wanted to explain the "natural" world. In this realm of nonmanufactured items, functions and roles are discovered, not created.

Although Plato thought he could answer the question concerning the nature of human beings, for the moment what concerns us is not the content of his answer, but the additional philosophical mileage we can expect from success in providing this type of answer. To be able to say what a thing is in terms of its function or purpose is simultaneously to set up standards for its evaluation. Once we can state the function of any "X," we can say what a good "X" is, or more precisely, we can say that "X" is good to the extent that it fulfills its function. We still have this use of "good" in English; we say, for example, that a good lawnmower is one that cuts grass well, that is, one that fulfills its function.

Plato's effort to apply this teleological framework to human beings consists of his functional analysis of the soul as reason, spirit, and desire. These are analogous to functioning units in the state, namely, philosopher-kings, soldiers, and artisans. Even as the function of a philosopher-king is to rule the state, implicit in the notion of reason as a function is the ability to rule, govern, or control the rest of the soul or personality. When anything does its work well, it is virtuous or excellent. In this case, when reason as well as every other functioning unit is working well and working together, the result is harmony or an order of soul to which Plato gives the name of the overarching virtue, justice. Reason, then, is the ordering principle; a good person is one who has an ordered soul, whose personality is controlled by reason.

Aristotle's agreement with both the teleological method and Plato's application of it to reason is evident when he says, "It is both natural and expedient for the body to be ruled by the mind, and for the emotional part of our natures to be ruled by that part which possesses reason, our intelligence."[5] But, for Aristotle, the soul's capacities vary for different classes of people. While the parts of the soul are present in women, slaves and children, "the slave has no deliberative faculty at all, the woman has, but it is without authority, and the child has, but it is immature."[6]

Plato may be the only philosopher to have held a doctrine of natural place which assigns social roles on the basis of individual merit rather than assigning places to whole classes of people as illustrated by the commonplace statement, "woman's place is in the home." According to Plato, the nature (distinctive function) of human beings is reason, and a whole spectrum of rational abilities are distributed among human beings. One's nature, then, can be determined only by discovering one's talents, and, as Plato put it, "many women are better than many men in many things."[7] Aris-

5. Aristotle, *The Politics,* 1254b5 (trans. T. A. Sinclair).

6. Aristotle, *The Politics,* 1260a13 (trans. Benjamin Jowett). Sinclair translates this passage: "the deliberative faculty in the soul is not present at all in a slave; in a female it is inoperative, in a child underdeveloped."

7. Plato, *Republic,* 455d (trans. Allan Bloom). A full discussion of Plato's argument appears in my essay, "Equality: *Republic V,*" *The Monist* 57:1, January, 1973.

totle believed the more familiar doctrine that whole classes of people—women, slaves—have their natural places: "as between male and female the former is by nature superior and the ruler, the latter inferior and subject."[8]

When the class of human beings is divided into men and women (or, perhaps better rendered, when women are not considered full human beings), the method of determining the essence of each often remains teleological, but for women the natural is no longer the rational but the biological. This type of move usually results in defining women as childbearers and reserving rationally oriented roles for men. The biological interpretation of women's nature distorts the Platonic enterprise insofar as reproduction is not a function peculiar to human beings.

Assigning to women the same function as would be appropriate to a female of any species has serious consequences, since in citing the function or role of something, we are setting certain standards which it must measure up to in order to be called good. If we are suspicious of teleology, the quarrel is not with the fact that a use of "good" is generated by defining things in terms of function; the quarrel concerns what sort of "good" we are talking about. Are the standards referred to in maintaining that a good "X" is one that functions well moral standards or simply standards of efficiency? They are at least the latter; the worry is they are perhaps only that. When we say a good lawnmower is one that cuts grass well, we clearly mean good in the sense of efficient or effective. If, to take another example, we define poison in terms of its function, good poison is that which does an effective, that is, quick and fatal, job. The good referred to is clearly not moral good. However, this does not imply that a teleological or instrumental use of "good" could not also be a moral use.

There may be cases where the word "good" serves both functions. For example, when Lon Fuller, a Professor of Jurisprudence at Harvard Law School, defines good law as laws that are clear, public, consistent, he is claiming that such standards are necessary for moral, that is fair, laws as well as effective ones. Laws that are unclear, secret, and inconsistent are not only ineffective, but unjust. Although some jurisprudential scholars have argued against Fuller by maintaining that an instrumental use of good cannot be a moral use, there seems to be no *a priori* reason why a word cannot function simultaneously in more than one way. Granting this, the criticism of teleology is not as dramatic as some would have it. Morality based on teleology cannot be scrapped merely because we claim to have discovered that the teleological use of "good" is not a moral use but simply means that things are efficient. However, we must

8. Aristotle, *The Politics,* 1254b14.

always be on guard to discover from context which use is intended since we can not assume that fulfilling a function or role is necessarily good in any moral sense.

For example, even if it is accepted that a good woman is one who fulfills her role, it may well be that "good" means nothing more than contributing to efficiency. Morton Hunt, in the May, 1970, issue of *Playboy*, argues against husband and wife sharing equally in all tasks (career and home) on the grounds that "when there is no specialization of function, there is inefficient performance. . . ."[9] Although specialization is supposedly one essential aspect of all successful human groups (the other being a system of leadership), it is quite conceivable that a group of two (as opposed to a large corporation) might not prize efficiency as its highest value.

Much depends upon what is meant by "success." Liberty or freedom of role choice may not be very "successful" if success is measured in terms of efficiency. Freedom has never been known for its efficiency; it is always getting in the way of the smooth operations of orderly systems. The conflict between freedom and efficiency can be illustrated by marriage, but is hardly confined to it. It may be inefficient for any one person (married, single, or living in a commune) to teach in a university, write articles, buy groceries, do karate, and demonstrate for political rights, but if a choice must be made between the freedom to do all these things and efficiency, the choice should at least be portrayed as a legitimate one.

Hunt argues not only that specific roles contribute to efficiency, but that they are (as opposed to unisex) attractive. "It feels good, and is productive of well-being, for man and woman to look different, smell different, act somewhat different."[10] He quotes Dr. Benjamin Spock to the effect that the sexes are "more valuable and more pleasing" to one another if they have "specialized traits and . . . roles to play for each other's benefit—gifts of function, so to speak, that they can give to each other." We cannot argue against the claim that specialization of function or role yields efficiency. We can, however, question the importance of efficiency; we can also ask, as we shall see later, efficient for whom? We cannot deny that many men and women find complementarity of role attractive. Some people even find inferiority attractive. Note once again the remarks of Mary Hemingway: "Equality! I didn't want to be Ernest's equal. I wanted him to be the master, to be the stronger and cleverer than I, to remember constantly how big he was and

9. Morton Hunt, "Up Against the Wall, Male Chauvinist Pig." *Playboy*, May, 1970, p. 209.

10. *Ibid.*, p. 207.

how small I was."[11] However, arguing that specific roles are efficient and attractive does not in and of itself determine who is to do what. Telling us in advance what woman's gift of function is going to be makes Hunt's argument typical of anti-women's liberation arguments that are couched in the language of role.

The *essential* content of woman's role is probably best characterized by the concept of "support"—a concept that usually does not get, but certainly deserves, much analysis. What do people mean by the "supportive role"? Why do they think it belongs to women? Hunt, after characterizing the roles of husband and wife as analogous to those of President and Speaker of the House respectively, concedes that "although the man is the head, he owes much to his wife's managerial support."[12] To prove the value of support, he appeals to a remark once made by Senator Maurine Neuberger that her greatest single need as a senator was for a good "wife." Neuberger's comment certainly proves that the supportive role aids efficiency; it is undeniably easier to be a senator if one has someone to shake hands, smile with you on campaign posters, repeat your ideas to groups you have not time for, and answer your dinner invitations. That playing the supporting role aids efficiency cannot be questioned; however, the question remains efficient for whom? It must be remembered that efficiency only requires that *someone* play the supportive role, belong to the maintenance class, devote [his or her life] psychologically and physically to making sure that other people get done whatever they want done. As long as women as a class play supportive roles, they contribute to the efficiency of a power structure that excludes them from freedom of role choice.

Carried to the harshest extreme, slaves played a very important supportive role for their masters; from the masters' point of view, society was the more efficient and hence more desirable for it. Aristotle attests to the efficiency, if not the morality, of his view of natural arrangements when he says that slaves would not be needed if looms would weave by themselves.[13] In its weakest version, playing the supportive role can mean as little as the truism that everyone likes to be fussed over. What Hunt has in mind is something between the two and closer to the former, since he points to the current system as admittedly unfair, but more workable and satisfying than any other alternatives. Part of what he means by "supportive" can be gleaned from the fact that for the most part he is thinking in terms of cases involving children (al-

11. Hemingway, p. 66.

12. Hunt, p. 209.

13. Politics, 1253b38.

though not all of his illustrations bear this out—for example, Neuberger). His perspective, then, centers around the social alternatives of the married woman. They are: the state may take care of the children, hired help may take care of the children, or we can introduce some notion of equality between men and women with regard to whatever tasks confront them, but this, as we have seen, will be inefficient.

Being an essentially pragmatic society, we often buy without question the latter half of the teleological framework: that good things are those that function well; we fail to scrutinize what we mean by "good." We easily overlook that having a function, even a so-called natural one, does not entail that those having it *ought* to use it. As we have seen, to use "X" when "X" is defined as functional is to have a good "X" in some sense of the word. We can explain what poison is by citing its function, but it does not necessarily follow that it ought (in any moral sense) to function. Having children is also a natural function; whether it is good to make use of this function is a separate issue. Given our current population problems, we might well decide that childbearing is not good in either the moral or efficient use of that word.

One might, at this point, legitimately object that the well-being of human beings is more complicated than that of lawnmowers and poisons. If a lawnmower does not function well or is never used to cut grass, the lawnmower is not worse off for it. However, one might say, indeed Freudian conservatives have said, that the human being's biological potential is so integrated that when it is not realized, some kind of "maladjustment" or "unhappiness" results. Of course, some maintain that no such frustration ensues; obviously, to the extent that this is correct, there is no problem, and, for example, people can decide whether or not to have children on the basis of values already discussed (efficiency, morality) since their "happiness" or "adjustment" is not at stake.

However, if we accept the Freudian conservatives' view, we must apply it consistently. Freudians have also taught us that suppression of sexual and aggressive impulses was necessary for the development of civilization. Even though suppression may result in frustration, we are told that in some cases this is the price that must be paid to purchase other goals. It is certainly not a new observation that one pays in some way for everything that one gets. Certainly, in recent times, humanity has paid in increased anxiety, frustration, and, most probably, neuroses, for its advanced technological society. Freudians must allow the same perspective on the question of childbearing as on the questions of sexuality and aggressiveness. In the latter case, we realize that some sort of suppression, probably resulting in some unhappiness, is required for civilization and/or technology. Some women's deliberate suppression of their biological potential should be regarded as an enhancement of the civilized and rational aspects of experience. If there is some biological or psychological frustration involved in the suppression of biological potential, only the individual woman should decide how she wishes to balance her desire for biological "completion" and her desire to experience the world as an independent human being. To recognize the possibility of such unhappiness is not to condone social arrangements which intensify the either/or character of this choice, but to elucidate once again the importance of liberty, and to complicate values (liberty, morality, efficiency) by which we decide which units capable of functioning ought to function.

In the conclusion of his article, Hunt once more calls upon natural law, assuring us that we need not fear the eradication of all sex-role differences because "nothing as joyless and contrary to our instincts is likely to become the pattern of the majority."[14] The language of "instinct," a somewhat modern way to refer to those things that we want to call "natural," is usually attached to some variation of philosophical determinism. "Instincts" are not considered to be matters of value choice, but a small class of desires that are somehow given. Some uses of "natural" lose their force without this built-in determinism; for example, excusing an action on the grounds that one was jealous, and "jealous is only natural," will work only if the people listening accept the reasoning, "I couldn't help myself." If we do not buy the determinism, we do not buy the excuse.

Hunt's argument, and similar arguments from instinct, assume that that which is not the result of human effort is impervious to human control, since he moves from the claim that these instincts are "natural" (meaning by "natural," something that happens without our doing anything to bring it about) to the claim that they are unalterable. That is an empirical assumption which is extremely dubious; it would commit us to the position that, since gravity "naturally" keeps us on the ground, we could never raise ourselves off the ground. Natural instinct may be just as open to control through education and training as our response to gravity is to the technology of air travel. However, if we assume that the behavior related to instincts is unalterable and inevitable, we can guarantee much more in that their obliteration will not become "the pattern of the majority." As John Stuart Mill argued a hundred years ago in *The Subjection of Women*, if the "proper sphere" of women is naturally determined, there will be no need for social and legal coercion to insure that women stay in that sphere. We need not fear that women will do what they cannot do. There is no point in recommending that people desire what they inevitably will desire,

14. Hunt, p. 209.

so, insofar as we recommend that people adopt certain roles, we are assuming that those roles are, at least to some extent, items of choice. So, he cannot have it both ways: as soon as one uses a claim of naturalness to entail a claim of inevitability, one shows it to be inappropriate as a support for a recommendation to be natural.

In psychoanalytic literature, the notion of instinct is frequently replaced by that of unconscious desire. Freud, in his *New Introductory Lectures on Psycho-Analysis,* defined the unconscious as follows: ". . . We call a psychical process unconscious whose existence we are obliged to assume—for some such reason as that we infer it from its effects—but of which we know nothing."[15] In other words, the unconscious is not a thing, not some kind of container filled with desires that "drive" us to do this or that, but rather an explanatory device, not itself empirically evident, but *needed* to explain certain behavior which is. "Needed," that is, in the sense that there are certain "effects" that defy explanation, that simply cannot be accounted for unless we posit an unconscious. For example, if people say they desire one thing, but act as if they desired the contrary, and we know they are not lying, we may be tempted to say that they are somehow unaware of what their "real" motivation is.

If Susan says she wants a career more than anything else in the world, but she does nothing all day except stay home and put on make-up, we are puzzled and desire an explanation. If she is not lying or frivolous, we still lack an explanation; anything, including childhood and gene structure, is fair game as far as possible explanations go. But if Leslie has spent eight years preparing for a career and assures a prospective employer that she is serious about it, she does not deserve as an answer: "I would like to believe you, my dear, but all women really desire to devote their lives to men and children. . . ." Such a remark is unwarranted because there are no "effects" in this case that need to be explained. (Of course, external evidence of competence, such as Ph.D.'s and M.D.'s, do help when one wants to be taken seriously. The undergraduate argument, "she only went to college to find a husband," does not seem so plausible when applied to Ph.D.'s. There simply has to be an easier way to get a husband!)

. . . .

15. Sigmund Freud, *New Introductory Lectures on Psycho-Analysis* (1933), reprinted in E. Kuykendall, *Philosophy in the Age of Crisis* (New York: Harper & Row, 1970), p. 122. To philosophers the above sounds like the kind of move John Locke made when he posited the existence of material substance as an explanatory account for why collections of qualities regularly occur together. To the extent that the move is similar to Locke's, it is, of course, subject to the same types of criticisms.

I have tried to show some of the muddles that language of the "natural" gets us into. Except in cases where the natural is defined in terms of purpose or function, it carries no automatic value tag, and in no case carries an automatic moral implication. After finding out what a person means by "natural," we then have to decide on independent grounds whether what is meant is in any sense good. For example, why is it good to do what animals do, or to avoid invented devices which interrupt what ordinarily happens? Why is what ordinarily happens considered to be a good thing? What is so good about order? Teleological uses of "natural" automatically set up an evaluative context; knowing the function of "X" makes it possible for us to evaluate "X" on grounds of functioning well. But as we have seen, teleological uses have to be morally evaluated: a good bomb is one that destroys, but is a good bomb morally good?

There is no reason to assume that the problem of evaluation would change because some things are created by persons and others are not. Many people, for example, argue that nature is good because God made it. This, of course, precipitates the old problem of evil. How can earthquakes and birth defects be good? The answer does not abandon the language of purpose, but rather tells us in Platonic fashion that all of "creation" functions for some good end; however, humans are incapable of knowing this end or purpose. Indeed, part of what it means to have faith is to believe that all natural (that is, created) purposes (in humans or otherwise) are good purposes, and work together toward some larger purpose. Since human beings cannot know this larger end, there is no way that they can evaluate it. This, however, does not eliminate the problem of evaluation. It does not eliminate the question, "In what sense are things that function well good?" It simply tells us that there is no cognitive answer, or more precisely, that only the faithful, after they have been faithful in believing the acceptability of God's answer, will receive an answer. The position comes to this: because we believe in God, we should believe that nature is good in some good sense.

Theological positions, however, in no way exempt us from either defining what we mean by "natural" or appraising it. Indeed, even if the ultimate evaluation is said to be a matter of faith, the task that Thomas Aquinas referred to as natural or rational theology (the spelling out of the ends of things that are imprinted on the natures of things) is something that human beings must be prepared to perform without divine assistance. This task brings us right back to the beginning of our inquiry, namely, what in the world do people mean when they say that "X" is natural"?

* * *

ELIZABETH V. SPELMAN

Elizabeth V. Spelman (1945–) has taught philosophy at Smith College since 1981. Unlike Russell, who developed his views on women only tangentially, without utilizing the skills of analysis he exhibits elsewhere, Spelman uses the tools of philosophical analysis to critique generalizations applied to women as a group and to minorities. Until recently, such generalizations have usually been formulated by white men who have no experience of what it means to be nonwhite or female. This lack of experiential grounding leads to what Spelman, in a 1983 article with Maria Lugones ("Have We Got A Theory for You!"), describes as "distrust of the male monopoly over accounts of women's lives." To avoid false accounts of women, those who have provided and who continue to transmit the accounts must learn to listen to women. Spelman's philosophical approach emphasizes differences among individuals and groups that cannot be fully revealed without the participation of the individuals or groups themselves.

"Part of human life," for Spelman and Lugones, "is talking about it, and we can be sure that being silenced in one's own account of one's life is a kind of amputation that signals oppression. . . . We can't separate lives from the accounts given of them; the articulation of our experience is part of our experience." In effect, silencing another—whether it comes from men who ignore women's experience, or from women who too quickly generalize from their own lives about the experience of all women—constitutes a denial of the other's personhood.

Woman: The One and the Many

I suspect it may be hard not to have the feeling that some philosophical sleight of hand is going on here, that there is something wantonly obscure in piling up argument after argument to the effect that it isn't as easy as one might think to talk coherently about a woman "as a woman," that attempts to isolate gender from race and class don't succeed in doing so. After all, most everyone has no trouble at all answering questions such as "What gender are you?" "What race are you?" and so on. This is not to say that there are not, for example, debates about the "racial" categories on United States census forms. Nor is it to forget that in countries like the United States the pretense of there being no class differences makes it very hard for many people to answer questions about what class they belong to. But I may seem to have forgotten that at least some of these questions about one's identity are easy to answer. I agree: I don't have any trouble answering that I am a woman and that I am white. These appear to be two separate questions, which I can answer separately; my brother answers one of them as I do, the other not. So it seems that I can easily pick out the "woman part" of me and the "white part" of me and, moreover, tell the difference between them.

But does this mean that there is a "woman part" of me, and that it is distinct, for example, from something that is the "white part" of me? If there is a "woman part" of me, it doesn't seem to be the kind of thing I could point to—not because etiquette demands that nice people don't point to their private or covered parts, but because even if I broke a social rule and did so, nothing I might point to would meet the requirements of being a "part" of me that was a "woman part" that was not also a "white part." Any part of my body is part of a body that is, by prevailing criteria, female and white. And now that I have moved surreptitiously from talking about a "woman part" to talking about a "female part," you will remember another reason why pointing to the "woman part" of myself would be no mean feat: being a "woman" is not the same thing as, nor is it reducible to, being a "female." "Women" are what females of the human species become, or are supposed to become, through learning how to think, act, and live in certain ways. What females in one society learn about how they are to think, act, and live, can differ enormously from what females in another society learn; in fact, as we have been reminded often, there can be very significant differences within a given society. Moreover, those females who don't learn their lessons very well, or who resist being and doing what they're taught, or who, as we saw in Aristotle's view, are born into the "wrong" group, may have their credentials as "real women" questioned even while their status as females remains intact. Indeed, unless their female status is assumed, there can be no grounds for wondering whether they are really "women." Being a woman—or a man, for that matter—is a complicated business, and apparently a precarious one, given the number of societal institutions instructing us about how to be women or men and punishing us for failing to act appropriately.

Maybe I could tell you better about that aspect of myself in virtue of which I am called a "woman" and show you how it is different from that aspect of myself in virtue of which I am called "white" by talking about how as a woman I am distinguished from men, while as a white person I am distinguished from, for example, Black people. I can metaphorically point to my womanness by reminding you of how I am different from men, to my whiteness by reminding you of how I am different from Black people. For example, I can attend to the different expectations my parents and teachers had for me and my two sisters, on the one hand, and our two brothers, on the other; or, *à la* Nancy Chodorow, I can try to describe the difference between how we three girls related to our mother and how our brothers related to her, and how that affected our senses of ourselves. And this might appear to have nothing to do with whether I am white or Black, Anglo or Hispana, Christian or Jewish. But it is only because whiteness is taken as a given that there is even the appearance of being able to distinguish simply between a person's being a woman and a person's being a man, and thus of being able somehow to point to the "woman part" of me in isolation from the "white part" of me. Even if the idea is that I am to be distinguished simply from men, it may turn out that I am distinguished from white men in ways different from the ways in which I am distinguished from Black men. We have discussed this before, but it's worth trying one more approach to it.

Let's suppose I have the chance to stand up on a stage next to James Baldwin. He is a man and I am a woman, but there are other differences between us, including of course the fact that he is Black and I am white. How, then, will contrasting myself to him enable you to see what my "woman part" is and how it is isolatable from my "white part"? Is my difference from him as a woman separable from my difference from him as a white person? To find out whether my gender difference is isolatable from my racial difference from him, it would help to add some more people on the stage. So now Angela Davis joins us. Is there some respect in which I am different from James Baldwin in just the same way Angela Davis is different from him—is there something she and I share such that we are different from him in just the same ways? And now let's add a white man up here—say my brother Jon. Are Angela Davis and I different from Jon in just the same way, since we both are women and he is a man?

Now in what respect could Angela and I be said to be different from Jon in just the same way? Well, we're both called "women" and he is not. But does our being called "women" mean the same thing to us and for us? Are there any situations in which my being white and her being Black does not affect what it means to us and for us to be women? To whom is it not going to make a difference that my "womanness" is the womanness of a white woman, that hers is the womanness of a Black woman? To our mothers? our fathers? our sisters? our brothers? our children? our teachers? our students? our employers? our lovers? ourselves?

If it were possible to isolate a woman's "womanness" from her racial identity, then we should have no trouble imagining that had I been Black I could have had just the same understanding of myself as a woman as I in fact do, and that no matter how differently people would have treated me had I been Black, nevertheless what it would have meant to them that I was a woman would have been just the same. To rehearse this imaginary situation is to expose its utter bizarreness.

The identities of persons are much more complicated than what might be suggested by the simple and straightforward use of terms like "Black," "white," "woman," "man." Conceptual tidiness would suggest that if Angela's a woman and I am too, while James is a man and so is Jon, then unless our language misleads us there must be something Angela and I share that distinguishes us from James and Jon and distinguishes us from them indistinguishably. Similarly, if Angela is Black and so is James, while Jon is white and so am I, then unless our language misleads us there must be something Angela and James share that distinguishes them from Jon and me and distinguishes them from us indistinguishably.

However, as some philosophers have been trying to tell us now for decades, we can't blame language for our failure to examine its use in context. And if we examine the use of "woman" in particular contexts, then we might be encouraged to ask when descriptions of what-it-is-to-be-a-woman really are descriptions of what-it-is-to-be-a-woman-in-culture-*X* or subculture-*Y*. Being a woman, as we surely know by now from cross-cultural studies, is something that is constructed by societies and differs from one society to another. Hence unless I know something more about two women than the fact that they are women, I can't say anything about what they might have in common. What is the "womanness" that Angela Davis and I are said to share? Prior to any actual investigation, all we can say for sure is that being a woman is constructed in contrast to (even if the contrast is minimal) being a man (or to some other gender as well—not all cultures are as stingy as those that countenance only "men" and "women").[1] While all women are gendered, and are gendered as women in contrast to men, nothing follows from that alone about what it means to be so gendered. For it is simply a tautology to say that all women are gendered, since women are by definition gendered females. (We are referring to gender and not to sex; not all human females end up gendered as women.)

It is thus evident that thinking about a person's identity as made up of neatly distinguishable "parts" may be very misleading, despite the impetus from philosophers such as Plato and Descartes to so describe ourselves. Just as in their cases we may get the impression that the whole person is a composite of soul (or mind) and body, so in the case of much feminist thought we may get the impression that a woman's identity consists of a sum of parts neatly

1. See, for example, Robert B. Edgerton, "Pokot Intersexuality: An East African Example of the Resolution of Sexual Incongruity," *American Anthropologist* 66, no. 1 (1964): 1288–99.

divisible from one another, parts defined in terms of her race, gender, class, and so on. We may infer that the oppressions she is subject to are (depending on who she is) neatly divisible into racism, sexism, classism, or homophobia, and that in her various political activities she works clearly now out of one part of herself, now out of another. This is a version of personal identity we might call tootsie roll metaphysics: each part of my identity is separable from every other part, and the significance of each part is unaffected by the other parts. On this view of personal identity (which might also be called pop-bead metaphysics), my being a woman means the same whether I am white or Black, rich or poor, French or Jamaican, Jewish or Muslim.[2] As a woman, I'm like other women; my difference from other women is only along the other dimensions of my identity. Hence it is possible on this view to imagine my being the same woman even if my race were different—the pop-bead or tootsie roll section labeled "woman" is just inserted into a different strand or roll. According to a powerful tradition within Western philosophy (though not limited to it), if my soul is separable from my body, it might become attached to or lodge in another body; and if my soul is who I really am, then this new combination of soul and body is still me. Similarly, if my "womanness" is separable from other aspects of my identity, then I as woman would still be the same woman I am even if I happen to have been born into a body of a different color, or even a body of the same color at a different moment in history.[3]

I

There is much new and recently recovered work by and about women, in history, anthropology, psychology, economics, and sociology, not to mention literature. It is the result of painstaking and often undervalued labor. Surely in such investigations we can expect to find people refusing to let either logical or political assump-

2. Many thanks to Barbara Cottle Johnson for the pop-bead imagery.

3. A white woman might think her gender is thoroughly distinct from her race because she appears to experience sexism in isolation from racism: she is subjected to sexism but not to racism. (I say "appears" because we cannot understand the sexism she experiences without understanding its connection to the racism she does not.) It does not follow from that apparent isolation that her gender is distinct from her race; but neither does it follow, from the fact that a woman experiences sexism *and* racism, that her gender is distinct from her race. . . .

It is important to note that this composite, collection-of-parts view of personhood, as well as its accompanying view of political activity, is held implicitly by a wide range of feminist political and social theorists—not only those who treat gender as distinct from and isolatable from racial, ethnic, or other identity, but those who treat racial, class, and ethnic identity as isolatable from gender identity.

tions of the kind we discussed in earlier chapters take the place of good empirical research: rather than assuming that women must have something in common as women, these researchers should help us look to see whether they do, to investigate not only the respects in which women of different races, classes, nationalities, historical periods, religions, sexual orientations, and so forth, are similar but the respects in which they are different. On the basis of such studies we may find a way to isolate what is true of women as women.

This way of trying to get at what is true about women is quite different from the two ways we have already explored: (1) To look within a single racial or ethnic or religious or cultural group for the effects of gender, eliminating other differences in an individual's development or treatment. (2) To examine the effects of gender on women not otherwise subject to oppression. Both of these methods are based on the unwarranted assumption that what is constant doesn't affect what is variable, that race or class disappear because they are held constant or because they are not a factor in a woman's oppression. Neither method requires us to investigate differences among women or to go beyond a single group of women.

This ought to tell us that rather than first finding out what is true of some women as women and then inferring that this is true of all women and thus is common to all women, we have to investigate different women's lives and see what they have in common *other* than being female and being called "women." Only then (if at all) can we talk about what is true of any and all of them as women.

Plato, as we saw, thought that only especially gifted thinkers could discern what differences between men and women, or differences among men and among women, mattered; only they could know how and why the differences made a difference; and only by virtue of such knowledge were they philosopher-rulers. If we take nothing else away from a reading of the *Republic*, surely we ought to question how the kind of authority about sameness and difference vested in philosopher-rulers ever becomes the bailiwick of any particular person or group (for example, of the justices of the Supreme Court of the United States, who are taken to have not merely the right but the obligation to decide what the relevant similarities and differences are between men and women, whites and Blacks, Christians and Jews, "normal" and mentally retarded people, etc., and what those similarities and differences mean).[4] The

4. For extremely illuminating accounts of the role of the judiciary in making such decisions, see Martha Minow, "When Difference Has Its Home: Group Homes for the Mentally Retarded, Equal Protection, and Legal Treatment of Difference," *Harvard Civil Rights Civil Liberties Review* 22, no. 1 (1987), 111–89; and her "Foreword: Justice Engendered," in "The Supreme Court 1986 Term," *Harvard Law Review* 101, no. 1 (1987): 10–95.

philosopher-rulers do not merely notice some interesting features about the world around them when they describe two people as being the same or different in particular ways—for example, when they claim that male and female philosopher-rulers are more alike than male philosophers and male cobblers. Whatever else they are doing, philosopher-rulers are implicitly insisting that this is the way the world really is. Moreover, they think that their actions and those of everyone else ought to be based on a picture of the way things really are and not on some less accurate account.

Reading Plato ought to encourage us to look at the degree of metaphysical and political authority presupposed by those who claim the right to point out commonality, who assert or exercise the privilege of determining just what it means in terms of others' identities, social locations, and political priorities. It is useful to remember, for example, that Plato didn't consult with women around him to find out if they thought they were like men in the significant ways he thought they were; he claimed to know how and to what extent men and women of a given class were similar and what that meant about how their lives ought to be organized. This as much as any other consideration should make us wonder about the extent to which Plato ought to be called a feminist. One can have a theory about the equality between men and women that itself violates the conditions under which real equality can exist: for simply telling a group of heretofore subjugated people "You are like us in the following respects and hence ought to be treated in the following way" is an assertion of the very power and authority that the claims about equality are supposed to make illicit. As James Baldwin said: "There is no reason for you to try to become like white people and there is no basis whatever for their impertinent assumption that *they* must accept *you*."[5]

It is no wonder, then, that women of color have been distrustful of white women who point to similarities between them when it seems politically expedient to do so and to dissimilarities when it does not.[6] They have wanted to know just why and when white women become interested in similarities and differences among women. At issue is not so much whether there are or are not similarities or differences, but about how white middle-class feminists try to use claims about similarity and differences among women in different directions, depending on what they believe such similarity or dissimilarity implies. For example, as we have seen, some-

5. *The Fire Next Time* (New York: Dell, 1962), 19. James Baldwin died while I was writing this book.

6. See Lorraine Bethel, "What Chou Mean *WE*, White Girl?" in *Conditions* 5 (1979): 86–92.

times feminists have insisted on the similarity between the treatment of "women" and that of "slaves"; other times they have insisted that the situation of free women and slave women is different enough that the situation of slave women cannot be a useful guide to that of free women. The issue is thus not so much a metaphysical one as a political one. Given the highly charged political atmosphere in which claims about sameness and difference are made, challenged and negotiated, and the consequences of such claims for access to resources, status, and power, we cannot assume that they are simple descriptive reports on the basis of which we can come to see what women of different races, cultures, and so on, have in common, what is true of them as women. Investigations into ways in which women are similar and ways we are different must always be looked at in the light of the following questions: Who is doing the investigating? Whose views are heard and accepted? Why? What criteria are used for similarity and difference? Finally, and most important, what is said to follow from the supposed existence of similarity or difference?[7] Have those under investigation been asked what they think?

Someone might tell me that we have something in common, but even if I agree, I may find that utterly insignificant in terms of my identity and my plans for action. This reminds us that the claim of commonality can be very arrogant indeed: the caller may be attempting to appropriate the other's identity. We are aware of this whenever we find it annoying for a stranger or even an acquaintance to claim something in common with us. In such cases we resent the implication that because we have something in common there is some special connection between us, some reason for spending time together, making plans together.

Nevertheless, not all claims about commonality are arrogant. Let us take for example the following case:

> You have described yourself as having certain properties or characteristics by virtue of which you justify the claim to a certain position or status or certain entitlements.
>
> I claim that I am like you in that respect and that I therefore also ought to be enjoying the status or those entitlements.
>
> You have the power and authority to recognize our similarity and your doing so will make a significant difference as to whether my claim is attended to.

7. See Minow references in note 4 above.

The history of the civil rights movement and women's rights movements provides familiar examples of this claim. A subordinated people insist that they have characteristics in common with their dominators (e.g., humanity, reason, vulnerability to suffering) and therefore that they are owed a higher regard than presently afforded them by the dominators.

In stark contrast we have the following case:

> You have described yourself as having certain properties or characteristics.
>
> You claim that I am like you in having the same characteristics, but you have not consulted me as to whether I think I am like you in this way or whether I attach the same significance you do to having such characteristics.
>
> You have more power and authority than I to make your claims heard and attended to.

White feminists have fallen into this trap whenever they have assumed that women of color are like themselves and hence ought to have the same priorities. Although it is not arrogant, for example, for a Black woman in the United States to claim that she is like me in having characteristics I say entitle me to citizenship, it is arrogant for me to simply declare to the same woman that she is like me and tell her what that means about the two of us. What makes my claim untenable is my presumption that I have the power and the authority to legislate her identity. She makes no such presumptions in her assertion of her rights; she merely refers to my own description of my identity and rights as a basis for asserting her own. Of course none of this means that I can't help but be arrogant in all ways or that she couldn't possibly be in any way. The two cases we've described do not exhaust the possibilities; variations along a spectrum of claims about commonality will be the more interesting cases for feminist examination.

We have begun to realize that I don't necessarily correct my picture of what is true of women "as women" by doing "empirical research" rather than simply generalizing from my own case.[8] For I can't simply "look and see" to find out what we have or don't have in common. First of all, I have to have decided what kind of similarity or difference I am interested in. It makes no sense to ask simply whether women are similar or different—I have to specify in what way they might be similar or different. Moreover, I have to

8. I hardly begin to dip into the issues raised by reflection on what actual or desirable social science methodology is.

employ criteria of sameness and difference—I have to use some measure by which I decide whether they are the same or different in the specified way. And finally, I have to determine the significance of the similarities and differences I find.

Let us suppose that I am interested in finding out how much economic and political power various groups of women have. Let us also suppose that the criterion for similarity or difference I use is whether women have as much economic and political power as the most powerful men. Using this criterion, I say I find—perhaps I may be challenged by some anthropologists—that there are no significant differences among women with respect to their having that degree of economic and political power. Finally, I judge that being the same in this way is a very significant fact about women, more significant than any other similarity or difference among us. The most important fact about us is what we have in common: namely, that none of us has the power the most powerful men do.

On the other hand, I might employ another criterion. I might ask not simply whether any women have as much power as the most powerful men, but rather investigate the degree to which and ways in which different groups of women have access to such power, even on borrowed terms. Using this criterion I am much more likely to see differences among women; and while I may not be sure just what significance to attach to those differences, I am at least prepared to give them some weight. For example, using the first criterion I cannot attach any significance to the fact that because the wives of white slaveowners in the United States were of a different race and class, they had many more privileges than the Black women who were their slaves (including the privilege of whipping their female slaves at will and with impunity). If my working criterion is the kind of power women lack rather than the degree of power they have, then I have to say that the wives did not have the economic and political power their husbands did, and hence that there is no significant difference between them and the Black slave women. But by the second criterion, I do not discount the power women have (however derivative it might be) in trying to see what women do or do not have in common. I note that while neither the white wife nor the Black female slave had the power the white male slaveowner did, this did not mean they were subject to the same abuses of his power, nor did it mean that the women were equally powerless in relation to each other.

Let us explore a related example. Suppose my criterion for deciding how similar women are with respect to economic and political power is whether they have as much power as men of their own racial, class, or ethnic group. Let us suppose—contrary to some anthropological findings and to the facts of slavery before us—that according to this criterion, all women are the same: none of us has as much or more power than the men of our group. But if we use this criterion for deciding how similar or different we are, then we completely leave aside the differences in power between men of different groups, between women of different groups, and between men of one group and women of another. If we suppose, for example, that upper-class white women in the United States are as subject to the whims of their husbands' desire to abuse them as poor white women are, we leave out of the picture the power upper-class white women and their husbands have over poor white men and poor white women.

[. . . An] example from Kenneth Stampp . . . brings to mind yet another decision that has to be made when I try to "look and see" what different groups of people have in common: how shall I describe what they share? You will recall that Stampp describes a working assumption of his investigations in this way:

> I have assumed that the slaves were merely ordinary human beings, that innately Negroes *are*, after all, only white men with black skins, nothing more, nothing less.[9]

What Blacks and whites have in common, according to Stampp, is an essential "whiteness." Stampp is willing to countenance similarity to members of a different racial group, historically despised by his own, as long as it is on his terms (he gets to decide who is like whom and what that means) and as long as it is favorable to him (it preserves his identity and erases that of the formerly despised group). He is hardly being "color-blind" here, but rather is insisting that Black people aren't the color some of us might have thought; they actually are white.

In short, I may have a great deal at stake when I explore similarities and differences among groups of people. Just what I have at stake may show up at the many points in my investigation at which I must make some crucial decisions: decisions about the kind of similarity or difference I am interested in, decisions about the criteria I will employ to see what similarities and differences there are, decisions about what I take them to mean, decisions about how I describe those similarities or differences. We feminists are no less subject to the biases such decisions can introduce than anyone else is. A description of the common world we share "as women" may be simply a description of my world with you now as an honorary member.

9. Kenneth Stampp, *The Peculiar Institution* (New York: Knopff, 1956): vii–viii.

II

Let us return for a moment to the knowledge about our identities that most of us find easy to express. Most of us (in perhaps most societies) are asked at regular intervals to indicate whether we are men or women, what racial or ethnic category describes us, and so on (what we are asked will depend on the society we live in). Indeed, our knowledge of such facts about our identities is called upon all the time—for example, in filling out new patient forms at the dentist's, in choosing which bathroom to enter, in providing information for demographic studies (to say nothing about the information we constantly give out to others about aspects of our identities, through our speech patterns, gestures, accents, inflections, gait, and clothing). No doubt we can lie about these identities—by checking the wrong box, for example. No doubt we can refuse to act the way we might be expected to on the basis of this self-knowledge—my knowing I'm a woman doesn't mean I won't use a bathroom marked "men." But lying and "misbehaving" presuppose the kind of knowledge in question, that is, knowledge of one's gender, one's race, one's ethnicity, one's nationality. What is it I know if I know that I am a woman or a man, Black or Hispana or white, Jewish or Christian, straight or gay or lesbian? Could I be wrong? If others disagree with me, is there a way of deciding which of us is right?

Descartes argued that given good grounds for doubt about anything else he might have come to believe, there was only one thing he could know for certain: that he existed.

> This proposition "I am," "I exist," whenever I utter it or conceive it in my mind, is necessarily true.[10]

Indeed, the fact of his doubting was the very condition of his certain knowledge—for doubting (itself a kind of thinking) couldn't take place unless there was someone to do the doubting. To paraphrase Walt Kelly's Pogo: I have met the doubter and he is I. I think, therefore I am. This knowledge of his own existence was something Descartes took himself to have apart from the mediation of his senses (those, he had satisfied himself, were deceptive until proven otherwise) and apart from the mediation of his culture (there was no good reason to believe anything he had been taught).[11]

10. René Descartes, *Meditations on First Philosophy*, in *Descartes: Philosophical Writings*, translated and edited by Elizabeth Anscombe and Peter Geach (London: Nelson, 1969). Meditation 2:67. Further citations are from this edition.

11. See Descartes, *Discourse on Method*.

And he was in many ways quite attuned to the reach of his senses and his culture: for having found the nugget of certainty in the fact that he existed, he was very cautious about describing who or what the "I" that exists *is:*

> But I do not yet sufficiently understand what is this "I" that necessarily exists. I must take care, then, that I do not rashly take something else for the "I," and thus go wrong even in the knowledge that I am maintaining to be the most certain and evident of all. . . . What, then, did I formerly think I was?[12]

He trots out, only to dismiss on the sceptical grounds he already has laid, several possible candidates for what he is—reasonable animal, man, body, soul. I can't say for certain that I have a face, hands, arms, Descartes reasoned, even though I can say for certain that I exist, because I have said that I have reason to doubt that such things exist.

I bring up Descartes here, not because I think a program of sceptical calisthenics along the lines he proposed is the right antidote for the habits of thought that lie at the root of tendencies toward ethnocentrism in dominant Western feminist thought. But I do find instructive his caution about *what* or *who* he is, as well as his general point about the deceptive ease with which we use words, the facile certainty with which we describe what we might think we know best—ourselves. Descartes—certain as he is about some facts about himself—is concerned about how much our understanding of ourselves is due, not to unmediated introspection, but to concepts and categories we inherit from other people, concepts and categories that presuppose the existence of the very things Descartes thinks we have reason to doubt.[13] I might well be a man, Descartes is saying, but I have to convince myself that I know some other things before I'll agree to this description of myself.

I say that I know I am a woman, I know that I am white, and so on. But if I know that, surely I know what I mean by saying these things. What properties am I ascribing to myself? Are there circumstances under which I might have doubts about what or who I am? Is being a woman something I could cease being? Is being

12. Meditation 2:67.

13. That is, he would agree with the later Wittgenstein (see, for example, *The Philosophical Investigations* [New York: Macmillan, 1953]) to some extent that the language we use to talk about ourselves is itself an intersubjective product and project and that therefore if we want to locate a kind of knowledge that does not depend on such products and projects we can't use language that imports them. Descartes does not realize how this undermines the method of the *Meditations.*

white something I could cease being? What have I learned, when I learn that I am a woman? When I learn that I am white? What have I agreed to, in agreeing to say that I am a woman? In agreeing to say that I am white? What am I refusing, if I were to insist that neither of these terms applies to me?

Imagine a huge customs hall with numerous doors, marked "women," "men," "Afro-American," "Asian-American," "Euro-American," "Hispanic-American," "working class," "middle class," "upper class," "lesbian," "gay," "heterosexual," and so forth. (You may add to or subtract from the number of doors to your heart's content; we'll return in a minute to the question of who decides how many doors there are, what the doors say, and other questions about the legislation and orchestration of identity.) The doors are arranged in banks, so that each person faces first a bank of doors that sort[s] according to gender, then a bank that sort[s] according to race, or alternatively sort[s] first according to race, then according to class, then according to gender, and so on. We'll all give notice of who we are by going through the requisite doors.

Assume that the doors at the first bank are marked

Women | Men

and at the second bank

Afro-American | Euro-American | Asian-American | Hispanic American

If the sorting done at the first bank is still in effect at the second, then there will have to be two sets of doors at the second, like so:

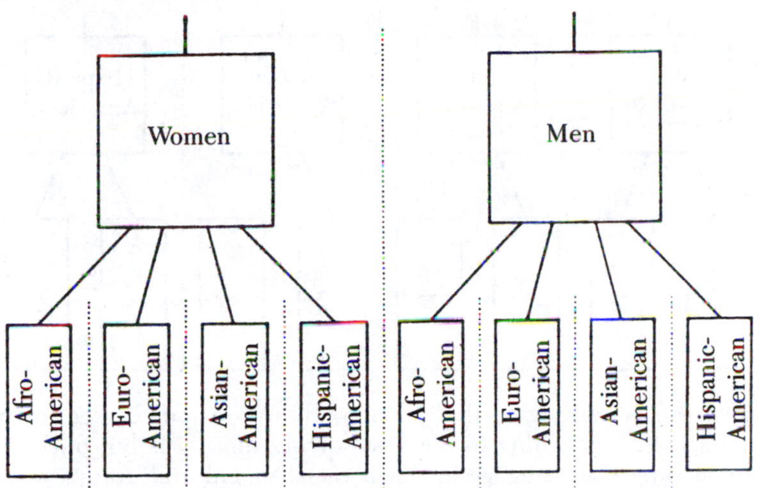

That is, if the original division is maintained between women and men, then Afro-American women and men will not go through the same doors—for there will be two doors marked "Afro-American," one the other side of the door marked "women," the other the other side of the door marked "men."[14] Notice that in this case whatever the Afro-Americans have in common, they will not end up on the other side of the same door; they won't be in the same place. For their Afro-Americanness, whatever that is, will be seen to exist in the context of their being women or men, and more particularly as in some sense subordinate to their being women or men. In accordance with this way of sorting people, there is only one category of "woman," but two categories of each racial or cultural identity.

Let us see what happens if we change the order of the doors or if we do not insist that one sorting have effect on the next: for example, the Afro-American men and women would have ended up on the other side of the same door marked "Afro-American" if after the division into women and men all the people involved in the sorting had come back together again in a big group and started afresh. Though they once would have been divided for another purpose, that fact about them does not show up in the next division. Or let us suppose that the first division was not between men and women but between Afro-American, Euro-American, and so forth. In this situation, Afro-American women and the other women would not end up in the same location after the first sorting.

14. This pattern of sorting was not used by those who constructed segregated bathrooms in the United States.

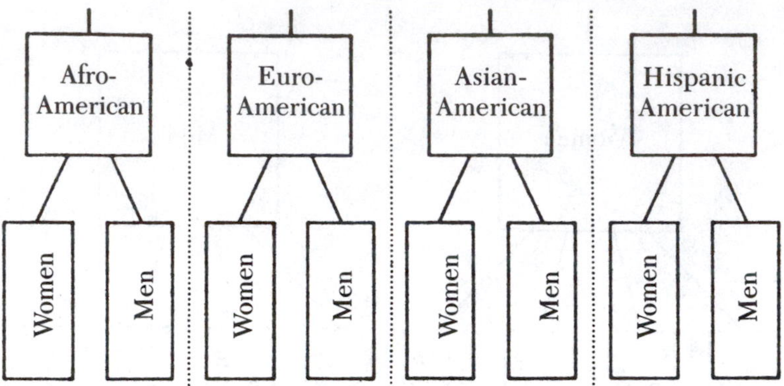

Notice that according to this schema, there are four categories of women, while according to the first sorting there was but one; and there is only one category for each racial or cultural group, while according to the first division there were several. Whether and how people are divided up further depends on what the next set of doors is.

As you already can see, we get different pictures of people's identities, and of the extent to which one person shares some aspect of identity with another, depending on what the doors are, how they are ordered, and how people are supposed to proceed through them. For example, according to the first schema, a woman who is "Asian-American" has more in common with all other women than she does with Asian-American men; while according to the second, Asian-American men and women have more in common than Asian-American women and other women. According to the first schema, I can in some sense think about myself as a woman in isolation from other facts about myself; if I couldn't, I wouldn't know how to go through the doors. Yet according to the second schema, my thinking about myself as a woman is in the context of being Asian-American or Afro-American, or some other racial group.

We will need to know more about these doors: Who makes them, and who guards them? That is, who decides what will be on them, how many there will be, in what order they occur? Who decides which one you are supposed to take if there is any doubt? Is one free to ignore a door or to go around a given set of doors? We surely also need to know what facts about you and your experiences and history make it seem likely—to you and others—that you will go through one door rather than another, or that you will find the order of the doors appropriate to your identity.

Questions will also arise about what the designations on the doors mean. For example, there is a certain ambiguity about the doors marked "men" and "women." That isn't the same as having them marked "male" and "female."[15] Many questions will come up about the accuracy of the designations: What if someone refused to go through a door marked simply "woman" or simply "Asian-American," on the grounds that she found those categories too crude and was suspicious of the point of being cataloged in these ways? Suppose someone didn't know what the point of door-dividing is and was not sure of what the designations mean? Moreover, if I think that things are better behind one door than another, I might try very hard to convince the guards and the people scheduled to be sorted that I ought to go behind that one even though I know it is not the one they expect me to go through. Do some people know better than I what doors I really belong behind? Is there any reason why I should not try to get on the far side of any door I want to? Are the doors there to pinpoint one's "true identity," if there is such a thing? Do people have identities independent of what proceeding through the doors would indicate? Are the doors there mainly to control access to some other place, or some other people? Why are they there? Do I have to go through them? What happens if I try not to? What happens if someone tries to claim an identity as an act of solidarity—by wearing a yellow star or a pink triangle, for example?

The doors imagery helps us to deal with some issues that have been plaguing us throughout this book and helps us also to see the point of questions raised earlier about what it is to have knowledge of one's gender, race, class or any other possible identifier. The alternative schemas (and we have only presented two of indefinitely many) present graphically for us the different things it can mean to talk about what is true of women "as women" and about what women have in common. According to the first schema, what is true of me "as a woman" seems to be what I have in common

15. This reminds us to ask whether the kinds of questions we referred to earlier that we are so adept at answering are questions about our sexual identity or our gender identity. It is worth thinking about why many bathroom doors are marked "men" and "women" rather than "male" and "female," since applications and census forms typically use the latter and seem to have to do simply with sexual identity. (Forms that ask one to pick from among "Mr.," "Mrs.," "Miss," and now "Ms." have more to do with gender identity and social role than sexual identity, since there are only two sexes referred to.) Perhaps it is because bathrooms have a lot to do with the maintenance of gender identity, insofar as they are places where females are expected to engage in the titivating activities necessary for maintaining one's womanly appearance—brushing one's hair, putting on makeup, adjusting one's skirt, attending to small children, spraying on perfume, and so forth.

In regard to accuracy of designation, one knows why doors are marked "men" and "women," and one knows what is in store behind those doors—even if one thinks bathrooms ought to be co-ed. I also note that it is perfectly within the rules about bathroom doors that humans below a certain age can go into either—or rather, that little boys can go into rooms marked "women" even though little girls don't usually go into rooms marked "men."

with all other women in contrast to all other men. According to the second schema, what is true of me "as a woman" would seem to be what I have in common with other women of my ethnic and racial background in contrast to men of the same background. The second schema suggests that one's womanness is to be understood in the context of one's ethnic and racial background, while the first makes it look as if one's womanness can be specified quite independently of such background. According to the second schema, even if a case could be made for there being a "woman part" of each woman that was isolatable from her other "parts," that wouldn't necessarily show that all women have something substantial in common "as women," that the "woman part" would be the same in all cases. In order to know whether all the people who end up behind the doors marked "women" share anything substantial in common, we'd have to know the criteria used for dividing women from men in each case and see if they were similar in all cases (and this, as noted earlier, will require us to decide in what respect and by what criteria we want to see whether they are similar). Of course we could assure that all women have something substantial in common by insisting that anyone who does not have some particular characteristic is not a "woman"; then "all women have something in common" would be as secure, and as trivial, as any other tautology.

The schemas enable us to see how the situation of white middle-class women can be conflated with the situation of "women," thus securing the privileged position of one group of women over others. If we use the first schema, differences among women are recognized but treated as secondary to whatever it is that distinguishes all women from all men. The first schema doesn't tell us what this common distinguishing feature is. But if our description of what distinguishes "women" from "men" in fact ends up being what distinguishes one group of women from the men like them, then what is true of that one group of women will be taken to characterize all women. This is in effect what we saw happening in de Beauvoir's account. If we keep the second schema in mind, we might be less likely to take the case of one group of women for the case of all, since the second schema implies that gender distinctions exist in the context of ethnic and racial distinctions. Indeed, it suggests that the distinctions between any two ethnic or racial groups are more significant (according to those who devise the system) than the distinctions between men and women within any such group. It makes it harder for us to take any particular group of women's experience as representative of all, but surely it does not prohibit us from asking what different groups of women have or might come to have in common.

Since people can be classified and cataloged in any number of ways, overlapping ways, how we catalog them, in particular how we sort out the overlapping distinctions, will depend on our purposes and our sense of what the similarities and differences among them are and how they ought to be weighed. (Think of the different classificatory schemas implicitly proposed by those who insist "I am a woman who is a writer," or "I am a writer who is a woman.") Purposes may clash, indeed may clash somewhat predictably along the lines of certain differences among us; and not all of us have the same degree of power and authority about which schema or schemas are the most appropriate or revealing means of presenting the significance of similarities and differences among people.

By thinking of cataloging schemes as being like doors in an imaginary customs house, or like doors in some version of the immigration bureau that existed at Ellis Island, or like bathroom doors in segregated areas of the United States, we may be more likely to keep in mind the constant human effort it takes to create and maintain classificatory schemes, the continual human battles over which schemes are to prevail, and the purposes of such schemes.

Perhaps we need to add a door that says "officials only" to remind us of another very important difference—that between people who create and maintain the schemes and those simply subject to them. On the other hand, it may well be that those with the most power of all don't have doors—especially not doors labeled "makers and keepers of the doors"—for that would only reveal that the scheme is not a "natural" one and also enable those upset with the scheme to know where to begin to look for its creators and enforcers.[16] This points to another useful feature of the doors analogy: it reminds us how certain human artifacts can come to be regarded as things found or forged in nature, facts to be discovered or unearthed by human investigators. It has been crucial for those who make much of certain differences among humans to portray those differences as givens that humanity disregards at its peril.[17]

Classificatory names on doors have an important kind of official status: while they reflect the particular purposes of powerful members of human communities (purposes that may be shared by less powerful members, a point to which we shall return below), they at the same time obscure those purposes through the suggestion that the categories are uncreated, that they exist in themselves. In this view, each of us is either man or woman, either white or Black or brown, either Jewish or Christian, heterosexual or gay or lesbian,

16. It is not without reason that trustees of colleges and universities typically don't have campus offices.

17. Sociobiology is perhaps the most recent field to define human differences in this way. For another illustration of the creation of difference in the guise of discovering it, see the legal and medical documents collected by Michel Foucault together with the memoirs of a nineteenth-century French hermaphrodite in *Herculine Barbin* (New York: Random, 1980).

and that like it or not, one or some of those elements of our identities are more fundamentally descriptive of us than others. No doubt it is true that once those categories have been created, and once social and political and economic institutions have been built around them, there will be criteria in accordance with which we can say with assurance into what categories any particular person fits. And even if we had no part in the creation of such categories, if we have learned the ways of our society, we have learned which doors we will be expected to pass through. Indeed, we may joyfully embrace the identities they draw attention to.

Our learning of the categories and where we fit into them is unlikely to include learning about their historical character. That is, it is unlikely that we learn about the point at which a category came into being. (For example, the creation of "homosexual" as a category of person as opposed to a category of action dates apparently from the late nineteenth century).[18] It is also unlikely that we learn about the battles over what the categories mean (for example, battles over definitions among white men about what constitutes "Negro blood," or over definitions among contemporary Blacks in the United States over what constitutes being "Black").[19]

If we think of such distinctions in terms of the doors, then we might begin to ask a number of questions that would challenge the assumption that the distinctions we make among people are simple and straightforward responses to the distinctions found among them in nature. (It also helps to challenge a somewhat more complicated assumption: that the categories are indeed created for human purposes, but not for those of any particular group—as if all humans have the same authority over the creation and maintenance of the categories.) First of all, the door imagery implies some ambiguity about whether the process of going (or being made to go) through the doors represents a recognition of differences among people or a creation of them. Insofar as there are criteria for the appropriateness of particular people passing through particular doors, and insofar as those who pass through and those who monitor their passage seem to have no questions about the passage, it looks as if the doors simply represent a moment at which people are processed in accordance with characteristics that inhere in them. More-

18. For a recent discussion of this, see Ian Hacking, "Making Up People," in *Reconstructing Individualism*, ed. Thomas C. Heller, Morton Sosna, and David E. Wellerby (Stanford: Stanford University Press, 1986), 222–36. See also "On 'Compulsory Heterosexuality and Lesbian Existence': Defining the Issues," a collection of comments by Ann Ferguson, Jacquelyn N. Zita, and Kathryn Pyne Addelson, *Signs* 7 (1981): 158–99.

19. See, for example, "Woman Seeks Change in Racial Designation," *The New York Times*, Friday, 28 November 1984, A28. Also see Michael Omi and Howard Winant, "By the Rivers of Babylon: Race in the United States," parts 1 and 2, *Socialist Review* 71 and 72 (1983).

over, the monitors or guards seem to be there, not to keep making up categories, but to make sure that the people whom the guards know (and whom the guards assume know they know) to belong to one category rather than another go through the right door. A further but only occasionally called-upon role of the monitors is to decide about borderline cases.

On the other hand, the process by which people are channeled into one category rather than another can be seen as creating distinctions. We need to ask why people are being processed through these doors, whether social and political positions and privileges are at stake in this processing. We need also to inquire whether (and how) those subject to such processing ever challenge the categories or their significance. It is important to know whether they are punished for questioning the appropriateness of the categories or challenging the authority of those who seem to have most power over the maintenance of them. Whether categories come into and go out of existence, and if so, why. We must ask whether there are battles over what the categories ought to be, or over what they mean, or over who gets to decide these issues.

We may also want to know more about just how people are processed through the doors: by this we mean to ask not simply whether people resist going through or help others who resist going through; but also whether if they do resist they are forced through anyway. It is not enough to know whether people do something without resistance to decide whether they are made to do it. For we can come to do without apparent coercion what we were encouraged to do and punished for not doing from an early age. We have to ask what happens when we do not do what we are expected to. I should be wary of describing my actions as "willing" if I would have been punished for not acting in that way. The existence of known punishments for failure to do something strongly suggests that one is being made to do that thing—that in the absence of such punishments one probably wouldn't do it.

In light of such considerations we might go back to some questions raised earlier in this chapter about what one knows when one answers such questions as "Are you a man or a woman?" "Are you white or Black or . . . ?" To answer the first by saying "I am a woman" is to agree to what one understands to be the criteria for being a woman and to say that one meets those criteria. But one could be challenged either on the grounds that one isn't using the right criteria or on the grounds that one doesn't meet them. And insofar as the doors analogy helps us to see the extent to which gender identity is, not only as de Beauvoir argued the ongoing creation of a society (women are made, not born), but something over which some members of society have more authority than others, my claim about being a woman may well be challenged by those who have that authority. Sojourner Truth had to argue for the proposition that she was a "woman." Someone who refuses to indicate whether one is a "woman" or a "man," or someone who refuses to specify their "race" or "ethnicity" on a census form, may be punished by those who distribute such forms. Some women may be told by white feminists that they aren't properly distinguishing their voices as "women" from their voices as "Afro-Americans" or "Jews" or members of the "working class."[20] Jan Morris decided that rather than contest the meaning of "woman" or "man" she would change her bodily appearance and her gestures and "life-style" so that she would be counted as a "woman."[21] (I don't know what it says on her passport about her sexual identity, or who exactly is in the position to decide what she is entitled to put there, but I feel certain she uses bathrooms marked "women" and presents herself in social life as a woman—indeed, as an upper-middle-class white English-woman.)

Given the possibility of questions about and challenges to the categories, it may be more important to ask, not what I know when I answer such questions about my identity, but what I acquiesce in, what I do not resist, when I agree to answer them. I am agreeing to some schema of identity, forged in accordance with some individual's or some group's or some society's classificatory purposes. Unless I register some kind of protest or qualification, I accept (willingly or not) the appropriateness of the classification and the significance attached to it. So, for example, I might gladly use the word "woman" to refer to myself but try in concert with others to resist what I take to be the prevailing meaning of the term or the prevailing significance attached to it. Or I might think it important to resist a term altogether—for example, "handicapped." I might think it important to embrace joyfully a term such as "lesbian" or "Black" and to try with others to invest it with new meaning.

Insofar as we don't regard the kinds of exercises in which we are asked to indicate our gender, race, and so on, as problematic, we may have forgotten to ask how we came to use those categories to refer to ourselves or to others. It may seem to us as if who we are, who others are, and what we do and don't have in common are matters of simple observation. Perhaps because we learn the categories so early and are continually asked to reflect our knowledge of them, they seem unproblematic. Ease of application of the categories can be confused with justified certainty about how "natural" they are.

20. See Maria Lugones and Elizabeth V. Spelman, "Have We Got a Theory for You!" in *Women's Studies International Forum* 6 (1983) 573–81.

21. Jan Morris, *Conundrum* (New York: Signet, 1974).

Furthermore, if we think about identities and points of similarity and difference as things that are always being negotiated and challenged, we may think more about ways in which these categories depend upon the particular purposes of those who create and maintain them. This is not to say that it is easy to identify those who create and maintain them. It often seems as if none of us created these categories but all of us help to maintain them. But insofar as we feel moved to do battle over them, we exhibit both a sense of being subject to them against our will and a sense of being able to do something about the power they have over the articulation of our identities and thus over our social and political positions to the extent that they depend on those identities.

In some ways it ought to be quite surprising that describing who we are and how we are like and unlike others is not always the straightforward process it appears to be. For first of all, the ability to compare and contrast things by seeing what categories they do or don't fit into is crucial to thinking and to using language. Second, in societies in which great significance is attached to sexual, racial, and class categories, we learn early and well which of those categories we and everyone around us belong to. Indeed, most of the time we probably are showing ourselves and others which of these categories we belong to, even when we are not explicitly saying so. Unless categorization is made problematic for us, we are not likely to raise questions about the categories we use; and it seems likely that the more a society has invested in its members' getting the categories right, the more occasions there will be for reinforcing them, and the fewer occasions there will be for raising questions about them.[22]

As noted right at the beginning of this book, feminists have rightly been concerned with how philosophers and other thinkers have spoken with great authority about the differences between men and women and what social and political significance those differences have. We have tried to lay bare how neatly their classificatory schemes conflate being a man with being human, how in subtle or not so subtle ways they show us that women are inferior specimens of humanity. But we feminists have not been free of classificatory schemes either—how could we be?—and many of us have not been attentive to the political priorities and race and class privileges imported by the schemes we use. The imagery of the doors can help us review some of the ways in which this importation works.

22. There will be tension between these two things, since being too obvious about reinforcing categories may make people suspicious.

III

According to Plato, in order to create and maintain the best possible state it is absolutely crucial that someone know the "proper divisions and distinctions" among its various members.[23] Such a person would know that the distinction between philosopher-rulers and cobblers is much more significant than that between male and female. Thus Plato might arrange the doors in the following fashion:

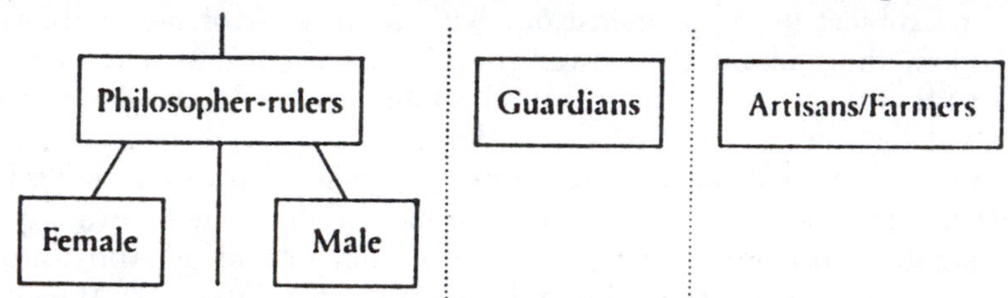

The purpose of such a division is the recognition of differences necessary for the creation of a just state. The divisions will be maintained by the philosopher-rulers with the aid of the guardians; and if child-rearing is done the way Plato prescribes, everyone will acquire the habits and desires appropriate to one's role, perpetuating the structure of the society. That is, people will come to understand that they wouldn't be better off trying to do the work assigned another group, that real happiness lies in knowing what one's nature is and doing the kind of work appropriate to it.

Where would Plato place slaves in this arrangement? Their position seems to be so taken for granted by Plato that they are hardly mentioned. In terms of the doors imagery, this is like finding no door with the term by which you expect to be called (whether or not you contest it). We may well wonder whether, whatever the difficulties about being classified in a particular way, there are worse difficulties in store for those not deemed worthy of the notice classificatory schemes provide.

Nor does the above schema capture everything Plato says about women. It does seem accurate as a representation of what Plato said about the possibility of female philosopher-rulers and their position vis-à-vis male philosopher-rulers as well as males belonging to other groups. But it leaves out what he took to be typical of Athenian women. We know he did not think of them as belonging to the same category as women who would be philosopher-rulers; the distinction between such women and other women was as important for Plato as that between males who would be philosopher-rulers and males who would be artisans or farmers. For Plato, the distinction between men and women is phrased in terms of distinc-

23. *Republic* 454a.

tions among philosopher-rulers, guardians, artisans. Women who are philosopher-rulers have an entirely different nature from those who are not, even though all women are alike in their bodily configuration. So were we to speak as if gender is the primary consideration in Plato's views of "women," we would not simply give an inaccurate account of his views; we would give notice that the only women worth knowing about are those belonging to a particular group. We would take Plato's views about an elite group of women to be all there is to his views about women.

On the face of it, Aristotle might arrange the doors in the following manner:

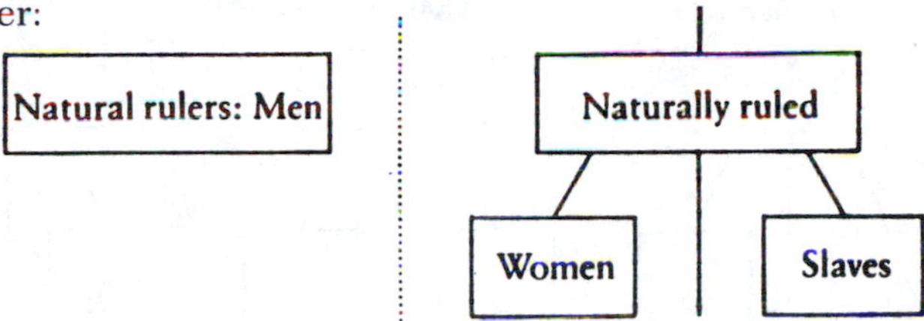

The distinctions between the rulers and the ruled are simply those intended by nature, according to Aristotle; and any well-ordered community will respect them, since they correspond to the different functions different people are fit to perform in the community.

But as we saw, there is something misleading about this way of representing Aristotle's views. First of all, there is the somewhat nagging problem of whether Aristotle thought there were some men who were by nature neither natural rulers nor naturally ruled. But more important for our purposes, the category "slaves" obscures the fact that even on Aristotle's own reckoning some of those slaves were female. So Aristotle, like Plato, really has two different categories of females or women. Indeed, in effect he puts females in two different gender categories: females with the gender "woman" and females with no gender at all. A slave woman trying to go through the door Aristotle marked "women" wouldn't be allowed through; she would have to go through the one marked "slave," along with males who are slaves.

As with Plato, so with Aristotle: We cannot fully represent his views about the significance of sex or gender by using the schema according to which the most significant distinction among people is that between men and women. It would be misleading to imply that we could get at his views about women by focusing simply on the distinctions he draws between men and women of a particular group. Moreover, it would show that we had decided that what he says about female slaves isn't important in trying to come to understand his views about the significance of sex and gender, that we only need to understand what he says about "free" women.

The tension we explored in de Beauvoir's account of the condition of women can be represented usefully through the analogy of the doors. On the one hand, de Beauvoir says much to suggest that in order to understand the condition of women we have to look at them in the context of the various racial and class groups to which they belong. That is, we have to look at the relative privileges they have vis-à-vis one another, which might be done in the following way:

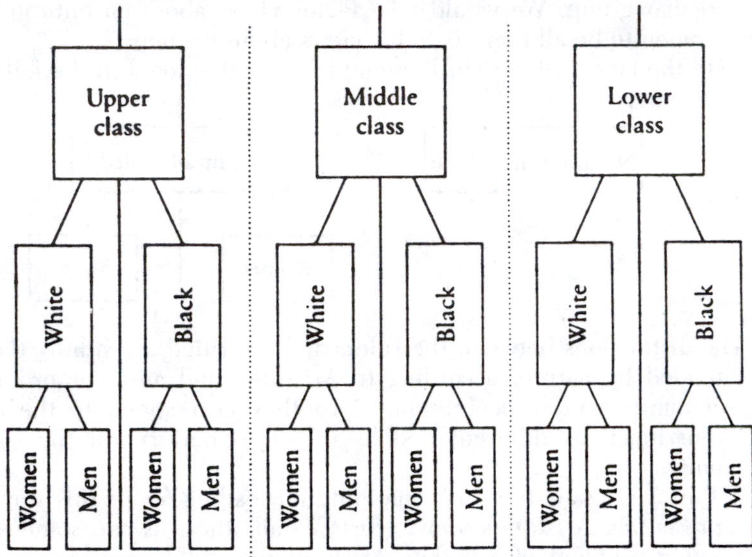

This is a way of representing her claim that in order to describe sexual privilege properly we have to keep the race and class of the men and women constant.

On the other hand, she also describes as the condition of women something that might best be represented by the schema in which the most important distinction is that between men and women. More accurately, given the contrasts she draws early in the book, it looks as if the first bank of doors includes not simply two categories

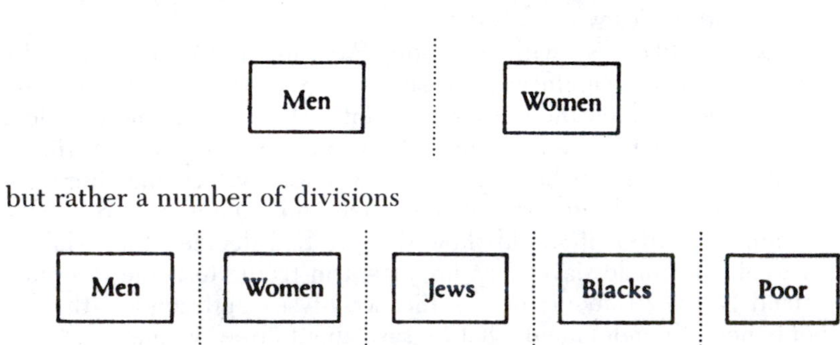

but rather a number of divisions

and so forth. Indeed, this latter schema best represents her conflation of the condition of "women" with that of white, middle-class, Christian women, for when she talks generally about relations between "men and women" she can only be referring to men and women who are not Jewish or Black or poor.

Which schema best represents what Chodorow has to say about distinctions among humans and the significance they have? The kind of similarity and differences she is interested in is the sense of self and relational stance toward others that humans develop; the significant division in this regard, she says, is

Or does she? Her claim is actually more cautious: It is that though there are interesting and important differences in the way different cultures assign work, they all assign it according to gender and in all cases women are assigned the major work of parenting. Hence her view is more like that represented in the schema according to which we ought to look at gender differences in the context of other differences.

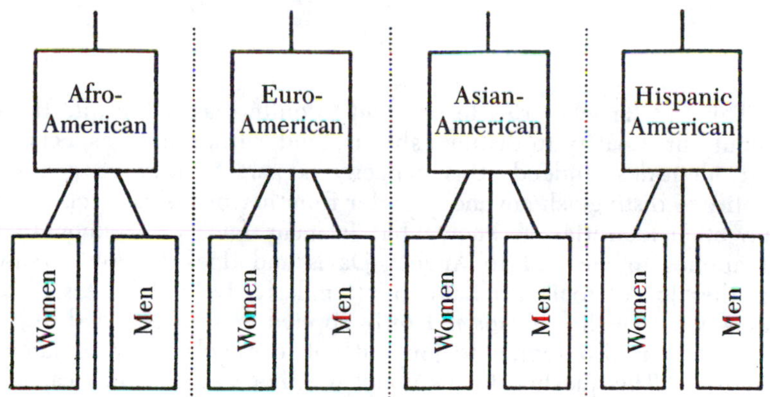

However, Chodorow implies that for the purpose of her study we can ignore the cultural differences: for the same thing that is true of the relationship between men and women of one group will be true of that between men and women of any other group. Mothers always do most of the parenting, and they do it always in the context of sexism. In this sense, the distinction between the first and second schemas collapses. And when it does, we lose sight of important features of the context of gender relations only visible in the second schema—namely, that women mother in a social and political context in which they not only are distinguished from men, but are, along with men of their same cultural background, distinguished from men and women of other cultural backgrounds.

It is also revealing to try to use the doors to represent Chodorow's fledgling account of the relation between sexism and other forms of oppression such as racism and classism. According to such an account, we recall, the attitudes that men have toward women as Other provide the model for the attitudes they come to have toward everyone else. Thus the relation between men and women in any one group is the same as the relation between any one group of men and women to any other group of men and women when one group is racist or classist toward the other. But this would mean that the relationship between whites and Blacks is in important ways the same as that between white men and white women, as well as that between Black men and Black women. . . . [F]or a variety of reasons this is an odd position to hold. It also suggests that white men and white women have the same attitude toward Black men and Black women as white men have toward white women (and as Black men have toward Black women). But if that is the case, Chodorow ought to pay more attention than she does to racist and classist attitudes among women and not portray them as belonging solely to men (or a particular group of men).

IV

This . . . [article] tries to respond to quite reasonable questions about our capacity to distinguish our gender from other aspects of our identities. Indeed, this capacity is part of a more general ability to distinguish anyone's gender from her or his race, class, or any other identities. To know what "woman" means is to know that it applies to me and to Angela Davis and doesn't apply to my brother Jon or to James Baldwin. (Similarly, I couldn't be said to know what "white" means if I only applied it to myself and didn't know how it also applies to Jon but not to Angela Davis or James Baldwin.) The question for us is not whether we have such capacities but what, if anything, follows from them.

It certainly doesn't follow that there is an essential "womanness" that Angela and I share and that Jon and James lack. That is, what makes it true that Angela and I are women is not some "woman" substance that is the same in each of us and interchangeable between us. Selves are not made up of separable units of identity strung together to constitute a whole person. It is not as if there is a goddess somewhere who made lots of little identical "woman" units and then, in order to spruce up the world a bit for herself, decided to put some of those units in black bodies, some in white bodies, some in the bodies of kitchen maids in seventeenth-century France, some in the bodies of English, Israeli, and Indian prime ministers.

Indeed, positing an essential "womanness" has the effect of making women inessential in a variety of ways. First of all, if there is an essential womanness that all women have and have always had, then we needn't know anything about any woman in particular. For the details of her situation and her experience are irrelevant to her being a woman. Thus if we want to understand what "being a woman" means, we needn't investigate her individual life or any other woman's individual life. All those particulars become inessential to her being and our understanding of her being a woman. And so she also becomes inessential in the sense that she is not needed in order to produce the "story of woman." If all women have the same story "as women," we don't need a chorus of voices to tell the story.

Moreover, to think of "womanness" in this way obscures three related facts about the meaning of being a woman: first of all, that whatever similarities there are between Angela Davis and me, they exist in the context of differences between us; second, that there is ongoing debate about what effect such differences have on those similarities (different arrangements of the doors express different positions on this matter); third, not all participants in that debate get equal air time or are invested with equal authority.

The problem with the "story of man" was that women couldn't recognize themselves in it. So those who produce the "story of woman" want to make sure they appear in it. The best way to ensure that is to be the storyteller and hence to be in a position to decide which of all the many facts about women's lives ought to go into the story, which ought to be left out. Essentialism works well in behalf of these aims, aims that subvert the very process by which women might come to see where and how they wish to make common cause. For essentialism invites me to take what I understand to be true of me "as a woman" for some golden nugget of womanness all women have as women; and it makes the participation of other women inessential to the production of the story. How lovely: the many turn out to be one, and the one that they are is me.

SUGGESTIONS FOR FURTHER READING

Philosophical Analysis

Durant, W. J. "Bertrand Russell on Marriage and Morals." In *Adventures in Genius.* New York: Simon and Schuster, 1931.

Ferguson, Ann. "Androgyny as an Ideal for Human Development." In *Feminism and Philosophy,* ed. by Mary Vetterling-Braggin, Frederick A. Elliston, and Jane English. Totowa, N.J.: Littlefield, Adams & Co., 1977, pp. 45–69.

Govier, Trudy. "Woman's Place." *Philosophy* 49 (1974), pp. 303–9.

Hein, Hilde. "Woman: A Philosophical Analysis." *The Holy Cross Quarterly* 4 (Fall 1971), pp. 18–23.

Kohl, Marvin. "Bertrand Russell's Characterization of Benevolent Love." *Russell* 12 (Winter 1992–93), pp. 117–34.

Korsmeyer, Carolyn. "The Hidden Joke: Generic Use of Masculine Terminology." In *Feminism and Philosophy,* ed. by Mary Vetterling-Braggin, Frederick A. Elliston, and Jane English. Totowa, N.J.: Littlefield, Adams & Co., 1977, pp. 138–53.

Lucas, Joseph R. "Because You Are a Woman." *Philosophy* 48 (1973), pp. 161–71.

Moran, Margaret, "Bertrand Russell Meets His Muse: The Impact of Lady Ottoline Morrell (1911–12)." *Russell* 11 (Winter 1991/92), pp. 180–92.

Moulton, Janice. "The Myth of the Neutral 'Man.'" In *Feminism and Philosophy,* ed. by Mary Vetterling-Braggin, Frederick A. Elliston, and Jane English. Totowa, N.J.: Littlefield, Adams & Co., 1977, pp. 124–53.

Munitz, Milton K. *Contemporary Analytic Philosophy.* Riverside, N.Y.: Macmillan, 1981.

Padia, Chandrakala. "Is Russell a Political Philosopher: A Critique of His Critiques." *Russell* 6 (Winter 1986/1987), pp. 134–43.

Pierce, Christine and Collins, Margery L. "Holes and Slime: Sexism in Sartre's Psychoanalysis." *The Philosophical Forum* 5 (1973–74), pp. 1–2.

Russell, Bertrand. "The Status of Women." *The Bertrand Russell Archives,* 1974, pp. 3–12.

Spelman, Elizabeth V. "On Treating Persons as Persons." *Ethics* 88 (Jan. 1978), pp. 150–61.

Tait, Katharine. "Russell and Feminism." *Russell* 29 (1978), pp. 5–16.

Trebilcot, Joyce. "Two Forms of Androgynism." In *Feminism and Philosophy,* ed. by Mary Vetterling-Braggin, Frederick A. Elliston, and Jane English. Totowa, N.J.: Littlefield, Adams & Co., 1977, pp. 70–78.

———. *Dyke Ideas: Process, Politics, Daily Life.* New York: State University of New York, 1994.

Valian, Virginia. "Linguistics and Feminisms." In *Feminism and Philosophy,* ed. by Mary Vetterling-Braggin, Frederick A. Elliston, and Jane English. Totowa, N.J.: Littlefield, Adams & Co., 1977, pp. 154–66.

III
FEMINIST PERSPECTIVES

THE DIVERSITY OF FEMINISM

Those unfamiliar with feminist literature sometimes think that the term "feminism" represents a single philosophical orientation. They are wrong. Just as there are multiple approaches to philosophy, there are different versions of feminism, embodying philosophical orientations that may be at odds with each other. Typically, the different forms of feminism agree in rejecting the oppression of women in theory or in practice, but they do not all agree in their views of women, the relationship of women to men, or how to promote equality between the sexes. A liberal version of feminism, for example, is at odds with a socialist version of feminism because the liberal view attributes more importance to individual liberty than to social equality, but both versions maintain that women should have opportunities and advantages comparable to their male counterparts.

The following selections are intended to illustrate the diversity of feminist accounts of women. Inevitably, they represent different views of human beings and of men as well. Although most feminists insist that women's experience is crucial to their analysis, at least one version of feminism repudiates attempts to conceptualize woman or women as inadequate and misleading. Some versions critique other versions of feminism as neglectful of women of color and of women whose cultural background differs from that which dominates Western philosophy. Still others insist that understanding woman or women requires a sense not only of relationships between women and men, but also of relationships among human beings, other animals, and their common environment.

Many of these selections draw on the work of authors included in previous sections of the book. They do so explicitly or implicitly, in either case selecting those concepts or arguments that refute or support their own point of view. In most cases, the argument is carried forward to a new level because the author is interested in developing her own account of feminism. Since all versions of feminism address or assume an understanding of women, scrutiny of the different perspectives is required for thorough, critical assessment of earlier as well as current sources.

ZILLAH R. EISENSTEIN

The Radical Future of Liberal Feminism

It is an oversimplification of liberal feminism to say that it is merely a reflection of the manipulation of women by the state. The hold that liberal feminism has on women reflects women's consciousness in a society that presents the ideology of liberalism as its world view. Therefore, the concern here is to examine why Friedan and the liberal feminist position she represents had such force in the 1960s and, to a lesser extent, in the 1970s. Although critics of Friedan's work argue that it applies to the white middle-class woman alone, I believe it can appeal to any woman who identifies with middle-class values and the liberal ideas of equality of opportunity and independence. One does not have to be white or middle class to aspire to these values, and therefore the ideas of liberal feminism are accepted by more women than is commonly thought. The political appeal of Friedan's writing lies in this fact; her analysis addresses the liberal individual consciousness of a majority of American women. . . .

THE LIBERAL FEMINIST MYSTIQUE

Friedan's analysis of women's oppression is best expressed through her discussion of the "feminine mystique." "The feminine mystique permits, even encourages, women to ignore the question of their identity."[1] It defines woman in terms of her femininity, and this is measured in relation to being a mother and a wife, not in terms of being an independent individual.[2] "The problem is always being the children's mommy, or the minister's wife and never being myself."[3] The concept of the autonomous independent self, which originates in liberal thought, appears once again in the feminist demand for selfhood. This time, the conception is not limited to a notion of citizen's rights but takes on a psychological dimension due to the influence of Freudian thinking. As a result, woman's self-identity takes center stage in Friedan's conception of the independent woman. She is concerned about woman's loss of identity.[4] She believes that the feminine mystique limits and curtails woman's

1. Betty Friedan, *The Feminine Mystique* (New York: Dell, 1963), p. 64.

2. Ibid., p. 41.

3. Ibid., p. 23.

4. Ibid., p. 312.

development as a person, with a separate ego and identity, in much the same way nineteenth-century feminists feared Victorian ideology's impact on woman's sexuality.

Friedan presents this problem, which is particular and specific to the suburban middle-class woman's identity, as though it is woman's problem in general. "It is my thesis that the core of the problem for women today is not sexual but a problem of identity—a stunting or evasion of growth that is perpetuated by the feminine mystique."[5] The feminine mystique is a generalized problem to the degree all women can identify with it as an ideology about femininity that applies to all women across economic class and race lines. Friedan misses the point that in actuality it applies differently to women of different economic classes and races, and that the way one relates to it is not a matter of individual choice. Friedan also seems to accept more of the picture of the nonworking woman presented in the mystique as true than, in reality, it was.

By the time Friedan wrote *The Feminine Mystique,* more than one-third of the nation's workers were women; 54 percent of these women were married, and 33 percent were mothers.[6] Actually, throughout the 1950s, women from middle-income families entered the labor force more rapidly than any other group.[7] By 1956, 70 percent of all families earning between $7,000 and $15,000 had two wage earners in the family.[8] The period from shortly before World War II through the 1960s showed a 34 percent increase in the number of women workers.

In 1945 women already accounted for 36 percent of the nation's labor force. By 1960, 42 percent of the families in the United States had two workers.[9] Since World War II, the majority of women entering the labor force have been married women.[10] Friedan discusses these women workers as if they were holding part-time jobs that were not financially essential to their families.[11] The data do

5. Ibid., p. 69.

6. Judith Hole and Ellen Levine, *Rebirth of Feminism* (New York: Quadrangle, 1971), p. 18.

7. Sara Evans, *Personal Politics* (New York: Knopf, 1979), p. 8.

8. Ibid., p. 9.

9. Congressional Quarterly, *The Women's Movement, Achievement and Effects* (Washington, D.C.: Government Printing Office, 1977), p. 27.

10. U.S. Department of Labor Employment Standards Administration, Women's Bureau, *Handbook on Women Workers,* 1975 (Washington, D.C.: Government Printing Office, 1975), p. 10.

11. Friedan, p. 13.

not bear this out. Most women who worked earned together *with* their husbands between $7,000 and $15,000 a year.

Although the "feminine mystique" presented the picture of woman as a nonworker, woman's wage labor was much more central to the economy than Friedan recognizes, even for middle-class women.[12] If she had recognized this, she would have been able to appreciate the need for connecting her analysis of the "feminine mystique" to woman's actual relation to the public (market) sphere. My criticism of Friedan is not only that she analyzes the white middle-class woman, to the exclusion of the working class and other racial groups, but that she wrongly interprets much of what is actually happening to middle-class women as well. If Friedan had looked at the *reality* of life for black women, working-class women, and the wage-earning working- or middle-class woman, she would have realized that it is not enough to ask for equality of opportunity in the public world without calling for a reorganization of the so-called private world of the family. The double-day of work, which results when the market is opened to women and at the same time the responsibilities of the home remain theirs, is no solution to woman's problem.

Friedan leaves women vulnerable to redefinitions of the feminine mystique because she does not explain the economic and social origins of the "mystique." It is therefore difficult to understand the reasons for the "mystique" and the reasons why it will continually be redefined in terms of the new emerging needs of capitalist patriarchy. As a result, Friedan cannot help women uncover the different and changing forms of the "feminine mystique" or prepare them to fight against changes within the "mystique" that are not in their interest.

She sees woman's acceptance of the feminine mystique, not the system of patriarchy and its economic expression in capitalism, as the greatest obstruction to woman's development. Because she has no structural analysis of woman's oppression, Friedan inadvertently ends up blaming women themselves for their condition. She asks,

12. Friedan frankly admits that she is speaking about the middle-class woman because it is this woman, according to Friedan, who is facing an identity crisis. For a discussion of some of these issues, but from a perspective that recognizes the married middle-class woman as a worker, see Milton Cantor and Bruce Laurie, eds., *Class, Sex and the Woman Worker* (Westport, Conn.: Greenwood, 1977); *Conference on Work in the Lives of Married Women, Columbia University, 1957* (New York: Columbia University Press, 1958); Jean Curtis, *Working Mothers* (New York: Doubleday, 1976); Ivan Nye and Lois Wladis Hoffman, *The Employed Mother in America* (Chicago: Rand McNally, 1963); Ann Oakley, *The Sociology of Housework* (Bath, England: Pitman, 1974); idem, *Woman's Work, The Housewife, Past and Present* (New York: Pantheon, 1974); Sheila Rowbotham, *Woman's Consciousness, Man's World* (London: Penguin, 1973); and Robert Smuts, *Women and Work in America* (New York: Columbia University Press, 1959).

"Why with the removal of all the legal, political, economic, and educational barriers that once kept woman from being man's equal, a person in her own right, an individual free to develop her own potential, should she accept this new image? . . ."[13] Instead of asking what the origins of the feminine mystique are, Friedan asks only why women accept it.

Although the cultural oppression of women is seriously harmful, Friedan makes it seem as though these ideas about femininity alone completely create the oppression of women. "I think all of these resistances are not that great. Our own self-denigration of ourselves as women and perhaps our own fears are the main problem."[14] The "feminine mystique," as a real ideological force, oppresses women in that they internalize these values. It then curtails women's options and by doing so impinges on their daily lives. But ideas do not come from the air. Their life force is not found in themselves or merely within those who believe them. There must be real needs in the society that reproduce these ideas and give them new life. The human mind plays a part in the process of reproducing ideas, but its part is affected by the cultural, economic, and sexual relations of society. Without connecting the "feminine mystique" to its ideological role—its political purpose in reproducing the relations of patriarchy—it is impossible to understand how it functions as part of the sexual oppression of patriarchy.

But Friedan lacks this understanding and therefore misconstrues the impact woman's liberation would have on both men and women. She thinks women fear it for what it will demand of them and thinks men support it for the freedom it will bring them.[15] This belief shows that Friedan does not see women's liberation involving a struggle for power. According to her view, men have nothing to lose and women have only to take the risk. Woman must question her own self-image and then act on this newly found independence. According to Friedan, there appear to be no constraints upon woman except the limitations she places on herself.

Although the conception one has of oneself makes activity possible, changing the conception of woman is not merely an individual matter. After all, one's conception of oneself as a woman is part of the larger reality of one's definition as a member of the sex-class woman. One's actual daily life activity affects the way one can think about oneself. To perceive oneself as active, independent, and creative, it helps, in fact, to be involved in creative activity. Thinking

13. Friedan, p. 61.

14. Betty Friedan, *It Changed My Life* (New York: Dell, 1977), p. 103.

15. Ibid., p. 40.

and acting affect each other. Friedan helps us understand that how we think about ourselves is important, but she does not help us understand that individual yearning is not enough. Individual activity is racially, economically, and sexually ordered with limitations and constraints. Woman does not have the freedom to act in the way Friedan assumes she does within this unequal structuring of patriarchal society. A woman may not have the education; she may have children to care for; she may not be able to earn a living wage.

Friedan envisions woman's problem as "a massive crisis of identity."[16] According to her, the attitudes of the 1950s caused women to seek the comfort of home and children. "After the loneliness of war and the unspeakableness of the bomb, against the frightening uncertainty, the cold immensity of the changing world, women as well as men sought the comforting reality of home and children."[17] Friedan's discussion of the feminine mystique suffers from an idealism that treats social reality as though it were made up of only ideas. In this view, social change requires only a change of ideas and consciousness. Therefore, when Friedan speaks of the dependence of the housewife created by the feminine mystique, she speaks of her dependence as though it were primarily a problem for woman's mind. "They are chains made up of mistaken ideas and misinterpreted facts, of incomplete truths and unreal choices."[18]

I do not mean to argue that women are merely passive subjects within a system of sexual oppression. Neither are they the free actors, which Friedan has made them. Given Friedan's lack of a power analysis, she thinks men have something to gain in women's equality. I would agree. But they also have much to lose—the sexual privilege they enjoy within the sexual hierarchy that divides home and work. Once men lose their male privilege, they will have to share the burdens and responsibilities of childrearing and domestic labor. They will lose privileges and freedoms that have existed as a result of patriarchal oppression. The destruction of a system of power and oppression does not result in everyone gaining equally and in the same way.

Because, for Friedan, so much rests in the realm of ideas (disconnected from the social structures they protect), she can believe that education is a major vehicle of social change. To free women from their secondary status, men will have to accept equal responsibility for the rearing of children. How this happens, or specifically what this means, is never made clear. However, she does see

16. Ibid., p. 23.

17. Friedan, *Feminine Mystique*, p. 174.

18. Ibid., p. 26.

this first of all as a challenge to education.[19] She does not view the reorganization and rearrangement of the care of children as involving a question of power and privilege, although in *The Feminine Mystique* she often demonstrates that this is in fact the case. She therefore thinks education can substitute for the struggle necessary to rearrange power relations. In speaking of the need to educate men to their childrearing role, she writes: "Man and society have to be educated to accept their responsibility for that role as well. And this is first of all a challenge to education."[20]

Although educating people to a new consciousness is part of social change, Friedan has not gone any further than Wollstonecraft here. A serious challenge to the ideas must *include* a challenge to the social structures they protect. Although Friedan does address the exclusionary nature of the female-centered parenting family, she does not discuss its fundamental reorganization as necessary to creating equality for women. It is not enough to ask men to help rear children without understanding that one is speaking of a fundamental reorganization of society. This will involve men in the *equal* sharing in the responsibility for child care. The entire social organization of the way people live their lives, as well as think about them, is involved.

The organization of wage labor, the relationship between home and work, the conception of public life, and the definition of masculine and feminine have to be completely rethought and restructured. This is the only way that daily life will be able to reinforce the idea of man as a childrearer. Friedan disconnects the relationship between ideas, social relations, power, and education in ways that merely obscure the way ideology affects and mirrors real life conditions.

It is therefore no surprise that Friedan emphasizes the importance of education as a way to broaden existing choices for women.[21] It would seem that Friedan should know that women are already overeducated for their jobs and for their work in the home. But she still offers individual solutions as political ones. My point is not that education is an irrelevant concern but that there is a difference between educating oneself—and helping others do the same—and accepting this as the political solution to the problem of woman's inequality. This liberal individualist attitude dominates her analysis.

19. Friedan, *Changed My Life*, p. 163.

20. Betty Friedan, "Our Revolution Is Unique," in *Voices of the New Feminism*, ed. Mary Lou Thompson (Boston: Beacon, 1970), p. 40.

21. Friedan, *Changed My Life*, p. 43.

As a result, Friedan often thinks that there is no political solution to an individual problem rather than understanding that there are no individual solutions to political problems.[22] The social connections between women are blurred so that Friedan thinks their only choice is to struggle individually. But this is not a totally accurate reading of Friedan because she does understand the necessity of political movement for women. In this sense, both her politics and her discussion of the "feminine mystique" recognize the social nature of woman's oppression, even though she usually reduces this problem to that of an individual's dilemma.

Friedan reflects these two tendencies when she argues that the educational attempts at social change must be backed up by women's struggle for political equality. Her conception of political equality, as I have noted, is narrow. It involves woman's equality within government, law, and the public arena in general. The problem that remains is that even when women are granted equality before the law, this does not necessarily create equality in their everyday lives. Women's inequality, rooted in her responsibility for rearing children, is not addressed (directly) by the law. Hence, equality before the law sidesteps this issue.

There are times when Friedan makes statements that beg for a fuller analysis. "It certainly did not occur to any of us then, even the most radical, that companies which made a big profit selling us all those washing machines, dryers, freezers and second cars, were overselling us on the bliss of domesticity in order to sell us more things."[23] But these insights remain underdeveloped in both *It Changed My Life* and her . . . article "Feminism Takes a New Turn."[24] In this article, she writes of the economic purposes the family fulfills for capitalist society. The problem is that there is little, if any, understanding on her part of the family as a unit of sexual oppression functioning in the interests of patriarchy. When Friedan asks, "Can American capitalism accommodate a strengthened, evolving American family?" she answers, "Why not? despite the rhetoric, the family has never ranked high on the American political agenda, except as a unit to which to sell things."[25]

22. Ti Grace Atkinson in *Amazon Odyssey* (New York: Links, 1974) has an excellent discussion of woman's oppression as a political problem needing a political solution.

23. Friedan, *Changed My Life*, p. 31.

24. Betty Friedan, "Feminism Takes a New Turn," *New York Times Magazine*, 18 November 1979, pp. 40–106.

25. Ibid., p. 106.

In her early writing of *The Feminine Mystique*, she recognized the importance of the patriarchal structure of the family, even if she did not term it as such. She criticizes Adlai Stevenson's commencement address at Smith College in 1955 for relegating woman's role to that of wife and mother and the family sphere. "Modern woman's participation in politics is through her role as wife and mother. . . . Women, especially educated women, have a unique opportunity to influence us, man and boy. The only problem is woman's failure to appreciate that her true part in the political crisis is as wife and mother."[26]

Friedan continued to write about the "feminine mystique," characterizing women as mothers and houseworkers with no independent lives, up until 1979. At this point, she recognized (although somewhat belatedly) that "the mystique" has changed. According to Friedan, the vision of the "super-professional" woman reflects the new cultural oppression of women. The interesting point is that Friedan does not discuss this new vision of woman as a redefinition of the "feminine mystique." She does not make the connections that would allow women to understand how this view of women reflects patriarchal ideology's manipulation of women's lives—their energy and their labor—as part of the same process of the 1950s and '60s. Without understanding that she is really criticizing her own analysis in *The Feminine Mystique*, which demanded woman's right to enter the public sphere, like men, she wrote in 1979:

> Why should women simply replace the glorification of domesticity with the glorification of work as their life and identity? Simply to reverse the roles of breadwinner and homemaker is no progress at all, not for women and not for men. The challenge of the 80's will be to transcend these polarities by creating new family patterns based on equality and full human identity for both sexes.[27]

Friedan is finally acknowledging the fact that the relationship between the family and the market needs discussion. She does not want to accept the relegation of women to the family sphere, but she does not want women to accept the ratrace of the market either. "Women's equality will have been for nothing if its beneficiaries, by trying to beat men at their old power games and aping their strenuous climb into and up that corporate ladder, fall into

26. Friedan, *Feminine Mystique*, p. 53.

27. Friedan, "Feminism Takes a New Turn," p. 98.

the traps men are beginning to escape."[28] Putting aside the above assumptions for the moment—that women's equality has been won or that men are beginning to escape the ugliness of the business world or that most working women are allowed to engage in the climb up the corporate ladder—it is not terribly clear what Friedan wants, other than to ease the pressures of the work world on women so that they will be free to choose motherhood if they wish it. "The great challenge we face in the 1980's is to frame a new agenda that makes it possible for women to be able to work and love in equality with men—and to choose, if they so desire, to have children."[29]

By 1979, Friedan argued that this challenge called for the restructuring of home and work life.[30] She defines this partially in terms of "balancing the demands of the workplace and the family" and "reconciling" the demands of family and career.[31] It remains unclear how one balances the demands between men and women within the hierarchical sexual structure of their homes and workforce. Friedan discusses reorganizing the workplace in terms of innovations like "flex-time," where one can arrange their starting and leaving hours according to their children's needs.[32] It is never clear whether this arrangement is supposed to ease women's double burden (of family and work) or significantly restructure *who* is responsible for child care and *how* this responsibility is carried out.

What happened throughout the 1960s and '70s was that the demands on women's time and for their labor increased. Instead of simply being mothers, as the "feminine mystique" presented women, today women are supposed to be "working mothers." They are to operate within the patriarchal sexual division of labor in both the public and private spheres. Although women have gained access to the public domain, they have done so while remaining responsible for the private life of their family members. Women are still defined by the sexual-class structure of their lives. As mothers, they have the added responsibility today to work for wages—to help feed, clothe, and educate their children. Unlike Friedan's description of the career and professional woman, well over two-thirds of the women in the labor force are wage laborers, not professionals climbing the corporate ladder. They are simply "work-

28. Ibid.

29. Ibid., p. 40.

30. Ibid., p. 92.

31. Ibid., p. 96.

32. Ibid.

ing mothers"; the "mystique" of the 1970s and '80s in new form. This time, instead of criticizing the mystique, Friedan ends up servicing it.

A CONCEPTION OF INDIVIDUALITY VS. LIBERAL INDIVIDUALISM FOR FEMINISM

In the late 1960s and early 1970s feminism revealed that a woman's problem was not merely a personal one; it was shared by many other women, in similar ways. Consciousness raising was an effective political strategy because of the social nature of woman's oppression. It helped unmask the social nature of woman's individual existence.[33] Becoming conscious as a feminist meant understanding that one was socially related to other women. A woman's feminist consciousness of herself as an individual was connected to her understanding of herself as part of a sexual class, women. Friedan discusses this reality when she says, "We identified as woman, with every woman."[34] She does not, however, see this statement as proof of the sex-class structure of society. Nor does she see the contradictions between her liberal individualism and the following statement: "But none of us could have found the power to organize a movement in ourselves alone."[35]

Whereas liberalism itself denies the connectedness and relatedness of individuals, liberal *feminism* cannot fully accept this view because its feminist priorities reflect an understanding of the social nature of woman's oppression. Although Friedan says she rejects the sex-class theory of woman's oppression, she cannot completely do so and remain a feminist. Without understanding woman's position qua other women, she would be unable to make the demands she does on behalf of women as a group. Liberal feminism, by dint of speaking of women as a group, is in contradiction with "the principles of liberalism," which do not see people as groups, only individuals. Therefore, her implicit acceptance of woman as part of a sexual class contradicts her explicit denial of it and her adherence to the liberal individualist theory of power.

The liberal individualist conception of human life disconnects one person from another and from the economic, sexual, and racial

33. For an excellent discussion of the radical-feminist and social conception of consciousness-raising, see Kathie Sarachild, "Consciousness Raising: A Radical Weapon," in Redstockings, *Feminist Revolution* (New Paltz, NY: Redstockings, 1975; reissued by Random House, 1978).

34. Friedan, *Changed My Life*, p. 110.

35. Ibid.

relations that define *his* (or her) life. Instead of seeing connection and relatedness between people, between politics and economics, between ideology and actual social constraints, they separate all these. The view of people or things as separate supports the dichotomized view of male and female worlds, public and private life, and politics as government, disconnected from the power relations of patriarchy, capitalism, and racism. This is the individualist view of liberalism that one must transcend as a feminist if one hopes to create the real equity between men and women.

At the same time that we can learn from Friedan that the ideology of liberal individualism is insufficient for a theory of women's liberation, we can recognize the necessity of a theory of individuality within Western feminism. This recognizes the individualist nature of Western liberal societies and the necessity that feminist theory must first recognize this before it can transcend it. I am writing of a feminist individualism that recognizes the necessity of independence and autonomy within women's (and men's) lives. Feminist politics requires a social collectivity that recognizes the independence and the interconnectedness of women. *This theory of individualism must recognize the individual character of our social nature and the social nature of our individuality.*

An understanding of the interconnection of power relations and the relatedness of human beings, each to the other, is also necessary to develop a social theory of feminist individuality. Once one understands that woman is embedded in a series of social relations, one sees the necessity of mapping out the relationship between one's individual life and the social and political structure that defines it. Only in this way can the real limitations of sex, race, and economic class on one's individuality be specified. In this way, a conception of woman's individuality will recognize her social and individual self.

Friedan sees the question of individualism for women as requiring "free choice" about decisions that affect their lives, such as abortion, and day care. Woman must be free to choose motherhood or abortion.[36] Child-care centers and maternity leaves are necessary for women to freely choose motherhood.[37] Friedan herself recognizes the social needs women have if they are to achieve individuality, even if she seems limited to the ideology of the liberal individualism most of the time. She sees abortion as "the final essential right of full personhood for women"[38] and knows it is a

36. Friedan, "Our Revolution Is Unique," p. 35.

37. Friedan, *Changed My Life*, p. 157.

38. Ibid., p. 167.

social as well as a personal question. Abortion raises the issue of women's individual right to self-determination, but it is also a social decision in that one does not decide how to exercise one's individual right to self-determination in a vacuum.

The social nature of woman's oppression shows that it is not an individual problem, but oppression is rather a socially constructed reality of which the individual is only a part. In other words, one can understand woman's oppression only by seeing woman's position in relation to other women, in relation to men, in relation to housework, in relation to childrearing. Being aware of the oppression of woman is understanding the social relations that define the total existence of being a woman. To the extent that feminism requires the recognition of woman's life within a sex class (however implicit and unformulated this understanding is), feminism lays the basis for the move beyond *liberal* individualism. And to the degree [that] feminism requires a recognition of the individuality of women (and men), it assures a place for the individual in the social collectivity.

HEIDI I. HARTMANN

The Unhappy Marriage of Marxism and Feminism: Towards a More Progressive Union

The "marriage" of marxism and feminism has been like the marriage of husband and wife depicted in English common law: marxism and feminism are one, and that one is marxism.[1] Recent attempts to integrate marxism and feminism are unsatisfactory to us as feminists because they subsume the feminist struggle into the "larger" struggle against capital. To continue our simile further, either we need a healthier marriage or we need a divorce.

The inequalities in this marriage, like most social phenomena, are no accident. Many marxists typically argue that feminism is at best less important than class conflict and at worst divisive of the working class. This political stance produces an analysis that absorbs feminism into the class struggle. Moreover, the analytic power

1. Often paraphrased as "the husband and wife are one and that one is the husband," English law held that "by marriage, the husband and wife are one person in law: that is, the very being or legal existence of the woman is suspended during the marriage, or at least is incorporated and consolidated into that of the Husband," I. Blackstone, *Commentaries*, 1965, pp. 442–45, cited in Kenneth M. Davidson, Ruth B. Ginsburg, and Herma H. Kay, *Sex Based Discrimination* (St. Paul, Minn.: West Publishing Co., 1974), p. 117.

of marxism with respect to capital has obscured its limitations with respect to sexism. We will argue here that while marxist analysis provides essential insight into the laws of historical development, and those of capital in particular, the categories of marxism are sex-blind. Only a specifically feminist analysis reveals the systemic character of relations between men and women. Yet feminist analysis by itself is inadequate because it has been blind to history and insufficiently materialist. Both marxist analysis, particularly its historical and materialist method, and feminist analysis, especially the identification of patriarchy as a social and historical structure, must be drawn upon if we are to understand the development of western capitalist societies and the predicament of women within them. In this essay we suggest a new direction for marxist feminist analysis. . . .

I. MARXISM AND THE WOMAN QUESTION

The woman question has never been the "feminist question." The feminist question is directed at the causes of sexual inequality between women and men, of male dominance over women. Most marxist analyses of women's position take as their question the relationship of women to the economic system, rather than that of women to men, apparently assuming the latter will be explained in their discussion of the former. Marxist analysis of the woman question has taken [several] forms. All see women's oppression in our connection (or lack of it) to production. Defining women as part of the working class, these analyses consistently subsume women's relation to men under workers' relation to capital. . . .All attempt to include women in the category working class and to understand women's oppression as another aspect of class oppression. In doing so all give short shrift to the object of feminist analysis, the relations between women and men. While our "problems" have been elegantly analyzed, they have been misunderstood. The focus of marxist analysis has been class relations; the object of marxist analysis has been understanding the laws of motion of capitalist society. While we believe marxist methdology *can* be used to formulate feminist strategy, these marxist feminist approaches discussed above clearly do not do so; their marxism clearly dominates their feminism. . . .

Marxism enables us to understand many aspects of capitalist societies: the structure of production, the generation of a particular occupational structure, and the nature of the dominant ideology. Marx's theory of the development of capitalism is a theory of the development of "empty places." Marx predicted, for example, the growth of the proletariat and the demise of the petit bourgeoisie. More precisely and in more detail, Braverman among others has explained the creation of the "places" clerical worker and service worker in advanced capitalist societies.[2] Just as capital creates these places indifferent to the individuals who fill them, the categories of marxist analysis, class, reserve army of labor, wage-laborer, do not explain why particular people fill particular places. They give no clues about why *women* are subordinate to *men* inside and outside the family and why it is not the other way around. *Marxist categories, like capital itself, are sex-blind.* The categories of marxism cannot tell us who will fill the empty places. Marxist analysis of the woman question has suffered from this basic problem. . . .

II. RADICAL FEMINISM AND PATRIARCHY

The great thrust of radical feminist writing has been directed to the documentation of the slogan "the personal is political." Women's discontent, radical feminists argued, is not the neurotic lament of the maladjusted, but a response to a social structure in which women are systematically dominated, exploited, and oppressed. Women's inferior position in the labor market, the male-centered emotional structure of middle class marriage, the use of women in advertising, the so-called understanding of women's psyche as neurotic—popularized by academic and clinical psychology—aspect after aspect of women's lives in advanced capitalist society was researched and analyzed. The radical feminist literature is enormous and defies easy summary. At the same time, its focus on psychology is consistent. The New York Radical Feminists' organizing document was "The Politics of the Ego." "The personal is political" means for radical feminists, that the original and basic class division is between the sexes, and that the motive force of history is the striving of men for power and domination over women, the dialectic of sex.[3]

We can usefully define patriarchy as a set of social relations between men, which have a material base, and which, though hierarchical, establish or create interdependence and solidarity among men that enable them to dominate women. Though patriarchy is hierarchical and men of different classes, races, or ethnic groups

2. Harry Braverman, *Labor and Monopoly Capital* (New York: Monthly Review Press, 1975).

3. "Politics of Ego: A Manifesto for New York Radical Feminists," can be found in *Rebirth of Feminism*, ed. Judith Hole and Ellen Levine (New York: Quadrangle Books, 1971), pp. 440–43. "Radical feminists" are those feminists who argue that the most fundamental dynamic of history is men's striving to dominate women. 'Radical' in this context does *not* mean anti-capitalist, socialist, counter-cultural, etc., but has the specific meaning of this particular set of feminist beliefs or group of feminists. Additional writings of radical feminists, of whom the New York Radical Feminists are probably the most influential, can be found in *Radical Feminism*, ed. Ann Koedt (New York: Quadrangle Press, 1972).

have different places in the patriarchy, they also are united in their shared relationship of dominance over their women; they are dependent on each other to maintain that domination. Hierarchies "work" at least in part because they create vested interests in the status quo. Those at the higher levels can "buy off" those at the lower levels by offering them power over those still lower. In the hierarchy of patriarchy, all men, whatever their rank in the patriarchy, are bought off by being able to control at least some women. There is some evidence to suggest that when patriarchy was first institutionalized in state societies, the ascending rulers literally made men the heads of their families (enforcing their control over their wives and children) in exchange for the men's ceding some of their tribal resources to the new rulers.[4] Men are dependent on one another (despite their hierarchical ordering) to maintain their control over women.

The material base upon which patriarchy rests lies most fundamentally in men's control over women's labor power. Men maintain this control by excluding women from access to some essential productive resources (in capitalist societies, for example, jobs that pay living wages) and by restricting women's sexuality.[5] Monogamous heterosexual marriage is one relatively recent and efficient form that seems to allow men to control both these areas. Controlling women's access to resources and their sexuality, in turn, allows men to control women's labor power, both for the purpose of serving men in many personal and sexual ways and for the purpose of

4. See Viana Muller, "The Formation of the State and the Oppression of Women: Some Theoretical Considerations and a Case Study in England and Wales," *Review of Radical Political Economics,* Vol. 9, no. 3 (Fall 1977), pp. 7–21.

5. The particular ways in which men control women's access to important economic resources and restrict their sexuality vary enormously, both from society to society, from subgroup to subgroup, and across time. The examples we use to illustrate patriarchy in this section, however, are drawn primarily from the experience of whites in western capitalist countries. The diversity is shown in *Toward an Anthropology of Women,* ed. Rayna Rapp Reiter (New York: Monthly Review Press, 1975), *Woman, Culture and Society,* ed. Michelle Rosaldo and Louise Lamphere (Stanford, California: Stanford University Press, 1974), and *Females, Males, Families: A Biosocial Approach,* by Liba Leibowitz (North Scituate, Massachusetts: Duxbury Press, 1978). The control of women's sexuality is tightly linked to the place of children. An understanding of the demand (by men and capitalists) for children is crucial to understanding changes in women's subordination.

Where children are needed for their present or future labor power, women's sexuality will tend to be directed toward reproduction and childrearing. When children are seen as superfluous, women's sexuality for other than reproductive purposes is encouraged, but men will attempt to direct it toward satisfying male needs. The Cosmo girl is a good example of a woman "liberated" from childrearing only to find herself turning all her energies toward attracting and satisfying men. Capitalists can also use female sexuality to their own ends, as the success of *Cosmo* in advertising consumer products shows.

rearing children. The services women render men, and which exonerate men from having to perform many unpleasant tasks (like cleaning toilets) occur outside as well as inside the family setting. Examples outside the family include the harrassment of women workers and students by male bosses and professors as well as the common use of secretaries to run personal errands, make coffee, and provide "sexy" surroundings. Rearing children, whether or not the children's labor power is of immediate benefit to their fathers, is nevertheless a crucial task in perpetuating patriarchy as a system. Just as class society must be reproduced by schools, work places, consumption norms, etc., so must patriarchal social relations. In our society children are generally reared by women at home, women socially defined and recognized as inferior to men, while men appear in the domestic picture only rarely. Children raised in this way generally learn their places in the gender hierarchy well. Central to this process, however, are the areas outside the home where patriarchal behaviors are taught and the inferior position of women enforced and reinforced: churches, schools, sports, clubs, unions, armies, factories, offices, health centers, the media, etc.

The material base of patriarchy, then, does not rest solely on childrearing in the family, but on all the social structures that enable men to control women's labor. The aspects of social structures that perpetuate patriarchy are theoretically identifiable, hence separable from their other aspects. Gayle Rubin has increased our ability to identify the patriarchal element of these social structures enormously by identifying "sex/gender systems":

> a "sex/gender system" is the set of arrangements by which a society transforms biological sexuality into products of human activity, and in which these transformed sexual needs are satisfied.[6]

We are born female and male, biological sexes, but we are created woman and man, socially recognized genders. *How* we are so created is that second aspect of the *mode* of production of which Engels spoke, "the production of human beings themselves, the propagation of the species."

How people propagate the species is socially determined. If, biologically, people are sexually polymorphous, and society were organized in such a way that all forms of sexual expression were equally permissible, reproduction would result only from some sexual encounters, the heterosexual ones. The strict division of labor by sex, a social invention common to all known societies, creates

6. Gayle Rubin, "The Traffic in Women," in *Anthropology of Women*, ed. Reiter, p. 159.

two very separate genders and a need for men and women to get together for economic reasons. It thus helps to direct their sexual needs toward heterosexual fulfillment, and helps to ensure biological reproduction. In more imaginative societies, biological reproduction might be ensured by other techniques, but the division of labor by sex appears to be the universal solution to date. Although it is theoretically possible that a sexual division of labor not imply inequality between the sexes, in most known societies, the socially acceptable division of labor by sex is one which accords lower status to women's work. The sexual division of labor is also the underpinning of sexual subcultures in which men and women experience life differently; it is the material base of male power which is exercised (in our society) not just in not doing housework and in securing superior employment, but psychologically as well.

How people meet their sexual needs, how they reproduce, how they inculcate social norms in new generations, how they learn gender, how it feels to be a man or a woman—all occur in the realm Rubin labels the sex/gender system. Rubin emphasizes the influence of kinship (which tells you with whom you can satisfy sexual needs) and the development of gender specific personalities via childrearing and the "oedipal machine." In addition, however, we can use the concept of the sex/gender system to examine all other social institutions for the roles they play in defining and reinforcing gender hierarchies. Rubin notes that theoretically a sex/gender system could be female dominant, male dominant, or egalitarian, but declines to label various known sex/gender systems or to periodize history accordingly. We choose to label our present sex/gender system patriarchy, because it appropriately captures the notion of hierarchy and male dominance which we see as central to the present system.

Economic production (what marxists are used to referring to as *the* mode of production) and the production of people in the sex/gender sphere both determine "the social organization under which the people of a particular historical epoch and a particular country live," according to Engels. The whole of society, then, can be understood by looking at both these types of production and reproduction, people and things.[7] There is no such thing as "pure cap-

7. Himmelweit and Mohun point out that both aspects of production (people and things) are logically necessary to describe a mode of production because by definition a mode of production must be capable of reproducing itself. Either aspect alone is not self-sufficient. To put it simply the production of things requires people, and the production of people requires things. Marx, though recognizing capitalism's need for people did not concern himself with how they were produced or what the connections between the two aspects of production were. See Susan Himmelweit and Simon Mohun, "Domestic Labour and Capital," *Cambridge Journal of Economics,* Vol. 1, no. 1 (March 1977), pp. 15–31.

italism," nor does "pure patriarchy" exist, for they must of necessity coexist. What exists is patriarchal capitalism, or patriarchal feudalism, or egalitarian hunting/gathering societies, or matriarchal horticultural societies, or patriarchal horticultural societies, and so on. There appears to be no necessary connection between *changes* in the one aspect of production and changes in the other. A society could undergo transition from capitalism to socialism, for example, and remain patriarchal.[8] Common sense, history, and our experience tell us, however, that these two aspects of production are so closely intertwined, that change in one ordinarily creates movement, tension, or contradiction in the other.

Racial hierarchies can also be understood in this context. Further elaboration may be possible along the lines of defining color/race systems, arenas of social life that take biological color and turn it into a social category, race. Racial hierarchies, like gender hierarchies, are aspects of our social organization, of how people are produced and reproduced. They are not fundamentally ideological; they constitute that second aspect of our mode of production, the production and reproduction of people. It might be most accurate then to refer to our societies not as, for example, simply capitalist, but as patriarchal capitalist white supremacist. In Part III below, we illustrate one case of capitalism adapting to and making use of racial orders and several examples of the interrelations between capitalism and patriarchy.

Capitalist development creates the places for a hierarchy of workers, but traditional marxist categories cannot tell us who will fill which places. Gender and racial hierarchies determine who fills the empty places. *Patriarchy is not simply hierarchical organization*, but hierarchy in which *particular* people fill *particular* places. It is in studying patriarchy that we learn why it is women who are dominated and how. While we believe that most known societies have been patriarchal, we do not view patriarchy as a universal, unchanging phenomenon. Rather patriarchy, the set of interrelations among men that allow men to dominate women, has changed in form and intensity over time. It is crucial that the hierarchy among men, and their differential access to patriarchal benefits, be examined. Surely, class, race, nationality, and even marital status and sexual orientation, as well as the obvious age, come into play here. And women of different class, race, national, marital status, or sexual orientation groups are subjected to different degrees of patriarchal power. Women may themselves exercise class, race, or national power, or even patriarchal power (through their family

8. For an excellent discussion of one such transition to socialism, see Batya Weinbaum, "Women in Transition to Socialism: Perspectives on the Chinese Case," *Review of Radical Political Economics*, Vol. 8, no. 1 (Spring 1976), pp. 34–58.

connections) over men lower in the patriarchal hierarchy than their own male kin.

To recapitulate, we define patriarchy as a set of social relations which has a material base and in which there are hierarchical relations between men and solidarity among them which enable them in turn to dominate women. The material base of patriarchy is men's control over women's labor power. That control is maintained by excluding women from access to necessary economically productive resources and by restricting women's sexuality. Men exercise their control in receiving personal service work from women, in not having to do housework or rear children, in having access to women's bodies for sex, and in feeling powerful and being powerful. The crucial elements of patriarchy as we *currently* experience them are: heterosexual marriage (and consequent homophobia), female childrearing and housework, women's economic dependence on men (enforced by arrangements in the labor market), the state, and numerous institutions based on social relations among men—clubs, sports, unions, professions, universities, churches, corporations and armies. All of these elements need to be examined if we are to understand patriarchal capitalism. . . .

III. THE PARTNERSHIP OF PATRIARCHY AND CAPITAL

How are we to recognize patriarchal social relations in capitalist societies? It appears as if each woman is oppressed by her own man alone; her oppression seems a private affair. Relationships among men and among families seem equally fragmented. It is hard to recognize relationships among men, and between men and women, as *systematically* patriarchal. We argue, however, that patriarchy as a system of relations between men and women exists in capitalism, and that in capitalist societies a healthy and strong partnership exists between patriarchy and capital.

. . . Although the terms of the bargain have altered over time, it is still true that the family and women's work in the family serve capital by providing a labor force and serve men as the space in which they exercise their privilege. Women, working to serve men and their families, also serve capital as consumers.[9] The family is also the place where dominance and submission are learned, as

9. See Batya Weinbaum and Amy Bridges, "The Other Side of the Paycheck: Monopoly Capital and the Structure of Consumption." *Monthly Review*, Vol. 28, no. 3 (July–August 1976), pp. 88–103, for a discussion of women's consumption work.

Firestone, the Frankfurt School, and many others have explained.[10] Obedient children become obedient workers; girls and boys each learn their proper roles.

While the family wage shows that capitalism adjusts to patriarchy, the changing status of children shows that patriarchy adjusts to capital. Children, like women, came to be excluded from wage labor. As children's ability to earn money declined, their legal relationship to their parents changed. At the beginning of the industrial era in the United States, fulfilling children's need for their fathers was thought to be crucial, even primary, to their happy development; fathers had legal priority in cases of contested custody. As children's ability to contribute to the economic well-being of the family declined, mothers came increasingly to be viewed as crucial to the happy development of their children, and gained legal priority in cases of contested custody.[11] Here patriarchy adapted to the changing economic role of children: when children were productive, men claimed them; as children became unproductive, they were given to women. . . .

The Family and the Family Wage Today

. . . Despite women's increased labor force participation, particularly rapid since World War II, the family wage is still, we argue, the cornerstone of the present sexual division of labor—in which women are primarily responsible for housework and men primarily for wage work. Women's lower wages in the labor market (combined with the need for children to be reared by someone) assure the continued existence of the family as a necessary income pooling unit. The family, supported by the family wage, thus allows the control of women's labor by men both within and without the family. . . .

. . . The sexual division of labor reappears in the labor market, where women work at women's jobs, often the very jobs they used to do only at home—food preparation and service, cleaning of all kinds, caring for people, and so on. As these jobs are low-status and low-paying patriarchal relations remain intact, though their mate-

10. For the view of the Frankfurt School, see Max Horkheimer, "Authority and the Family," in *Critical Theory* (New York: Herder & Herder, 1972) and Frankfurt Institute of Social Research, "The Family," in *Aspects of Sociology* (Boston: Beacon, 1972).

11. Carol Brown, "Patriarchial Capitalism and the Female-Headed Family," *Social Scientist* (India); no. 40–41 (November–December 1975), pp. 28–39.

rial base shifts somewhat from the family to the wage differential, from family-based to industrially-based patriarchy.[12]

Industrially-based patriarchal relations are enforced in a variety of ways. Union contracts which specify lower wages, lesser benefits, and fewer advancement opportunities for women are not just atavistic hangovers—a case of sexist attitudes or male supremacist ideology—they maintain the material base of the patriarchal system. While some would go so far as to argue that patriarchy is already absent from the family . . . , we would not. Although the terms of the compromise between capital and patriarchy are changing as additional tasks formerly located in the family are capitalized, and the location of the deployment of women's labor power shifts,[13] it is nevertheless true, as we have argued above, that the wage differential caused by extreme job segregation in the labor market reinforces the family, and, with it, the domestic division of labor, by encouraging women to marry. The "ideal" of the family wage—that a man can earn enough to support an entire family—may be giving way to a new ideal that both men and women contribute through wage earning to the cash income of the family. The wage differential, then, will become increasingly necessary in perpetuating patriarchy, the male control of women's labor power. The wage differential will aid in *defining* women's work as secondary to men's at the same time it necessitates women's actual continued economic dependence on men. The sexual division of labor in the labor market and elsewhere should be understood as a manifestation of patriarchy which serves to perpetuate it.

Many people have argued that though the partnership between capital and patriarchy exists now, it may *in the long run* prove intolerable to capitalism; capital may eventually destroy both familial relations and patriarchy. The argument proceeds logically that capitalist social relations (of which the family is not an example)

12. Carol Brown, in "Patriarchal Capitalism," argues, for example, that we are moving from "family based" to "industrially-based" patriarchy within capitalism.

13. Jean Gardiner, in "Women's Domestic Labour," *New Left Review*, no. 89 (January–February 1975), pp. 47–58, clarifies the cause for the shift in location of women's labor, from capital's point of view. She examines what capital needs (in terms of the level of real wages, the supply of labor, and the size of markets) at various stages of growth and of the business cycle. She argues that in times of boom or rapid growth it is likely that socializing housework (or more accurately capitalizing it) would be the dominant tendency, and that in times of recession, housework will be maintained in its traditional form. In attempting to assess the likely direction of the British economy, however, Gardiner does not assess the economic needs of patriarchy. We argue in this essay that unless one takes patriarchy as well as capital into account one cannot adequately assess the likely direction of the economic system.

tend to become universalized, that women will become increasingly able to earn money and will increasingly refuse to submit to subordination in the family, and that since the family is oppressive particularly to women and children, it will collapse as soon as people can support themselves outside it.

We do not think that the patriarchal relations embodied in the family can be destroyed so easily by capital, and we see little evidence that the family system is presently disintegrating. Although the increasing labor force participation of women has made divorce more feasible, the incentives to divorce are not overwhelming for women. Women's wages allow very few women to support themselves and their children independently and adequately. The evidence for the decay of the traditional family is weak at best. The divorce rate has not so much increased, as it has evened out among classes; moreover, the remarriage rate is also very high. Up until the 1970 census, the first-marriage age was continuing its historic decline. Since 1970 people seem to have been delaying marriage and childbearing, but most recently, the birth rate has begun to increase again. It is true that larger proportions of the population are now living outside traditional families. Young people, especially, are leaving their parents' homes and establishing their own households before they marry and start traditional families. Older people, especially women, are finding themselves alone in their own households, after their children are grown and they experience separation or death of a spouse. Nevertheless, trends indicate that the new generations of young people will form nuclear families at some time in their adult lives in higher proportions than ever before. The cohorts, or groups of people, born since 1930 have much higher rates of eventual marriage and childrearing than previous cohorts. The duration of marriage and childrearing may be shortening, but its incidence is still spreading.[14]

The argument that capital destroys the family also overlooks the social forces which make family life appealing. Despite critiques of nuclear families as psychologically destructive, in a competitive society the family still meets real needs for many people. This is true not only of long-term monogamy, but even more so for raising

14. For the proportion of people in nuclear families, see Peter Uhlenberg, "Cohort Variations in Family Life Cycle Experiences of U.S. Females," *Journal of Marriage and the Family*, Vol. 36, no. 5 (May 1974), pp. 284–92. For remarriage rates see Paul C. Glick and Arthur J. Norton, "Perspectives on the Recent Upturn in Divorce and Remarriage," *Demography*, Vol. 10 (1974), pp. 301–14. For divorce and income levels see Arthur J. Norton and Paul C. Glick, "Marital Instability: Past, Present, and Future," *Journal of Social Issues*, Vol. 32, no. 1 (1976), pp. 5–20. Also see Mary Jo Bane, *Here to Stay: American Families in the Twentieth Century* (New York: Basic Books, 1976).

children. Single parents bear both financial and psychic burdens. For working class women, in particular, these burdens make the "independence" of labor force participation illusory. Single parent families have . . . been seen by policy analysts as transitional family formations which become two-parent families upon remarriage.[15]

It could be that the effects of women's increasing labor force participation are found in a declining sexual division of labor within the family, rather than in more frequent divorce, but evidence for this is also lacking. Statistics on who does housework, even in families with wage-earning wives, show little change . . . women still do most of it.[16] The double day is a reality for wage-working women. This is hardly surprising since the sexual division of labor outside the family, in the labor market, keeps women financially dependent on men—even when they earn a wage themselves. The future of patriarchy does not, however, rest solely on the future of familial relations. For patriarchy, like capital, can be surprisingly flexible and adaptable.

Whether or not the patriarchal division of labor, inside the family and elsewhere, is "ultimately" intolerable to capital, it is shaping capitalism now. As we illustrate below, patriarchy both legitimates capitalist control and delegitimates certain forms of struggle against capital.

Ideology in the Twentieth Century

Patriarchy, by establishing and legitimating hierarchy among men (by allowing men of all groups to control at least some women), reinforces capitalist control, and capitalist values shape the definition of patriarchal good.

. . . If we examine the characteristics of men as radical feminists describe them—competitive, rationalistic, dominating—they are much like our description of the dominant values of capitalist society.

This "coincidence" may be explained in two ways. In the first instance, men, as wage laborers, are absorbed in capitalist social relations at work, driven into the competition these relations pre-

15. Heather L. Ross and Isabel B. Sawhill, *Time of Transition: The Growth of Families Headed by Women* (Washington, D.C.: The Urban Institute, 1975).

16. See Kathryn E. Walker and Margaret E. Woods *Time Use: A Measure of Household Production of Family Goods and Services* (Washington D.C.: American Home Economics Association, 1976); and Heidi I. Hartmann, "The Family as the Locus of Gender, Class, and Political Struggle: The Example of Housework," *Signs: Journal of Women in Culture and Society*, Vol. 6, no. 3 (Spring 1981).

scribe, and absorb the corresponding values.[17] The radical feminist description of men was not altogether out of line for capitalist societies. Secondly, even when men and women do not actually behave in the way sexual norms prescribe, men *claim for themselves* those characteristics which are valued in the dominant ideology. So, for example, the authors of *Crestwood Heights* found that while the men, who were professionals, spent their days manipulating subordinates (often using techniques that appeal to fundamentally irrational motives to elicit the preferred behavior), men and women characterized men as "rational and pragmatic." And while the women devoted great energies to studying scientific methods of childrearing and child development, men and women in Crestwood Heights characterized women as "irrational and emotional.[18]

This helps to account not only for "male" and "female" characteristics in capitalist societies, but for the particular form sexist ideology takes in capitalist societies. Just as women's work serves the dual purpose of perpetuating male domination and capitalist production, so sexist ideology serves the dual purpose of glorifying male characteristics/capitalist values, and denigrating female characteristics/social need. If women were degraded or powerless in other societies, the reasons (rationalizations) men had for this were different. Only in a capitalist society does it make sense to look down on women as emotional or irrational. As epithets, they would not have made sense in the renaissance. Only in a capitalist society does it make sense to look down on women as "dependent." "Dependent" as an epithet would not make sense in feudal societies. Since the division of labor ensures that women as wives and mothers in the family are largely concerned with the production of use values, the denigration of these activities obscures capital's inability to meet socially determined need at the same time that it degrades women in the eyes of men, providing a rationale for male dominance. An example of this may be seen in the peculiar ambivalance of television commercials. On one hand, they address themselves to the real obstacles to providing for socially determined needs:

17. This should provide some clues to class differences in sexism, which we cannot explore here.

18. See John R. Seeley et al., *Crestwood Heights* (Toronto: University of Toronto Press, 1956), pp. 382–94. While men's place may be characterized as "in production" this does not mean that women's place is simply "not in production"—her tasks, too, are shaped by capital. Her nonwage work is the resolution, on a day-to-day basis, of production for exchange with socially determined need, the provision of use values in a capitalist society (this is the context of consumption). See Weinbaum and Bridges, "The Other Side of the Paycheck," for a more complete discussion of this argument. The fact that women provide "merely" use values in a society dominated by exchange values can be used to denigrate women.

detergents that destroy clothes and irritate skin, shoddily made goods of all sorts. On the other hand, concern with these problems must be denigrated; this is accomplished by mocking women, the workers who must deal with these problems.

A parallel argument demonstrating the partnership of patriarchy and capitalism may be made about the sexual division of labor in the work force. The sexual division of labor places women in low-paying jobs, and in tasks thought to be appropriate to women's role. Women are teachers, welfare workers, and the great majority of workers in the health fields. The nurturant roles that women play in these jobs are of low status because capitalism emphasizes personal independence and the ability of private enterprise to meet social needs, emphases contradicted by the need for collectively provided social services. As long as the social importance of nurturant tasks can be denigrated because women perform them, the confrontation of capital's priority on exchange value by a demand for use values can be avoided. In this way, it is not feminism, but sexism that divides and debilitates the working class. . . .

The struggle against capital and patriarchy cannot be successful if the study and practice of the issues of feminism is abandoned. A struggle aimed only at capitalist relations of oppression will fail, since their underlying supports in patriarchal relations of oppression will be overlooked. And the analysis of patriarchy is essential to a definition of the kind of socialism useful to women. While men and women share a need to overthrow capitalism they retain interests particular to their gender group. It is not clear—from our sketch, from history, or from male socialists—that the socialism being struggled for is the same for both men and women. For a humane socialism would require not only consensus on what the new society should look like and what a healthy person should look like, but more concretely, it would require that men relinquish their privilege.

As women we must not allow ourselves to be talked out of the urgency and importance of our tasks, as we have so many times in the past. We must fight the attempted coercion, both subtle and not so subtle, to abandon feminist objectives.

This suggests two strategic considerations. First, a struggle to establish socialism must be a struggle in which groups with different interests form an alliance. Women should not trust men to liberate them after the revolution, in part, because there is no reason to think they would know how; in part, because there is no necessity for them to do so. In fact their immediate self-interest lies in our continued oppression. Instead we must have our own organizations and our own power base. Second, we think the sexual division of labor within capitalism has given women a practice in which we have learned to understand what human interdependence and needs are. While men have long struggled *against* capital, women know what to struggle *for*.[19] As a general rule, men's position in patriarchy and capitalism prevents them from recognizing both human needs for nurturance, sharing, and growth, and the potential for meeting those needs in a nonhierarchical, nonpatriarchal society. But even if we raise their consciousness, men might assess the potential gains against the potential losses and choose the status quo. Men have more to lose than their chains.

As feminist socialists, we must organize a practice which addresses both the struggle against patriarchy and the struggle against capitalism. We must insist that the society we want to create is a society in which recognition of interdependence is liberation rather than shame, nurturance is a universal, not an oppressive practice, and in which women do not continue to support the false as well as the concrete freedoms of men.

CHARLENE HADDOCK SEIGFRIED

Where Are All the Pragmatist Feminists?

In the first part of this article, I point out the absence of the American tradition of pragmatism in most feminist discourse and make some suggestions to account for this fact. I then seek to encourage the rediscovery of women pragmatists as a first step in examining their contributions to both feminism and pragmatism. Pragmatism seems to me to exhibit a recognizably feminine style, a point developed in the third part of the article, partly in order to help account for its marginalization but also to encourage feminist appropriation of this neglected aspect. Finally, I mention a few features feminism and pragmatism share as a way of arousing interest in exploring them in greater depth. Particularly significant is their recourse to the practices and institutions of everyday life, both to dismantle the social and political structures of oppression and to develop better alternatives.

I. THE ECLIPSE OF PRAGMATISM

It is sometimes incorrectly assumed that pragmatism is missing from theoretical classifications of feminism because it continues liberal assertions of the isolated individual, advocates the public-

19. Lise Vogel, "The Earthly Family," *Radical America* Vol. 7, no. 4–5 (July–October 1973), pp. 9–50.

private split, or is scientistic. Richard Rorty's neopragmatism gives some substance to these assumptions, but he has been vigorously criticized by other pragmatist philosophers for distorting, among other things, the social and political dimensions of the pragmatist tradition.[1] A more likely hypothesis is that the ascendancy of logical positivism after World War II eclipsed pragmatism for reasons that feminists would reject. Pragmatism never disappeared, but it was marginalized. Generations of philosophy students grew up mostly ignorant of it, or worse, were inoculated against it by the newly dominant philosophical mainstream of analytic philosophy, the assumption being that anything worthwhile about pragmatism had already been assimilated into the very different agendas of Wilfred Sellars, W. V. O. Quine, Nelson Goodman, and Hilary Putnam.

On the other hand, it has sometimes been claimed that all feminists are pragmatists.[2] This assertion could be explored as part of feminist reconstructions of pragmatism, but in this article *pragmatism, pragmatic,* and *pragmatist* refer to a historically specific philosophical movement that originated in America in the nineteenth century in response to multiple intellectual and social upheavals. It began with Charles Sanders Peirce and William James, was developed further by Josiah Royce, John Dewey and George Herbert Mead, and continues in those who still find in the works of these authors a sufficiently coherent and attractive philosophical perspective to serve as a basis for their own analyses.[3] Since pragmatism is a living tradition and not a deductive system, there are many varieties of pragmatist theory, ranging from the more architectonic semiotics based on Peirce to a fallibilist pluralism derived from James. For the sake of simplicity, *pragmatism* is being used in the minimalist sense of "positions developed in dialogue with the philosophic tradition of American pragmatism." Specific claims will be more true or false of some pragmatists than others. The usage is merely a convenient starting point. In order to engage significantly

1. See Brodsky (1982), McDermott et al. (1985), and Bernstein (1987; 1990). (A reference list appears at the end of this selection.)

2. Denise Riley, for instance, uses pragmatism in this wider sense (Riley 1988, 112).

3. I am deliberately excluding women from the pantheon of pragmatist philosophers to make both a historical and a political point. Historically, classical American philosophy—as it has been handed down in publications and taught in the universities—excludes women pragmatists. Until I began this project, I was not even aware that there were any women pragmatists beyond my own immediate contemporaries. I begin with this tradition in which women are invisible as a heuristic device which enables me to subvert it as the article develops. However, on the level of theory and in my own development as a philosopher, what comes from feminist and what from pragmatist sensibilities cannot easily be distinguished.

the varieties of feminist theory—once it is agreed that such an undertaking is worthwhile—a particular constellation of pragmatist themes must be adopted, defended, and developed further, as I do in my other writings and as I intimate in questioning some features of Rorty's version of pragmatism.[4]

Pragmatism influenced the development of the humanities and social sciences in America, particularly philosophy, psychology, sociology, political science, American studies, and education. Therefore, feminists seeking to ground our analyses in their historical, cultural context can further develop the objective basis of our revisioning of these same disciplines by examining pragmatism's theoretical contributions. Like Marxism, what has been developed in its name has sometimes been antithetical to its best original insights. Just as feminists are questioning the assumptions and omissions of the various disciplines, so are contemporary pragmatists (Burnett 1981; Hickman 1990) questioning the disciplinary developments falsely attributed to pragmatist theory.

. . . There is a bit of social Darwinist in all of us that assumes that it [pragmatism] was a tradition that was tried and found wanting and therefore ceased to be a central part of the philosophy curriculum. But from my perspective it seems that it was criticized and eventually relegated to the margins for holding the very positions that today feminists would find to be its greatest strengths. These include early and persistent criticisms of positivist interpretations of scientific methodology; disclosure of the value dimension of factual claims; reclaiming aesthetics as informing everyday experience; linking of dominant discourses with domination; subordinating logical analysis to social, cultural, and political issues; realigning theory with praxis; and resisting the turn to epistemology and instead emphasizing concrete experience.[5] Thomas McCarthy, for instance, recently noted the enormous influence of the human sciences and the liberating potential of sociohistorical research on Continental philosophy and American pragmatism and suggests that James and Dewey were ignored by analytic philosophers because "it was not always possible to overlook [their] appropriation of the human sciences," as it was possible in the case of Peirce.[6]

The early pragmatists located reflection in its actual historical, psychological, economic, political, and cultural context and defined

4. My own reconstruction of pragmatism is developed most fully in Seigfried (1990c).

5. See Thayer (1981), Smith (1983), and Bernstein (1983).

6. Thomas McCarthy, "Philosophy and Social Practice: Avoiding the Ethnocentric Predicament," paper read at symposium on "Analysis, Interpretation, and the End of Philosophy," Purdue University, March 17, 1989, pp. 2–3.

its goal as the intelligent overcoming of oppressive conditions. This is reflected in Cornel West's (1989) comment that they influenced engaged public philosophers as much as they did professional philosophers. Pragmatists also hastened the demise of their own movement by inspiring their students to abandon purely conceptual philosophical analysis. West points out that C. Wright Mills, a student of Dewey, gave up philosophy after earning his M.A. and turned to social theory, declaring war on Talcott Parsons's sociology because it supported the corporate liberal establishment. W. E. B. Du Bois "also gave up philosophy after studying under William James at Harvard, turning to the study of history and society" (West 1989, 113). The retreat of academic philosophers to their ivory tower and away from the pragmatists' active engagement in the problems of their day is an indictment, not of pragmatism, but of academic philosophy. James (1968, 329–47) anticipated this development and warned against it to no avail in "The Ph.D. Octopus." If the pragmatists had succeeded in stopping philosophers from turning their backs on active engagement in solving society's most pressing problems, then feminists of our generation would not have had the continuing struggle both to break into academia and to deinstitutionalize and open up academic deliberations to the wider community.

Against the newly ascendant positivist model legislating value neutrality for the social sciences, the pragmatists called for active engagement.[7] They both attacked the supposed neutrality as a self-deceptive mask for unacknowledged interests and advocated a radical social agenda. The social sciences themselves were to be advocates for transformation rather than upholders of the status quo and instruments for the enhancement of power of one segment of the society against another. The subtitle to Dewey's *Human Nature and Conduct*, for instance, is *An Introduction to Social Psychology*. The great issues of self-determination, exploration of values, and problems of community living are not taken as addenda to the science of social psychology; they are its very subject matter. In Dewey's words: "Why employ language, cultivate literature, acquire and develop science, sustain industry, and submit to the refinements of art? To ask these questions is equivalent to asking: Why live? . . . The only question having sense which can be asked is *how* we are going to use and be used by these things, not whether we are going to use them. Reason, moral principles, cannot in any case be shoved behind these affairs, for reason and morality grow out of them" (Dewey 1983, 57–58). The first internationally acclaimed book in American psychology, James's (1890) *The Principles of Psychology*, was also criticized in early reviews for intruding moral issues into a

7. See Seigfried (1984b; 1990a) and Alexander (1987, 119–82).

book whose purpose was to distinguish a separate, empirical psychology from armchair philosophical psychology.

Since the pragmatists aimed at democratic inclusiveness, they—with the notable exception of Peirce—fought the development of a specialized disciplinary jargon inaccessible except to a specialist elite.[8] Marilyn French (1990, 39–42) shows how such mechanisms of exclusion have unfairly impacted on women over the centuries.[9] In connecting "high style" with patriarchy, she renders plausible my contention that this is one more factor in the displacement of pragmatism by theories elaborated in increasingly technical vocabularies. One need only compare Dewey's *Logic: The Theory of Inquiry* (1986) with the dominant position now accorded symbolic logic. James held that "*technical* writing on *philosophical* subjects . . . is certainly a crime against the human race" (quoted in Perry 1935, 387). And Dewey criticized science for being highly abstract and technically specialized and utilizing vocabularies and symbol systems that are impenetrable to the uninitiated. He calls this state of affairs a disaster because it renders "the things of the environment unknown and incommunicable by human beings in terms of their own activities and sufferings" (Dewey 1985a, 173).

In seeking to answer the question of why pragmatism was marginalized from mainstream philosophy, I have drawn on my feelings and recollections of how feminism was rediscovered a few decades after World War II. The first responses to accusations that there were no great women artists, scientists, writers, etc., was to point out their exclusion from the social, educational, and professional ambience of male productivity. This early response led to critical and detailed studies of the mechanisms of exclusion. Closely following on this early response was the claim that there were talented women, maybe even women of genius in the past, but they tended to be exceptionally situated and spokeswomen for the establishment, such as Queen Elizabeth I. But the search was on. Mary Wollstonecraft's *A Vindication of the Rights of Woman*, published in 1792, for instance, was at first thought to be one of the earliest voices raised in explicit protest. But by dint of research to recover our heritage, we have come to see that she did not spring up out of nowhere but was herself part of a long line of feminist voices that receded into the dim past. Each new discovery raised new questions. If feminist women existed in the past, why didn't we know

8. Peirce's infatuation with systematically technical systems is one reason why he hardly figures in my own reconstruction of pragmatism, although other aspects of Peirce's philosophy are certainly amenable to feminist revisioning.

9. French begins by asserting that "a third feminist principle, to which I myself am committed, is accessibility, language and style that aim at comprehensibility" (French 1990, 39).

about them? How had they become invisible? The answers have given concrete content to the theoretical claim that women's intellectual contributions were not just forgotten but were actively suppressed.[10]

The recovery of a history of feminist writings has also contributed to defining some common features of feminist thought, which is otherwise extremely diverse. These two features are (1) the identification and investigation of the oppressive structures that contribute to women's subordination in order to actively dismantle them and (2) the development of analyses of women's experiences that are not systematically distorted by sexist assumptions.

I am not arguing that the loss of influence of pragmatism is comparable to the suffering of women under various forms of patriarchal domination and millennia of misogynist beliefs and practices. I am suggesting that unless we continue to explore the reasons for the absence of pragmatism in core curricula of philosophy, the myth will persist that something vital is lacking in pragmatism itself, rather than in the philosophical milieu, that accounts for its neglect. It would be a shame if the same forces that succeeded for so long in denying that feminist issues were properly philosophical were to succeed in convincing feminists to neglect that very part of our American philosophical tradition that radically joined theory with praxis. If it is true that pragmatism declined in influence just to the extent that it challenged the rejection by professional philosophers of their role as cultural critic and scorned the pseudoscientism that reduced philosophy to supposedly value-free epistemology, then feminists have good reasons for reclaiming it as an ally.[11] Moreover, if the history of feminism is any precedent, we should also expect to generate an evolving redefinition of pragmatism, one that explicitly raises feminist issues and that includes women's contributions.

II. CHALLENGING THE CANON: WOMEN PRAGMATISTS

If my assumption that pragmatism is congenial to feminism is correct, then one would expect to find enthusiastic women pragmatists in the heyday of pragmatism in the late nineteenth and early twentieth centuries. My limited research indicates that this is indeed the case but that these women have fallen through the cracks of patriarchal public memory and need to be rediscovered. In the absence of any feminist biography of Jane Addams, for instance, who was "the most outstanding progressive activist in the U.S."

10. See Spender (1983) and Russ (1983).

11. For corroboration, see Wilson (1990).

(Cook 1991, 61), how can we assess her influence on Dewey and vice versa?[12] Pragmatism's white, male pantheon needs to be expanded to include women's contributions, including those of people of color, much as Cornel West does in *The American Evasion of Philosophy* (1989).

. . . I suspect that the pragmatist influence on some current feminist positions is not so much absent as invisible. Just recently I serendipitously discovered such a hidden connection. Only when Sidney Ratner received the Herbert Schneider Award in 1989 for his contributions to American philosophy did I find out that his wife, Louise M. Rosenblatt (1983), was the first person to develop the "reader-response" theory of literature in her 1938 book, *Literature as Exploration.*[13] It is an interesting case of degrees of marginalization and the mechanisms of disappearance. Rosenblatt is virtually unknown in philosophy, either to feminist or pragmatist philosophers, despite the fact that her literary theory is based on pragmatism, specifically, on Dewey's theory of transaction, and despite the fact that reader-response theory is so central to feminist theories of literature (see Fetterly 1978).

Dewey's theory of transaction replaces that of the Cartesian isolated ego that inaugurated the modern alienation of subject and object. Both subject and object are interactively constituted within a horizon of social praxis. By changing the gender in Dewey's explanation we get:

> An experience is always what it is because of a transaction taking place between an individual and what, at the time, constitutes her environment, whether the latter consists of persons with whom she is talking about some topic or event, the subject talked about being also a part of the situation; or the toys with which she is playing; the book she is reading . . . ; or the materials of an experiment she is performing. The environment, in other words, is whatever conditions interact with personal needs, desires, purposes, and capacities to create the experience which is had. (Dewey 1938, 43–44)

Rosenblatt herself did not fully explore the radical consequences of either pragmatism or feminism, but this alone cannot account for her neglect. Her disappearance is a salutary reminder that not only does the dominant philosophic discourse marginalize other discourses, such as feminism, pragmatism, phenomenology, and

12. But see Deegan (1988).

13. For confirmation, see Tomkins (1980, x and xxvi, n1). See also Rosenblatt (1985).

Marxism, but that the groups so marginalized also have their centers and margins (Seigfried 1987).

. . . [T]he very effort needed to recover women pragmatists points to a more substantial reason for the dearth of pragmatist feminists. With the exception of Dewey's brief polemical addresses supporting women's issues, women as such do not figure much in pragmatist writings, not even in those of the women pragmatists just mentioned. Moreover, James's views of women were typically Victorian, which is to say patriarchal. Pragmatists often criticize the social and political oppressions of class, race, nationalism, ethnic origin, and monopolistic capitalism, but not of sex. This absence may be partially ameliorated by widening the circle of those who are considered pragmatists, as Maureen L. Egan does in including Charlotte Perkins Gilman because she shared some of the ideas and interests that would eventually be known as pragmatist (Egan 1989, 103). However, the lack of specific analyses of women's oppression in pragmatism will only be overcome by explicitly feminist reconstructions of pragmatist theory.

III. FEMININE STYLE

Two aspects of pragmatist theory, in particular, which I suspect contributed to the marginalization of pragmatism, should also make the theory particularly attractive to feminist reconstruction. One is its explicit linkage of categorizations with value judgments. The pragmatists' position that human knowledge always instantiates particular perspectives, including values, ran strongly counter to the rising tide of positivist ideology espousing the neutrality of science and the objectivity of pure observation. Claims about reality are political. The power to name is exercised most extensively by the dominant forces—individual and institutional—that seek to control society, but it rightly belongs to every human being.

The other feature of pragmatism is more subtle. Indeed, without recent feminist analyses uncovering the gender assumptions and relations influencing modes of discourse, it could not even be recognized or named. On a scale of traits, assumptions, and positions that range from stereotypically masculine to feminine, pragmatism (again excepting Peirce) appears far more feminine than masculine. Among the various aspects contributing to this feeling are a penchant for indirect, metaphorical discourse rather than a deductive and reductively symbolic one, the concreteness of pragmatist methodology, philosophizing out of one's own experience and everyday problems, the priority of human relations and actual experiences over abstract conceptual distinctions, shared understanding and communal problem-solving rather than rationally forced conclusions as the goal of philosophical discourse, the valuing of inclusiveness and community over exaggerated claims of autonomy and detachment, and developmental rather than rule-governed ethics.

This feminine rather than masculine style may help account for why I was drawn to pragmatism in the first place and have continued to find it emotionally sustaining as well as intellectually attractive. I am not the only one to make these connections. Mahowald (1987, 415) also finds feminine elements in pragmatism and suggests that this may have been due to direct feminist influence. She cites Royce's emphasis on community, which refers "more to the relationships that exist among individuals than to their collective or aggregate status," as what attracted her to his writings (Mahowald 1987, 413). She also cautions against confusing feminine characteristics with feminist analyses, which explicitly expose and reject the sexist oppression of women.

Femininity and masculinity are social and psychological interpretations of gender that both instantiate and mask unequal power relations. Feminism exposes the negative impact of such stereotypical attributions of gender characterizations. However, some aspects of experience that have been associated with women, labeled "feminine," and consequently devalued in patriarchal cultures have also been positively revalued by feminists. A nonauthoritarian leadership style comes to mind as an example of feminine behavior that has been revalued and redefined as a feminist method. That I find James's metaphorical and suggestive rather than analytic and explicit style congenial to my own way of thinking can be understood as the expression of a feminine style without implying that all women think this way or that no men do. James (1978, 168; Seigfried 1990c, 181–83), for instance, rejects the polemically virulent style of philosophic argumentation that seeks to triumph over an opponent by convicting them of errors and argues instead for shared understanding as the goal of philosophic discourse. From my point of view, he is rejecting a prevalent form of masculine style for a feminine one.

Before filling in the claim that pragmatism seems more feminine than masculine, something needs to be said about how an intellectual schema can be gendered. What constitutes femininity or masculinity varies over time and among cultures, even taking on opposite characteristics according to what is most valued at particular times and places. The kernel of gender differences may be biological, but the nature and extent of this biological substrate are difficult, and perhaps impossible, to determine given the context of beliefs, values, and expectations that inform the differential psychological developmental patterns that are discussed.[14] According to

14. For a pragmatist analysis of the intertwining of biological and normative descriptions of gender, see Seigfried (1990b).

characteristics that have been associated with women and men in late nineteenth- and twentieth-century America, pragmatism appears far more feminine than what replaced it.

In *The Flight to Objectivity* Susan Bordo draws on Carol Gilligan, Evelyn Fox Keller, and Nancy Chodorow to attribute the configuration of masculine traits she identifies as prominent in modern, Western rationalism to the "more rigorous individuation from the mother [which] is demanded of boys (as a requisite to their attaining a 'masculine' identity in a culture in which masculinity is defined in opposition to everything that the mother represents" (Bordo 1987, 6–7). Whether one agrees with this psychological explanation or finds the origins of misogyny in specific cultural, economic, and political conditions, the list of masculine traits that results is recognizably plausible. They are "detachment, autonomy, and a clear sense of boundaries between self and world, self and others. This has resulted, in our male-dominated intellectual traditions in the fetishization of detachment and 'objectivity' in ethical reasoning and scientific rationality" (Bordo 1987, 6-7).

Thomas Nagel's *The View from Nowhere* (1986) is the logical conclusion of a long process, which extends back to Descartes, of distancing self from world. He is also heir to a shift in mainstream philosophizing that was inaugurated by the arrival of members of the Vienna school of logical positivism in America. It is this movement that eventually displaced pragmatism. Bordo connects the extreme mind/body dualism in Descartes's philosophy with separation anxiety. His disconnectedness from both the natural world and his own body reflects "separation from the *maternal*—the immanent realms of earth, nature, the authority of the body—and a compensatory turning toward the *paternal* for legitimation through external regulation, transcendent values, and the authority of law" (Bordo 1987, 58).

Against such a background understanding of the polarization of masculinity and femininity in Western thinking, it is possible to see how pragmatism would be implicitly categorized with feminine rather than masculine traits, even if such a connection was not made in print or on a conscious level. Descartes reacted to the Galilean and Newtonian displacement of the human. Dewey, on the other hand, responded to the Darwinian reconnection of humans with all of organic life. When separation, generalization, sharp boundaries, and the drive to reduce the multiplicity of experience into as few categories as possible are categorized as masculine, then inclusiveness, concreteness, vagueness, tolerance of ambiguities, and pluralism are seen as feminine. But these latter traits are also characteristic of pragmatist thinking (Seigfried 1982). Compare Bordo's description of Cartesian separation anxiety, for instance, with one of Dewey's early articles, explaining his "New Psychology" as a better starting point for philosophizing than abstract analysis of language or of theoretical terms:

> The New Psychology is content to get its logic from . . . experience, and not do violence to the sanctity and integrity of the latter by forcing it to conform to certain preconceived abstract ideas. It wants the logic of fact, of process, of life. It has within its departments of knowledge no psycho-statics, for it can nowhere find spiritual life at rest. For this reason, it abandons all legal fiction of logical and mathematical analogies and rules; and is willing to throw itself upon experience, believing that the mother which has borne it will not betray it. But it makes no attempts to dictate to this experience, and to tell it what it *must* be in order to square with a scholastic logic. Thus the New Psychology bears the realistic stamp of the contact with life. (quoted in Bernstein 1966, 12)

Whereas contemporary philosophers often privilege physics as the most rational model of science, one which should be imitated by philosophers, pragmatists consistently use biological models and examples drawn from ordinary experience and the human sciences. Pragmatism's pervasive metaphors are often as characteristic of women's experiences as of men's. Dewey's are organic and developmental; many were drawn from his involvement with early childhood education, while James's metaphors, which are as striking as Nietzsche's, include the stream of thought, truth as the marriage function of our beliefs with sensory experiences, and the organization of experience as weaving chaos into order. Imagine the reaction of philosophers of the late nineteenth century, who not only prided themselves on their rigorous argumentative form but were also suffering from an acute case of science-envy, to James's exposure of the false objectivity of positivist science:

> It is absurd for Science to say that the egoistic elements of experience should be suppressed. The axis of reality runs solely through the egotistic places—they are strung on it like so many beads. To describe the world with all the various feelings of the individual pinch of destiny, all the various spiritual attitudes, left out from the description . . . would be something like offering a printed bill of fare as the equivalent for a solid meal. . . . A bill of fare with one real raisin in it instead of the word "raisin," with one real egg instead of the word "egg," might be an inadequate meal, but it would at least be a commencement of reality. (James 1985, 394)[15]

15. See also Heldke (1988).

It may seem odd that I am pointing out some feminine aspects of pragmatism because it is so often dismissed as an irresponsible instrumentalism. Martin Heidegger, for instance, once contemptuously dismissed it as a philosophy for engineers. But this is a self-indictment, both of his ignorance of pragmatism as a philosophy and of his disinterest in social and political reconstruction. One need only recall Dewey's (1982) definition of philosophy as "reconstruction through criticism" to recognize that he aligned himself with neither a reductionist instrumentalism nor a fatalistic openness to being. He says in "Context and Thought" that "philosophy is criticism; criticism of the influential beliefs that underlie culture; a criticism which traces the beliefs to their generating conditions as far as may be, which tracks them to their results, which considers the mutual compatibility of the elements of the total structure of beliefs. Such an examination terminates, whether so intended or not, in a projection of them into a new perspective which leads to new surveys of possibilities" (Dewey 1985b, 19). Far from blindly advocating a ruthless application of the most efficient means to accomplish predetermined ends, Dewey's pragmatic instrumentalism advocates criticizing the beliefs that have led to presently unsatisfactory conditions in order to radically reconstruct our society according to nonoppressive and cooperative standards.

IV. THE CONTEXT OF OPPRESSION

I would like to conclude with pragmatism's criticism of philosophy as traditionally practiced and its plea to turn away from the problems found only in academic philosophy journals and toward the problems that arise in actual experience. For pragmatists, philosophical reflection begins and ends with experience, as it also does for many feminists. For both, experience is inextricably personal and social. Pragmatism needs feminism to carry out its own stated program, since feminists are in the forefront of philosophers addressing social and political issues that affect women. On the other hand, the three features that Sandra Harding (1987, 6–9) suggests best characterize feminist analysis have also been developed in pragmatism as ones that should characterize any defensible inquiry. They are related as the specific to the general. Feminist theory distinctively urges women's points of view. Pragmatism argues for the inclusion of diverse communities of interest, particularly marginalized ones.

According to Harding (1987, 6–9) the three distinctive features of feminist research are: (1) it begins with women's experiences as the basis for social analysis, (2) the aim of the research is to benefit women, and (3) the researcher is not a neutral observer, but is on the same critical plane as the subject matter. Support for and development of these three themes can be found throughout pragmatist philosophy, which emphasizes that reflection ought to begin with experience, which is irreducibly plural; that the goal of reflection is to satisfactorily resolve the problematic situations which arise within particular experiences, as these are defined by those involved; and that knowledge is always shaped by—in Harding's words—the "concrete, specific desires and interests" of the investigator (Harding 1987, 9).

Pragmatism and feminism reject philosophizing as an intellectual game that takes purely logical analysis as its special task. For both, philosophical techniques are means, not ends. The specific, practical ends are set by various communities of interest, the members of which are best situated to name, resist, and overcome the oppressions of class, sex, race, and gender. The problem with philosophy's enchantment with "the logic of general notions" is that it forces specific situations into predetermined, abstract categories. Pragmatism's fundamental criticism of traditional philosophy is that it "substitutes discussion of the meaning of concepts and their dialectical relationship to one another" for knowledge of specific groups of individuals, concrete human beings, and special institutions or social arrangements (Dewey 1982, 188).

Dewey says that "we want to know about the worth of the institution of private property as it operates under given conditions of definite time and place" (Dewey 1982, 189). Instead, we get discussions of "*the* state, *the* individual, the nature of institutions as such, society in general" (Dewey 1982, 188). Instead of assisting inquiry, the disregard of specific historical phenomena for general answers with supposedly universal meaning closes it. "In transferring the issue from concrete situations to definitions and conceptual deductions, the effect . . . is to supply the apparatus for intellectual justification of the established order" (Dewey 1982, 189–90). Women are members of all the categories mentioned, but how specific is pragmatist analysis of women's situation, individually, socially, and institutionally? According to its own logic, to the extent to which pragmatists do not actually reflect on the status of women and the oppressions of race, class, sexual orientation, and economic forces which women suffer, they are contributing to the justification of the established order.

Feminists, on the other hand, can benefit from such specific theoretical analyses, as that by which pragmatism radically revisions the task of philosophy. Dewey, for instance, argues that "neglect of context is the greatest single disaster which philosophic thinking can incur" (Dewey 1985b, 11). Philosophy and other reflective endeavors have their own context of discourse, which is narrowly constrained within disciplinary concerns and which is only tenuously, if at all, connected with everyday life. He insists that the strategic research of the sciences and other disciplines gains its meaning and value from its relation to what is taken to be the purpose of human life as such. What this purpose is cannot be imposed from above, by experts, but must be decided from below, by all those affected. Disciplinary contexts are necessarily narrowly strategic and strategic thinking becomes dangerous to the extent that it is not guided by more encompassing purposes that are agreed upon as being mutually beneficial. It is dangerous for the disciplines to neglect context in a way that is not the case in less explicitly structured situations because "in the face to face communications of everyday life, context may be safely ignored . . . [because] it is irrevocably there" (Dewey 1985b, 5). In everyday life it is taken for granted, but it can be explicitly retrieved when the need arises. "But in philosophizing there is rarely an immediately urgent context which controls the course of thought" (Dewey 1985b, 6).

This "neglect of specific acknowledgement" of context in philosophizing "is, then, too readily converted into virtual denial" (Dewey 1985b, 6). Context includes both the temporal and spatial background which are not consciously attended to and selective interest. It includes the horizon of meaning and value that gives point to everything said. If context is being denied, then the actually informing meanings and values remain unrecognized, uncriticized, and thus unreconstructed. We then passively acquiesce in the operative structures of power rather than participate in setting the conditions for our own being in the world.

In fighting the entrenched belief that it is "derogatory to link a body of philosophic ideas to the social life and culture of their epoch" (Dewey 1985b, 17), pragmatism is a helpful ally of feminist criticism. I think that both feminism and pragmatism have much to offer each other. Pragmatist philosophy, for instance, explains why the neglect of context is the besetting fallacy of philosophical thought.[16] Feminism cogently and extensively shows how gender, race, class, and sexual preference are crucial parts of context that philosophy has traditionally neglected.

To answer the question posed in the title of this paper: Pragmatist feminists and feminist pragmatists exist among us but in surprisingly small numbers. Pragmatists might be predisposed to be

16. "Thinking takes place in a scale of degrees of distance from the urgencies of an immediate situation in which something is to be done. The greater the degree of remoteness, the greater is the danger that a temporary and legitimate failure of express reference to context will be converted into a virtual denial of its place and import. Thinking is always thinking, but philosophic thinking is, upon the whole, at the extreme end of the scale of distance from the active urgency of concrete situations" (Dewey 1985b, 17).

sympathetic to feminism, but too often they do not directly engage in feminist analysis. This is a loss for both pragmatist and feminist theory and praxis. Likewise, many feminists know little about pragmatism, but I think they would find it congenial and helpful. West, unfortunately, exhibits a widespread pragmatist ignorance of feminist analyses of the pervasiveness of sex when he expresses the opinion that American culture "cuts deeper than sexual identity" (West 1989, 181). But he also expresses pragmatism's openness to revision, its recognition of cultural specificity, and its refusal to speak for those who can more authentically speak for themselves when he follows this statement by saying that "the issue is how American women will reshape and revise pragmatism," through reflections on their own experiences. "For the difference pragmatism makes is always the difference people make with it."

References

Alexander, Thomas M. 1987. *John Dewey's theory of art, experience and nature: The horizons of feeling*. Albany: State University of New York Press.

Antler, Joyce. 1988. The educational biography of Lucy Sprague Mitchell: A case study in the history of women's higher education. In *Women and higher education in American history*. John Mack Faragher and Florence Howe, eds. New York: W. W. Norton.

Ayim, Maryann. 1983. The implications of sexually stereotypic language as seen through Peirce's theory of signs. *Transactions of the Charles S. Peirce Society* 19(2) 183–97.

Bernstein, Richard J. 1966. *John Dewey*. Atascadero, CA: Ridgeview.

———. 1983. *Beyond objectivism and relativism: Science, hermeneutics, and praxis*. Philadelphia: University of Pennsylvania Press.

———. 1987. One step forward, two steps backward: Richard Rorty on liberal democracy and philosophy. *Political Theory* 15(4): 538–63.

———. 1990. Rorty's liberal utopia. *Social Research* 57(1): 31–72.

Bordo, Susan. 1987. *The flight to objectivity*. Albany: State University of New York Press.

Brodsky, Garry. 1982. Rorty's interpretation of pragmatism. *Transactions of the Charles S. Peirce Society* 18(4): 311–37.

Burnett, Joe R. 1981. Whatever happened to John Dewey? In *Philosophy of education since mid-century*, 64–82. Jonas F. Soltis, ed. New York: Teachers College Press.

Cook, Blanche Wiesen. 1991. Books: The womanly art of biography. *Ms.* 1(4): 60–62.

Deegan, Mary Jo. 1988. *Jane Addams and the men of the Chicago school, 1892–1918*. New Brunswick: Transaction Books.

Dewey, John. 1938. *Experience and education.* New York: Macmillan.

______. 1982. *Reconstruction in philosophy.* In *John Dewey, the middle works. Vol. 12, 1920,* 77–201. Jo Ann Boydston, ed. Carbondale: Southern Illinois University Press.

______. 1983. *John Dewey, the middle works. Vol. 14, 1922. Human nature and conduct.* Jo Ann Boydston, ed. Carbondale: Southern Illinois University Press.

______. 1985a (1927). *The public and its problems.* Athens, OH: Swallow Press.

______. 1985b. "Context and thought." In *John Dewey, the later works. Vol. 6, 1931–1932,* 3–21. Carbondale: Southern Illinois University Press.

______. 1986. *John Dewey, the later works. Vol. 12, 1938. Logic, the theory of inquiry.* Carbondale: Southern Illinois University Press.

______. 1988. *Individualism, old and new.* In *John Dewey, the later works. Vol. 5, 1929–1930,* 41–123. Jo Ann Boydston, ed. Carbondale: Southern Illinois University Press.

Egan, Maureen. 1989. Evolutionary theory in the social philosophy of Charlotte Perkins Gilman. *Hypatia* 4(1): 102–19.

Fetterly, Judith. 1978. *The resisting reader.* Bloomington and Indianapolis: Indiana University Press.

French, Marilyn. 1990. Is there a feminist aesthetic? *Hypatia* 5(2): 33–42.

Harding, Sandra, ed. 1987. *Feminism and methodology.* Bloomington and Indianapolis: Indiana University Press.

Heldke, Lisa. 1987. John Dewey and Evelyn Fox Keller: A shared epistemological tradition. *Hypatia* 2(3): 129–40.

______. 1988. Recipes for theory making. *Hypatia* 3(2): 15–29.

Hickman, Larry A. 1990. *John Dewey's pragmatic technology.* Bloomington and Indianapolis: Indiana University Press.

James, William. 1890. *The principles of psychology.* 2 vol., New York: Henry Holt.

______. 1968 (1903). *Memories and studies.* Westport, CT: Greenwood Press.

______. 1978. *Essays in philosophy.* In *The works of William James.* Cambridge: Harvard University.

______. 1985 (1902). *The varieties of religious experience.* In *The works of William James.* Cambridge: Harvard University Press.

McDermott, John J., R. W. Sleeper, Abraham Edel, and Richard Rorty. 1985. Symposium on Rorty's *Consequences of pragmatism. Transactions of the Charles S. Peirce Society* 21(1): 1–48.

Mahowald, Mary B. 1987. A majority perspective: Feminine and feminist elements in American philosophy. *Cross Currents* 36(4): 410–17.

Miranda, Wilma R. 1980. Implications in Dewey for feminist theory in education. *Educational Horizons* 58(Summer): 197–202.

Nagel, Thomas. 1986. *The view from nowhere.* Oxford: Oxford University Press.

Perry, Ralph Barton. 1935. *The thought and character of William James.* Vol. 2. Boston: Little, Brown.

Riley, Denise. 1988. *"Am I that name?"* Minneapolis: University of Minnesota Press.

Rosenblatt, Louise M. 1983 (1938). *Literature as exploration.* 3d ed. New York: Modern Language Association.

———. 1985. Viewpoints: Transaction versus interaction—a terminological rescue operation. *Research in the Teaching of English,* 96–107.

Russ, Joanna. 1983. *How to suppress women's writing.* Austin: University of Texas Press.

Seigfried, Charlene Haddock. 1982. Vagueness and the adequacy of concepts: In defense of William James's picturesque style. *Philosophy Today* 26(Winter): 357–67.

———. 1984a. Gender-specific values. *The Philosophical Forum* 15(4): 425-42.

———. 1984b. Extending the Darwinian model: James's struggle with Royce and Spencer. *Idealistic Studies* 14(Sept.): 259–72.

———. 1987. Feminist aesthetics and marginality. *Resources for Feminist Research* 16(4): 10–15.

———. 1989. Pragmatism, feminism, and sensitivity to context. In *Who cares? Theory, research, and educational implications of the ethic of care,* 63–83. Mary M. Brabeck, ed. New York: Praeger Press.

———. 1990a. Poetic invention and scientific observation: James's model of "sympathetic concrete observation." *Transactions of the Charles S. Peirce Society* 26(1): 115–30.

———. 1990b (1985). *Second sex: Second thoughts.* Reprinted in *Hypatia reborn: Essays in feminist philosophy,* 305–22. Azizah Y. al-Hibri and Margaret A. Simons, eds. Bloomington and Indianapolis: Indiana University Press.

———. 1990c. *William James's radical reconstruction of philosophy.* Albany: State University of New York Press.

Smith, John E. 1983. *The spirit of American philosophy.* Rev. ed. Albany: State University of New York Press.

Spender, Dale. 1983. *Women of ideas (and what men have done to them).* London: Ark.

Thayer, H. S. 1981. *Meaning and action.* 2d ed. Indianapolis: Hackett.

Tomkins, Jane P., ed. 1980. *Reader-response criticism.* Baltimore: Johns Hopkins University Press.

West, Cornel. 1989. *The American evasion of philosophy: A genealogy of pragmatism.* Madison: University of Wisconsin Press.

Wilson, Daniel J. 1990. *Science, community, and the transformation of American philosophy, 1860–1930*. Chicago: University of Chicago Press.

SARA RUDDICK

Maternal Thinking

MATERNAL PRACTICE

Maternal practice begins in a response to the reality of a biological child in a particular social world. To be a "mother" is to take upon oneself the responsibility of child care, making its work a regular and substantial part of one's working life.

Mothers, as individuals, engage in all sorts of other activities, from farming to deep sea diving, from astrophysics to elephant training. Mothers as individuals are not defined by their work; they are lovers and friends; they watch baseball, ballet, or the soaps; they run marathons, play chess, organize church bazaars and rent strikes. Mothers are as diverse as any other humans and are equally shaped by the social milieu in which they work. In my terminology they are "mothers" just because and to the degree that they are committed to meeting demands that define maternal work.

Both her child and the social world in which a mother works make these demands. "Demands" is an artificial term. Children demand all sorts of things—to eat ice cream before dinner, stay up all night, take the subway alone, watch the latest horror show on TV. A mother's social group demands of her all sorts of behavior—that she learn to sew or get a high school degree, hold her tongue or speak wittily in public, pay her taxes or go to jail for refusing to do so, sit ladylike in a restaurant or sit in at a lunch counter. A mother will decide in her own way which of these demands she will meet.

But in my discussion of maternal practice, I mean by "demands" those requirements that are imposed on anyone doing maternal work, in the way respect for experiment is imposed on scientists and racing past the finish line is imposed on jockeys. In this sense of demand, children "demand" that their lives be preserved and their growth fostered. In addition, the primary social groups with which a mother is identified, whether by force, kinship, or choice, demand that she raise her children in a manner acceptable to them. These three demands—for *preservation*, *growth*, and *social acceptability*—constitute maternal work; to be a mother is to be committed to meeting these demands by works of preservative love, nurturance, and training.

MATERNAL THINKING

Daily, mothers think out strategies of protection, nurturance, and training. Frequently conflicts between strategies or between fundamental demands provoke mothers to think about the meaning and relative weight of preservation, growth, and acceptability. In quieter moments, mothers reflect on their practice as a whole. As in any group of thinkers, some mothers are more ambitiously reflective than others, either out of temperamental thoughtfulness, moral and political concerns, or, most often, because they have serious problems with their children. However, maternal thinking is no rarity. Maternal work itself demands that mothers think; out of this need for thoughtfulness, a distinctive discipline emerges.

I speak about a mother's thought—the intellectual capacities she develops, the judgments she makes, the metaphysical attitudes she assumes, the values she affirms. Like a scientist writing up her experiment, a critic working over a text, or a historian assessing documents, a mother caring for children engages in a discipline. She asks certain questions—those relevant to her aims—rather than others; she accepts certain criteria for the truth, adequacy, and relevance of proposed answers; and she cares about the findings she makes and can act on. The discipline of maternal thought, like other disciplines, establishes criteria for determining failure and success, sets priorities, and identifies virtues that the discipline requires. Like any other work, mothering is prey to characteristic temptations that it must identify. To describe the capacities, judgments, metaphysical attitudes, and values of maternal thought presumes not maternal achievement, but a *conception* of achievement.

FEMINIST POLITICS

There is no litmus test for identifying a "feminist." Internationally and in the United States, feminism is a multifaceted social movement in the process of change and self-creation. When I speak of feminism I refer, minimally, to a politics that is dedicated to transforming those social and domestic arrangements that deliberately or unwittingly penalize women because of their sex. Second, whatever their other politics and interests, feminists focus seriously on the ways that gender—the social construction of masculinity and femininity—organizes political, personal, and intellectual life. The feminist assumption is that gender divisions of work, pleasure, power, and sensibility are socially created, detrimental to women and, to a lesser degree, to men, and therefore can and should be changed. Most important, though perhaps controversially, feminists are partisans of women,[1] fighting on their side, sometimes against, often with, men. As women, or in solidarity with them, feminists struggle against any social, racial, economic, or physical abuse that threatens women's capacity to work and to love.

This is a general and elastic definition that leaves open virtually every specific disagreement among feminists about policy or theory. It is a definition that in no way commits feminists to antimilitarism. In many parts of the world, feminist women organize to procure arms in defense of themselves and their people and in despair of getting powerful, violent men to disarm. Some feminists support military recruitment in less desperate circumstances, arguing that women benefit from the wages, work, travel, and education military life offers; moreover, they insist, if allowed to prepare for and participate in combat, women could acquire the courage and skills fostered by battle.

More politically, many feminists believe that it is a part of citizenship in a democratic society to assume the privileges and burdens a military state imposes on its citizens. In the United States, individual men have bought and begged their way out of combat; Black Americans and other men of "minority" races have had to fight to be included in combat and command; "minority" and poor men are selectively conscripted for unpopular wars. Nonetheless, despite these violations, many North American feminists endorse an ideal of civic virtue according to which no class of people, whether marked by race, sex, or ethnicity, should be excluded or exempted from military combat and command.

Whether they are sober liberals or struggling liberationists, feminists can take heart from a developing feminist *women's* militarist politics. The feminist soldier heroine may be most perfectly represented by a young woman with a baby in her arms and a gun over her shoulder, although an armed girl dressed as and sometimes passing for a comely man is a close second. The many distinctly feminine, and often distinctly sexy, soldier heroines of exemplary spirit simultaneously domesticate violence, expand women's imaginative aggressiveness, and rewrite, in a manner titillating and scary, the sexual scripts of battle.

Whether or not feminists are militarist, feminist politics transforms maternal militarism. Like a women's politics of resistance, feminism shifts the balance within maternal practice from denial to

1. The phrase "partisans of women" is Terry Winant's in "The Feminist Standpoint: A Matter of Language," *Hypatia*, vol. 2, no. 1, Winter 1987.

lucid knowledge, from parochialism to awareness of others' suffering, and from compliance to stubborn, decisive capacities to act. This transformation begins, paradoxically, in a tense relationship between feminists and women who are mothers. Mothers and feminists cannot leave each other alone. Almost every feminist had a mother; many are mothers; few think coolly about the institutions and passions of mothering that shaped their mothers' and often their own lives. For their part, many mothers, even those who are feminists, fear that feminism offers heartless or oversimple solutions to the social and personal dilemmas of mothering.

Nonetheless, the actual confrontation of mothers and feminists—whether practical or psychological—is deeply beneficial to mothering. Although some feminists have indeed been guilty of contempt for mothers, no other movement has taken so seriously or worked so effectively to ensure women's economic and psychological ability to engage in mothering without undue sacrifice of physical health and nonmaternal projects. Organizing women workers, fighting for day-care centers, adequate health care, and maternal and paternal leave, demanding birthgivers' right to participate in mothering as and when they choose—in these and many other struggles feminists have proved many times over that, as partisans of women, they are sturdy allies of mothers. In this practical support of mothers in their daily work the feminist transformation of maternal militarism is rooted.

Either because of their own experience of sexual prejudice and abuse or because they are heartened by particular feminist policies and fights on their behalf, many previously skeptical mothers become feminists. That is, with varying degrees of conviction, they tend to become partisans of women, able to focus on the impact of gender on their lives and to set themselves to change the sexual and domestic arrangements that oppress them. In becoming feminists, mothers acquire a "feminist consciousness," a confusing, often painful, but irresistible recognition that the stories they have told themselves about "being a woman" are self-deceptive and do not serve their interests. With this new knowledge comes an unsettling conviction that certain realities of their lives are intolerable and must be changed.

Sandra Bartky's early account of feminist consciousness—suggestive of the later standpoint theory—is especially useful:

> Coming to have a feminist consciousness is the experience of coming to know the truth about oneself and one's society. . . . The very *meaning* of what the feminist apprehends is illuminated by the light of what ought to be. . . . The feminist apprehends certain features of reality *as* intolerable, as to be rejected in behalf of a transforming project for the future. . . .

> Social reality is revealed as deceptive. . . . What is really happening is quite different from what appears to be happening.[2]

For a mother, "coming to know the truth" includes looking at the real feelings and conflicts of mothering. It is a feminist project to describe realistically the angers and ambivalences of maternal love. A feminist consciousness also requires mothers to look undefensively at women's social status and the political relations between men and women, which exact from mothers—even those who are men—unnecessary and unacceptable sacrifices of power and pleasures.

A feminist mother's growing ability to name and resist the forces ranged within and against her undermines many varieties of self-denial to which maternal thinking is susceptible. This does not mean that cheery denial, inauthenticity, or self-loss in attentive love—to take only three examples—can be "cured" by feminism. These are temptations endemic to maternal work. But a clear-sighted rather than mystifying apprehension of "oneself and one's society," combined with real increases in women's opportunities and self-respect, shifts the balance away from illusion and passivity toward active responsibility and engagement. A mother acquiring feminist consciousness ferrets out the meaning of dominant values, asking whose interests they serve and how they affect her children. To be a feminist mother is to recognize that many dominant values—including, but not limited to, the subordination of women—are unacceptable and need not be accepted.

These feminist habits of lucidity strengthen maternal nonviolence in distinctive ways. Although mothers are committed to resisting violence directed against their children, children themselves often remember being betrayed by mothers who blamed them for "provoking" the violence they suffered or who asked them to "understand" the violator. Nearly as frightening are memories of protective mothers unable to protect themselves from physical abuse or from silencing and contempt that borders on violence. Feminists name the many kinds of violence women suffer—from lovers, employers, husbands, and strangers—and recognize women's tendencies to "submit" or take the blame for men's violence, or, worse, get their children to do so.

Although feminists may be appalled when mothers abuse or neglect their children, and although feminist voices are prominent in protesting the poverty and desperation that often lie behind abuse and neglect, it is sometimes harder for feminists to see violence

2. Sandra Lee Bartky, "Toward a Phenomenology of Feminist Consciousness" in *Feminism and Philosophy*, ed. Mary Vetterlin-Braggin, Frederick A. Elliston and Jane English (Totowa, NJ: Littlefield Adams, 1977), pp. 22–34.

clearly and condemn it unequivocally when it is committed by women. Nonetheless, in scholarly works, fiction, and letters to the editors, feminists have insisted on looking at maternal violence in order to understand and take action against it. It is a feminist task to identify the violence involved when mothers take nature as an enemy, breaking the wills and sometimes the bodies of children. More generally, when feminists analyze the effects of repressive sexuality or a maternal rage for order born of fear and deprivation, they also write about and against maternal violence. Feminists do all this as partisans of women, not only analyzing but also creating policies and spaces that give women the economic possibility and physical safety to take care of themselves and those they care for—to start again.

In sum, a feminist mother becomes increasingly clear-sighted about the violences she has suffered or inflicted and increasingly able to resist them. As she develops a critical stance toward violences that she previously accepted, she is also likely to become suspicious of the fantasies and theories that dominate organized, public violence. Myths of beastly males, alluring warriors, omniscient defense intellectuals, conspiracies, emergencies, and nuclear protection are all vulnerable to the lucid, knowing gaze. When conjoined with the commitment to protect, lucid, suspicious knowledge may in itself be sufficient to inspire a mother's resistance to militarist plans and "strategic defense initiatives" that threaten her children.

But lucid knowledge cannot in itself inspire a mother's resistance to violence that threatens "other" children, not even when it is violence funded and perpetrated by her own government. For extended maternal antimilitarism, the best knowledge must be motivated and tested by a sympathetic apprehension of *others'* suffering as "intolerable, to be rejected in behalf of a transforming project for the future." . . . [T]here is a basis in maternal practice for extending the range of domestic nonviolence through maternal identification with other mothers' particular commitments to protect and cherish lives. I have . . . celebrated the extension of sympathy in Argentinian and Chilean women's politics of resistance. Feminist politics too makes a distinctive contribution to transnational and transcultural solidarity among mothers.

Unlike maternal thinking, which is rooted in particular passions and loyalties, feminism explicitly proclaims an ideal of solidarity and loudly rues its failures to implement the ideal. The ideal of solidarity is a successor to an earlier ideal of "sisterhood," which some feminists espoused . . . [more than] a decade ago.[3] The sister-

3. My discussion here is directly indebted to Bell Hooks's discussion of solidarity in *Feminist Theory: From the Margin to the Center* (Boston: South End Press, 1984).

hood of women was based on allegedly shared oppression and shared responsibility for caring labor. The romantic hope of sisterhood did not survive class and racial division, the marked disparity between the kind and degree of women's oppression, and the myriad cultural and individual varieties of women's participation in caring labor. Along with the ideal of sisterhood the idea that men were other and enemy briefly held sway. This militarist construction belied the alliances of women with men of their race and class and the affectionate camaraderie that often flourishes among women and men who are colleagues and friends. Nor could a feminism that identified men as enemies enlist the allegiance of countless women who, whatever their sexuality, loved men—brothers, fathers, sons, other kin, friends, and sometimes lovers.

The feminist ideal of identifying with women's struggles quite different from one's own survived romantic and militarized sisterhood. While feminists no longer claimed that all women shared a common oppression or common experiences of mothering and tending, they did develop an alternative ideal based on solidarity with women who suffered from and resisted sexual, racial, intellectual, economic, or other abuse. The ideal of solidarity does not reflect an attitude feminists have to any or all women. Most obviously, the subjects of feminist solidarity are women who suffer abuse from individual men or from sexist and heterosexist institutions. Second, whatever their individual experiences, feminists tend to ally themselves politically with women who are abused—out of whatever combination of class, race, and sexual oppression—as birthgivers, mothers, or female kin. Solidarity extends indefinitely with different emphases depending on the feminist. But it does not extend to "women" in general, but rather to women in particular situations of struggle.

A mother who is a woman acquiring feminist consciousness will likely encounter the ideal of solidarity among women, especially if she finds herself in the company of other feminists. Whether they meet in a shelter, reading group, health center, union, or peace action, feminists proclaim ideals of solidarity in explicit ideological statements, often through bitter recriminations and acknowledgments of failure that attest to the force of the ideal. To the extent that a mother herself acquires the ideal of solidarity, the purview of her lucid knowledge will extend to "other" women, including often mothers who are targets of her own government's violence. Solidarity with women in struggle tends to undercut military loyalty to states. It eschews abstract labels of cause or party—"communist," "fascist," "democrat"—in favor of a closer look at what women actually suffer and how they act. Military loyalties require women and men to kill—or at least to pay for and train killers—in the name of abstract enmity. Feminist solidarity searches among these abstract enemies and allies to identify with women's culturally specific struggles to work, care, and enjoy, to think and speak freely, and to resist abuse.

As feminism transforms the denial and parochialism that encourage maternal militarism, mothers are likely to act first against particular policies and forces of violence that threaten them and their children, then against those that are deployed by their own government against others, and finally on behalf of children anywhere who suffer violence. Mothers are not especially altruistic; nonetheless they are capable of responsibility and solidarity. Mothers engage in various kinds of action, from writing letters to blockading a military base, usually in concert with women and men who are not mothers, sometimes in groups that are specifically maternal or feminist. Insofar as they become publicly visible *as mothers* who are resisting violence and inventing peace, they transform the meaning of "motherhood."

It is also true that when mothers become publicly visible as peace activists, feminists may prove reluctant to support them. As many feminists have pointed out, women can act individually or collectively as women without making for themselves or for women generally typical feminist claims such as for the right to equal pay, promotion, and management, self-respecting sexual pleasure, control of the conditions of giving birth, or autonomy within marriage and the option of fair divorce. Any politics that does not make explicit claims about injustice to women will be seen by many feminists as diverting women's energies from feminist demands. Many feminists will be especially skeptical of a maternal antimilitarist politics that turns on women's identities as mothers, caretakers, kin workers, and shelterers. In drawing strength from women's work, this politics seems to ignore the exploitation of the workers and to reinforce a conception of women's responsibility that has boded ill for women themselves. Unlike a women's politics of resistance that proudly draws on traditional identities even as it transforms them, a feminist politics subjects all traditional womanly roles to critical reflection.

Nonetheless, despite these inevitable tensions I believe that feminists strengthen mothers' power to act whether as individuals, in mixed groups, or in a women's politics of resistance. Feminists themselves point out that whenever women act publicly or in conjunction with other women they tend to acquire the self-respect and skills that feminists wish for all women. Feminist literature and art celebrate these strengths and consequently legitimate them for the women themselves and often in the eyes of their culture, whatever the cause in which they are developed. Less happily, it is also true that women acting militantly, once they are at all effective, are invariably subject to misogynist insult from strangers and political opponents and often from the men they live among. Despite local variations in vocabulary and emphasis, there is a depressing redundancy in the vocabulary of abuse: women's judgment is impugned as "crazy," "hysterical," naive, and sentimental; their "castrating" anger arises from sexual envy or deprivation; they are witches, whores, and lesbians. It is feminists who have deconstructed these terms of abuse, revealing the ways in which psychiatric insult, sexual superstition, and homophobia have been tools of intimidation that separate women from each other and deny them confidence in their minds, angers, and desires. In a feminist culture, even without explicit feminist support, contempt that would otherwise be dispiriting can issue in appropriate anger and pride.

In sum, mothers who acquire a feminist consciousness and engage in feminist politics are likely to become more effectively nonviolent and antimilitarist. By increasing mothers' powers to know, care, and act, feminism actualizes the peacefulness latent in maternal practice. Feminism has these transformative powers whether or not feminists are antimilitarist. As I have insisted, in any generous understanding of feminism, it is possible to applaud organized violence without violating feminist commitments.

It does not, however, follow that feminism and peace politics are opposed. Indeed, it is my belief that feminism is already conjoined with a peace politics that is marked by its double origins in women's traditional work and feminist resistance to abuse against women. It should be obvious that insofar as feminist mothers are antimilitarist, so too is that part of the feminist movement made up of mothers and mother-identified men and women. Quite aside from its maternal membership, there are inherently antimilitarist features of feminism. In revealing connections between making "masculine" men and making war, feminists cut beneath the abstractions of just-war theory to the sexual fantasies and fears that sustain the allure of violence. Often feminists take violence against women both as emblematic of military and ecological violence and as causally responsible for them; to resist the one is to resist the other. Feminism is a global movement committed to a solidarity that respects differences despite anger and bitterness. Even in their efforts to support one another effectively, feminists have to invent the techniques of "peace."

It is not surprising that a distinctly *feminist* peace politics is one of the most vital parts of the international peace movement. If feminism at its most militarist challenges maternal militarism, is it unreasonable to hope that an antimilitarist feminism can effectively transform a latent maternal peacefulness into an instrument of peace? Feminist peace activists offer peacemaking mothers resources, theoretical insights, psychological support and solidarity in action. The direction is not only one way. Mothers strengthen even as they are strengthened by feminism, bringing to a collective peace politics distinctive habits of mind and principles of nonviolence honed by daily use.

I do not want to suggest that feminism assimilates either to mothering or to peace politics. Many feminists are appalled by the conditions of mothering and by the women who submit to them; many feminist women are engaged in organized violence as part of their resistance to the unrelenting economic and racial violence they suffer. Nonetheless, there is truth—and hope—in the poster slogan "A feminist world is a peaceful world." A feminist consciousness can be both antimilitarist and maternal; the standpoint achieved in the feminist transformation of mothering is also a distinct and powerful antimilitarist vision.

SARAH HOAGLAND

Lesbian Ethics

Understanding sexism involves analyzing how institutional power is in the hands of men, how men discriminate against women, how society classifies men as the norm and women as passive and inferior, how male institutions objectify women, how society excludes women from participation as full human beings, and how what has been perceived as normal male behavior is also violence against women. In other words, to analyze sexism is to understand primarily how women are victims of institutional and ordinary male behavior.

Understanding heterosexism, as well as homophobia, involves analyzing, not just women's victimization, but also how women are defined in terms of men or not at all, how lesbians and gay men are treated—indeed scapegoated—as deviants, how choices of intimate partners for both women and men are restricted or denied through taboos to maintain a certain social order. (For example, if sexual relations between men were openly allowed, then men could do to men what men do to women[1] and, further, [some] men could become what women are. This is verboten. In addition, if love between women were openly explored, women might simply walk away from men, becoming 'not-women'. This, too, is verboten.) Focusing on heterosexism challenges heterosexuality as an institu-

1. Conversation, Marilyn Frye. Note Andrea Dworkin, *Pornography: Men Possessing Women* (New York: G. P. Putnam's Sons, 1979), p. 61.

tion, but it can also lead lesbians to regard as a political goal our acceptance, even assimilation, into heterosexual society: we try to assure heterosexuals we are normal people (that is, just like them), that they are being unjust in stigmatizing us, that ours is a mere sexual preference.

In her ground-breaking work on compulsory heterosexuality, Adrienne Rich challenges us to address heterosexuality as a political institution which ensures male right of physical, economical, and emotional access to women.[2] Jan Raymond develops a theory of hetero-reality and argues: "While I agree that we are living in a heterosexist society, I think the wider problem is that we live in a hetero-relational society where most of women's personal, social, political, professional, and economic relations are defined by the ideology that woman is for man."[3] I go a bit further.

Understanding heterosexualism involves analyzing the relationship between men and women in which both men and women have a part. Heterosexualism is men dominating and de-skilling women in any of the number of forms, from outright attack to paternalistic care, and women devaluing (of necessity) female bonding as well as finding inherent conflicts between commitment and autonomy and consequently valuing an ethics of dependence. Heterosexualism is a way of living (which actual practitioners exhibit to a greater or lesser degree) that normalizes the dominance of one person in a relationship and the subordination of another. As a result, it undermines female agency.

What I am calling 'heterosexualism' is not simply a matter of males having procreative sex with females.[4] It is an entire way of living which involves a delicate, though at times indelicate, balance between masculine predation upon and masculine protection of a feminine object of masculine attention. Heterosexualism is a particular economic, political, and emotional relationship between men and women: men must dominate women and women must subordinate themselves to men in any of a number of ways. As a result, men presume access to women while women remain riveted on men and are unable to sustain a community of women.

In the u.s., women cannot appear publicly without some men advancing on them, presuming access to them. In fact, many women will think something is wrong if this doesn't happen. A woman simply is someone toward whom such behavior is appropriate. When

2. Adrienne Rich, "Compulsory Heterosexuality and Lesbian Existence," *Signs* 5, no. 4 (Summer 1980): 647; reprinted in *Women-Identified-Women,* ed. Trudy Darty and Sandee Potter (Palo Alto, Calif.: Mayfield Publishing Co., 1984), p. 133.

3. Janice G. Raymond, *A Passion for Friends* (Boston: Beacon Press, 1986), p. 11.

4. Conversation, Ariane Brunet.

a woman is accompanied by a man, however, she is usually no longer considered fair game. As a result, men close to individual women—fathers, boyfriends, husbands, brothers, escorts, colleagues—become protectors (theoretically), staving off advances from other men.

The value of special protection for women is prevalent in this society. Protectors interact with women in ways that promote the image of women as helpless: men open doors, pull out chairs, expect women to dress in ways that interfere with their own self-protection.[5] And women accept this as attentive, complimentary behavior and perceive themselves as persons who need special attention and protection.

What a woman faces in a man is either a protector or a predator, and men gain identity through one or another of these roles.[6] This has at least five consequences. First, there can be no protectors unless there is a danger. A man cannot identify himself in the role of protector unless there is something which needs protection. So it is in the interest of protectors that there be predators. Secondly, to be protected, women must be in danger. In portraying women as helpless and defenseless, men portray women as victims . . . and therefore as targets.

Thirdly, a woman (or girl) is viewed as the object of male passion and thereby its cause. This is most obvious in the case of rape: she must have done something to tempt him—helpless hormonal bundle that he is. Thus if women are beings who by nature are endangered, then, obviously, they are thereby beings who by nature are seductive—they actively attract predators. Fourthly, to be protected, women must agree to act as men say women should: to appear feminine, prove they are not threatening, stay at home, remain only with the protector, devalue their connections with other women, and so on.

Finally, when women step out of the feminine role, thereby becoming active and "guilty," it is a mere matter of logic that men will depict women as evil and step up overt physical violence against them in order to reaffirm women's victim status. For example, as the demand for women's rights in the u.s. became publicly perceptible, the depiction of lone women as "sluts" inviting attack also became prevalent. A lone female hitchhiker was perceived, not as someone to protect, but as someone who had given up her right

5. For further development of this point, note Marilyn Frye, "Oppression," in *The Politics of Reality: Essays in Feminist Theory* (Trumansburg, N.Y.: The Crossing Press, 1983, now in Freedom, Calif.), pp. 5–6.

6. Note Susan Griffin, "Rape: The All-American Crime," in *Feminism and Philosophy,* ed. Mary Vetterling-Braggin, Frederick A. Elliston, & Jane English (Totowa, N.J.: Littlefield, Adams & Co., 1977), especially p. 320.

to protection and thus as someone who was a target for attack. The rampant increase in pornography—entertainment by and for men about women—is men's general response to the u.s. women's liberation movement's demand of integrity, autonomy, and dignity for women.

What radical feminists have exposed through all the work on incest (daughter rape) and wife-beating is that protectors are also predators. Of course, not all men are wife- or girlfriend-beaters, but over half who live with women are. And a significant number of u.s. family homes shelter an "incestuous" male.[7]

Although men may exhibit concern over womanabuse, they have a different relationship to it than women; their concerns are not women's concerns. For example, very often men become irate at the fact that a woman has been raped or beaten by another man. But this is either a man warming to his role of protector—it rarely, if ever, occurs to him to teach her self-defense—or a man deeply affected by damage done to his "property" by another man. And while some men feel contempt for men who batter or rape, Marilyn Frye suggests it is quite possible their contempt arises, not from the fact that womanabuse is happening, but from the fact that the batterer or rapist must accomplish by force what they themselves can accomplish more subtly by arrogance.[8]

7. Sonia Johnson, presidential campaign speech, Chicago, Ill., 1984; conversation, Pauline Bart. The figure on wife-beating comes from the "Uniform Crime Reports of 1982," federal reports on incidences of domestic crime. According to a fact sheet from the Illinois Coalition on Domestic Violence, "National Domestic Violence Statistics, 1/84," ten to twenty percent of American children are abused. Another fact sheet, "Verified Domestic Statistics," researched and compiled by the Western Center on Domestic Violence (San Francisco, Calif.), cites estimates of Maria Roy, *The Abusive Partner* (New York: Van Nostrand Rernhold, 1982) as indicating that violence against wives will occur at least once in two-thirds of all marriages. Another fact sheet, "Wife Abuse: The Facts" (Center for Woman Policy Studies, 2000 P. Street N.W., Washington, D.C. 20036), cites Murray Straus, Richard Gelles, and Suzanne Steinmetz, *Beyond Closed Doors: Violence in the American Family* (Garden City, N.Y.: Doubleday, 1980) as saying that twenty-five percent of wives are severely beaten during their marriage. There are many more statistics . . . you get the idea. Bette S. Tallen was extremely helpful in obtaining some of this information. Note also Del Martin, *Battered Wives,* revised and updated (Volcano Press, Inc., 330 Ellis St., #518, Dept. B, San Francisco, CA 94102, 1976, 1981); Leonore Walker, *The Battered Woman* (New York: Harper & Row, 1979); Florence Rush, *The Best Kept Secret: The Sexual Abuse of Children* (Englewood Cliffs, N.J.: Prentice-Hall, Inc., 1980); Diana E. H. Russell, *Sexual Exploitation: Rape, Child Sexual Abuse, and Workplace Harassment* (Beverly Hills, Calif.: Sage Publications, 1984); and Elizabeth A. Stanko, *Intimate Intrusions: Women's Experience of Male Violence* (Boston, Mass.: Routledge & Kegan Paul, 1985) among others.

8. Marilyn Frye, "In and Out of Harm's Way: Arrogance and Love," *Politics of Reality,* p. 72.

The current willingness of men in power to pass laws restricting pornography is a matter of men trying to reestablish the asexual, virginal image of (some) women whom they can then protect in their homes. And they are using as their excuse right-wing women as well as feminists who appear to be asking for protection, like proper women, rather than demanding liberation. Men use violence when women don't pay attention to them. Then, when women ask for protection, men can find meaning by turning on the predators—particularly ones of a different race or class.

In other words, the logic of protection is essentially the same as the logic of predation. Through predation, men do things to women and against women all of which violate women and undermine women's integrity. Yet protection objectifies just as much as predation. To protect women, men do things to women and against women; acting "for a woman's own good," they violate her integrity and undermine her agency. . . .

Heterosexualism has certain similarities to colonialism, particularly in its maintenance through force when paternalism is rejected (that is, the stepping up of male predation when women reject male protection) and in its portrayal of domination as natural (men are to dominate women as naturally as colonizers are to dominate the colonized, and without any sense of themselves as oppressing those they dominate except during times of overt aggression) and in the de-skilling of women. And just as it is colonizers who cannot survive as colonizers without the colonized, so it is men who cannot survive as men (protectors or predators) without women.

Complementing the protector/predator function of men is the concept of 'woman', particularly as it functions in mainstream U.S. society. Consider what the concept lacks. It lacks (1) a sense of female power, (2) any hint that women as a group have been the targets of male violence, (3) any hint either of collective or individual female resistance to male domination and control, and (4) any sense of lesbian connection.

The concept of 'woman' includes no real sense of female power. Certainly, it includes no sense of women as conquering and dominating forces. More significantly, it includes no sense of strength and competence. I am not denying that there are many strong women. And where women encourage each other in defiance of the dominant valuation, significant images appear. But over time, under heterosexualism, these images tend to be modified by appeals to femininity or are used against women. Without sufficient deference to men, women will find 'castrating bitch' or 'dyke' or comparable concepts used to keep them in line.

Men of a given group will partially modify 'femininity' in order to emphasize female competence and skill when they absolutely need extra help: during wars—Rosie the riveter, for example—or on small nebraska farms or in revolutionary movements or in kibbutzim when the state is unstable or in a community deeply split under oppression. But once their domain is more firmly established, men drag up the feminine stereotype (while nevertheless expecting women to do most of the work with none of the benefits). . . .

Because there is no sense that violence has ever been directed at women as a group, it is difficult to gain a perspective on the magnitude of the force used against women now. While u.s. women may be horrified at the specter of african genital mutilation and indian dowry deaths, african (particularly nigerian) and indian students in my classes are no less horrified at the incidence of rape and the amount of pornography which form a daily part of u.s. women's lives. Except for radical feminists, no one in the united states perceives the phenomenal rate of incest (daughter rape), wife-beating, rape, forced prostitution, and the ideology of pornography—depicted not only in men's magazines but on television, billboards, in grocery stores, in schools, and in general in every public and private sector a woman goes—as any kind of concerted assault on women. There is no general sense that, as Sonia Johnson points out, men have declared war on women,[9] rather this assault—because men are paying attention to women—is called "attraction," even "admiration."

Thirdly, the concept of 'woman' includes no sense of female resistance—either collective or individual—to male domination. While there is evidence that amazons once lived in north africa, in china, in anatolia (turkey), and between the black and the caspian seas, amazons are repeatedly treated as a joke or buried. Yet as Helen Diner writes:

> At the celebrations in honor of the dead, Demosthenes, Lysias, Himerios, Isocartes, and Aristeides praise the victory over the Amazons as more important than that over the Persians or any other deed in history. . . . The wars between the Greeks and Persians were wars between two male-dominated societies. In the Amazon war, the issue was which of the two forms of life was to shape European civilization in its image.[10]

Significantly, even feminists and lesbian-feminists shun amazons, apparently for fear of appearing out of touch with reality (with the

9. Sonia Johnson, presidential campaign speech, Chicago, Ill., 1984; also *Going Out of Our Minds: The Metaphysics of Liberation* (Freedom, Calif.: The Crossing Press, 1987), p. 244.

10. Helen Diner, *Mothers and Amazons* (New York: Doubleday, 1973), pp. 95–105.

consensus). With a few notable exceptions, we are not responding to Maxine Feldman's call, "Amazon women rise."[11] There is little celebration of amazons (even though we are beginning to hear again of goddesses and witches). We do not acknowledge the amazons even as symbolic defenders of womanhood—and this at a time when male violence against women is blatant. Instead, even radical feminists push for greater police and state protection. The amazons—as well as female warriors such as those of the dahomey or the nootka societies—simply do not fit within the concept of 'woman' of mainstream u.s. society.[12]

Because there is no mythological, much less historical, memory of female resistance to male domination, isolated and individual acts of female resistance are also rendered imperceptible as resistance, particularly, as I argue below, through the concept of 'femininity'. A 'woman' is one whose identity comes through her alliance with a man to such an extent that any woman who resists male violence, male advances, and male access is not a real woman.

The value of 'woman', thus, excludes a sense of female presence, skill, and power, an awareness that violence has been and is perpetrated against women as a group, and a sense of female resistance to male domination. It also excludes a sense of lesbian connection. Adrienne Rich took on the task of addressing (1) the bias "through which lesbian experience is perceived on a scale ranging from deviant to abhorrent, or simply rendered invisible;" (2) "how and why women's choice of women as passionate comrades, life partners, coworkers, lovers, tribe, has been crushed, invalidated, forced into

11. Maxine Feldman, "Amazon," recorded on the album *Closet Sale* (Galaxia, P.O. Box 212, Woburn, MA 01801). Some exceptions include Susan Cavin, *Lesbian Origins* (San Francisco: Jism Press, 1985); Mary Daly, *Gyn/Ecology;* Audre Lorde, *The Black Unicorn* (New York: W. W. Norton & Co., 1978); Merlin Stone, *When God Was a Woman* (New York: Harcourt, Brace, Jovanovich/Harvest, 1976); Monique Wittig, *Les Guérillères* (New York: Avon, 1969), and Monique Wittig and Sande Zeig, *Lesbian Peoples: Material for a Dictionary* (New York: Avon, 1979); Carol Moorefield and Kathleen Valentine, "Matriarchy: A Guide to the Future?," in *For Lesbians Only: A Separatist Anthology,* ed. Sarah Lucia Hoagland and Julia Penelope, Onlywomen Press, London; "Amazons," in *The Woman's Encyclopedia of Myths and Secrets,* Barbara G. Walker (New York: Harper & Row, 1983), p. 24–7; Judy Grahn, *Another Mother Tongue: Gay Words, Gay Worlds* (Boston: Beacon Press, 1984); Anne Cameron, *Daughters of Copper Woman* (Vancouver, B.C.: Press Gang Publishers, 1981); Micheline Grimard-Leduc, "The Mind-Drifting Islands," *Trivia* 8 (Winter 1986): 28–36, published in *l'île des amantes: essai/poèmes,* Micheline Grimard-Leduc, C.P. 461, Station N, Montréal, Québec, H2X 3N3, Canada, 1982; and Jeffner Allen, *Lesbian Philosophy: Explorations* (Palo Alto, Calif.: Institute of Lesbian Studies, 1986).

12. For reference to the Dahomey, note Audre Lorde, *The Black Unicorn,* p. 119; also Carol Moorefield and Kathleen Valentine, "Matriarchy: A Guide to the Future?;" for reference to the Nootka, note Anne Cameron, *Daughters of Copper Woman.*

hiding and disguise;" and (3) "the virtual or total neglect of lesbian existence in a wide range of writings, including feminist scholarship."[13] As Harriet Ellenberger writes:

> A central taboo in patriarchy is the taboo against women consorting with women—and yet that tabooed consorting, allying, connecting has gone on and goes on in front of their noses, and men and most women don't think it's real.[14]

What the concept of 'woman' includes is equally significant. Given the masculinist naming of women, a 'woman' is (1) male-identified, someone whose identity emerges through her relationship to a man, (2) someone who makes herself attractive to men, (3) an object to be conquered by men, and (4) a breeder (of boys).

A woman's identity is incorporated in her relationship with a man: she is first and foremost some man's but not some woman's mother, wife, mistress, or daughter. As the radicalesbians argued in 1970:

> We are authentic, legitimate, real to the extent that we are the property of some man whose name we bear. To be a woman who belongs to no man is to be invisible, pathetic, inauthentic, unreal.[15]

A woman belonging to no man either doesn't exist or is trying to be a man. Further, a 'woman' is responsible for the sexual servicing of men.[16] Her goodness or badness, her ethical status, is based on her sexual availability, cost, and fidelity to men.[17] Ultimately, a 'woman' is a virgin or a whore—that is, related through sex to a man.

Secondly, a 'woman' is someone who is attractive to men. If she does not try to make herself attractive to men, she is considered to have a serious problem. In mainstream u.s. society, attractiveness

13. Adrienne Rich, "Compulsory Heterosexuality and Lesbian Existence," p. 632 or pp. 119–20.

14. Harriet Desmoines [Ellenberger], "There Goes the Revolution . . . ," *Sinister Wisdom* 9 (Spring 1979): 22.

15. Radicalesbians, "The Woman Identified Woman," in *Notes From the Third Year*, 1971, reprinted in *Radical Feminism*, p. 244. Note also Anita Cornwell, "Some Notes on the Black Lesbian and the Womin-Identified Womin Concept," in *Black Lesbian in America* (Tallahassee, Fla.: The Naiad Press, 1983), pp. 26–30.

16. Kathleen Barry, *Female Sexual Slavery* (Englewood Cliffs, N.J.: Prentice-Hall, 1979).

17. Julia P. Stanley [Julia Penelope], "Paradigmatic Woman: The Prostitute," in *Papers in Language Variation*, ed. David L. Shores and Carole P. Hines (Birmingham: University of Alabama Press, 1977), pp. 303–21.

means she is white anglo, upper middle class, virtually anorexic (that is, unhealthy), and young enough to have no character lines on her face, though occasionally she may be dark and "exotic." Those women who fall outside these categories, while not entirely discounted as women, are nevertheless made to feel poor substitutes for a woman. Further, a 'woman' is one who must be protected from what is evil (that is, dark) unless she is dark (that is, evil) herself—in which case, other women must be protected from her. The whiter she is, the purer she is. The darker she is, the more dangerously sexual she is. Again, she is a virgin or a whore—that is, white or black.

Thirdly, a 'woman' is someone who must be conquered by a man. The ideology of pornography, from soft porn to snuff, portrays a woman as an object (someone to be acted upon—in this case, attacked and overcome), someone who exists to be dominated. through violation—which violation she will ultimately crave. The ideology of romanticism (popularly portrayed in the harlequin romances) is the same: A woman is an object (someone to be acted upon—in this case, protected and seduced), someone who exists to be conquered. She is characterized by her lack of sexual desire—she is to reject (male) sexual advances in order to display her modesty; and hence men know that when she says "no," she really means "yes." Thus she, too, is to be dominated through violation—violation of her integrity—which violation she suddenly starts to crave. Both pornography and romanticism tell us that a woman is to be conquered and dominated by the force of masculine will.

Finally, a 'woman' is a breeder. A woman is fulfilled through breeding, her basic ethical possibility is selfless giving and nurturing, and anything which interferes with this process is suspect. Further, whenever a people are in jeopardy because men play war, men stress breeding to the exclusion of all else, and carefully supervise it. In anglo-european, eurasian, and all mainstream american societies (central, south, and north), this function cannot be entrusted to her. Her body is not hers to determine. For example, the issue of abortion, as it is being played out in the u.s., is not a woman's issue. For the question concerns, simply, which men will control women's abortions—the state or individual men.[18] And doctors exercising their paternalistic concern for social order sterilize women they deem inappropriate mothers, such as poor black and poor puerto rican women.[19] A 'woman' is a breeder, and breeders

18. This point was made in a talk by Marilyn Frye.

19. Claudia Dreifus, "Sterilizing the Poor," in *Seizing Our Bodies: The Politics of Women's Health*, ed. Claudia Dreifus (New York: Vintage Books/Random House, 1978), pp. 105–20.

need caretakers who make breeding decisions, including genetic reconstruction. Further, of course, when a woman breeds successfully, what she breeds is male—that is, someone who carries on her husband's line.

A 'woman', thus, is a sex object essentially submissive to and dependent on men, one whose function is to perpetuate the race (while protectors and predators engage in their project of destroying it). No, one is not born a woman.

I want a moral revolution.

The primary concept used to interpret and evaluate individual women's choices and actions is 'femininity'. 'Femininity' normalizes male domination and paints a portrait of women as subordinate and naively content with being controlled. Thus patrihistorians claim that women have remained content with their lot, accepting male domination throughout time, with the exception of a few suffragists and now a few aberrant feminists. . . .

'Femininity' is a concept which goes a long way in the social construction of heterosexual reality. A movement of women could withdraw from that framework and begin to revalue that reality and women's choices within it. A movement of women can challenge the feminine stereotype, dis-cover women's resistance, and provide a base for more effective resistance. A movement of women can challenge the consensus that made the individual act of sabotage plausible.

Yet if that movement does not challenge the concept of 'femininity', ultimately it will not challenge the consensus, it will not challenge the dominance and subordination of heterosexualism. For example, radical feminists and revolutionary feminists in england criticize the women's work at greenham common for appealing too much to traditional feminine stereotypes, including woman as nurturer and peacemaker as well as sacrificer for her children. As a result, they argue, the peace movement coopts feminism.[20]

Further, feminism itself is in danger of perpetuating the value of 'femininity' in interpreting and evaluating individual women's choices. Feminists continue to note how women are victims of institutional and ordinary behavior, but many have ceased to challenge the concept of 'woman' and the role men and male institutions play as "protectors" of women. . . .

A movement which challenges the dominant valuation of women will focus on women as agents in a relationship rather than as a type. A woman is not a passive being to whom things unfortunately or intentionally happen. She is a breathing, judging being, acting in coerced and oppressive circumstances. Her judgments and choices

20. Note, for example, *Breaching the Peace: A Collection of Radical Feminist Papers* (London: Onlywomen Press, 1983).

may be ineffective on any given occasion, or wrong, but they are decisions nevertheless. She is an agent and she is making choices. More than a victim, Kathleen Barry suggests, a woman caught in female sexual slavery is a survivor, making crucial decisions about what to do in order to survive. She is a moral agent who makes judgments within a context of oppression in consideration of her own needs and abilities.

By perceiving women's behavior, not through the value of 'femininity', but rather as actions of moral agents making judgments about their own needs and abilities in coerced and oppressive circumstances, we can begin to conceive of ourselves and each other as agents of our actions (though not creators of the circumstances we face under oppression). And this is a step toward realizing an ethical existence under oppression, one not caught up with the values of dominance and subordination. . . .

Heterosexualism is a conceptual framework within which the concept of 'moral agency' independent of the master/slave virtues cannot find fertile ground. And it combines with ethical judgments to create a value whose primary function is not the moral development of individuals but rather the preservation of a patriarchal social control. Thus I want to challenge our acceptance and use of that ethics. . . .

In discussing what I call Lesbian Ethics, I do not claim that lesbians haven't made many of the choices (heterosexual) women have made or that lesbians haven't participated in the consensus of straight thinking or that lesbians have withdrawn from the value of dominance and subordination and the security of established meaning we can fine therein. I am not claiming that lesbians have lived under different conceptual or material conditions. I am claiming, however, that lesbian choice holds certain possibilities. It is a matter of further choice whether we go on to develop these possibilities or whether instead we try to fit into the existing heterosexual framework in any one of a number of ways.

Thus I am claiming that the conceptual category 'lesbian'—unlike the category 'woman'—is not irretrievably tied up with dominance and subordination as norms of behavior. And I am claiming that by attending each other, we may find the possibility of ethical values appropriate to lesbian existence, values we can choose as moral agents to give meaning to our lives as lesbians. In calling for withdrawal from the existing heterosexual value system, I am calling for a moral revolution, a revolution of lesbianism. . . .

Understanding choice as creation, not sacrifice, helps us better understand choices we make typically considered "altruistic." We often are drawn to helping others. That's one reason so many are drawn to healing, to teaching, to volunteering to work at shelters, to practicing therapy, to working at community centers or in political campaigns, to going to nicaragua—to all kinds of political work. In doing such work, we feel we are creating something, that we are participating in something; we engage and we make a difference.

However, there remains the danger that we treat choice and engagement as "handing our identity over to individuals or institutions," or even as "acting as though in my own behalf, but in behalf of the other." To choose and engage, we are both separate and related. In heteropatriarchy, engagement and creation for women amount to mothering. Mothering, perhaps, most clearly embodies the feminine virtues, is itself a feminine virtue. And appealing once again to the 'feminine', we tend to romanticize 'mothering' as women's function and regard it as unconditional loving, as a matter of selflessly protecting and nurturing all life.

In the first place, mothering is women's *function* only given the values of heterosexualism. Church fathers (inspired by Thomas Aquinas among others) and state fathers (such as Hitler and Mussolini) argue that the function of a woman is to bear and raise children. They thereby conclude that women ought to bear and raise children.

Certainly it is true that some women have borne and raised children, many women are capable of it. Nevertheless, we cannot conclude that something a woman is capable of is women's function or that women ought to do it unless we add a premise to the effect that women ought to do what they're capable of. Now, women are capable of many things, and women actually do many things—kill battering husbands, for example, or avenge the rape of daughters. Yet christian fathers are not prepared to assert that women ought to do all they're capable of, they are not prepared to add any such premise. As a result, what appears to be a factual statement about women's function is actually a disguised value statement in that men have picked one of the many things women do and decided to call *that* women's function.[21]

If I were to pick one thing and claim it is women's function these days, I would suggest it is amazoning. Some women do it, and many women are capable of it. And, in my opinion, it is far more necessary than mothering. While some might focus on mothering, the vast majority might answer the call to amazon. Further, they would accomplish through amazoning what they keep trying to accomplish through mothering—appropriate atmosphere for children, self-esteem for girls, caring, room to grow and flourish.

Other fathers in patriarchy, scientific fathers, claim that women's function is to bear and raise children because, they claim, the species will not survive otherwise. As a result they target women who cannot or who do not bear children as "abnormal" women.

21. This function argument comes from the work of Jim Kimble, University of Colorado.

Given the population, we can only conclude that these fathers are actually thinking of maintaining dominance of their race (which they equate with its survival) and—to touch on finer points—maintenance of their class. Concomitantly, white men institute programs of forced sterilization against women of color. Further, as Marilyn Frye writes:

> In the all white or mostly white environments I have usually lived and worked in, when the women start talking up feminism and lesbian feminism, we are very commonly challenged with the claim that if we had our way, the species would die out. (The assumption our critics make here is that if women had a choice, we would never have intercourse and never bear children. This reveals a lot about the critics' own assessment of the joys of sex, pregnancy, birthing and motherhood.) They say the species would die out. What I suspect is that the critics confuse the white race with the human species. . . . What the critics are saying, once it is decoded, is that the white race might die out. The demand that white women make white babies to keep the race afloat has not been overt. . . . [White] women have generally interpreted our connections with these men solely in terms of gender, sexism, and male dominance. We have to figure their desire for racial dominance in their equations.[22]

Men stress women's breeding function when they want cannon fodder or a larger pool of unemployed through which they can drive wages down and exploit the labor force. Women may find that the species will survive only if women refuse to bear and raise children, particularly when under pressure from men to breed. Certainly, as Sally Gearhart convincingly argues,[23] the survival of the species may depend on women reducing drastically the number of male children they bear. It is not at all clear that the survival of the species depends on women bearing and raising children. As Elsa Gidlow writes, "ask no man pardon."[24]

The idea that mothering is women's function also appears in women's spirituality, which is rushing to claim the 'feminine'. Wom-

22. Marilyn Frye, "On Being White: Toward a Feminist Understanding of Race and Race Supremacy," in *The Politics of Reality*, p. 124.

23. Sally Gearhart, "The Future—If There Is One—Is Female," in *Reweaving the Web of Life: Feminism and Nonviolence*, ed. Pam McAllister (Philadelphia: New Society Publishers, 1982), pp. 266–84.

24. Elsa Gidlow, *Ask No Man Pardon: The Philosophical Significance of Being a Lesbian* (Druid Heights Books, 685 Camino del Canyon, Mill Valley, CA 94941).

en's spirituality embraces mothering as nurturing and as an ideal for all women. Mothering, for many, is the paradigm of women's creativity and power, whether mothering takes the form of nurturing children (boys or girls or men) or saving the world and being the buttress of civilization. As one author writes:

> Women's power is the power to give birth whether we are birthing children or ideas. Our power is the power to nurture, to nourish, to take care and protect all life.[25]

The idea that all women are or should be mothers in one way or another is not only not challenged, it is pursued.

To begin with, actual mothering is not simply a matter of protecting and nurturing all life. The choice to feed children is the choice to interrupt the life process of something or someone else (whether or not that action is with its consent). The choice to mother is also a choice to protect one's own against others when necessary. The choice to mother can involve the choice to destroy destructive forces, from bacteria to batterers: a mother, like others, may have to kill to survive. Mothering may also involve the choice not to bring a child into the world so long as society won't let a lesbian be the kind of mother she chooses to be.[26] The choice to mother can involve the choice to abort.

I think mothers can claim both the power (enabling) of life and the power (enabling) of death. Many feminists, for example, attempt to deny the depth of the choice to abort by claiming that a zygote is nothing but a clump of cells or that, while a fetus may be a potential person, it is not morally significant. I think this is an error. The choice to abort a fetus is morally significant. To legitimize the choice we need not deny its moral import. As a moral agent, a mother who makes such a choice is making a choice about what is possible.

Mothering is one way of embracing and developing one ability to make a difference in this living; it is creating a quality of life through choice. As such, it does not always involve protecting living things, nor is the energy involved only nurturing energy. More significantly, we must challenge the concept of mothering as it is institutionalized in heteropatriarchy.[27]

25. Diane Mariechild, "Interview on 'Womanpower,'" *Woman of Power: A Magazine of Feminism, Spirituality, and Politics* (Spring 1984): 18–21.

26. Conversation, Florencia Carolina.

27. Note for example, Adrienne Rich, *Of Woman Born: Motherhood as Experience and Institution* (New York: W. W. Norton & Co., Inc., 1976).

JANE FLAX

Postmodernism and Gender Relations in Feminist Theory

Feminist theory seems to me to belong within two, more inclusive, categories with which it has special affinity: the analysis of social relations and postmodern philosophy.[1] Gender relations enter into and are constituent elements in every aspect of human experience. In turn, the experience of gender relations for any person and the structure of gender as a social category are shaped by the interactions of gender relations and other social relations such as class and race. Gender relations thus have no fixed essence; they vary both within and over time.

As a type of postmodern philosophy, feminist theory reveals and contributes to the growing uncertainty within Western intellectual circles about the appropriate grounding and methods for explaining and/or interpreting human experience. Contemporary feminists join other postmodern philosophers in raising important metatheoretical questions about the possible nature and status of theorizing itself. Given the increasingly fluid and confused status of Western self-understandings, it is not even clear what would constitute the basis for satisfactory answers to commonly agreed upon questions within feminist (or other forms of social) theory.

Postmodern discourses are all "deconstructive" in that they seek to distance us from and make us skeptical about beliefs concerning truth, knowledge, power, the self, and language that are often taken for granted within and serve as legitimation for contemporary Western culture.

Postmodern philosophers seek to throw into radical doubt beliefs still prevalent in (especially American) culture but derived from the Enlightenment, such as:

1. Sources for and practitioners of postmodernism include Friedrich Nietzsche, *On the Genealogy of Morals* (New York: Vintage, 1969), and *Beyond Good and Evil* (New York: Vintage, 1966); Jacques Derrida, *L'écriture et la difference* (Paris: Editions du Seuil, 1967); Michel Foucault, *Language, Counter-Memory, Practice* (Ithaca, N.Y.: Cornell University Press, 1977); Jacques Lacan, *Speech and Language in Psychoanalysis* (Baltimore: Johns Hopkins University Press, 1968), and *The Four Fundamental Concepts of Psychoanalysis* (New York: W. W. Norton & Co., 1973); Richard Rorty, *Philosophy and the Mirror of Nature* (Princeton, N.J.: Princeton University Press, 1979); Paul Feyerabend, *Against Method* (New York: Schocken Books, 1975); Ludwig Wittgenstein, *On Certainty* (New York: Harper & Row, 1972), and *Philosophical Investigations* (New York: Macmillan Publishing Co., 1970); Julia Kristeva, "Women's Time," *Signs: Journal of Women in Culture and Society* 7, no. 1 (Autumn 1981): 13–35; and Jean-François Lyotard, *The Postmodern Condition* (Minneapolis: University of Minnesota Press, 1984).

1. The existence of a stable, coherent self. Distinctive properties of this Enlightenment self include a form of reason capable of privileged insight into its own processes and into the "laws of nature."

2. Reason and its "science"—philosophy—can provide an objective, reliable, and universal foundation for knowledge.

3. The knowledge acquired from the right use of reason will be "True"—for example, such knowledge will represent something real and unchanging (universal) about our minds and/or the structure of the natural world.

4. Reason itself has transcendental and universal qualities. It exists independently of the self's contingent existence (e.g., bodily, historical, and social experiences do not affect reason's structure or its capacity to produce atemporal knowledge).

5. There are complex connections between reason, autonomy, and freedom. All claims to truth and rightful authority are to be submitted to the tribunal of reason. Freedom consists in obedience to laws that conform to the necessary results of the right use of reason. (The rules that are right for me as a rational being will necessarily be right for all other such beings.) In obeying such laws, I am obeying my own best transhistorical part (reason) and hence am exercising my own autonomy and ratifying my existence as a free being. In such acts, I escape a determined or merely contingent existence.

6. By grounding claims to authority in reason, the conflicts between truth, knowledge, and power can be overcome. Truth can serve power without distortion; in turn, by utilizing knowledge in the service of power both freedom and progress will be assured. Knowledge can be both neutral (e.g., grounded in universal reason, not particular "interests") and also socially beneficial.

7. Science, as the exemplar of the right use of reason, is also the paradigm for all true knowledge. Science is neutral in its methods and contents but socially beneficial in its results. Through its process of discovery we can utilize the "laws of nature" for the benefit of society. However, in order for science to progress, scientists must be free to follow the rules of reason rather than pander to the "interests" arising from outside rational discourse.

8. Language is in some sense transparent. Just as the right use of reason can result in knowledge that represents the real, so, too, language is merely the medium in and through which such representation occurs. There is a correspondence between "word" and "thing" (as between a correct truth claim and the real). Objects are not linguistically (or socially) constructed, they are merely *made present* to consciousness by naming and the right use of language.

The relation of feminist theorizing to the postmodern project of deconstruction is necessarily ambivalent. Enlightenment philosophers such as Kant did not intend to include women within the population of those capable of attaining freedom from traditional forms of authority. Nonetheless, it is not unreasonable for persons who have been defined as incapable of self-emancipation to insist that concepts such as the autonomy of reason, objective truth, and beneficial progress through scientific discovery ought to include and be applicable to the capacities and experiences of women as well as men. It is also appealing, for those who have been excluded, to believe that reason will triumph—that those who proclaim such ideas as objectivity will respond to rational arguments. If there is no objective basis for distinguishing between true and false beliefs, then it seems that power alone will determine the outcome of competing truth claims. This is a frightening prospect to those who lack (or are oppressed by) the power of others.

Nevertheless, despite an understandable attraction to the (apparently) logical, orderly world of the Enlightenment, feminist theory more properly belongs in the terrain of postmodern philosophy. Feminist notions of the self, knowledge, and truth are too contradictory to those of the Enlightenment to be contained within its categories. The way(s) to feminist future(s) cannot lie in reviving or appropriating Enlightenment concepts of the person or knowledge.[2]

Feminist theorists enter into and echo postmodernist discourses as we have begun to deconstruct notions of reason, knowledge, or the self and to reveal the effects of the gender arrangements that lay beneath their "neutral" and universalizing facades.[3] Some feminist theorists, for example, have begun to sense that the motto of Enlightenment, "*sapere aude*—'Have courage to use your own reason,'"[4] rests in part upon a deeply gender-rooted sense of self and self-deception. The notion that reason is divorced from "merely contingent" existence still predominates in contemporary Western thought and now appears to mask the embeddedness and depen-

2. In "The Instability of the Analytical Categories of Feminist Theory," *Signs* 11, no. 4 (Summer 1986): 656–64, Sandra Harding discusses the ambivalent attraction of feminist theorizing to both sorts of discourse. She insists that feminist theorists should live with the ambivalence and retain both discourses for political and philosophical reasons. However, I think her argument rests in part on a too uncritical appropriation of a key Enlightenment equation of knowing, naming, and emancipation.

3. Examples of such work include Alice A. Jardine, *Gynesis: Configurations of Woman and Modernity* (Ithaca, N.Y.: Cornell University Press, 1985); Donna Haraway, "A Manifesto for Cyborgs: Science, Technology, and Socialist Feminism in the 1980s," *Socialist Review* 80 (1983): 65–107; Kristeva; Kathy E. Ferguson, *The Feminist Case against Bureaucracy* (Philadelphia: Temple University Press, 1984); and Luce Irigaray, *Speculum of the Other Woman* (Ithaca, N.Y. Cornell University Press, 1985).

4. Immanuel Kant, "What Is Enlightenment?" in *Foundations of the Metaphysics of Morals* (Indianapolis: Bobbs-Merrill Co., 1959), 85.

dence of the self upon social relations, as well as the partiality and historical specificity of this self's existence. What Kant's self calls its "own" reason and the methods by which reason's contents become present or "self-evident," it now appears, are no freer from empirical contingency than is the so-called phenomenal self.[5]

In fact, feminists, like other postmodernists, have begun to suspect that all such transcendental claims reflect and reify the experience of a few persons—mostly white, Western males. These transhistoric claims seem plausible to us in part because they reflect important aspects of the experience of those who dominate our social world.

A FEMINIST PROBLEMATIC

This excursus into metatheory has now returned us to the opening of my paper—that the fundamental purpose of feminist theory is to analyze how we think, or do not think, or avoid thinking about gender. Obviously, then, to understand the goals of feminist theory we must consider its central subject—gender.

Here, however, we immediately plunge into a complicated and controversial morass. For among feminist theorists there is by no means consensus on such (apparently) elementary questions as: What is gender? How is it related to anatomical sexual differences? How are gender relations constituted and sustained (in one person's lifetime and more generally as a social experience over time)? How do gender relations relate to other sorts of social relations such as class or race? Do gender relations have a history (or many)? What causes gender relations to change over time? What are the relationships between gender relations, sexuality, and a sense of individual identity? What are the relationships between heterosexuality, homosexuality, and gender relations? Are there only two genders? What are the relationships between forms of male dominance and gender relations? Could/would gender relations wither away in egalitarian societies? Is there anything distinctively male or female in modes of thought and social relations? If there is, are these distinctions in-

5. For critiques of the mind (reason)/body split, see Naomi Scheman, "Individualism and the Objects of Psychology," in Sandra Harding and Merrill B. Hintikka, eds., *Discovering Reality: Feminist Perspectives on Epistemology, Metaphysics, Methodology, and Philosophy of Science* (Boston: D. Reidel Publishing Co., 1983); Susan Bordo, "The Cartesian Masculinization of Thought," *Signs* 11, no. 3 (Spring 1986): 439–56; Nancy C. M. Hartsock, "The Feminist Standpoint: Developing the Ground for a Specifically Feminist Historical Materialism," in Harding and Hintikka, eds.; Caroline Whitbeck, "Afterword to the 'Maternal Instinct,'" in Joyce Trebilcot, ed. *Mothering: Essays in Feminist Theory* (Totowa, N.J.: Rowman & Allanheld, 1984); and Dorothy Smith, "A Sociology for Women," in *The Prison of Sex: Essays in the Sociology of Knowledge*, ed. J. Sherman and E. T. Beck (Madison: University of Wisconsin Press, 1979).

nate and/or socially constituted? Are gendered distinctions socially useful and/or necessary? If so, what are the consequences for the feminist goal of attaining gender justice?[6]

Confronted with such a bewildering set of questions, it is easy to overlook the fact that a fundamental transformation in social theory has occurred. The single most important advance in feminist theory is that the existence of gender relations has been problematized. Gender can no longer be treated as a simple, natural fact. The assumption that gender relations are natural, we can now see, arose from two coinciding circumstances: the unexamined identification and confusion of (anatomical) sexual differences with gender relations, and the absence of active feminist movements. I will return to a consideration of the connections between gender relations and biology later in the paper.

Contemporary feminist movements are in part rooted in transformations in social experience that challenge widely shared categories of social meaning and explanation. In the United States, such transformations include changes in the structure of the economy, the family, the place of the United States in the world system, the declining authority of previously powerful social institutions, and the emergence of political groups that have increasingly more divergent ideas and demands concerning justice, equality, social legislation, and the proper role of the state. In such a "decentered" and unstable universe it seems plausible to question one of the most natural facets of human existence—gender relations. On the other hand, such instability also makes old modes of social relations more attractive. The new right and Ronald Reagan both call upon and reflect a desire to go back to a time when people and countries were in their "proper" place. The conflicts around gender arrangements become both the locus for and symbols of anxieties about all sorts of social-political ideas, only some of which are actually rooted primarily in gender relations.[7]

The coexistence of such social transformations and movements makes possible an increasingly radical and social, self-conscious questioning of previously unexamined "facts" and "explanations." Thus, feminist theory, like all other forms of theory (including gender-biased ones), is dependent upon and reflects a certain set of social experiences. Whether, to what extent, and why feminist theory can be "better" than the gender-biased theories it critiques are

6. These questions are suggested by Judith Stacey, "The New Conservative Feminism," *Feminist Studies* 9, no. 3 (Fall 1983): 559–83; and Nancy Chodorow, "Gender, Relation, and Difference in Psychoanalytic Perspective," in *The Future of Difference*, ed. Hester Eisenstein and Alice Jardine (1980; reprint, New Brunswick, N.J.: Rutgers University Press, 1985).

7. On the appeal of new right ideology to women, see Stacey.

questions that vex many writers.[8] In considering such questions feminist theorists invariably enter the epistemological terrain shared in part with other postmodern philosophies. Hence, I wish to bracket these questions for now in order to consider more closely a fundamental category and object of investigation of feminist theory—gender relations.

THINKING IN RELATIONS

"Gender relations" is a category meant to capture a complex set of social relations, to refer to a changing set of historically variable social processes. Gender, both as an analytic category and a social process, is relational. That is, gender relations are complex and unstable processes (or temporary "totalities" in the language of dialectics) constituted by and through interrelated parts. These parts are interdependent, that is, each part can have no meaning or existence without the others.

Gender relations are differentiated and (so far) asymmetric divisions and attributions of human traits and capacities. Through gender relations two types of persons are created: man and woman. Man and woman are posited as exclusionary categories. One can be only one gender, never the other or both. The actual content of being a man or woman and the rigidity of the categories themselves are highly variable across cultures and time. Nevertheless, gender relations so far as we have been able to understand them have been (more or less) relations of domination. That is, gender relations have been (more) defined and (imperfectly) controlled by one of their interrelated aspects—the man.

These relations of domination and the existence of gender relations themselves have been concealed in a variety of ways, including defining women as a "question" or the "sex" or the "other"[9] and

8. Harding discusses these problems in detail. See n. 2 above. See also Sandra Harding, "Is Gender a Variable in Conceptions of Rationality? A Survey of Issues," in Carol C. Gould, *Beyond Domination: New Perspectives on Woman and Philosophy* (Totowa, N.J.: Rowman & Allanheld, 1984), and "Why Has the Sex/Gender System Become Visible Only Now?" in Harding and Hintikka, eds.; and Allison M. Jaggar, *Feminist Politics and Human Nature* (Totowa, N.J.: Rowman & Allanheld, 1983), 353–94. Since within modern Western cultures science is the model for knowledge and is simultaneously neutral/objective yet socially useful/powerful (or destructive), much epistemological inquiry has focused on the nature and structure of science. Compare Hilary Rose, "Hand, Brain, and Heart: A Feminist Epistemology for the Natural Sciences," *Signs* 9, no. 1 (Autumn 1983): 73–90; and Helen Longino and Ruth Doell, "Body, Bias, and Behavior: A Comparative Analysis of Reasoning in Two Areas of Biological Science," *Signs* 9, no. 2 (Winter 1983): 206–27.

9. For example, the Marxist treatments of the "woman question" from Engels onward, or existentialist, or Lacanian treatment of woman as the "other" to man.

men as the universal (or at least without gender). In a wide variety of cultures and discourses, men tend to be seen as free from or as not determined by gender relations. Thus, for example, academics do not explicitly study the psychology of men or men's history. Male academics do not worry about how being men may distort their intellectual work, while women who study gender relations are considered suspect (of triviality, if not bias). Only recently have scholars begun to consider the possibility that there may be at least three histories in every culture—"his," "hers," and "ours." "His" and "ours" are generally assumed to be equivalents, although in contemporary work there might be some recognition of the existence of that deviant—woman (e.g., women's history).[10] However, it is still rare for scholars to search for the pervasive effects of gender relations on all aspects of a culture in the way that they feel obligated to investigate the impact of relations of power or the organization of production.

To the extent that feminist discourse defines its problematic as "woman," it, too, ironically privileges the man as unproblematic or exempted from determination by gender relations. From the perspective of social relations, men and women are both prisoners of gender, although in highly differentiated but interrelated ways. That men appear to be and (in many cases) are the wardens, or at least the trustees within a social whole, should not blind us to the extent to which they, too, are governed by the rules of gender. (This is not to deny that it matters a great deal—to individual men, to the women and children sometimes connected to them, and to those concerned about justice—where men as well as women are distributed within social hierarchies.)[11]

FEMINIST THEORIZING AND DECONSTRUCTION

The study of gender relations entails at least two levels of analysis: of gender as a thought construct or category that helps us to make sense out of particular social worlds and histories; and of gender as a social relation that enters into and partially constitutes all other social relations and activities. As a practical social relation, gender can be understood only by close examination of the mean-

10. On this point, see Joan Kelly, "The Doubled Vision of Feminist Theory," *Feminist Studies* 6, no. 2 (Summer 1979): 216–27; and also Judith Stacey and Barrie Thorne, "The Missing Feminist Revolution in Sociology," *Social Problems* 32, no. 4 (April 1985): 301–16.

11. Compare Phyllis Marynick Palmer, "White Women/Black Women: The Dualism of Female Identity and Experience in the United States," *Feminist Studies* 9, no. 1 (Spring 1983): 151–70.

ings of "male" and "female" and the consequences of being assigned to one or the other gender within concrete social practices.

Obviously, such meanings and practices will vary by culture, age, class, race, and time. We cannot presume a priori that in any particular culture there will be a single determinant or cause of gender relations, much less that we can tell beforehand what this cause (or these causes) might be. Feminist theorists have offered a variety of interesting causal explanations including the "sex/gender system," the organization of production or sexual division of labor, childrearing practices, and processes of signification or language. These all provide useful hypotheses for the concrete study of gender relations in particular societies, but each explanatory scheme also seems to me to be deeply flawed, inadequate, and overly deterministic.

For example, Gayle Rubin locates the origin of gender systems in the "transformation of raw biological sex into gender."[12] However, Rubin's distinction between sex and gender rests in turn upon a series of oppositions that I find very problematic, including the opposition of "raw biological sexuality" and the social. This opposition reflects the idea predominant in the work of Freud, Lacan, and others that a person is driven by impulses and needs that are invariant and invariably asocial. This split between culture and "natural" sexuality may in fact be rooted in and reflect gender arrangements.

As I have argued elsewhere,[13] Freud's drive theory reflects in parts an unconscious motive: to deny and repress aspects of infantile experience which are relational (e.g., the child's dependence upon and connectedness with its earliest caregiver, who is almost always a woman). Hence, in utilizing Freud's concepts we must pay attention to what they conceal as well as reveal, especially the unacknowledged influences of anxieties about gender on his supposedly gender-neutral concepts (such as drive theory).

Socialist feminists locate the fundamental cause of gender arrangements in the organization of production or the sexual division of labor. However, this explanatory system also incorporates the historical and philosophical flaws of Marxist analysis. As Balbus convincingly argues,[14] Marxists (including socialist feminists) un-

12. This is Gayle Rubin's claim in "The Traffic in Women: Notes on the 'Political Economy' of Sex," in *Toward an Anthropology of Women*, ed. Rayna Rapp Reiter (New York: Monthly Review Press, 1975).

13. I develop this argument in "Psychoanalysis as Deconstruction and Myth: On Gender, Narcissism and Modernity's Discontents," in *The Crisis of Modernity: Recent Theories of Culture in the United States and West Germany*, ed. Kurt Shell (Boulder, Colo.: Westview Press, 1986).

14. See Isaac D. Balbus, *Marxism and Domination* (Princeton, N.J.: Princeton University Press, 1982), chap. 1, for a further development of these arguments. Despite Balbus's critique of Marx, he still seems to be under Marx's spell on a

critically apply the categories Marx derived from his description of a particular form of the production of commodities to all areas of human life at all historical periods. Socialist feminists replicate this privileging of production and the division of labor with the concomitant assumptions concerning the centrality of labor itself. Labor is still seen as the essence of history and human being. Such conceptions distort life in capitalist society and surely are not appropriate to all other cultures.[15]

An example of the problems that follow from this uncritical appropriation of Marxist concepts can be found in the attempts by socialist feminists to "widen" the concept of production to include most forms of human activity. These arguments avoid an essential question: why "widen" the concept of production instead of dislodging it or any other singularly central concept from such authoritative power?

This question becomes more urgent when it appears that, despite the best efforts of socialist feminists, the Marxist concepts of labor and production invariably exclude or distort many kinds of activity, including those traditionally performed by women. Pregnancy and child rearing or relations between family members more generally cannot be comprehended merely as "property relations in action."[16] Sexuality cannot be understood as an "exchange" of physical energy, with a "surplus" (potentially) flowing to an "exploiter."[17] Such concepts also ignore or obscure the existence and activities of other persons as well—children—for whom at least a part of their formative experiences has nothing to do with production.

However, the structure of child-rearing practices also cannot serve as *the* root of gender relations. Among the many problems with this approach is that it cannot explain why women have the primary

---

metatheoretical level when he tries to locate a root of all domination—child-rearing practices. I have also discussed the inadequacy of Marxist theories in "Do Feminists Need Marxism?" in *Building Feminist Theory*, ed. Quest Staff (New York: Longman, Inc., 1981), and "The Family in Contemporary Feminist Thought: A Critical Review," in Jean Bethke Elshtain, ed., *The Family in Political Thought* (Amherst: University of Massachusetts Press, 1982), 232–39.

15. Marx may replicate rather than deconstruct the capitalist mentality in his emphasis on the centrality of production. Compare Albert O. Hirschman, *The Passions and the Interests* (Princeton, N.J.: Princeton University Press, 1977) for a very interesting discussion of the historical emergence and construction of specifically *capitalist* mentality.

16. Annette Kuhn, "Structures of Patriarchy and Capital in the Family," in Annette Kuhn and Anne Marie Wolpe, eds., *Feminism and Materialism* (Boston: Routledge & Kegan Paul, 1978), 53.

17. Ann Ferguson, "Conceiving Motherhood and Sexuality: A Feminist Materialist Approach," in Trebilcot, ed. (n. 5 above), 156–58.

responsibility for child rearing; it can explain only some of the consequences of this fact. In other words, the child-rearing practices taken as causal already presuppose the very social relations we are trying to understand: a gender-based division of human activities and hence the existence of socially constructed sets of gender arrangements and the (peculiar and in need of explanation) salience of gender itself.

The emphasis that (especially) French feminists place on the centrality of language (e.g., chains of signification, signs, and symbols) to the construction of gender also seems problematic.[18] A problem with thinking about (or only in terms of) texts, signs, or signification is that they tend to take on a life of their own or become the world, as in the claim that nothing exists outside of a text; everything is a comment upon or a displacement of another text, as if the modal human activity is literary criticism (or writing).

Such an approach obscures the projection of its own activity onto the world and denies the existence of the variety of concrete social practices that enter into and are reflected in the constitution of language itself (e.g., ways of life constitute language and texts as much as language constitutes ways of life). This lack of attention to concrete social relations (including the distribution of power) results, as in Lacan's work, in the obscuring of relations of domination. Such relations (including gender arrangements) then tend to acquire an aura of inevitability and become equated with language or culture (the "law of the father") as such.

Much of French (including feminist) writing also seems to assume a radical (even ontological rather than socially constructed) disjunction between sign/mind/male/world and body/nature/female.[19] The prescription of some French feminists for the recovery (or reconstitution?) of female experience—"writing from the body"—seems incoherent given this sort of (Cartesian) disjunction. Since "the body" is presocial and prelinguistic, what could it say?

All of these social practices posited as explanations for gender arrangements may be more or less important, interrelated, or themselves partially constituted in and through gender relations depending upon context. As in any form of social analysis, the study of gender relations will necessarily reflect the social practices it at-

18. The theories of French feminists vary, of course. I am focusing on a predominant and influential approach within the variations. For further discussion of French feminisms, see the essays in *Signs*, vol. 7, no. 1 (Autumn 1981) and *Feminist Studies*, vol. 7, no. 2 (Summer 1981).

19. Domna Stanton, in "Difference on Trial: A Critique of the Maternal Metaphor in Cixous, Irigaray, and Kristeva," in *The Poetics of Gender*, ed. Nancy Miller (New York: Columbia University Press, 1986), discusses the ontological and essentialist aspects of these writers' work.

tempts to understand. There cannot, nor should we expect there to be, a feminist equivalent to (a falsely universalizing) Marxism; indeed, the epistemologies of feminism undercut all such claims, including feminist ones.[20]

It is on the metatheoretical level that postmodern philosophies of knowledge can contribute to a more accurate self-understanding of the nature of our theorizing. We cannot simultaneously claim (1) that the mind, the self, and knowledge are socially constituted and that what we can know depends upon our social practices and contexts *and* (2) that feminist theory can uncover the Truth of the whole once and for all. Such an absolute truth (e.g., the explanation for all gender arrangements at all times is *X* . . .) would require the existence of an "Archimedes point" outside of the whole and beyond our embeddedness in it from which we could see (and represent) the whole. What we see and report would also have to be untransformed by the activities of perception and of reporting our vision in language. The object seen (social whole or gender arrangement) would have to be apprehended by an empty (ahistoric) mind and perfectly transcribed by/into a transparent language. The possibility of each of these conditions existing has been rendered extremely doubtful by the deconstructions of postmodern philosophers.

Furthermore, the work of Foucault (among others) should sensitize us to the interconnections between knowledge claims (especially to the claim of absolute or neutral knowledge) and power. Our own search for an "Archimedes point" may conceal and obscure our entanglement in an "episteme" in which truth claims may take only certain forms and not others.[21] Any episteme requires the suppression of discourses that threaten to differ with or undermine the authority of the dominant one. Hence within feminist theory a search for a defining theme of the whole or a feminist viewpoint may require the suppression of the important and discomforting voices of persons with experiences unlike our own. The suppression of these voices seems to be a necessary condition for the (apparent) authority, coherence, and universality of our own.

Thus, the very search for a root or cause of gender relations (or more narrowly, male domination) may partially reflect a mode of

20. Catherine MacKinnon, in "Feminism, Marxism, Method, and the State: An Agenda for Theory," *Signs* 7, no. 3 (Spring 1982): 515–44, seems to miss this basic point when she makes claims such as: "The defining theme of the whole is the male pursuit of control over women's sexuality—men not as individuals nor as biological beings, but as a gender group characterized by maleness as socially constructed, of which this pursuit is definitive" (532).

21. On the problem of the "Archimedes point," see Myra Jehlen, "Archimedes and the Paradox of Feminist Criticism," *Signs* 6, no. 4 (Summer 1981): 575–601. Compare Michel Foucault, *Power/Knowledge*, ed. Colin Gordon (New York: Random House, 1981).

thinking that is itself grounded in particular forms of gender (and/or other) relations in which domination is present. Perhaps reality can have "a" structure only from the falsely universalizing perspective of the dominant group. That is, only to the extent that one person or group can dominate the whole, will reality appear to be governed by one set of rules or be constituted by one privileged set of social relations. Criteria of theory construction such as parsimony or simplicity may be attained only by the suppression or denial of the experiences of the "other(s)."

THE NATURAL BARRIER

Thus, in order for gender relations to be useful as a category of social analysis we must be as socially and self-critical as possible about the meanings usually attributed to those relations and the ways we think about them. Otherwise, we run the risk of replicating the very social relations we are attempting to understand. We have to be able to investigate both the social and philosophical barriers to our comprehension of gender relations.

One important barrier to our comprehension of gender relations has been the difficulty of understanding the relationship between gender and "sex." In this context, sex means the anatomical differences between male and female. Historically (at least since Aristotle), these anatomical differences have been assigned to the class of "natural facts" of biology. In turn, biology has been equated with the pre- or nonsocial. Gender relations then become conceptualized as if they are constituted by two opposite terms or distinct types of being—man and woman. Since man and woman seem to be opposites or fundamentally distinct types of being, gender cannot be relational. If gender is as natural and as intrinsically a part of us as the genitals we are born with, it follows that it would be foolish (or even harmful) to attempt either to change gender arrangements or not to take them into account as a delimitation on human activities.

Even though a major focus of feminist theory has been to "denaturalize" gender, feminists as well as nonfeminists seem to have trouble thinking through the meanings we assign to and the uses we make of the concept "natural."[22] What after all, is the "natural" in the context of the human world?[23] There are many aspects of our

22. But see the work of Evelyn Fox Keller on the gendered character of our views of the "natural world," especially her essays "Gender and Science," in Harding and Hintikka, eds., and "Cognitive Repression in Physics," *American Journal of Physics* 47 (1979): 718–21.

23. In *Public Man, Private Woman,* Jean Bethke Elshtain provides an instructive instance of how allegedly natural properties (of infants) can be used to limit what a

embodiedness or biology that we might see as given limits to human action which Western medicine and science do not hesitate to challenge. For example, few Westerners would refuse to be vaccinated against diseases that our bodies are naturally susceptible to, although in some cultures such actions would be seen as violating the natural order. The tendency of Western science is to "disenchant" the natural world.[24] More and more the "natural" ceases to exist as the opposite of the "cultural" or social. Nature becomes the object and product of human action; it loses its independent existence. Ironically, the more such disenchantment proceeds, the more humans seem to need something that remains outside our powers of transformation. Until recently one such exempt area seemed to be anatomical differences between males and females.[25] Thus in order to "save" nature (from ourselves) many people in the contemporary West equate sex/biology/nature/gender and oppose these to the cultural/social/human. Concepts of gender then become complex metaphors for ambivalences about human action in, on, and as part of the natural world.

But in turn the use of gender as a metaphor for such ambivalences blocks further investigation of them. For the social articulation of these equations is not really in the form I stated above but, rather, sex/biology/nature/woman:cultural/social/man. In the contemporary West, women become the last refuge from not only the "heartless" world but also an increasingly mechanized and fabricated one as well.[26] What remains masked in these modes of

---

"reflective feminist" ought to think. In Elshtain's recent writings it becomes (once again) the responsibility of *women* to rescue children from an otherwise instrumental and uncaring world. Elshtain evidently believes that psychoanalytical theory is exempt from the context-dependent hermeneutics she believes characterize all other kinds of knowledge about social relations. She utilizes psychoanalytic theory as a warrant for absolute or foundational claims about the nature of "real human needs" or "the most basic human relationships" and then bases political conclusions on these "natural" facts. See Jean Bethke Elshtain, *Public Man, Private Woman* (Princeton, N.J.: Princeton University Press, 1981), 314, 331.

24. See Max Weber, "Science as a Vocation," in *From Max Weber*, ed. H. H. Gerth and C. Wright Mills (New York: Oxford University Press, 1958); and Max Horkheimer and Theodor W. Adorno, *Dialectic of Enlightenment* (New York: Herder & Herder, 1972).

25. I say "until recently" because of developments in medicine such as "sex change" operations and new methods of conception and fertilization of embryos.

26. As in the work of Christopher Lasch, *Haven in a Heartless World* (New York: Basic Books, 1977). Lasch's work is basically a repetition of the ideas stated earlier by members of the "Frankfurt School," especially Horkheimer and Adorno. See, e.g., the essay, "The Family," in *Aspects of Sociology*, Frankfurt Institute for Social Research (Boston: Beacon Press, 1972).

thought is the possibility that our concepts of biology/nature are rooted in social relations; they do not merely reflect the given structure of reality itself.

Thus, in order to understand gender as a social relation, feminist theorists need to deconstruct further the meanings we attach to biology/sex/gender/nature. This process of deconstruction is far from complete and certainly is not easy. Initially, some feminists thought we could merely separate the terms "sex" and "gender." As we became more sensitive to the social histories of concepts, it became clear that such an (apparent) disjunction, while politically necessary, rested upon problematic and culture-specific oppositions, for example, the one between "nature" and "culture" or "body" and "mind." As some feminists began to rethink these "oppositions," new questions emerged: does anatomy (body) have no relation to mind? What difference does it make in the constitution of my social experiences that I have a specifically female body?

Despite the increasing complexity of our questions, most feminists would still insist that gender relations are not (or are not only) equivalent to or a consequence of anatomy. Everyone will agree that there are anatomical differences between men and women. These anatomical differences seem to be primarily located in or are the consequence of the differentiated contributions men and women make to a common biological necessity—the physical reproduction of our species.

However, the mere existence of such anatomical differentiation is a descriptive fact, one of many observations we might make about the physical characteristics of humans. Part of the problem in deconstruction of the meaning of biology/sex/gender/nature is that sex/gender has been one of the few areas in which (usually female) embodiment can be discussed at all in (nonscientific) Western discourses. There are many other aspects of our embodiedness that seem equally remarkable and interesting, for example, the incredible complexity of the structure and functioning of our brains, the extreme and relatively prolonged physical helplessness of the human neonate as compared to that of other (even related) species, or the fact that every one of us will die.

It is also the case that physically male and female humans resemble each other in many more ways than we differ. Our similarities are even more striking if we compare humans to (say) toads or trees. So why ought the anatomical differences between male and female humans assume such significance in our sense of our selves as persons? Why ought such complex human social meanings and structures be based on or justified by a relatively narrow range of anatomical differences?

One possible answer to these questions is that the anatomical differences between males and females are connected to and are partially a consequence of one of the most important functions of the species—its physical reproduction. Thus, we might argue, because reproduction is such an important aspect of our species life, characteristics associated with it will be much more salient to us than, say, hair color or height.

Another possible answer to these questions might be that in order for humans physically to reproduce the species, we have to have sexual intercourse. Our anatomical differences make possible (and necessary for physical reproduction) a certain fitting together of distinctively male and female organs. For some humans this "fitting together" is also highly desirable and pleasurable. Hence our anatomical differences seem to be inextricably connected to (and in some sense, even causative of) sexuality.

Thus, there seems to be a complex of relations that have associated, given meanings: penis or clitoris, vagina, and breasts (read distinctively male or female bodies), sexuality (read reproduction—birth and babies), sense of self as a distinct, differentiated gender—as either (and only) a male or female person (read gender relations as a "natural" exclusionary category). That is, we believe there are only two types of humans, and each of us can be only one of them.

A problem with all these apparently obvious associations is that they may assume precisely what requires explanation—that is, gender relations. We live in a world in which gender is a constituting social relation and in which gender is also a relation of domination. Therefore, both men's and women's understanding of anatomy, biology, embodiedness, sexuality, and reproduction is partially rooted in, reflects, and must justify (or challenge) preexisting gender relations. In turn, the existence of gender relations helps us to order and understand the facts of human existence. In other words, gender can become a metaphor for biology just as biology can become a metaphor for gender.

PRISONERS OF GENDER: DILEMMAS IN FEMINIST THEORY

The apparent connections between gender relations and such important aspects of human existence as birth, reproduction, and sexuality make possible both a conflating of the natural and the social *and* an overly radical distinction between the two. In modern Western culture and sometimes even in feminist theories, "natural" and "social" become conflated in our understanding of "woman." In nonfeminist and some feminist writings about men a radical disjunction is frequently made between the "natural" and the "social." Women often stand for/symbolize the body, "difference," the concrete. These qualities are also said by some feminist as well as nonfeminist writers to suffuse/define the activities most associated with women: nurturing, mothering, taking care of and being in relation with others, "preserving."[27] Women's minds are also often seen as reflecting the qualities of our stereotypically female activities and bodies. Even feminists sometimes say women reason and/or write differently and have different interests and motives than men.[28] Men are said to have more interest in utilizing the power of abstract reason (mind), to want mastery over nature (including bodies), and to be aggressive and militaristic.

The reemergence of such claims even among some feminists needs further analysis. Is this the beginning of a genuine transvaluation of values and/or a retreat into traditional gendered ways of understanding the world? In our attempts to correct arbitrary (and gendered) distinctions, feminists often end up reproducing them. Feminist discourse is full of contradictory and irreconcilable conceptions of the nature of our social relations, of men and women and the worth and character of stereotypically masculine and feminine activities. The positing of these conceptions such that only one perspective can be "correct" (or properly feminist) reveals, among other things, the embeddedness of feminist theory in the very social processes we are trying to critique and our need for more systematic and self-conscious theoretical practice.

As feminist theorizing is presently practiced, we seem to lose sight of the possibility that each of our conceptions of a practice (e.g., mothering) may capture an aspect of a very complex and contradictory set of social relations. Confronted with complex and changing relations, we try to reduce these to simple, unified, and undifferentiated wholes. We search for closure, or the right answer, or the "motor" of the history of male domination. The complexity of our questions and the variety of the approaches to them are taken by some feminists as well as nonfeminists as signs of weakness or failure to meet the strictures of preexisting theories rather than as symptoms of the permeability and pervasiveness of gender relations and the need for new sorts of theorizing.

Some of the reductive moves I have in mind include the constricting of "embodiedness" to a glorification of the distinctively

27. Compare Sara Ruddick's essays, "Maternal Thinking," and "Preservative Love and Military Destruction: Some Reflections on Mothering and Peace," both in Trebilcot, ed. (n. 5 above).

28. On women's "difference," see the essays in Eisenstein and Jardine, eds. (n. 6 above); and Elaine Marks and Isabelle de Courtivron, eds., *New French Feminisms* (New York: Schocken Books, 1981); also Carol Gilligan, *In a Different Voice* (Cambridge, Mass.: Harvard University Press, 1982); and Stanton (n. 19 above).

female aspects of our anatomy.[29] This reduction precludes considering the many other ways in which we experience our embodiedness (e.g., nonsexual pleasures, or the processes of aging, or pain). It also replicates the equating of women with the body—as if men did not have bodies also! Alternatively, there is a tendency simply to deny or neglect the meaningfulness or significance of any bodily experience within both women's and men's lives or to reduce it to a subset of "relations of production" (or reproduction).

Within feminist discourse, women sometimes seem to become the sole "bearers" of both embodiedness and difference. Thus we see arguments for the necessity to preserve a gender-based division of labor as our last protection from a state power that is depersonalizing and atomizing.[30] In such arguments the family is posited as an intimate, affective realm of natural relations—of kinship ties, primarily between mothers, children, and female kin—and it is discussed in opposition to the impersonal realms of the state and work (the worlds of men). Alternatively, feminists sometimes simply deny that there are any significant differences between women and men and that insofar as such differences exist, women should become more like men (or engage in men's activities). Or, the family is understood only as the site of gender struggle and the "reproduction" of persons—a miniature political economy with its own division of labor, source of surplus (women's labor), and product (children and workers).[31] The complex fantasies and conflicting wishes and experiences women associate with family/home often remain unexpressed and unacknowledged. Lacking such self-analysis, feminists find it difficult to recognize some of the sources of our differences or to accept that we do not necessarily share the same past or share needs in the present.[32]

Female sexuality is sometimes reduced to an expression of male

29. As in e.g., Hélène Cixous, "Sorties," in *The Newly Born Woman*, ed. Hélène Cixous and Catherine Clement (Ithaca, N.Y.: Cornell University Press, 1986).

30. See, for instance, Elshtain (n. 23 above), and Elshtain, ed. (n. 14 above), 7–30.

31. This seems to be the basic approach characteristic of socialist-feminist discussions of the family. See, e.g., the essays by A. Ferguson (n. 17 above); and Kuhn (n. 16 above).

32. See, e.g., Barbara Smith's discussion of the meanings of "home" to her in the "Introduction" to *Home Girls: A Black Feminist Anthology* (New York: Kitchen Table; Women of Color Press, 1983). Smith's definition contrasts strongly with the confinement and exploitation some middle-class white women associate with "home." See, e.g., Michele Barrett and Mary McIntosh, *The Anti-social Family* (London: Verso, 1983); and Heidi I. Hartmann, "The Family as the Locus of Gender, Class, and Political Struggle: The Example of Housework," *Signs* 6, no. 3 (Spring 1981): 366–94.

dominance, as when Catherine MacKinnon claims "gender socialization is the process through which women come to identify themselves as sexual beings, as beings that exist for men."[33] Among many other problems such a definition leaves unexplained how women could ever feel lust for other women and the wide variety of other sensual experiences women claim to have—for example, in masturbation, breast feeding, or playing with children. Alternatively, the "essence" of female sexuality is said to be rooted in the quasi-biological primal bonds between mother and daughter.[34]

For some theorists, our fantasy and internal worlds have expression only in symbols, not in actual social relations. For example, Iris Young claims that gender differentiation as a "category" refers only to "ideas, symbols and forms of consciousness."[35] In this view, fantasy, our inner worlds, and sexuality may structure intimate relations between women and men at home, but they are rarely seen as also entering into and shaping the structure of work and the state. Thus feminist theory recreates its own version of the public/private split. Alternatively, as in some radical feminist accounts, innate male drives, especially aggression and the need to dominate others are posited as the motor that drives the substance and teleology of history.[36]

Feminist theorists have delineated many of the ways in which women's consciousness is shaped by mothering, but we often still see "fathering" as somehow extrinsic to men's and children's consciousness.[37] The importance of modes of child rearing to women's status and to women's and men's sense of self is emphasized in feminist theory; yet we still write social theory in which everyone is presumed to be an adult. For example, in two recent collections of feminist theory focusing on mothering and the family,[38] there is

33. MacKinnon (n. 20 above), 531.

34. This seems to be Adrienne Rich's argument in "Compulsory Heterosexuality and Lesbian Existence," *Signs* 5, no. 4 (Summer 1980): 631–60. See also Stanton (n. 19 above) on this point.

35. Iris Young, "Is Male Gender Identity the Cause of Male Domination?" in Trebilcot, ed. (n. 5 above), 140. In this essay, Young replicates the split Juliet Mitchell posits in *Psychoanalysis and Feminism* (New York: Pantheon Books, 1974) between kinship/gender/superstructure and class/production/base.

36. As in Shulamith Firestone, *The Dialectic of Sex* (New York: Bantam Books, 1970); and MacKinnon (n. 20 above).

37. On this point, see the essay by Nancy Chodorow and Susan Contratto, "The Fantasy of the Perfect Mother," in *Rethinking the Family*, ed. Barrie Thorne with Marilyn Yalom (New York: Longman, Inc., 1983).

38. Trebilcot, ed. (n. 5 above); and Thorne and Yalom, eds.

almost no discussion of children as human beings or mothering as a relation between persons. The modal "person" in feminist theory still appears to be a self-sufficient individual adult.

These difficulties in thinking have social as well as philosophical roots, including the existence of relations of domination and the psychological consequences of our current modes of child rearing. In order to sustain domination, the interrelation and interdependence of one group with another must be denied. Connections can be traced only so far before they begin to be politically dangerous. For example, few white feminists have explored how our understandings of gender relations, self, and theory are partially constituted in and through the experiences of living in a culture in which asymmetric race relations are a central organizing principle of society.[39]

Furthermore, just as our current gender arrangements create men who have difficulties in acknowledging relations between people and experiences, they produce women who have difficulties in acknowledging differences within relations. In either gender, these social relations produce a disposition to treat experience as all of one sort or another and to be intolerant of differences, ambiguity, and conflict.

The enterprise of feminist theory is fraught with temptations and pitfalls. Insofar as women have been part of all societies, our thinking cannot be free from culture-bound modes of self-understanding. We as well as men internalize the dominant gender's conceptions of masculinity and femininity. Unless we see gender as a social relation, rather than as an opposition of inherently different beings, we will not be able to identify the varieties and limitations of different women's (or men's) powers and oppressions within particular societies. Feminist theorists are faced with a fourfold task. We need to (1) articulate feminist viewpoints of/within the social worlds in which we live; (2) think about how we are affected by these worlds; (3) consider the ways in which how we think about them may be implicated in existing power/knowledge relationships; and (4) imagine ways in which these worlds ought to/can be transformed.

Since within contemporary Western societies gender relations have been ones of domination, feminist theories should have a

39. But see the dialogues between Gloria I. Joseph and Jill Lewis, *Common Differences: Conflicts in Black and White Feminist Perspectives* (New York: Doubleday & Co., 1981); and Marie L. Lugones and Elizabeth V. Spelman, "Have We Got a Theory for You," in *Women and Values,* ed. Marilyn Pearsall (Belmont, Calif.: Wadsworth Publishing Co., 1986); and Palmer (n. 11 above). Women of color have been insisting on this point for a long time. Compare the essays in B. Smith, ed. (n. 32 above); and Cherríe Moraga and Gloria Azaldúa, eds., *This Bridge Called My Back* (Watertown, Mass.: Persephone Press, 1981). See also Audre Lorde, *Sister Outsider* (Trumansburg, N.Y.: Crossing Press, 1984).

compensatory as well as a critical aspect. That is, we need to recover and explore the aspects of social relations that have been suppressed, unarticulated, or denied within dominant (male) viewpoints. We need to recover and write the histories of women and our activities into the accounts and stories that cultures tell about themselves. Yet, we also need to think about how so-called women's activities are partially constituted by and through their location within the web of social relations that make up any society. That is, we need to know how these activities are affected but also how they effect, or enable, or compensate for the consequences of men's activities, as well as their implication in class or race relations.

There should also be a transvaluation of values—a rethinking of our ideas about what is humanly excellent, worthy of praise, or moral. In such a transvaluation, we need to be careful not to assert merely the superiority of the opposite. For example, sometimes feminist theorists tend to oppose autonomy to being-in-relations. Such an opposition does not account for adult forms of being-in-relations that can be claustrophobic without autonomy—an autonomy that, without being-in-relations, can easily degenerate into mastery. Our upbringing as women in this culture often encourages us to deny the many subtle forms of aggression that intimate relations with others can evoke and entail. For example, much of the discussion of mothering and the distinctively female tends to avoid discussing women's anger and aggression—how we internalize them and express them, for example, in relation to children or our own internal selves.[40] Perhaps women are not any less aggressive than men; we may just express our aggression in different, culturally sanctioned (and partially disguised or denied) ways.

Since we live in a society in which men have more power than women, it makes sense to assume that what is considered to be more worthy of praise may be those qualities associated with men. As feminists, we have the right to suspect that even "praise" of the female may be (at least in part) motivated by a wish to keep women in a restricted (and restrictive) place. Indeed, we need to search into all aspects of a society (the feminist critique included) for the expressions and consequences of relations of domination. We should insist that all such relations are social, that is, they are not the result of the differentiated possession of natural and unequal properties among types of persons.

However, in insisting upon the existence and power of such relations of domination, we should avoid seeing women/ourselves as totally innocent, passive beings. Such a view prevents us from seeing the areas of life in which women have had an effect, in

40. Compare the descriptions of mothering in Trebilcot, ed. (n. 5 above); especially the essays by Whitbeck and Ruddick.

which we are less determined by the will of the other(s), and in which some of us have and do exert power over others (e.g., the differential privileges of race, class, sexual preference, age, or location in the world system).

Any feminist standpoint will necessarily be partial. Thinking about women may illuminate some aspects of a society that have been previously suppressed within the dominant view. But none of us can speak for "woman" because no such person exists except within a specific set of (already gendered) relations—to "man" and to many concrete and different women.

Indeed, the notion of *a* feminist standpoint that is truer than previous (male) ones seems to rest upon many problematic and unexamined assumptions. These include an optimistic belief that people act rationally in their own interests and that reality has a structure that perfect reason (once perfected) can discover. Both of these assumptions in turn depend upon an uncritical appropriation of the Enlightenment ideas discussed earlier. Furthermore, the notion of such a standpoint also assumes that the oppressed are not in fundamental ways damaged by their social experience. On the contrary, this position assumes that the oppressed have a privileged (and not just different) relation and ability to comprehend a reality that is "out there" waiting for our representation. It also presupposes gendered social relations in which there is a category of beings who are fundamentally like each other by virtue of their sex—that is, it assumes the otherness men assign to women. Such a standpoint also assumes that women, unlike men, can be free of determination from their own participation in relations of domination such as those rooted in the social relations of race, class, or homophobia.[41]

I believe, on the contrary, that there is no force or reality "outside" our social relations and activity (e.g., history, reason, progress, science, some transcendental essence) that will rescue us from partiality and differences. Our lives and alliances belong with those who seek to further decenter the world—although we should reserve the right to be suspicious of their motives and visions as well.[42] Feminist theories, like other forms of postmodernism, should encourage us to tolerate and interpret ambivalence, ambiguity, and

41. For contrary arguments, see Jaggar (n. 8 above); and also Hartsock, "The Feminist Standpoint" (n. 5 above).

42. I discuss the gender biases and inadequacies of postmodern philosophy in "Freud's Children" in *Thinking Fragments: Psychoanalysis, Feminism, and Postmodernism in the Contemporary West* (Berkeley: University of California Press, 1990). See also Naomi Schor, "Dreaming Dissymmetry: Barthes, Foucault, and Sexual Difference" (paper delivered to the Boston Area Colloquium on Feminist Theory, Northeastern University, Fall 1986).

multiplicity as well as to expose the roots of our needs for imposing order and structure no matter how arbitrary and oppressive these needs may be.

If we do our work well, "reality" will appear even more unstable, complex, and disorderly than it does now. In this sense, perhaps Freud was right when he declared that women are the enemies of civilization.[43]

BELL HOOKS

Black Women: Shaping Feminist Theory

A central tenet of modern feminist thought has been the assertion that "all women are oppressed." This assertion implies that women share a common lot, that factors like class, race, religion, sexual preference, etc. do not create a diversity of experience that determines the extent to which sexism will be an oppressive force in the lives of individual women. Sexism as a system of domination is institutionalized but it has never determined in an absolute way the fate of all women in this society. Being oppressed means the *absence of choices.* It is the primary point of contact between the oppressed and the oppressor. Many women in this society do have choices (as inadequate as they are), therefore exploitation and discrimination are words that more accurately describe the lot of women collectively in the United States. Many women do not join organized resistance against sexism precisely because sexism has not meant an absolute lack of choices. They may know they are discriminated against on the basis of sex, but they do not equate this with oppression. Under capitalism, patriarchy is structured so that sexism restricts women's behavior in some realms even as freedom from limitations is allowed in other spheres. The absence of extreme restrictions leads many women to ignore the areas in which they are exploited or discriminated against; it may even lead them to imagine that no women are oppressed.

There are oppressed women in the United States, and it is both appropriate and necessary that we speak against such oppression. French feminist Christine Delphy makes the point in her essay, "For a Materialist Feminism," that the use of the term oppression is important because it places feminist struggle in a radical political framework:

43. Sigmund Freud, *Civilization and Its Discontents* (New York: W. W. Norton & Co., 1961), 50–51.

> The rebirth of feminism coincided with the use of the term "oppression." The ruling ideology, i.e. common sense, daily speech, does not speak about oppression but about a "feminine condition." It refers back to a naturalist explanation: to a constraint of nature, exterior reality out of reach and not modifiable by human action. The term "oppression," on the contrary, refers back to a choice, an explanation, a situation that is political. "Oppression" and "social oppression" are therefore synonyms or rather social oppression is a redundance: the notion of a political origin, i.e. social, is an integral part of the concept of oppression.

However, feminist emphasis on "common oppression" in the United States was less a strategy for politicization than an appropriation by conservative and liberal women of a radical political vocabulary that masked the extent to which they shaped the movement so that it addressed and promoted their class interests.

Although the impulse towards unity and empathy that informed the notion of common oppression was directed at building solidarity, slogans like "organize around your own oppression" provided the excuse many privileged women needed to ignore the differences between their social status and the status of masses of women. It was a mark of race and class privilege, as well as the expression of freedom from the many constraints sexism places on working class women, that middle class white women were able to make their interests the primary focus of feminist movement and employ a rhetoric of commonality that made their condition synonymous with "oppression." Who was there to demand a change in vocabulary? What other group of women in the United States had the same access to universities, publishing houses, mass media, money? Had middle class black women begun a movement in which they had labeled themselves "oppressed," no one would have taken them seriously. Had they established public forums and given speeches about their "oppression," they would have been criticized and attacked from all sides. This was not the case with white bourgeois feminists for they could appeal to a large audience of women, like themselves, who were eager to change their lot in life. Their isolation from women of other class and race groups provided no immediate comparative base by which to test their assumptions of common oppression. . . .

Feminists in the United States are aware of the contradictions. Carol Ehrlich makes the point in her essay, "The Unhappy Marriage of Marxism and Feminism: Can It Be Saved?," that "feminism seems more and more to have taken on a blind, safe, nonrevolutionary outlook" as "feminist radicalism loses ground to bourgeois feminism," stressing that "we cannot let this continue":

> Women need to know (and are increasingly prevented from finding out) that feminism is *not* about dressing for success, or becoming a corporate executive, or gaining elective office; it is *not* being able to share a two career marriage and take skiing vacations and spend huge amounts of time with your husband and two lovely children because you have a domestic worker who makes all this possible for you, but who hasn't the time or money to do it for herself; it is *not* opening a Women's Bank, or spending a weekend in an expensive workshop that guarantees to teach you how to become assertive (but not aggressive); it is most emphatically *not* about becoming a police detective or CIA agent or marine corps general.
>
> But if these distorted images of feminism have more reality than ours do, it is partly our own fault. We have not worked as hard as we should have at providing clear and meaningful alternative analyses which relate to people's lives and at providing active, accessible groups in which to work.

It is no accident that feminist struggle has been so easily co-opted to serve the interests of conservative and liberal feminists since feminism in the United States has so far been a bourgeois ideology. Zillah Eisenstein discusses the liberal roots of North American feminism in *The Radical Future of Liberal Feminism*, explaining in the introduction:

> One of the major contributions to be found in this study is the role of the ideology of liberal individualism in the construction of feminist theory. Today's feminists either do not discuss a theory of individuality or they unself-consciously adopt the competitive, atomistic ideology of liberal individualism. There is much confusion on this issue in the feminist theory we discuss here. Until a conscious differentiation is made between a theory of individuality that recognizes the importance of the individual within the social collectivity and the ideology of individualism that assumes a competitive view of the individual, there will not be a full accounting of what a feminist theory of liberation must look like [in] our Western society.

The ideology of "competitive, atomistic liberal individualism" has permeated feminist thought to such an extent that it undermines the potential radicalism of feminist struggle. The usurpation of feminism by bourgeois women to support their class interests has been to a very grave extent justified by feminist theory as it has so far been conceived. (For example, the ideology of "common oppression.") Any movement to resist the co-optation of feminist struggle must begin by introducing a different feminist perspective—a new theory—one that is not informed by the ideology of liberal individualism.

The exclusionary practices of women who dominate feminist discourse have made it practically impossible for new and varied theories to emerge. Feminism has its party line and women who feel a need for a different strategy, a different foundation, often find themselves ostracized and silenced. Criticisms of or alternatives to established feminist ideas are not encouraged, e.g. recent controversies about expanding feminist discussions of sexuality. Yet groups of women who feel excluded from feminist discourse and praxis can make a place for themselves only if they first create, via critiques, an awareness of the factors that alienate them. Many individual white women found in the women's movement a liberatory solution to personal dilemmas. Having directly benefited from the movement, they are less inclined to criticize it or to engage in rigorous examination of its structure than those who feel it has not had a revolutionary impact on their lives or the lives of masses of women in our society. Non-white women who feel affirmed within the current structure of feminist movement (even though they may form autonomous groups) seem to also feel that their definitions of the party line, whether on the issue of black feminism or on other issues, is the only legitimate discourse. Rather than encourage a diversity of voices, critical dialogue, and controversy, they, like some white women, seek to stifle dissent. As activists and writers whose work is widely known, they act as if they are best able to judge whether other women's voices should be heard. Susan Griffin warns against this overall tendency towards dogmatism in her essay, "The Way of All Ideology":

> . . . when a theory is transformed into an ideology, it begins to destroy the self and self-knowledge. Originally born of feeling, it pretends to float above and around feeling. Above sensation. It organizes experience according to itself, without touching experience. By virtue of being itself, it is supposed to know. To invoke the name of this ideology is to confer truthfulness. No one can tell it anything new. Experience ceases to surprise it, inform it, transform it. It is annoyed by any detail which does not fit into its world view. Begun as a cry against the denial of truth, now it denies any truth which does not fit into its scheme. Begun as a way to restore one's sense of reality, now it attempts to discipline real people, to remake natural beings after its own image. All that it fails to explain it records as its enemy. Begun as a theory of liberation, it is threatened by new theories of liberation; it builds a prison for the mind.

We resist hegemonic dominance of feminist thought by insisting that it is a theory in the making, that we must necessarily criticize, question, re-examine, and explore new possibilities. My persistent critique has been informed by my status as a member of an oppressed group, experience of sexist exploitation and discrimination, and the sense that prevailing feminist analysis has not been the force shaping my feminist consciousness. This is true for many women. There are white women who had never considered resisting male dominance until the feminist movement created an awareness that they could and should. My awareness of feminist struggle was stimulated by social circumstance. Growing up in a Southern, black, father-dominated, working class household, I experienced (as did my mother, my sisters, and my brother) varying degrees of patriarchal tyranny and it made me angry—it made us all angry. Anger led me to question the politics of male dominance and enabled me to resist sexist socialization. Frequently, white feminists act as if black women did not know sexist oppression existed until they voiced feminist sentiment. They believe they are providing black women with "the" analysis and "the" program for liberation. They do not understand, cannot even imagine, that black women, as well as other groups of women who live daily in oppressive situations, often acquire an awareness of patriarchal politics from their lived experience, just as they develop strategies of resistance (even though they may not resist on a sustained or organized basis).

These black women observed white feminist focus on male tyranny and women's oppression as if it were a "new" revelation and felt such a focus had little impact on their lives. To them it was just another indication of the privileged living conditions of middle and upper class white women that they would need a theory to inform them that they were "oppressed." The implication being that people who are truly oppressed know it even though they may not be engaged in organized resistance or are unable to articulate in written form the nature of their oppression. These black women saw nothing liberatory in party line analyses of women's oppression. Neither the fact that black women have not organized collectively in huge numbers around the issues of "feminism" (many of us do not know or use the term) nor the fact that we have not had access to the machinery of power that would allow us to share our analyses or theories about gender with the American public negate its presence in our lives or place us in a position of dependency in relationship to those white and non-white feminists who address a large audience.

The understanding I had by age thirteen of patriarchal politics created in me expectations of the feminist movement that were quite different from those of young, middle class, white women. When I entered my first women's studies class at Stanford University in the early 1970s, white women were revelling in the joy of being together—to them it was an important, momentous occasion. I had not known a life where women had not been together, where women had not helped, protected, and loved one another deeply. I had not known white women who were ignorant of the impact of race and class on their social status and consciousness (Southern white women often have a more realistic perspective on racism and classism than white women in other areas of the United States). I did not feel sympathetic to white peers who maintained that I could not expect them to have knowledge of or understand the life experiences of black women. Despite my background (living in racially segregated communities) I knew about the lives of white women, and certainly no white women lived in our neighborhood, attended our schools, or worked in our homes.

When I participated in feminist groups, I found that white women adopted a condescending attitude towards me and other non-white participants. The condescension they directed at black women was one of the means they employed to remind us that the women's movement was "theirs"—that we were able to participate because they allowed it, even encouraged it; after all, we were needed to legitimate the process. They did not see us as equals. They did not treat us as equals. And though they expected us to provide first hand accounts of black experience, they felt it was their role to decide if these experiences were authentic. Frequently, college-educated black women (even those from poor and working class backgrounds) were dismissed as mere imitators. Our presence in movement activities did not count, as white women were convinced that "real" blackness meant speaking the patois of poor black people, being uneducated, streetwise, and a variety of other stereotypes. If we dared to criticize the movement or to assume responsibility for reshaping feminist ideas and introducing new ideas, our voices were tuned out, dismissed, silenced. We could be heard only if our statements echoed the sentiments of the dominant discourse.

Attempts by white feminists to silence black women are rarely written about. All too often they have taken place in conference rooms, classrooms, or the privacy of cozy living room settings, where one lone black woman faces the racist hostility of a group of white women. From the time the women's liberation movement began, individual black women went to groups. Many never returned after a first meeting. Anita Cornwall is correct in "Three for the Price of One: Notes from a Gay Black Feminist," when she states, ". . . sadly enough, fear of encountering racism seems to be one of the main reasons that so many black womyn refuse to join the women's movement."[1] Recent focus on the issue of racism has generated discourse but has had little impact on the behavior of white feminists toward black women. Often the white women who are busy publishing papers and books on "unlearning racism" remain patronizing and condescending when they relate to black women. This is not surprising given that frequently their discourse is aimed solely in the direction of a white audience and the focus solely on changing attitudes rather than addressing racism in a historical and political context. They make us the "objects" of their privileged discourse on race. As "objects," we remain unequals, inferiors. Even though they may be sincerely concerned about racism, their methodology suggests they are not yet free of the type of paternalism endemic to white supremacist ideology. Some of these women place themselves in the position of "authorities" who must mediate communication between racist white women (naturally they see themselves as having come to terms with their racism) and angry black women whom they believe are incapable of rational discourse. Of course, the system of racism, classism, and educational elitism remain intact if they are to maintain their authoritative positions.

In 1981, I enrolled in a graduate class on feminist theory where we were given a course reading list that had writings by white women and men, one black man, but no material by or about black, Native American Indian, Hispanic, or Asian women. When I criticized this oversight, white women directed an anger and hostility at me that was so intense I found it difficult to attend the class. When I suggested that the purpose of this collective anger was to create an atmosphere in which it would be psychologically unbearable for me to speak in class discussions or even attend class, I was told that they were not angry. *I* was the one who was angry. Weeks after class ended, I received an open letter from one white female student acknowledging her anger and expressing regret for her attacks. She wrote:

> I didn't know you. You were black. In class after a while I noticed myself, that I would always be the one to respond to whatever you said. And usually it was to contradict. Not that the argument was always about racism by any means. But I think the hidden logic was that if I could prove you wrong about one thing, then you might not be right about anything at all.

1. Anita Cornwall, "Three for the Price of One" in *Lavendar Culture*, ed. by Karla Jay and Alice Young (New York: Jove Publications, 1979), p. 471.

And in another paragraph:

> I said in class one day that there were some people less entrapped than others by Plato's picture of the world. I said I thought we, after fifteen years of education, courtesy of the ruling class, might be more entrapped than others who had not received a start in life so close to the heart of the monster. My classmate, once a close friend, sister, colleague, has not spoken to me since then. I think the possibility that we were not the best spokespeople for all women made her fear for her self-worth and for her Ph.D.

Often in situations where white feminists aggressively attacked individual black women, they saw themselves as the ones who were under attack, who were the victims. During a heated discussion with another white female student in a racially mixed women's group I had organized, I was told that she had heard how I had "wiped out" people in the feminist theory class, that she was afraid of being "wiped out" too. I reminded her that I was one person speaking to a large group of angry, aggressive people; I was hardly dominating the situation. It was I who left the class in tears, not any of the people I had supposedly "wiped out."

Racist stereotypes of the strong, superhuman black woman are operative myths in the minds of many white women, allowing them to ignore the extent to which black women are likely to be victimized in this society and the role white women may play in the maintenance and perpetuation of that victimization. In Lillian Hellman's autobiographical work *Pentimento,* she writes, "All my life, beginning at birth, I have taken orders from black women, wanting them and resenting them, being superstitious the few times I disobeyed." The black women Hellman describes worked in her household as family servants and their status was never that of an equal. Even as a child, she was always in the dominant position as they questioned, advised, or guided her; they were free to exercise these rights because she or another white authority figure allowed it. Hellman places power in the hands of these black women rather than acknowledge her own power over them; hence she mystifies the true nature of their relationship. By projecting onto black women a mythical power and strength, white women both promote a false image of themselves as powerless, passive victims and deflect attention away from their aggressiveness, their power (however limited in a white supremacist, male-dominated state), their willingness to dominate and control others. These unacknowledged aspects of the social status of many white women prevent them from transcending racism and limit the scope of their understanding of women's overall social status in the United States.

Privileged feminists have largely been unable to speak to, with, and for diverse groups of women because they either do not understand fully the inter-relatedness of sex, race, and class oppression or refuse to take this inter-relatedness seriously. Feminist analyses of woman's lot tend to focus exclusively on gender and do not provide a solid foundation on which to construct feminist theory. They reflect the dominant tendency in Western patriarchal minds to mystify woman's fate. Certainly it has been easier for women who do not experience race or class oppression to focus exclusively on gender. Although socialist feminists focus on class and gender, they tend to dismiss race or they make a point of acknowledging that race is important and then proceed to offer an analysis in which race is not considered.

As a group, black women are in an unusual position in this society, for not only are we collectively at the bottom of the occupational ladder, but our overall social status is lower than that of any other group. Occupying such a position, we bear the brunt of sexist, racist, and classist oppression. At the same time, we are the group that has not been socialized to assume the role of exploiter/oppressor in that we are allowed no institutionalized "other" that we can exploit or oppress. (Children do not represent an institutionalized other even though they may be oppressed by parents.) White women and black men have it both ways. They can act as oppressor or be oppressed. Black men may be victimized by racism, but sexism allows them to act as exploiters and oppressors of women. White women may be victimized by sexism, but racism enables them to act as exploiters and oppressors of black people. Both groups have led liberation movements that favor their interests and support the continued oppression of other groups. Black male sexism has undermined struggles to eradicate racism just as white female racism undermines feminist struggle. As long as these two groups or any group defines liberation as gaining social equality with ruling class white men, they have a vested interest in the continued exploitation and oppression of others.

Black women with no institutionalized "other" that we may discriminate against, exploit, or oppress often have a lived experience that directly challenges the prevailing classist, sexist, racist social structure and its concomitant ideology. This lived experience may shape our consciousness in such a way that our world view differs from those who have a degree of privilege (however relative within the existing system). It is essential for continued feminist struggle that black women recognize the special vantage point our marginality gives us and make use of this perspective to criticize the dominant racist, classist, sexist hegemony as well as to envision and create a counter-hegemony. I am suggesting that we have a central role to play in the making of feminist theory and a contribution to

offer that is unique and valuable. The formation of a liberatory feminist theory and praxis is a collective responsibility, one that must be shared. Though I criticize aspects of feminist movement as we have known it so far, a critique which is sometimes harsh and unrelenting, I do so not in an attempt to diminish feminist struggle but to enrich, to share in the work of making a liberatory ideology and a liberatory movement.

KAREN J. WARREN

Feminism and the Environment: An Overview of the Issues

INTRODUCTION

The past few decades have witnessed an enormous interest in the women's movement and the ecology (or environmental) movement. Many feminists have argued that the goals of these two movements are mutually reinforcing and ultimately involve the development of worldviews and practices which are not based on models of domination. One of the first feminists to do so was Rosemary Radford Ruether who, in 1975, wrote in *New Women/New Earth*,

> Women must see that there can be no liberation for them and no solution to the ecological crisis within a society whose fundamental model of relationships continues to be one of domination. They must unite the demands of the women's movement with those of the ecological movement to envision a radical reshaping of the basic socioeconomic relations and the underlying values of this [modern industrial] society. (204)

Subsequent feminist writings by animal rights activists, ecological and other environmental feminists have reinforced Ruether's basic point: there are important connections between feminism and environmentalism, an appreciation of which is essential for the success of the women's and ecological movements.

Just what are some of the connections between "feminism and the environment"? How has recognition of these connections affected and informed the theoretical perspectives of feminism and environmental ethics? What is the philosophical significance of the topic "feminism and the environment"?

In this essay I attempt to answer these questions by doing three things: First, I identify some of the connections between the domination of women and the domination of nature which have been suggested in the scholarly literature on "feminism and the environment." Second, I identify a range of philosophical positions which have emerged, particularly in the field of environmental ethics, in an attempt to provide a theoretical framework for understanding the connections between feminism and the environment. Third, I suggest what the philosophical significance of this emerging literature is, not only for feminism and environmental ethics but for mainstream philosophy as well. While no attempt is made to provide an exhaustive account, hopefully this overview highlights some of the relevant issues and acquaints the newcomer with the nature and range of philosophical positions on "feminism and the environment."

SOME ALLEGED CONNECTIONS BETWEEN FEMINISM AND THE ENVIRONMENT

In what follows I identify eight sorts of connections which feminists, particularly "ecological feminists" (ecofeminists), have identified as important to understanding the connections between feminism and the environment. No attempt is made here to critically assess the claims made about these connections. Furthermore, these eight categories are not to be viewed as competing or mutually exclusive. Indeed, many of the important claims made about one kind of connection (e.g., conceptual and theoretical) often depend on insights gleaned from others (e.g., historical and empirical). The aim in this section is simply to present for consideration the various elements of the overall "feminism and the environment" picture.

1. Historical and causal. One sort of alleged connection between feminism and the environment discussed is historical. When historical data is used to generate theories concerning the sources of the twin dominations of women and nature, it is also causal. In fact, some feminists characterize ecofeminism in terms of just such historical and causal claims: "Eco-feminism is a recent development in feminist thought which argues that the current global environmental crisis is a predictable outcome of patriarchal culture" (Salleh 1988, 138, n.1). What are some of these historical and causal claims?

Some feminists (e.g., Spretnak 1990) trace the historical and causal connections to prototypical patterns of domination begun with the invasion of Indo-european societies by nomadic tribes from Eurasia about 4500 B.C. (Lahar 1991). Riane Eisler describes the time before these invasions as a "matrilocal, matrilineal, peaceful agrarian era." Others (e.g., Griffin 1978; Plumwood 1991; Ruether 1975) focus on the historical role played by rationalism and important conceptual dualisms (discussed at 2, below) in classical Greek philosophy. Still other feminists (e.g., Merchant 1980; Shiva 1988) focus on cultural and scientific changes that occurred during the scientific revolution and sanctioned the exploitation of nature, unchecked commercial and industrial expansion, and the subordination of women.

What prompts and explains these alleged historical and causal connections between the domination of women and the domination of nature? What *else* was in place to permit and sanction these twin dominations? To answer these questions, many have turned to the conceptual props which keep the historical dominations of women and nature in place.

2. Conceptual. Many feminists (e.g., Cheney 1987; Gray 1981; Griffin 1978; King 1981, 1983, 1989; Merchant 1980, 1990; Plumwood 1986, 1991; Ruether 1975; Salleh, 1984; Warren 1987, 1988, 1990) have argued that, ultimately, historical and causal links between the dominations of women and of nature are located in conceptual structures of domination and in the way women and nature have been conceptualized, particularly in the western intellectual tradition. Four such conceptual links have been suggested.

One account locates the conceptual basis of the twin dominations of women and nature in *value dualisms*, i.e., disjunctive pairs in which the disjuncts are seen as oppositional (rather than as complementary) and exclusive (rather than as inclusive), and *value hierarchies*, i.e., perceptions of diversity organized by a spatial Up-Down metaphor which attribute higher value (status, prestige) to that which is higher ("Up") (see Gray 1981; Griffin 1978, 1989a; King 1981, 1983, 1990; Ruether 1975; Zimmerman 1987). Frequently cited examples of these hierarchically organized value dualisms include reason/emotion, mind/body, culture/nature, human nature, and man/woman dichotomies. These theorists argue that whatever is (historically) associated with emotion, body, nature, and women is regarded as inferior to that which is (historically) associated with reason, mind, culture, human (i.e., male) and men. One role of feminism and environmental ethics, then, is to expose and dismantle these dualisms, and to rethink and reconceive those mainstay philosophical notions (e.g., reason, rationality, knowledge, objectivity, the self as knower and moral agent) which rely on them.

A second, related account houses the value dualistic, value hierarchical thinking (described above) in larger, oppressive patriarchal conceptual frameworks—ones undergirding *all* social "isms of domination," e.g., racism, classicism, heterosexism, as well as sexism as well as "naturism" or, the unjustified domination and subordination. An oppressive conceptual framework is patriarchal when it explains, justifies and maintains the subordination of women by men. Oppressive and patriarchal conceptual frameworks are characterized not only by value dualisms and value hierarchies, but also by "power-over" conceptions of power and relationships of domination (Warren 1991) and by a "logic of domination," i.e., a structure of argumentation which justifies subordination on the grounds that *superiority justifies subordination* (Warren, 1987, 1990). On this view, it is oppressive and patriarchal conceptual frameworks (and the behaviors which they give rise to) which sanction, maintain, and perpetuate the twin dominations of women and nature. Revealing and overcoming oppressive and patriarchal conceptual frameworks as they are manifest in theories and practices regarding women and nature are important tasks of feminism, environmentalism, and environmental ethics.

A third account locates the conceptual basis in sex-gender differences, particularly in differentiated personality formation or consciousness (see Cheney 1987; Gray 1981; Salleh 1984). The claim is that female bodily experiences (e.g., of reproduction and childbearing), not female biology *per se,* situate women differently with respect to nature than men. This difference is revealed in a different consciousness in women than men; it is rooted conceptually in "paradigms that are uncritically oriented to the dominant western masculine forms of experiencing the world: the analytic, nonrelated, delightfully called 'objective' or 'scientific' approaches" (Salleh 1988, 130)—just the sort of value dualisms which are claimed (above) to separate and inferiorize what is historically female-gender identified. These sociopsychological factors provide a conceptual link insofar as they are embedded in different conceptualization structures and strategies (different "ways of knowing"), coping strategies and ways of relating to nature for women and men. A goal of feminism and environmental ethics, then, is to develop gender-sensitive language, theory, and practices which do not further the exploitative experiences and habits of dissociated, male-gender identified culture toward women and nature.

A fourth account draws on some of the historical connections mentioned earlier (at 1). It locates the conceptual link between feminism and the environment in the metaphors and models of mechanistic science which began during both the Enlightenment and pre-Enlightenment period (see Merchant 1980; Easlea 1981). The claim is that prior to the seventeenth century, nature was conceived on an organic model as a benevolent female, a nurturing mother; after the scientific revolution, nature was conceived on a mechanistic model as a (mere) machine, inert, dead. On both models, nature was female. The claim is that the move from the organic to the mechanistic model conceptually permitted and ethically justified the exploitation of the (female) earth, by removing the sorts of barriers to such treatment that the metaphor of nature as a living organism previously prevented. The challenge to feminists, environmentalists, and the environmental ethicists, then, is to overcome metaphors and models which feminize nature *and* naturalize women to the mutual detriment of both nature and women.

3. Empirical and experimental. Many feminists have documented empirical evidence linking feminism and the environment. Some point to various health and risk factors caused by the presence of low-level radiation, pesticides, toxics, and other pollutants and borne disproportionately by women and children (see Diamond 1990; Kheel 1989; Philpose 1989). Others provide data to show that First World development policies foster practices regarding food, forests, and water which directly contribute to the inability of women to provide adequately for themselves and their families (e.g., Mies 1986; Salleh 1990; Shiva 1988; Warren 1988, 1989). Feminist animal rights scholars argue that factory farming, animal experimentation, hunting, and meat-eating are tied to patriarchal concepts and practices (Adams 1988, 1991; Collard with Contrucci 1988; Kheel 1985, 1987–88). Appeal[s] to such empirical data are intended to document the very real, felt, lived connections between the dominations of women and nature and to motivate the need for feminist critical analysis of environmental concerns.

Some feminists cite experiential connections which honor and celebrate important cultural and spiritual ties of women and indigenous peoples to the earth (see Allen 1986, 1990; Bagby 1990; Doubiago 1989; LaChapelle 1978; *Woman of Power* 1988). Indeed documenting such connections and making them integral to the project of "feminism and the environment" is often heralded as one of the most important contributions to the creation of liberating, life-affirming and post-patriarchal worldviews and earth-based spirituality or theology (see Christ 1990; McDaniel 1989, 1990; Ruether 1989; Spretnak 1989a, 1990; Starhawk 1989, 1990). Appreciating these connections and understanding the "politics of women's spirituality" is viewed as an important aspect of feminism, environmentalism, and environmental ethics.

4. Epistemological. The various historical, conceptual, and empirical/experimental connections which have been claimed to link feminism and the environment (discussed at 1–3, above) have also motivated the need for different feminist environmental epistemologies. Typically these emerging epistemologies build on scholarship currently underway in feminist philosophy which challenges mainstream views of reason, rationality, knowledge, and the nature of knower (see APA *Newsletter on Feminism and Philosophy* 1989; Cheney 1989a; Code 1987; Garry and Pearsall 1989; Harding and Hintikka 1983; Jaggar and Bordo 1989). Douglas Buege, for instance, argues for a feminist environmental epistemology that builds on Lorraine Code's responsibilist epistemology (Buege 1991). As Val Plumwood suggests, if one mistakenly construes environmental philosophy as only or mainly concerned with ethics, one will neglect "a key aspect of the overall problem which is concerned with the definition of the human self as separate from nature, the connection between this and the instrumental view of nature, and broader *political* aspects of the critique of instrumentalism" (Plumwood 1991). A feminist environmental epistemology would address these political aspects of the human/nature dichotomy.

Other feminists appeal to the Critical Theory of Horkheimer (1974), Balbus (1982) and the Frankfurt circle, claiming that "their epistemology and substantive analysis both point to a convergence of feminist and ecological concerns, anticipating the more recent arrival of eco-feminism" (Salleh 1988, 131). For those feminists, Critical Theory provides a critique of the "nature versus culture" and an epistemological structure for critiquing the relationship between the domination of women and the domination of nature (see Salleh 1988; Mills 1987, 1991).

5. Symbolic. Many theorists (see, e.g., *Heresies #13;* Bell 1988; Salleh 1988) explore the symbolic association and devaluation of women and nature that appears in art, literature, religion, and theology. Drawing on feminist literature (e.g., the literature of Atwood 1985; Bagby 1990; Corrigan and Hoppe 1989, 1990; Doubiago 1990; Gearhart 1979; Kolodny 1975; LeGuin 1985, 1987, 1988; Piercy 1976; Rich 1986; Silko 1987; Zahava 1988), some argue that patriarchal conceptions of nature and women have justified "a two-pronged rape and domination of the earth and the women who live on it" (Murphy 1988, 87), often using this as background for developing an ecofeminist literary theory (Murphy 1991). Others explore the potential of (eco)feminism for creating alternative languages (e.g., Daly 1978; Griffin 1978), religious/spiritual symbols (e.g., "Goddess" symbols), hypotheses (e.g., feminist-inspired interpretations of the "Gaia hypothesis"), theologies (e.g., Christ 1990; Daly 1978; Gray 1988; Ruether 1989; Spretnak 1982, 1989a; Starhawk 1989, 1990) and societies (e.g., the feminist utopias suggested by Gearhart 1979 and Piercy 1976).

Other theorists explore the symbolic connections between sexist and naturalist language, i.e., language which inferiorizes women and nonhuman nature. This may involve raising questions about whether the sex-gendered language used to describe "Mother nature" is, in Ynestra King's words, "potentially liberating or simply a rationale for the continued subordination of women (King 1981, 12; see also Griscom 1981; Ortner 1974; Roach 1991). It may involve establishing connections between the languages used to describe women, nature, and nuclear weaponry (see Cohn 1989; Strange 1989). For instance, women are often described in animal terms (e.g., as cows, foxes, chicks, serpents, bitches, beavers, old bats, pussycats, cats, bird-brains, hare-brains). Nature is often described in female and sexual terms: Nature is raped, mastered, conquered, controlled, mined. Her secrets are penetrated and her womb is put into the services of the "man of science." Virgin timber is felled, cut down. Fertile soil is tilled and land that lies fallow is "barren," useless. The claim is that language which so feminizes nature and naturalizes women describes, reflects, and perpetuates the domination and inferiorization of both by failing to see the extent to which the twin dominations of women and nature (including animals) are, in fact, culturally (and not merely figuratively) analogous. The development of feminist theory and praxis which does not perpetuate this language and the power-over systems of domination they reinforce is, therefore, a goal of feminist environmentalism.

6. Ethical. Much of the philosophical literature on feminism and the environment has linked the two ethically. The claim is that the interconnections among the conceptualizations and treatment of women, animals, and (the rest of) nonhuman nature require a feminist ethical analysis and response. Minimally, the goal of feminist environmental ethics is to develop theories and practices concerning humans and the natural environment which are not male-biased and which provide a guide to action in the pre-feminist present (see Warren 1990; Warren and Cheney 1991b). Since a discussion of ethical concerns is intimately tied with alleged theoretical connections between feminism and the environment, consider now the range of theoretical positions which have emerged.

7. Theoretical. The varieties of alleged connections between feminism and the environment (identified at 1–6, above) have generated different, sometimes competing, theoretical positions in all areas of feminist and environmental scholarship. Nowhere is this more evident than in the field of environmental ethics. For reasons of space and audience, the discussion of "theoretical connections" is limited here to the field of environmental ethics.

In many respects, contemporary environmental ethics reflects the range of positions in contemporary normative philosophical ethics. The latter includes traditional consequentialist (e.g., ethical egoist, utilitarian) and non-consequentialist or deontological (e.g. Kantian, rights-based, virtue-based) positions, as well as challenges to them by non-traditional (e.g., some feminist, existentialist, Marxist, Afrocentric) positions. Similarly with environmental ethics. There are consequentialist (e.g., eco-utilitarian, utilitarian-based animal liberation, land stewardship) positions that extend traditional ethical considerations to animals and the nonhuman environment. There also are non-traditional approaches (e.g., holistic Leopoldian land ethics, social ecology, deep ecology, ecological feminism). Feminists who address environmental issues can be found defending each of these sorts of positions.

However, one position stands out as being expressly committed to making visible the nature of the connections between feminism and the environment: ecological feminism. Is there, then, one ecofeminism and one ecofeminist ethic?

In each case the answer is "No." Just as there is not one feminism, there is not one ecofeminism. 'Ecological feminism' is the name of a variety of different feminist perspectives on the nature of the connections between the domination of women (and other oppressed humans) and the domination of nature. These different perspectives reflect not only different feminist perspectives (e.g., liberal, traditional Marxist, radical, socialist); they also reflect different understandings of the nature, and solution to, pressing environmental problems (see Warren 1987). By extension, there is not one ecofeminist ethic. Given the newness of ecofeminism as a theoretical position, the nature of ecofeminist ethics is still emerging. Among the most visible feminist-inspired positions are feminist animal rights positions (e.g., Adams 1991; Kheel 1985; Slicer 1991) and feminist environmental ethics based on an ethic of care themes in social ecology (e.g., King 1981, 1983, 1989, 1990) and themes in bioregionalism (e.g., Cheney 1989b; Plant 1990). They all recognize important connections between the indefensible treatment of women and of nature, and involve a commitment to developing ethics which are not male-biased. It remains an open question how many, which, and on what ground *any* of the various positions in environmental ethics which acknowledge such feminist concerns are ecofeminist positions.

8. Political (Praxis). Francoise d'Eaubonne introduced the term 'ecofeminisme' in 1974 to bring attention to women's potential for bringing about an ecological revolution (1974, 213–52). Ecofeminist and other feminist concerns for women and the environment have always grown out of pressing political and practical concerns. These range from issues of health concerning women and the natural environment, to development and technology, the treatment of animals, and peace, anti-nuclear, anti-militarism activism (see Griffin 1989b; Lahar 1991; Spretnak 1989b). The varieties of feminist theoretical perspectives on the environment are properly seen as an attempt to take seriously such grassroots activism and political concerns by developing analyses of domination which explain, clarify, and guide that praxis (see *The Ecofeminist Newsletter;* King 1981, 1983, 1989, 1990; Spretnak 1989b; Warren 1991).

PHILOSOPHICAL IMPORTANCE OF THE LITERATURE CONNECTING FEMINISM AND THE ENVIRONMENT

In the preceding I have identified eight sorts of connections between feminism and the environment in the literature. I have indicated why and how, if indeed there are these connections, feminism, environmentalism, and environmental ethics will need to take them seriously. What are some of the implications of these connections for mainstream philosophy? I suggest a few here.

The conceptual links (given above at 2) suggest that philosophical conceptions of the self, knowledge and the "knower," reason and rationality, objectivity, and "nature versus culture"—mainstay philosophical notions in ethics, epistemology, metaphysics, philosophy of science, history of philosophy, political philosophy—will need to be reconceived. The value dualisms which seem to pervade the western philosophical tradition since the early Greeks (e.g., reason/emotion, mind/body, culture/nature, human/nature) and the historical sex-gendered assocation of women with emotion, body, and nature, will need to be examined for male-gender bias.

The historical and empirical links (given at 1 and 3, above) suggest that social scientific data on women and the environment is relevant to theoretical undertakings in many areas of philosophy. For example, in ethics, this data . . . raises issues of anthropocentric and androcentric bias. Can mainstream normative ethical theories generate an environmental ethic which is not male biased? In epistemology, data on the "indigenous technical knowledge" (see Warren 1988) of women who globally constitute the main agricultural production force (e.g., at least 80% of the farmers in Africa are women) raises issues about women's "epistemic privilege" about farming and forestry (see Warren 1988). If there is such privilege, does it generate the need for "feminist standpoint epistemologies" (see Garry and Pearsall 1989; Harding 1986; Harding and Hintikka 1983; Jaggar and Bordo 1989)? In metaphysics, data of the cross-cultural variability of women-nature connections raises issues about the concept of nature and the nature/cultural dichotomy. Is "nature" a given, a cross-cultural constant that stands in contrast to socially evolving and created "culture"? Or is nature, like culture, a social construct? That is, even if there really are material trees, rivers, and ecosystems, does the way nature is conceived and theorized about reflect historical, socioeconomic factors in much the same way that, according to many feminists, conceptions and theories about "humans" and "human nature" do? In political philosophy, data about the inferior standards of living of women globally raises issues about political theories and theorizing. What roles do unequal distributions of power and privilege play in the maintenance of systems of domination over both women and nature? How do they affect the content and methodology of political theories and theorizing? In the history of philosophy, data on the historical interiorization and associations of women and nature raises issues about . . . the philosophical theories advanced in any given time period. Do these theories contain biases against women and nature which bear on the substantive content of the theories themselves? In philosophy of science, particularly philosophy of biology, such data raises issues about the relationships between feminism and science, particularly the science of ecology. As Carolyn Merchant asks, "Is there a set of assumptions basic to the science of ecology that also holds implications for the status of women? Is there an ecological ethic that is also a feminist ethic?" (Merchant 1985, 229). Are there important parallels between contemporary feminist environmental ethics and ecosystems ecology which suggest ways in which they are engaged in mutually supportive projects (see King 1989; Warren and Cheney 1991)? These are the sort of questions raised by a philosophical look at the significance of issues concerning "feminism and the environment."

CONCLUSION

In this essay I have identified some of the alleged connections between "feminism and the environment" and discussed some of the issues these connections raise for feminism, environmentalism, environmental ethics, and mainstream philosophy. Presumably, taking these issues seriously involves revising the courses we teach and rethinking much of our scholarship. As with any attempt to incorporate the scholarship on women and feminism into our curricula and scholarship, such revising projects may be quite challenging. With regard to feminism and the environment, they also may be vital—not only for women, animals, and planet Earth, but for the development of worldviews and practices which are ecologically responsible and socially just for us all.

Works Cited

Adams, Carol J. 1991. "Ecofeminism and the Eating of Animals," *Hypatia*, Special Issue on Ecological Feminism. 6(1).

———. 1990. *The Sexual Politics of Meat: A Feminist-Vegetarian Critical Theory*. New York: Continuum.

Adorno, Theodor W. 1974. *Minima Moralia: Reflections from Damaged Life*. Trans. E.F.M. Jephcott. London: New Left Books.

———. 1973. *Negative Dialectics*. Trans. E.B. Ashton. New York: Seabury Press.

Allen, Paula Gunn. 1990. "The Woman I Love is a Planet; The Planet I Love is a Tree," in *Reweaving the World: The Emer-*

gence of Ecofeminism, eds. Irene Diamond and Gloria Femen Orenstein. San Francisco: Sierra Club Books: 52–58.

———. 1986. *The Sacred Hoop: Recovering the Feminine in American Indian Tradition*. Boston: Beacon Press.

American Philosophical Association (APA) *Newsletter on Feminism and Philosophy*. 1989. Special Issue on Reason, Rationality, and Gender. 88(2).

Atwood, Margaret. 1985. *The Handmaid's Tale*. New York: Fawcett Crest.

Bagby, Rachel L. 1990. "Daughters of Growing Things," in *Reweaving the World: The Emergence of Ecofeminism*, eds. Irene Diamond and Gloria Femen Orenstein. San Francisco: Sierra Club Books: 231–48.

Balbus, Isaac. 1982. *Marxism and Domination: A Neo-Hegelian, Feminist, Psychoanalytic Theory of Sexual, Political, and Technological Liberation*. Princeton: Princeton University Press.

Bell, Barbara Currier. 1988. "Cable of Blue Fire: Glimpsing a Group Identity for Mankind," in *Studies in the Humanities*. Special Issue on Feminism, Ecology and the Future of the Humanities, ed. Patrick Murphy. 15(2): 90–107.

Buege, Douglas. 1991. "Epistemic Responsibility to the Natural: Toward a Feminist Epistemology for Environmental Philosophy," APA *Newsletter on Feminism and Philosophy*. October.

Cheney, Jim. 1989a. "The Neo-Stoicism of Radical Environmentalism," *Environmental Ethics* 11: 293–326.

———. 1989b. "Postmodern Environmental Ethics: Ethics as Bioregional Narrative," *Environmental Ethics* 11(2): 117–34.

———. 1987. "Eco-feminism and Deep Ecology," *Environmental Ethics* 9(2): 115–45.

Christ, Carol P. 1990. "Rethinking Theology and Nature," in *Reweaving the World: The Emergence of Ecofeminism*, eds. Irene Diamond and Gloria Femen Orenstein. San Francisco: Sierra Club Books: 58–69.

Code, Lorraine. 1987. *Epistemic Responsibility*. Hanover, NH: University Press of New England.

Cohn, Carol. 1989. "Sex and Death in the Rational World of Defense Intellectuals," in *Exposing Nuclear Phallacies*, ed. Diana Russell. New York: Pergamon Press: 127–59.

Collard, Andree with Joyce Contrucci. 1988. *Rape of the Wild: Man's Violence Against Animals and the Earth*. Bloomington, IN: Indiana University Press.

Corrigan, Theresa, and Stephanie T. Hoppe. 1990. *And a Deer's Ear, Eagle's Sond, and Bear's Graces: Relationships Between Animals and Women*. Pittsburgh, PA: Cleis Press.

———. 1989. *With a Fly's Eye, Whale's Wit, and Woman's Heart: Animals and Women*. Pittsburgh, PA: Cleis Press.

Daly, Mary. 1978. *Gyn/Ecology: The Metaphysics of Radical Feminism.* Boston: Beacon Press.

Devall, Bill and George Sessions. 1985. *Deep Ecology: Living as if Nature Mattered.* Salt Lake City: Peregrine Smith Books.

Diamond, Irene. 1990. "Babies, Heroic Experts, and a Poisoned Earth," in *Reweaving the World: The Emergence of Ecofeminism,* eds. Irene Diamond and Gloria Femen Orenstein. San Francisco: Sierra Club Books: 201–10.

Diamond, Irene, and Gloria Femen Orenstein, eds. 1990. *Reweaving the World: The Emergence of Ecofeminism.* San Francisco: Sierra Club Books.

Doubiago, Sharon. 1990. "Mama Coyote Talks to the Boys," in *Healing the Wounds: The Promise of Ecofeminism,* ed. Judith Plant. Santa Cruz, CA: New Society Publishers: 40–44.

Easlea, Brian. 1981. *Science and Sexual Oppression: Patriarchy's Confrontation with Women and Nature.* London: Weidenfeld & Nicholson.

d'Eaubonne, Françoise. 1974. *Le Feminisme ou la Mort.* Paris: Pierre Horay.

The Ecofeminist Newsletter: A Publication of the National Women Studies Association (NWSA) Ecofeminist Task Force, ed. Noel Sturgeon. Middletown, CT: Center for the Humanities, Wesleyan University.

Eisler, Riane. 1990. "The Gaia Tradition and the Partnership Future," in *Reweaving the World: The Emergence of Ecofeminism,* eds. Irene Diamond and Gloria Femen Orenstein. San Francisco: Sierra Club Books, 23–34.

———. 1988. *The Chalice & the Blade: Our History, Our Future.* San Francisco: Harper and Row.

Fox, Warwick. 1989. "The Deep Ecology-Ecofeminism Debate and its Parallels," *Environmental Ethics* 11(1):5–25.

———. 1985. "A Postscript on Deep Ecology and Intrinsic Value," *The Trumpeter* 2: 20–23.

Garry, Ann and Marilyn Pearsall, eds. 1989. *Women, Knowledge, and Reality.* Boston: Unwin Hyman.

Gearhart, Sally. 1979. *The Wanderground: Stories of the Hill Women.* Boston: Alyson Publications.

Gray, Elizabeth Dodson. 1981. *Green Paradise Lost.* Wellesley, MA: Roundtable Press.

Gray, Elizabeth Dodson, ed. 1988. *Sacred Dimensions of Women's Experience.* Wellesley, MA: Roundtable Press.

Griffin, Susan. 1989a. "Split Culture," in *Healing the Wounds: The Promise of Ecofeminism,* ed. Judith Plant. Santa Cruz, CA: New Society Publishers: 7–17.

———. 1989b. "Ideologies of Madness," in *Exposing Nuclear Phallacies.* New York: Pergamon Press: 75–83.

———. 1978. *Women and Nature: The Roaring Inside Her.* San Francisco: Harper & Row.

Griscom, Joan L. 1981. "On Healing the Nature/History Split in Feminist Thought," *Heresies #13*. Special Issue on Feminism and Ecology. 4: 4–9.

Gwaganad. 1989. "Speaking for the Earth The Haida Way," in *Reweaving the World: The Emergence of Ecofeminism,* eds. Irene Diamond and Gloria Femen Orenstein. San Francisco: Sierra Club Books: 76–89.

Harding, Sandra. 1986. *The Science Question in Feminism.* Ithaca, NY: Cornell University Press.

Harding, Sandra, and Merrill Hintikka, eds. 1983. *Discovering Reality: Feminist Perspectives on Epistemology, Metaphysics, Methodology and the Philosophy of Science.* Dordrecht: Reidel Publishing Company.

Hargrove, Eugene. 1989. "Beginning the Next Decade: Taking Stock," *Environmental Ethics* 11: 3–4.

Harris, Adrienne and Ynestra King. 1990. *Rocking the Ship of State: Toward a Feminist Peace Politics.* Boulder, CO: Westview Press.

Heresies #13: Feminism and Ecology. 1981. 4(1).

Horkheimer, Max. 1974. *Eclipse of Reason.* New York: Seabury Press.

Jaggar, Alison M., and Susan R. Bordo, eds. 1989. *Gender/Body/Knowledge: Feminist Reconstructions of Being and Knowing.* New Brunswick, NJ: Rutgers University Press.

Kheel, Marti. 1989. "From Healing Herbs to Deadly Drugs: Western Medicine's War Against the Natural World," in *Healing the Wounds: The Promise of Ecofeminism,* ed. Judith Plant. Santa Cruz, CA: New Society Publishers: 96–111.

———. 1987–88. "Animal Liberation is a Feminist Issue," *The New Catalyst Quarterly* 10: 8–9.

———. 1985. "The Liberation of Nature: A Circular Affair," *Environmental Ethics* 7(2): 135–49.

King, Ynestra. 1990. "Healing the Wounds: Feminism, Ecology, and the Nature/Culture Dualism," in *Reweaving the World: The Emergence of Ecofeminism,* eds. Irene Diamond and Gloria Femen Orenstein. San Francisco: Sierra Club Books: 106–21.

———. 1989. "The Ecology of Feminism and the Feminism of Ecology," in *Healing the Wounds: The Promise of Ecofeminism,* ed. Judith Plant. Santa Cruz, CA: New Society Publishers: 18–28.

———. 1983. "The Eco-feminist Imperative," in *Reclaim the Earth,* eds. Leonie Caldecott and Stephanie LeLand. London: The Women's Press: 9–14.

———. 1981. "Feminism and the Revolt of Nature," in *Heresies #13: Feminism and Ecology* 4(1): 12–16.

Kolodny, Annette. 1975. *The Lay of the Land: Metaphor as Experience and History in American Life and Letters.* Chapel Hill: University of North Carolina Press.

LaChapelle, Dolores. 1978. *Earth Wisdom.* Silverton, CO: Way of the Mountain Learning Center and International College.

Lahar, Stephanie. 1991. "Ecofeminist Theory and Grassroots Politics," *Hypatia,* Special Issue on Ecological Feminism 6(1).

LeGuin, Ursula K. 1989. "Women/Wilderness," in *Healing the Wounds: The Promise of Ecofeminism,* ed. Judith Plant. Santa Cruz, CA: New Society Publishers: 45–50.

———. 1988. *Wild Oats and Fireweed.* New York: Harper and Row.

———. 1987. *Buffalo Gals and Other Animal Presences.* Santa Barbara, CA: Capra Press.

———. 1985. *Always Coming Home.* New York: Bantam Books.

McDaniel, Jay B. 1990. *Earth, Sky, God and Mortals: Developing an Ecological Spirituality.* Mystic, CT: Twenty-Third Publications.

———. 1989. *Of God and Pelicans: A Theology of Reverence for Life.* Louisville, KY: Westminster/John Knox Press.

Merchant, Carolyn. 1990. "Ecofeminism and Feminist Theory," in *Reweaving the World: The Emergence of Ecofeminism,* eds. Irene Diamond and Gloria Femen Orenstein. San Francisco: Sierra Club Books: 100–05.

———. 1985. "Feminism and Ecology," in *Deep Ecology: Living as if Nature Mattered,* eds. Bill Devall and George Session. Salt Lake City: Peregrine Smith Books: 229–31.

———. 1980. *The Death of Nature: Women, Ecology, and the Scientific Revolution.* San Francisco: Harper and Row.

Mies, Maria. 1986. *Patriarchy and Accumulation on a World Scale.* London: Zed Books Ltd.

Mills, Patricia. 1991. "Feminism and Ecology: On the Domination of Nature," *Hypatia,* Special Issue on Ecological Feminism. 6(1).

———. 1987. *Woman, Nature, and Psyche.* New Haven: Yale University Press.

Murphy, Patrick. 1991. "Ground, Pivot, Motion: Ecofeminist Theory, Dialogics, and Literary Practice," *Hypatia,* Special Issue on Ecological Feminism. 6(1).

———. 1988. "Introduction: Feminism, Ecology, and the Future of the Humanities," *Studies in the Humanities.* Special Issue on Feminism, Ecology, and the Future of the Humanities. 15(2): 85–89.

Naess, Arne. 1986. "The Deep Ecological Movement: Some Philosophical Aspects," *Philosophical Inquiry* 8: 10–31.

———. 1985. "Identification as a Source of Deep Ecological Attitudes," *Deep Ecology,* ed. Michael Tobias. San Diego, CA: Avant Books: 256–70.

———. 1973. "The Shallow and the Deep, Long-Range Ecology Movement: A Summary," *Inquiry* 16: 95–100.

Ortner, Sherry B. 1974. "Is Female to Male as Nature is to Culture?" in *Woman, Culture and Society*, eds. Michelle Rosaldo and Louise Lamphere. Stanford: Stanford University Press: 67–87.

Philipose, Pamela. 1989. "Women Act: Women and Environmental Protection in India," in *Reweaving the World: The Emergence of Ecofeminism*, eds. Irene Diamond and Gloria Femen Orenstein. San Francisco: Sierra Club Books: 67–75.

Piercy, Marge. 1976. *Women on the Edge of Time*. New York: Fawcett Crest.

Plant, Judith. 1990. "Searching for Common Ground: Ecofeminism and Bioregionalism," in *Reweaving the World: The Emergence of Ecofeminism*, eds. Irene Diamond and Gloria Femen Orenstein. San Francisco: Sierra Club Books: 155–61.

Plant, Judith, ed. 1989. *Healing the Wounds: The Promise of Ecofeminism*, Santa Cruz, CA: New Society Publishers.

Plumwood, Val. 1991. "Nature, Self, and Gender: Feminism, Environmental Philosophy and the Critique of Rationalism," *Hypatia*, Special Issue on Ecological Feminism. 6(1).

———. 1986. "Ecofeminism: An Overview and Discussion of Positions and Arguments," *Australasian Journal of Philosophy*, Supplement to Vol. 64: 120–37.

Rich, Adrienne. 1986. *Your Native Land, Your Life*. New York: Norton.

Roach, Catherine. 1991. "Loving Your Mother: On the Woman-Nature Relation," in *Hypatia*, Special Issue on Ecological Feminism. 6(1).

Ruether, Rosemary Radford. 1989. "Toward an Ecological-Feminist Theology of Nature," in *Healing the Wounds: The Promise of Ecofeminism*, ed. Judith Plant. Santa Cruz, CA: New Society Publishers: 145–50.

———. 1975. *New Woman/New Earth: Sexist Ideologies and Human Liberation*. New York: The Seabury Press.

Salleh, Ariel Kay. 1990. "Living with Nature: Reciprocity or Control?" in *Ethics of Environment and Development*, eds. R. and J. Engel: Tucson: University of Arizona Press.

———. 1988. "Epistemology and the Metaphors of Production: An Eco-feminist Reading of Critical Theory," in *Studies in the Humanities*. Special Issue on Feminism, Ecology, and the Future of the Humanities, ed. Patrick Murphy. 15(2): 130–39.

———. 1984. "Deeper than Deep Ecology: The Eco-Feminist Connection," *Environmental Ethics* 6(4): 339–45.

Shiva, Vandana. 1988. *Staying Alive: Women, Ecology and Development*. London: Zed Books.

Silko, Leslie Marmon. 1987. "Landscape, History and the Pueblo

Imagination," in *On Nature: Nature, Landscape, and Natural History*, ed. Daniel Halpern. San Francisco: North Point.

Slicer, Deborah. 1991. "Your Daughter or Your Dog? A Feminist Assessment of Animal Research Issues," *Hypatia*, Special Issue on Ecological Feminism. 6(1).

Spretnak, Charlene. 1990. "Ecofeminism: Our Roots and Flowering," in *Reweaving the World: The Emergence of Ecofeminism*, ed. Irene Diamond and Gloria Femen Orenstein. San Francisco: Sierra Club Books: 3–14.

———. 1989a. "Toward an Ecofeminist Spirituality," in *Healing the Wounds: The Promise of Ecofeminism*, ed. Judith Plant. Santa Cruz, CA: New Society Publishers: 127–32.

———. 1989b. "Naming the Cultural Forces that Push Us Toward War," in *Exposing Nuclear Phallacies*, ed. Diana Russell. New York: Pergamon Press: 53–62.

Spretnak, Charlene, ed. 1982. *The Politics of Women's Spirituality*. Garden City, NY: Anchor Press.

Starhawk. 1990. "Power, Authority, and Mystery: Ecofeminism and Earth-Based Spirituality," in *Reweaving the World: The Emergence of Ecofeminism*, eds. Irene Diamond and Gloria Femen Orenstein. San Francisco: Sierra Club Books: 73–86.

———. 1989. "Feminist Earth-Based Spirituality and Ecofeminism," in *Healing the Wounds: The Promise of Ecofeminism*, ed. Judith Plant. Santa Cruz, CA: New Society Publishers: 174–88.

Strange, Penny. 1989. "It'll Make a Man of You: A Feminist View of the Arms Race," in *Exposing Nuclear Phallacies*, ed. Diana Russell. New York: Pergamon Press: 104–26.

Warren, Karen J. 1991. "Toward a Feminist Peace Politics," *Journal of Peace and Justice Studies*.

———. 1990. "The Power and the Promise of Ecological Feminism." *Environmental Ethics* 12(2): 125–46.

———. 1989. "Water and Streams: An Ecofeminist Perspective," *Imprint* (June): 5–7.

———. 1988. "Toward and Ecofeminist Ethic," *Studies in the Humanities*. Special Issue on Feminism, Ecology, and the Future of the Humanities, ed. Patrick Murphy. 15(2): 140–56.

———. 1987. "Feminism and Ecology: Making Connections," *Environmental Ethics* 9(1): 3–20.

Warren, Karen J., and Jim Cheney. 1991. "Ecofeminism and Ecosystem Ecology," *Hypatia*, Special Issue on Ecological Feminism. 6(1).

Woman of Power. 1988. Nature Issue. 9(Spring).

Zahava, Irene. 1988. *Through Other Eyes: Animal Stories by Women*. Freedom, CA: The Crossing Press.

Zimmerman, Michael. 1987. "Feminism, Deep Ecology, and Environmental Ethics." *Environmental Ethics* 9(1): 21–44.

SUGGESTIONS FOR FURTHER READING

Feminist Perspectives

Addelson, Kathryn Pyne. *Impure Thoughts: Essays on Philosophy, Feminism, and Ethics.* Philadelphia: Temple University Press, 1991.

Andre, Judith. "Power, Oppression and Gender." *Social Theory and Practice* 11 (Spring 1985), pp. 107–21.

Ashton-Jones, Evelyn and Olson, Gary A. *The Gender Reader.* New York: Simon & Schuster, 1991.

Bartky, Sandra Lee. *Femininity and Domination: Studies in the Phenomenology of Oppression.* New York: Routledge, 1990.

Battersby, Christine. "Recent Work in Feminist Philosophy." *Philosophical Books* (Oct. 1991), pp. 193–201.

Benhabib, Seyla. *Situating the Self: Gender, Community and Postmodernism in Contemporary Ethics.* New York: Routledge, 1992.

Bleier, Ruth. *Science and Gender: A Critique of Biology and Its Theories on Women.* New York: Pergamon, 1984.

Bordo, Susan. "Feminist Skepticism and the 'Maleness' of Philosophy." *Journal of Philosophy* 85 (Nov. 1988), pp. 619–29.

———. "Postmodern Subjects, Postmodern Bodies." *Feminist Studies* 18 (Spring 1992), pp. 159–75.

Braidotti, Rosi. "The Subject in Feminism." *Hypatia* 6 (Summer 1991), pp. 155–72.

Cade, Toni (ed.). *The Black Woman: An Anthology.* New York: New American Library Mentor Books, 1970.

Cahill, Lisa Sowell. "Women, Marriage, Parenthood: What Are Their 'Natures.'" *Logos* 9 (1988), pp. 11–35.

Card, Claudia (ed.). *Feminist Ethics.* Lawrence, Kans.: University Press of Kansas, 1991.

Chandler, John. "Feminism and Epistemology." *Metaphilosophy* 21 (Oct. 1990), pp. 367–81.

Clatterbaugh, Kenneth. "Contemporary Perspectives on Masculinity: Men, Women, and Politics." In *Modern Society.* Boulder, Colo.: Westview Press, 1990.

Code, Lorraine. *What Can She Know? Feminist Theory and the Construction of Knowledge.* Ithaca: Cornell University Press, 1991.

Crouch, Margaret A. "Feminist Philosophy and the Genetic Fallacy." *Hypatia* 6 (Summer 1991), pp. 104–17.

Curtin, Deane. "Toward an Ecological Ethic of Care." *Hypatia* 6 (Spring 1991), pp. 60–74.

Dietz, Mary G. "Citizenship with a Feminist Face: The Problem with Maternal Thinking." *Political Theory* 13 (Feb. 1985), pp. 19–38.

Dillon, Robin. "Toward a Feminist Conception of Self-Respect." *Hypatia* 7 (Winter 1992), pp. 52–69.

Di Stefano, Christine. *Configurations of Masculinity: A Feminist*

Perspective on Modern Political Theory. Ithaca: Cornell University Press, 1991.

Duhan, Laura. "Feminism and Peace Theory: Women as Nurturers versus Women as Public Citizens." In *The Interest of Peace: A Spectrum of Philosophical Views,* ed. by Kenneth H. Klein and Joseph C. Kunkel. Wakefield, N.H.: Longwood, 1990.

Duran, Jane. "Ecofeminism and Androcentric Epistemology." *International Journal of Applied Philosophy* (Fall 1990), pp. 9–14.

Eames, Elizabeth R. "Sexism and Woman as Sex Object." *Journal of Thought* 11 (April 1976), pp. 140–43.

Elshtain, Jean Bethke. "Women as Mirror and Other: Toward a Theory of Women, War, and Feminism. *Human Soc.* 5 (Winter–Spring 1982), pp. 29–44.

Ferguson, Ann. "Motherhood and Sexuality: Some Feminist Questions." *Hypatia* 1 (Fall 1986), pp. 3–22.

Fischer, Linda. "Feminist Theory and the Politics of Inclusion." *Journal of Social Philosophy* (Fall–Winter 1990), pp. 174–83.

Fox-Genovese, Elizabeth. "The Feminist Challenge to the Canon." *National Forum* 69 (Summer 1989), pp. 32–34.

Friedman, Marilyn A. and May, Larry. "Harming Women as a Group." *Social Theory and Practice* 11 (Summer 1985), pp. 207–34.

Fuss, Diana. *Essentially Speaking: Feminism, Nature and Difference.* New York: Routledge, 1990.

Gatens, Moira. *Feminism and Philosophy: Perspectives on Difference and Equality.* Bloomington: Indiana University Press, 1991.

Genova, Judith (ed.). *Power, Gender, Values.* Edmonton: Academic Printing and Publishing, 1987.

Gilligan, Carol. *In a Different Voice: Psychological Theory and Women's Development.* Cambridge, Mass.: Harvard University Press, 1982.

Gould, Carol and Wartofsky, M. *Women and Philosophy.* New York: G. P. Putnam and Sons, 1976.

Govier, Trudy. "Trust, Distrust, and Feminist Theory." *Hypatia* 7 (Winter 1992), pp. 16–33.

Gregory, Ann. "Are Women Different and Why are Women Thought to Be Different? Theoretical and Methodological Perspectives." *Journal of Business Ethics* 9 (April–May 1990), pp. 257–66.

Griffiths, Morwenna and Whitford, Margaret (eds.). *Feminist Perspectives in Philosophy.* Bloomington: Indiana University Press, 1988.

Grimshaw, Jean. *Philosophy and Feminist Thinking.* Minneapolis: University of Minnesota Press, 1986.

Haack, Susan. "Science from a Feminist Perspective." *Philosophy* 67 (Jan. 1992), pp. 5–18.

Harding, Sandra. *The Science Question in Feminism.* Ithaca, New York: Cornell University Press, 1986.

Hartsock, Nancy C. M. *Money, Sex, and Power: Toward a Feminist Historical Materialism.* New York: Longman, 1983.

Hekman, Susan. "Reconstructing the Subject: Feminism, Modernism, and Postmodernism." *Hypatia* 6 (Summer 1991), pp. 44–63.

Held, Virginia. "Feminist Transformations of Moral Theory." *Philosophy and Phenomenological Research* (Fall 1990), pp. 321–44.

Hernandez, Adriana. "Feminist Theory, Plurality of Voices and Cultural Imperialism." *Philosophical Studies in Education* (1989), pp. 59–71.

Hoagland, Sarah Lucia. *Lesbian Ethics.* Palo Alto, Calif.: Basic Books, Inc., 1989.

Holmstrom, Nancy. "Do Women Have a Distinct Nature?" *Philosophical Forum* 14 (Fall 1982), pp. 25–42.

Howell, Nancy R. "Radical Relatedness and Feminist Separatism." *Process Studies* 18 (Summer 1989), pp. 118–26.

Hubbard, Ruth, Henifin, Mary Sue and Fried, Barbara (eds.). *Women Look at Biology Looking at Women: A Feminist Critique.* Cambridge: Schenkman Publishing Company, 1979.

Irigaray, Luce. *This Sex Which Is Not One,* trans. by Catherine Porter and Carolyn Burke. Ithaca: Cornell University Press, 1985.

Jaggar, Alison M. *Feminist Politics and Human Nature.* Totowa, N.J.: Rowman & Allanheld, 1983.

Jaggar, Alison M. and Rothenberg, Paula S. *Feminist Frameworks: Aternative Theoretical Accounts of the Relations between Women and Men.* New York: McGraw-Hill, 3rd ed., 1993.

Kaplan, Laura Duhan. "On the Compatibility of Pacifism and Care." *Hypatia* 7 (Winter 1992), pp. 133–34.

Keller, Evelyn Fox. "The Gender/Science System: Or Is Sex to Gender as Nature Is to Science?" *Hypatia* 2 (Fall 1987), pp. 37–49.

King, Roger J. H. "Caring About Nature: Feminist Ethics and the Environment." *Hypatia* 6 (Spring 1991), pp. 75–89.

Kittay, Eva Feder and Meyers, Diana T. (eds.). *Women and Moral Theory.* Totowa, N.J.: Littlefield, 1987.

Kourany, Janet A., Sterba, James P., and Tong, Rosemarie (eds.). *Feminist Philosophies.* Englewood Cliffs, N.J.: Prentice Hall, 1992.

Larrabee, Mary Jeanne. "Feminism and Parental Roles: Possibilities for Change." *Journal of Social Philosophy* 14 (May 1983), pp. 18–30.

Leach, Mary S. "Towards Caring about the Feminine." *Philosophy of Education, Proceedings of the Education Society* 41 (1985), pp. 359–63.

Lloyd, Genevieve. *The Man of Reason: "'Male' and 'Female' in Western Philosophy.* Minneapolis: University of Minnesota Press, 1984.

Longino, Helen E. "Feminism and Philosophy of Science." *Journal of Social Philosophy* (Fall–Winter 1990), pp. 150–59.

MacGuigan, Maryellen. "Is Woman a Question?" *International Philosophical Quarterly* 13 (1973), pp. 485–505.

MacKinnon, Catherine A. *Toward a Feminist Theory of the State.* Cambridge: Harvard University Press, 1991.

Mahowald, Mary B. "To Be or Not Be a Woman: Anorexia Nervosa, Normative Gender Roles, and Feminism." *Journal of Medicine and Philosophy* 17 (1992), pp. 233–51.

Mills, Patricia Jagentowicz. "Feminism and Ecology: On the Domination of Nature." *Hypatia* 6 (Spring 1991), pp. 162–78.

Nicholson, Linda J. (ed.). *Feminism/Postmodernism.* New York: Routledge, 1990.

Noddings, Nel. *Caring: A Feminine Approach to Ethics and Moral Education.* Berkeley: University of California Press, 1984.

Nye, Andrea. *Feminist Theory and the Philosophies of Man.* London: Croom Helm, 1988.

Okin, Susan Moller. *Justice, Gender, and the Family.* New York: Basic Books, Inc., 1989.

Overall, Christine. "Heterosexuality and Feminist Theory." *Canadian Journal of Philosophy* 20 (March 1990), pp. 1–17.

Palmer, Phyllis Marynick. "White Women/Black Women: The Dualism of Identity and Experience in the United States." *Feminist Studies* 9 (Spring 1983), pp. 151–70.

Pearsall, Marilyn (ed.). *Women and Values.* Belmont, Calif.: Wadsworth Publishing Company, 1986.

Plumwood, Val. "Nature, Self, and Gender: Feminism, Environmental Philospohy, and the Critique of Rationalism." *Hypatia* 6 (Spring 1991), pp. 3–27.

Purdy, Laura M. "Nature and Nurture." *Hypatia* 1 (Spring 1986), pp. 167–74.

Raymond, Janice G. "Reproductive Gifts and Gift Giving: The Altruistic Woman." *Hastings Center Report* 20 (Nov.–Dec. 1990), pp. 7–11.

Roach, Catherine. "Loving Your Mother: On the Woman-Nature Relationship." *Hypatia* 6 (Spring 1991), pp. 46–59.

Ruddick, Sara. *Maternal Thinking: Toward a Politics of Peace.* Boston: Beacon Press, 1989.

Russell, Denise. "Feminism and Relativism." *Methodology and Science* (1989), pp. 149–58.

Schedler, George. "The Radical Feminist View of Motherhood: Epistemological Issues and Political Implications." *International Journal of Applied Philosophy* 4 (Fall 1989), pp. 25–34.

Scheman, Naomi. "The Unavoidability of Gender." *Journal of Social Philosophy* (Fall–Winter 1990), pp. 34–39.

Seigfried, Charlene H. "Gender-Specific Values." *Philosophical Forum* 15 (Summer 1984), pp. 425–42.

Spelman, Elizabeth V. *Inessential Woman: Problems of Exclusion in Feminist Thought.* Boston: Beacon Press, 1988.

Stenger, Mary Ann. "Feminism and Pluralism in Contemporary Theology." *Laval Theologique et Philosophique* (Oct. 1990), pp. 291–305.

Tapper, Marion. "Can a Feminist be a Liberal?" *Australasian Journal of Philosophy* Suppl. 64 (June 1986), pp. 37–47.

Tong, Rosemarie. *Feminist Thought: A Comprehensive Introduction.* Boulder, Colo. Westview Press, 1989.

Tress, Daryl McGowan. "Feminist Theory and Its Discontents." *Interpretation* (Winter 1990–1991), pp. 293–311.

Tuana, Nancy. "The Radical Future of Feminist Empiricism." *Hypatia* 7 (Winter 1992), pp. 100–14.

Vetterling, May, Elliston, Frederick, and English, Jane (eds.). *Feminism and Philosophy.* Totowa, N.J.: Littlefield, Adams and Company, 1977.

Waithe, Mary Ellen (ed.). *A History of Women Philosophers,* vol. II: *Medieval, Renaissance and Enlightenment,* A.D. *500–1600.* Norwell, Mass.: Kluwer, 1989.

Wendell, Susan. "Toward a Feminist Theory of Disability." *Hypatia* 4 (Summer 1989), pp. 104–24.

Winant, Terry. "Rationality, Relativism, Feminism." In *Writing the Politics of Difference.* Albany: State University of New York Press, 1991.

Young, Iris Marion. *Justice and the Politics of Difference.* Princeton: Princeton University Press, 1990.

Zita, Jacquelyn. "Lesbian Angels and Other Matters." *Hypatia* 5 (Spring 1990), pp. 133–39.

[illegible]. "[illegible]." [illegible].

Wollstonecraft, Mary. [illegible] (2nd ed. [illegible]). *A Vindication of the Rights of Woman* [illegible]. New York: [illegible], 1988(?).

Acknowledgments

Not surprisingly, each edition of this book has extended the list of people I wish to thank. Let me reiterate my gratitude to all of those who have helped me in the past: family, friends, and colleagues. In preparing this third edition, however, Joan Hives, my faithful and persistent assistant at the University of Chicago, is at the top of the list of new people to thank. Alison Jaggar and Jane Martin were helpful in determining the rationale and outline of this edition, and Charlene Haddock Seigfried offered needed advice regarding the section on pragmatism. I am grateful to many people who contribute to the E-mail network for the Society for Women in Philosophy, who have provided bibliographic and other suggestions for updating the material included here. Jay Hullett and Deborah Wilkes, at the Cambridge office of Hackett Publishing Co., Inc., have been most cooperative in their editorial assistance. Dan Kirklin has been diligent and critical, while remaining reasonable and gracious, in his editing of the manuscript. The meticulous copyediting of Sonya Manes has saved me from numerous mistakes, greatly improving the quality of the final product.

I am also indebted to the authors and publishers who have allowed me to quote from the material they published. In addition to listing material requiring permission for use, the following list includes works in the public domain.

The Plato excerpts are from Plato's *Republic,* Book V, translated by G. M. A. Grube. (Indianapolis: Hackett Publishing Co., 1974).

Aristotle's "On the Generation of Animals" is reprinted by permission of the publishers and the Loeb Classical Library from Aristotle: *Generation of Animals,* translated by A. L. Peck, Cambridge, Mass.: Harvard University Press, 1942.

Aristotle's "Politics" is excerpted from *Aristotle's Politics,* translated by W. Bolland (London: Longman, Green, 1877).

The biblical excerpts Genesis 1–5, The Song of Solomon, Ephesians 5, and 1 Corinthians 7 and 11 are excerpted from *The Holy Bible,* Revised Standard Version.

The Augustine excerpts from *The Trinity* (Book XII), "Treatises on Marriage and Other Subjects," and *Confessions* (Book XIII) are reprinted from The Fathers of the Church series, Catholic University Press of America.

Aquinas' *The City of God* and "On the First Man" are excerpted from *The Basic Writings of St. Thomas Aquinas,* edited by Anton Pegis.

John Locke's "Of Paternal Power" and "Of Political and Civil Society" are excerpted from *Two Treatises of Government,* Book II: Of Civil Government, in *The Works of John Locke, Esq.*, Vol. II, ch. VI and VII. London: Printed for S. Birt, D. Browne, T. Longman, J. Shuckburgh, C. Hitch and L. Hawes, J. Hodges, J. Oswald, A. Millar, J. and J. Rivington, J. Ward, and M. Cooper. 1751, pp. 181–82, 184–85, 188–91.

David Hume's "Of Love and Marriage" and "Of Polygamy and Divorce" are excerpted from *Essays, Moral, Political and Literary,* edited by T. H. Green and T. H. Gross.

David Hume's "Of Chastity and Modesty" is excerpted from Hume's *Treatise of Human Nature,* edited by L. A. Selby-Bigge. Oxford at the Clarendon Press, 1888.

Jean-Jacques Rousseau's "Marriage" is reprinted with the permission of the publisher from William Boyd (trans. and ed.), "Marriage" from *The Emile of Jean-Jacques Rousseau.* (New York: Teachers College Press, 1962; by arrangement with William Heinemann, Ltd.).

Immanuel Kant's "Of the Distinction of the Beautiful and the Sublime in the Interrelations of the Two Sexes" is copyright © 1960 by the Regents of the University of California; excerpts from Immanuel Kant, *Observations on the Feeling of the Beautiful and the Sublime,* translated by John T. Goldthwait.

The Wollstonecraft excerpts are from *Vindication of the Rights of Woman,* ed. by Miriam Kramnick (Middlesex: Penguin Books, 1975).

G. W. F. Hegel's "The Ethical World" is excerpted from G. W. F. Hegel, *Phenomenology of Mind,* translated by J. B. Baillie, with the permission of Allen and Unwin.

Arthur Schopenhauer's "On Women" is excerpted from *Studies on Pessimism,* translated by Thomas Bailey Sanders (1860–1928).

The John Stuart Mill excerpts are from *Subjection of Women,* edited by Susan Moller Okin (Indianapolis and Cambridge: Hackett Publishing Co., 1988.).

Harriet Taylor Mill's "Enfranchisement of Women" is excerpted from *The Westminster and Foreign Quarterly Review,* Vol. LV (April–July 1851), pp. 291–311. London: Groombridge and Sons, 5, Paternoster Row.

Søren Kierkegaard's "Diary of the Seducer" is excerpted from Kierkegaard, Søren: *Either/Or,* Volume One, translated by David F. Swenson and Lillian Marvin Swenson, with revisions and foreword by Howard A. Johnson. Copyright © 1959, renewed, by Princeton University Press. Reprinted by permission of Princeton University Press.

Friedrich Nietzsche's "Of Womenkind, Old and Young," "Of Child and Marriage," and "Our Virtues" are excerpted from *Beyond Good and Evil,* by Friedrich Nietzsche, translated by Walter Kaufmann. Copyright © 1966 by Random House, Inc. Reprinted by Permission of Random House, Inc.

The Simone de Beauvoir excerpt is from *The Second Sex* by Simone de Beauvoir, trans. H. M. Parshley. Copyright 1952 and renewed 1980 by Alfred A. Knopf, Inc. Reprinted by permission of the publisher.

Sigmund Freud's "Femininity" is excerpted from Sigmund Freud, *New Introductory Lectures in Psychoanalysis,* translated and edited by James Strachey, by permission of W. W. Norton and Company, The Institute of Psychoanalysis and the Hogarth Press.

C. G. Jung's "Marriage as a Psychological Relationship" is excerpted from Jung, Carl, *The Collected Works of C. J. Jung,* translated by R. F. C. Hull, Bollingen Series XX, vol 17. Copyright © 1982 by Princeton University Press. Reprinted with permission of Princeton University Press.

Karen Horney's "Feminine Psychology" is reprinted from *New Ways in Psychoanalysis,* by Karen Horney, M.D., with the permission of W. W. Norton & Company, Inc., renewed © 1966 by Marianne von Eckardt, Renate Mintz, and Brigitte Swarzenski.

Juliet Mitchell's "Femininity" is excerpted from *Psychoanalysis and Feminism* by Juliet Mitchell. Copyright © 1974 Juliet Mitchell. Reprinted by permission of Pantheon Books, a division of Random House, Inc.

Friedrich Engels's "Origin of the Family" is excerpted from Friedrich Engels, *Origin of the Family, Private Property and the State,* by permission of International Publishers.

V. I. Lenin's *The Emancipation of Women* is excerpted from V. I. Lenin, *The Emancipation of the State,* by permission of International Publishers.

The Charlotte Perkins Gilman selection is excerpted from *Women and Economics* (Boston: Small, Maynard & Co., 1898).

Herbert Marcuse's "Nature and Revolution" is excerpted from *Counterrevolution and Revolt,* by Herbert Marcuse. Copyright © 1975 by Herbert Marcuse, reprinted by permission of Beacon Press.

The Jessie Taft selection is excerpted from *The Woman Movement from the Point of View of Social Consciousness,* Department of Philosophy, The University of Chicago, 1915. (Menasha, Wis.: George Banta Publishing Co., 1915 [The Collegiate Press]), 24–25.

The Jane Addams selections are excerpted from *Democracy and Social Ethics.* (New York: The Macmillan Company, 1902), 89–90 and from *Peace and Bread in Time of War,* Anniversary Edition 1915–1945 (New York: King's Crown Press, 1945), 77–83.

The Bertrand Russell selection is excerpted from Bertrand Russell, *Marriage and Morals,* by permission of Unwin Hyman.

The Joyce Trebilcot excerpt is from "Sex Roles: the Argument from Nature," by Joyce Trebilcot, reprinted from *Ethics* 85 (1975), by permission of the University of Chicago Press.

The Christine Pierce selection is from "Natural Law Language and Women" by Christine Pierce from *Women in Sexist Society* by Vivian Gornick and Barbara K. Moran. © 1971 by Basic Books, Inc. Reprinted by permission of Basic Books, a division of HarperCollins Publishers, Inc.

Elizabeth V. Spelman's "Woman: The One and the Many" is excerpted from *Inessential Woman*, by Elizabeth V. Spelman. Copyright © 1988 by Elizabeth V. Spelman. Reprinted by permission of Beacon Press.

The Zillah R. Eisenstein selection is excerpted from *The Radical Future of Liberal Feminism* by Zillah R. Eisenstein. Copyright 1981, 1993 by Zillah R. Eisenstein. Reprinted with the permission of Northeastern University Press, Boston.

The Heidi I. Hartmann selection is excerpted from Heidi Hartmann, "The Unhappy Marriage of Marxism and Feminism: Towards a More Progressive Union" from *Women and Revolution*, by Lydia Sargent, 1981, South End Press.

Charlene Haddock Seigfried's "Where Are All the Pragmatist Feminists?" is excerpted from "Where Are All the Pragmatist Feminists?" by permission of the author.

The Sara Ruddick selection is excerpted from *Maternal Thinking*, by Sara Ruddick. Copyright © 1989 by Sara Ruddick. Reprinted by permission of Beacon Press.

The Sarah Hoagland selection is excerpted from Sarah Hoagland, *Lesbian Ethics*, 1991, by permission of the Institute of Lesbian Studies, P.O. Box 2556, Chicago, Illinois 60625.

The Jane Flax selection is excerpted from Jane Flax, "Postmodernism and Gender Relations in Feminist Theory," from *Signs*, 1987, vol. 12, no. 4. By permission of the author.

bell hooks's "Black Women: Shaping Feminist Theory" is excerpted from bell hooks, *Feminist Theory from Margin to Center*, 1984, South End Press. Reprinted by permission of the publisher.

The Karen J. Warren selection is reprinted from "Feminism and the Environment," APA Newsletter, 90, 3 (Fall 1991), by permission of the author and the American Philosophical Association.